Rosalind Fergusson was born in Liverpool in 1953 and obtained her degree in French from Exeter University. From here she took a teaching certificate and became an assistant teacher at a school in West Sussex. From 1978 to 1984 she worked for Market House Books where she trained as an assistant editor and rose to the position of Senior Editor. During this time she worked on a range of reference books. Since leaving Market House Books she has worked as a freelance editor.

Her other publications include The Penguin Dictionary of Proverbs (1983), The Penguin Rhyming Dictionary (1985), Choose your Baby's Name (1987), The Hamlyn Dictionary of Quotations (1989), The Penguin Dictionary of English Synonyms and Antonyms (1992) and Chambers Dictionary of Foreign Words and Phrases (1995). Rosalind Fergusson has also edited and co-edited a number of dictionaries and reference books, and has contributed to The Bloomsbury Good Word Guide (1988) and Brewer's Dictionary of 20th-Century Phrase and Fable (1991), among others.

Rosalind Fergusson is married and lives in Kent. Her leisure interests include walking, sailing and music.

The New Penguin Dictionary of

Abbreviations

From A to zz

Rosalind Fergusson

PENGUIN BOOKS

PENGUIN BOOKS

Published by the Penguin Group
Penguin Books Ltd, 27 Wrights Lane, London W8 5TZ, England
Penguin Putnam Inc., 375 Hudson Street, New York, New York 10014, USA
Penguin Books Australia Ltd, Ringwood, Victoria, Australia
Penguin Books Canada Ltd, 10 Alcorn Avenue, Toronto, Ontario, Canada M4V 3B2
Penguin Books (NZ) Ltd, Private Bag 102902, NSMC, Auckland, New Zealand

Penguin Books Ltd, Registered Offices: Harmondsworth, Middlesex, England

First published 2000
10 9 8 7 6 5 4 3 2 1

Set in ITC Stone
Typeset by Rowland Phototypesetting Ltd, Bury St Edmunds, Suffolk
Printed in England by Clays Ltd, St Ives plc

Contents

The New Penguin Dictionary of Abbreviations contains over 40,000 entries, listed under more than 20,000 headwords. Abbreviations abound in all walks of modern life, and no dictionary of abbreviations can hope to be fully comprehensive, but users of this book should find in its pages most of the abbreviations they are likely to encounter, whether they are reading a magazine, listening to the news, browsing on the Internet, buying a house, or applying for a job.

Abbreviations fall into five main categories. There are *shortenings*, in which a word is simply truncated, as in **Co.** and **technol.**; *contractions*, which contain the first and last letters of the full word, as in **Ltd** and **Dr**; *initialisms*, made up of the first letters of a series of words, as in **BBC** and **e.g.**; *acronyms*, in which the first letters or syllables of a name or phrase are pronounced as a word, as in **NATO** and **Ofsted**; and *symbols*, which often belong to the fields of science and technology and may or may not be related to the words they represent, such as **km** and **Pb** (meaning 'lead'). The scope of *The New Penguin Dictionary of Abbreviations* has been broadened to include some items that are not classified as abbreviations in many standard dictionaries because they are – or have become – part of the English language as words in their own right, such as the acronyms **radar** and **laser** and informal short forms such as **fridge** and **pub**.

Abbreviations are perhaps most frequently used to save time and space in writing and printing, and the form that they take may vary from person to person, or from publication to publication. Some acronyms can appear in print either as a lower-case word with a capital initial or as a string of capitals, as in **Unesco** or **UNESCO**. Initialisms may often be capital or lower-case, with or without full stops or other punctuation, as in **ASAP** or **a.s.a.p.** (In *The New Penguin Dictionary of Abbreviations* we have tended to prefer the all-capital form of acronyms, unless an alternative form is known to be more frequent or favoured by the organization concerned; for lower-case initialisms we have usually retained the full stops.) Many users of British English signal the difference between shortenings and contractions by putting a full stop at the end of the former but not the latter, a convention that has been followed in this dictionary.

Order of entries

The abbreviations are listed in alphabetical order. Where two or more abbreviations differ only in capitalization and/or punctuation, all the forms containing capitals precede those in lower case, and unpunctuated forms precede those with slashes, full stops, spaces, etc. Abbreviations containing numbers follow those made up of the letter or letters before (or after) the number: **3M** comes between **M**, **m.**, etc. and **MA**, and **Y2K** comes between **Y**, **y.**, etc. and **YA**. The ampersand symbol has been alphabetized as 'and', so **R&A** follows **RANCOM**.

Within each entry, the full forms are listed in character-by-character alphabetical order, ignoring any letters or words in brackets.

Abbreviations used in advertisements

personal

ALA	all letters answered	**PA**	photograph appreciated
ALAWP	all letters answered with photograph	**SOH**	sense of humour
		TDH	tall, dark and handsome
ARA	all replies answered	**TLEH**	true love and everlasting happiness
GL	good-looking		
GSOH	good sense of humour	**VGL**	very good-looking
n/m	not married	**VGSOH**	very good sense of humour
NS	nonsmoker		
n/s	nonsmoker	**VYAH**	very young at heart
NSP	nonsmoker preferred	**WLTM**	would like to meet
NTW	no time wasters	**YAH**	young at heart
OHAC	own house and car		

for cars

a/b	airbag(s)	**FAR**	front arm rests
a/con.	air conditioning	**FSH**	full service history
AT	automatic transmission	**g/box**	gearbox
AW	alloy wheels	**h'back**	hatchback
b/bar	bull-bar	**HFS**	heated front seats
b/kit	body kit	**HLW**	headlamp wipers
C/C	cruise control	**HLWW**	headlamp wash and wipe
CDL	central door locking	**HRW**	heated rear window
ch.	chassis	**HWW**	headlamp wash and wipe
CL	central locking	**IRL**	infrared (remote) locking
c/lock.	central locking	**IS**	independent suspension
COL	centrally operated locking	**l.h.d.**	left-hand drive
EDS	electrically adjusted driver's seat	**LSW**	lights spray and wipe
		LUD	leather-upholstered dashboard
EFW	electric front windows		
EPS	electrically positioned seats	**LW&S**	lights wipe and spray
		MDS	memory-adjusted driver's seat
ESC	electric seat control; etched security code	**mlg.**	mileage
ESR	electric sunroof	**MSR**	manual sunroof
EW	electric windows	**OBC**	on-board computer

OTG	outside temperature gauge	**s/hist.**	service history
p.a.s.	power-assisted steering	**spd**	speed
PS	power steering	**s/r**	sunroof
PW	power windows	**s/roof**	sunroof
r/belt	rear seat belt	**s/susp.**	sports suspension
r.h.d.	right-hand drive	**T&T**	taxed and tested
RHR	rear head restraints	**WW**	walnut wood (trim)

for houses, flats, etc.

balc.	balcony	**lhld**	leasehold
bath.	bathroom	**lnge**	lounge
bed.	bedroom	**LU**	lock-up
bedrm	bedroom	**magnif.**	magnificent
beds	bedrooms	**mais.**	maisonette
bung.	bungalow	**mod.**	modernized
c&c	carpets and curtains	**OCH**	oil central heating
CH	central heating	**o'lkng**	overlooking
c.h.	central heating	**o.p.**	open-plan
clkrm	cloakroom	**ORP**	off-road parking
conserv.	conservatory	**OSCH**	off-peak (or overnight) storage central heating
CW	cavity wall		
det.	detached	**OSP**	off-street parking
d-f	double-fronted	**p/b**	purpose-built
DG	double glazed (or glazing)	**p.p.**	planning permission
DR	dining room	**ptr**	porter
ens.	en suite	**rec.**	reception room
EOT	end of terrace	**recpt.**	reception room
e/s	en suite	**rest.**	restored
FCH	full central heating	**rm**	room
FF	fixtures and fittings; fully fitted	**SD**	semi-detached
		sh.	shower
FGCH	full gas central heating	**shwr**	shower
F/H	freehold	**sit.**	sitting room
fhld	freehold	**sitt.**	sitting room
FTB	first-time buyer	**SOF**	share of freehold
fttgs	fittings	**spac.**	spacious
GCH	gas central heating	**s/pool**	swimming pool
g/f	ground floor	**SSTC**	sold subject to contract
GFCH	gas-fired central heating	**STC**	subject to contract
gge	garage	**t&s**	toilet and shower
K	kitchen	**terrd**	terraced
k&b	kitchen and bathroom	**unmod.**	unmodernized
kit.	kitchen	**util.**	utility room
lge	lounge	**W/W**	wall-to-wall
L/H	leasehold		

for rented accommodation, hotels, etc.

B	bathroom	**BBEM**	bed, breakfast and evening meal
b.	bedroom		
BB	bed and breakfast	**DBB**	dinner, bed and breakfast
BBB	bed, breakfast and bath	**ED**	evening dinner

EM	evening meal	**SD**	spin dryer
ens.	en suite	**sh.**	shower
e/s	en suite	**shwr**	shower
f.	furnished	**SWF**	single white female
FB	full board	**SWM**	single white male
f.b.	full board	**SWPF**	single white professional female
FF	fully furnished		
f/furn	fully furnished	**SWPM**	single white professional male
furn.	furnished		
p.a.x.	per annum, exclusive	**t&s**	toilet and shower
penthse	penthouse	**u/f**	unfurnished
SC	self-contained	**unfurn.**	unfurnished
s/c	self-catering; self-contained	**WM**	washing machine

general

a/nw	as new	**o.v.n.o.**	or very near offer
g.c.	good condition	**P/E**	part exchange
immac.	immaculate	**POA**	price on application
neg.	negotiable	**pt ex.**	part exchange
o.b.o.	or best offer	**PX**	part exchange
OIEO	offers in excess of	**v.g.c.**	very good condition
OIRO	offers in the region of	**WM**	well maintained
o.n.o.	or near(est) offer	**WTP**	willing to pay
o/o	offers over		

Abbreviations used on the Internet

.ac.uk	UK academic institution (in Internet address)
AFK	away from the keyboard (in Internet chat)
ANSI	American National Standards Institute
ARPANET	Advanced Research Projects Agency Network
ASCII	American Standard Code for Information Interchange
.at	Austria (in Internet address)
ATK	at the keyboard (in Internet chat)
ATM	asynchronous transfer mode; at the moment (in Internet chat and e-mail)
.au	Australia (in Internet address)
BBL	be back later (in Internet chat)
BBS	be back soon (in Internet chat); bulletin board system
BCNU	be seein' you (in Internet chat)
.be	Belgium (in Internet address)
BITNET	Because It's Time Network
BRB	be right back (in Internet chat)
BTDT	been there, done that (in Internet chat)
BTW	by the way (in Internet chat and e-mail)
.ca	Canada (in Internet address)
.com	(US) commercial organization (in Internet address)
.co.uk	UK commercial organization (in Internet address)
.de	Germany (in Internet address)
.dk	Denmark (in Internet address)
DL	download

DNS	domain name system
EBCDIC	extended binary-coded decimal-interchange code
EOF	end of file
EOM	end of message
.es	Spain (in Internet address)
FAQ	frequently asked question
FOAF	friend of a friend
FOHCL	falls off her/his chair laughing (in Internet chat)
.fr	France (in Internet address)
FTP	file-transfer protocol
FWIW	for what it's worth (in Internet chat and e-mail)
GIF	graphics interchange format
GMTA	great minds think alike (in Internet chat)
.gov	government (in Internet address)
.gov.uk	UK government (in Internet address)
.gr	Greece (in Internet address)
.hk	Hong Kong (in Internet address)
HTML	hypertext markup language
HTTP	hypertext transfer protocol
IAB	Internet architecture board
IAP	Internet access provider
.ie	Ireland (in Internet address)
IETF	Internet Engineering Task Force
IMHO	in my humble opinion (in Internet chat and e-mail)
IMO	in my opinion (in Internet chat and e-mail)
IOW	in other words (in Internet chat and e-mail)
IP	Internet protocol
IRC	Internet relay chat
IRL	in real life (in Internet chat)
ISDN	Integrated Services Digital Network
ISP	Internet service provider
.it	Italy (in Internet address)
IVL	in virtual life (in Internet chat)
.jp	Japan (in Internet address)
LOL	laughs out loud (in Internet chat)
.lu	Luxembourg (in Internet address)
.mil	US military (in Internet address)
MIME	multipurpose Internet mail extension
.mod.uk	Ministry of Defence (in Internet address)
MUD	multi-user dungeon (or dimension) (in game)
.mx	Mexico (in Internet address)
.net	network (in Internet address)
.nl	Netherlands (in Internet address)
NNTP	net(work) news transfer protocol
.nz	New Zealand (in Internet address)
.org	noncommercial organization (in Internet address)
OTOH	on the other hand (in Internet chat and e-mail)
PC	personal computer
POP	point of presence; post office protocol
PPP	point-to-point protocol
.pt	Portugal (in Internet address)
ROTFL	rolls on the floor laughing (in Internet chat)

.ru	Russia (in Internet address)
.sg	Singapore (in Internet address)
SGML	standard generalized markup language
SLIP	serial line Internet protocol
SMTP	simple mail transfer protocol
TCP	transmission control protocol
TCP/IP	transmission control protocol/Internet protocol
.uk	United Kingdom (in Internet address)
UL	upload
URL	Uniform Resource Locator (address of Internet location)
.us	United States of America (in Internet address)
WAIS	wide-area information service
WAN	wide-area network
WLAN	wireless local area network
WWW	World Wide Web
wysiwyg	what you see is what you get
XML	extensible markup language

Foreign business abbreviations

a.	*accepté* (French: accepted); *akzeptiert* (German: accepted)
A/B	*Aktiebolaget* (Swedish: joint-stock company)
a.B	*auf Bestellung* (German: on order)
abb.	*abbuono* (Italian: allowance, discount)
abl	*abril* (Spanish: April)
a.b.s.	*aux bons soins (de)* (French: care of, c/o) (in postal addresses)
a/c	*ai cuidado (de)* (Portuguese: care of, c/o) (in postal addresses)
a.c.	*à compte* (French: on account); *année courante* (French: this year)
a cta	*a cuenta* (Spanish: on account)
AG	*Aktiengesellschaft* (German: public limited company, plc)
ago.	*agosto* (Italian or Spanish: August)
Akt	*Aktiebolaget* (Swedish: joint-stock company)
Aktb	*Aktiebolaget* (Swedish: joint-stock company)
a.l.	*après livraison* (French: after delivery)
AM	*assurance mutuelle* (French: mutual insurance)
anme	*anonyme* (French: limited liability; of company)
AP	*à protester* (French: to be protested; on bill of exchange)
Apr.	*April* (German: April)
apr.	*aprile* (Italian: April)
A/S	*Aksjeselskap* (Norwegian: limited company, Ltd); *Aktieselskab* (Danish: joint-stock company)
a/s de	*aux soins (de)* (French: care of, c/o) (in postal addresses)
ASP	*accepté sous protêt* (French: accepted under protest)
ASPC	*accepté sous protêt pour compte* (French: accepted under protest for account)
Aug.	*August* (German: August)
av.	*avril* (French: April)
b. à p.	*billets à payer* (French: bills payable)
b. à r.	*billets à recevoir* (French: bills receivable)
Best.	*Bestellung* (German: order)
b.p.f.	*bon pour francs* (French: value in francs)

BV	*Besloten Vennootschap* (Dutch: limited company, Ltd)
Ca	*compagnia* (Italian: company, Co.); *companhia* (Portuguese: company, Co.); *compañía* (Spanish: company, Co.)
CAF	*coût, assurance, fret* (French: cost, insurance, freight, CIF)
c/c	*compte courant* (French: current account); *conto corrente* (Italian: current account)
ccc	*cwmni cyfyngedig cyhoeddus* (Welsh: public limited company, plc)
cedex	*courrier d'entreprise à distribution exceptionnelle* (French: special business postal code)
Cia	*compagnia* (Italian: company, Co.); *companhia* (Portuguese: company, Co.); *compañía* (Spanish: company, Co.)
Cie	*compagnie* (French: company, Co.)
CO	*compte ouvert* (French: open account)
cour.	*courant* (French: current, this month, inst.) (in correspondence)
ct	*courant* (French: current, this month, inst.) (in correspondence)
dbre	*diciembre* (Spanish: December)
déc.	*décembre* (French: December)
Dez.	*Dezember* (German: December)
dic.	*dicembre* (Italian: December)
dim.	*dimanche* (French: Sunday)
d.M	*dieses Monats* (German: this month, inst.)
Do.	*Donnerstag* (German: Thursday)
dom.	*domenica* (Italian: Sunday); *domingo* (Spanish: Sunday)
Dtg	*Dienstag* (German: Tuesday)
EGmbH	*Eingetragene Gesellschaft mit beschränkter Haftung* (German: registered limited company)
eno	*enero* (Spanish: January)
e.o.o.e.	*erreur ou omission exceptée* (French: errors and omissions excepted)
Fa	*Firma* (German: firm, business)
fa	*factura* (Spanish: invoice)
f. à b.	*franco à bord* (French: free on board)
facta	*factura* (Spanish: invoice)
fbro.	*febrero* (Spanish: February)
febb.	*febbraio* (Italian: February)
Febr.	*Februar* (German: February)
fév.	*février* (French: February)
Fr.	*Frau* (German: Mrs)
Fre.	*Freitag* (German: Friday)
fre	*facture* (French: invoice)
Frk.	*Fröken* (Swedish: Miss); *Frøken* (Danish or Norwegian: Miss)
Frl.	*Fräulein* (German: Miss)
genn.	*gennaio* (Italian: January)
Ges.	*Gesellschaft* (German: company, society)
gio.	*giovedì* (Italian: Thursday)
giu.	*giugno* (Italian: June)
GmbH	*Gesellschaft mit beschränkter Haftung* (German: limited company, Ltd)
H/F	*Hlutafjelagid* (Icelandic: limited company, Ltd)
Hr	*Herr* (German: Mr, Sir)
Jan.	*Januar* (German: January)
janv.	*janvier* (French: January)
jeu.	*jeudi* (French: Thursday)
juev.	*jueves* (Spanish: Thursday)

juil.	*juillet* (French: July)
jul.	*julio* (Spanish: July)
jun.	*junio* (Spanish: June)
KG	*Kommanditgesellschaft* (German: limited partnership)
KK	*Kabushiki Kaisha* (Japanese: joint-stock company)
Komp.	*Kompanie* (German: company)
Kto	*Konto* (German: account)
Lda	*Sociedade de responsabilidade limitada* (Portuguese: limited company, Ltd)
liv.	*livraison* (French: delivery)
L/L	*Lutlang* (Norwegian: limited company, Ltd)
l/o	*leur ordre* (French: their order)
l.R	*laufen der Rechnung* (German: current account)
lu.	*luglio* (Italian: July)
lun.	*lundi* (French: Monday); *lunedì* (Italian: Monday); *lunes* (Spanish: Monday)
M	*Monsieur* (French: Mr, Sir)
magg.	*maggio* (Italian: May)
mar.	*mardi* (French: Tuesday); *martedì* (Italian: Tuesday); *martes* (Spanish: Tuesday); *marzo* (Italian or Spanish: March)
mbH	*mit beschränkter Haftung* (German: with limited liability) (of company)
m.c.	*mois courant* (French: current month)
mer.	*mercoledì* (Italian: Wednesday); *mercredi* (French: Wednesday)
miér.	*miércoles* (Spanish: Wednesday)
Mit.	*Mittwoch* (German: Wednesday)
Mlle	*Mademoiselle* (French: Miss)
Mme	*Madame* (French: Mrs)
Mmes	*Mesdames* (French: plural of Mme)
moms	*mervaerdiomsaetningsskat* (Danish: value-added tax); *mervardesomsattningsskatt* (Swedish: value-added tax)
Mon.	*Montag* (German: Monday)
Mpy	*Maatschappij* (Dutch: company, Co.)
nbre	*noviembre* (Spanish: November)
Nov.	*November* (German: November)
nov.	*novembre* (French or Italian: November)
NV	*Naamloze Vennootschap* (Dutch: public limited company, plc)
obre	*octobre* (French: October)
oct.	*octubre* (Spanish: October)
OHG	*Offene Handelsgesellschaft* (German: partnership)
Okt.	*Oktober* (German: October)
ott.	*ottobre* (Italian: October)
p.A	*per Adresse* (German: care of, c/o) (in postal addresses)
p. Adr.	*per Adresse* (German: care of, c/o) (in postal addresses)
SA	*sociedad anónima* (Spanish: (public) limited company, plc or Ltd); *sociedade anónima* (Portuguese: (public) limited company, plc or Ltd); *società anonima* (Italian: (public) limited company, plc or Ltd); *société anonyme* (French: (public) limited company, plc or Ltd)
sab.	*sabato* (Italian: Saturday)
sáb.	*sábado* (Spanish: Saturday)
Sam.	*Samstag* (German: Saturday)
sam.	*samedi* (French: Saturday)
Sarl	*société à responsabilité limitée* (French: limited company, Ltd)
Sas	*società in accomandita semplice* (Italian: limited partnership)

sbre	*septiembre* (Spanish: September)
S en C	*sociedad en comandita* (Spanish: limited partnership); *société en commandite* (French: limited partnership)
S en NC	*société en nom collectif* (French: partnership)
Sept.	*September* (German: September)
sept.	*septembre* (French: September)
sett.	*settembre* (Italian: September)
s.f.	*sans frais* (French: no expenses)
So.	*Sonntag* (German: Sunday)
Soc.	*società* (Italian: company)
SpA	*società per azioni* (Italian: public limited company, plc)
sprl	*société de personnes à responsabilité limitée* (French: limited company, Ltd)
SRC	*sociedad regular colectiva* (Spanish: partnership)
Srl.	*società a responsabilità limitata* (Italian: limited company, Ltd)
Sté	*société* (French: company, Co.)
t.p.	*tout payé* (French: all (expenses) paid)
TVA	*taxe à la valeur ajoutée* (French: value-added tax, VAT)
ven.	*vendredi* (French: Friday); *venerdì* (Italian: Friday)
Ver.	*Verein* (German: association, company)
vier.	*viernes* (Spanish: Friday)
z.H	*zu Händen* (German: for the attention of, f.a.o., care of, c/o) (in postal addresses)

Symbols for chemical elements

Ac	actinium	**Dy**	dysprosium
Ag	silver (from Latin *argentum*)	**Er**	erbium
Al	aluminium	**Es**	einsteinium
Am	americium	**Eu**	europium
Ar	argon	**F**	fluorine
As	arsenic	**Fe**	iron (from Latin *ferrum*)
At	astatine	**Fm**	fermium
Au	gold (from Latin *aurum*)	**Fr**	francium
B	boron	**Ga**	gallium
Ba	barium	**Gd**	gadolinium
Be	beryllium	**Ge**	germanium
Bh	bohrium	**H**	hydrogen
Bi	bismuth	**Ha**	hahnium
Bk	berkelium	**He**	helium
Br	bromine	**Hf**	hafnium
C	carbon	**Hg**	mercury (from Latin *hydrargyrum*)
Ca	calcium		
Cd	cadmium	**Ho**	holmium
Ce	cerium	**Hs**	hassium
Cf	californium	**I**	iodine
Cl	chlorine	**In**	indium
Cm	curium	**Ir**	iridium
Co	cobalt	**K**	potassium (from Latin *kalium*)
Cr	chromium		
Cs	caesium	**Kr**	krypton
Cu	copper (from Latin *cuprum*)		

Ku	kurchatovium (alternative name for rutherfordium)	**Re**	rhenium
		Rf	rutherfordium
La	lanthanum	**Rh**	rhodium
Li	lithium	**Rn**	radon
Lr	lawrencium	**Ru**	ruthenium
Lu	lutetium	**S**	sulphur
Md	mendelevium	**Sb**	antimony (from Latin
Mg	magnesium		*stibium*)
Mn	manganese	**Sc**	scandium
Mo	molybdenum	**Se**	selenium
Mt	meitnerium	**Sg**	seaborgium
N	nitrogen	**Si**	silicon
Na	sodium (from Latin	**Sm**	samarium
	natrium)	**Sn**	tin (from Latin *stannum*)
Nb	niobium	**Sr**	strontium
Nd	neodymium	**Ta**	tantalum
Ne	neon	**Tb**	terbium
Ni	nickel	**Tc**	technetium
No	nobelium	**Te**	tellurium
Np	neptunium	**Th**	thorium
O	oxygen	**Ti**	titanium
Os	osmium	**Tl**	thallium
P	phosphorus	**Tm**	thulium
Pa	protactinium	**U**	uranium
Pb	lead (from Latin *plumbum*)	**V**	vanadium
Pd	palladium	**W**	tungsten (from former
Pm	promethium		name wolfram)
Po	polonium	**Xe**	xenon
Pr	praseodymium	**Y**	yttrium
Pt	platinum	**Yb**	ytterbium
Pu	plutonium	**Zn**	zinc
Ra	radium	**Zr**	zirconium
Rb	rubidium		

UK vehicle registration letters

AA	Bournemouth	**AP**	Brighton
AB	Worcester	**AR**	Chelmsford
AC	Coventry	**AS**	Inverness
AD	Gloucester	**AT**	Hull
AE	Bristol	**AU**	Nottingham
AF	Truro	**AV**	Peterborough
AG	Hull	**AW**	Shrewsbury
AH	Norwich	**AX**	Cardiff
AJ	Middlesbrough	**AY**	Leicester
AK	Sheffield	**AZ**	Belfast
AL	Nottingham	**BA**	Manchester
AM	Swindon	**BB**	Newcastle upon Tyne
AN	Reading	**BC**	Leicester
AO	Carlisle	**BD**	Northampton

BE	Lincoln	**DJ**	Liverpool
BF	Stoke-on-Trent	**DK**	Manchester
BG	Liverpool	**DL**	Portsmouth
BH	Luton	**DM**	Chester
BJ	Ipswich	**DN**	Leeds
BK	Portsmouth	**DO**	Lincoln
BL	Reading	**DP**	Reading
BM	Luton	**DR**	Exeter
BN	Manchester	**DS**	Glasgow
BO	Cardiff	**DT**	Sheffield
BP	Portsmouth	**DU**	Coventry
BR	Newcastle upon Tyne	**DV**	Exeter
BS	Aberdeen	**DW**	Cardiff
BT	Leeds	**DX**	Ipswich
BU	Manchester	**DY**	Brighton
BV	Preston	**DZ**	Antrim
BW	Oxford	**EA**	Dudley
BX	Haverfordwest	**EB**	Peterborough
BY	northwest London	**EC**	Preston
BZ	Down	**ED**	Liverpool
CA	Chester	**EE**	Lincoln
CB	Manchester	**EF**	Middlesbrough
CC	Bangor	**EG**	Peterborough
CD	Brighton	**EH**	Stoke-on-Trent
CE	Peterborough	**EJ**	Haverfordwest
CF	Reading	**EK**	Liverpool
CG	Bournemouth	**EL**	Bournemouth
CH	Nottingham	**EM**	Liverpool
CJ	Gloucester	**EN**	Manchester
CK	Preston	**EO**	Preston
CL	Norwich	**EP**	Swansea
CM	Liverpool	**ER**	Peterborough
CN	Newcastle upon Tyne	**ES**	Dundee
CO	Exeter	**ET**	Sheffield
CP	Huddersfield	**EU**	Bristol
CR	Portsmouth	**EV**	Chelmsford
CS	Glasgow	**EW**	Peterborough
CT	Lincoln	**EX**	Norwich
CU	Newcastle upon Tyne	**EY**	Bangor
CV	Truro	**EZ**	Belfast
CW	Preston	**FA**	Stoke-on-Trent
CX	Huddersfield	**FB**	Bristol
CY	Swansea	**FC**	Oxford
CZ	Belfast	**FD**	Dudley
DA	Birmingham	**FE**	Lincoln
DB	Manchester	**FF**	Bangor
DC	Middlesbrough	**FG**	Brighton
DD	Gloucester	**FH**	Gloucester
DE	Haverfordwest	**FJ**	Exeter
DF	Gloucester	**FK**	Dudley
DG	Gloucester	**FL**	Peterborough
DH	Dudley	**FM**	Chester

FN	Maidstone	**HS**	Glasgow
FO	Gloucester	**HT**	Bristol
FP	Leicester	**HU**	Bristol
FR	Preston	**HV**	central London
FS	Edinburgh	**HW**	Bristol
FT	Newcastle upon Tyne	**HX**	central London
FU	Lincoln	**HY**	Bristol
FV	Preston	**HZ**	Tyrone
FW	Lincoln	**IA**	Antrim
FX	Bournemouth	**IB**	Armagh
FY	Liverpool	**IJ**	Down
FZ	Belfast	**IL**	Fermanagh
GA	Glasgow	**IW**	Londonderry
GB	Glasgow	**J**	Durham
GC	southwest London	**JA**	Manchester
GD	Glasgow	**JB**	Reading
GE	Glasgow	**JC**	Bangor
GF	southwest London	**JD**	central London
GG	Glasgow	**JE**	Peterborough
GH	southwest London	**JF**	Leicester
GJ	southwest London	**JG**	Maidstone
GK	southwest London	**JH**	Reading
GL	Truro	**JI**	Tyrone
GM	Reading	**JJ**	Maidstone
GN	southwest London	**JK**	Brighton
GO	southwest London	**JL**	Lincoln
GP	southwest London	**JM**	Reading
GR	Newcastle upon Tyne	**JN**	Chelmsford
GS	Luton	**JO**	Oxford
GT	southwest London	**JP**	Liverpool
GU	southeast London	**JR**	Newcastle upon Tyne
GV	Ipswich	**JS**	Inverness
GW	southeast London	**JT**	Bournemouth
GX	southeast London	**JU**	Leicester
GY	southeast London	**JV**	Lincoln
GZ	Belfast	**JW**	Birmingham
HA	Dudley	**JX**	Huddersfield
HB	Cardiff	**JY**	Exeter
HC	Brighton	**JZ**	Down
HD	Huddersfield	**K**	Liverpool
HE	Sheffield	**KA**	Liverpool
HF	Liverpool	**KB**	Liverpool
HG	Preston	**KC**	Liverpool
HH	Carlisle	**KD**	Liverpool
HJ	Chelmsford	**KE**	Maidstone
HK	Chelmsford	**KF**	Liverpool
HL	Sheffield	**KG**	Cardiff
HM	central London	**KH**	Hull
HN	Middlesbrough	**KJ**	Maidstone
HO	Bournemouth	**KK**	Maidstone
HP	Coventry	**KL**	Maidstone
HR	Swindon	**KM**	Maidstone

KN	Maidstone	MT	northeast London
KO	Maidstone	MU	northeast London
KP	Maidstone	MV	southeast London
KR	Maidstone	MW	Swindon
KS	Edinburgh	MX	southeast London
KT	Maidstone	MY	southeast London
KU	Sheffield	MZ	Belfast
KV	Coventry	NA	Manchester
KW	Sheffield	NB	Manchester
KX	Luton	NC	Manchester
KY	Sheffield	ND	Manchester
KZ	Antrim	NE	Manchester
LA	northwest London	NF	Manchester
LB	northwest London	NG	Norwich
LC	northwest London	NH	Northampton
LD	northwest London	NJ	Brighton
LE	northwest London	NK	Luton
LF	northwest London	NL	Newcastle upon Tyne
LG	Chester	NM	Luton
LH	northwest London	NN	Nottingham
LJ	Bournemouth	NO	Chelmsford
LK	northwest London	NP	Worcester
LL	northwest London	NR	Leicester
LM	northwest London	NS	Glasgow
LN	northwest London	NT	Shrewsbury
LO	northwest London	NU	Nottingham
LP	northwest London	NV	Northampton
LR	northwest London	NW	Leeds
LS	Edinburgh	NX	Dudley
LT	northwest London	NY	Cardiff
LU	northwest London	NZ	Londonderry
LV	Liverpool	OA	Birmingham
LW	northwest London	OB	Birmingham
LX	northwest London	OC	Birmingham
LY	northwest London	OD	Exeter
LZ	Armagh	OE	Birmingham
MA	Chester	OF	Birmingham
MB	Chester	OG	Birmingham
MC	northeast London	OH	Birmingham
MD	northeast London	OI	Belfast
ME	northeast London	OJ	Birmingham
MF	northeast London	OK	Birmingham
MG	northeast London	OL	Birmingham
MH	northeast London	OM	Birmingham
MJ	Luton	ON	Birmingham
MK	northeast London	OO	Chelmsford
ML	northeast London	OP	Birmingham
MM	northeast London	OR	Portsmouth
MO	Reading	OS	Glasgow
MP	northeast London	OT	Portsmouth
MR	Swindon	OU	Bristol
MS	Edinburgh	OV	Birmingham

OW	Portsmouth	**SA**	Aberdeen
OX	Birmingham	**SB**	Glasgow
OY	northwest London	**SC**	Edinburgh
OZ	Belfast	**SCY**	Truro (Isles of Scilly)
PA	Guildford	**SD**	Glasgow
PB	Guildford	**SE**	Aberdeen
PC	Guildford	**SF**	Edinburgh
PD	Guildford	**SG**	Edinburgh
PE	Guildford	**SH**	Edinburgh
PF	Guildford	**SJ**	Glasgow
PG	Guildford	**SK**	Inverness
PH	Guildford	**SL**	Dundee
PJ	Guildford	**SM**	Carlisle
PK	Guildford	**SN**	Dundee
PL	Guildford	**SO**	Aberdeen
PM	Guildford	**SP**	Dundee
PN	Brighton	**SR**	Dundee
PO	Portsmouth	**SS**	Aberdeen
PP	Luton	**ST**	Inverness
PR	Bournemouth	**SU**	Glasgow
PS	Aberdeen	**SV**	Carlisle
PT	Newcastle upon Tyne	**SW**	Glasgow
PU	Chelmsford	**SX**	Edinburgh
PV	Ipswich	**SZ**	Down
PW	Norwich	**TA**	Exeter
PX	Portsmouth	**TB**	Liverpool
PY	Middlesbrough	**TC**	Bristol
PZ	Belfast	**TD**	Manchester
RA	Nottingham	**TE**	Manchester
RB	Nottingham	**TF**	Reading
RC	Nottingham	**TG**	Cardiff
RD	Reading	**TH**	Swansea
RE	Stoke-on-Trent	**TJ**	Liverpool
RF	Stoke-on-Trent	**TK**	Exeter
RG	Newcastle upon Tyne	**TL**	Lincoln
RH	Hull	**TM**	Luton
RJ	Manchester	**TN**	Newcastle upon Tyne
RK	northwest London	**TO**	Nottingham
RL	Truro	**TP**	Portsmouth
RM	Carlisle	**TR**	Portsmouth
RN	Preston	**TS**	Dundee
RO	Luton	**TT**	Exeter
RP	Northampton	**TU**	Chester
RR	Nottingham	**TV**	Nottingham
RS	Aberdeen	**TW**	Chelmsford
RT	Ipswich	**TX**	Cardiff
RU	Bournemouth	**TY**	Newcastle upon Tyne
RV	Portsmouth	**TZ**	Belfast
RW	Coventry	**UA**	Leeds
RX	Reading	**UB**	Leeds
RY	Leicester	**UC**	central London
RZ	Antrim	**UD**	Oxford

UE	Dudley	**WD**	Dudley
UF	Brighton	**WE**	Sheffield
UG	Leeds	**WF**	Sheffield
UH	Cardiff	**WG**	Sheffield
UI	Londonderry	**WH**	Manchester
UJ	Shrewsbury	**WJ**	Sheffield
UK	Birmingham	**WK**	Coventry
UL	central London	**WL**	Oxford
UM	Leeds	**WM**	Liverpool
UN	Exeter	**WN**	Swansea
UO	Exeter	**WO**	Cardiff
UP	Newcastle upon Tyne	**WP**	Worcester
UR	Luton	**WR**	Leeds
US	Glasgow	**WS**	Bristol
UT	Leicester	**WT**	Leeds
UU	central London	**WU**	Leeds
UV	central London	**WV**	Brighton
UW	central London	**WW**	Leeds
UX	Shrewsbury	**WX**	Leeds
UY	Worcester	**WY**	Leeds
UZ	Belfast	**WZ**	Belfast
VA	Peterborough	**XI**	Belfast
VB	Maidstone	**XZ**	Armagh
VC	Coventry	**YA**	Taunton
VE	Peterborough	**YB**	Taunton
VF	Norwich	**YC**	Taunton
VG	Norwich	**YD**	Taunton
VH	Huddersfield	**YE**	central London
VJ	Gloucester	**YF**	central London
VK	Newcastle upon Tyne	**YG**	Leeds
VL	Lincoln	**YH**	central London
VM	Manchester	**YJ**	Brighton
VN	Middlesbrough	**YK**	central London
VO	Nottingham	**YL**	central London
VP	Birmingham	**YM**	central London
VR	Manchester	**YN**	central London
VS	Luton	**YO**	central London
VT	Stoke-on-Trent	**YP**	central London
VU	Manchester	**YR**	central London
VV	Northampton	**YS**	Glasgow
VW	Chelmsford	**YT**	central London
VX	Chelmsford	**YU**	central London
VY	Leeds	**YV**	central London
VZ	Tyrone	**YW**	central London
WA	Sheffield	**YX**	central London
WB	Sheffield	**YY**	central London
WC	Chelmsford	**YZ**	Londonderry

International vehicle registration marks

A	Austria		
AFG	Afghanistan	EAU	(East Africa) Uganda
AL	Albania	EAZ	(East Africa) Tanzania
AND	Andorra		(formerly Zanzibar)
AUS	Australia	EC	Ecuador
AZ	Azerbaijan	ES	El Salvador
B	Belgium	EST	Estonia
BD	Bangladesh	ET	(Arab Republic of) Egypt
BDS	Barbados	ETH	Ethiopia
BF	Burkina Faso	F	France
BG	Bulgaria	FIN	Finland
BIH	Bosnia-Herzegovina	FJI	Fiji
BOL	Bolivia	FL	Liechtenstein (from
BR	Brazil		German *Fürstentum*
BRN	Bahrain		*Liechtenstein*)
BRU	Brunei	FR	Faeroe Islands
BS	Bahamas	G	Gabon
BUR	Myanmar (from former	GB	Great Britain
	name Burma)	GBA	Alderney
BVI	British Virgin Islands	GBG	Guernsey
BY	Belarus (from alternative	GBJ	Jersey
	name Byelorussia)	GBM	Isle of Man
BZ	Belize	GBZ	Gibraltar
C	Cuba	GCA	Guatemala (Central
CAM	Cameroon		America)
CDN	Canada	GE	Georgia
CH	Switzerland (from French	GH	Ghana
	Confédération Helvétique or	GR	Greece
	Latin *Confederatio*	GUY	Guyana
	Helvetica)	H	Hungary
CI	Côte d'Ivoire (Ivory Coast)	HK	Hong Kong
CL	Sri Lanka (from former	HKJ	(Hashemite Kingdom of)
	name Ceylon)		Jordan
CO	Colombia	HR	Croatia (from Croatian
CR	Costa Rica		*Hrvatska*)
CY	Cyprus	I	Italy
CZ	Czech Republic	IL	Israel
D	Germany (from German	IND	India
	Deutschland)	IR	Iran
DK	Denmark and Greenland	IRL	Ireland
DOM	Dominican Republic	IRQ	Iraq
DY	Benin (from former name	IS	Iceland (from Icelandic
	Dahomey)		*Ísland*)
DZ	Algeria (from Arabic	J	Japan
	Djazïr)	JA	Jamaica
E	Spain (from Spanish	K	Cambodia (from former
	España)		name Kampuchea)
EAK	(East Africa) Kenya	KS	Kyrgyzstan
EAT	(East Africa) Tanzania	KWT	Kuwait

KZ	Kazakhstan	**RIM**	(Islamic Republic of)
L	Luxembourg		Mauritania (from French
LAO	Laos		*République Islamique de*
LAR	Libya (Arab Republic)		*Mauritanie*)
LB	Liberia	**RL**	(Republic of) Lebanon
LS	Lesotho	**RM**	(Republic of) Madagascar
LT	Lithuania	**RMM**	(Republic of) Mali
LV	Latvia	**RN**	(Republic of) Niger
M	Malta	**RO**	Romania
MA	Morocco	**ROK**	(Republic of) Korea
MAL	Malaysia	**ROU**	(Republic of) Uruguay
MC	Monaco	**RP**	(Republic of the)
MD	Moldova		Philippines
MEX	Mexico	**RSM**	(Republic of) San Marino
MK	Macedonia	**RU**	(Republic of) Burundi
MOC	Mozambique (from		(from former name
	Portuguese *Moçambique*)		Urundi)
MS	Mauritius	**RUS**	Russia
MW	Malawi	**RWA**	Rwanda
N	Norway	**S**	Sweden
NA	Netherlands Antilles	**SA**	Saudi Arabia
NAM	Namibia	**SD**	Swaziland
NAU	Nauru	**SGP**	Singapore
NEP	Nepal	**SK**	Slovakia
NGR	Nigeria	**SLO**	Slovenia
NIC	Nicaragua	**SME**	Suriname
NL	Netherlands	**SN**	Senegal
NZ	New Zealand	**SO**	Somalia
P	Portugal	**SUD**	Sudan
PA	Panama	**SY**	Seychelles
PE	Peru	**SYR**	Syria
PK	Pakistan	**T**	Thailand
PL	Poland	**TCH**	Chad (from French *Tchad*)
PNG	Papua New Guinea	**TG**	Togo
PY	Paraguay	**TJ**	Tajikistan
Q	Qatar	**TM**	Turkmenistan
RA	(Republic of) Argentina	**TN**	Tunisia
RB	(Republic of) Botswana	**TR**	Turkey
RC	Taiwan (Republic of	**TT**	Trinidad and Tobago
	China)	**UA**	Ukraine
RCA	Central African Republic	**USA**	United States of America
	(from French *République*	**V**	Vatican City State
	Centrafricaine)	**VN**	Vietnam
RCB	(Republic of) Congo (from	**WAG**	(West Africa) Gambia
	former name	**WAL**	(West Africa) Sierra Leone
	Congo-Brazzaville)	**WD**	(Windward Islands)
RCH	(Republic of) Chile		Dominica
RG	(Republic of) Guinea	**WG**	(Windward Islands)
RH	(Republic of) Haiti		Grenada
RI	(Republic of) Indonesia	**WL**	(Windward Islands)
			St Lucia
		WS	(Western) Samoa

WV	(Windward Islands)	**Z**	Zambia
	St Vincent	**ZA**	South Africa (from
YAR	Yemen (Arab Republic)		Afrikaans *Zuid Afrika*)
YU	Yugoslavia	**ZW**	Zimbabwe
YV	Venezuela		

UK postcodes

AB	Aberdeen	**HA**	Harrow
AL	St Albans	**HD**	Huddersfield
B	Birmingham	**HG**	Harrogate
BA	Bath	**HP**	Hemel Hempstead
BB	Blackburn	**HR**	Hereford
BD	Bradford	**HU**	Hull
BH	Bournemouth	**HX**	Halifax
BL	Bolton	**IG**	Ilford
BN	Brighton	**IM**	Isle of Man
BR	Bromley	**IP**	Ipswich
BS	Bristol	**IV**	Inverness
BT	Belfast	**JE**	Jersey
CA	Carlisle	**KA**	Kilmarnock
CB	Cambridge	**KT**	Kingston-upon-Thames
CF	Cardiff	**KW**	Kirkwall (Orkney)
CH	Chester	**KY**	Kirkcaldy
CM	Chelmsford	**L**	Liverpool
CO	Colchester	**LA**	Lancaster
CR	Croydon	**LD**	Llandrindod Wells
CT	Canterbury	**LE**	Leicester
CV	Coventry	**LL**	Llandudno
CW	Crewe	**LN**	Lincoln
DA	Dartford	**LS**	Leeds
DD	Dundee	**LU**	Luton
DE	Derby	**M**	Manchester
DG	Dumfries	**ME**	Medway
DH	Durham	**MK**	Milton Keynes
DL	Darlington	**ML**	Motherwell
DN	Doncaster	**N**	north London
DT	Dorchester	**NE**	Newcastle upon Tyne
DY	Dudley	**NG**	Nottingham
E	east London	**NN**	Northampton
EC	east central London	**NP**	Newport
EH	Edinburgh	**NR**	Norwich
EN	Enfield	**NW**	northwest London
EX	Exeter	**OL**	Oldham
FK	Falkirk	**OX**	Oxford
FY	Blackpool	**PA**	Paisley
G	Glasgow	**PE**	Peterborough
GL	Gloucester	**PH**	Perth
GU	Guildford	**PL**	Plymouth
GY	Guernsey	**PO**	Portsmouth

PR	Preston	**TD**	Galashiels
RG	Reading	**TF**	Telford
RH	Redhill	**TN**	Tonbridge
RM	Romford	**TQ**	Torquay
S	Sheffield	**TR**	Truro
SA	Swansea	**TS**	Cleveland
SE	southeast London	**TW**	Twickenham
SG	Stevenage	**UB**	Uxbridge
SK	Stockport	**W**	west London
SL	Slough	**WA**	Warrington
SM	Sutton (Surrey)	**WC**	west central London
SN	Swindon	**WD**	Watford
SO	Southampton	**WF**	Wakefield
SP	Salisbury	**WN**	Wigan
SR	Sunderland	**WR**	Worcester
SS	Southend-on-Sea	**WS**	Walsall
ST	Stoke-on-Trent	**WV**	Wolverhampton
SW	southwest London	**YO**	York
SY	Shrewsbury	**ZE**	Lerwick
TA	Taunton		

US postcodes (zip codes)

AK	Alaska	**MT**	Montana
AL	Alabama	**NC**	North Carolina
AR	Arkansas	**ND**	North Dakota
AZ	Arizona	**NE**	Nebraska
CA	California	**NH**	New Hampshire
CO	Colorado	**NJ**	New Jersey
CT	Connecticut	**NM**	New Mexico
DC	District of Columbia	**NV**	Nevada
DE	Delaware	**NY**	New York
FL	Florida	**OH**	Ohio
GA	Georgia	**OK**	Oklahoma
HI	Hawaii	**OR**	Oregon
IA	Iowa	**PA**	Pennsylvania
ID	Idaho	**RI**	Rhode Island
IL	Illinois	**SC**	South Carolina
IN	Indiana	**SD**	South Dakota
KS	Kansas	**TN**	Tennessee
KY	Kentucky	**TX**	Texas
LA	Louisiana	**UT**	Utah
MA	Massachusetts	**VA**	Virginia
MD	Maryland	**VT**	Vermont
ME	Maine	**WA**	Washington
MI	Michigan	**WI**	Wisconsin
MN	Minnesota	**WV**	West Virginia
MO	Missouri	**WY**	Wyoming
MS	Mississippi		

A

A [fishing port] Aberdeen; [physics] absolute (temperature); academician; academy; [card games] ace; acre; acreage; adjutant; admiral; [cinema] adult (former film classification); [education] advanced (as in **A level**); air; *Altesse* (French: Highness); [music] alto; amateur; America; American; ammeter (in circuit diagrams); [Bible] Amos; ampere; ampere-turn; analog; [botany] androecium (in floral formula); angstrom; [horticulture] annual; anode; answer; anterior; April; area; armoured; art; arterial road (as in **A27**); article; artillery; assault (as in **A-day**); assistant; associate; athletic; atom(ic) (as in **A-bomb**); atomic weight; August; Australia; Australian; [international vehicle registration] Austria; *avancer* (French: go faster) (on clock or watch regulator); [medicine] blood group; [education] highest grade or mark; managerial or professional (occupational group); [physics] mass number; [music] note of scale; ten (in hexadecimal notation)

A [physics] absorbance; [chemistry] activity; [chemistry] affinity; [mathematics] area

a *année* (French: year); *annus* (Latin: year); are (unit of area); atto- (indicates 10^{-18}, as in **am** = attometre)

a [physics] acceleration; [physics] amplitude

a. about; absent; accepted; [finance] *accepté* (French: accepted) (on bill of exchange); acre; acreage; acting; [grammar] active; actual; address; adjective; advance; advanced; afternoon; age; [finance] *akzeptiert* (German: accepted) (on bill of exchange); [music] alto; amateur; *anno* (Latin: in the year); anonymous; answer; *ante* (Latin: before); anterior; *aqua* (Latin: water); arrive; arriving; [baseball] assist

A0 [paper size] 841 × 1189 mm

A1 [paper size] 594 × 841 mm; in first-class condition

A2 [paper size] 420 × 594 mm; [civil aircraft marking] Botswana

a2 [music] *a due* (Italian: for two (instruments or voices))

A3 [paper size] 297 × 420 mm; [civil aircraft marking] Tonga

A4 [paper size] 210 × 297 mm

A5 [paper size] 148 × 210 mm; [civil aircraft marking] Bhutan

A6 [paper size] 105 × 148 mm; [civil aircraft marking] United Arab Emirates

A7 [paper size] 74 × 105 mm; [civil aircraft marking] Qatar

A8 [paper size] 52 × 74 mm

A9 [paper size] 37 × 52 mm

A9C [civil aircraft marking] Bahrain

A10 [paper size] 26 × 37 mm

A40 [civil aircraft marking] Oman

3A [civil aircraft marking] Monaco

5A [civil aircraft marking] Libya

9A [civil aircraft marking] Croatia

AA [cinema] accompanied by adult (former film classification); achievement age; administrative assistant; advertising agency; Advertising Association; [taxation] age allowance; air attaché; Alcoholics Anonymous; [fishing port] Alloa; American Aviation; [biochemistry] amino acid; Anglers' Association; [military] anti-aircraft; Architectural Association; Army Act; [biochemistry] ascorbic acid; Associate in Accounting; Associate in Agriculture; Associate in Arts; Association of Agriculture; *Astronautica Acta* (journal of IAF); [physics] atomic absorption; [physics] atomic adsorption; Augustinians of the Assumption; Australian Army; author's alteration; Automobile Association; [vehicle registration] Bournemouth

a.a. absolute alcohol; acting appointment; after arrival; [shipping] always afloat; approximate absolute; area administrator; arithmetic average; attendance allowance; author's alteration

AAA [medicine] abdominal aortic aneurysm; [USA] Agricultural Adjustment Act; [USA] Agricultural Adjustment Administration; Allied Artists of America; Amateur Athletic Association; American Accounting Association; American Automobile Association; [biochemistry] amino acid analogue; [military] anti-aircraft artillery; [USA] Army Audit Agency; Association of Average Adjusters; Australian Association of Accountants; Australian Automobile Association; Automobile Association of America

AAAA Amateur Athletic Association of America; American Association of Advertising Agencies; Associated Actors and Artistes of America; Australian Association of Advertising Agencies

AAAC all-aluminium alloy conductor

AAAI American Association for Artificial Intelligence

AAAL American Academy of Arts and Letters

AAAM American Association of Aircraft Manufacturers

AA&QMG Assistant Adjutant and Quartermaster-General

AAAS American Academy of Arts and Sciences; American Academy of Asian Studies; American Association for the Advancement of Science; Associate of the American Antiquarian Society

AAB Aircraft Accident Board; Association of Applied Biologists

AABC American Amateur Baseball Congress

AABL Associated Australian Banks in London

AABM Australian Association of British Manufacturers

AABT American Association of Behavior Therapists

AABW Antarctic Bottom Water

AAC Aeronautical Advisory Council; Agricultural Advisory Council; [US air force] Alaskan Air Command; amateur athletic club; *anno ante Christum* (Latin: in the year before Christ); Army Air Corps; [electronics] automatic amplitude control

AACB [USA] Aeronautics and Astronautics Coordinating Board; Association of African Central Banks

AACC American Association of Clinical Chemists; [aeronautics] area-approach control centre

AACP American Association for Child Psychiatry; Anglo-American Council on Productivity

AACR [bibliography] Anglo-American Cataloguing Rules

AACS Aberdeen-Angus Cattle Society; [USA] Airways and Air Communications Service; [computing] automated-access control system

AAD [medicine] atlantoaxial dislocation

AADC air aide-de-camp; [USA] Army–Air Defense Command

AADFI Association of African Development Finance Institutions

AADS [USA] Army–Air Defense System

AAE American Association of Engineers

AAEC Australian Atomic Energy Commission

AAEE Aircraft and Armament Experimental Establishment

AAeE Associate in Aeronautical Engineering

AAES Association of Agricultural Education Staffs; Australian Army Education Service

AAEW [military] Atlantic airborne early warning

AAF Allied Air Forces; [USA] Army Air Forces

AAFC [military] anti-aircraft fire control

AAFCE Allied Air Forces in Central Europe

AAFIS Army and Air Force Intelligence Staff

AAFNE Allied Air Forces in Northern Europe

AAFSE Allied Air Forces in Southern Europe

AAG Air Adjutant-General; Assistant Adjutant-General; Association of American Geographers

AAgr Associate in Agriculture

AAGS Association of African Geological Surveys

AAHPER American Association for Health, Physical Education, and Recreation

AAIA Associate of the Association of International Accountants; Associate of the Australian Institute of Advertising; Association of American Indian Affairs

AAIB Air Accidents Investigation Branch

AAII Associate of the Australian Insurance Institute

AAIL American Academy and Institute of Arts and Letters

AAL [meteorology] above aerodrome level; Academy of Art and Literature; [USA] Arctic Aeromedical Laboratory; Association of Assistant Librarians

AALA American Association for Laboratory Accreditation

AALD Australian Army Legal Department

AALL American Association of Law Libraries

AAM air-to-air missile; American Association of Microbiology; American Association of Museums; Anti-Apartheid Movement; Association of Assistant Mistresses in Secondary Schools; Australian Air Mission

AAMI [medicine] age-associated memory impairment

AAMW [USA] Association of Advertising Men and Women

AAMWS Australian Army Medical Women's Service

AANA Australian Association of National Advertisers

A&A additions and amendments

A&AEE Aeroplane and Armament Experimental Establishment

a&b assault and battery

A&C addenda and corrigenda

A&E [medicine] accident and emergency (hospital department)

a&h [insurance] accident and health

A&I [USA] Agricultural and Industrial (college)

a&i [insurance] accident and indemnity

A&M [USA] Agricultural and Mechanical

(college); Ancient and Modern (hymn book)

A&N Army and Navy (stores or club)

A&NI Andaman and Nicobar Islands

A&P [commerce] advertising and promotion; [New Zealand] Agricultural and Pastoral (show or association)

A&R artists and recording; artists and repertoire (as in **A&R man**)

a&r assault and robbery

a&s [insurance] accident and sickness

A&SH [military] Argyll and Sutherland Highlanders

A&W alive and well

AANS Australian Army Nursing Service

AAO American Association of Orthodontists; Anglo-Australian Observatory

aaO am angeführten Orte (German: at the place quoted)

AAOC Australian Army Ordnance Corps

AAOM American Academy of Occupational Medicine

AAP affirmative action programme; [US astronautics] Apollo Applications Program; Association of American Publishers; Australian Associated Press (news agency)

AAPA Advertising Agency Production Association; American Association of Port Authorities

AAPB American Association of Pathologists and Bacteriologists

AAPC All African People's Conference

AAPE American Academy of Physical Education

AAPG American Association of Petroleum Geologists

AAPHI Associate of the Association of Public Health Inspectors

AAPM American Association of Physicists in Medicine

AAPS American Association for the Promotion of Science

AAPSO Afro-Asian People's Solidarity Organization

AAPSS American Academy of Political and Social Science

AAPSW Associate of the Association of Psychiatric Social Workers

AAPT American Association of Physics Teachers

AAR Association of American Railroads

a.a.r. after action report; [insurance]

against all risks; aircraft accident record; aircraft accident report; average annual rainfall

AARP American Association of Retired Persons

AAS *Academiae Americanae Socius* (Latin: Fellow of the American Academy (of Arts and Sciences)); *Acta Apostolicae Sedis* (Latin: Acts of the Apostolic See) (publication of Roman Catholic Church); American Academy of Sciences; American Antiquarian Society; American Astronautical Society; American Astronomical Society; Andersen air sampler; Army Air Service; Associate in Applied Science; Association of Architects and Surveyors; Association of Asian Studies; atomic absorption spectrometry; Australian Academy of Science; Auxiliary Ambulance Service

AASA Associate of the Australian Society of Accountants

AASB [aeronautics] aerodynamically air-staged burner; American Association of Small Businesses

AASC Allied Air Support Command; Australian Army Service Corps

AASF Advanced Air Striking Force

AASG Association of American State Geologists

A'asia Australasia

AASM Associated African States and Madagascar (treaty)

AASR Airport and Airways Surveillance Radar

AASS *Americanae Antiquarianae Societatis Socius* (Latin: Associate of the American Antiquarian Society)

AAT [psychology] achievement anxiety test; Anglo-Australian Telescope (Siding Spring, Australia); Association of Accounting Technicians; [medicine] asymptomatic autoimmune thyroiditis; Australian Antarctic Territory

AATA Anglo-American Tourist Association

AATNU *Administration de l'assistance technique des Nations Unies* (French: United Nations Technical Assistance Administration)

AATT American Association of Textile Technology

AATTA Arab Association of Tourism and Travel Agents

AATUF All-African Trade Union Federation (replaced by OATUU)

AAU [USA] Amateur Athletic Union; Association of American Universities

AAUN American Association for United Nations; Australian Association for United Nations

AAUP American Association of University Presses; American Association of University Professors

AAUW American Association of University Women

AAV [medicine] adeno-associated virus; assault amphibious vehicle

AAVC Australian Army Veterinary Corps

AAVS American Anti-Vivisection Society

AAWC Australian Advisory War Council

AAZPA American Association of Zoological Parks and Aquariums

AB [UK postcode] Aberdeen; [fishing port] Aberystwyth; able-bodied seaman; advisory board; air board; airborne; [US air force] Airman Basic; Alberta; *Alliance balkanique* (French: Balkan Alliance); ammonia for bees (used to treat stings); antiballistic (missile); [medicine] asthmatic bronchitis; [baseball] at bat; [USA] Bachelor of Arts (from Latin *Artium Baccalaureus*); [medicine] blood group; [vehicle registration] Worcester

A/B [commerce] *Aktiebolaget* (Swedish: joint-stock company)

Ab antibody

a.B [commerce] *auf Bestellung* (German: on order)

a/b airbag(s) (in car advertisement); airborne

ab. about; abridgment

a.b. anchor bolt; [baseball] at bat

ABA Amateur Boxing Association; American Badminton Association; American Bankers' Association; American Bar Association; American Basketball Association (became part of NBA); American Book Award; American Booksellers Association; Antiquarian Booksellers Association; Associate in Business Administration; Association of British Archaeologists; Australian Bankers' Association

ABAA Antiquarian Booksellers Association of America

ABAC Association of British Aero Clubs and Centres

ABB [accounting] activity-based budgeting

Abb. Abbess; Abbey; Abbot

abb. abbey; [commerce] *abbuono* (Italian: allowance, discount)

ABBA Amateur Basketball Association; American Board of Bio-Analysis

abbr. abbreviated; abbreviation

abbrev. abbreviated; abbreviation

ABC [accounting] activity-based costing (as in **ABC method**); Advance Booking Charter (airline ticket); advanced biomedical capsule; Aerated Bread Company; air bridge to Canada; [medicine] airway, breathing, circulation (in first aid); America–Britain–Canada; American book-prices current; American Broadcasting Companies; analysis of benefits and costs; animal birth control; Arab Banking Corporation; Argentina–Brazil–Chile; Aruba, Bonaire, Curaçao (group of islands); Associated British Cinemas; [computing] Atanasoff–Berry computer; atomic, biological, and chemical (weapons or warfare); Audit Bureau of Circulation; Australian Broadcasting Corporation; [computing] automatic binary computer; automatic brake control

ABCA American Business Communication Association; Army Bureau of Current Affairs

ABCB Association of Birmingham Clearing Banks

ABCC Association of British Chambers of Commerce; Association of British Correspondence Colleges

ABCD [military] American, British, Chinese, Dutch (in World War II); atomic, biological and chemical protection and damage control

ABCFM American Board of Commissioners for Foreign Missions

ABCM Associate of the Bandsmen's College of Music

ABD [US military] advanced base depot; all but dissertation (of higher degree candidate); average body dose (of radiation)

abd abdicated; abridged

abd. abdicate; abdomen; abdominal

ABDA [military] American, British, Dutch, Australian (in World War II)

abdom. abdomen; abdominal

ABDP Association of British Directory Publishers

ABE acetone–butanol–ethanol (solvent)

ABEd [USA] Bachelor of Arts in Education

Aber. Aberdeen; Aberdonian

ABERCOR Associated Banks of Europe Corporation

ABF [informal] absolute bloody final (drink); Actors' Benevolent Fund; Associated British Foods

Abf. *Abfahrt* (German: departure)

ABFD Association of British Factors and Discounters

ABFM American Board of Foreign Missions

ABGB [Austria] *Allgemeines Bürgerliches Gesetzbuch* (German: General Civil Code)

abgk. *abgekürzt* (German: abbreviated)

ABGWIU [USA] Aluminum Brick and Glass Workers International Union

ABH actual bodily harm

Abh. *Abhandlungen* (German: transactions, treatises)

ABI [computing] application binary interface; Associate of the Institute of Book-keepers; Association of British Insurers

ABIA Association of British Introduction Agencies

ab init. *ab initio* (Latin: from the beginning)

ABINZ Associate of the Bankers' Institute of New Zealand

ABL atmospheric boundary layer

abl *abril* (Spanish: April)

abl. [grammar] ablative

ABLA American Business Law Association

ablat. [grammar] ablative

ABLJ adjustable buoyancy lifejacket

ABLS Association of British Library Schools; [USA] Bachelor of Arts in Library Science

ABM antiballistic missile; Associate in Business Management; Australian Board of Missions; automatic batch mix

ABMA Army Ballistic Missile Agency

ABMAC Association of British Manufacturers of Agricultural Chemicals

ABMEWS antiballistic missile early warning system

ABMPM Association of British Manufacturers of Printers' Machinery

ABMT [medicine] autologous bone marrow transplant(ation)

ABN [chemistry] acid–base–neutral; Anti-Bolshevik Bloc of Nations

Abn Aberdeen

abn airborne

ABNE Association for the Benefit of Non-contract Employees

ABO American Board of Ophthalmology; American Board of Orthodontics; American Board of Otolaryngology; [medicine] blood group system

ABOF Association of British Organic Fertilizers

ABOG American Board of Obstetrics and Gynecology

A-bomb atomic bomb

ABOS American Board of Oral Surgery; American Board of Orthopedic Surgery

ABP American Board of Pathology; American Board of Pediatrics; American Board of Peridontology; American Board of Prosthodontics; [biochemistry] androgen-binding protein; [medicine] arterial blood pressure; Associated Book Publishers; Associated British Ports

Abp Archbishop

ABPA Australian Book Publishers' Association

ABPC American Book Publishers' Council; Associated British Picture Corporation

ABPI Association of the British Pharmaceutical Industry

ABPN American Board of Psychiatry and Neurology; Association of British Paediatric Nurses

ABPO Advanced Base Personnel Officer

ABPS American Board of Plastic Surgery

ABPVM Association of British Plywood and Veneer Manufacturers

ABR American Board of Radiology; [medicine] auditory brainstem recording

abr. abridge; abridged; abridgment

ABRACADABRA Abbreviations and Related Acronyms Associated with Defense, Astronautics, Business and Radio-electronics (US publication)

ABRC Advisory Board for the Research Councils

ABRES advanced ballistic re-entry system

ABRO Animal Breeding Research Organization; Army in Burma Reserve of Officers

ABRS Association of British Riding Schools

ABRSM Associated Board of the Royal Schools of Music

ABRV [military] advanced ballistic re-entry vehicle

ABS acrylonitrile–butadiene–styrene (type of plastic); [chemistry] alkyl benzene sulphonate; American Bible Society; American Board of Surgery; American Bureau of Shipping; *Antiblockiersystem* (German: antilocking system (for brakes)); antilock braking system; Architects' Benevolent Society; Association of Broadcasting Staff; Australian Bureau of Statistics

abs. absence; absent; absolute; absolutely; absorbent; abstract

a.b.s. *aux bons soins* (*de*) (French: care of, c/o) (in postal addresses)

ABSA Association of Business Sponsorship of the Arts

abse. re. [law] *absente reo* (Latin: the defendant being absent)

abs. feb. [medicine] *absente febre* (Latin: when there is no fever)

ABSIE American Broadcasting Station in Europe (in World War II)

ABSM Associate of the Birmingham School of Music

ABSM(TTD) Associate of the Birmingham School of Music (Teacher's Training Diploma)

absol. absolute; absolutely

abs. re. [law] *absente reo* (Latin: the defendant being absent)

abstr. abstract; abstracted

abs. visc. absolute viscosity

ABSW Association of British Science Writers

ABT advanced backplane technology; [computing] advanced bi-CMOS technology; Association of Building Technicians

Abt. *Abteilung* (German: division, part)

abt about

ABTA Allied Brewery Traders' Association; Association of British Travel Agents Limited; Australian British Trade Association

ABTAC Australian Book Trade Advisory Committee

ABTUC All-Burma Trade Union Congress

ABU Asian Broadcasting Union; Assembly of the Baptist Union

A-BU Anglo-Belgian Union

abv. above

ABWR [nuclear technology] advanced boiling-water reactor

AC [chemistry] activated carbon; [chemistry] activated charcoal; [medicine] acute cholecystitis; adult contemporary (music); [computing] advanced CMOS; aero club; Air Command; Air Commodore; air conditioning; air control; Air Corps; Air Council; aircraftman; Alcohol Concern; Alpine Club; [physics] alternating current; Ambulance Corps; analogue computer; analytical chemist; angular correlation; annual conference; *ante Christum* (Latin: before Christ, BC); [law] Appeal Case; appeal court; *appellation contrôlée* (French: name controlled) (wine classification); Army Corps; Army Council; artillery college; Arts Council; Assistant Commissioner; athletic club; Atlantic Charter; *Auditor Camerae* (Latin: Auditor of the Papal Treasury); *Azione Cattolica* (Italian: Catholic Action) (social organization); Companion of the Order of Australia; [vehicle registration] Coventry

A/C account; account current; air conditioning; aircraft; aircraftman

Ac [chemistry] acetyl; [chemical element] actinium

Ac [meteorology] altocumulus

aC *antes de Cristo* (Portuguese: before Christ, BC); *avanti Cristo* (Italian: before Christ, BC)

a/c account; account current; *ai cuidado (de)* (Portuguese: care of, c/o) (in postal addresses)

ac. acre; activity

a.c. *a capo* (Italian: new line); *à compte* (French: on account); advisory committee; [physics] alternating current; *année courante* (French: this year); *anno corrente* (Latin: this year); [medicine] *ante cibum* (Latin: before meals) (in prescriptions); [finance] *assegno circolare* (Italian: banker's draft); author's correction

ACA [telecommunications] adjacent-channel attenuation; advanced combat aircraft; Agricultural Cooperative Association; American Camping Association; American Canoe Association; Anglers' Cooperative Association; Arts Council of America; Associate of the Institute of Chartered Accountants; Association of Consulting Actuaries; Australian Consumers' Association; Australian Council for Aeronautics

ACAA Agricultural Conservation and Adjustment Administration; American Coal Ash Association

ACAB [USA] Army Contract Adjustment Board

Acad. Academy

acad. academic; academy

Acad. fran. *Académie française* (French: French academy)

ACADI *Association des cadres dirigeants de l'industrie* (French: Association of Industrial Executives)

ACAE Advisory Council for Adult and Continuing Education

ACAL Advanced Computer Architecture Laboratory

AC&U [USA] Association of Colleges and Universities

ACAO Assistant County Advisory Officer

Acap. Acapulco

ACARD Advisory Council for Applied Research and Development

ACAS Advisory, Conciliation, and Arbitration Service; Assistant Chief of Air Staff

ACB *Association canadienne des bibliothèques* (French: Canadian Library Association)

ACBG [medicine] aorto-coronary bypass graft

ACBS Accrediting Commission for Business Schools

ACBSI Associate of the Chartered Building Societies Institute

ACBWS automatic chemical–biological warning system

ACC [New Zealand] Accident Compensation Corporation; [computing] accumulator; [medicine] acute cardiovascular collapse; Administrative Coordination Committee; advanced communication course; Agricultural Credit Corporation Limited; Anglican Consultative Council; annual capital charge; army cadet college; Army Catering Corps; Assistant County Commissioner (in Scouting); Associated Chemical Companies; Association of County Councils

acc. accelerate; acceleration; accent; [commerce] acceptance; [commerce] accepted; [music] accompanied (by); [music] accompaniment; according (to); account; accountant; [grammar] accusative

ACCA Aeronautical Chamber of Commerce of America; Agricultural Central Cooperative Association; Associate of the Chartered Association of Certified Accountants; Association of Certified and Corporate Accountants

ACCC Association of Canadian Community Colleges

ACCD American Coalition of Citizens with Disabilities

acce [commerce] acceptance

accel. [music] *accelerando* (Italian: with increasing speed)

access. accessory

ACCHAN Allied Command Channel (in NATO)

ACCM Advisory Council for the Church's Ministry

ACCO Association of Child Care Officers

accom. accommodation

accomp. accompanied; accompaniment; accompany

ACCP American College of Chest Physicians

accred. accredited

ACCS Associate of the Corporation of Secretaries (formerly Associate of the Corporation of Certified Secretaries)

ACCT Association of Cinematograph, Television and Allied Technicians

acct account; accountant

acct. accounting

acctd accented

accum. accumulative

accus. [grammar] accusative

accy accountancy; accuracy

ACD [medicine] acid citrate dextrose (as in

ACD solution); [medicine] acquired cystic disease of the kidney

acd accord

ACDA Advisory Committee on Distinction Awards; [USA] Arms Control and Disarmament Agency; Aviation Combat Development Agency

ACDAS automatic control and data acquisition system

AC/DC [physics] alternating current/direct current; [informal] bisexual

ACDCM Archbishop of Canterbury's Diploma in Church Music

ACdre Air Commodore

ACDS Assistant Chief of Defence Staff

acdt accident

ACE [astronomy] Advanced Composition Explorer; advanced computing environment; [engineering] advanced cooled engine; Advisory Centre for Education; [medicine] alcohol–chloroform–ether (anaesthetic); Allied Command Europe; American Council on Education; [medicine] angiotensin-converting enzyme (as in **ACE inhibitor**); [USA] Army Corps of Engineers; Association for the Conservation of Energy; Association of Conference Executives; Association of Consulting Engineers; Association of Cultural Exchange; Australian College of Education; [computing] Automatic Computing Engine

ACEA Action Committee for European Aerospace

ACEd. Associate in Commercial Education

ACEEE American Council for an Energy-Efficient Economy

ACEF Australian Council of Employers' Federations

ACER Australian Council for Educational Research

ACERT Advisory Council for the Education of Romanies and other Travellers

ACET Advisory Committee on Electronics and Telecommunications; [medicine] Aids care, education and treatment

acet. acetate; acetone

ACEWEX Allied Command Europe Weather Exchange

ACF *Académie Canadienne Française* (French: French Canadian Academy); [South Africa] Active Citizen Force; Army

Cadet Force; *Automobile Club de France* (French: Automobile Club of France)

ACFA Army Cadet Force Association

ACFAS *Association canadienne-française pour l'avancement des sciences* (French: French-Canadian Association for the Advancement of Science)

ACFHE Association of Colleges of Further and Higher Education

ACFI Associate of the Clothing and Footwear Institute

acft aircraft

ACG *An Comunn Gaidhealach* (Gaelic: The Gaelic Society); Assistant Chaplain-General; automatic control gear

ACGB Arts Council of Great Britain

ACGBI Automobile Club of Great Britain and Ireland

ACGI Associate of the City and Guilds (of London) Institute

ACGME Accreditation Council for Graduate Medical Education

ACGS Assistant Chief of the General Staff

ACH [banking] automated clearing house

ach [building] air changes per hour

ACHR American Convention on Human Rights

AChS Associate of the Society of Chiropodists

ACI *Alliance coopérative internationale* (French: International Cooperative Alliance); Alloy Castings Institute; American Concrete Institute; army council instruction; Associate of the Institute of Commerce; *Automobile Club d'Italia* (Italian: Automobile Club of Italy)

ACIA Associate of the Corporation of Insurance Agents; [computing] asynchronous communications interface adapter

ACIAA Australian Commercial and Industrial Artists' Association

ACIArb Associate of the Chartered Institute of Arbitrators

ACIB Associate of the Chartered Institute of Bankers; Associate of the Corporation of Insurance Brokers

ACIC [USA] Aeronautical Charting and Information Center

ACIGS Assistant Chief of the Imperial General Staff

ACII Associate of the Chartered Insurance Institute

ACILA Associate of the Chartered Institute of Loss Adjusters

ACINF [USA] Advisory Committee on Irradiated and Novel Foods

ACIOPJF *Association catholique internationale des œuvres de protection de la jeune fille* (French: International Catholic Girls' Society)

ACIS American Committee for Irish Studies; Associate of the Institute of Chartered Secretaries and Administrators (formerly Associate of the Chartered Institute of Secretaries)

ACIT Associate of the Chartered Institute of Transport

ACJP airways corporations joint pensions

ACK [telecommunications] acknowledgment

ack. acknowledge; acknowledgment

ack-ack anti-aircraft (from former phonetic alphabet for AA)

ackgt acknowledgment

ackt acknowledgment

ACL [computing] access control list; action-centred leadership; Analytical Chemistry Laboratory; Atlas Computer Laboratory

ACLA Anti-Communist League of America

ACLANT Allied Command Atlantic

ACLC Air Cadet League of Canada

ACLP Association of Contact Lens Practitioners

ACLS American Council of Learned Societies

ACLS automatic carrier landing system

ACLU American Civil Liberties Union; American College of Life Underwriters

ACM Air Chief Marshal; air combat manœuvring; American Campaign Medal; asbestos-containing material; [USA] Assistant Chief of Mission; Association for Computing Machinery; authorized controlled material

ACMA Agricultural Cooperative Managers' Association; Associate of the Chartered Institute of Management Accountants

ACMC Association of Canadian Medical Colleges

ACME [USA] Advisory Council on Medical Education; [USA] Association of Consulting Management Engineers

ACMET Advisory Council on Middle East Trade

ACMF [USA] Air Corps Medical Forces; Allied Central Mediterranean Forces; Australian Commonwealth Military Forces

ACMM Associate of the Conservatorium of Music, Melbourne

ACMP Advisory Committee on Marine Pollution; Assistant Commissioner of the Metropolitan Police

acmp. accompany

ACMRR Advisory Committee on Marine Resources Research

ACMT American College of Medical Technologies

ACN [chemistry] alkane carbon number; American College of Neuropsychiatrists; *ante Christum natum* (Latin: before the birth of Christ)

a.c.n. all concerned notified

ACNA [USA] Advisory Council on Naval Affairs; Arctic Institute of North America

ACNS Assistant Chief of Naval Staff; Associated Correspondents News Service

ACNY Advertising Club of New York

ACO Admiralty Compass Observatory; Association of Children's Officers

AC of S Assistant Chief of Staff

ac.o.g. aircraft on ground

ACom Associate in Commerce

AComm Associate in Commerce

a/con. air conditioning (in car advertisement)

ACOPS Advisory Commission on Pollution of the Sea

ACOR American Center for Oriental Research

ACORD Advisory Council on Research and Development

ACORN *A Classification of Residential Neighbourhoods* (directory); [computing] associative content retrieval network; [computing] automatic checkout and recording network

ACOS Advisory Committee on Safety; American College of Osteopathic Surgeons; Assistant Chief of Staff

ACOST Advisory Council on Science and Technology

ACP advanced computer program; advanced computer project; African, Caribbean and Pacific (countries);

American College of Pharmacists; American College of Physicians; Associate of the College of Preceptors; Association of Circus Proprietors of Great Britain; Association of Clinical Pathologists; *Automóvel Clube de Portugal* (Portuguese: Automobile Club of Portugal)

ACPM American Congress of Physical Medicine and Rehabilitation

ACPO Association of Chief Police Officers

acpt. [commerce] acceptance

ACPU auxiliary computer power unit

acq. acquire; acquisition; acquittal

ACR Admiral Commanding Reserves; advanced capabilities radar; aircraft control room; American College in Rome; [aeronautics] approach control radar; Association of College Registrars; audio cassette recorder

ACRB *Aero-Club royal de Belgique* (French: Royal Belgian Aero Club)

acrd accrued

ACRE Action with Communities in Rural England; Advisory Committee on Releases to the Environment; automatic climatological recording equipment

ACRF Advanced Computing Research Facility

acrg. acreage

ACRI [USA] Air-Conditioning and Refrigeration Institute

ACRL [USA] Association of College and Research Libraries

acron. acronym

ACRR American Council on Race Relations

ACRS [taxation] accelerated cost recovery system; Advisory Committee on Reactor Safeguards

ACS [aeronautics] active control system; Admiral Commanding Submarines; Admiralty computing service; advanced communications system; air-conditioning system; airport catering services; [aeronautics] altitude control system; American Cancer Society; American Ceramic Society; American Chemical Society; American College of Surgeons; assembly control system; Associate in Commercial Science; Association of Caribbean States; Association of Commonwealth Students; Australian

Computer Society; [finance] automated confirmation service; [computing] automated control system

ACSA Allied Communications Security Agency; Associate of the Institute of Chartered Secretaries and Administrators

ACSE [Australia] Association of Consulting Structural Engineers

ACSEA Allied Command South East Asia

ACSL [computing] advanced continuous simulation language; assistant Cub Scout leader

ACSM American Congress on Surveying and Mapping

ACSN Association of Collegiate Schools of Nursing

ACSPA Australian Council of Salaried and Professional Associations

a/cs pay. accounts payable

a/cs rec. accounts receivable

ACSS [printing] automated colour separation system

ACSTT Advisory Committee on the Supply and Training of Teachers

ACT activated-complex theory; [aeronautics] active control technology; advance corporation tax; [computing] advanced CMOS with TTL inputs; advanced coal technology; Advisory Council on Technology; Agricultural Central Trading Limited; Air Council for Training; American College Test; [computing] analogical circuit technique; Associate of the College of Technology; Associated Container Transportation; Association of Corporate Treasurers; Australian Capital Territory; Australian College of Theology

act. acting; [grammar] active; activities; actor; actual; actuary

a cta *a cuenta* (Spanish: on account)

ACTC Art Class Teacher's Certificate

actg acting

ACTH [biochemistry] adrenocorticotrophic hormone

ACTO Advisory Council on the Treatment of Offenders

ACTP American College Testing Program

ACTS [USA] Acoustic Control and Telemetry System; Action of Churches Together in Scotland; Australian Catholic Truth Society

ACTT Association of Cinematograph, Television and Allied Technicians (became part of BECTU)

ACTU Australian Council of Trade Unions

ACTWU [USA] Amalgamated Clothing and Textile Workers Union

ACU Actors' Church Union; American Congregational Union; Asian Clearing Union; Association of Commonwealth Universities; Auto-Cycle Union; [computing] automatic calling unit

ACUA Association of Cambridge University Assistants

ACUE American Committee of United Europe

.ac.uk UK academic institution (in Internet address)

ACUS Atlantic Council of the United States

ACV actual cash value; air-cushion vehicle; Associate of the College of Violinists; Associated Commercial Vehicles

ACW agricultural crop waste; Air Command and Warning; Air Control and Warning; aircraftwoman; [physics] alternating continuous wave; automatic car wash

ACWS aircraft control and warning system

ACWW Associated Country Women of the World

ACY average crop yield

AD [insurance] accidental damage; *Acción Democrática* (Spanish: Democratic Action Party) (in Venezuela); accumulated dose (of radiation); [military] active duty; administrative department; [military] air defence; air dried; [currency] Algerian dinar; [medicine] Alzheimer's disease; *anno Domini* (Latin: in the year of the Lord, AD) (in dates); [fishing port] Ardrossan; armament depot; art director; assembly district; assistant director; Australian Democrat (or Democrats); autograph document; average deviation; Dame of the Order of Australia; [vehicle registration] Gloucester

A-D Albrecht Dürer (German artist)

A/D aerodrome; after date; [computing] analog–digital (conversion or converter)

a.D *ausser Dienst* (German: retired, on half pay)

ad [US short form] advantage (in tennis); [short form] advertisement

ad. adapt; adaptation; adapted; adapter; [medicine] *addantur* (Latin: let there be added) (in prescriptions); [medicine] *adde* (Latin: add) (in prescriptions); [grammar] adverb; advertisement

.ad Andorra (in Internet address)

a.d. after date; *ante diem* (Latin: before the day); autograph document

ADA [medicine] adenosine deaminase (as in **ADA deficiency**); Agricultural Development Association; [USA] Air Defense Agency; Aluminium Development Association; American Dental Association; American Diabetes Association; Americans for Democratic Action; Association of Drainage Authorities; Atomic Development Authority; Australian Dental Association

ADAA Art Dealers Association of America

ADAD [USA] automatic telephone dialing – announcing device

adag. [music] *adagio* (Italian: slowly)

adap. adapted

Adapt Access for Disabled People to Arts Today

ADAPTS [USA] Air-Deliverable Antipollution Transfer System (in Coast Guard)

ADAS Agricultural Development and Advisory Service; [computing] automatic data acquisition system; [computing] auxiliary data annotation set

ADAWS [military] action data automation and weapons systems; Assistant Director of Army Welfare Services

A-day assault day

ADB accidental death benefit; African Development Bank; Asian Development Bank; Associate of the Drama Board; [USA] Bachelor of Domestic Arts

ADC advanced developing country (or countries); [telecommunications] advice of duration and charge; aerodrome control; [Jamaica] Agricultural Development Corporation; aide-de-camp; [medicine] Aids dementia complex; Aid to Dependent Children; [USA] Air Defense Command; amateur dramatic club; [computing] analog–digital converter; apparent diffusion coefficient; Art Directors' Club; Assistant District Com-

missioner (in Scouting); Association of District Councils; [computing] automated distribution control; automatic digital calculator

ADCC [USA] Air Defense Control Center

ADCCP [computing] advanced data communication control procedure

ADCI American Die Casting Institute

ADCM Archbishop of Canterbury's Diploma in Church Music

ADCONSEN [USA] advice and consent of the Senate

ADCP personal aide-de-camp (to the monarch)

ADCT Art Directors' Club, Toronto

ADD [aeronautics] airstream direction detector; [medicine] attention deficit disorder

add. [medicine] *addantur* (Latin: let there be added) (in prescriptions); [medicine] *adde* (Latin: add) (in prescriptions); addenda; addendum; addition; additional; address; addressed

ADDC [USA] Air Defense Direction Center

ADDF Abu Dhabi Defence Force

addl additional

addn addition

addnl additional

addsd addressed

ADEF *Agence d'évaluation financière* (French: financial rating agency)

ad effect. [medicine] *ad effectum* (Latin: until effective) (in prescriptions)

ADEME Assistant Director, Electrical and Mechanical Engineering

ad eund. *ad eundem gradum* (Latin: to the same degree)

ADF [Australia] approved deposit fund; Asian Development Fund; Australian Defence Force; [navigation] automatic direction finder

a.d.f. after deducting freight

ad fin. *ad finem* (Latin: at the end, near the end)

ADFManc Art and Design Fellow, Manchester

ADFW Assistant Director of Fortifications and Works

ADG Assistant Director-General

ADGB Air Defence of Great Britain

ADGMS Assistant Director-General of Medical Services

ad gr. acid. [medicine] *ad gratam acidit-atem* (Latin: to an agreeable acidity) (in prescriptions)

ad gr. gust. [medicine] *ad gratam gustum* (Latin: to an agreeable taste) (in prescriptions)

ADH [biochemistry] antidiuretic hormone; Assistant Director of Hygiene; Association of Dental Hospitals

ADHD [medicine] attention deficit hyperactivity disorder

ad h.l. *ad hunc locum* (Latin: at this place, on this passage)

ADI [medicine] acceptable daily intake (of toxic substance); approved driving instructor

ad inf. *ad infinitum* (Latin: to infinity)

ad init. *ad initium* (Latin: at the beginning)

ad int. *ad interim* (Latin: in the meantime)

ADIZ [USA] air defense identification zone

ADJ [meteorology] adjacent

adj. adjacent; [grammar] adjective; adjoining; [mathematics] adjoint; adjourned; adjudged; adjunct; [insurance, banking] adjustment; adjutant

AdjA [USA] Adjunct in Arts

ADJAG Assistant Deputy Judge Advocate-General

Adj-Gen Adjutant-General

adjt adjutant

Adjt-Gen Adjutant-General

ADL [electronics] acoustic delay line; [medicine] activities of daily living (or life); [computing] ADA design language; [USA] Anti-Defamation League (of B'nai B'rith); Assistant Director of Labour

ad lib. *ad libitum* (Latin: according to pleasure, freely)

ad loc. *ad locum* (Latin: at the place, on this passage)

ADLP Australian Democratic Labor Party

ADM Advanced Diploma in Midwifery; annual delegate meeting; Association of Domestic Management; atomic demolition munitions; average daily membership

Adm. Admiral; Admiralty

adm. administration; administrative; administrator; admission; admitted

ADMA American Drug Manufacturers' Association; [USA] Aviation Distributors' and Manufacturers' Association

admin [short form] administration

admin. administration; administrative; administrator

Adml Admiral

ADMO(CA) Assistant Director of the Meteorological Office (Civil Aviation)

ADMOS [computing] automatic device for mechanical order selection

admov. [medicine] *admoveatur* (Latin: let it be applied) (in prescriptions)

Adm. Rev. *Admodum Reverendus* (Latin: Very Reverend)

ADMS Assistant Director of Medical Services

ADMT Association of Dental Manufacturers and Traders of the United Kingdom

admx administratrix

ADN *Allgemeiner deutscher Nachrichtendienst* (German news agency)

ADNA Assistant Director of Naval Accounts

ADNC Assistant Director of Naval Construction

ad neut. [medicine] *ad neutralizandum* (Latin: until neutral)

ADNI Assistant Director of Naval Intelligence

ADNOC Abu Dhabi National Oil Company

ADNS Assistant Director of Nursing Services

ADO [USA] advanced development objective; air defence officer; assistant district officer; Association of Dispensing Opticians; automotive diesel oil

ADOF Assistant Director of Ordnance Factories

ADOS Assistant Director of Ordnance Services

ADP [biochemistry] adenosine diphosphate; air defence position; [physics] area density of particles; Association of Dental Prosthesis; [computing] automatic data processing

ADPA Associate Diploma of Public Administration

ADPCM [computing] adaptive differential pulse code modulation

ADPLAN advanced planning

ADPR Assistant Director of Public Relations

ADPSO Association of Data Processing Service Organizations

ADR accident data recorder; [law] alternative dispute resolution; [stock exchange] American Depository Receipt

ADRA Animal Diseases Research Association (Edinburgh)

ADS [computing] accurately defined systems; advanced dressing station; [USA] air defense sector; American Dialect Society; [engineering] articulated drill string; Astrophysics Data System; [engineering] automatic depressurization system

A.d.S. *Académie des sciences* (French: Academy of Sciences)

a.d.s. autograph document signed

ad s. [law] *ad sectam* (Latin: at the suit of)

ad saec. *ad saeculum* (Latin: to the century)

ADS&T Assistant Director of Supplies and Transport

ad sat. [medicine] *ad saturandum* (Latin: to saturation)

ADSOC [USA] Administrative Support Operations Center

ADSS Association of Directors of Social Services; Australian Defence Scientific Service

ADST [finance] approved deferred share trust

adst. feb. [medicine] *adstante febre* (Latin: when fever is present)

ADT American District Telegraph; Assistant Director of Transport; Atlantic Daylight Time; [electronics] automatic double tracking; average daily traffic

ADTECH advanced decoy technology

ADTS Automated Data and Telecommunications Service

ad us. *ad usum* (Latin: according to the custom)

ad us. ext. [medicine] *ad usum externum* (Latin: for external use) (in prescriptions)

Adv. Advent; Advocate

adv. advance; [grammar] adverb; [grammar] adverbial; *adversus* (Latin: against); advertisement; advertising; advice; advise; adviser; advisory; advocate

ad val. *ad valorem* (Latin: according to value)

advb [grammar] adverb

adven. adventure

adv. pmt advance payment

ADVS Advanced Diploma in Voice Studies; Assistant Director of Veterinary Services

advt advertisement

advv. [grammar] adverbs

ADW air defence warning; Assistant Director of Works

ADWE&M Assistant Director of Works, Electrical and Mechanical

ADX [computing] automatic data exchange; [telecommunications] automatic digital exchange

AE account executive; [physics] acoustic emission; adult education; aeronautical engineer; aeronautical engineering; [taxation] age exemption; *Agence Europe* (news agency); agricultural engineer; agricultural engineering; Air Efficiency Award; *Aktiebolaget Atomenergi* (Swedish: Atomic Energy Corporation); All England; American English; army education; Associate in Education; Associate in Engineering; atomic energy; [photography] autoexposure; [vehicle registration] Bristol; pen-name of George Russell (Irish poet)

ae. [numismatics] *aeneus* (Latin: made of copper); *aetatis* (Latin: at the age of, aged)

.ae United Arab Emirates (in Internet address)

AEA [physics] acoustic emission analysis; [USA] Actors' Equity Association; [engineering] air entraining agent; American Economic Association; [USA] Atomic Energy Act; Atomic Energy Authority

AEAA *Asociación de Escritores y Artistas Americanos* (Spanish: Association of Spanish-American Writers and Artists)

AEAF Allied Expeditionary Air Force

AE&MP Ambassador Extraordinary and Minister Plenipotentiary

AE&P Ambassador Extraordinary and Plenipotentiary

AEAUSA Adult Education Association of the United States of America

AEB Area Electricity Board; Associated Examining Board

AEBP atmospheric equivalent boiling point

AEC [insurance] additional extended cover(age); Agricultural Executive Council; American Express Company; Army Electronics Command; Associated Equipment Company; Association of Education Committees; [USA] Atomic Energy Commission; [South Africa] Atomic Energy Corporation; [USA] Atomic Energy Council; [photography] automatic exposure control

a.e.c. at earliest convenience

AECB [USA] Atomic Energy Control Board

AECCG African Elephant Conservation Coordinating Group

AECI African Explosives and Chemical Industries; Associate of the Institute of Employment Consultants

AECL Atomic Energy of Canada Limited

AED advanced electronics design; Algol Extended for Design (computer programming language); Association of Engineering Distributors; automated engineering design; Doctor of Fine Arts (from Latin *Artium Elegantium Doctor*)

AEd Associate in Education

AEDE *Association européenne des enseignants* (French: European Teachers' Association)

AEDOT Advanced Energy Design and Operation Technologies

AEDP [USA] Alternative Energy Development Program

AEDS [USA] Association for Educational Data Systems; Atomic Energy Detection Systems

AEDU Admiralty Experimental Diving Unit

AEE airborne evaluation equipment; Atomic Energy Establishment

AeE aeronautical engineer

AEEC [USA] Airlines Electronic Engineering Committee

AEEE [Canada] Army Equipment Engineering Establishment

AEEN *Agence européenne pour l'energie nucléaire* (French: European Agency for Atomic Energy)

AEEU Amalgamated Engineering and Electrical Union

AEF Allied Expeditionary Force; American Expeditionary Force(s); Australian Expeditionary Force

A-effect [theatre] alienation effect

AEFM *Association européenne des festivals de musique* (French: European Association of Music Festivals)

AEG *Allgemeine Elektrizitäts-Gesellschaft* (German manufacturer of electrical goods)

a.e.g. *ad eundem gradum* (Latin: to the same degree); [bookbinding] all edges gilt

AEGIS Aid for the Elderly in Government Institutions; [computing] an existing general information system

AEGM Anglican Evangelical Group Movement

AEH A(lfred) E(dward) Housman (British poet)

AEI [USA] Alternative Energy Institute; American Express International; Associated Electrical Industries; *Association des écoles internationales* (French: International Schools Association)

AEIOU *Austriae Est Imperare Orbi Universi* (Latin: it is given to Austria to rule the whole world); *Austria Erit In Orbe Ultima* (Latin: Austria will be the world's last survivor)

AEJ Association for Education in Journalism

AEL Admiralty Engineering Laboratory; aeronautical engine laboratory; aircraft engine laboratory; Associated Engineering Limited; automation engineering laboratory

AELE *Association européenne de libre-échange* (French: European Free Trade Association, EFTA)

AELTC All England Lawn Tennis Club

AEM Air Efficiency Medal; analytical electron microscope (or microscopy)

AEMT Association of Electrical Machinery Trades

AEMU [astronautics] Advanced Extra-vehicular Mobility Unit

AEn Associate in English

Aen. *The Aeneid* (epic poem by Virgil)

aen. [numismatics] *aeneus* (Latin: made of copper)

AENA All England Netball Association

AEng Associate in Engineering

AEO Assistant Education Officer; Assistant

Experimental Officer; Association of Exhibition Organizers

AEP *Agence européenne de productivité* (French: European Production Agency); American Electric Power

AEPI American Educational Publishers Institute

aeq. *aequalis* (Latin: equal)

AER Army Emergency Reserve

aer. aeronautics; aeroplane

AERA American Educational Research Association; Associate Engraver, Royal Academy

aera. aeration

AERE Atomic Energy Research Establishment (Harwell)

AerE aeronautical engineer

AERI Agricultural Economics Research Institute (Oxford University)

AERNO aeronautical equipment reference number

AERO Air Education and Recreation Organization

aero. aeronautic(al)

Aeroflot Aero Flotilla (Russian airline company)

aeron. aeronautic(al); aeronautics

aerosp. aerospace

AES advanced energy system; [USA] Aerospace Electrical Society; Agricultural Economics Society (Reading University); [USA] Airways Engineering Society; [physics] atomic emission spectrum; Audio Engineering Society

Aes. Aesop (ancient Greek writer of fables)

AESE [USA] Association of Earth Science Editors

AESL [USA] Aerospace Energy Systems Laboratory

aesth. aesthetics

AET Associate in Electrical (or Electronic) Technology

aet. *aetatis* (Latin: at the age of, aged)

a.e.t. after extra time

aetat. *aetatis* (Latin: at the age of, aged)

AEU Amalgamated Engineering Union (became part of AEEU); American Ethical Union

AEV aerothermodynamic elastic vehicle; air evacuation; [microbiology] avian erythroblastosis virus

AEW Admiralty Experimental Works; airborne early warning (aircraft)

AEW&C airborne early warning and control

AEWHA All England Women's Hockey Association

AEWLA All England Women's Lacrosse Association

AEWS advanced earth satellite weapons system; aircraft early warning system

AF *Académie française* (French: French Academy); Admiral of the Fleet; air force; [USA] Air Foundation; Anglo-French; *Armée française* (French: French Army); Associated Fisheries; Associate Fellow; audiofrequency; [photography] autofocus; automatic (smoke) filter; [vehicle registration] Truro

A/F antiflooding; as found (in auction catalogue)

Af [currency] afgháni (used in Afghanistan)

Af. Africa; African; Afrikaans; [currency] Aruban florin

a/f [commerce] *a favor* (Spanish: in favour); as found (in auction catalogue)

.af Afghanistan (in Internet address)

a.f. advanced freight; [commerce] *a favor* (Spanish: in favour); *anno futuro* (Latin: next year); audiofrequency

AFA [nuclear technology] advanced fuel assembly; African Football Association; Air Force Act; [USA] Air Force Association; Amateur Fencing Association; Amateur Football Alliance; American Foundrymen's Association; Associate in Fine Arts; Associate of the Faculty of Actuaries

AFAC American Fisheries Advisory Committee

AFAEP Association of Fashion Advertising and Editorial Photographers

AFAFC [USA] Air Force Accounting and Finance Center

AFAIAA Associate Fellow of the American Institute of Aeronautics and Astronautics

AFAIM Associate Fellow of the Australian Institute of Management

AFAITC [USA] Armed Forces Air Intelligence Training Center

AFAL [USA] Air Force Astronautical Laboratory

AFAM Ancient Free and Accepted Masons

AF&AM Ancient Free and Accepted Masons

AFAS *Association française pour l'avancement des sciences* (French: French Association for the Advancement of the Sciences)

AFASIC Association for all Speech-Impaired Children

AFB [USA] Air Force Base; American Federation for the Blind

AFBD Association of Futures Brokers and Dealers

AFBF American Farm Bureau Federation

AFBMD [USA] Air Force Ballistic Missile Division

AFBPsS Associate Fellow of the British Psychological Society

AFBS American and Foreign Bible Society

AFC Air Force Cross; amateur football club; American Football Conference; [immunology] antibody-forming cell; association football club; Australian Flying Corps; automatic flight control; automatic frequency control; average fixed costs

a.f.c. automatic flight control; automatic frequency control

AFCAI Associate Fellow of the Canadian Aeronautical Institute

AFCE Associate in Fuel Technology and Chemical Engineering; automatic flight control equipment

AFCEA [USA] Armed Forces Communications and Electronics Association

AFCent Allied Forces in Central Europe

AFCO Admiralty Fleet Confidential Order

afco [engineering] automatic fuel cut-off

AFCRL [USA] Air Force Cambridge Research Laboratories

AFCS Air Force Communications Service; automatic flight control system

AFCU American and Foreign Christian Union

AFCW Association of Family Case Workers

AFD accelerated freeze dried; accelerated freeze drying; air force depot; [USA] Doctor of Fine Arts

AFDC [USA] Aid to Families with Dependent Children

AFDCS Association of First Division Civil Servants (formerly FDA)

AFDM [engineering] advanced fluid-dynamics model

AFDS Air Fighting Development Squadron

AFEA American Farm Economics Association; American Film Export Association

AFEE Airborne Forces Experimental Establishment

AFEIS Advanced Further Education Information Service

AFERO Asia and the Far East Regional Office

AFES Admiralty Fuel Experimental Station

AFESC [USA] Air Force Engineering and Services Center

AFESD Arab Fund for Economic and Social Development

AFEX [USA] Air Forces Europe Exchange; [USA] Armed Forces Exchange

AFF [photography] aberration-free focus

aff. affairs; affectionate; affectionately; affiliate; affiliated; affirmative; affix

affil. affiliate; affiliated

Aff.IP Affiliate of the Institute of Plumbing

AFFL Agricultural Finance Federation Limited

afft affidavit

AFFTC [USA] Air Force Flight Test Center

AFG [international vehicle registration] Afghanistan

Afg. Afghan; Afghanistan

AFGE American Federation of Government Employees

Afgh. Afghan; Afghanistan

Afghan. Afghanistan

AFGL [USA] Air Force Geophysics Laboratory

AFGM American Federation of Grain Millers

AFH American Foundation for Homeopathy

AFHC Air Force Headquarters Command

AFHQ Allied Forces Headquarters; Armed Forces Headquarters

AFI American Film Institute

AFIA American Foreign Insurance Association; Apparel and Fashion Industry

AFIAP *Artiste de la Fédération internationale de l'art photographique* (French: Artist of the International Federation of Photographic Art)

AFICD Associate Fellow of the Institute of Civil Defence

AFII American Federation of International Institutes

AFIIM Associate Fellow of the Institution of Industrial Managers

AFIMA Associate Fellow of the Institute of Mathematics and its Applications

AFIPS American Federation of Information Processing Societies (Incorporated)

AFK away from the keyboard (in Internet chat)

AFL [computing] abstract family of languages; Air Force List; American Federation of Labor; American Football League; *Associação de Futebol de Lisboa* (Portuguese: Lisbon Football Association)

AFLA Amateur Fencers' League of America; Asian Federation of Library Associations

AFLC [USA] Air Force Logistics Command

AFL-CIO American Federation of Labor and Congress of Industrial Organizations

aflt afloat

AFM [engineering] abrasive flow machining; Air Force Medal; American Federation of Musicians of the United States and Canada; assistant field manager; Associated Feed Manufacturers; [physics] atomic force microscope (or microscopy); [telecommunications] audiofrequency modulation

AFMA Armed Forces Management Association; Artificial Flower Manufacturers' Association of Great Britain

AFMDC [USA] Air Force Missile Development Center

AFMEC African Methodist Episcopal Church

AFMed Allied Forces in Mediterranean

afmo *afectísimo* (Spanish: very affectionately) (in correspondence)

AFMTC [USA] Air Force Missile Test Center

AFN American Forces Network; Armed Forces Network; Association of Free Newspapers

AFNIL *Agence francophone pour la numérotation internationale du livre* (French: French Agency for International Book Numbering, ISBN)

AFNOR *Association française de normalisation* (French: French Standardization Association)

AFNorth Allied Forces in Northern Europe

AFO Admiralty Fleet Order; army forwarding officer

AFOAR [USA] Air Force Office of Aerospace Research

AFOAS [USA] Air Force Office of Aerospace Sciences

AF of M American Federation of Musicians of the United States and Canada

AFOM Associate of the Faculty of Occupational Medicine

AFOSR [USA] Air Force Office of Scientific Research

AFP *Agence France Presse* (French news agency); [medicine] alpha-fetoprotein

AFPRB Armed Forces Pay Review Board

AFR accident frequency rate; air-fuel ratio; automatic fingerprint recognition

AFr. Anglo-French

Afr. Africa; African; Afrikaans

AFRA American Farm Research Association

AFRAeS Associate Fellow of the Royal Aeronautical Society

AFRC Agricultural and Food Research Council (formerly ARC)

Afrik. Afrikaans

AFRO African Regional Office

AFRTS [USA] Armed Forces Radio and Television Service

AFS Advanced Flying School; air force station; Alaska Ferry Service; American Field Service; Army Fire Service; Atlantic Ferry Service; auxiliary fire service

AFSA American Foreign Service Association; [USA] Armed Forces Security Agency

AFSBO American Federation of Small Business Organizations

AFSC Air Force Systems Command; American Friends Service Committee; Armed Forces Staff College

AFSCME American Federation of State, County and Municipal Employees

afsd aforesaid

AFSIL Accommodation for Students in London

AFSLAET Associate Fellow of the Society

of Licensed Aircraft Engineers and Technologists

AFSouth Allied Forces in Southern Europe

AFT American Federation of Teachers; axial-flow turbine

aft. after; afternoon

AFTA ASEAN Free Trade Area

AFTE American Federation of Technical Engineers

AFTM American Foundation of Tropical Medicine; [computing] anonymous file transfer protocol

AFTN Aeronautical Fixed Telecommunications Network

aftn afternoon

AFTR American Federal Tax Reports

AFTRA American Federation of Television and Radio Artists

AFU advanced flying unit

AFULE Australian Federated Union of Locomotive Enginemen

AFV armoured fighting vehicle; armoured force vehicle

AFVG [aeronautics] Anglo-French variable geometry

AFVPA Advertising Film and Videotape Producers' Association

AFW army field workshop

AFWAL [USA] Air Force Wright Aeronautical Laboratories

AG Accountant-General; Action Group Party (in Nigeria); Adjutant-General; Agent-General (of colonies); air gunner; [commerce] *Aktiengesellschaft* (German: public limited company, plc); *Alberghi per la Gioventù* (Italian: Youth Hostels); art gallery; Attorney-General; [vehicle registration] Hull

Ag antigen; [chemical element] silver (from Latin *argentum*)

Ag. August

ag. against; agent; agreement; agricultural; agriculture

.ag Antigua and Barbuda (in Internet address)

a.g. anti-gas

AGA air-to-ground-to-air; *Aktiebolaget Gas-accumulator* (Swedish gas company, original manufacturer of stoves); Amateur Gymnastics Association; American Gas Association; American Genetic Association; [obstetrics] appropriate for gesta-

tional age; Australian Garrison Artillery

AGAC American Guild of Authors and Composers

AGACS automatic ground-to-air communications system

AGARD Advisory Group for Aerospace Research and Development (in NATO)

a.g.b. a good brand; any good brand

AGBI Artists' General Benevolent Institution

AGC [USA] advanced graduate certificate; American Grassland Council; [electronics] automatic gain control

AGCA [aeronautics] automatic ground-controlled approach

AGCAS Association of Graduate Careers Advisory Service

AGCC Arab Gulf Cooperation Council

AGCL [aeronautics] automatic ground-controlled landing

AGCM [meteorology] atmospheric general circulation model

agcy agency

agd agreed

a.g.d. [engineering] axial gear differential

AGDC [Freemasonry] Assistant Grand Director of Ceremonies

AGDL Attorney-General of the Duchy of Lancaster

AGE Admiralty Gunnery Establishment; aerospace ground equipment; Associate in General Education; automatic guidance electronics

AgE agricultural engineer

AGES Association of Agricultural Education Staffs

AGF Adjutant-General to the Forces; army ground forces

Agfa *Aktiengesellschaft für Anilinfabrikation* (German chemical company)

ag. feb. [medicine] *aggrediente febre* (Latin: when the fever increases)

agg. aggregate

aggr. aggregate

AGH Australian General Hospital

AGI [USA] adjusted gross income (in tax returns); American Geographical Institute; American Geological Institute; annual general inspection; *Artistes graphiques internationaux* (French: International Graphic Artists); Associate of the Institute of Certificated Grocers

AGIP *Agenzia Generale Italiana Petroli* (Italian oil company)

agit. [medicine] *agitatum* (Latin: shaken)

agit. ante sum. [medicine] *agita ante sumendum* (Latin: shake before taking) (in prescriptions)

Agitprop *Agitpropbyuro* (Russian: Agitation and Propaganda Bureau) (former bureau of Soviet Communist Party)

AGK *Astronomische Gesellschaft Katalog* (German: Astronomical Society Catalogue)

AGL above ground level

aglm. agglomerate

AGM advisory group meeting; [medicine] African green monkey; air-to-ground missile; annual general meeting; Award of Garden Merit (Royal Horticultural Society award)

AGMA American Guild of Musical Artists; Athletic Goods Manufacturers' Association

AGN [astronomy] active galactic nucleus

agn again; agnomen

agnos. agnostic

ago. *agosto* (Italian or Spanish: August)

AGOR Auxiliary-General Oceanographic Research

AGP Academy of General Practice; [computing] accelerated graphics port; [computing] advanced graphics port; aviation general policy

AGPA American Group Psychotherapy Association

AGPL *Administração-Geral do Pôrto de Lisboa* (Portuguese: Port of Lisbon Authority)

AGR [nuclear technology] advanced gas-cooled reactor; Association of Graduate Recruiters

agr. agreed; agreement; agricultural; agriculture; agriculturist

AGRA Army Group Royal Artillery; Association of Genealogists and Record Agents

AGREE Advisory Group on Reliability of Electronic Equipment

AGRF American Geriatric Research Foundation

agric. agricultural; agriculture; agriculturist

AGRM Adjutant-General, Royal Marines

agron. agronomy

AGS [astronautics] abort guidance system; aircraft general standard; Air Gunnery School; Alpine Garden Society; American Geographical Society; Associate in General Studies

AGSM Associate of the Guildhall School of Music (and Drama); Australian Graduate of the School of Management

AGSRO Association of Government Supervisors and Radio Officers

AGSS American Geographical and Statistical Society

agst against

AGT advanced gas turbine; Art Gallery of Toronto; [USA] Association of Geology Teachers

agt agent; agreement

AGU American Geophysical Union

AGV [pharmacology] aniline gentian violet; automated guided vehicle; [electronics] autonomous guided vehicle

AGVA American Guild of Variety Artists

AGW actual gross weight

AGWAC Australian Guided Weapons and Analogue Computer

AGWY [insurance] Atlantic, Gulf, West Indies

agy agency

AH *anno Hebraico* (Latin: in the Jewish year); *anno Hegirae* (Latin: in the year of the Hegira) (in Muslim calendar); [insurance] Antwerp–Hamburg coastal ports; [fishing port] Arbroath; [chemistry] aromatic hydrocarbon; [medicine] artificial hyperglycaemia; [vehicle registration] Norwich

a.h. [shipping] after hatch; [shipping] aft hatch; ampere-hour; armed helicopter

AHA American Heart Association; American Historical Association; American Hospitals Association; area health authority; Australian Hotels Association

AHAM [USA] Association of Home Appliance Manufacturers

AH&FITB Agricultural, Horticultural and Forestry Industry Training Board

AHAUS Amateur Hockey Association of the United States

AHC Accepting Houses Committee; American Horticultural Council; Army Hospital Corps

AHD *American Heritage Dictionary*

ahd ahead

AHDL [medicine] alveolar hydatid disease of the liver

AHE [USA] Associate in Home Economics; [USA] Association for Higher Education

AHEM Association of Hydraulic Equipment Manufacturers

AHF [medicine] antihaemophilic factor

AHG [medicine] antihaemophilic globulin

AHGMR Ad Hoc Group on Missile Reliability

AHI American Health Institute; American Hospital Institute

AHIL [USA] Association of Hospital and Institutional Libraries

AHL American Hockey League

a.h.l. *ad hunc locum* (Latin: at this place, on this passage)

AHMC Association of Hospital Management Committees

AHMPS Association of Headmistresses of Preparatory Schools

AHMS American Home Mission Society

AHNCV Area of High Nature Conservation Value

AHP [engineering] absorption heat pump; assistant house physician

ahp air horsepower

AHPR Association of Health and Pleasure Resorts

AHQ Air Headquarters; Allied Headquarters; Army Headquarters

a.h.r. acceptable hazard rate (in risk analysis)

AHRC Australian Humanities Research Council

AHRHS Associate of Honour of the Royal Horticultural Society

AHRIH [New Zealand] Associate of Honour of the Royal Institute of Horticulture

AHS adult health study; American Helicopter Society; *anno humanae salutis* (Latin: in the year of human salvation); annual housing survey; assistant house surgeon

AHSA American Horse Shows Association

AHSB Authority, Health and Safety Branch (of Atomic Energy Authority)

AHSM Associate of the Institute of Health Services Management

AHT absorption heat transformer; acoustic homing torpedo; Animal Health Trust; Association of Highway Technicians

a.h.v. *ad hanc vocem* (Latin: at this word) (in reference book)

AHWA Association of Hospital and Welfare Administrators

AI Admiralty instruction; Admiralty Islands; [computing] Adobe Illustrator; air interception; air interdiction; *Altesse Impériale* (French: Imperial Highness); American Institute; Amnesty International; *anno inventionis* (Latin: in the year of the discovery); Anthropological Institute; Army Intelligence; artificial insemination; artificial intelligence

a.i. *ad interim* (Latin: for the meantime)

AIA Abrasive Industries Association; [USA] Aerospace Industries Association; American Institute of Aeronautics; American Institute of Architects; American Insurance Association; Anglo-Indian Association; Archeological Institute of America; Associate of the Institute of Actuaries; Association of International Accountants; Association of International Artists; automated image analysis; [New Zealand] Aviation Industry Association

AIAA Aircraft Industries Association of America; American Institute of Aeronautics and Astronautics; Association of International Advertising Agencies

AIAB Associate of the International Association of Book-keepers

AIAC Air Industries Association of Canada; *Association internationale d'archéologie classique* (French: International Association for Classical Archaeology)

AIAE Associate of the Institution of Automobile Engineers

AIAgrE Associate of the Institution of Agricultural Engineers

AIAL Associate Member of the International Institute of Arts and Letters

AIAS Australian Institute of Agricultural Science

AIB [insurance] accidents investigation branch (of insurance company); American Institute of Banking; Association of Independent Businesses; *Associazione Italiana Biblioteche* (Italian: Italian Library Association)

AIBA *Association internationale de boxe*

amateur (French: International Amateur Boxing Association)

AIBC Architectural Institute of British Columbia

AIBD Associate of the Institute of British Decorators; Association of International Bond Dealers

AIBM *Association internationale des bibliothèques musicales* (French: International Association of Music Libraries)

AIBP Associate of the Institute of British Photographers

AIBS American Institute of Biological Sciences

AIBScot Associate of the Institute of Bankers in Scotland

AIC Agricultural Improvement Council; Agricultural Institute of Canada; American Institute of Chemists; artificial insemination centre; Art Institute of Chicago

AICA Associate Member of the Commonwealth Institute of Accountants; *Association internationale des critiques d'art* (French: International Association of Art Critics)

AICB *Association internationale contre le bruit* (French: International Association Against Noise)

AICBM anti-intercontinental ballistic missile

AICC All India Congress Committee

AICE American Institute of Chemical Engineers; American Institute of Consulting Engineers; Associate of the Institution of Civil Engineers

AIChE American Institute of Chemical Engineers

AICMA *Association internationale des constructeurs de matériel aérospatial* (French: International Association of Aerospace Equipment Manufacturers)

AICRO Association of Independent Contract Research Organizations

AICS Associate of the Institute of Chartered Shipbrokers; *Association internationale du cinéma scientifique* (French: International Scientific Film Association)

AICTA Associate of the Imperial College of Tropical Agriculture

AICV armoured infantry combat vehicle

AID [medicine] acute infectious disease; Aeronautical Inspection Directorate;

[USA] Agency for International Development; agricultural industrial development; Aircraft Intelligence Department; American Institute of Decorators; American Institute of Interior Designers; Army Intelligence Department; [medicine] artificial insemination by donor; *Association internationale pour le développement* (French: International Development Association)

AIDA *Association internationale de droit africain* (French: International African Law Association); *Association internationale de la distribution alimentaire* (French: International Association of Food Distribution); [marketing] attention, interest, desire, action (of customer)

AIDAS Agricultural Industry Development Advisory Service

AIDD American Institute for Design and Drafting

AIDF African Industrial Development Fund

AIDL [New Zealand] Auckland Industrial Development Laboratory

AIDP Associate of the Institute of Data Processing; *Association internationale de droit pénal* (French: International Association of Penal Law)

AIDS accident information display system; [medicine] acquired immune deficiency syndrome; aircraft integrated data system; air force intelligence data-handling system

Aids [medicine] acquired immune deficiency syndrome

AIEA *Agence internationale de l'énergie atomique* (French: International Atomic Energy Agency)

AIED *Association internationale des étudiants dentaires* (French: International Association of Dental Students)

AIEE Associate of the Institution of Electrical Engineers; *Association des instituts d'études européennes* (French: Association of Institutes for European Studies)

AIEP [USA] Association of Independent Electricity Producers

AIF *Alliance internationale des femmes* (French: International Alliance of Women); [USA] Atomic Industrial Forum; Australian Imperial Forces

AIFA Associate of the International Faculty of Arts

AIFF Associate of the Institute of Freight Forwarders

AIFireE Associate of the Institution of Fire Engineers

AIFM *Association internationale des femmes médecins* (French: International Association of Women Doctors)

AIG Adjutant Inspector-General; Assistant Inspector-General; Assistant Instructor of Gunnery

AIGA American Institute of Graphic Arts

AIGCM Associate of the Incorporated Guild of Church Musicians

AIGS Agricultural Investment Grant Schemes

AIH all in hand; [medicine] artificial insemination by husband; *Association internationale de l'hôtellerie* (French: International Hotel Association)

AIHA American Industrial Hygiene Association

AIIA Australian Institute of International Affairs

AIIE American Institute of Industrial Engineers

AIIExE Associate of the Institution of Incorporated Executive Engineers

AIInfSc Associate of the Institute of Information Scientists

AIITech Associate Member of the Institute of Industrial Technicians

AIJD *Association internationale des juristes démocrates* (French: International Association of Democratic Lawyers)

AIJPF *Association internationale des journalistes de la presse féminine et familiale* (French: International Association of Women's Press Journalists)

AIL air intelligence liaison; Associate of the Institute of Linguists

AILAS [aeronautics] automatic instrument-landing approach system

AILO air intelligence liaison officer

AILocoE Associate of the Institution of Locomotive Engineers

AIM Africa Inland Mission; Alternative Investment Market; American Indian Movement (civil-rights organization); American Institute of Management; Amsterdam International Market; analytical ion microscopy; Australian

Inland Mission (in Presbyterianism); Australian Institute of Management

a.i.m.a. as interest may appear

AIMarE Associate of the Institute of Marine Engineers

AIMCO [USA] Association of Internal Management Consultants

AIME American Institute of Mechanical Engineers; American Institute of Mining Engineers

AIMechE Associate of the Institution of Mechanical Engineers

AIMI Associate of the Institute of the Motor Industry

AIMM Australasian Institute of Mining and Metallurgy

AIMO Association of Industrial Medical Officers

AIMPA *Association internationale de météorologie et de physique de l'atmosphère* (French: International Association of Meteorology and Atmospheric Physics)

AIMS Association for Improvement in Maternity Services

AIMU American Institute of Marine Underwriters

AIN American Institute of Nutrition

AINEC All-India Newspaper Editors' Conference

AInstP Associate of the Institute of Physics

AInstPI Associate of the Institute of Patentees and Inventors

AINucE Associate of the Institution of Nuclear Engineers

AIP American Institute of Physics; Associate of the Institute of Plumbing; Association of Independent Producers

AIPA Associate of the Institute of Practitioners in Advertising; *Association internationale de psychologie appliquée* (French: International Association of Applied Psychology)

AIPO American Institute of Public Opinion

AIPR Associate of the Institute of Public Relations

AIPS *Association internationale de la presse sportive* (French: International Sports Press Association); astronomical image-processing system

AIQS Associate of the Institute of Quantity Surveyors

AIR All India Radio; American Institute of Refrigeration

a-i-r artist-in-residence

AIRA [USA] air attaché

AIRC Association of Independent Radio Companies

AIRCENT Allied Air Forces, Central Europe

AIRCOM airways communications system

air con. air conditioning

AIRG Agency for Intellectual Relief in Germany

AIRH *Association internationale de recherches hydrauliques* (French: International Association of Hydraulic Research)

AIRPASS aircraft interception radar and pilots attack sight system

AIRS [physics, electronics] acoustic-imaging recognition system

AIRTE Associate of the Institute of Road Transport Engineers

AIRTO Association of Independent Research and Technology Organizations

AIS [commerce] agreed industry standard; androgen insensitivity syndrome; Anglo-Italian Society; *Association internationale de sociologie* (French: International Sociological Association); Australian Illawarra Shorthorn (breed of cattle)

AISA Associate of the Incorporated Secretaries Association

AISE *Association internationale des sciences économiques* (French: International Economics Association)

AISI American Iron and Steel Institute

AISJ *Association internationale des sciences juridiques* (French: International Association of Legal Science)

AISS *Association internationale de la sécurité sociale* (French: International Social Security Association)

AIST [USA] Agency of Industrial Science and Technology

AIStructE Associate of the Institution of Structural Engineers

AIT *Alliance internationale de tourisme* (French: International Tourism Alliance); [meteorology] artificial ionospheric turbulence; Asian Institute of Technology; Association of HM Inspec-

tors of Taxes; Association of Investment Trusts

AITA *Association internationale du théâtre d'amateurs* (French: International Amateur Theatre Association)

AITC *Association internationale des traducteurs de conférence* (French: International Association of Conference Translators); Association of Investment Trust Companies

AITO Association of Independent Tour Operators

AIU *Association internationale des universités* (French: International Association of Universities)

AIV *Association internationale de volcanologie* (French: International Association of Volcanology)

AIW (International Union of) Allied Industrial Workers of America; Atlantic-Intercoastal Waterway (from Cape Cod to Florida Bay)

AIWC All-India Women's Conference

AIWEM Associate of the Institution of Water and Environmental Management

AIWM American Institute of Weights and Measures

AIX [computing] advanced interactive executive

AJ ankle jerk; [telecommunications] anti-jam; *Archaeological Journal*; Associate in Journalism; [vehicle registration] Middlesbrough

AJA American of Japanese ancestry; Anglo-Jewish Association; Australian Journalists' Association

AJAG Assistant Judge Advocate-General

AJC Australian Jockey Club

AJCC American Joint Committee on Cancer

AJE [accounting] adjusting journal entry

AJEX Association of Jewish Ex-Service Men and Women

AJPM *ad Jesum per Mariam* (Latin: to Jesus through Mary)

AJR Association of Jewish Refugees; Australian Jurist Reports

AJY Association for Jewish Youth

AK above knee; [US postcode] Alaska; automatic Kalashnikov (type of rifle, as in **AK-47**); Knight of the Order of Australia; [vehicle registration] Sheffield

a.k.a. also known as

Akad. *Akademie* (German: academy)

AKC American Kennel Club; Associate of King's College (London)

AKEL *Anorthotikon Komma Ergazomanou Laou* (Greek: Progressive Party of the Working People) (in Cyprus)

AKOE Anti-Killer Organization of Expatriates (in Cyprus)

AKR auroral kilometric radiation (from the earth)

Akt [commerce] *Aktiebolaget* (Swedish: joint-stock company)

Aktb [commerce] *Aktiebolaget* (Swedish: joint-stock company)

Aktieb [commerce] *Aktiebolaget* (Swedish: joint-stock company)

AL Abraham Lincoln (US president); [medicine] activity of living; Admiralty letter; [US postcode] Alabama; [international vehicle registration] Albania; *América Latina* (Spanish: Latin America); [baseball] American League; American Legion; Anglo-Latin; *anno lucis* (Latin: in the year of light); army list; [vehicle registration] Nottingham; [UK postcode] St Albans

Al [chemical element] aluminium

al. alcohol; alcoholic; *alia* (Latin: other things); *alii* (Latin: others)

.al Albania (in Internet address)

a.l. [finance] allotment letter; [commerce] *après livraison* (French: after delivery); autograph letter

ALA Air Licensing Authority; all letters answered (in personal advertisement); American Library Association; Associate in Liberal Arts; Associate of the Library Association; Association of London Authorities; Authors' League of America

Ala. Alabama

ALAA Associate of the Library Association of Australia

ALAC Artificial Limb and Appliance Centre

ALACP American League to Abolish Capital Punishment

ALADI *Asociación Latino-Americana de Integración* (Spanish: Latin-American Integration Association)

ALAI *Association littéraire et artistique internationale* (French: International Literary and Artistic Association)

ALA-ISAD American Library Association–Information Science and Automation Division

ALAM Associate of the London Academy of Music (and Dramatic Art)

ALAP as low as practicable (referring to radiation level or dose)

ALARA as low as reasonably achievable (referring to radiation level or dose)

Alas. Alaska

ALAWP all letters answered with photograph (in personal advertisement)

Alb. Albania; Albanian; Alberta; Albion

alb. [medicine] albumin

Alba Alberta

Alban. *Albanensis* (Latin: (Bishop) of St Albans)

ALBM air-launched ballistic missile

Albq. Albuquerque

ALBSU Adult Literacy and Basic Skills Unit

ALC Agricultural Land Commission

alc. alcohol

a.l.c. à la carte

ALCAN Aluminium Company of Canada

ALCD Associate of the London College of Divinity

alch. alchemy

ALCM air-launched cruise missile; Associate of London College of Music

ALCS Authors' Lending and Copyright Society

ALD [medicine] adrenoleukodystrophy; [computing] automatic line drawing

Ald. Alderman

ALDEV African Land Development

Aldm. Alderman

ALE [insurance] additional living expense; Association for Liberal Education

A level [education] Advanced level

ALF Animal Liberation Front; Arab Liberation Front (in Iraq); automatic letter facer (machine for sorting mail)

ALFSEA Allied Land Forces South-East Asia

ALG [medicine] antilymphocyte globulin

Alg. Algeria; Algerian; Algiers

alg. algebra; algebraic

a.l.g. advanced landing ground

ALGES Association of Local Government Engineers and Surveyors

ALGFO Association of Local Government Financial Officers

Algol [computing] algorithmic language

ALH Australian Light Horse

ALI American Library Institute; Argyll Light Infantry; Associate of the Landscape Institute

ALICE Autistic and Language-Impaired Children's Education

algn. alignment

ALJ Administration Law Judge; Australian Law Journal

ALJR Australian Law Journal Reports

alk. alkali; alkaline

ALL [medicine] acute lymphatic leukaemia

ALLC Association for Literary and Linguistic Computing

alleg. allegation; allegorical; allegory

All H. All Hallows

all'ingr. *all'ingrosso* (Italian: wholesale)

allo [music] *allegro* (Italian: quickly)

all'ott. [music] *all'ottava* (Italian: an octave higher)

All S. All Souls

All SS All Saints

ALM [medicine] alveolar lining material; Association of Lloyd's Members; audio-lingual method (in foreign-language teaching); Master of the Liberal Arts (from Latin *Artium Liberalium Magister*)

ALN [medicine] axillary lymph nodes

ALNA *Armée de libération nationale d'Angola* (French: Angolan National Liberation Army)

ALO air liaison officer; allied liaison officer

ALOE A Lady of England (pen-name of Charlotte M. Tucker, British novelist)

ALP American Labor Party; Australian Labor Party; automated language processing; automated learning process; [USA] automated library program

alp. alpine

ALPA Air Line Pilots' Association

ALPAL [computing] A Livermore Physics Applications Language

alph. alphabetic(al)

alphanum. alphanumeric

ALPO Association of Land and Property Owners; Association of Lunar and Planetary Observers

ALPSP Association of Learned and Professional Society Publishers

ALPURCOMS all-purpose communications system

ALR American Law Reports

alr *aliter* (Latin: otherwise)

ALRC Anti-Locust Research Centre

ALRI airborne long-range input

ALS accident localization system; Agricultural Land Service; [medicine] amyotrophic lateral sclerosis; [immunology] antilymphocytic serum; [aeronautics] approach lighting system(s); Associate of the Linnean Society; autograph letter signed; automated library system

a.l.s. autograph letter signed

Alsat. Alsatian

al seg. [music] *al segno* (Italian: to the sign, at the sign)

ALSEP Apollo Lunar Surface Experiment Package

ALT Agricultural Land Tribunal

Alt [computing] alternate (key)

Alt. *Altesse* (French: Highness)

alt. alteration; altered; alternate; alternative; alternator; altimeter; altitude; [music] alto

Alta Alberta

alt. dieb. [medicine] *nis diebus* (Latin: every other day)

alter. alteration

alt. hor. [medicine] *alternis horis* (Latin: every other hour)

alt. noct. [medicine] *alternis noctibus* (Latin: every other night)

ALTPR Association of London Theatre Press Representatives

ALTU Association of Liberal Trade Unionists

ALU [computing] arithmetic and logic unit

alum. aluminium; alumna(e); alumnus (or alumni)

ALV [microbiology] avian leucosis virus

ALWR [nuclear technology] advanced light-water reactor

AM Academy of Management; administrative memorandum; [astronautics] airlock module; air mail; Air Marshal; Air Ministry; Albert Medal; Alpes-Maritimes (French department); [radio] amplitude modulation; [physics] angular momentum; *anno mundi* (Latin: in the year of the world); *annus mirabilis* (Latin: year of wonders, 1666); *ante meridiem* (Latin: before noon); area manager;

army manual; assistant manager;
Associate Member; [insurance] *assurance
mutuelle* (French: mutual insurance); *Ave
Maria* (Latin: Hail Mary); Award of
Merit; [USA] Master of Arts (from Latin
Artium Magister); Member of the Order
of Australia; [vehicle registration]
Swindon

Am [chemical element] americium

Am. America; American; [Bible] Amos

aM *am Main* (German: on the River Main)
(in place-names)

am attometre

a/m above-mentioned

am. amateur; ammeter; ammunition

.am Armenia (in Internet address)

a.m. [radio] amplitude modulation; *ante
meridiem* (Latin: before noon)

AMA against medical advice; American
Management Association; American
Marketing Association; American
Medical Association; American
Missionary Association; American Motor-
cycle Association; Assistant Masters
Association; Associate of the Museums
Association; Association of Metropolitan
Authorities; Australian Medical
Association

AMAB Army Medical Advisory Board

AMAE American Museum of Atomic
Energy

amal. amalgamated

amalg. amalgamated

AMAmIEE Associate Member of the
American Institute of Electrical
Engineers

AMARC Associated Marine and Related
Charities

AMASCE Associate Member of the
American Society of Civil Engineers

amat. amateur

AMAusIMM Associate Member of the Australasian Institute of Mining and
Metallurgy

AMB Air Ministry bulletin; [USA] Airways
Modernization Board

Amb. Ambassador; ambulance

AMBAC Associate Member of the British
Association of Chemists

Ambas. Ambassador

ambig. ambiguity; ambiguous

AMBIM Associate Member of the British
Institute of Management

AMC [USA] Aerospace Manufacturers'
Council; Agricultural Mortgage Corpor-
ation Limited; American Motors Corpor-
ation; [USA] Army Missile Command;
[USA] Army Mobile Command; [USA]
Army Munitions Command; Art
Master's Certificate; Association of Man-
agement Consultants; Association of
Municipal Corporations

AMCA Architectural Metal Craftsmen's
Association

AMCIB Associate Member of the Corporation of Insurance Brokers

AMCIOB Associate Member of the
Chartered Institute of Building

AMCL Association of Metropolitan Chief
Librarians

AMCS airborne missile control system

AMCT Associate of the Manchester College of Technology

am. cur. [law] *amicus curiae* (Latin: friend
of the court)

AMD acid-mine drainage; Admiralty
machinery depot; aerospace medical division; [meteorology] air movement data;
Army Medical Department

amd amend

AMDB Agricultural Machinery Development Board

AMDEA Association of Manufacturers of
Domestic Electrical Appliances

AMDEC Agricultural Marketing Development Executive Committee

AMDG *ad majorem Dei gloriam* (Latin: to
the greater glory of God) (motto of
Jesuits)

amdt amendment

AME [USA] Advanced Master of Education; African Methodist Episcopal;
Association of Municipal Engineers

AMEC Australian Minerals and Energy
Council

AMEDS [USA] Army Medical Service

AMEE Admiralty Marine Engineering
Establishment; Association of Managerial Electrical Executives

AMEIC Associate Member of the Engineering Institute of Canada

AMEM African Methodist Episcopal
Mission

Am. Emb. American Embassy

AMEME Association of Mining Electrical
and Mechanical Engineers

amend. amendment
amendt amendment
Amer. America; American
Amer. Ind. American Indian
Amer. Std American Standard
AMES Air Ministry Experimental Station; Association of Marine Engineering Schools
AMet Associate of Metallurgy
AMETS Association for Management Education and Training in Scotland
AMEWA Associated Manufacturers of Electric Wiring Accessories
Amex American Express; American Stock Exchange
AMEZC African Methodist Episcopal Zion Church
AMF Allied Mobile Force (of NATO); Australian Marine Force; Australian Military Forces
AMG Allied Military Government
amg among
a.m.g. [aeronautics] automatic magnetic guidance
AMGO Assistant Master-General of Ordnance
AMGOT Allied Military Government of Occupied Territory (in World War II)
AMI [medicine] acute myocardial infarction; American Meat Institute; American Military Institute; Ancient Monuments Inspectorate; *Association Montessori internationale* (French: International Montessori Association)
a.m.i. [military] advanced manned interceptor; [aeronautics] air mileage indicator
AMIAE Associate Member of the Institution of Automobile Engineers
AMIAP Associate Member of the Institution of Analysts and Programmers
AMIBF Associate Member of the Institute of British Foundrymen
AMICE Associate Member of the Institution of Civil Engineers
AMICEI Associate Member of the Institution of Civil Engineers of Ireland
AMIChemE Associate Member of the Institution of Chemical Engineers
AMICW Associate Member of the Institute of Clerks of Works of Great Britain
AMIED Associate Member of the Institution of Engineering Designers

AmIEE American Institute of Electrical Engineers
AMIEI Associate Member of the Institution of Engineering Inspection
AMIEx Associate Member of the Institute of Export
AMIFireE Associate Member of the Institution of Fire Engineers
AMIGasE Associate Member of the Institution of Gas Engineers
AMIHT Associate Member of the Institution of Highways and Transportation
AMII Association of Musical Instrument Industries
AMIIE Associate Member of the Institution of Incorporated Engineers
AMIIM Associate Member of the Institution of Industrial Managers
AMILocoE Associate Member of the Institution of Locomotive Engineers
AMIMarE Associate Member of the Institute of Marine Engineers
AMIMechE Associate Member of the Institution of Mechanical Engineers
AMIMGTechE Associate Member of the Institution of Mechanical and General Technician Engineers
AMIMI Associate Member of the Institute of the Motor Industry
AMIMM Associate Member of the Institution of Mining and Metallurgy
Am. Ind. American Indian
AMInIsTech Associate in Minerals Technology
AMInstBE Associate Member of the Institution of British Engineers
AMInstR Associate Member of the Institute of Refrigeration
AMINucE Associate Member of the Institution of Nuclear Engineers
AMIOP Associate Member of the Institute of Printing
AMIPA Associate Member of the Institute of Practitioners in Advertising
AMIPRE Associate Member of the Incorporated Practitioners in Radio and Electronics
AMIQA Associate Member of the Institute of Quality Assurance
AMIRA Australian Mineral Industries Research Association
AMIRSE Associate Member of the Institute of Railway Signalling Engineers

AMIStructE Associate Member of the Institution of Structural Engineers

AMITA Associate Member of the Industrial Transport Association

AMIWEM Associate Member of the Institution of Water and Environmental Management

AMJ *Assemblée mondiale de la jeunesse* (French: World Assembly of Youth)

AML abandoned mine land; [medicine] acute myeloid leukaemia; Admiralty materials laboratory; [New Zealand] applied mathematics laboratory

AMLS [USA] Master of Arts in Library Science

AMM antimissile missile; assistant marketing manager; *Association médicale mondiale* (French: World Medical Association)

amm. ammunition

AMMA Assistant Masters' and Mistresses' Association

AMMI American Merchant Marine Institute

amn ammunition

AMNECInst Associate Member of the North East Coast Institution of Engineers and Shipbuilders

AMNILP Associate Member of the National Institute of Licensing Practitioners

AMO Air Ministry order; area medical officer; assistant medical officer; Association of Managerial Officers

AMOB automatic meteorological oceanographic buoy

AMORC Ancient Mystical Order Rosae Crucis (= Rosicrucians)

amort. amortization

AMOS automatic meteorological observing station

AMP [biochemistry] adenosine monophosphate; Air Member for Personnel (in RAF); Associated Master Plumbers and Domestic Engineers; Australian Mutual Provident Society

amp [short form] ampere; [short form] amplifier

amp. amperage; ampere; amplification; amplified; amplifier; amplitude

AMPAS [USA] Academy of Motion Picture Arts and Sciences

AMPC [USA] automatic message processing center; auxiliary military pioneer corps

amph. amphibian; amphibious

AMPHIBEX amphibious exercise

ampl. amplifier

AMPS [finance] auction market preferred stock; automatic message processing system

AMPSS advanced manned precision strike system

AMQ American medical qualification

AMR Atlantic missile range; automated meter reading; automatic message routing

AMRAAM advanced medium-range air-to-air missile

AMRINA Associate Member of the Royal Institution of Naval Architects

Amrit. Amritsar

AMRO Association of Medical Record Officers

AMRS Air Ministry radio station

AMS accident-monitoring system; [USA] Agricultural Marketing Service; American Mathematical Society; American Meteorological Society; American Microscopical Society; American Musicological Society; Ancient Monuments Society; [astronautics] Apollo mission simulator; army map service; army medical services; army medical staff; assistant military secretary; Australian medical services; automatic music search

AMSA advanced manned strategic aircraft

AMSAM antimissile surface-to-air missile

Am. Sam. American Samoa

AMSE Associate Member of the Society of Engineers

AMSEF anti-minesweeping explosive float

AMSERT Associate Member of the Society of Electronic and Radio Technicians

AMSGA Association of Manufacturers and Suppliers for the Graphic Arts

AMSL above mean sea level

AMSO Air Member for Supply and Organization (in RAF); Association of Market Survey Organizations

AMSST Associate Member of the Society of Surveying Technicians

Amst. Amsterdam

Amstrad Alan Michael Sugar Trading (computer manufacturer)

AMSW [USA] Master of Arts in Social Work

AMT Academy of Medicine, Toronto; air-mail transfer; Air Member for Training (in RAF); [USA] alternative minimum tax; area management team; Associate in Mechanical Technology; Associate in Medical Technology; Association of Marine Traders; [USA] Master of Arts in Teaching

amt amount

AMTA Association of Multiple Travel Agents

AMTC Art Master's Teaching Certificate

AMTDA Agricultural Machinery Tractor Dealers' Association

AMTE Admiralty Marine Technology Establishment

AMTI airborne moving target indicator

AMTRI Advanced Manufacturing Technology Research Institute

AMTS Associate Member of the Television Society

AMU Associated Metalworkers' Union; [USA] Associated Midwestern Universities; Association of Master Upholsterers

amu [physics] atomic mass unit

AMUA Associate of Music, University of Adelaide

AMus Associate in Music

AMusD Doctor of Musical Arts

AMusLCM Associate in Music, London College of Music

AMusTCL Associate in Music, Trinity College of Music, London

AMV *Association mondiale vétérinaire* (French: World Veterinary Association); [microbiology] avian myeloblastosis virus

AMVAP Associated Manufacturers of Veterinary and Agricultural Products

AMVERS automated merchant vessel report system

AMVETS American Veterans (of World War II etc.)

AMW average molecular weight

AN [chemistry] acid number; [chemistry] ammonium nitrate; Anglo-Norman; [medicine] antenatal; Associate in Nursing; [physics] audible noise; [medicine] avascular necrosis; [civil aircraft marking] Nicaragua; [vehicle registration] Reading

A/N advice note; alphanumeric

An [chemistry] actinon

An. Annam

an. *anno* (Latin: in the year); anonymous; answer

.an Netherlands Antilles (in Internet address)

a.n. above named

ANA All Nippon Airways; American Nature Association; American Neurological Association; American Newspaper Association; American Numismatic Association; American Nurses' Association; [commerce] Article Number Association; [USA] Associate National Academician; Association of Nurse Administrators; Australian Natives' Association

anaes. anaesthesia; anaesthetic

anag. anagram

anal. analogous; analogy; analyse; analysis; analytic(al)

ANAPO *Allianza Nacional Popular* (Spanish: National Popular Alliance) (in Colombia)

ANARE Australian National Antarctic Research Expedition

anat. anatomic(al); anatomy

ANC advanced nuclear computer; African National Congress; Army Nurse Corps; Australian Newspapers Council

anc. ancient

anch. anchored

ANCUN Australian National Committee for the United Nations

AND [international vehicle registration] Andorra

And [astronomy] Andromeda

and. [music] *andante* (Italian: at moderate speed)

ANDB [USA] Air Navigation Development Board

ANDI [medicine] abnormal development and involution

ANEC American Nuclear Energy Council

ANECInst Associate of the North East Coast Institution of Engineers and Shipbuilders

ANERI [USA] Advanced Nuclear Equipment Research Institute

ANF [USA] Advanced Nuclear Fuels (Corporation); antinuclear factor; Atlantic Nuclear Force; [medicine] atrial natriuretic factor; Australian National Flag Association

ANG [USA] Air National Guard; Australian Newspaper Guild

Ang. Anglesey; *Anglice* (Latin: in English)

ang. angle; angular

ANGB [USA] Air National Guard Base

Angl. *Angleterre* (French: England); Anglican; Anglicized

Anglo-Fr. Anglo-French

Anglo-Ind. Anglo-Indian

Anglo-Ir. Anglo-Irish

Anglo-L Anglo-Latin

Anglo-Sax. Anglo-Saxon

ANGUS Air National Guard of the United States

Anh. *Anhang* (German: appendix) (of book etc.)

anhyd. [chemistry] anhydrous

anhydr. [chemistry] anhydrous

ANI *Agência Nacional de Informações* (Portuguese: National Information Agency); American Nuclear Insurers

anim. [music] *animato* (Italian: in a lively manner)

Ank. *Ankunft* (German: arrival)

ANL Anti-Nazi League; *Archaeological News Letter*; [USA] Argonne National Laboratory; [engineering] automatic noise limiting; National Library of Australia

ANM Admiralty Notices to Mariners

Anm. *Anmerkung* (German: note) (in book etc.)

anme [commerce] *anonyme* (French: limited liability) (of company)

ANN [telecommunications] all-figure numbers now; [computing] artificial neural network

ann. annals; *anni* (Latin: years); *anno* (Latin: in the year); annual; annuity

ANNA [USA] Army–Navy–NASA–Air Force satellite

anniv. anniversary

annot. annotate; annotation; annotator

annuit. annuitant

annul. annulled; annulment

Annunc. Annunciation

ANO [USA] Association of Nuclear Operators

anon. anonymous; anonymously

ANOVA [mathematics] analysis of variance

ANP advanced nursing practice; aircraft nuclear propulsion; *Algemeen Nederlands Persbureau* (Dutch news agency); ammonium nitrate–phosphate (fertilizer); Australian National Party

ANPA American Newspaper Publishers' Association; Australian National Publicity Association

anr another

anrac aids navigation radio control

ANRC American National Red Cross; Australian National Research Council

ANRE advanced nuclear rocket engine

ANRPC Association of Natural Rubber Producing Countries

ANS [physics] advanced neutron source; American Nuclear Society; Army News Service; Army Nursing Service; [computing] artificial neural system; Astronomical Netherlands Satellite; [anatomy] autonomic nervous system

ans. answer

a.n.s. autograph note signed

ANSA *Agenzia Nazionale Stampa Associata* (Italian news agency); Independent Union for Abbey National Staff (formerly Abbey National Staff Association)

ANSI American National Standards Institute

ANSI–SPARC American National Standards Institute/Systems Planning and Requirements Committee

ANSL Australian National Standards Laboratory

ANSP Academy of Natural Sciences of Philadelphia; Australian National Socialist Party

ANSR [nuclear technology] advanced neutron-source reactor

ANSTI African Network of Scientific and Technological Institutions

ANSTO Australian Nuclear Science and Technology Organization

Ant [astronomy] Antlia

Ant. Antarctica; Antigua; Antrim

ant. antenna; anterior; anticipated; antilogarithm; antiquarian; antique; antiquity; antonym

ANTA American National Theater and Academy; Australian National Travel Association

Antarc. Antarctic

anthol. anthology

anthrop. anthropological; anthropology

anthropol. anthropological; anthropology

Antig. Antigua

antilog [short form] antilogarithm

antiq. antiquarian; antiquities

antiq. antiquity

Ant. Lat. antique Latin

ant. ld antique laid (paper)

anton. antonym

ANTOR Association of National Tourist Office Representatives

Antr. Antrim

ant. wo. antique wove (paper)

ANU Australian National University

a/nw as new (in advertisement)

ANWR Arctic National Wildlife Refuge

anx annex

ANZ Australia and New Zealand

ANZAAS Australia and New Zealand Association for the Advancement of Science

Anzac Australia and New Zealand Army Corps (in World War I)

ANZAM Australia, New Zealand and Malaysia (defence strategy)

ANZAMRS Australia and New Zealand Association for Medieval and Renaissance Studies

ANZCAN Australia, New Zealand and Canada

ANZIA Associate of the New Zealand Institute of Architects

ANZUK Australia, New Zealand and United Kingdom (defence force)

ANZUS Australia, New Zealand and the United States (defence alliance)

AO accountant officer; Air Officer; air ordnance; *anno ordinis* (Latin: in the year of the order); [chemistry] anthracene oil; area office; army order; Australian Opera; [vehicle registration] Carlisle; Officer of the Order of Australia

A/O [accounting] account of; and others

aO *an der Oder* (German: on the River Oder) (in place-names)

a/o [accounting] account of

.ao Angola (in Internet address)

AOA activity-on-arrow; [USA] Administration on Aging; Aerodrome Owners' Association; Air Officer in charge of Administration; American Ordnance Association; American Orthopedic Association; American Osteopathic Association; American Overseas Association

AOB advanced operational base; Antediluvian Order of Buffaloes; any other business

a.o.b. any other business; at or below

AOC Air Officer Commanding; *anno orbis Conditi* (Latin: in the year of the Creation); any other colour; *appellation d'origine contrôlée* (French: name of origin controlled) (wine classification); Army Ordnance Corps; Artists of Chelsea

AOCB any other competent business

AOC-in-C Air Officer Commanding-in-Chief

AOCM [US air force] aircraft out of commission for maintenance

AOD acousto-optic device; advanced ordnance depot; Ancient Order of Druids; Army Ordnance Department

AOER Army Officers' Emergency Reserve

AOF *Afrique Occidentale Française* (French: French West Africa); Ancient Order of Foresters; Australian Olympic Federation

A of F Admiral of the Fleet

AOFP absolute open-flow potential

A of S Academy of Science

AOG aircraft on ground

AOH Ancient Order of Hibernians

AoI aims of industry

aoi angle of incidence

a.o.i.v. [engineering] automatically operated inlet valve

A-OK [USA] all OK

AOL [USA] absent over leave; Admiralty Oil Laboratory; America Online (Internet service provider); [USA] Atlantic Oceanographic Laboratories; [Canada] Atlantic Oceanographic Laboratory

AOM amorphous organic matter

AON activity-on-node

AONB area of outstanding natural beauty

AOP Association of Optical Practitioners

AOPU Asian Oceanic Postal Union

AOQ average outgoing quality

AOQL average outgoing quality limit

AOR [music] adult-oriented rock; [US law] advice of rights; [USA] album-oriented radio; [music] album-oriented rock

aor angle of reflection

a/or and/or

aor. aorist

AOS [astronautics] acquisition of signal; American Opera Society; American Ophthalmological Society; Ancient Order of Shepherds; automated office system

AOSIS Association of Small Island States

AOSO advanced orbiting solar observatory

AOSS *Americanae Orientalis Societatis Socius* (Latin: Fellow of the American Oriental Society)

AOSTRA Alberta Oil Sands Technology and Research Authority

AOSW Association of Official Shorthand Writers

AOT [engineering] allowed outage time; [engineering] allowed out-of-service time

AOTA American Occupational Therapy Association

AOU American Ornithologists' Union

AOV any other variety

AP [insurance] additional premium; [grammar] adjective phrase; aerosol particle; [USA] airplane; [USA] Air Police; air pollution; air publication (of Ministry of Defence); *Alianza Popular* (Spanish: Popular Alliance) (political party); [USA] American plan (for payment of hotel bills); [surveying] *Amsterdamsch Peil* (German: Amsterdam level) (mean level used in parts of northern Europe); Andhra Pradesh; [medicine] angina pectoris; [medicine] anterior pituitary; [medicine] anteroposterior; antipersonnel; [commerce] *à protester* (French: to be protested) (on bill of exchange); armour-piercing; [computing] array processor; [medicine] arterial (blood) pressure; Associated Presbyterian; Associated Press (news agency); atomic power; authority to pay; authority to purchase; automotive products; [insurance] average payable; [vehicle registration] Brighton; [civil aircraft marking] Pakistan

Ap. apostle; Apostolic; April

ap. apostle; apothecaries' (weight or measure); apothecary; apparent; apparently; *apud* (Latin: in the works of, according to)

a.p. above proof; [insurance] additional premium; advanced post; [medicine] *ante prandium* (Latin: before meals) (in prescriptions); [mathematics] arithmetical progression; author's proof

APA [taxation] additional personal allowance; Alaska Power Authority; [Australia] All Parties Administration; [computing] all points addressable (as in **APA mode**); American Philological Association; American Physicists Association; American Pilots Association; American Press Association; American Protestant Association; American Psychiatric Association; American Psychological Association; [telecommunications] annular phased array; Associate in Public Administration; Association for the Prevention of Addiction; Association of Public Analysts; Australian Physiotherapy Association; *Austria Presse Agentur* (Austrian news agency)

APACL Asian People's Anti-Communist League

APACS Association for Payment Clearing Services

APAE Association of Public Address Engineers

apart. apartment

APB Accounting Principles Board; [USA] all-points bulletin (police alert); Auditing Practices Board

APBA American Power Boat Association

APBF Accredited Poultry Breeders' Federation

APC [engineering] advanced process control; air-pollution control; All People's Congress (in Sierra Leone); American Philatelic Congress; [immunology] antigen-presenting cell; Appalachian Power Company; armoured personnel carrier; aspirin, phenacetin and caffeine; Assistant Principal Chaplain; Associated Portland Cement; Auditing Practices Committee; automatic phase control; [electronics] automatic power control; automatic public convenience

a.p.c. average propensity to consume

APCA [USA] Air Pollution Control Association; Anglo-Polish Catholic Association

APCIMS Association of Private Client Investment Managers and Stockbrokers

APCK Association for Promoting Christian Knowledge (in Church of Ireland)

APCN *anno post Christum natum* (Latin: in the year after the birth of Christ)

APCO Association of Pleasure Craft Operators

APCOL All-Pakistan Confederation of Labour

APD Administrative Planning Division; [USA] Air Pollution Division; Army Pay Department

apd approved

APDC Apple and Pear Development Council

Ap. Deleg. Apostolic Delegate

AP/DOS [computing] advanced pick/disk operating system

APE Amalgamated Power Engineering; automatic photomapping equipment; [physics] available potential energy

APEC Asia-Pacific Economic Cooperation Conference

APEX advance-purchase excursion (reduced fare on train or aeroplane); Association of Professional, Executive, Clerical and Computer Staff (became part of GMB)

APF Association for the Propagation of the Faith

APFC Asia-Pacific Forestry Commission

APG [US air force] air proving ground

APGA American Public Gas Association

APH A(lan) P(atrick) Herbert (British writer and politician); [medicine] ante-partum haemorrhage; [biochemistry] anterior pituitary hormone

aph. aphorism

APHA American Public Health Association

APHC Association of Plumbing and Heating Contractors

aphet. aphetic

APHI Association of Public Health Inspectors

APHIS [USA] Animal and Plant Health Inspection Service

API air-pollution index; air-position indicator; American Petroleum Institute (as in **API scale** for measuring specific gravity of petroleum products); [computing] application program(mer) interface; *Association phonétique internationale* (French: International Phonetic Association); atmospheric pressure ionization

APIS Army Photographic Intelligence Service

ap. J-C *après Jésus-Christ* (French: after Jesus Christ, AD)

APL Alberta Power Limited; alternating polarization laser; [USA] Applied Physics Laboratory (Johns Hopkins University); [computing] A Programming Language

Apl April

APLA Azanian People's Liberation Army

APLE Association of Public Lighting Engineers

APM [USA] Academy of Physical Medicine; airborne particulate matter; Assistant Paymaster; Assistant Provost-Marshal; [astronomy] automatic plate-measuring machine

APMC Allied Political and Military Commission

APMG Assistant Postmaster-General

APMI Associate of the Pensions Management Institute

apmt appointment

APNEC All-Pakistan Newspaper Employees' Confederation

APO Acting Pilot Officer; African People's Organization; Armed Forces Post Office; Army Post Office; Asian Productivity Organization

apo. apogee

Apoc. Apocalypse; Apocrypha; Apocryphal

Apocr. Apocrypha; Apocryphal

apog. apogee

Apos. Apostolic

apos. apostrophe

APOTA automatic positioning tele-metering antenna

apoth. apothecary

APP African People's Party (became part of KANU); [computing] application portability profile

App. Apostles

app. apparatus; apparent; apparently; appeal; appended; appendix (of book); applied; appointed; appointment; appreciated; apprentice; approval; approved; approximate; approximately

APPA African Petroleum Producers Association

appar. apparatus; apparent; apparently

app. crit. *apparatus criticus* (Latin: critical apparatus) (list of variant readings)

appd approved

APPITA Australian Pulp and Paper Industries Technical Association

appl appeal

appl. appellant; applicable; applied

appos. appositive

APPR [USA] Army Package Power Reactor

appr. apprentice; approved

appro [short form] approval

approx. approximate; approximately; approximation

apps appendices

appt appoint; appointment

apptd appointed

APPU Australian Primary Producers' Union

appurts appurtenances

appx appendix (of book)

APR Accredited Public Relations Practitioner; annual percentage rate (of interest); annual progress report; annual purchase rate (on hire purchase)

Apr. April; *April* (German: April)

apr. *aprile* (Italian: April)

APRA Air Public Relations Association

APRC *anno post Romam conditam* (Latin: in the year from the foundation of Rome)

A/Prin. Assistant Principal

apr. J-C *après Jésus-Christ* (French: after Jesus Christ, AD)

APRS [navigation] acoustic position reference system; Association for the Protection of Rural Scotland; Association of Professional Recording Studios

APS [Australia] Aborigines' Protection Society; Advanced Photo System; Algeria Press Service (news agency); American Peace Society; American Philatelic Society; American Philosophical Society; American Physics Society; American Physiological Society; American Protestant Society; Arizona Public Service (Company); army postal service; assistant private secretary; Associate of the Pharmaceutical Society; Associate of the Philosophical Society

Aps [astronomy] Apus

a.p.s. autograph poem signed; average propensity to save

APSA American Political Science Association; Associate of the Photographic Society of America; Australian Political Studies Association

APSE [computing] Ada programming support environment

APSL Acting Paymaster Sublieutenant

APST Association of Professional Scientists and Technologists

APSW Association of Psychiatric Social Workers

APT advanced passenger train; advanced process technology; [nautical] after peak tank; [medicine] alum-precipitated (diphtheria) toxoid; Association of Polytechnic Teachers; Association of Printing Technologists; Association of Private Traders; automatic picture transmission (from satellite)

apt apartment

APTC Army Physical Training Corps

APTI Association of Principals of Technical Institutions

APTIS all-purpose ticket-issuing systems

APTS [astronautics] Automatic Picture Transmission Subsystem

APTU African Postal and Telecommunications Union

APU acute psychiatric unit; Arab Postal Union; [education] Assessment of Performance Unit; [aeronautics] auxiliary power unit

APUC Association for Promoting Unity of Christendom

APUD amine-precursor uptake and decarboxylation (as in **APUD cell**)

a.p.v. adjusted present value

APWA All Pakistan Women's Association; American Public Welfare Association; American Public Works Association

APWR [nuclear technology] advanced pressurized-water reactor

APWU American Postal Workers Union

apx. approximately

AQ [psychology] accomplishment quotient; [psychology] achievement quotient; [military] Administration and Quartering

Aq. [horticulture] aquatic

aq. *aqua* (Latin: water); aqueous

.aq Antarctica (in Internet address)

aq. bull. [pharmacology] *aqua bulliens* (Latin: boiling water)

AQC Associate of Queen's College (London)

aq. cal. [pharmacology] *aqua calida* (Latin: warm water)

aq. com. [pharmacology] *aqua communis* (Latin: tap water)

aq. dest. [pharmacology] *aqua destillata* (Latin: distilled water)

aq. ferv. [pharmacology] *aqua fervens* (Latin: hot water)

aq. frig. [pharmacology] *aqua frigida* (Latin: cold water)

AQI air-quality index

AQL acceptable quality level

Aql [astronomy] Aquila

AQMG Assistant Quartermaster-General

aq. m. pip. [pharmacology] *aqua menthae piperitae* (Latin: peppermint water)

AQPS *autre que pur sang* (French: other than pure blood) (in horse-breeding)

aq. pur. [pharmacology] *aqua pura* (Latin: pure water)

Aqr [astronomy] Aquarius

aq. tep. [pharmacology] *aqua tepida* (Latin: tepid water)

aque. aqueduct

AR [psychology] accomplishment ratio; account receivable; [psychology] achievement ratio; acid resisting; acrylic rubber; [medicine] acute rejection; [physiology] adrenergic receptor; advice of receipt; *Agencja Robotnicza* (Polish workers' news agency); [USA] airman recruit; *Altesse Royale* (French: Royal Highness); [physiology] androgen receptor; *Anna Regina* (Latin: Queen Anne); *anno regni* (Latin: in the year of the reign); annual register; *Annual Register of World Events*; annual report; [taxation] annual return; [medicine] aortic regurgitation; [numismatics] *argentum* (Latin: silver); [US postcode] Arkansas; Army Regulation(s); artificial respiration; [image technology] aspect ratio; Assistant Resident; Associated Rediffusion; Autonomous Region; Autonomous Republic; [fishing port] Ayr; [vehicle registration] Chelmsford

Ar [chemical element] argon

Ar. Arab; Arabia; Arabian; Arabic; Aramaic

aR *am Rhein* (German: on the River Rhine) (in place-names)

a/r [insurance] all risks

ar. arrival; arrive(s); arrived

.ar Argentina (in Internet address)

a.r. [insurance] all risks; *anno regni* (Latin: in the year of the reign)

ARA Aircraft Research Association; all replies answered (in personal advertisement); Amateur Rowing Association; American Railway Association; Army Rifle Association; Associate of the Royal Academy; Association of the River Authorities; [New Zealand] Auckland Regional Authority

Arab. Arabia; Arabian; Arabic

ARAC Associate of the Royal Agricultural College

arach. arachnology

ARACI Associate of the Royal Australian Chemical Institute

ARAD Associate of the Royal Academy of Dancing

ARAeS Associate of the Royal Aeronautical Society

ARAIA Associate of the Royal Australian Institute of Architects

ARAM Associate of the Royal Academy of Music

Aram. Aramaic

ARAMCO Arabian-American Oil Company

ARAS Associate of the Royal Astronomical Society

ARB Air Registration Board (in civil aviation); Air Research Bureau

arb. arbiter; arbitrageur; arbitrary; arbitration; arbitrator

ARBA Associate of the Royal Society of British Artists

ARBE *Académie royale des beaux-arts, école supérieure des arts décoratifs et école supérieure d'architecture de Bruxelles* (French: Brussels Royal Academy of Fine Arts)

arbor. arboriculture

ARBS Associate of the Royal Society of British Sculptors

ARC Aeronautical Research Council; Agricultural Research Council (former name of AFRC); [medicine] Aids-related complex; American Red Cross; [USA] Ames Research Center; Archaeological Resource Centre (York); Architects' Registration Council; Arthritis and Rheumatism Council; Astrophysical Research Consortium; Atlantic Research Corporation

arc. [music] *arcato* (Italian: bowed);

[music] *coll'arco* (Italian: with the bow)

ARCA Associate of the Royal Cambrian Academy; Associate of the Royal Canadian Academy of Arts; Associate of the Royal College of Art

ARCamA Associate of the Royal Cambrian Academy

arccos [mathematics] arc cosine

arccosec [mathematics] arc cosecant

arccot [mathematics] arc cotangent

Arch. Archbishop; Archdeacon; Archduke

arch. archaic; archaism; archery; archipelago; architect; architectural; architecture

archaeol. archaeology

Archbp Archbishop

Archd. Archdeacon; Archduke

archit. architect; architectural; architecture

archt architect

ARCIC Anglican/Roman Catholic International Commission

ARCM Associate of the Royal College of Music

Arcnet attached resource computing network

ARCO Associate of the Royal College of Organists

ARCO(CHM) Associate of the Royal College of Organists with Diploma in Choir Training

ARCOS Anglo-Russian Cooperative Society

ARCPsych Associate of the Royal College of Psychiatrists

ARCS Associate of the Royal College of Science; Associate of the Royal College of Surgeons (of England); Australian Red Cross Society

arcsec [mathematics] arc secant; arc second

arcsin [mathematics] arc sine

ARCST Associate of the Royal College of Science and Technology (Glasgow)

arctan [mathematics] arc tangent

ARCUK Architects' Registration Council of the United Kingdom

ARCVS Associate of the Royal College of Veterinary Surgeons

ARD [medicine] acute radiation disease; [medicine] acute respiratory disease

ARDC [USA] Air Research and Development Command

ARDEC [USA] Army Research Development and Engineering Center

ARDMS automated route design and management system

ARDS [medicine] adult respiratory distress syndrome

ARE activated reactive evaporation; Admiralty Research Establishment; Arab Republic of Egypt; Associate of the Royal Society of Painter-Printmakers (formerly Associate of the Royal Society of Painter-Etchers and Engravers)

ARELS Association of Recognized English Language Schools

ARENA *Aliança Renovadora Nacional* (Spanish: National Renewal Alliance) (in Brazil)

ARF [medicine] acute renal failure; [medicine] acute respiratory failure; Advertising Research Foundation

Arg. [heraldry] argent; Argentina; Argentine; Argentinian; Argyll(shire)

aRh. *am Rhein* (German: on the River Rhine) (in place-names)

ARHA Associate of the Royal Hibernian Academy

ARHS Associate of the Royal Horticultural Society

ARI [medicine] acute respiratory infection

Ari [astronomy] Aries

ARIA automated radioimmunoassay

ARIAS Associate of the Royal Incorporation of Architects in Scotland

ARIBA Associate of the Royal Institute of British Architects

ARICS Professional Associate of the Royal Institution of Chartered Surveyors

ARIEL Automated Real-time Investments Exchange Limited (former share-dealing system)

ARIMA [computing] autoregressive integrated moving average

ARINA Associate of the Royal Institution of Naval Architects

ARIPHH Associate of the Royal Institute of Public Health and Hygiene

ARIS advanced range instrumentation ship

Arist. Aristotle (ancient Greek philosopher)

Aristoph. Aristophanes (ancient Greek dramatist)

arith. arithmetic; arithmetical; arithmetician

Ariz. Arizona
Ark. Arkansas
ARL Admiralty Research Laboratory; Aeronautical Research Laboratory; Arctic Research Laboratory; [USA] Association of Research Libraries; Australian Rugby League
ARLA Association of Residential Letting Agents
ARLL [computing] advanced run length limited
ARM [USA] adjustable-rate mortgage; *Alliance réformée mondiale* (French: Worldwide Presbyterian Alliance); antiradar missile; antiradiation missile; [medicine] artificial rupture of membranes; atomic resolution microscope; Australian Republican Movement
ArM Master of Architecture (from Latin *Architecturae Magister*)
Arm. Armagh; Armenia; Armenian; Armorica; Armorican
ARMA Association of Residential Managing Agents; [computing] autoregressive moving average
ARMCM Associate of the Royal Manchester College of Music
armd armoured
ARMIT Associate of the Royal Melbourne Institute of Technology
ARMS Action for Research into Multiple Sclerosis; Associate of the Royal Society of Miniature Painters
ARNA Arab Revolution News Agency
ARO army routine order; Asian Regional Organization; Associate Member of the Register of Osteopaths
AROD airborne remote operated device
AROS African Regional Organization for Standardization
ARP [US finance] adjustable rate preferred (stock); air-raid precautions; Associated Reformed Presbyterian
arp. [music] *arpeggiato* (Italian: played as arpeggio); [music] arpeggio
ARPA Advanced Research Projects Agency (former name of DARPA)
ARPANET [computing] Advanced Research Projects Agency Network
ARPO Association of Resort Publicity Officers
ARPS Associate of the Royal Photographic Society; Association of Railway Preservation Societies
ARR accounting rate of return; *anno regni Reginae* (Latin: in the year of the Queen's reign); *anno regni Regis* (Latin: in the year of the King's reign); Association of Radiation Research
arr. [music] arranged (by); [music] arrangement; [music] arranger; arrival; arrive(s); arrived
ARRC Associate of the Royal Red Cross
arrd arrived
arron. *arrondissement* (French: administrative district)
ARRS American Roentgen Ray Society
ARS [medicine] acute radiation syndrome; [USA] Agricultural Research Service; American Records Society; American Recreation Society; American Rocket Society; *anno reparatae salutis* (Latin: in the year of our redemption); [medicine] aortic regurgitation and stenosis; Army Radio School
ARSA Associate of the Royal Scottish Academy; Associate of the Royal Society of Arts
ARSAP [USA] Advanced Reactor Severe Accident Program
ARSCM Associate of the Royal School of Church Music
ARSH Associate of the Royal Society of Health
ARSL Associate of the Royal Society of Literature
ARSM Associate of the Royal School of Mines
ARSR air route surveillance radar
ARSW Associate of the Royal Scottish Water Colour Society
ART [computing] algebraic reconstruction technique; [computing] automated reasoning tool
Art. Artemis (ancient Greek goddess)
art. article; artificer; artificial; artillery; artist
ARTC air route traffic control
artic [short form] articulated truck
artic. articulated
artif. artificer
art. pf artist's proof
arty artillery
ARU American Railway Union; [computing] audio response unit

ARV [medicine] Aids-associated retrovirus; [Bible] American (Standard) Revised Version

ARVA Associate of the Rating and Valuation Association

ARWA Associate of the Royal West of England Academy

ARWS Associate of the Royal Watercolour Society

AS Academy of Science; Admiral Superintendent; [education] Advanced Supplementary (as in **AS level**); air speed; air staff; [insurance] all sections; [music] *al segno* (Italian: to the sign, at the sign); [geology] aluminium silicate; American Samoa; [computing] analogue states; Anglo-Saxon; *anno salutis* (Latin: in the year of salvation); *anno Salvatoris* (Latin: in the year of the Saviour); antisubmarine; assistant secretary; assistant surgeon; Associate in Science; [vehicle registration] Inverness; [taxation] personal allowance

A/S account sales; [education] Advanced Supplementary (as in **A/S level**); [banking] after sight; [commerce] *Aksjeselskap* (Norwegian: limited company, Ltd); [commerce] *Aktieselskab* (Danish: joint-stock company); alongside

As [chemical element] arsenic

As [meteorology] altostratus

As. Asia; Asian; Asiatic

a.s. account sales; aggregate supply

ASA Acoustical Society of America; [USA] Addiction Services Agency; Advertising Standards Authority; Amateur Swimming Association; American Sociological Association; American Standards Association; American Statistical Association; Army Sailing Association; [USA] Associate of the Society of Actuaries; Australian Society of Accountants

ASAA Associate of the Society of Incorporated Accountants and Auditors

ASAB Association for the Study of Animal Behaviour

ASAI Associate of the Society of Architectural Illustrators

ASAM Associate of the Society of Art Masters

AS&TS of SA Associated Scientific and Technical Societies of South Africa

ASAP as soon as possible; automated shipboard aerological programme

a.s.a.p. as soon as possible

ASAT [military] antisatellite (interceptor)

ASB Accounting Standards Board; [South Africa] *Afrikaanse Studentebond* (Afrikaans: South African students' union); Alternative Service Book (in Church of England); American Society of Bacteriologists; [medicine] anencephaly and spina bifida

asb. asbestos

a.s.b. aircraft safety beacon

ASBAH Association for Spina Bifida and Hydrocephalus

ASBM air-to-surface ballistic missile

ASBSBSW Amalgamated Society of Boilermakers, Shipwrights, Blacksmiths and Structural Workers

ASC Accounting Standards Committee; Administrative Staff College (Henley); [USA] Air Service Command; altered state of consciousness; American Society of Cinematographers; Anglo-Soviet Committee; Asian Socialist Conference

ASc Associate in Science

Asc. [astrology] Ascendant

asc. ascend; ascent

ASCA Associate of the Society of Company and Commercial Accountants

ASCAB Armed Services Consultant Approval Board

ASCAP American Society of Composers, Authors, and Publishers

ASCC Accounting Standards Steering Committee; Association of Scottish Climbing Clubs; [computing] Automatic Sequence Controlled Calculator

ASCE American Society of Civil Engineers

ASCII [computing] American Standard Code for Information Interchange

ASCM Australian Student Christian Movement

ASCS [engineering] advanced Stirling conversion system

ASCU [USA] Association of State Colleges and Universities

ASD [engineering] adjustable speed drive; Admiralty Salvage Department; [engineering] antislip drive; Armament Supply Department; [medicine] atrial septal defect

Asda Associated Dairies

ASDAR aircraft-to-satellite data relay

ASDC Associate of the Society of Dyers and Colourists

ASDE Airport Surface Detection Equipment

a/s de *aux soins de* (French: care of, c/o) (in postal addresses)

ASDIC Allied Submarine Detection Investigation Committee (early form of sonar); [USA] Armed Services Documents Intelligence Center

ASE Admiralty Signal Establishment; American Stock Exchange; [physics] amplified spontaneous emission; Army School of Education; Associate of the Society of Engineers; Association for Science Education; automotive Stirling engine

ASEA Association of South East Asia

ASEAN Association of South East Asian Nations

ASEC [USA] Applied Solar Energy Corporation

ASEE American Society for Engineering Education; Association of Supervisory and Executive Engineers (became part of IIExE)

ASF [computing] aspect source flag; Associate of the Institute of Shipping and Forwarding Agents

ASG Acting Secretary-General; Assistant Secretary-General

ASGB Aeronautical Society of Great Britain; Anthroposophical Society of Great Britain

ASGBI Anatomical Society of Great Britain and Ireland

asgd assigned

asgmt assignment

ASH Action on Smoking and Health

ashp airship

ASHRAE American Society of Heating, Refrigeration and Air-Conditioning Engineers

ASI airspeed indicator; *Association soroptimiste internationale* (French: Soroptimist International Association)

ASIA Airlines Staff International Association

ASIC [electronics] application-specific integrated circuit

ASIF Amateur Swimming International Federation

ASIO Australian Security Intelligence Organization

ASIP [astronomy] all-sky imaging photometer

ASIRC [USA] Aquatic Sciences Information Retrieval Center (Rhode Island)

ASIS [astronautics] abort sensing and implementation system; American Society for Information Science

ASL above sea level; Acting Sublieutenant; Advanced Student in Law; American Sign Language; American Soccer League; assistant Scout leader

ASLA American Society of Landscape Architects

ASLB [USA] Atomic Safety and Licensing Board

ASLE American Society of Lubrication Engineers

ASLEF Associated Society of Locomotive Engineers and Firemen

ASLEP [astronautics] Apollo surface lunar experiments package

AS level [education] Advanced Supplementary level

A/S level [education] Advanced Supplementary level

ASLIB Association for Information Management (formerly Association of Special Libraries and Information Bureaux)

ASLO American Society of Limnology and Oceanography; Australian Scientific Liaison Office

ASLP Amalgamated Society of Lithographic Printers

ASLW Amalgamated Society of Leather Workers

ASM Acting Sergeant-Major; air-to-surface missile; [computing] algorithmic state machine; American Society for Metals; assistant sales manager; assistant Scoutmaster; assistant stage manager; assistant station master; Association of Senior Members

ASME American Society of Mechanical Engineers; Association for the Study of Medical Education

As. Mem. Associate Member

ASMO Arab Organization for Standardization and Metrology

ASMP American Society of Magazine Photographers

ASN army service number; average sample number

ASNE American Society of Newspaper Editors

ASO Air Staff Officer; American Symphony Orchestra; area supplies officer

ASOS automatic storm observation service

ASP [commerce] *accepté sous protêt* (French: accepted under protest); [US air force] aerospace plane; African Special Project (of IUCN); Afro-Shirazi Party (in Tanzania); American selling price; [USA] Anglo-Saxon Protestant; Astronomical Society of the Pacific

ASPA Australian Sugar Producers' Association

ASPAC Asian and Pacific Council

ASPC [commerce] *accepté sous protêt pour compte* (French: accepted under protest for account); Association of Swimming Pool Contractors

ASPCA American Society for the Prevention of Cruelty to Animals

ASPEP Association of Scientists and Professional Engineering Personnel

ASPF Association of Superannuation and Pension Funds

ASPI [computing] advanced SCSI programming interface

ASR airport surveillance radar; air-sea rescue; [meteorology] altimeter setting region; answer, send and receive; [computing] automatic send and receive

ASRE Admiralty Signal and Radar Establishment

A/SRS air-sea rescue service

ASS automatic space station

Ass. Associate; Associated; Association

ass. assembly; assistance; assistant; association; assurance

ASSC Accounting Standards Steering Committee

Ass-Com-Gen Assistant-Commissary-General

ASSET [US air force] aero-thermodynamic-elastic structural systems environmental tests

ASSGB Association of Ski Schools in Great Britain

assigt assignment

assim. assimilate; assimilated

assmt assessment

assn association

assoc. associate; associated; association

AssocEng Associate of Engineering

AssocMCT Associateship of Manchester College of Technology

assocn association

AssocSc Associate in Science

ASSR Autonomous Soviet Socialist Republic

asst assistant

asstd assorted

ASSU American Sunday School Union

assy assembly

Assyr. Assyrian

AST above-ground storage tank; advanced supersonic transport; air service training; assured shorthold tenancy; Atlantic Standard Time; automated screen trading; automatic station tuning

ASTA American Society of Travel Agents; [New Zealand] Auckland Science Teachers' Association

ASTC Administrative Service Training Course; Associate of the Sydney Technical College

ASTIA [USA] Armed Services Technical Information Agency

ASTM American Society for Testing and Materials

ASTMS Association of Scientific, Technical and Managerial Staffs

ASTOR antisubmarine torpedo ordnance rocket

ASTP Apollo–Soyuz test project

astr. astronomer; astronomical; astronomy

ASTRO [USA] Air Space Travel Research Organization

astro. astronautics; astronomer; astronomy

astrol. astrologer; astrological; astrology

astron. astronomer; astronomical; astronomy

astrophys. astrophysical

Ast. T astronomical time

ASU American Students Union; Arab Socialist Union

ASUA Amateur Swimming Union of the Americas

ASV aircraft-to-surface vessel; [Bible] American Standard Version; [microbiology] avian sarcoma virus

ASVA Associate of the Incorporated Society of Valuers and Auctioneers

ASVU Army Security Vetting Unit

ASW Amalgamated Society of Wood Workers; antisubmarine warfare; antisubmarine work; Association of Scientific Workers; Association of Social Workers

ASWDU Air Sea Warfare Development Unit

ASWE Admiralty Surface Weapons Establishment

AT achievement test; administrative trainee; Advanced Technologies; [immunology] agglutination test; alternative technology; *Angling Times*; antitank; apparent time; [USA] appropriate technology; arrival time; [medicine] ataxia telangiectasia; Atlantic Time; [education] attainment target; Australia Telescope; automatic transmission (in car advertisement); [vehicle registration] Hull

A/T American terms

At ampere-turn; [chemical element] astatine; [informal] (member of the) Auxiliary Territorial Service

at. atmosphere; atomic; [navigation] attitude; attorney

.at Austria (in Internet address)

ATA [computing] Advanced Technologies attachment; [nuclear technology] advanced test accelerator; Air Transport Association; Air Transport Auxiliary; American Translators' Association; Amusement Trades Association; Animal Technicians' Association; Associate Technical Aide; Atlantic Treaty Association

ATAC Air Transport Advisory Council

ATAE Association of Tutors in Adult Education

ATAF Allied Tactical Air Force

ATAM Association for Teaching Aids in Mathematics

AT&T American Telephone and Telegraph Company

Atapi [computing] Advanced Technologies attachment packet interface

ATAS Air Transport Auxiliary Service

ATB advanced technology bomber; all-terrain bike; at the time of the bomb(ing)

ATBM antitactical ballistic missile

ATC acid-treated coal; air traffic control; Air Training Command; Air Training

Corps; Air Transport Command; [law] Annotated Tax Cases; Art Teacher's Certificate; [computing] authorization to copy (software); automatic temperature control; automatic train control

a.t.c. average total costs

ATCC air traffic control centre

ATCE [astronautics] ablative thrust chamber engine

atchd attached

ATCL Associate of Trinity College of Music, London

ATCO Air Traffic Control Officer

ATCRBS air traffic control radar beacon system

ATCSP Association of Teachers of the Chartered Society of Physiotherapy

ATD actual time of departure; advanced technology development; Art Teacher's Diploma; Australian Tax Decisions

ATDS Association of Teachers of Domestic Science

ATE Amusement Trades Exhibition; Automatic Telephone and Electric (Company); [electronics] automatic test equipment

ATEC Air Transport Electronics Council

a tem. [music] *a tempo* (Italian: in time)

ATF [nuclear technology] accelerator test facility; [nuclear technology] advanced toroidal facility

ATFS Association of Track and Field Statisticians

ATG [medicine] antithymocyte globulin

ath. athlete; athletic

ATHE Association of Teachers in Higher Education

Athen. Athenian

athl. athlete; athletic

ATI Associate of the Textile Institute; Association of Technical Institutions

ATII Associate of the Taxation Institute, Incorporated (member of Chartered Institute of Taxation)

ATK at the keyboard (in Internet chat)

ATL [insurance] actual total loss; [medicine] adult T-cell leukaemia; Association of Teachers and Lecturers; [computing] automated (or automatic) tape library

Atl. Atlantic

ATLAS [astronomy] airborne tunable laser absorption spectrometer; [USA] Argonne tandem-linac accelerator system; auto-

matic tabulating, listing and sorting
package; automatic telephone line
address system

ATLB Air Transport Licensing Board

ATLV [medicine] adult T-cell leukaemia
virus

ATM [computing] Adobe Type Manager;
air training memorandum; antitank
missile; approved testing material;
Association of Teachers of Management;
Association of Teachers of Mathematics;
[computing] asynchronous transfer
mode; at the moment (in Internet chat
and e-mail); [banking] automated teller
machine

atm atmosphere (unit of pressure)

atm. atmospheric

ATMS assumption-based truth maintenance system

ATN [medicine] acute tubular necrosis;
[mathematics] arc tangent; [telecommuni-
cations] augmented transition
network

ATNA Australasian Trained Nurses'
Association

ATNF Australia Telescope National
Facility

at. no. atomic number

ATO Ammunition Technical Officer
(bomb-disposal officer); [aeronautics]
assisted take-off

A to A air-to-air

A to J [New Zealand] Appendices to Journals (of parliament)

ATOL Air Travel Organizers' Licence

ATP [biochemistry] adenosine tri-
phosphate; [aeronautics] advanced tur-
boprop; [commerce] aid trade provision;
Air Technical Publications; Associated
Theatre Properties; Association of Tennis
Professionals; [railways] automatic train
protection

ATPAS Association of Teachers of
Printing and Allied Subjects

ATPC Association of Tin Producing
Countries

ATPG automatic test-pattern generation

ATPL(A) Airline Transport Pilot's Licence
(Aeroplanes)

ATPL(H) Airline Transport Pilot's Licence
(Helicopters)

ATR [nuclear technology] advanced test
reactor; [nuclear technology] advanced

thermal reactor; [aeronautics] air
turbo-ram (jet engine); [radar] anti-
transmit-receive (as in **ATR tube**);
Association of Teachers of Russian; [mili-
tary] automatic target recognition

ATRAN automatic terrain recognition
and navigation

a.t.r.i.m.a. [law] as their respective interests may appear

ATS [Australia] Amalgamated Television
Services; American Temperance Society;
American Tract Society; American Trans-
port Service; [medicine] antitetanus
serum; [USA] Army Transport Service;
Associate of Theological Study; auto-
mated trade system; Auxiliary Territorial
Service (in World War II)

a.t.s. [law] at the suit of

ATSC Associate of the Tonic Sol-Fa
College

ATSDR [USA] Agency for Toxic Substances and Disease Registry

ATSIS [computing] automated technical-
specification information system

ATSS Association for the Teaching of
Social Sciences

ATT antitetanus toxoid

att. attached; attention; attorney

Att-Gen Attorney-General

attn attention; for the attention of

attrac. attractive

attrib. attribute; attributed (to); attri-
bution; [grammar] attributive; attribu-
tively

atty attorney

Atty-Gen Attorney-General

ATU [USA] Amalgamated Transit Union

ATUC African Trade Union Confederation

ATV all-terrain vehicle; Associated Television

at. wt atomic weight

AU [USA] Actors' Union; [printing] all up
(i.e. all set in type); angstrom unit; arith-
metic(al) unit; astronomical unit;
[vehicle registration] Nottingham

Au [chemical element] gold (from Latin
aurum)

.au Australia (in Internet address)

AUA [finance] agricultural unit of account
(in EU); American Unitarian Association; American Urological Association

AUBC Association of Universities of the
British Commonwealth

AUBTW Amalgamated Union of Building Trade Workers

AUC *ab urbe condita* (Latin: (in the year) from the founding of the city (of Rome)); *anno urbis conditae* (Latin: in the year from the founding of the city (of Rome)); [mathematics] area under the curve (on graph); Association of Underwater Contractors; Australian Universities Commission

AUCAS Association of University Clinical Academic Staff

aud. audit; audited; auditor

Aud-Gen Auditor-General

AUEW Amalgamated Union of Engineering Workers (became part of AEEU)

Aufl. *Auflage* (German: edition)

AUFW Amalgamated Union of Foundry Workers

Aug. August; *August* (German: August)

aug. augment; [grammar] augmentative; augmented

augm. augment; [grammar] augmentative; *augmenté* (French: enlarged)

AUI [computing] attachment unit interface

AULLA Australasian Universities Language and Literature Association

AUM air-to-underwater missile

AUMLA Australian Universities Modern Language Association

a.u.n. *absque ulla nota* (Latin: with no identifying mark)

AUO African Unity Organization

AUP Aberdeen University Press; acceptable use policy; Australian United Press (news agency)

Aur [astronomy] Auriga

AUS Army of the United States; assistant undersecretary; [international vehicle registration] Australia

Aus. Australia; Australian; Austria; Austrian

AUSA Association of the United States Army

Ausg. *Ausgabe* (German: edition)

Aust. Australia; Australian; Austria; Austrian

Austral. Australasia; Australasian; Australia; Australian

AUT Association of University Teachers

Aut. *Autriche* (French: Austria)

aut. autograph; autumn

AUTA Association of University Teachers of Accounting

AUTEC [US navy] Atlantic Underwater Test Evaluation Center

auth. authentic; author; authority; authorize; authorized

Auth. Ver. [Bible] Authorized Version

AUTIF Association of Unit Trusts and Investment Funds

auto. automatic; automobile; automotive

autobiog. autobiographical; autobiography

autog. autograph

AUT(S) Association of University Teachers (Scotland)

a.u.w. all-up-weight

AUWE Admiralty Underwater Weapons Establishment

AUX [linguistics] auxiliary verb

aux. auxiliary

AV [chemistry] acid value; [finance] *ad valorem* (Latin: according to value); [photography] aperture value; Artillery Volunteers; [medicine] atrioventricular (as in **AV node**); audiovisual; [numismatics] *aurum* (Latin: gold); [Bible] Authorized Version; average value; [vehicle registration] Peterborough

Av. Avenue; *Avocat* (French: lawyer)

a/v [finance] *ad valorem* (Latin: according to value)

av. avenue; average; avoirdupois; *avril* (French: April)

a.v. *annos vixit* (Latin: (he/she) lived . . . years); [finance] asset value

AVA Alberta Veterinary Association; Amateur Volleyball Association (of Great Britain); audiovisual aids; Audiovisual Association; Australian Veterinary Association

avail. available

AVB [medicine] atrioventricular block

AVC additional voluntary contribution (to pension scheme); American Veterans' Committee; [electronics] automatic volume control

av. C *avanti Cristo* (Italian: before Christ, BC)

a.v.c. [electronics] automatic volume control; average variable costs

Av. Cert. Aviator's Certificate

AVCM Associate of Victoria College of Music

AVCO [accounting] average cost

AVD Army Veterinary Department

avdp. avoirdupois

Ave. Avenue

ave. average

AVF [US military] all-volunteer force

avg. average

AVGAS aviation gasoline

avge [cricket] average

AVI Association of Veterinary Inspectors; audio-video interleaved; automatic vehicle identification

avia. aviation

av. J-C *avant Jésus-Christ* (French: before Jesus Christ, BC)

AVL [computing] Adel'son-Vel'skii-Landis (as in **AVL tree**); automatic vehicle location

AVLA Audio Visual Language Association

AVLIS atomic vapour laser isotope separation

AVM Air Vice-Marshal; [medicine] arteriovenous malformation; automatic vending machine

AVMA Action for the Victims of Medical Accidents; Automatic Vending Machine Association

AVN [medicine] atrioventricular node

avn aviation

AVO administrative veterinary officer; average vehicle occupancy

avoir. avoirdupois

AVR Army Volunteer Reserve

AVRI Animal Virus Research Institute

AVRO A. V. Roe and Company Limited (aircraft manufacturer)

AVRP audiovisual recording and presentation

AVS Anti-Vivisection Society

AVSL assistant Venture Scout leader

AVTRW Association of Veterinary Teachers and Research Workers

AW added water (in food); Alfred Wainwright (British walker and writer); alloy wheels (in car advertisement); Armstrong Whitworth (aircraft manufacturer); Articles of War; atomic warfare; [vehicle registration] Shrewsbury

a/w actual weight; airworthy; artwork

.aw Aruba (in Internet address)

a.w. actual weight; [shipping] all water; atomic weight

AWACS airborne warning and control system

AWAM Association of West African Merchants

AWAS Australian Women's Army Service

AWB [South Africa] *Afrikaner Weerstandsbeweging* (Afrikaans: Afrikaner Resistance Movement) (right-wing political party); Agricultural Wages Board; [USA] air waybill; Australian Wages Board

AWC Allied Works Council; [USA] Army War College; Australian Wool Corporation

AWE Atomic Weapons Establishment

AWEA American Wind Energy Association

AWeldI Associate of the Welding Institute

AWG American Wire Gauge; Art Workers' Guild

AWHA Australian Women's Home Army

AWJ [engineering] abrasive water jet

AWL absent with leave

AWMC Association of Workers for Maladjusted Children

AWNL Australian Women's National League

AWO American Waterways Operators (Incorporated)

AWOL absent without (official) leave

AWP amusements with prizes (in British Gaming Acts); annual wood production

AWPR Association of Women in Public Relations

AWR Association for the Study of the World Refugee Problem

AWRA Australian Wood Realization Agency

AWRE Atomic Weapons Research Establishment

AWS [geology] acoustic well sounding; Agricultural Wholesale Society; American Welding Society; automatic warning system

AWSA American Water Ski Association

AWU Australian Workers' Union

AX [vehicle registration] Cardiff

ax. axiom

AXAF Advanced X-ray Astrophysical Facility (at NASA)

AY [vehicle registration] Leicester
AYH American Youth Hostels
AYM [Freemasonry] Ancient York Mason
Ayr. Ayrshire
AZ [US postcode] Arizona; [international vehicle registration] Azerbaijan; [vehicle registration] Belfast
az. azimuth; azure

.az Azerbaijan (in Internet address)
Azapo [South Africa] Azanian People's Organization
az. ld [printing] azure laid (paper)
Azo. Azores
AZT [medicine] azidothymidine (used to treat Aids)
az. wo. [printing] azure wove (paper)

B

B administrative or professional (occupational group); Bachelor; [currency] baht (used in Thailand); [currency] balboa (used in Panama); [fishing port] Ballina; Baptist; Baron; [physics] baryon number; [chemistry] base-catalysed reaction; [music] bass; [music] basso; bathroom (in accommodation advertisement); battle; Baumé (temperature scale); bay (on map); *Beatus* (Latin: Blessed); [fishing port] Belfast; [international vehicle registration] Belgium; Benediction; best (wrought iron); Bey; Bible; billion; [UK postcode] Birmingham; Bishop; [chess] bishop; black (soft pencil lead); Blessed; [medicine] blood group; blue; board; boatswain; [currency] bolívar (used in Venezuela); bomber (aircraft) (as in **B-52**); [immunology] bone marrow (as in **B-cell**); book; [chemical element] boron; breadth; Britain; British; brotherhood; [photography] B-setting (shutter setting); building; [civil aircraft marking] China; eleven (in hexadecimal notation); [music] note of scale; of secondary importance (as in **B-side**); secondary road (as in **B5053**); [education] second highest grade or mark; [civil aircraft marking] Taiwan
b [physics] barn (unit of nuclear cross-section); [meteorology] blue sky; [physics] bottom (quark flavour)
b. bag; bale; ball; barrel; base; [music] bass; [music] basso; bath; batsman; bay; beam; bedroom (in accommodation advertisement); before; billion; *bis* (Latin: twice); bitch; bloody; book; born; bound; [medicine] bowels; [cricket]

bowled (by); breadth; brother; [informal] bugger; bust; by; [cricket] bye
B0 [paper size] 1000 × 1414 mm
B1 [paper size] 707 × 1000 mm
B2 [paper size] 500 × 707 mm
B3 [paper size] 353 × 500 mm
B4 [paper size] 250 × 353 mm
B5 [paper size] 176 × 250 mm
B6 [paper size] 125 × 176 mm
B7 [paper size] 88 × 125 mm
B8 [paper size] 62 × 88 mm
B9 [paper size] 44 × 62 mm
B10 [paper size] 31 × 44 mm
2B double black (very soft pencil lead)
3B [civil aircraft marking] Mauritius; treble black (very soft pencil lead)
5B [civil aircraft marking] Cyprus
BA able-bodied seaman; Bachelor of Arts; [fishing port] Ballantrae; [finance] bank acceptance; [finance] banker's acceptance; [UK postcode] Bath; [medicine] biliary atresia; [USA] *Biological Abstracts*; Board of Agriculture; Booksellers' Association (of Great Britain and Ireland); [chemistry] boric acid; British Academy; British Airways; British America; British Association (for the Advancement of Science); [medicine] bronchial asthma; Buenos Aires; [computing] bus automaton; [vehicle registration] Manchester
Ba [chemical element] barium
.ba Bosnia-Herzegovina (in Internet address)
b.a. [taxation] balancing allowance; blind approach
BAA Bachelor of Applied Arts; Booking Agents' Association of Great Britain; British Accounting Association; British

Airports Authority; British Archaeological Association; British Astronomical Association

BAA&A British Association of Accountants and Auditors

BAAB British Amateur Athletic Board

BA(Admin) Bachelor of Arts in Administration

BAAF British Agencies for Adoption and Fostering

BAAL British Association for Applied Linguistics

BA(Art) Bachelor of Arts in Art

BAAS British Association for the Advancement of Science

Bab. Babylonia; Babylonian

BABIE British Association for Betterment of Infertility and Education

BABS [aeronautics] beam approach beacon system; [aeronautics] blind approach beacon system

BAC biologically active compound(s); blood-alcohol concentration; blood-alcohol content; British Aircraft Corporation; British Association of Chemists; [medicine] bronchoalveolar cell(s); Business Archives Council

BAc Bachelor of Acupuncture

Bac. Baccalauréat (French school-leaving examination); *Baccalaureus* (Latin: Bachelor)

BACAH British Association of Consultants in Agriculture and Horticulture

BACAN British Association for the Control of Aircraft Noise

BACAT barge aboard catamaran; barge canal traffic

BAcc Bachelor of Accountancy

bach. bachelor

BACIE British Association for Commercial and Industrial Education

BACM British Association of Colliery Management

BACO British Aluminium Company (Limited)

BACS Bankers Automated Clearing System

bact. bacteria; bacterial; bacteriological; bacteriology; bacterium

bacteriol. bacteriological; bacteriology

BAD base air depot; British Association of Dermatology

BADA British Antique Dealers' Association

BADGE base air defence ground environment

BAdmin Bachelor of Administration

BAE Bachelor of Aeronautical Engineering; Bachelor of Arts in Education; Badminton Association of England; Belfast Association of Engineers; [USA] Bureau of Agricultural Economics

BAe British Aerospace

BAEA British Actors' Equity Association

BAEC Bangladesh Atomic Energy Commission; British Agricultural Export Council

BA(Econ) Bachelor of Arts in Economics

BA(ED) Bachelor of Arts in Environmental Design

BA(Ed) Bachelor of Arts in Education

BAEF Belgian-American Educational Foundation

BAF biological aerated filter; British Athletics Federation

BAFM British Association of Forensic Medicine; British Association of the Friends of Museums

BAFMA British and Foreign Maritime Agencies

BAFO British Air Forces of Occupation; British Army Forces Overseas

BAFRA British Antique Furniture Restorers' Association

BAFSC British Association of Field and Sports Contractors

BAFSV British Armed Forces Special Vouchers

BAFTA British Academy of Film and Television Arts

BAG Bank Action Group

BAGA British Amateur Gymnastics Association

BAGB Bicycle Association of Great Britain

BAgEc Bachelor of Agricultural Economics

BAgr Bachelor of Agriculture

BAgrSc Bachelor of Agricultural Science

Bah. Bahamas

BAHA British Association of Hotel Accountants

BAHOH British Association for the Hard of Hearing

BAHS British Agricultural History Society

BAI Bachelor of Engineering (from Latin *Baccalaureus Artis Ingeniariae*); [military] battlefield air interdiction; Book Association of Ireland; [medicine] bronchial arterial infusion

BAIE British Association of Industrial Editors

BAIR British Airports Information Retrieval

BAJ Bachelor of Arts in Journalism

BAL blood alcohol level; British antilewisite (antidote to gas and metal poisoning); [medicine] bronchoalveolar lavage

Bal. Ballarat

bal. [accounting] balance

balc. balcony (in property advertisement)

BALH British Association for Local History

ball. ballast; ballistics

BALPA British Air Line Pilots' Association

bals. balsam

Balt. Baltic; Baltimore

balun [telecommunications] balanced unbalanced (transformer)

BAM Bachelor of Applied Mathematics; Bachelor of Arts in Music

BaM [medicine] barium meal

BAMA British Aerosol Manufacturers' Association; British Amsterdam Maritime Agencies; British Army Motoring Association

BAMBI ballistic missile boost intercept

BAMTM British Association of Machine Tool Merchants

BA(Mus) Bachelor of Arts in Music

BAMW British Association of Meat Wholesalers

BAN British Association of Neurologists

Ban. Bangor; Bantu

BANC British Association of National Coaches; British Association of Nature Conservationists

Banc. Sup. [law] *Bancus Superior* (Latin: higher bench, Queen's Bench, King's Bench)

B&B bed and breakfast

B&C [insurance] building and contents

B&D bondage and discipline; bondage and domination

b&e beginning and ending

B&FBS British and Foreign Bible Society

B&Q (Richard) Block and (David) Quayle (British founders of chain of DIY stores)

B&S brandy and soda; Browne and Sharpe (wire gauge)

B&W black and white

B&WE Bristol and West of England

BANS British Association of Numismatic Societies

BANZARE British, Australian, New Zealand Antarctic Research Expedition

BAO Bachelor of Arts in Obstetrics; Bankruptcy Annulment Order; British American Oil

BAOD British Airways Overseas Division

BA of E Badminton Association of England

BAOMS British Association of Oral and Maxillofacial Surgeons

BAOR British Army of the Rhine

Bap. Baptist

bap. baptize; baptized

b. à p. *billets à payer* (French: bills payable)

BAPA British Amateur Press Association

BAPC British Aircraft Preservation Council

BAPCO Bahrain Petroleum Company

BA(PE) Bachelor of Arts in Physical Education

BAPL Bettis Atomic Power Laboratory

BAPLA British Association of Picture Libraries and Agencies

BAPM British Association of Physical Medicine

BAppArts Bachelor of Applied Arts

BAppSc Bachelor of Applied Science

BAppSc(MT) Bachelor of Applied Science (Medical Technology)

BAPS beacon automated processing system (for lighthouses); British Association of Paediatric Surgeons; British Association of Plastic Surgeons

BAPT British Association for Physical Training

Bapt. Baptist

bapt. baptism; baptized

BAR [computing] base address register; *Book Auction Records*; British Association of Removers; Browning Automatic Rifle; [computing] buffer address register

Bar. Baritone; Barrister; [Bible] Baruch (book of Apocrypha)

bar. baritone; barleycorn (former unit of

length); barometer; barometric; barrel; barrister

b. à r. *billets à recevoir* (French: bills receivable)

BARB British Association of Rose Breeders; British Audience Research Bureau; Broadcasters' Audience Research Board

Barb. Barbados

barbie [Australian short form] barbecue

BARC British Automobile Racing Club

BArch Bachelor of Architecture

BArchE Bachelor of Architectural Engineering

barg. bargain

barit. baritone

BARLA British Amateur Rugby League Association

BARP British Association of Retired Persons

BARR British Association of Rheumatology and Rehabilitation

Barr. Barrister

BARS [commerce] behaviourally anchored rating scales; British Association of Residential Settlements

Bart Baronet

Bart's St Bartholomew's Hospital (London)

BAS Bachelor of Agricultural Science; Bachelor of Applied Science; British Antarctic Survey

BASA British Architectural Students' Association; British Australian Studies Association

BASAF British and South Africa Forum

BASC British Association for Shooting and Conservation

BASc Bachelor of Agricultural Science; Bachelor of Applied Science

BASCA British Academy of Songwriters, Composers and Authors

BASF *Badische Anilin- und Soda-Fabrik* (German chemical and electronics company)

BASI British Association of Ski Instructors

Basic beginners' all-purpose symbolic instruction code (computer programming language); British-American scientific international commercial (as in **Basic English**)

BASMA Boot and Shoe Manufacturers' Association and Leather Trades Protection Society

bass. con. [music] *basso continuo* (Italian: continuous bass)

BASW British Association of Social Workers

BAT best available technology; British Aerial Transport; British-American Tobacco Company; [medicine] brown adipose tissue

Bat. Batavia

bat. battalion; battery; battle

BATF [USA] Bureau of Alcohol, Tobacco and Firearms

bath. bathroom (in property advertisement)

BA(Theol) Bachelor of Arts in Theology

bathrm bathroom (in property advertisement)

BATO [aeronautics] balloon-assisted take-off

BA(TP) Bachelor of Arts in Town and Country Planning

BATS [ecology] biosphere–atmosphere transfer scheme

batt. battalion; [military] battery

battn battalion

BAU British Association Unit; business as usual

BAUA Business Aircraft Users' Association

BAUS British Association of Urological Surgeons

Bav. Bavaria; Bavarian

b. à v. [finance] *bon à vue* (French: good at sight)

BAWA British Amateur Wrestling Association

BAWLA British Amateur Weightlifters' Association

BAYS British Association of Young Scientists

BB bail bond; balloon barrage; bank book; bed and breakfast (in accommodation advertisement); best best (wrought iron); [UK postcode] Blackburn; Blue Book; B'nai B'rith (Jewish society); Boys' Brigade; Brigitte Bardot (French actress); double black (very soft pencil lead); [vehicle registration] Newcastle upon Tyne

Bb. bishops

bb. books

.bb Barbados (in Internet address)

b.b. ball bearing; bearer bonds; [nautical] below bridges

BBA Bachelor of Business Administration; [obstetrics] born before arrival; British Backgammon Association; British Bankers' Association; British Beekeepers' Association; British Bloodstock Association; British Board of Agrément; British Bobsleigh Association

BBAC British Balloon and Airship Club

b/bar bull-bar (in car advertisement)

BBB bed, breakfast and bath (in accommodation advertisement); [USA] Better Business Bureau; [physiology] blood–brain barrier; treble black (very soft pencil lead)

BBBC British Boxing Board of Control

BBC British Broadcasting Corporation

BBCC British Bottle Collectors' Club

BBCCS British Beer Can Collectors Society

BBCM Bandmaster of the Bandsmen's College of Music

BBCMA British Baby Carriage Manufacturers' Association

BBCS British Beer Mat Collectors Society; British Butterfly Conservation Society

BBEM bed, breakfast and evening meal (in accommodation advertisement)

BBF British Baseball Federation

BBFC British Board of Film Classification (formerly British Board of Film Censors)

BBI British Bottlers' Institute

BBIP *British Books in Print*

BBIRA British Baking Industries' Research Association

B Bisc. Bay of Biscay

BBL be back later (in Internet chat); British Bridge League

bbl barrel

BBMA British Brush Manufacturers' Association; British Button Manufacturers' Association

BBMC British Board of Marbles Control

BBQ barbecue

BBQC British Board of Quality Control

BBS Bachelor of Business Science; Bachelor of Business Studies; be back soon (in Internet chat); [computing] bulletin board system

BBSR Bermuda Biological Station for Research

BBSRC Biotechnology and Biological Sciences Research Council

BBT [medicine] basal body temperature

BC Bachelor of Chemistry; Bachelor of Commerce; Bachelor of Surgery (from Latin *Baccalaureus Chirurgiae*); badminton club; [taxation] balancing charge; bank clearing; bankruptcy court; basketball club; [music] *basso continuo* (Italian: continuous bass); Battery Commander; battle cruiser; bayonet cap (on light bulb); before Christ (in dates); bicycle club; billiards club; bills for collection; birth control; bishop and confessor; [medicine] blood consumption; board of control; boat club; boating club; [biochemistry] body composition; [astronomy] bolometric correction; Bomber Command; borough council; bowling club; bowls club; boxing club; boys' club; Bristol Channel; British Coal; British Columbia; British Commonwealth; British Council; [medicine] bronchial carcinoma; budgeted cost; [education] Burnham Committee; [vehicle registration] Leicester

B/C bills for collection

b.c. [music] *basso continuo* (Italian: continuous bass); blind copy; bulk carrier

BCA [New Zealand] Bachelor of Commerce and Administration; Book Club Associates; Boys' Clubs of America; British-Caribbean Association; [angling] British Casting Association; British Chicken Association; British Chiropractic Association

BCAB Birth Control Advisory Bureau; British Computer Association for the Blind

BCAC British Conference on Automation and Computation

BC&T [USA] Bakery, Confectionery and Tobacco Workers International Union

BCAP British Code of Advertising Practice

BCAR British Civil Airworthiness Requirements; British Council for Aid to Refugees

BCAS British Compressed Air Society

BCAT Birmingham Centre for Art Therapies

BCBC British Cattle Breeders' Club; British Citizens Band Council

BCC [medicine] basal-cell carcinoma; British Caravanners Club; British Coal Corporation (replacement for NCB); British Colour Council; British Copyright Council; British Council of Churches; British Crown Colony; Bus and Coach Council

b.c.c. blind carbon copy

BCCA British Cyclo-Cross Association

BCCG British Cooperative Clinical Group

BCCI Bank of Credit and Commerce International

BCD [USA] bad conduct discharge; [computing] binary coded decimal; [astronomy] blue compact dwarf

BCDP [medicine] balloon catheter dilation of the prostate

BCDTA British Chemical and Dyestuffs Traders' Association

BCE Bachelor of Chemical Engineering; Bachelor of Civil Engineering; before Christian Era (in dates); before Common Era (in dates); Board of Customs and Excise

BCEAO *Banque centrale des états de l'Afrique de l'Ouest* (French: Central Bank of West African States)

BCECC British and Central European Chamber of Commerce

BCF battle cruiser force; billion cubic feet; British Chess Federation; British Cycling Federation; [chemistry] bromochlorodifluoromethane (used in fire extinguishers); [textiles] bulked continuous filament; [USA] Bureau of Commercial Fisheries

BCFA British–China Friendship Association

BCG [medicine] bacille Calmette–Guérin (vaccine against tuberculosis); [medicine] ballistocardiography; [astronomy] blue compact galaxy

BCGA British Commercial Gas Association; British Cotton Growing Association

BCH [computing] Bose–Chaudhuri–Hocquenghem (code)

BCh Bachelor of Surgery (from Latin *Baccalaureus Chirurgiae*)

bch branch; bunch

BChD Bachelor of Dental Surgery (from Latin *Baccalaureus Chirurgiae Dentalis*)

BChE Bachelor of Chemical Engineering

BChemEng Bachelor of Chemical Engineering

BChir Bachelor of Surgery (from Latin *Baccalaureus Chirurgiae*)

BCINA British Commonwealth International Newsfilm Agency

BCIRA British Cast-Iron Research Association

BCIS Building Cost Information Service; *Bureau central international de séismologie* (French: International Central Bureau of Seismology)

BCK [fishing port] Buckie

BCL Bachelor of Canon Law; Bachelor of Civil Law

BCM [USA] Boston Conservatory of Music; British Commercial Monomark; British Consular Mail

BCMA British Colour Makers' Association; British Columbia Medical Association; British Complementary Medicine Association; British Country Music Association

BCMD biological and chemical munitions disposal

BCMF British Ceramic Manufacturers' Federation

BCMG Birmingham Contemporary Music Group

BCMS Bible Churchmen's Missionary Society

BCN British Commonwealth of Nations

bcn beacon

BCNU be seein' you (in Internet chat)

BCNZ Broadcasting Corporation of New Zealand

BCO [medicine] bilateral carotid (artery) occlusion; British College of Optometrists (or Ophthalmic Opticians)

BCOG British College of Obstetricians and Gynaecologists

BCom Bachelor of Commerce

BComm Bachelor of Commerce

BComSc Bachelor of Commercial Science

BCP Book of Common Prayer; Bulgarian Communist Party (former name of BSP)

BCPC British Crop Protection Council

BCPIT British Council for the Promotion of International Trade

BCPL [computing] Basic Combined Programming Language; [computing] Basic Computer Programming Language

BCPMA British Chemical Plant Manufacturers' Association

BCR battlefield casualty replacement

BCRA British Carbonization Research Association; British Ceramic Research Association

BCRC British Cave Rescue Council; British Columbia Research Council

BCRD British Council for the Rehabilitation of the Disabled

BCRU British Committee on Radiological Units

BCRUM British Committee on Radiation Units and Measurements

BCS Bachelor of Chemical Science; Bachelor of Commercial Science; [physics] Bardeen–Cooper–Schrieffer (theory of superconductivity); battle cruiser squadron; Bengal Civil Service; British Calibration Service; British Cardiac Society; British Computer Society; British Crossbow Society; [USA] Bureau of Criminal Statistics

BCSA British Constructional Steelwork Association

bcst broadcast

BCT Belfast Chamber of Trade; [medicine] body computer tomograph; Building Conservation Trust

BCTA British Canadian Trade Association; British Children's Theatre Association

BCTGA British Christmas Tree Growers Association

BCTV [microbiology] beet curly top virus

BCU [cinema] big close-up; British Canoe Union; British Commonwealth Union

BCURA British Coal Utilization Research Association

BCVA British Columbia Veterinary Association

BCWMA British Clock and Watch Manufacturers' Association

BCYC British Corinthian Yacht Club

BD Bachelor of Divinity; [currency] Bahraini dinar; [international vehicle registration] Bangladesh; battle dress; [physics] beam deflection; [fishing port] Bideford; [medicine] bile duct; [commerce] bill(s) discounted; bomb disposal; [medicine] bone density; [astronomy] Bonner Durchmusterung (star catalogue); boom defence; [UK postcode] Bradford; *Bundesrepublik Deutschland* (German: Federal Republic of Germany); [vehicle registration] Northampton

B/D bank draft; banker's draft; [commerce] bill(s) discounted; [book-keeping] brought down

Bd *Band* (German: volume); [computing] baud; Board; Boulevard

bd board; [printing] bold; [finance] bond; [bookbinding] bound; broad

b/d barrels per day; [book-keeping] brought down

bd. bundle

.bd Bangladesh (in Internet address)

b.d. [commerce] bill(s) discounted; [medicine] *bis (in) die* (Latin: twice a day) (in prescriptions)

BDA Bachelor of Domestic Arts; Bachelor of Dramatic Art; bomb damage assessment; British Deaf Association; British Decorators Association; British Dental Association; British Diabetic Association; British Dyslexia Association

BDBJ Board of Deputies of British Jews

BDC Book Development Council

b.d.c. [engineering] bottom dead centre

BDCC British Defence Coordinating Committee

Bde *Bände* (German: volumes); Brigade

BDentSc Bachelor of Dental Science

BDes Bachelor of Design

BDF [computing] backward differentiation formulae (as in **BDF methods**); Ballroom Dancers Federation; Botswana Defence Force

BDFA British Dairy Farmers' Association

bd ft board foot (unit of timber length)

BDG [bookbinding] binding

BDG/ND [bookbinding] binding, no date (given)

BDH British Drug Houses

BDI British Dyslexia Institute; *Bundesverband der deutschen Industrie* (German: Federal Association of German Industry)

b.d.i. bearing deviation indicator; both dates (or days) included

BDL below detectable limits; British Drama League

bdl. bundle

bdle bundle

BDM births, deaths, marriages; bomber defence missile; branch delegates' meeting

BDMA British Direct Marketing Association; British Disinfectant Manufacturers' Association

BDMAA British Direct Mail Advertising Association

Bdmr Bandmaster

BDNF [medicine] brain-derived neuro-trophic factor

BDO Boom Defence Officer; British Darts Organization

BDP breakdown pressure

Bdr Bombardier; Brigadier

BDRA British Drag Racing Association

bdrm bedroom (in property or accommodation advertisement)

BDS Bachelor of Dental Surgery; [international vehicle registration] Barbados; bomb disposal squad; British Deer Society; British Dragonfly Society; British Driving Society

bds [bookbinding] boards; bundles

b.d.s. [medicine] *bis (in) die sumendus* (Latin: to be taken twice a day) (in prescriptions)

BDSA [USA] Business and Defense Services Administration

BDSc Bachelor of Dental Science

BDST British Double Summer Time

BDU [astronomy] baryon-dominated universe; bomb disposal unit

BDV breakdown voltage; [accounting] budget day value

Bdx Bordeaux

BE Bachelor of Economics; Bachelor of Education; Bachelor of Engineering; Bank of England; [fishing port] Barnstaple; best estimate; bill of exchange; [computing] binary encounter; [physics] binding energy; [USA] Board of Education; borough engineer; [physics] Bose–Einstein; British Element; British Embassy; British Empire; [vehicle registration] Lincoln

B/E bill of entry; bill of exchange

Be [chemical element] beryllium

Bé Baumé (temperature scale)

be. *bezüglich* (German: with reference to)

.be Belgium (in Internet address)

b.e. bill of entry; bill of exchange; binding edge

BEA British East Africa; British Epilepsy Association; British Esperanto Association; British European Airways (former airline company)

BEAB British Electrical Approvals Board

BEAC *Banque des états de l'Afrique centrale* (French: Bank of Central African States)

BEAIRE British Electrical and Allied Industries' Research Association

BEAM [medicine] brain electrical activity mapping

BEAMA (Federation of) British Electrotechnical and Allied Manufacturers' Associations

bearb. *bearbeitet* (German: compiled, edited)

BEAS British Educational Administration Society

BEC Building Employers' Confederation; *Bureau européen du café* (French: European Coffee Bureau); [USA] Bureau of Employees' Compensation

BEc Bachelor of Economics

bec. because

BECA British Exhibition Contractors' Association

Bech. Bechuanaland (former name of Botswana)

BE(Chem) Bachelor of Chemical Engineering

BECO booster-engine cut-off

BEcon Bachelor of Economics

BEcon(IA) Bachelor of Economics in Industrial Administration

BEcon(PA) Bachelor of Economics in Public Administration

BECTU Broadcasting, Entertainment, Cinematograph and Theatre Union

BEd Bachelor of Education

bed. bedroom (in property advertisement)

BEDA British Electrical Development Association; Bureau of European Designers' Associations

BEd(Com) Bachelor of Education in Commerce

BEd(HEc) Bachelor of Education in Home Economics

BEd(N) Bachelor of Education in Nursing

BEd(PE) Bachelor of Education in Physical Education

bedrm bedroom (in property advertisement)

Beds Bedfordshire

beds bedrooms (in property advertisement)

BEd(Sc) Bachelor of Education in Science

BEE Bachelor of Electrical Engineering

Beeb [short form] British Broadcasting Corporation

BEEL biological equivalent exposure limit (of radiation)

BEF British Equestrian Federation; British Expeditionary Force

bef. before

b.e.f. blunt end first

BEFA British Emigrant Families Association

BEG [USA] Bureau of Economic Geology

beg. beginning

BEHA British Export Houses Association

BEI Bachelor of Engineering (Dublin); *Banque européenne d'investissement* (French: European Investment Bank, EIB)

Beibl. *Beiblatt* (German: supplement)

BEIC British Egg Industry Council

beigeb. *beigebunden* (German: bound, in with something else)

beil. *beiliegend* (German: enclosed)

BEIR biological effects of ionizing radiation

BEL British Electrotechnical Committee

Bel. Belgian; Belgium

bel ex. *bel exemplaire* (French: fine copy) (of book or engraving)

Belf. Belfast

Belfox Belgian Futures and Options Exchange

Belg. Belgian; Belgic; Belgium

BEM British Empire Medal; bug-eyed monster

BEMA British Essence Manufacturers' Association

BEMAC British Exports Marketing Advisory Committee

BEMAS British Education Management and Administration Society

BEMB British Egg Marketing Board

BEME Brigade Electrical and Mechanical Engineer

BEMSA British Eastern Merchant Shippers' Association

BEN [electronics] broadband electrostatic noise

ben. *benedictio* (Latin: blessing); benediction

Bend. Bendigo (Australia)

BenDr *Bachelier en droit* (French: Bachelor of Law)

benef. benefice

Benelux Belgium, Netherlands, Luxembourg

BEng Bachelor of Engineering

Beng. Bengal; Bengali

BEngr Bachelor of Engraving

BenH *Bachelier en humanité* (French: Bachelor of Humanities)

BEO Base Engineer Officer

BEPC British Electrical Power Convention

beq. bequeath

beqt bequest

Ber. Berlin

BERCO British Electric Resistance Company

Berks Berkshire

Berl. Berlin

Berm. Bermuda

BERSA British Elastic Rope Sports Association

Berw. Berwick(shire)

BES Bachelor of Engineering Science; Bachelor of Environmental Studies; Biological Engineering Society; British Ecological Society; Business Expansion Scheme (replaced by EIS)

bes. *besonders* (German: especially)

BESA British Esperanto Scientific Association

BèsA *Bachelier ès arts* (French: Bachelor of Arts)

BESI bus electronic scanning indicator

BèsL *Bachelier ès lettres* (French: Bachelor of Letters)

BESO British Executive Service Overseas

BESS Bank of England Statistical Summary; bottom environmental sensing system (in oceanography)

BèsS *Bachelier ès sciences* (French: Bachelor of Science)

BEST British Expertise in Science and Technology (database)

Best. [commerce] *Bestellung* (German: order)

BET British Electric Traction Company; buildings energy technology

bet. between

BETA Broadcasting and Entertainment Trades Alliance (became part of BECTU); Business Equipment Trades' Association

BETAA British Export Trade Advertising Association

BETRO British Export Trade Research Organization

betw. between

BEU [engineering] batch extraction unit; Benelux Economic Union

BEUC *Bureau européen des unions de consommateurs* (French: European Bureau of Consumers' Unions)

BEV Black English Vernacular

BeV [USA] billion electronvolts

bev. bevel; beverage

BEVA British Exhibition Venues' Association

BEXA British Exporters Association

bez. *bezahlt* (German: paid); *bezüglich* (German: with reference to)

bezw. *beziehungsweise* (German: respectively)

BF Bachelor of Forestry; [fishing port] Banff; *Banque de France* (French: Bank of France); [currency] Belgian franc; black face (sheep); blast furnace; [informal] bloody fool; body fat; breathing frequency; British Funds; [international vehicle registration] Burkina Faso; [vehicle registration] Stoke-on-Trent

B/F bring forward; [book-keeping] brought forward

bf brief

b/f bring forward; [book-keeping] brought forward

.bf Burkina Faso (in Internet address)

b.f. bankruptcy fee; base frequency; beer firkin; [informal] bloody fool; [printing] bold face; bona fide

BFA Bachelor of Fine Arts; British Film Academy

BFAP British Forces Arabian Peninsula

BFASS [nuclear technology] BWR fuel assembly sealing system

b'fast breakfast

BFAWU Bakers', Food and Allied Workers' Union

BFBB British Federation of Brass Bands

BFBPW British Federation of Business and Professional Women

BFBS British and Foreign Bible Society; British Forces Broadcasting Service

BFCA British Federation of Commodity Associations

BFCS British Friesian Cattle Society

BFEBS British Far Eastern Broadcasting Service

BFET [electronics] ballistic field-effect transistor

BFFA British Film Fund Agency

BFFC British Federation of Folk Clubs

BFFS British Federation of Film Societies

BFG Big Friendly Giant (in children's book by Roald Dahl)

BFI British Film Institute

BFIA British Flower Industry Association

BFMA British Farm Mechanization Association

BFMF British Federation of Music Festivals; British Footwear Manufacturers' Federation

BFMIRA British Food Manufacturing Industries' Research Association

BFMP British Federation of Master Printers

BFN [informal] bye for now

Bfn Bloemfontein; British Forces Network

BFO beat-frequency oscillator

BFor Bachelor of Forestry

BForSc Bachelor of Forestry Science

BFP Bureau of Freelance Photographers

BFPA British Film Producers' Association

BFPC British Farm Produce Council

BFPO British Forces Post Office

BFr [currency] Belgian franc

BFS [mining] blast-furnace slag; British Fuchsia Society

BFSA British Fire Services' Association

BFSS British and Foreign Sailors' Society; British Field Sports Society

BFT biofeedback training

BFTA British Fur Trade Alliance

BFUW British Federation of University Women

BFV [military] Bradley fighting vehicle

BG Birmingham (Wire) Gauge; blood group; Brigadier-General; British Guiana (former name of Guyana); [international vehicle registration] Bulgaria; [vehicle registration] Liverpool

bg [commerce] bag

b/g bonded goods

.bg Bulgaria (in Internet address)

b.g. [horseracing] bay gelding

BGA [USA] Better Government Association; British Gliding Association; British Graduates Association

BGB *Bürgerliches Gesetzbuch* (German: code of civil law)

BGC bank giro credit

BGCS Botanic Gardens Conservation Secretariat

BGEA Billy Graham Evangelistic Association

BGenEd Bachelor of General Education

BGF [Australia] Banana Growers' Federation

BGH [biochemistry] bovine growth hormone

BGIRA British Glass Industry Research Association

BGL Bachelor of General Laws

b.g.l. below ground level

bglr bugler

BGM Bethnal Green Museum

BGMA British Gear Manufacturers' Association

BGMV [microbiology] bean golden mosaic virus

BGRB British Greyhound Racing Board

BGS Brigadier General Staff; British Geological Survey; British Geriatrics Society; British Goat Society; Brothers of the Good Shepherd

bgt bought

BGV below-ground vault

BH base hospital; [astronomy] black hole; [fishing port] Blyth; [UK postcode] Bournemouth; [metallurgy] Brinell hardness; British Honduras (former name of Belize); British Hovercraft; Burlington House (London) (home of Royal Academy); [vehicle registration] Luton

B/H bill of health

Bh [chemical element] bohrium

b/h barrels per hour

.bh Bahrain (in Internet address)

b.h. [informal] bloody hell

BHA [mining] bottom-hole assembly; British Handball Association; British Homeopathic Association; British Humanist Association

B'ham Birmingham

BHB British Hockey Board

BHC [medicine] benign hereditary chorea; benzene hexachloride (insecticide); British High Commissioner

bhd beachhead; billhead; bulkhead

BHDF British Hospital Doctors' Federation

BHE Bachelor of Home Economics

B'head Birkenhead

BHF British Hardware Federation; British Heart Foundation

Bhf *Bahnhof* (German: railway station)

BHGA British Hang Gliding Association

BHI British Horological Institute; *Bureau hydrographique international* (French: International Hydrographic Bureau)

BHL biological half-life

Bhm Birmingham

BHMRA British Hydromechanics' Research Association

BHN [metallurgy] Brinell hardness number

BHort Bachelor of Horticulture

BHortSc Bachelor of Horticultural Science

BHP [Australia] Broken Hill Proprietary

bhp brake horsepower

bhpric bishopric

BHQ Brigade Headquarters

BHRA British Hydromechanics' Research Association

BHRCA British Hotels, Restaurants and Caterers' Association

BHS boys' high school; British Home Stores; British Horse Society

BHT [electronics] bipolar heterojunction transistor; [mining] bottom-hole temperature

BHTA British Herring Trade Association

Bhu. Bhutan

BHy Bachelor of Hygiene

BI background information; Bahama Islands; Balearic Islands; base ignition; Befrienders International; Bermuda Islands; [medicine] bone injury; bulk issue

Bi [chemical element] bismuth

.bi Burundi (in Internet address)

BIA British Institute of Acupuncture; British Insurance Association; British Ironfounders' Association; [USA] Bureau of Indian Affairs

BIAA British Industrial Advertising Association

BIAC Business and Industry Advisory Committee

BIAE British Institute of Adult Education

BIAS Bristol Industrial Archaeological Society

BIAT British Institute of Architectural Technologists

BIATA British Independent Air Transport Association

BIB [military] baby incendiary bomb

Bib. Bible; Biblical

bib. [medicine] *bibe* (Latin: drink); biblical; *bibliothèque* (French: library)

BIBA British Insurance Brokers' Association (former name of BIIBA)

BIBC British Isles Bowling Council

BIBF British and Irish Basketball Federation

bibl. biblical; bibliographer; bibliographical; bibliography

biblio. bibliography

bibliog. bibliographer; bibliographical; bibliography

BIBRA British Industrial Biological Research Association

BIC Bahá'í International Community; [electronics] biased ion collector; *Bureau international du cinéma* (French: International Cinema Bureau); Butter Information Council

bicarb [short form] bicarbonate of soda

BICC Berne International Copyright Convention; British Insulated Callender's Cables Limited

BICE *Bureau international catholique de l'enfance* (French: International Catholic Child Bureau)

BICEMA British Internal Combustion Engine Manufacturers' Association

BICEP British Industrial Collaborative Exponential Programme

BICERI British Internal Combustion Engine Research Institute

BICFET [electronics] bipolar inversion-channel field-effect transistor

bi-CMOS [electronics] (merged) bipolar/complementary metal oxide semiconductor

BICS British Institution of Cleaning Science

BID Bachelor of Industrial Design; Bachelor of Interior Design; [medicine] brought in dead

b.i.d. [medicine] *bis in die* (Latin: twice a day) (in prescriptions)

BIDS British Institute of Dealers in Securities

BIE Bachelor of Industrial Engineering; [mathematics] boundary integral equation; *Bureau international d'éducation* (French: International Bureau of Education); *Bureau international des expositions* (French: International Exhibition Bureau)

BIEE British Institute of Energy Economics

bien. biennial

bienn. biennial

BIET British Institute of Engineering Technology

BIF [geology] banded iron formation; British Industries Fair

BIFFEX Baltic International Freight Futures Market (formerly Baltic International Freight Futures Exchange)

BIFU Banking, Insurance and Finance Union

BIH [medicine] benign intracranial hypertension; [international vehicle registration] Bosnia-Herzegovina; *Bureau international de l'heure* (French: International Time Bureau)

BIHA British Ice Hockey Association

BIIBA British Insurance and Investment Brokers' Association (formerly BIBA)

BIM [mathematics] boundary integral method; British Institute of Management; British Insulin Manufacturers

bim. *bimestrale* (Italian: bimonthly); *bimestre* (Italian: two-month period)

BIMA [astronomy] Berkeley–Illinois–Maryland Association (array)

BIMBO buy-in management buyout

BIMCAM British Industrial Measuring and Control Apparatus Manufacturers' Association

BIN *Bulletin of International News*

bin. [mathematics] binary

BINC Building Industries' National Council

bind. binding

BIO [Canada] Bedford Institute of Oceanography

biochem. biochemical; biochemistry

biodeg. biodegradable

biog. biographer; biographical; biography

biogeog. biogeography

biol. biological; biologist; biology

BIOS [computing] basic input–output system; Biological Investigation of Space; [astronautics] biological satellite; British Intelligence Objectives Subcommittee

BIOT British Indian Ocean Territory

BIP Botswana Independence Party; British

Industrial Plastics; British Institute in Paris

BIPCA *Bureau international permanent de chimie analytique pour les matières destinées à l'alimentation de l'homme et des animaux* (French: Permanent International Bureau of Analytical Chemistry of Human and Animal Food)

BIPL Burmah Industrial Products Limited

BIPM *Bureau international des poids et mésures* (French: International Bureau of Weights and Measures)

BIPP [medicine] bismuth iodoform paraffin paste (formerly applied to wounds); British Institute of Practical Psychology

BIR Board of Inland Revenue; British Institute of Radiology

BIRD *Banque internationale pour la reconstruction et le développement* (French: International Bank for Reconstruction and Development, IBRD)

BIRF Brewing Industry Research Foundation

Birm. Birmingham

BIRMO British Infra-Red Manufacturers' Organization

BIRS British Institute of Recorded Sound

BIS Bank for International Settlements; British Information Services; British Interplanetary Society; *Bureau international du scoutisme* (French: Boy Scouts International Bureau); business information system

bis. bissextile

BISA British International Studies Association

Bisc. Biscayan

BISF British Iron and Steel Federation

BISFA British Industrial and Scientific Film Association

bish. bishop

bis in 7d. [medicine] *bis in septem diebus* (Latin: twice a week) (in prescriptions)

BISPA British Independent Steel Producers' Association

BISRA British Iron and Steel Research Association

BISYNC [computing] binary synchronous communications

BIT *Bureau international du travail* (French: International Labour Office)

bit [computing] binary digit

bit. bitumen; bituminous

BITA British Industrial Truck Association

bitm. bituminous

BITNET [computing] Because It's Time Network

BITO British Institution of Training Officers

BITOA British Incoming Tour Operators' Association

bitum. bituminous

BIU Bermuda Industrial Union; *Bureau international des universités* (French: International University Bureau)

biv. bivouac

BIWF British–Israel World Federation

BIWS Bureau of International Whaling Statistics

BIZ *Bank für internationalen Zahlungsausgleich* (German: Bank for International Settlements)

BJ Bachelor of Journalism; [vehicle registration] Ipswich

.bj Benin (in Internet address)

BJA British Judo Association

BJCEB British Joint Communications Electronics Board

BJJ [electronics] boundary Josephson junction

BJJA British Ju Jitsu Association

BJOS *British Journal of Occupational Safety*

BJP [India] Bharatiya Janata Party

BJSM British Joint Services Mission

BJT [electronics] bipolar junction transistor

BJTRA British Jute Trade Research Association

BJur Bachelor of Jurisprudence

BJuris Bachelor of Jurisprudence

BK [fishing port] Berwick-on-Tweed; [trademark] Burger King; [vehicle registration] Portsmouth

Bk [chemical element] berkelium

bk backwardation; bank; bark; barrack; black; block; book; break

BKA British Karate Association; *Bundeskriminalamt* (German: criminal investigations office)

bkble bookable

bkcy bankruptcy

BKD [medicine] bacterial kidney disease

bkd blackboard; booked

bkfst breakfast

bkg banking; booking; book-keeping

bkgd background
b/kit body kit (in car advertisement)
bkkg book-keeping
bklr [printing] black letter
bklt booklet
Bklyn [USA] Brooklyn
bkm buckram
bkpg book-keeping
bkpt bankrupt
bkrpt bankrupt
bks barracks; books
BKSTS British Kinematograph, Sound and Television Society
bkt basket; bracket; bucket
BL Bachelor of Law; Bachelor of Letters; Bachelor of Literature; Barrister-at-Law; base line; bill lodged; bill of lading; [printing] black letter; [medicine] blood lead; Boatswain Lieutenant; Bodleian Library (Oxford); [UK postcode] Bolton; [fishing port] Bristol; British Legion; British Leyland (former vehicle manufacturer); British Library; [medicine] Burkitt's lymphoma; [vehicle registration] Reading
B/L bill of lading
Bl. *Blatt* (German: newspaper); Blessed
bl barrel
bl. bale; black; blue
b.l. bill of lading; breech-loading (rifle)
BLA Bachelor of Landscape Architecture; Bachelor of Liberal Arts; British Legal Association; British Liberation Army
BLACC British and Latin American Chamber of Commerce
BLAISE British Library Automated Information Service
BLAVA British Laboratory Animals Veterinary Association
BLB [horticulture] bacterial leaf blight; [medicine] Boothby, Lovelace and Bulbulian (nasal oxygen mask)
BLBSD British Library, Bibliographic Services Division
BLC British Lighting Council
bld [printing] bold (face)
bldg building
BLDSC British Library, Document Supply Centre
BLE [USA] Brotherhood of Locomotive Engineers
bleaters [informal] born losers expending all their energy rubbishing success

BLESMA British Limbless Ex-Servicemen's Association
BLEU Belgo-Luxembourg Economic Union; [aeronautics] Blind Landing Experimental Unit
BLG *Burke's Landed Gentry*
BLH British Legion Headquarters
BLHSS British Library, Humanities and Social Sciences
BLI British Lighting Industries
BLib Bachelor of Library Science
BLibSc Bachelor of Library Science
BLIC *Bureau de liaison des industries du caoutchouc de la CE* (French: Rubber Industries Liaison Bureau of the EU)
BLIS [USA] Bibliographic Literature Information System
Bliss baby life support systems; [military] bend, low silhouette, irregular shape, small, secluded (pilots' escape technique)
BLit Bachelor of Literature
BLitt Bachelor of Letters (from Latin *Baccalaureus Litterarum*)
blk black; blank; block; bulk
BLL Bachelor of Laws
BLLD British Library, Lending Division
BLM blind landing machine; [USA] Bureau of Land Management
BLMA British Lead Manufacturers' Association
BLMAS Bible Lands Missions' Aid Society
BLMRA British Leather Manufacturers' Research Association
BLNL British Library Newspaper Library
BLOF British Lace Operatives' Federation
BLOX [finance] block order exposure system
BLP Barbados Labour Party
b.l.r. breech-loading rifle
BLRA British Launderers' Research Association
BLRD British Library, Reference Division
BLRG [astronomy] broad-line radio galaxy
BLS Bachelor of Library Science; basic life support; *benevolenti lectori salutem* (Latin: greeting to the well-wishing reader); Branch Line Society; [USA] Bureau of Labor Statistics
BLSN [meteorology] blowing snow
BLT bacon, lettuce and tomato (sandwich)
blt built

BLV [microbiology] bovine leukaemia virus; British Legion Village

Blvd Boulevard

BLWA British Laboratory Ware Association

BLWN [electronics] band-limited white noise

BM Bachelor of Medicine; Bachelor of Music; bandmaster; [medicine] basal metabolism; base metal; *beatae memoriae* (Latin: of blessed memory); *Beata Maria* (Latin: Blessed Mary); [surveying] benchmark; Bishop and Martyr; *bonae memoriae* (Latin: of happy memory); [medicine] bone marrow; [computing] Boyer–Moore (algorithm); brigade major; British Monomark; British Museum; [fishing port] Brixham; bronze medal; bronze medallist; [USA] Bureau of Mines; [vehicle registration] Luton

b.m. *bene merenti* (Latin: to the well-deserving); [horseracing] black mare; board measure (of wood); [medicine] bowel movement; breech mechanism (of firearm)

BMA Bahrain Monetary Agency; British Manufacturers' Association; British Medical Association; British Midland Airways

BMath Bachelor of Mathematics

BMATT British Military Advisory and Training Team

BMBF British Mountain Bike Federation

BMC [medicine] bone marrow cell(s); [medicine] bone mineral content (or concentration); Book Marketing Council; British Match Corporation; British Medical Council; British Metal Corporation; British Motor Corporation (vehicle manufacturer); British Mountaineering Council; British Museum Catalogue (of 15th-century books)

BMCIS Building Maintenance Cost Information Service

BMD ballistic missile defence; births, marriages and deaths; [medicine] bone mineral density

BMDM [medicine] bone-marrow-derived macrophage(s); British Museum Department of Manuscripts

BMDO [USA] Ballistic Missile Defense Organization

Bmdr Bombardier

BME Bachelor of Mechanical Engineering; Bachelor of Mining Engineering; Bachelor of Music Education; [medicine] benign myalgic encephalomyelitis

BMEC British Marine Equipment Council

BMed Bachelor of Medicine

BMedSci Bachelor of Medical Science

BMEF British Mechanical Engineering Federation

BMEG Building Materials Export Group

BMEO British Middle East Office

BMEP [engineering] brake mean effective pressure

BMet Bachelor of Metallurgy

BMetE Bachelor of Metallurgical Engineering

BMEWS ballistic missile early warning system

BMF Builders Merchants Federation

BMFA Boston Museum of Fine Arts

BMH British Military Hospital

BMI ballistic missile interceptor; Birmingham and Midland Institute; body-mass index; Broadcast Music Incorporated

BMJ *British Medical Journal*

BML Bachelor of Modern Languages; British Museum Library

BMM British Military Mission

BMMA Bacon and Meat Marketing Association

b.m.o. business machine operator

B'mouth Bournemouth

BMP biochemical methane potential; biochemical methane production; [computing] bitmap (format)

bmp brake mean power

BMPA British Metalworking Plantmakers' Association

BMPS British Musicians' Pension Society

BMR [physiology] basal metabolic rate

BMRA Brigade Major Royal Artillery

BMRB British Market Research Bureau

BMRMC British Motor Racing Marshals' Club

BMRR [USA] Brookhaven Medical Research Reactor

BMS Bachelor of Marine Science; Baptist Missionary Society; British Mycological Society; building management system; business modelling system

BMSE Baltic Mercantile and Shipping Exchange

BMT basic motion time-study; bone-marrow transplant; borehole-mining tool; British Mean Time

BMTA British Motor Trade Association

BMus Bachelor of Music

BMusEd Bachelor of Music Education

BMV Blessed Mary the Virgin; [microbiology] brome mosaic virus

BMW *Bayerische Motorenwerke* (German vehicle manufacturer)

BMWE [USA] Brotherhood of Maintenance of Way Employees

BMWS ballistic missile weapon system

BMX bicycle motocross

BN Bachelor of Nursing; bank note; [astronomy] Becklin–Neugebauer (object); [fishing port] Boston; [UK postcode] Brighton; Britten–Norman (aircraft); [vehicle registration] Manchester

Bn Baron; Battalion

bn bassoon; battalion; beacon; been; billion; born

.bn Brunei (in Internet address)

BNA British Naturalists' Association; British North America; [insurance] British North Atlantic; British Nursing Association

BNAF British North Africa Force

BNB [physiology] blood–nerve barrier; *British National Bibliography*

BNBC British National Book Centre

BNC [computing] bayonet nut couplers; [linguistics] British National Corpus

BNCAR British National Committee for Antarctic Research

BNCC British National Committee for Chemistry

BNCI *Banque nationale pour le commerce et l'industrie* (French: National Bank for Commerce and Industry) (in Madagascar)

BNCM *Bibliothèque nationale du conservatoire de musique* (French: National Library of Music) (in Paris)

BNCS British National Carnation Society

BNCSAA British National Committee on Surface-Active Agents

BNCSR British National Committee on Space Research

BND *Bundesnachrichtendienst* (German: national intelligence service)

B/ND [bookbinding] binding, no date (given)

BNDD [USA] Bureau of Narcotics and Dangerous Drugs

Bndr Bandmaster

BNEC British National Export Council; British Nuclear Energy Conference

BNES British Nuclear Energy Society

BNF [computing] Backus–Naur form; [computing] Backus normal form; [pharmacology] British National Formulary; British Nuclear Fuels; British Nutrition Foundation

BnF *Bibliothèque nationale de France* (French: National Library of France)

BNFC British National Film Catalogue

BNFL British Nuclear Fuels Limited

BNFMF British Non-Ferrous Metals Federation

BNGA British Nursery Goods Association

BNGM British Naval Gunnery Mission

BNHQ battalion headquarters

bnkg banking

BNL *Banca Nazionale del Lavoro* (Italian: National Bank of Labour); Brookhaven National Laboratory

BNM *Bureau national de métrologie* (French: National Bureau of Metrology)

BNO [medicine] bowels not opened

BNOC British National Oil Corporation; British National Opera Company

BNP *Banque nationale de Paris* (French: National Bank of Paris); Barbados National Party; British National Party

BNS Bachelor of Natural Science; Bathymetric Navigation System; British Numismatic Society; buyer no seller

BNSC British National Space Centre

BNSc Bachelor of Nursing Science

BNTA British Numismatic Trade Association

BNurs Bachelor of Nursing

BNX British Nuclear Export Executive

bnzn [chemistry] benzoin

BO Bachelor of Oratory; biological oceanography; [informal] body odour; [fishing port] Borrowstounness (Bo'ness); [medicine] bowels opened; box office; branch office; [vehicle registration] Cardiff

B/O [book-keeping] brought over; buyer's option

b/o [book-keeping] brought over

.bo Bolivia (in Internet address)

b.o. back order; blackout; broker's order; buyer's option

BOA British Olympic Association; British Optical Association; British Orthopaedic Association; broad ocean area

BOAC British Overseas Airways Corporation (former airline company)

BOAD *Banque ouest-africaine de développement* (French: West African Development Bank)

BOA(Disp) British Optical Association, Dispensing Certificate

BOAI [medicine] balloon occluded arterial infusion

BOAT byroad open to all traffic

BOBA British Overseas Banks' Association

BOBMA British Oil Burner Manufacturers' Association

BOBS Board of Banking Supervision

BOC [computing] beginning of cycle; [computing] bimodal optical computer; British Oxygen Corporation; Burmah Oil Company

BOCE Board of Customs and Excise

BOCM British Oil and Cake Mills Limited

BOD biochemical oxygen demand

Bod. Bodleian Library (Oxford)

Bodl. Bodleian Library (Oxford)

BODMAS brackets, of, division, multiplication, addition, subtraction (mnemonic for order of arithmetical operations)

Body British Organ Donor Society

BOE Bank of England; Board of Education; [building] brick on edge (as in **BOE sill**)

BOF basic oxygen furnace; [computing] beginning of file; British Orienteering Federation; British Overseas Fairs

B of E Bank of England

B of H Band of Hope Union

BOGMC Bangladesh Oil, Gas and Minerals Corporation

Boh. Bohemia; Bohemian

BOHA [medicine] balloon occlusion hepatic angiography

BOJ Bank of Japan

BOL beginning of life; [international vehicle registration] Bolivia

Bol. (Simon) Bolívar (South American statesman); Bolivia; Bolivian

bol. [medicine] bolus (large pill)

BOLTON better on lips than on notepaper (on envelope of love letter)

BOM bill of materials; [USA] Bureau of Mines

Bom. Bombay

b.o.m. bill of materials

Bomb. Bombardier; Bombay

BomCS Bombay Civil Service

BomSC Bombay Staff Corps

BON British Organization of Non-Parents

bon *bataillon* (French: battalion)

BONUS [finance] Borrower's Option for Notes and Underwritten Standby

Boo [astronomy] Bootes

BOP [chemistry] basic oxygen process; [mining] blowout preventer; *Boy's Own Paper*

BOptom Bachelor of Optometry

BOQ [US military] bachelor officers' quarters; base officers' quarters

BOr Bachelor of Orientation

bor. borough

BORAD British Oxygen Research and Development Association

boro. borough

BOS basic oxygen steelmaking; [computing] business operating system

bos'n boatswain

Bos Pops [USA] Boston Pops Orchestra

BOSS Bioastronautic Orbiting Space Station; [South Africa] Bureau of State Security

Boswash [USA] Boston–Washington, DC (urban area)

BOT [computing] beginning of tape (marker); Board of Trade (became part of DTI)

bot bought

bot. botanic(al); botanist; botany; bottle; bottom

BOTB British Overseas Trade Board

BOU British Ornithologists' Union

Boul. Boulevard

BOV brown oil of vitriol (commercial sulphuric acid)

BOWO Brigade Ordnance Warrant Officer

BP Bachelor of Pharmacy; Bachelor of Philosophy; back projection; (Robert) Baden Powell (founder of Scout movement); barometric pressure; [finance] basis point; [military] beach party; before present (in dates); be prepared (motto of Scout movement); [shipping] between perpendiculars; [medicine] blood pressure; *Blue Peter* (television programme);

Boerenpartij (Dutch: Farmers' Party); boiling point; British Patent; British Petroleum; British Pharmacopoeia; British Public; [vehicle registration] Portsmouth

B/P bills payable

Bp Bishop

b/p bills payable; blueprint

bp. baptized; birthplace

b.p. below proof (of alcohol); bills payable; [medicine] blood pressure; boiling point; *bonum publicum* (Latin: the public good)

BPA Bachelor of Professional Arts; *Bahnpostamt* (German: railway post office); [USA] Biological Photographic Association; Bookmakers' Protection Association; British Paediatric Association; British Parachute Association; British Philatelic Association; [USA] Brookhaven (National Laboratory) Plant Analyzer; [USA] Business Publications Audit of Circulation

BPAA British Poster Advertising Association

BPAGB Bicycle Polo Association of Great Britain

BPAS British Pregnancy Advisory Service

b.p.b. bank post bills

BPBF British Paper Box Federation

BPBIRA British Paper and Board Industry Research Association

BPBMA British Paper and Board Makers' Association

BPC Book Prices Current; British Pharmaceutical Codex; British Pharmacopoeia Commission; British Printing Corporation; British Productivity Council; [USA] Business and Professional Code

BPCA British Pest Control Association

BPCC British Printing and Communication Corporation

bpcd barrels per calendar day

BPCF British Precast Concrete Federation

BPCR Brakes on Pedal Cycle Regulations

BPCRA British Professional Cycle Racing Association

BPd Bachelor of Pedagogy

bpd barrels per day

BPDB Bangladesh Power Development Board

BPDMS [military] basic point defence missile system

BPE Bachelor of Physical Education

BPEd Bachelor of Physical Education

BPF bottom pressure fluctuation; British Plastics Federation; British Polio Fellowship

b.p.f. [commerce] *bon pour francs* (French: value in francs)

BPG Broadcasting Press Guild

BPH Bachelor of Public Health; [medicine] benign prostatic hypertrophy (or hyperplasia)

BPh Bachelor of Philosophy

bph barrels per hour

BPharm Bachelor of Pharmacy

BPhil Bachelor of Philosophy

BPI Booksellers' Provident Institution; British Pacific Islands

bpi [computing] bits per inch; [computing] bytes per inch

BPICA *Bureau permanent international des constructeurs d'automobiles* (French: International Permanent Bureau of Motor Manufacturers)

BPIF British Printing Industries' Federation

Bpl. Barnstaple

bpl. birthplace

bpm barrels per minute; [music] beats per minute

BPMA British Premium Merchandise Association; British Pump Manufacturers' Association

BPMF British Postgraduate Medical Federation; British Pottery Manufacturers' Federation

BPO base post office; Berlin Philharmonic Orchestra

BPOE Benevolent and Protective Order of Elks

BPP Botswana People's Party

BPPMA British Power-Press Manufacturers' Association

BPR business process re-engineering

BPRA Book Publishers' Representatives' Association

BPRO Blind Persons Resettlement Officer

BPS [medicine] blood-pool scintigraphy; border patrol sector; border patrol station; British Pharmacological Society; British Psychological Society; [USA] Bureau of Professional Standards (Internal Affairs)

BPs Bachelor of Psychology

bps [computing] bits per second; [computing] bytes per second
BPsS British Psychological Society
Bp Suff. Bishop Suffragan
BPsych Bachelor of Psychology
BPT Bachelor of Physiotherapy; battle practice target; British Petroleum Tanker
bpt [computing] bits per track
BPV [microbiology] bovine papilloma virus
BQ *bene quiescat* (Latin: may he/she rest well)
Bq becquerel (unit of radioactivity)
bq. barque
BQA British Quality Association
BQMS Battery Quartermaster-Sergeant
bque barque
BR [law] *Bancus Reginae* (Latin: Queen's Bench); [law] *Bancus Regis* (Latin: King's Bench); bioaccumulation ratio; [medicine] blink reflex; [education] block release; book of reference; [international vehicle registration] Brazil; [nuclear technology] breeder reactor; breeding ratio; [physics] bremsstrahlung radiation; [fishing port] Bridgwater; British Rail; [UK postcode] Bromley; (poly)butadiene rubber; butyl rubber; [vehicle registration] Newcastle upon Tyne
B/R bills receivable; Bordeaux or Rouen (in grain trade); [insurance] builders' risks
Br [currency] birr (used in Ethiopia); Bombardier; [chemical element] bromine; [Roman Catholic Church] Brother; [military] Bugler
Br. Branch; Brazil; Breton; Britain; British
br. bearing; branch; bridge; brief; brig; bronze; brother; brown
.br Brazil (in Internet address)
b.r. bank rate; bills receivable
BRA Bee Research Association; Brigadier Royal Artillery; British Records Association; British Rheumatism and Arthritis Association
bra [short form] brassière
BRAD *British Rates and Data* (directory of publications)
Brad. Bradford
Br. Am. British America
BRAS ballistic rocket air suppression
Braz. Brazil; Brazilian
Brazza. Brazzaville

BRB be right back (in Internet chat); [medicine] blood retinal barrier
BRC [USA] base residence course; Biological Records Centre (Nature Conservancy Council); British Radio Corporation; business reply card
Br. C British Columbia
brch branch
BRCS British Red Cross Society
BRD [fishing port] Broadford; [USA] Building Research Division (National Bureau of Standards)
brd board
BRDC British Racing Drivers' Club
brdcst broadcast
BRE Bachelor of Religious Education; British Rail Engineering; Building Research Establishment
Brec. Brecon
b. rec. bills receivable
BREL British Rail Engineering Limited
BREMA British Radio Equipment Manufacturers' Association
Bren Brno and Enfield (places of manufacture of Bren gun)
Br'er Brother
Bret. Breton
brev. brevet; *breveté* (French: patent); *brevetto* (Italian: patent)
brew. brewer; brewery; brewing
BRF Bible Reading Fellowship; British Road Federation
brf [law] brief
BRFC [angling] British Record Fish Committee
brg bearing
br. g. [horseracing] brown gelding
BRI *Banque des règlements internationaux* (French: Bank for International Settlements, BIS); [computing] basic-rate ISDN; [USA] Biological Research Institute; [USA] Brain Research Institute
Br. I British India; British Isles
Brig. Brigade; Brigadier
Brig-Gen Brigadier-General
brill [short form] brilliant
brill. [music] *brillante* (Italian: brilliant)
BRIMEC British Mechanical Engineering Confederation
BRINCO British Newfoundland Corporation Limited
Brisb. Brisbane

Brist. Bristol
Brit. Britain; Britannia; British; Briton
Brit. Mus. British Museum
Brit. Pat. British Patent
brk brick
brkf. breakfast
brklyr bricklayer
brkt bracket
brkwtr breakwater
BRL Ballistic Research Laboratory; [USA] Bible Research Library
brl barrel
BRM [computing] binary-rate multiplier; [medicine] biological response modifier; British Racing Motors
BRMA Board of Registration of Medical Auxiliaries; British Rubber Manufacturers' Association
BRMCA British Ready-Mixed Concrete Association
BRMF British Rainwear Manufacturers' Federation
BRN [international vehicle registration] Bahrain
brn brown
BRNC Britannia Royal Naval College
brng [navigation] bearing; burning
BRO brigade routine order
Bro. Brotherhood
bro. brother
brom. [chemistry] bromide
Bros. Brothers
bros. brothers
BRP biological reclamation process
BRS British Record Society; British Road Services; Building Research Station
BRSA British Rail Staff Association
BRSCC British Racing and Sports Car Club
BRT *Belgische Radio en Televisie* (Belgian broadcasting company); [shipping] *Brutto-Registertonnen* (German: gross register tons)
brt bright
BRTA British Racing Toboggan Association; British Regional Television Association; British Road Tar Association
BRU [international vehicle registration] Brunei
Brum Brummagem (informal name for Birmingham)
Brunsw. Brunswick
BRurSc Bachelor of Rural Science

Brux. *Bruxelles* (French: Brussels)
BRW British Relay Wireless
bry. bryology
bryol. bryology
brz. bronze
BS [vehicle registration] Aberdeen; [USA] Bachelor of Science; Bachelor of Surgery; [international vehicle registration] Bahamas; battleship; battle squadron; [fishing port] Beaumaris; below specification; Bibliographical Society; bill of sale; [computing] binary state; Biochemical Society; Blackfriars Settlement; Blessed Sacrament; [medicine] blood sugar; Boy Scouts; [angling] breaking strain (of line); [medicine] breath sounds; [UK postcode] Bristol; [aeronautics] Bristol Siddeley; British Standard; British Steel (plc); Budgerigar Society; building society; [slang] bullshit; [computing] bus switch
B/S bill of sale; [commerce] bill of store
Bs [currency] bolívar (used in Venezuela)
bs bags; bales
.bs Bahamas (in Internet address)
b.s. backstage; balance sheet; bill of sale; [slang] bullshit
BSA Bachelor of Science in Agriculture; Bachelor of Scientific Agriculture; Bibliographical Society of America; Birmingham Small Arms Company; [medicine] body surface area; [medicine] bovine serum albumin; Boy Scouts' Association; Boy Scouts of America; British School at Athens; British Speleological Association; Building Societies' Association
BSAA Bachelor of Science in Applied Arts; British School of Archaeology at Athens
BSAC British Sub-Aqua Club
BSAdv Bachelor of Science in Advertising
BSAE Bachelor of Science in Aeronautical Engineering; Bachelor of Science in Agricultural Engineering
BSAeEng Bachelor of Science in Aeronautical Engineering
BSAgE Bachelor of Science in Agricultural Engineering
BSAgr Bachelor of Science in Agriculture
BS&W basic (or bottom) sediment and water
BSAP British Society of Animal Production

BSArch Bachelor of Science in Architecture

BSAS British Ship Adoption Society

BSAVA British Small Animals Veterinary Association

BSB British Satellite Broadcasting (became part of BSkyB); British Standard brass (screw thread)

Bsb. Brisbane

BSBA Bachelor of Science in Business Administration

BSBC British Social Biology Council

BSBI Botanical Society of the British Isles

BSBus Bachelor of Science in Business

BSC Bachelor of Science in Commerce; Bengal Staff Corps; Bibliographical Society of Canada; [computing] binary symmetric channel; [computing] binary synchronous communications; Biomedical Sciences Corporation; British Safety Council; British Shoe Corporation; British Society of Cinematographers; British Standard Channel; British Stationery Council; British Steel Corporation; British Sugar Corporation; British Supply Council; Broadcasting Standards Council; Building Societies Commission

BSc Bachelor of Science

bsc basic

BSCA British Swimming Coaches' Association; [USA] Bureau of Security and Consular Affairs

BSc(A) Bachelor of Science in Agriculture

BSc(Acc) Bachelor of Science in Accounting

BSc(Ag) Bachelor of Science in Agriculture

BScApp Bachelor of Applied Science

BSc(Arch) Bachelor of Science in Architecture

BSCC British Society of Clinical Cytology; British Synchronous Clock Conference

BSc(ChemE) Bachelor of Science in Chemical Engineering

BScD Bachelor of Dental Science

BSc(Dent) Bachelor of Science in Dentistry

BSCE Bachelor of Science in Civil Engineering

BSc(Econ) Bachelor of Science in Economics

BSc(Ed) Bachelor of Science in Education

BSc(Eng) Bachelor of Science in Engineering

BSChE Bachelor of Science in Chemical Engineering

BSc(Hort) Bachelor of Science in Horticulture

BScMed Bachelor of Medical Science

BSc(Nutr) Bachelor of Science in Nutrition

BSCP British Standard Code of Practice

BSCRA British Steel Castings Research Association

BScSoc Bachelor of Social Science

BScTech Bachelor of Technical Science

BSD Bachelor of Science in Design; ballistic system division; [computing] Berkeley Systems Distribution; British Society of Dowsers; British Space Development

BSDes Bachelor of Science in Design

b.s.d.l. boresight datum line

BSE Bachelor of Science in Education; Bachelor of Science in Engineering; [veterinary science] bovine spongiform encephalopathy; [medicine] breast self-examination

b.s.e. base support equipment

BSEc Bachelor of Science in Economics

BSECP Black Sea Economic Cooperation Project

BSEd Bachelor of Science in Education

BSEE Bachelor of Science in Electrical Engineering; Bachelor of Science in Elementary Education

BSEEng Bachelor of Science in Electrical Engineering

BSEIE Bachelor of Science in Electronic Engineering

BSEM Bachelor of Science in Engineering of Mines

BSEng Bachelor of Science in Engineering

BSES Bachelor of Science in Engineering Sciences; British Schools Exploring Society

BSF Bachelor of Science in Forestry; British Salonica Force; British Shipping Federation (Limited); British Slag Federation; British Standard fine (screw thread); British Stone Federation

BSFA British Science Fiction Association; British Steel Founders' Association

b.s.f.c. brake specific fuel consumption

BSFL British Shipping Federation Limited

BSFM Bachelor of Science in Forestry Management

BSFor Bachelor of Science in Forestry

BSFS Bachelor of Science in Foreign Service; British Soviet Friendship Society

BSFT Bachelor of Science in Fuel Technology

BSG British Standard Gauge

b.s.g.d.g. *breveté sans garantie du gouvernement* (French: patented without government guarantee)

BSGE Bachelor of Science in General Engineering

BSH British Society of Hypnotherapists; British Standard Hardness

bsh. bushel

BSHA Bachelor of Science in Hospital Administration

BSHE Bachelor of Science in Home Economics

BSHEc Bachelor of Science in Home Economics

BSHS British Society for the History of Science

BSHyg Bachelor of Science in Hygiene

BSI British Sailors' Institute; British Standards Institution; Building Societies' Institute

BSIA British Security Industry Association

BSIB Boy Scouts International Bureau

BSIC British Ski Instruction Council

BSIE Bachelor of Science in Industrial Engineering

BSIP British Solomon Islands Protectorate

BSIRA British Scientific Instrument Research Association

BSIS Business Sponsorship Incentive Scheme

BSIU British Society for International Understanding

BSJ Bachelor of Science in Journalism

BSJA British Show Jumping Association

bsk. basket

bskt basket

BSkyB British Sky Broadcasting

BSL Bachelor of Sacred Literature; Bachelor of Science in Linguistics; [medicine] bacterial skin lesion; Boatswain Sublieutenant; British Sign Language

Bs/L bills of lading

BSLS Bachelor of Science in Library Science

BSM Bachelor of Sacred Music; Bachelor of Science in Medicine; Battery Sergeant-Major; branch sales manager; British School of Motoring; [USA] bronze star medal

BSMA British Skate Makers' Association

BSME Bachelor of Science in Mechanical Engineering; Bachelor of Science in Mining Engineering

BSMedTech Bachelor of Science in Medical Technology

BSMet Bachelor of Science in Metallurgy

BSMetE Bachelor of Science in Metallurgical Engineering

BSMGP British Society of Master Glass-Painters

BSMT Bachelor of Science in Medical Technology

bsmt basement

BSMV [microbiology] barley stripe mosaic virus

BSN Bachelor of Science in Nursing

BSNE Bachelor of Science in Nuclear Engineering

BSNS Bachelor of Naval Science

BSO base supply officer; Boston Symphony Orchestra; Bournemouth Symphony Orchestra; Business Statistics Office

BSocSc Bachelor of Social Science

BSOT Bachelor of Science in Occupational Therapy

BSP Bachelor of Science in Pharmacy; Bering Sea Patrol; [computing] binary space-partitioning (as in **BSP tree**); Birmingham School of Printing; [printing] bleached sulphite pulp; British Standard pipe (screw thread); Bulgarian Socialist Party (formerly BCP); business systems planning

BSPA Bachelor of Science in Public Administration

BSPE Bachelor of Science in Physical Education

BSPH Bachelor of Science in Public Health

BSPhar Bachelor of Science in Pharmacy

BSPharm Bachelor of Science in Pharmacy

BSPhTh Bachelor of Science in Physical Therapy

BSPT Bachelor of Science in Physical Therapy

BSR Birmingham Sound Reproducers;

[medicine] blood sedimentation rate; Board for Social Responsibility (in Church of England); British School at Rome

BSRA British Ship Research Association; British Society for Research on Ageing; British Sound Recording Association

BSRAE British Society for Research in Agricultural Engineering

BSRC [USA] Biological Serial Record Center

BSRT Bachelor of Science in Radiological Technology

BSS Bachelor of Secretarial Science; Bachelor of Social Science; [medicine] balanced salt solution; basic safety standards; Bibliothèque Saint-Sulpice (Montreal library); [geology] borehole seismic system; British Sailors' Society; British Standard size; British Standards Specification

BSSA Bachelor of Science in Secretarial Administration

BSSc Bachelor of Social Science

BSSE Bachelor of Science in Secondary Education

BSSG [USA] Biomedical Sciences Support Grant

BSSO British Society for the Study of Orthodontics

BSSS Bachelor of Science in Secretarial Studies; Bachelor of Science in Social Science; British Society of Soil Science

BST Bachelor of Sacred Theology; bovine somatotrophin; British Standard Time; British Summer Time; bulk supply tariff

B/St bill of sight

BSTA British Surgical Trades' Association

BSTC British Student Travel Centre

bstd bastard

bstr booster

bstr rkt booster rocket

BSU [engineering] bench scale unit

BSurv Bachelor of Surveying

BSW Bachelor of Social Work; British Standard Whitworth (screw thread)

b.s.w. barrels of salt water

BSWB Boy Scouts World Bureau

BSWE British Scouts in Western Europe

BSWIA British Steel Wire Industries' Association

BT Bachelor of Teaching; Bachelor of Theology; basic trainer; basic training; [psychology] behaviour therapy; [UK postcode] Belfast; [medicine] benign tumour; bishop's transcript; British Telecommunications (plc) (formerly British Telecom); [vehicle registration] Leeds

Bt [currency] baht (used in Thailand); Baronet; [military] brevet

bt beat; benefit; bent; bought

.bt Bhutan (in Internet address)

BTA Billiards Trade Association; [USA] Blood Transfusion Association; British Theatre Association; British Tourist Authority (formerly British Travel Association); British Tuberculosis Association

BTAC [computing] binary tree algebraic computation

BTASA Book Trade Association of South Africa

BTB [medicine] blood–tumour barrier; [medicine] breakthrough bleeding

BTBA British Tenpin Bowling Association

BTBS Book Trade Benevolent Society

BTC [USA] Bankers' Trust Company; [USA] basic training center; British Textile Confederation; British Transport Commission

btca *biblioteca* (Spanish: library)

BTCC Board of Transportation Commissioners of Canada

BTCh Bachelor of Textile Chemistry

BTCP Bachelor of Town and Country Planning

BTCV British Trust for Conservation Volunteers

b.t.d. bomb testing device

BTDB Bermuda Trade Development Board

b.t.d.c. [engineering] before top dead centre

BTDT been there, done that (in Internet chat)

BTE Bachelor of Textile Engineering

bté *breveté* (French: patent)

BTEC Business and Technology Education Council

BTech Bachelor of Technology

BTechEd Bachelor of Technical Education

BTechFood Bachelor of Food Technology

BTEF Book Trade Employers' Federation

BTEMA British Tanning Extract Manufacturers' Association

BTEX benzene, toluene, ethylbenzene and xylene (solvents)

BTF British Trawlers Federation; British Turkey Federation

b.t.f. balance to follow; barrels of total fuel; bomb tail fuse

BTG British Technology Group

BTH British Thomson-Houston Company

BTh Bachelor of Theology

bth bath; berth

bth. bathroom (in property or accommodation advertisement)

BTHMA British Toy and Hobby Manufacturers' Association

BthU British thermal unit

BTI *British Technology Index*

BTIA British Tar Industries' Association

btk buttock

btl. bottle

BTM bromotrifluoromethane (used in firefighting)

btm bottom

BTMA British Typewriter Manufacturers' Association

BTN Brussels Tariff Nomenclature

btn baton; button

BTO big-time operator; British Trust for Ornithology; Brussels Treaty Organization (replaced by WEU)

BTP Bachelor of Town Planning

BTR [physics] bimetric theory of relativity; *British Tax Review*; British Telecommunications Research

BTRA Bombay Textile Industry's Research Association

BTRP Bachelor of Town and Regional Planning

btry [military] battery

BTS Blood Transfusion Service; British Telecommunications Systems

Btss Baroness

BTTA British Thoracic and Tuberculosis Association

BTU Board of Trade unit; [USA] British thermal unit

Btu British thermal unit

BTUC Bahamas Trade Union Congress

BTW by the way (in Internet chat and e-mail)

btw. between

btwn between

BTX benzene, toluene and xylene (solvents)

bty [military] battery

BU Bakers, Food and Allied Workers Union; Baptist Union (of Great Britain and Ireland); Brown University (Rhode Island); [fishing port] Burntisland; [vehicle registration] Manchester

Bu. Bureau

bu. bureau; bushel

b.u. base unit; [finance] break-up

BuAer [USA] Bureau of Aeronautics

BUAF British United Air Ferries

BUA of E Badminton Umpires' Association of England

BUAV British Union for the Abolition of Vivisection

BUC Bangor University College

buck. buckram

Bucks Buckinghamshire

BUCOP *British Union Catalogue of Periodicals*

Bud. Buddhism; Buddhist

bud. budget

Budd. Buddhism; Buddhist

BuDocks [US navy] Bureau of Yards and Docks

Budpst Budapest

BUF British Union of Fascists

BUIC back-up interceptor control

BUJ Bachelor of Canon and Civil Law (from Latin *Baccalaureus Utriusque Juris*)

bul. bulletin

Bulg. Bulgaria; Bulgarian

bull. bulla (seal on papal bull); bulletin; [medicine] *bulliat* (Latin: let it boil)

buloga business logistics game

BULVA Belfast and Ulster Licensed Vintners' Association

BuMed [US navy] Bureau of Medicine and Surgery

BUN [medicine] blood urea nitrogen

Buna [trademark] butadiene and natrium (synthetic rubber)

BUNAC British Universities North America Club

BUNCH Burroughs, Univac, NCR, Control Data, Honeywell (computer manufacturers)

bung. bungalow (in property advertisement)

BuOrd [US navy] Bureau of Ordnance

BUP British United Press

BUPA British United Provident Association (company providing health insurance)

BuPers [US navy] Bureau of Naval Personnel

BuPubAff [USA] Bureau of Public Affairs

BUR [international vehicle registration] Myanmar (from former name Burma)

Bur. Burma; Burmese

bur. bureau; buried

BuRec [USA] Bureau of Reclamation

burg. burgess; burgomaster

burl. burlesque

Burm. Burma; Burmese

BURMA be undressed ready, my angel (on envelope of love letter)

burp [informal] bankrupt unemployed rejected person

Burs. Bursar

bus [short form] omnibus

bus. bushel; business

BuS&A [US navy] Bureau of Supply and Accounts

BUSF British Universities' Sports Federation

bush. bushel

BuShips [US navy] Bureau of Ships

bus. mgr business manager

BUSWE British Union of Social Work Employees

but. butter; button

buy. buyer; buying

BV *Beata Virgo* (Latin: Blessed Virgin); *Beatitudo Vestra* (Latin: Your Holiness); *bene vale* (Latin: farewell); [commerce] *Besloten Vennootschap* (Dutch: limited company, Ltd); Bible Version (of Psalms); Blessed Virgin; [medicine] blood vessel; [medicine] blood volume; [shipping] *Bureau Veritas* (French shipping classification society); [vehicle registration] Preston

b.v. balanced voltage; [accounting] book value

BVA British Veterinary Association

BVD [veterinary science] bovine virus diarrhoea

BVetMed Bachelor of Veterinary Medicine

BVetSc Bachelor of Veterinary Science

BVI [international vehicle registration] British Virgin Islands

BVJ *British Veterinary Journal*

BVK *Bundesverdienstkreuz* (German: Federal Cross of Merit)

BVM Bachelor of Veterinary Medicine; *Beata Virgo Maria* (Latin: Blessed Virgin Mary); Blessed Virgin Mary

BVMA British Valve Manufacturers' Association

BVMS Bachelor of Veterinary Medicine and Surgery

BVO *Bundesverdienstorden* (German: Federal Order of Merit)

BVP British Visitors' Passport; British Volunteer Programme

BVRLA British Vehicle Rental and Leasing Association Limited

BVS Bachelor of Veterinary Surgery

BVSc Bachelor of Veterinary Science

BVSc&AH Bachelor of Veterinary Science and Animal Husbandry

bvt brevet

BW bacteriological warfare; [fishing port] Barrow; Bath and Wells (bishop's see); biological warfare; black and white; Black Watch; Board of Works; body water; [medicine] body weight; bonded warehouse; British Waterways; business week; [vehicle registration] Oxford

B/W black and white

b/w black and white

.bw Botswana (in Internet address)

b.w. *bitte wenden* (German: please turn over, PTO); bridleway(s)

BWA backward wave amplifier; Baptist World Alliance; British Waterworks Association; British West Africa

B-way [USA] Broadway

BWB British Waterways Board

BWC [USA] Board of War Communications; British War Cabinet

BWCC British Weed Control Conference

BWD [veterinary science] bacillary white diarrhoea

bwd backward

BWF British Whiting Federation; British Wool Federation

BWG Birmingham Wire Gauge

BWI British West Indies

BWIA British West Indian Airways

BWIR British West India Regiment

BWISA British West Indies Sugar Association

bwk brickwork; bulwark

BWM British War Medal

BWMA British Woodwork Manufacturers' Association

BWMB British Wool Marketing Board

BWO backward wave oscillator

BWP basic war plan

BWPA backward wave power amplifier; British Waste Paper Association; British Word Preserving Association

bwpd barrels of water per day

bwph barrels of water per hour

BWPUC British Wastepaper Utilization Council

BWR [nuclear technology] boiling-water reactor

BWS [medicine] battered wife (or woman) syndrome; British Watercolour Society

BWSF British Water Ski Federation

BWTA British Women's Temperance Association

BWU Barbados Workers' Union

BWV [music] *Bach Werke-Verzeichnis* (German: Catalogue of (J. S.) Bach's Works)

b.w.v. back water valve

BWVA British War Veterans of America

BWWA British Waterworks Association

BX [US air force] Base Exchange; British Xylonite; [vehicle registration] Haverfordwest

bx box

BY [international vehicle registration] Belarus (from alternative name Byelorussia); [vehicle registration] northwest London

By Barony

.by Belarus (in Internet address)

b.y. billion years

BYDV [microbiology] barley yellow dwarf virus

BYO bring your own

Byo Bulawayo

BYOB bring your own beer; bring your own booze; bring your own bottle

BYOG bring your own girl

byr billion years

BYT [informal] bright young things

BYU [USA] Brigham Young University

Byz. Byzantine; Byzantium

BZ [international vehicle registration] Belize; B'nai Zion; Brazil; British Zone; [vehicle registration] Down

Bz [chemistry] benzene (used in formulae)

.bz Belize (in Internet address)

BZH Brittany (from Breton *Breizh*)

bzw. *beziehungsweise* (German: respectively)

C

C *Caballeros* (Spanish: gentlemen); Caesar; *caldo* (Italian: hot); *caliente* (Spanish: hot); *calle* (Spanish: street); [geology] Cambrian; [civil aircraft marking] Canada; [informal] cancer; candle; canon; canto; Cape; Captain; [chemical element] carbon; [geology] Carboniferous; Cardinal; [USA] cargo transport (aircraft); [chess] castle; catechism; Catholic; Celsius; Celtic; centigrade; [theatre] centre (of stage); century; Chancellor; Chancery; *chaud* (French: hot); chief; Christ; Christian; circuit; *ciudad* (Spanish: town); [card games] clubs; [slang] cocaine; cold (water); Commander; Command Paper (1870–99) (in parliamentary procedure); commended; Commodore; Companion; [immunology] complement; Confessor; [pharmacology] *congius* (Latin: gallon); Congregation; Congregational; Congress; Conservative; contract; copyright; [fishing port] Cork; [botany] corolla (in floral formula); Corps; coulomb; council; Count; [music] countertenor; county; coupon; cross; [paper size] crown; cruiser; [international vehicle registration] Cuba; curacy; curate; current (electricity); [Roman numeral] hundred; [music] note of scale

C [physics] capacitance; [physics] charm quantum number; [physics] compliance; [physics] heat capacity; [chemistry] molecular concentration

© copyright

c centi- (indicates one-hundredth, as in **cl** = centilitre); [physics] charm (quark flavour); [chemistry] concentration; [mathematics] constant; cubic; [Roman numeral] hundred

c [physics] specific heat capacity; [physics] speed of light in vacuum

c. canine (tooth); capacity; *caput* (Latin: chapter); carat; carbon (paper); carton; case; [baseball] catcher; cathode; cattle; [cricket] caught (by); [currency] cent (hundredth of dollar etc.); [currency] centavo (hundredth of peso etc.); [currency] centime (hundredth of franc etc.); central; centre; century; chairman; chairwoman; chapter; charge; chest; child; church; [medicine] *cibus* (Latin: meal); *circiter* (Latin: approximately); *circum* (Latin: around); city; class; cloudy; cold; collected; college; colt; compound; conductor; constable; consul; *contra* (Latin: against); contralto; contrast; convection; copy; copyright; court; cousin; crowned; [medicine] *cum* (Latin: with) (in prescriptions); cup; currency; current (electricity); cycle(s)

c. *circa* (Latin: about) (in dates)

c/- [Australia, New Zealand] care of (in postal addresses); case; coupon; currency

C1 supervisory or clerical (occupational group)

C2 [civil aircraft marking] Nauru; skilled manual (occupational group)

C3 [civil aircraft marking] Andorra

C³I [military] command, control, communications and intelligence

C4 Channel Four (television company); [paper size] crown quarto (7.5 × 10 in)

C5 Channel Five (television company); [civil aircraft marking] Gambia

C6 [civil aircraft marking] Bahamas

C8 [paper size] crown octavo (5 × 7.5 in)

C9 [civil aircraft marking] Mozambique

C16 [paper size] crown 16mo (3.75 × 5 in)

C32 [paper size] crown 32mo (2.5 × 3.75 in)

3C [civil aircraft marking] Equatorial Guinea

CA [US postcode] California; Canadian army; capital account; [taxation] capital allowances; cardiac arrest; [fishing port] Cardigan; [UK postcode] Carlisle; Caterers' Association; Catholic Association; [chemistry] cellulose acetate; Central America; certificate of airworthiness; chargé d'affaires; [Scotland] Chartered Accountant; *Chemical Abstracts*; [vehicle registration] Chester; chief accountant; [genetics] chromosomal aberration; chronological age; Church Army; Church Assembly; citric acid; city architect; city attorney; civil affairs; civil aviation; Classical Association; clean air; coast artillery; College of Arms; commercial agent; community association; Companies Act; [USA] Confederate Army; constituent assembly; consular agent; Consumers' Association; [medicine] contrast angiography; Contributions Agency; controlled atmosphere; controller of accounts; cooperative agreement; *Corps d'armée* (French: Army Corps); county alderman; county architect; Court of Appeal; Croquet Association; Crown Agent; Cruising Association; [commerce] current assets

C/A capital account; credit account; current account

Ca [chemical element] calcium; [commerce] *compagnia* (Italian: company, Co.); [commerce] *companhia* (Portuguese: company, Co.); [commerce] *compañia* (Spanish: company, Co.)

Ca. California; Canada; Canadian

ca centiare (unit of area)

c/a cash account

ca. [medicine] carcinoma; [law] case(s)

ca. *circa* (Latin: about) (in dates)

.ca Canada (in Internet address)

c.a. [commerce] capital asset; [engineering] close annealed; [music] *coll'arco* (Italian: with the bow); [physics] *corriente alterna* (Spanish: alternating current); [physics] *courant alternatif* (French: alternating current)

CAA Campaign for the Abolition of Angling; Canadian Authors' Association; [commerce] Capital Allowances Act; Central African Airways Corporation; [USA] Civil Aeronautics Administration; [USA] Civil Aeronautics Administrator; Civil Aviation Authority; Clean Air Act; Commonwealth Association of Architects; [USA] Community Action Agency; Concert Artists' Association; [medicine] coronary artery aneurysm; Cost Accountants' Association; County Agricultural Adviser

CAAA Canadian Association of Advertising Agencies

CAADRP civil aircraft airworthiness data recording program

CAAE Canadian Association of Adult Education

CAAIS computer-aided (or -assisted) action information system(s)

CAAR compressed-air accumulator rocket

CAARC Commonwealth Advisory Aeronautical Research Council

CAAT Campaign Against Arms Trade; [Canada] College of Applied Arts and Technology; [accounting] computer-aided (or -assisted) audit technique

CAAtt Civil Air Attaché

CAAV Central Association of Agricultural Valuers

CAB Canadian Association of Broadcasters; [chemistry] cellulose acetate butyrate; Citizens' Advice Bureau; [USA] Civil Aeronautics Board; Commonwealth Agricultural Bureaux (former name of CABI)

cab. cabalistic; cabin; cabinet; cable

CABAS City and Borough Architects' Society

CABEI Central American Bank for Economic Integration

CABG [medicine] coronary artery bypass graft

CABI CAB International (formerly Commonwealth Agricultural Bureaux)

CABM Commonwealth of Australia Bureau of Meteorology

CABMA Canadian Association of British Manufacturers and Agencies

CABS [medicine] coronary artery bypass surgery

cabtmkr cabinetmaker

CAC Campaign Against Censorship; Canadian Armoured Corps; Central Advisory Committee; Central Arbitration Committee; [USA] Climate Analysis Center; Colonial Advisory Council; *Compagnie des agents de change* (French: stockbrokers' association); [USA] Consumer Advisory Council; County Agricultural Committee

CACA Canadian Agricultural Chemicals Association

CAC&W continental aircraft control and warning

CACC Civil Aviation Communications Centre; Council for the Accreditation of Correspondence Colleges (former name of ODLQC)

CACD computer-aided (or -assisted) circuit design

CACDS Centre for Advanced Computing and Decision Support

CACE Central Advisory Council for Education

CACGP Commission on Atmospheric Chemistry and Global Pollution

CACLB Churches' Advisory Committee on Local Broadcasting

CACM Central Advisory Council for the Ministry; Central American Common Market

CACSD computer-aided (or -assisted) control system design

CACUL Canadian Association of College and University Libraries

CAD cash against documents; [USA] civil air defense; *comité d'aide au développement* (French: development assistance committee); compact audio disc; computer-aided (or -assisted) design; computer-aided (or -assisted) drawing; contract award date; [medicine] coronary artery disease; Crown Agent's Department

Cád. Cádiz

cad. *cadauno* (Italian: each); [medicine] cadaver; [music] cadenza; cadet

c.a.d. cash against disbursements; cash against documents

c-à-d *c'est-à-dire* (French: that is to say)

cadav. [medicine] cadaver

CADC central air-data computer; colour analysis display computer

CADCAM computer-aided (or -assisted) design and manufacture

CADD computer-aided (or -assisted) drafting and design

CADF Commutated Antenna Direction Finder

CADIN [USA] continental air defense integration north

CADIS computer-aided (or -assisted) design information system

CADMAT computer-aided (or -assisted) design, manufacture and testing

CADO [USA] central air documents office

CADPO communications and data-processing operation

CADPOS communications and data-processing operations system

CADS computer-aided (or -assisted) design system

CAE Canadian Aviation Electronics; Chartered Automobile Engineer; *cóbrese al entregar* (Spanish: cash on delivery, COD); [Australia] College of Advanced Education; computer-aided (or -assisted) education; computer-aided (or -assisted) engineering

Cae [astronomy] Caelum

CAEC Central American Economic Community; County Agricultural Executive Committee

CAEM *Conseil d'assistance économique mutuelle* (French: Council for Mutual Economic Aid, COMECON)

CAER Conservative Action for Electoral Reform

Caern. Caernarvon(shire)

Caerns Caernarvonshire

CAES compressed-air energy storage

Caes. Caesar

CAEU Council of Arab Economic Unity

CAF [medicine] cardiac assessment factor; Central African Federation; charities aid foundation; charities aid fund; clerical, administrative and fiscal; [commerce] cost and freight; [commerce] *coût, assurance, fret* (French: cost, insurance, freight, CIF)

caf. cafeteria

c.a.f. [commerce] cost and freight; [commerce] *coût, assurance, fret* (French: cost, insurance, freight, c.i.f.)

CAFE [USA] Corporate Average Fuel Economy (fuel consumption standard for cars)

CAFEA-ICC Commission on Asian and Far Eastern Affairs of the International Chamber of Commerce

CAFIC Combined Allied Forces Information Centre

c.a.f.m. commercial air freight movement

Cafod Catholic Fund for Overseas Development

CAFR [accounting] comprehensive annual financial report

CAFS [computing] content-addressable file system

CAFU civil aviation flying unit

CAG Canadian Association of Geogra-phers; [US navy] carrier air group; [USA] civil air guard; commercial arbitration group; Commercial Artists' Guild; Concert Artists' Guild

CAGI [USA] Compressed Air and Gas Institute

CAGR [nuclear technology] civil advanced gas-cooled reactor; [nuclear technology] commercial advanced gas-cooled reactor

CAGS [USA] Certificate of Advanced Graduate Study

CAH [medicine] chronic active hepatitis; [medicine] congenital adrenal hyperplasia; [chemistry] cyanacetic hydrazide

CAI Canadian Aeronautical Institute; *Club Alpino Italiano* (Italian: Italian Alpine Club); colour alteration indices; computer-aided (or -assisted) instruction; Confederation of Aerial Industries Limited; [chemical engineering] controlled air incineration (or incinerator); [forestry] current annual increment

Cai. Caithness

CAIRC [USA] Caribbean Air Command

CAISM Central Association of Irish Schoolmistresses

CAISSE computer-aided (or -assisted) information system on solar energy

Caith. Caithness

CAL computer-aided (or -assisted) learning; Continental Airlines; [computing] conversational algebraic language; [USA] Cornell (University) Aeronautical Laboratory

Cal kilocalorie (from alternative name Calorie)

Cal. Calcutta; Caledonia; Calends; California

cal calorie

cal. [music] *calando* (Italian: lowering, falling away); calendar; calibre

CALA Civil Aviation Licensing Act

CALANS Caribbean and Latin American News Service

Calc. Calcutta

Calç. *Calçada* (Portuguese: street)

calc. calculate; calculated; calculation; calculator; calculus

cald calculated

CALE Canadian Army Liaison Executive

Calg. Calgary

calg calculating

calibr. calibrate; calibration

Calif. California

Cal. Mac. Caledonian MacBrayne (Scottish ferry company)

caln calculation

CALPA Canadian Air Line Pilots' Association

Caltech California Institute of Technology

Caltex California Texas Petroleum Corporation

Calv. (John) Calvin (French theologian); Calvinism; Calvinistic

Calz. *Calzada* (Spanish: boulevard)

CAM [international vehicle registration] Cameroon; [computing] cellular automata machine; commercial air movement; Commonwealth Association of Museums; communication, advertising and marketing (as in **CAM Foundation**); computer-aided (or -assisted) manufacture; [computing] content-addressable memory; continuous air monitor

Cam [astronomy] Camelopardalis

Cam. Cambodia; Cambodian; Cambrian; Cambridge; Cameroon

cam. camber; camouflage

CAMA Civil Aerospace Medical Association

CAMAL continuous airborne missile-launched and low-level system

Camb. Cambrian; Cambridge(shire)

Cambs Cambridgeshire

CAMC Canadian Army Medical Corps

CAMD [chemistry] computer-aided (or -assisted) molecular design

CAMDA Car and Motorcycle Drivers' Association

CAMDS chemical agent munitions disposal system

CAMM computer-aided (or -assisted) maintenance management

CAMRA Campaign for Real Ale

CAMRIC Campaign for Real Ice Cream

CAMS Certificate of Advanced Musical Study; [engineering] computer-aided (or -assisted) manipulation system

CaMV [microbiology] cauliflower mosaic virus

CAMW Central Association for Mental Welfare

CAN Committee on Aircraft Noise; customs-assigned number

Can. Canada; Canadian; Canal; Canberra; Canon; Canonry; *Cantoris* (Latin: of the precentor) (side of church choir)

can. canal; cancel; cannon; canon; canto; canton

CANA Caribbean News Agency; Clergy Against Nuclear Arms

Canad. Canada; Canadian

Canc. *Cancellarius* (Latin: Chancellor)

canc. cancellation; cancelled

CANCIRCO Cancer International Research Cooperative

CAND Campaign Against Nuclear Dumping

cand. candidate

C&A Clemens and Auguste (Breeninkmeyer) (Dutch founders of chain store)

c&b [cricket] caught and bowled (by)

c&c carpets and curtains (in property advertisement); command and control

c&d collection and delivery

C&E Customs and Excise

c&e consultation and education

c&f cost and freight

C&G Cheltenham and Gloucester (Building Society); City and Guilds

C&I commerce and industry; commercial and industrial

c&i cost and insurance

C&J clean and jerk (in weightlifting)

c&m care and maintenance

c&p carriage and packing; [bookbinding] collated and perfect

c&r convalescence and rehabilitation

CANDU [nuclear technology] Canadian Deuterium Uranium Reactor

C&W country and western (music)

C&W Ck caution and warning (system) check

CANEL [USA] Connecticut Advanced Nuclear Engineering Laboratory

Can. Fr. Canadian French

Can. I Canary Islands

CANO chief area nursing officer

Can. Pac. Canadian Pacific

CANSG Civil Aviation Navigational Services Group

Cant. Canterbury; [Bible] Canticles; Cantonese

cant. cantilever

Cantab. *Cantabrigiensis* (Latin: of Cambridge (University))

canton. [military] cantonment

CANTRAN cancel in transmission

Cantuar. *Cantuariensis* (Latin: (Archbishop) of Canterbury)

CANUS [military] Canada–United States

canv. canvas

CAO chief accountant officer; chief administrative officer; county advisory officer; county agricultural officer; Crimean Astrophysical Laboratory

CAORB Civil Aviation Operational Research Branch

CAORG Canadian Army Operational Research Group

CAOT Canadian Association of Occupational Therapy

CAP Canadian Association of Physicists; [genetics] catabolite activator protein; Church Action on Poverty; [USA] civil air patrol; Code of Advertising Practice; College of American Pathologists; [USA] combat air patrol; Common Agricultural Policy (in EU); [USA] Community Action Program; computer-aided (or -assisted) planning; computer-aided (or -assisted) production

Cap [astronomy] Capricornus

Cap. Captain

cap. capacity; [medicine] *capiat* (Latin: let him/her take) (in prescriptions); capital; capitalize; capital letter; *capitulum* (Latin: chapter, heading); *caput* (Latin: chapter, heading); foolscap

c.a.p. *codice di avviamento postale* (Italian: postcode number)

CAPA Canadian Association of Purchasing Agents

CAPAC Composers', Authors' and Publishers' Association of Canada

CAPCOM capsule communicator (in NASA)

CAPD [medicine] continuous ambulatory peritoneal dialysis

CAPE Clifton Assessment Procedures for the Elderly

CAPM [accounting] capital asset pricing model; computer-aided (or -assisted) production management

Capn Captain

CAPO Canadian Army Post Office; Chief Administrative Pharmaceutical Officer

CAPP computer-aided (or -assisted) process planning

Capric. Capricorn

CAPS Captive Animals' Protection Society; [USA] Center for Analysis of Particle Scattering

caps. capital letters; capsule

Capt. Captain

capt. caption

CAR Canadian Association of Radiologists; Central African Republic; Civil Air Regulations; [aeronautics] cloudtop altitude radiometer; [nuclear technology] collisionally activated reaction; [Australia] *Commonwealth Arbitration Reports*; [finance] compound annual return; compounded annual rate (of interest); computer-aided (or -assisted) retrieval; [computing] contents of address register

Car [astronomy] Carina

Car. Carlow; *Carolus* (Latin: Charles)

car. carat

CARA combat air rescue aircraft

CARAC Civil Aviation Radio Advisory Committee

CARAF Christians Against Racism and Fascism

CARB California Air Resources Board

carb [short form] carburettor

carb. carbon; [chemistry] carbonate

CARD Campaign Against Racial Discrimination; compact automatic retrieval device; computer-augmented road design

Card. Cardinal

card. cardinal

CARDE Canadian Armament Research and Development Establishment

Cards Cardiganshire (former name of Ceredigion)

CARE Christian Action for Research and Education; [psychology] communicated authenticity, regard, empathy; computer-aided (or -assisted) risk evaluation; continuous aircraft reliability evaluation; Cooperative for American Relief Everywhere; Cottage and Rural Enterprises

CAREC Caribbean Epidemiology Centre

Carib. Caribbean

CARIBANK Caribbean Investment Bank

CARICAD Caribbean Centre for Administration Development

CARICOM Caribbean Community and Common Market

CARIFTA Caribbean Free Trade Area

Carliol. *Carlioliensis* (Latin: (Bishop) of Carlisle)

Carms Carmarthenshire

carn. carnival

Carns Caernarvonshire

Carp. Carpathian (Mountains); Carpentaria

carp. carpenter; carpentry

carr. fwd [commerce] carriage forward

CARS Canadian Arthritis and Rheumatism Society

CART collision avoidance radar trainer

cart. cartage; carton

Carth. Carthage

cartog. cartographer; cartographic; cartography

CAS Cambridge Antiquarian Society; Carib Advertising Services (in Guyana); Centre for Administrative Studies; CERN Accelerator School; [USA] Certificate of Advanced Studies; Chemical Abstracts Service; Chief of Air Staff; Children's Aid Society; close air support; [aeronautics] collision avoidance system; *Connecticutensis Academiae Socius* (Latin: Fellow of the Connecticut Academy of Arts and Sciences); controlled airspace; [medicine] coronary arterial stenosis

Cas [astronomy] Cassiopeia

cas. castle; casual; casualty

CASA [USA] Coal Advisory Service Association; Contemporary Art Society of Australia

CA(SA) Chartered Accountant (South Africa)

ca. sa. [law] *capias ad satisfaciendum* (Latin: writ of execution)

CASAC [USA] Clean Air Scientific Advisory Committee

CASE Campaign for State Education; Centre for Advanced Studies in Environment; [USA] Committee on Academic Science and Engineering; computer-aided (or -assisted) software engineering; computer-aided (or -assisted) system engineering; Confederation for the Advancement of State Education; Cooperative Awards in Science and Engineering

casevac [military] casualty evacuation

cash. cashier

CASI Canadian Aeronautics and Space Institute

CASIG Careers Advisory Service in Industry for Girls

CASLE Commonwealth Association of Surveying and Land Economy

Caspar [physics] Cambridge analog simulator for predicting atomic reactions

cass. cassette

CAST Consolidated African Selection Trust

Cast. Castile; Castilian

CASTE Civil Aviation Signals Training Establishment

CASU Cooperative Association of Suez Canal Users

CASW [USA] Council for the Advancement of Scientific Writing

CAT Centre for Alternative Technology; [psychology] Children's Apperception Test; Civil Air Transport; [aeronautics] clear-air turbulence; College of Advanced Technology; compressed-air tunnel; [medicine] compute(rize)d axial tomography (as in **CAT scanner**); computer-aided (or -assisted) teaching; computer-aided (or -assisted) testing; [medicine] computer-aided (or -assisted) tomography; computer-aided (or -assisted) trading; computer-aided (or -assisted) training; computer-aided (or -assisted) translation; computer-aided (or -assisted) typesetting; low charges, easy access, fair terms (as in **CAT standard** for ISAs)

Cat. Catalan; Catholic; Catullus (Roman poet)

cat [short form] catalytic converter; [short form] catamaran

cat. catalogue; catamaran; [medicine] cataplasm (poultice); catapult; catechism; category; cattle

CATA Commonwealth Association of Tax Administration

catachr. catachresis; catachrestic

Catal. Catalan; Catalonian

CATC Commonwealth Air Transport Commission

CATCC Canadian Association of Textile Colorists and Chemists

CATE Committee for the Accreditation of Teacher Education

Cath. Cathedral; Catholic

cath. cathedral; cathode

CATI computer-aided (or -assisted) telephone interviewing

CATOR Combined Air Transport Operations Room

CATRA Cutlery and Allied Trades Research Association

CATS [education] credit accumulation transfer scheme

CATU Ceramic and Allied Trade Union

CATV community antenna television (= cable television)

caus. causation; causative

CAV constant air-volume (control system); [computing] constant angular velocity; [law] *curia advisari vult* (Latin: the court wishes to consider it) (used in reports when judgment follows hearing); [medicine] cyclophosphamide, adriamycin and vincristine (used in chemotherapy)

Cav. *Cavaliere* (Italian: Knight); Cavalry; Cavan

cav. cavalier; cavalry; [law] caveat

CAVD Completion, Arithmetic Problems, Vocabulary, Following Directions (intelligence test)

CAVI *Centre audio-visuel international* (French: International Audio-Visual Centre)

Caviar Cinema and Video Industry Audience Research

CAWU Clerical and Administrative Workers' Union (became part of GMB)

Cay. Cayenne; Cayman Islands

CAYA Catholic Association of Young Adults

CB [civil aircraft marking] Bolivia; [UK postcode] Cambridge; Cape Breton (Canada); carbon black; carte blanche; cash book; cavalry brigade; [USA] Census Bureau; [theatre] centre back (of stage); centre of buoyancy; chemical and biological (weapons or warfare); Chief Baron; chlorobromomethane (used in firefighting); Citizens' Band (radio); Coal Board; [law] Common Bench; Companion of the Order of the Bath; [physics] conduction band; confidential book (in Royal Navy); confined to barracks; construction battalion; *contrabasso* (Italian: double bass); cost-benefit; county borough; [chemistry] covalent bonding; currency bond; [vehicle registration] Manchester

Cb [chemical element] columbium (former name of niobium)

Cb [meteorology] cumulonimbus

c/b [cricket] caught and bowled; cost-benefit

c.b. cash book; cast brass; centre of buoyancy; circuit breaker; compass bearing; continuous breakdown

CBA [physics] colliding-beam accelerator; Commercial Bank of Australia; Commonwealth Broadcasting Association; [USA] Community Broadcasters' Association; cost-benefit analysis; Council for British Archaeology

CBAA Canadian Business Aircraft Association

CB&PGNCS circuit breaker and primary guidance navigation control system

CBAT [USA] College Board Achievement Test

CBB Campaign for Better Broadcasting

CBBC Children's BBC

CBC Canadian Broadcasting Corporation; Caribbean Broadcasting Company; [USA] Children's Book Council; [Australia] Christian Brothers' College; [computing] cipher block chaining; [medicine] complete blood count; county borough council

CBCRL Cape Breton Coal Research Laboratory

CBCS [Australia] Commonwealth Bureau of Census and Statistics

CBD cash before delivery; central business district; [anatomy] common bile duct

c.b.d. cash before delivery

CBDC Cape Breton Development Corporation

CBE chemical, biological and environmental (weapons or warfare); Commander of the Order of the British Empire; Council for Basic Education

CBEL *Cambridge Bibliography of English Literature*

CBEVE Central Bureau for Educational Visits and Exchanges

CBF Central Board of Finance; [medicine] cerebral blood flow

CBI Cape Breton Island; computer-based information; computer-based instruction; Confederation of British Industry; [USA] *Cumulative Book Index*

c.b.i. complete background investigation

CBIM Companion of the British Institute of Management

CBiol Chartered Biologist

CBIS computer-based information system

CBIV computer-based interactive video-disc

CBJO Coordinating Board of Jewish Organizations

cbk chequebook

CBL commercial bill of lading; computer-based learning; [meteorology] convective boundary layer

cbl. cable

CBM Californian Business Machines; confidence building measure; conveyor belt monitor(ing)

CBMIS computer-based management information system

CBMM Council of Building Materials Manufacturers

CBMPE Council of British Manufacturers of Petroleum Equipment

CBMS [USA] Conference Board of Mathematical Sciences

CBNM [USA] Central Bureau for Nuclear Measurements

CBNS Commander British Navy Staff

CBO Conference of Baltic Oceanographers; [USA] Congressional Budget Office; Counter-Battery Officer

Cbo Colombo (Sri Lanka)

CBOE Chicago Board of Options Exchange

C-bomb cobalt bomb

CBOT Chicago Board of Trade

CBPC Canadian Book Publishers' Council

CBQ civilian bachelor quarters

CBR [USA] Center for Brain Research; chemical, bacteriological and radiation (weapons or warfare); [aeronautics] cloud base recorder; [immunology] complement-binding reaction; [medicine] complete bed rest; [computing] constant bit rate; [astronomy] cosmic background radiation; crude birth rate

CBRI [India] Central Building Research Institute

CBS Canadian Biochemical Society; *Centraal Bureau voor de Statistiek* (Dutch: Central Statistical Bureau); Church Building Society; [medicine] citrate-buffered saline; [computing] close binary system; [USA] Columbia Broadcasting System;

[medicine] computerized bone scanning; [Roman Catholic Church] Confraternity of the Blessed Sacrament

CBSA Clay Bird Shooting Association

CBSI Chartered Building Societies Institute

CBSM conveyor-belt service machine

CBSO City of Birmingham Symphony Orchestra

CBT Chicago Board of Trade; computer-based teaching; computer-based training

CBU Clearing Banks Union; [commerce] completely built-up (goods for immediate use)

c.b.u. cluster(ed) bomb unit; [commerce] completely built-up (goods for immediate use)

CBV [medicine] cerebral blood volume

CBW chemical and biological warfare

CBX [telecommunications] company branch exchange

CBZ coastal boundary zone

CC [vehicle registration] Bangor; Cape Colony; Caribbean Commission; central committee; Chamber of Commerce; Charity Commission; chess club; chief clerk; [civil aircraft marking] Chile; circuit court; city council; city councillor; [insurance] civil commotion; civil court; [physics] close coupling; closed circuit (transmission); collision course; colour centre; [photography] colour conversion; [photography] colour correction; community council; [genetics] compact chromosome; Companion of the Order of Canada; company commander; [electronics] compensating current; computer code; concave; [military] confined to camp; consular clerk; [commerce] continuation clause; control computer; [medicine] corpus callosum; [medicine] corpus cardiacum; [physics] correction coil; [physics] *corriente continua* (Spanish: direct current); Countryside Commission; county clerk; county commissioner; county council; county councillor; county court; [electronics] coupled channel; credit card; cricket club; croquet club; Crown Clerk; cruise control (in car advertisement); cruising club; Curate in Charge; cushion craft; cycling club

C/C cruise control (in car advertisement)

Cc [meteorology] cirrocumulus

cc carbon copy (or copies); cruise control (in car advertisement); cubic centimetre

c/c *compte courant* (French: current account); *conto corrente* (Italian: current account)

cc. centuries; chapters

c.c. carbon copy (or copies); cash credit; change course; chronometer correction; close control; colour code; *compte courant* (French: current account); *conto corrente* (Italian: current account); contra credit; [physics] *courant continu* (French: direct current); cubic centimetre

CCA Canadian Construction Association; [US navy] carrier-controlled approach; Chief Clerk of the Admiralty; [USA] Circuit Court of Appeals; [medicine] common carotid artery; Commonwealth Correspondents' Association; [USA] Consumers' Cooperative Association; continental control area; [USA] Council for Colored Affairs; County Councils' Association; [USA] County Court of Appeals; current-cost accounting

CCAB Canadian Circulations Audit Board; Consultative Committee of Accountancy Bodies

CCAFS [USA] Cape Canaveral Air Force Station

CCAHC Central Council for Agricultural and Horticultural Cooperation

CCAM Canadian Congress of Applied Mechanics

CCAMLR Commission for the Conservation of Antarctic Marine Living Resources

CCAT Central Council for the Amateur Theatre

CCB [South Africa] Civil Cooperation Bureau

c.c.b. cubic capacity of bunkers

CCBI Council of Churches for Great Britain and Ireland

CCBN Central Council for British Naturism

CCBW Committee on Chemical and Biological Warfare

CCC Camping and Caravanning Club (of Great Britain and Ireland); Canadian Chamber of Commerce; Central Control Commission; Central Criminal Court; [USA] Chemical Control Corporation; [USA] Civilian Conservation Corps; Club Cricket Conference; Commodity Credit Corporation; *Conseil de coopération culturelle* (French: European Council for Cultural Cooperation); Council for the Care of Churches; county cricket club; cross-country club; Customs Cooperation Council

ccc [commerce] *cwmni cyfyngedig cyhoeddus* (Welsh: public limited company, plc)

CCCA Cocoa, Chocolate and Confectionery Alliance; Corps Commander, Coast Artillery

CCCBR Central Council of Church Bell Ringers

CCCC Charity Christmas Card Council

CCCI [military] command, control, communications and intelligence

CCCM Central Committee for Community Medicine

CCCO Committee on Climatic Changes and the Ocean

CCCP *Soyuz Sovietskikh Sotsialisticheskikh Respublik* (Russian: Union of Soviet Socialist Republics, USSR) (transcription of Cyrillic characters, transliterated as SSSR)

CCCR [medicine] closed-chest cardiac resuscitation; Coordinating Committee for Cancer Research

CCCS Commonwealth and Continental Church Society

CCD Central Council for the Disabled; [electronics] charge-coupled device; *Conseil de coopération douanière* (French: Customs Cooperation Council)

CCDA [USA] Commercial Chemical Development Association

CCE [chemistry] carbon-chloroform extract; Chartered Civil Engineer; compound-cycle engine; *Conseil des communes d'Europe* (French: Council of European Municipalities); [USA] Council of Construction Employers; [accounting] current cash equivalent; [electronics] current-carrying element

c.c.e.i. composite cost-effectiveness index

CCETSW Central Council for Education and Training in Social Work

CCETT *Centre commun d'études de télédiffusion et télécommunications* (French:

Television and Telecommunications
Research Centre)

CCF central computing facility; central
control function; Combined Cadet
Force; common-cause failure; Common
Cold Foundation; concentrated complete fertilizer; [medicine] congestive cardiac failure; [Canada] Cooperative
Commonwealth Federation; [statistics]
cross-correlation function

CCFA Combined Cadet Force Association

CCFD [statistics] complementary cumulative frequency distribution

CCFL [electronics] counter-current flow
limit

CCFM Combined Cadet Forces Medal

CCFP Certificate of the College of Family
Physicians

CCG Control Commission for Germany

CCGB Cycling Council of Great Britain

c.c.h. commercial clearing house; cubic
capacity of holds

CCHE Central Council for Health Education

CChem Chartered Chemist

CCHF Children's Country Holidays Fund

CCHMS Central Committee for Hospital
Medical Services

CCI Calculated Cetane Index; *Chambre de
commerce internationale* (French: International Chamber of Commerce)

CCIA Commission of the Churches on
International Affairs; [USA] Consumer
Credit Insurance Association

CCIC *Comité consultatif international du
coton* (French: International Cotton
Advisory Committee)

CCIE [computing] Cisco Certified Internet-
working Expert

CCIR Catholic Council for International
Relations; *Comité consultatif international
des radiocommunications* (French: International Radio Consultative Committee)

CCIS command control information
system

CCITT *Comité consultatif international télégraphique et téléphonique* (French: International Telegraph and Telephone
Consultative Committee)

CCITU Coordinating Committee of Independent Trade Unions

CCIVS Coordinating Committee for International Voluntary Service

CCJ circuit court judge; Council of Christians and Jews; county court judge;
[medicine] cranio-cervical junction

CCJO Consultative Council of Jewish
Organizations

CCK [biochemistry] cholecystokinin

CCL Canadian Congress of Labour; [USA]
commodity control list

CCLGF Consultative Committee on Local
Government Finance

CCLRC Council for the Central Laboratory of the Research Councils

CCM [medicine] caffeine clearance
measurement; [physics] constant current
modulation; [physics] controlled carrier
modulation; Cornish Chamber of
Mines

CCMA Call Centre Management Association; Commander, Corps Medium
Artillery; Contract Cleaning and Maintenance Association

CCMD [USA] Carnegie Committee for
Music and Drama; [physics] continuous-
current monitoring device

CCMS Committee on the Challenge of
Modern Society (in NATO)

CCN [meteorology] cloud condensation
nuclei; command control number; contract change notice; contract change
notification

CCNDT Canadian Council for Non-
Destructive Technology

CCNR Consultative Committee for
Nuclear Research (in Council of Europe)

CCNSC [USA] Cancer Chemotherapy
National Service Center

CCNY Carnegie Corporation of New York;
City College of the City University of
New York

CCO Central Coding Office; current-
controlled oscillator

CCOA County Court Officers' Association

CCOFI California Cooperative Oceanic
Fisheries Investigations

CCP Chinese Communist Party; Code of
Civil Procedure; Committee on Commodity Problems; Court of Common
Pleas; [nuclear technology] critical compression pressure

c.c.p. credit-card purchase

CCPE Canadian Council of Professional
Engineers

CCPF *Comité central de la propriété forestière*

de la CE (French: Central Committee on Forest Property for the EU)

CCPI Cyanamid Canada Pipeline Incorporated

CCPIT China Committee for the Promotion of International Trade

CCPL [USA] Computer Center Program Library

CCPO *Comité central permanent de l'opium* (French: Permanent Central Opium Board)

CCPR Central Council of Physical Recreation

CCPS Consultative Committee for Postal Studies

CCR cassette camera recorder; [USA] Commission of Civil Rights; Common Centre of Research; [law] contract change request; [medicine] cranial cavity ratio; critical compression ratio

CCRA Commander Corps of Royal Artillery

CCRE Commander Corps of Royal Engineers

CCREME Commander Corps of Royal Electrical and Mechanical Engineers

CCRSigs Commander Corps of Royal Signals

CCRU [USA] Common Cold Research Unit

CCS [computing] calculus of communicating systems; Canadian Cancer Society; Canadian Ceramic Society; casualty clearing station; child-care service; collective call sign; [USA] Combined Chiefs of Staff; controlled combustion system

CCSA Canadian Committee on Sugar Analysis

CCSATU Coordinating Council of South African Trade Unions

CCSC Central Consultants and Specialists Committee (in BMA)

CCSD [computing] coupled-cluster single and double

CCSEM computer-controlled scanning electron microscope (or microscopy)

CCSS centrifugally cast stainless steel

CCST [USA] Center for Computer Sciences and Technology

CCSU Council of Civil Service Unions

CCT [medicine] cerebral circulation time; [USA] clean coal technology; common customs tariff (in EU); compulsory competitive tendering; [electronics] contact charge-transfer; correct corps time; [medicine] cranial compute(rize)d tomography

CCTA Central Computer and Telecommunications Agency; *Commission de coopération technique pour l'Afrique* (French: Commission for Technical Cooperation in Africa); Coordinating Committee of Technical Assistance

CCTG constant concentration tracer gas (system)

CCTR [nuclear technology] cassette compact toroid reactor

CCTS [USA] Canaveral Council of Technical Societies; Combat Crew Training Squadron

CCTV closed-circuit television

CCU [medicine] coronary care unit

CCUS Chamber of Commerce of the United States

CCV [aeronautics] control-configured vehicle

CCW [nuclear technology] component cooling water; Curriculum Council for Wales

ccw. counterclockwise

CCWS [nuclear technology] component cooling water system

CD [vehicle registration] Brighton; Canadian Forces Decoration; [electronics] carrier density; certificate of deposit; [law] Chancery Division; Civil Defence; civil disobedience; closing date; [immunology] cluster of differentiation; coal dust; College Diploma; [Jamaica] Commander of the Order of Distinction; commercial dock; compact disc; Conference on Disarmament (of UN); confidential document; [USA] Congressional District; [medicine] contagious disease; [image technology] contrast detail; [astronomy] Córdoba Durchmusterung (star catalogue); [nuclear technology] core damage; *Corps diplomatique* (French: Diplomatic Corps); countdown; [Freemasonry] Court of Deliberation; cross-dresser (= transvestite); [electronics] current density

C/D consular declaration; customs declaration

Cd [chemical element] cadmium; [military]

Command; Command Paper (1900–18) (in parliamentary procedure); [military] Commissioned

cd candela (unit of luminous intensity); *ciudad* (Spanish: city); command; cord; could

c/d [book-keeping] carried down

c.d. [book-keeping] carried down; cash discount; [finance] cum dividend (i.e. with dividend)

CDA Canadian Dental Association; *Centre de données astronomiques* (French: Centre for Astronomical Data); [South Africa] Christian Democratic Alliance; Civil Defence Act; College Diploma in Agriculture; [computing] compound document architecture; [Canada] Conference of Defence Associations; Copper Development Association

CDAA Churches Drought Action in Africa

CDAAA Committee to Defend America by Aiding the Allies

CD&G compact disc and graphics

Cd Armn Commissioned Airman

CDAS Civil Defence Ambulance Service

CDB [computing] comprehensive database

Cd B Commissioned Boatswain

cdbd cardboard

Cd Bndr Commissioned Bandmaster

CDC Canada Development Corporation; canister decontamination cell (or chamber); [chemistry] carbon derived from coal; Caribbean Defence Command; [USA] Center for Disease Control; [USA] Combat Development Command; [computing] command and data-handling console; Commissioners of the District of Columbia; [computing] common development cycle; Commonwealth Development Corporation; Control Data Corporation (computer manufacturer); cost determination committee; [electronics] critical density of current

Cd CO Commissioned Communication Officer

Cd Con. Commissioned Constructor

CDD [USA] certificate of disability for discharge; [electronics] charge-density distribution

CDDI [computing] copper distributed data interface

CDE chemical defence ensemble; compact disc erasable

CD-E compact disc erasable

CDEE Chemical Defence Experimental Establishment

C de G *Croix de Guerre* (French: War Cross) (military decoration)

CDEM crop disease environment monitor

Cd Eng. Commissioned Engineer

CDEU Christian Democratic European Union

CDF [computing] central database facility; Collider Detector at Fermilab; [nuclear technology] core-damage frequency

c.d.f. [statistics] cumulative distribution function

CDFC Commonwealth Development Finance Company

Cdg. Cardigan

Cd Gr Commissioned Gunner

CDH College Diploma in Horticulture; [medicine] congenital disease of the heart; [medicine] congenital dislocation of the hip

CDHS California Department of Health Services

CDI compact disc interactive

CD-I compact disc interactive

CDIC [USA] Carbon Dioxide Information Center

CDIF [computing] CASE data interchange format

Cd In. O Commissioned Instructor Officer

CDipAF Certified Diploma in Accounting and Finance

c. div. [finance] cum dividend (i.e. with dividend)

CDL Central Dockyard Laboratory (in Ministry of Defence); central door locking (in car advertisement); [chemistry] coal-derived liquid; Council of the Duchy of Lancaster; [Australia] County and Democratic League

Cdl Cardinal

CDLD [medicine] chronic diffuse liver disease

CDM [astronomy] cold dark matter (as in **CDM theory**)

Cd MAA Commissioned Master-at-Arms

CDN [international vehicle registration] Canada; *Chicago Daily News*

Cdn Canadian

cDNA [biochemistry] complementary DNA

Cd O Commissioned Officer

Cdo Commando
Cd Obs. Commissioned Observer
Cd OE Commissioned Ordnance Engineer
CDOI Colorado Department of Institutions
Cd OO Commissioned Ordnance Officer
CDOS [computing] concurrent disk operating system
CDP Committee of Directors of Polytechnics
CDPE continental daily parcels express
CDPS [computing] compound document protocol specification
CDR carbon dioxide research; Committees for the Defence of the Revolution (in Cuba); compact disc recordable; [computing] contents of decrement register; critical design review; crude death rate
CD-R [computing] compact disc recordable
Cdr Commander; Conductor
CDRA Committee of Directors of Research Associations
Cd Rad. O Commissioned Radio Officer
CDRB Canadian Defence Research Board
CDRC Civil Defence Regional Commissioner
CDRD [USA] Carbon Dioxide Research Division
Cdre Commodore
CDRF Canadian Dental Research Foundation
CDRH [USA] Center for Devices and Radiological Health
CDRI [India] Central Drug Research Institute
CD-ROM [computing] compact disc read-only memory
CD-ROM XA [computing] CD-ROM extended architecture
CDRS Civil Defence Rescue Service
CD-RW [computing] compact disc rewritable
CDS Chief of the Defence Staff; Civil Defence Services
CDSC Communicable Disease Surveillance Centre
CDSE computer-driven simulation environment
Cd Sh. Commissioned Shipwright
CDSO Companion of the Distinguished Service Order

Cd SO Commissioned Stores Officer; Commissioned Supply Officer
CDT Carnegie Dunfermline Trust; [USA, Canada] Central Daylight Time; craft, design and technology (school subject)
Cdt Cadet; Commandant
Cdt Mid. Cadet Midshipman
CDTV [computing] Commodore Dynamic Total Vision; compact-disc television
CDU *Christlich-Demokratische Union* (German: Christian Democratic Union) (political party)
CDUCE Christian Democratic Union of Central Europe
CDV [microbiology] canine distemper virus; Civil Defence Volunteers; compact-disc video; current domestic value
c.d.v. *carte-de-visite* (French: visiting card)
CDW [USA] collision damage waiver (in car insurance)
c.d.w. chilled drinking water; cold drinking water
Cd Wdr Commissioned Wardmaster
CD-WO [computing] compact disc write once
CDWR California Department of Water Resources
CDWS Civil Defence Wardens' Service
Cdz Cádiz
CE Canada East; carbon equivalent; centre of effort; [medicine] cerebral embolism; Chancellor of the Exchequer; chemical engineer; chief engineer; Christian Endeavour; Christian Era (in dates); Church of England; [computing] circular error; civil engineer; [medicine] clinical evaluation; [fishing port] Coleraine; Combustion Engineering (Incorporated); [education] Common Entrance; Common Era (in dates); *Communauté européenne* (French: European Community); community education; compass error; compression engine; [computing] computing efficiency; contrast-enhanced (of picture image); Corps of Engineers; Council of Europe; counter-espionage; [electronics] current efficiency; [vehicle registration] Peterborough
Ce [chemical element] cerium
c.e. [law] *caveat emptor* (Latin: let the buyer beware); centre of effort; [computing] circular error; compass error; critical examination

CEA Canadian Electrical Association; [medicine] carcino-embryonic antigen; Central Electricity Authority; Cinematograph Exhibitors Association; Combustion Engineering Association; *Comité européen des assurances* (French: European Insurance Committee); [commerce] commodity exchange authority; *Confédération européenne de l'agriculture* (French: European Confederation of Agriculture); Conference of Educational Associations; control electronics assembly; [USA] Council of Economic Advisors; Council of Educational Advance

CEAA [USA] Center for Editions of American Authors; Council of European-American Associations

CEAC [USA] Citizens Energy Advisory Committee; *Commission européenne de l'aviation civile* (French: European Civil Aviation Commission)

CEB Central Electricity Board

CEBAR chemical, biological and radiological warfare

CEC California Energy Commission; Canadian Electrical Code (of standardization); Catholic Education Council; Central Ethical Committee (in BMA); Centre for Economic Cooperation (in UN); Church Education Corporation; Civil Engineering Corps; Clothing Export Council; Commission of the European Communities; Commonwealth Economic Committee; Commonwealth Education Conference; Commonwealth Engineering Conference; Community Education Centre; Council for Exceptional Children

CECA *Communauté européenne du charbon et de l'acier* (French: European Coal and Steel Community)

CECD *Confédération européenne du commerce de détail* (French: European Confederation of Retail Trades)

CECE Committee for European Construction Equipment

CECG Consumers in the European Community Group

CECLES *Conseil européen pour la construction de lanceurs d'engins spatiaux* (French: European Space Launching Development Organization)

CECS Church of England Children's Society; civil engineering computing system; Communications Electronics Coordination Section

CED Committee for Economic Development; computer entry device; [USA] Council for Economic Development

CEDA Committee for Economic Development of Australia

CEDAR coupling, energetics and dynamics of atmospheric regions

CEDC Committee on Economic Cooperation among Developing Countries

CEDEL *Centrale de livraison de valeurs mobilières* (French: eurobond settlement service)

cedex *courrier d'entreprise à distribution exceptionnelle* (French: special business postal code)

CEDI *Centre européen de documentation et d'information* (French: European Documentation and Information Centre)

CEDIC Church Estates Development and Improvement Company

CEDO Centre for Educational Development Overseas

CEDR Centre for Dispute Resolution

CEE Central Engineering Establishment; Certificate of Extended Education; *Commission économique pour l'Europe* (French: Economic Commission for Europe); *Commission internationale de réglementation en vue de l'approbation de l'équipement électrique* (French: International Commission on Rules for the Approval of Electrical Equipment); Common Entrance Examination; *Communauté économique européenne* (French: European Economic Community); Council for Environmental Education

CEEA *Communauté européenne de l'énergie atomique* (French: European Atomic Energy Community)

CEEB [USA] College Entrance Examination Board

CEEC Council for European Economic Cooperation

CEED Centre for Economic and Environmental Development

CEEP *Centre européen d'études de population* (French: European Centre for Population Studies)

CEF Canadian Expeditionary Force; Chinese Expeditionary Force; [chemistry] crystalline electric field

CEFTA Central European Free Trade Area

CEFTRI [India] Central Food Technological Research Institute

CEG *collège d'enseignement général* (French: college of general education); Computer Education Group

CEGB Central Electricity Generating Board

CEGGS Church of England Girls' Grammar School

CEGS Church of England Grammar School

CEI [Switzerland] *Centre d'études industrielles* (French: Centre for Industrial Studies); *Commission électrotechnique internationale* (French: International Electrotechnical Commission); Committee for Environmental Information; communications-electronics instructions; cost-effectiveness index; Council of Engineering Institutions

CEIF Council of European Industrial Federations

CEIR Corporation for Economic and Industrial Research

CEL [USA] Constitutional Educational League

Cel. Celsius

cel. celebrate; celebrated; celebration; celery; [music] celesta; celibate

CELA Council for Exports to Latin America

CELC Commonwealth Education Liaison Committee

celeb [short form] celebrity

celest. celestial

CELEX *Communitatis Europeae Lex* (Latin: European Community Law) (computerized documentation system)

CELJ Conference of Editors of Learned Journals

cello [short form] violoncello

Cels. Celsius

CELSS controlled ecological life-support system

Celt. Celtic

CEM *Companhia Electricidade de Macáu* (Macao electricity company); [physics] continuous emission monitoring; cost and effectiveness method; [astronautics] crew-escape module

cem. cement; cemetery

CEMA Canadian Electrical Manufacturers' Association; Catering Equipment Manufacturers' Association; Conveyor Equipment Manufacturers' Association; Council for Economic Mutual Assistance; Council for the Encouragement of Music and the Arts

CEMAC Committee of European Associations of Manufacturers of Active Electronic Components; *Communauté économique et monétaire de l'Afrique central* (French: Central African Economic and Monetary Community)

CEMAP *Commission européenne des méthodes d'analyse des pesticides* (French: Collaborative Pesticides Analytical Committee)

CEMF [electronics] counter-electromotive force

CEMLA *Centro de Estudios Monetarios Latino-Americanos* (Spanish: Latin-American Centre for Monetary Studies)

CEMR Council of European Municipalities and Regions

CEMS Church of England Men's Society

CEN *Comité européen de normalisation* (French: European Standardization Committee)

Cen [astronomy] Centaurus

cen. central; centre; century

CEND Civil Engineers for Nuclear Disarmament

CENELEC *Comité européen de normalisation électrotechnique* (French: European Electrotechnical Standardization Committee)

CEng Chartered Engineer

cens. censor; censored; censorship

cent. [currency] centavo (hundredth of peso etc.); [currency] centesimo (hundredth of peso etc.); centigrade; [currency] centime (hundredth of franc etc.); central; centrifugal; *centum* (Latin: hundred); century

CENTA Combined Edible Nut Trade Association

CENTAG Central (European) Army Group (in NATO)

centenn. centennial

centig. centigrade

Cento Central Treaty Organization

CEO chief education officer; chief executive officer; Confederation of Employee Organizations

CEOA Central European Operating Agency (in NATO)

CEP [computing] circular error probability

Cep [astronomy] Cepheus

CEPCEO *Comité d'études des producteurs de charbon d'Europe occidentale* (French: Western European Coal Producers' Association)

CEPES *Comité européen pour le progrès économique et social* (French: European Committee for Economic and Social Progress)

CEPIS Council of European Professional Informatics Societies

CEPO Central European Pipeline Office

CEPR Centre for Economic Policy Research

CEPS Central European Pipeline System; Centre for European Policy Studies; Cornish Engine Preservation Society

CEPT *Conférence européenne des administrations des postes et des télécommunications* (French: European Conference of Postal and Telecommunications Administrations)

CEQ [USA] Council on Environmental Quality

CEQA [USA] California Environmental Quality Act

CER carbon dioxide evolution rate; carbon dioxide exchange rate; [Australia, New Zealand] closer economic relations; Community of European Railways

cer. ceramic

ceram. ceramic

CERC [USA] Center for Energy Research Computation; Civil Engineering Research Council

CERCA Commonwealth and Empire Radio for Civil Aviation

CERCLA [USA] Comprehensive Environmental Response, Compensation and Liability Act

Cerdip [computing] ceramic dual in-line package

CERES [USA] Coalition for Environmentally Responsible Economies; Consumers for Ethics in Research Group

CERG Conservative European Reform Group

CERI Centre for Educational Research and Innovation (of OECD)

CERL Central Electricity Research Laboratories

CERN *Conseil européen pour la recherche nucléaire* (French: European Organization for Nuclear Research)

CERP *Centre européen des relations publiques* (French: European Centre of Public Relations)

CERT Charities Effectiveness Review Trust; computer emergency response team

cert [short form] certainty

cert. certain; certificate; certificated; certification; certified; certify

CertCAM Certificate in Communication, Advertising and Marketing

CertEd Certificate in Education

CertHE Certificate in Higher Education

certif. certificate; certificated; certified

cert. inv. certified invoice

cerv. [medicine] cervical

CES [USA] Center for Energy Studies; Centre for Environmental Studies; Christian Evidence Society; *collège d'enseignement secondaire* (French: college of secondary education); community energy system; cost-estimating system

CESAR [USA] Center for Engineering Systems Advanced Research

CESC Conference on European Security and Cooperation

CESE [USA] Center for Earth Science and Engineering

CESP Confederation of European Socialist Parties

CESR [USA] Cornell electron storage ring

CESSAC Church of England Soldiers', Sailors' and Airmen's Clubs

CESSI Church of England Sunday School Institution

CEST Centre for Exploitation of Science and Technology

Cestr. *Cestrensis* (Latin: (Bishop) of Chester)

CET Central European Time; *collège d'enseignement technique* (French: college of technical education); Common External Tariff; Council for Educational Technology

Cet [astronomy] Cetus

CETA [USA] Comprehensive Employment and Training Act

CETEX Committee on Extra-Terrestrial Exploration

CETHV Council for the Education and Training of Health Visitors

CETI communications with extraterrestrial intelligence

CETO Centre for Educational Television Overseas

cet. par. *ceteris paribus* (Latin: other things being equal)

CETS chemical energy transmission systems; Church of England Temperance Society

CEU Christian Endeavour Union

CEUS Central and Eastern United States

CEUSA Committee for Exports to the United States of America

CEVS [USA] controlled environment vitrification system

CEWC Council for Education in World Citizenship

CEWMS Church of England Working Men's Society

Cey. Ceylon

CEYC Church of England Youth Council

Ceyl. Ceylon

CEZMS Church of England Zenana Missionary Society

CF calibration factor; [civil aircraft marking] Canada; Canadian Forces; capacity factor; [fishing port] Cardiff; [UK postcode] Cardiff; [commerce] carried forward; centre of flotation; Chaplain to the Forces; charcoal-filtered; *Comédie Française* (French national theatre); Commonwealth Fund; [currency] Comorian franc; compensation fee; [medicine] conventional fractionation radiotherapy; Corresponding Fellow; cost and freight; [chemistry] crystal field (as in **CF theory**); [medicine] cystic fibrosis; [vehicle registration] Reading

Cf [chemical element] californium

Cf. [Roman Catholic Church] Confessions

c/f [book-keeping] carried forward; cost and freight

cf. [bookbinding] calfskin; *confer* (Latin: compare)

.cf Central African Republic (in Internet address)

c.f. [music] *cantus firmus* (Latin: fixed song); [book-keeping] carried forward; [sports] centre field; [baseball] centre fielder; [sports] centre forward; centre of flotation; *chemin de fer* (French: railway);

communication factor; context free; cost and freight; cubic feet

CFA Canadian Federation of Agriculture; Canadian Field Artillery; Canadian Forestry Association; cash-flow accounting; [USA] Chartered Financial Analyst; Commission of Fine Arts; Commonwealth Forestry Association; *Communauté financière africaine* (French: African Financial Community, as in **CFA franc**); [medicine] complete Freund's adjuvant; Consumer Federation of America; Contract Flooring Association Limited; Cookery and Food Association; Council for Acupuncture; Council of Foreign Affairs; [electrical engineering] cross-field amplifier; [medicine] cryptogenic fibrosing alveolitis

CFAF [currency] CFA franc (used in some countries of Africa)

CFAL current food additives legislation

CFAM cogeneration feasibility analysis model

CFAP Canadian Foundation for the Advancement of Pharmacy

CFAR constant false alarm rate

CFAT Carnegie Foundation for the Advancement of Teaching

CFB [computing] cipher feedback; [USA] Consumer Fraud Bureau; Council of Foreign Bondholders

CFBAC Central Fire Brigade Advisory Council (of England and Wales)

CFBS Canadian Federation of Biological Sciences

CFC carbon-fibre composite; chlorofluorocarbon (chemical harmful to ozone layer); [microbiology] colony-forming cell; Common Fund for Commodities (in UN); *Congregatio Fratrum Christianorum* (Latin: Congregation of Christian Brothers); consolidation freight classification

CFCE *Conseil des fédérations commerciales d'Europe* (French: Council of European Commercial Federations)

CFD [computing] compact floppy disk; [engineering] computational fluid dynamics

cfd cubic feet per day

CFDC Canadian Film Development Corporation

CFDT *Confederation française démocratique*

du travail (French: Democratic Federation of Labour)

CFE Central Fighter Establishment; College of Further Education; [microbiology] colony-forming efficiency; [physics] control fuel element; Conventional (Armed) Forces in Europe (as in **CFE treaty**)

CFF *Chemins de fer fédéraux suisses* (French: Swiss federal railways); [computing] critical flicker frequency; [physics] critical fusion frequency

CFFLS [USA] Consortium for Fossil Fuel Liquefaction Science

c.f.g. cubic feet of gas

cfh cubic feet per hour

CFHT Canada–France–Hawaii Telescope (Mauna Kea, Hawaii)

CFI Campaign for Freedom of Information; chief flying instructor; cost, freight and insurance; Court of First Instance (in EU)

c.f.i. cost, freight and insurance

CFL Canadian Football League; ceasefire line; Central Film Library

CFLP Central Fire Liaison Panel

CFM Cadet Forces Medal; [chemistry] chlorofluoromethane; Council of Foreign Ministers

cfm confirm; cubic feet per minute

cfm. confirmation

CfN Council for Nature

CFO [meteorology] Central Forecasting Office; chief financial officer; chief fire officer

c.f.o. calling for orders; channel for orders

CFOA Chief Fire Officers' Association

CFOD Catholic Fund for Overseas Development

CFP Common Fisheries Policy (of EU); *Communauté financière du Pacifique* (French: Pacific Financial Community, as in **CFP franc**); *Compagnie française des pétroles* (French petroleum company)

CFPF [currency] CFP franc (used in some countries of Pacific)

CFPP coal-fired power plant

CFR [USA] Code of Federal Regulations; Commander of the Order of the Federal Republic of Nigeria; [nuclear technology] commercial fast reactor; [engineering] Cooperative Fuel Research (Committee) (as in **CFR engine**); [medicine] coronary flow reserve; [metallurgy]

corrosion-fatigue resistance; Council on Foreign Relations

cfr chauffeur

cfr. *confronta* (Italian: compare)

CFRI [USA] Central Fuel Research Institute

CFRP carbon-fibre reinforced plastic

CFS central flying school; [medicine] chronic fatigue syndrome; Clergy Friendly Society; [telecommunications] combination frequency signal; [computing] common file system

cfs cubic feet per second

CFSAN [USA] Center for Food Safety and Applied Nutrition

CFSL Central Forensic Science Laboratory

CFSP Common Foreign and Security Policy (in EU)

CFSTI [USA] Clearinghouse for Federal Scientific and Technical Information

CFT *Compagnie française de télévision* (French television company); [medicine] complement fixation test; [engineering] cross-flow turbine; Cystic Fibrosis Trust

cft craft

CFTB Commonwealth Forestry and Timber Bureau

CFTC [USA] Commodity Futures Trading Commission; Commonwealth Fund for Technical Cooperation

cftmn craftsman

CFU [microbiology] colony-forming unit

CFV continuous-flow ventilation

CFWI County Federation of Women's Institutes

CFX [Roman Catholic Church] *Congregatio Fratrum Xaverianorum* (Latin: Congregation of Xaverian Brothers)

CG [vehicle registration] Bournemouth; Captain-General; Captain of the Guard; centre of gravity; Chaplain-General; [aeronautics] cloud-to-ground; coastguard; Coldstream Guards; [US army] Commanding General; Commissary-General; computer graphics; concentration guide; conjugate gradient; Consul-General; Covent Garden (opera house); *Croix de Guerre* (French: War Cross) (military decoration)

C-G Chaplain-General

cg centigram

.cg (Republic of) Congo (in Internet address)

c.g. centre of gravity

CGA [commerce] cargo's proportion of general average; Certified General Accountant; [USA] Coast Guard Academy; [USA] Coast Guard Auxiliary; [computing] colour graphics adapter; Community of the Glorious Ascension; Country Gentlemen's Association

CGAT City Gallery Arts Trust

CGB Commonwealth Geographical Bureau

CGBR central government borrowing requirement

CGC [USA] Coast Guard cutter; Commonwealth Games Council; *Confédération générale des cadres* (French: General Confederation of Executive Staff); Conspicuous Gallantry Cross

CGD [medicine] chronic granulomatous disease

CGDK Coalition Government of Democratic Kampuchea

CGE Conservative Group for Europe

cge carriage; charge

cge fwd carriage forward

cge pd carriage paid

CGF Commonwealth Games Federation

CGH Cape of Good Hope; computer-generated hologram

CGI Catholic Guides of Ireland; chief ground instructor; chief gunnery instructor; City and Guilds Institute; commercial grade item; [computing] common gateway interface; computer graphics interface

c.g.i. corrugated galvanized iron

CGIA City and Guilds (of London) Insignia Award

CGIAR Consultative Group in International Agricultural Research

CGIL *Confederazione Generale Italiana del Lavoro* (Italian: General Italian Confederation of Labour)

CGLI City and Guilds of London Institute

CGM computer graphics metafile; Conspicuous Gallantry Medal

cgm centigram

CGMW Commission for the Geological Map of the World

cgo cargo; [finance] contango

CGOU [USA] Coast Guard Oceanographic Unit

CGP College of General Practitioners

CGPM *Conférence générale des poids et mesures* (French: General Conference of Weights and Measures); *Conseil général des pêches pour la Méditerranée* (French: General Fisheries Council for the Mediterranean)

CGPS Canadian Government Purchasing System

CGRI [India] Central Glass and Ceramic Research Institute

CGRM Commandant-General, Royal Marines

CGRO Compton Gamma Ray Observatory

CGS central gunnery school; Chief of the General Staff; Coast and Geodetic Survey; [US army] Commissary General of Subsistence; Cottage Gardens Society

cgs centimetre-gram-second (as in **cgs units**)

CGSB Canadian Government Specifications Board

CGSC [USA] Command and General Staff College

CGSS [USA] Command and General Staff School

CGSUS Council of Graduate Schools in the United States

CGT capital gains tax; ceramic gas turbine; closed gas turbine; *Compagnie générale transatlantique* (French shipping company); compressed-gas turbometer; *Confederación general del trabajo* (Spanish: General Confederation of Labour) (in Argentina); *Confédération générale du travail* (French: General Confederation of Labour)

CGTB Canadian Government Travel Bureau

CGT-FO *Confédération générale du travail–force ouvrière* (French: General Confederation of Labour/Workers' Force)

c.g.u. ceramic glazed units

CH [military] Captain of the Horse; [Freemasonry] Captain of the Host; Carnegie Hall; central heating (in property advertisement); [medicine] cerebral haemorrhage; chapter house; [fishing port] Chester; [UK postcode] Chester; Christ's Hospital; clearing house; Companion of Honour; [medicine] contact hypersensitivity; [astronomy] coronal hole; corporate hospitality; custom(s) house; [vehicle registration] Nottingham; [international vehicle registration] Switzerland (from French *Confédération Helvétique* or Latin *Confederatio Helvetica*)

C/H central heating (in property advertisement)

Ch. chairman; chairwoman; Chaldean; Chaldee; Chamber; Champion; Chancellor; Chancery; Chapter; Chile; Chilean; China; Chinese; *Chirurgiae* (Latin: of Surgery) (in academic degrees); Christ; [Bible] Chronicles; Church

ch [mathematics] hyperbolic cosine

.ch Switzerland (in Internet address)

ch. chain (crochet stitch); chain (unit of length); chaldron (unit of capacity); *chambre(s)* (French: room(s)); champion; chaplain; chapter; charge(s); chart; [horseracing] chase; chassis (in car advertisement); [chess] check; cheese; chemical; chemistry; cheque; [horseracing] chestnut; *cheval-vapeur* (French: horsepower); chief; child; children; choir; choke; church

c.h. candle hour; central heating (in property advertisement); [sports] centre half; clearing house; club house; compass heading; court house; custom(s) house

CHA Catholic Hospital Association; Chest and Heart Association; Community Health Association; Countrywide Holidays Association

Cha [astronomy] Chamaeleon

chacom chain of command

Chal. Chaldaic; Chaldean; Chaldee

chal. chaldron (unit of capacity); *chaleur* (French: heat); challenge

Chald. Chaldaic; Chaldean; Chaldee

Chamb. Chamberlain; Chambers

Chan. Chancellor; Chancery

chan. chancel; channel

Chanc. Chancellor; Chancery

CHANCOM Channel Committee (in NATO)

chap. chapel; chaplain; chaplaincy; chapter

CHAPS Clearing House Automated Payment System

chapt. chapter

CHAR Campaign for Homeless People (formerly Campaign for the Homeless and Rootless)

char. character; characteristic; characterize; charity; charter

charc. charcoal

CHAS Catholic Housing Aid Society

Chas. Charles

Chauc. (Geoffrey) Chaucer (English poet)

CHB Companion of Honour of Barbados; [medicine] complete heart block

ChB Bachelor of Surgery (from Latin *Chirurgiae Baccalaureus*); [USA] Chief of the Bureau

Chb. Cherbourg

CHC child health clinic; choke coil; Clerk to the House of Commons; Community Health Council; [USA] Confederate High Command; [chemistry] cyclohexylamine carbonate

ch. cent. *chauffage central* (French: central heating)

Ch. Clk Chief Clerk

CHD [medicine] congenital heart disease; [medicine] coronary heart disease

ChD Doctor of Chemistry; Doctor of Surgery (from Latin *Chirurgiae Doctor*)

Ch. Div. [law] Chancery Division

CHDL computer hardware description language

CHE Campaign for Homosexual Equality

ChE chemical engineer; chief engineer

CHEAR Council on Higher Education in the American Republics

CHEC Commonwealth Human Ecology Council

Cheka *Chrezvychainaya Comissiya* (Russian: Special Commission (for fighting counter-revolution and sabotage)) (former Soviet security organization)

CHEL *Cambridge History of English Literature*

Chelm Cheltenham

CHEM chemical health effects (assessment) methodology

chem. chemical; chemically; chemist; chemistry

ChemE chemical engineer

Ches. Cheshire

CHESS [USA] Cornell high-energy synchrotron source

Chev. Chevalier

chev. chevron

CHF Carnegie Hero Fund; [medicine] congestive heart failure

ChF Chaplain of the Fleet

chf chief

ch. fwd charges forward

chg. change; charge
chgd charged
chge charge
chgph. choreographer; choreographic; choreography
Chi. Chicago; Chichester; China; Chinese
Chic. Chicago
Chich. Chichester
Chicom Chinese communist
childn children
CHILL [computing] CCITT high-level language
Chin. China; Chinese
CHIPS Clearing House Inter-Bank Payments System
CHIRP Confidential Human Incidence Reporting Programme (civil aviation safety scheme)
Chi. Trib. *Chicago Tribune*
chiv. chivalry
Ch. J Chief Justice
Ch. K Christ the King
chk check
chkd checked
chkpt checkpoint
chkr checker
Chl [botany] chlorophyll
chl. chloride; chloroform
Ch. Lbr chief librarian
ChLJ Chaplain of the Order of St Lazarus of Jerusalem
chlo. chloride; chloroform
CHLW [nuclear technology] commercial high-level waste
ChM Master of Surgery (from Latin *Chirurgiae Magister*)
chm. chairman; [chess] checkmate; choirmaster
CHMC [USA] Children's Hospital Medical Center
chmn chairman
CHMR [USA] Center for Hazardous Materials Research
CHNT Community Health Nurse Tutor
CHO Confederation of Healing Organizations; Crop Husbandry Officer
cho. choral; chorister; chorus
choc. chocolate
Ch. of S Chamber of Shipping
Ch. of the F Chaplain of the Fleet
CHOGM Commonwealth Heads of Government Meeting
choirm. choirmaster

chor. choral; chorister; chorus
CHP chemical heat pump; combined heat and power; *Cumhuriyet Halk Partisi* (Turkish: Republican People's Party)
ch. pd charges paid
ch. ppd charges prepaid
CHQ Commonwealth Headquarters (of Girl Guides Association); [military] Corps Headquarters
chq. cheque
Chr. Christ; Christian; Christianity; Christmas; [Bible] Chronicles
CHRI Commonwealth Human Rights Initiative
chrm. chairman
Chron. [Bible] Chronicles
chron. chronicle; chronological; chronologically; chronology; chronometry
chronol. chronological; chronologically; chronology
Chrs Chambers
CHS Canadian Hydrographic Service; Church Historical Society; [computing] cylinders, heads and sectors
chs chapters
CHSA Chest, Heart and Stroke Association
CHSC Central Health Services Council
ch'ship championship
Ch. Skr chief skipper
ChStJ Chaplain of the Order of St John of Jerusalem
c.h.t. cylinder-head temperature
chtg charting
ch. v. check valve
c.h.w. constant hot water
chwdn churchwarden
chyd churchyard
Chy Div. [law] Chancery Division
CI [medicine] cardiac index; [medicine] cerebral infarction; Channel Islands; [Freemasonry] Chapter of Instruction; chemical inspectorate; chemical ionization; Chief Inspector; chief instructor; [astronomy] Colour Index; [medicine] combined injury; [chemistry] combustion index; Commonwealth Institute; Communist International; compression-ignition (as in **CI engine**); [statistics] confidence interval; [chemistry] configuration interaction; consular invoice; [commerce] continuous improvement; [photography] contrast index;

[astronomy] coronal index (of solar activity); [engineering] corrosion inhibitor; [international vehicle registration] Côte d'Ivoire (Ivory Coast); counter-intelligence; (Imperial Order of the) Crown of India

Ci curie (unit of radioactivity)

Ci [meteorology] cirrus

.ci Côte d'Ivoire (Ivory Coast, in Internet address)

c.i. cast iron

CIA Cancer Information Association; cash in advance; [USA] Central Intelligence Agency; Chemical Industries' Association; Chief Inspector of Armaments; *Conseil international des archives* (French: International Council on Archives); Corporation of Insurance Agents; Culinary Institute of America

Cia [commerce] *compagnia* (Italian: company, Co.); [commerce] *companhia* (Portuguese: company, Co.); [commerce] *compañia* (Spanish: company, Co.)

CIAA *Centre international d'aviation agricole* (French: International Agricultural Aviation Centre); Coordinator of Inter-American Affairs

CIAB [USA] Coal Industry Advisory Board; *Conseil international des agences bénévoles* (French: International Council of Voluntary Agencies)

CIAC Construction Industry Advisory Council

CIAgrE Companion of the Institution of Agricultural Engineers

CIAI Commerce and Industry Association Institute

CIAL Corresponding Member of the International Institute of Arts and Letters

CIAPG *Confédération internationale des anciens prisonniers de guerre* (French: International Confederation of Former Prisoners of War)

CIArb Chartered Institute of Arbitrators

CIAS Conference of Independent African States

CIB Campaign for an Independent Britain; Central Intelligence Board; Chartered Institute of Bankers (formerly IOB); Corporation of Insurance Brokers; [New Zealand] Criminal Investigation Branch

CIBS Chartered Institute of Building Services (former name of CIBSE); Chartered Institution of Building Societies

CIBSE Chartered Institution of Building Services Engineers (formerly CIBS)

CIC Capital Issues Committee; Chemical Institute of Canada; Cinema International Corporation; [immunology] circulating immune complexes; [USA] Combat Information Center; Commander-in-Chief; [USA] Command Information Center; Commonwealth Information Centre; [USA] Counterintelligence Corps; [USA] Critical Issues Council

Cic. (Marcus Tullius) Cicero (Roman orator)

CICA Canadian Institute of Chartered Accountants

CICADA central instrumentation control and data acquisition

CICAR Cooperative Investigations of the Caribbean and Adjacent Regions

CICB Criminal Injuries Compensation Board

CICC [electronics] cable-in-conduit conductor; *Conférence internationale des charités catholiques* (French: International Conference of Catholic Charities)

Cicestr. *Cicestrensis* (Latin: (Bishop) of Chichester)

CICG *Centre international du commerce de gros* (French: International Centre for Wholesale Trade)

CICHE Committee for International Cooperation in Higher Education

CICI Confederation of Information Communication Industries

CICP [USA] Committee to Investigate Copyright Problems

CICR *Comité international de la Croix-Rouge* (French: International Committee of the Red Cross)

CICRC *Commission internationale contre le régime concentrationnaire* (French: International Commission Against Concentration Camp Practices)

CICRIS Cooperative Industrial and Commercial Reference and Information Service

CICS [computing] customer information control system

CICT *Conseil international du cinéma et de*

la télévision (French: International Film and Television Council)

CID [electronics] charge injection device; Committee for Imperial Defence; Council of Industrial Design; Criminal Investigation Department

CIDA Canadian International Development Agency; *Comisión interamericano de desarrollo agricola* (Spanish: Inter-American Committee for Agricultural Development); *Comité intergouvernemental du droit d'auteur* (French: Intergovernmental Copyright Committee)

CIDADEC *Confédération internationale des associations d'experts et de conseils* (French: International Confederation of Associations of Experts and Consultants)

CIDE *Comisión de inversion y desarrollo económico* (Spanish: Commission for Investment and Economic Development) (in Uruguay)

CIDESA *Centre international de documentation économique et sociale africaine* (French: International Centre for African Social and Economic Documentation)

CIDNP chemically induced dynamic nuclear polarization

CIDOC [Mexico] Centre for Intercultural Documentation

CIE captain's imperfect entry; *Centre international de l'enfance* (French: International Children's Centre); *Commission internationale de l'éclairage* (French: International Commission on Illumination, ICI); Companion of the Order of the Indian Empire; *Confédération internationale des étudiants* (French: International Confederation of Students); [Ireland] *Córas Iompair Éireann* (Gaelic: Transport Organization of Ireland)

Cie [commerce] *compagnie* (French: company, Co.)

CIEC *Centre international d'études criminologiques* (French: International Centre of Criminological Studies); *Commission internationale de l'état civil* (French: International Commission on Civil Status)

CIEE Companion of the Institution of Electrical Engineers

CIEO Catholic International Education Office

CIEPS *Conseil international de l'éducation*

physique et sportive (French: International Council of Sport and Physical Education)

CIF Canadian Institute of Forestry; *Clube internacional de futebol* (Portuguese: International Football Club); *Conseil international des femmes* (French: International Council of Women); [commerce] cost, insurance and freight

c.i.f. [commerce] cost, insurance and freight

CIFA Corporation of Insurance and Financial Advisers

c.i.f.c. [commerce] cost, insurance, freight and commission

c.i.f.c.i. [commerce] cost, insurance, freight, commission and interest

CIFE Colleges and Institutes for Further Education; *Conseil des fédérations industrielles d'Europe* (French: Council of European Industrial Federations); *Conseil international du film d'enseignement* (French: International Council for Educational Films)

c.i.f.e. [commerce] cost, insurance, freight and exchange

c.i.f.i. [commerce] cost, insurance, freight and interest

CIFJ *Centre international du film pour la jeunesse* (French: International Centre of Films for Children)

c.i.f.L.t. [commerce] cost, insurance and freight, London terms

CIG *Comité international de géophysique* (French: International Geophysical Committee)

cig [short form] cigarette

CIGA *Compagnia Italiana dei Grandi Alberghi* (Italian hotel company)

CIGAR [nuclear technology] channel inspection and gauging apparatus of reactors

CIGAS Cambridge Intercollegiate Graduate Application Scheme

CIGasE Companion of the Institution of Gas Engineers

CIGR *Commission internationale du génie rural* (French: International Commission of Agricultural Engineering)

CIGS Chief of the Imperial General Staff

CIH Certificate in Industrial Health; Chartered Institute of Housing; [medicine] chronic inactive hepatitis

CIHA *Comité international d'histoire de l'art* (French: International Committee on the History of Art)

CIHE Council for Industry and Higher Education

CII Centre for Industrial Innovation (of University of Strathclyde); Chartered Insurance Institute; *Conseil international des infirmières* (French: International Council of Nurses)

CIIA Canadian Institute of International Affairs; *Commission internationale des industries agricoles* (French: International Commission for Agricultural Industries)

CIIR Catholic Institute for International Relations

CIJ Chartered Institute of Journalists; *Commission internationale de juristes* (French: International Commission of Jurists)

CIL Confederation of Irish Labour

CILB *Commission internationale de lutte biologique contre les ennemis des plantes* (French: International Commission for Biological Control)

CILECT *Centre international de liaison des écoles de cinéma et de télévision* (French: International Association of National Film Schools)

CILG Construction Industry Information Liaison Group

CIM Canadian Institute of Mining; Chartered Institute of Marketing; China Inland Mission; Commission for Industry and Manpower; computer input on microfilm; computer-integrated manufacturing; *Conférence islamique mondial* (French: World Muslim Conference); *Conseil international de la musique* (French: International Music Council); Cooperative Investment Management

CIMA Chartered Institute of Management Accountants; [USA] Construction Industry Manufacturers' Association

CIMarE Companion of the Institute of Marine Engineers

CIMAS continuous iron-making and steel-making

CIMB Construction Industry Manpower Board

CIME *Comité intergouvernemental pour les migrations européennes* (French: Intergovernmental Committee for European Migration); Council of Industry for Management Education

CIMechE Companion of the Institution of Mechanical Engineers

CIMGTechE Companion of the Institution of Mechanical and General Technician Engineers

CIMM Canadian Institute of Mining and Metallurgy

CIMPM *Comité international de médecine et de pharmacie militaires* (French: International Committee of Military Medicine and Pharmacy)

CIMS [USA] chemical information management systems

CIMTP *Congrès international de médecine tropicale et de paludisme* (French: International Congress of Tropical Medicine and Malaria)

CIN [medicine] cervical intraepithelial neoplasia (in cervical smear); *Commission internationale de numismatique* (French: International Numismatic Commission)

C-in-C Commander-in-Chief

CINCENT Commander-in-Chief Allied Forces Central Europe

CINCLANT Commander-in-Chief Atlantic

CINCNORTH Commander-in-Chief Allied Forces Northern Europe

CINCPAC Commander-in-Chief Pacific

CINCSOUTH Commander-in-Chief Allied Forces Southern Europe

CINFO Chief of Information

Cinn. Cincinnati

CINO Chief Inspector of Naval Ordnance

CINR [USA] Central Institute for Nuclear Research

CINS [USA] child(ren) in need of supervision

CInstR Companion of the Institute of Refrigeration

CIO Church Information Office; *Comité international olympique* (French: International Olympic Committee); *Commission internationale d'optique* (French: International Commission for Optics); [USA] Congress of Industrial Organizations

CIOB Chartered Institute of Building (formerly IOB)

CIOMS Council for International Organizations of Medical Sciences

CIOS Combined Intelligence Objectives

Subcommittee; *Conseil international pour l'organisation scientifique* (French: International Committee of Scientific Management)

CIOT Chartered Institute of Taxation

CIP [mining] carbon-in-pulp; Cataloguing in Publication; *Centre d'information de la presse* (Belgian news agency); [engineering] cold isostatic pressing; Common Industrial Policy (of EU); [engineering] constant-injection pressure

CIPA Canadian Industrial Preparedness Association; Chartered Institute of Patent Agents

CIPFA Chartered Institute of Public Finance and Accountancy

CIPL *Comité international permanent des linguistes* (French: International Standing Committee of Linguists)

CIPM *Commission internationale des poids et mesures* (French: International Committee on Weights and Measures); [USA] Council for International Progress in Management

CIPO *Comité international pour la préservation des oiseaux* (French: International Committee for Bird Preservation)

CIPP *Conseil indo-pacifique des pêches* (French: Indo-Pacific Fisheries Council)

CIPR *Commission internationale de protection contre les radiations* (French: International Commission on Radiological Protection)

CIPS Central Illinois Public Service (Company); Chartered Institute of Purchasing and Supply; Choice in Personal Safety

CIPSH *Conseil international de la philosophie et des sciences humaines* (French: International Council for Philosophy and the Humanities)

CIR Canada India reactor; Commission (or Council) on Industrial Relations; Commissioners of Inland Revenue; cost information report; [computing] current instruction register

Cir [astronomy] Circinus

cir. circle; circuit; circular; circulation; circumference; circus

cir. circa (Latin: about) (in dates)

CIRA Conference of Industrial Research Associations

circ. circle; circuit; circular; circulation; circumcision; circumference; circus

circ. circa (Latin: about) (in dates)

CIRCCE *Confédération internationale de la représentation commerciale de la communauté européenne* (French: International Confederation of Commercial Representation in the European Community)

circs [short form] circumstances

circum. circumference

CIRF *Centre international d'information et de recherche sur la formation professionelle* (French: International Vocational Training Information and Research Centre); Corn Industries Research Foundation

CIRIA Construction Industry Research and Information Association

CIRIEC *Centre international de recherches et d'information sur l'économie collective* (French: International Centre of Research and Information on Collective Economy)

CIRP *Collège international pour recherche et production* (French: International Institution for Production Engineering Research)

CIRRPC [USA] Committee on Interagency Radiation Research and Policy Coordination

CIRS [computing] cross-interleaved Reed-Solomon (as in **CIRS scheme**)

CIRT Community Initiative Research Trust

CIS [medicine] carcinoma in situ; cataloguing in source; [USA] Catholic Information Society; [USA] Center for International Studies; Central Information Service on Occupational Health and Safety (of RoSPA); Chartered Institute of Secretaries (former name of ICSA); Coal Industry Society; [medicine] combined-injury syndrome; Commonwealth of Independent States (former Soviet republics); Cooperative Insurance Society

CISA Canadian Industrial Safety Association

CISAC Centre for International Security and Arms Control; *Confédération internationale des sociétés d'auteurs et compositeurs* (French: International Confederation of Societies of Authors and Composers)

CISBH *Comité international de standardis-*

ation en biologie humaine (French: International Committee for Standardization in Human Biology)

CISC complex instruction-set chip; complex instruction-set computer

CISCO City Group for Smaller Companies; Civil Service Catering Organization

CIS-COBOL [computing] compact interactive standard Cobol

CISF *Confédération internationale des sages-femmes* (French: International Confederation of Midwives)

CISL *Confédération internationale des syndicats libres* (French: International Confederation of Free Trade Unions); *Confederazione Italiana Sindacati Lavoratori* (Italian: Italian Confederation of Workers' Trade Unions)

CISM *Conseil international du sport militaire* (French: International Military Sports Council)

CISPR *Comité international spécial des perturbations radioélectriques* (French: International Special Committee on Radio Interference)

CISS Centre for International Sports Studies; *Conseil international des sciences sociales* (French: International Social Science Council)

Cist. Cistercian

CISTI Canadian Institute for Scientific and Technological Information

CISV Children's International Summer Village Association

CIT [USA] California Institute of Technology; [USA] Carnegie Institute of Technology; [New Zealand] Central Institute of Technology; Chartered Institute of Transport; [astronomy] circumstellar imaging telescope; *Comité international des transports par chemin de fer* (French: International Railway Transport Committee); [nuclear technology] compact ignition tokamak; *Compagnia Italiana Turismo* (Italian tourism company)

cit. citadel; citation; cited; citizen; citrate

c.i.t. compression in transit

CITB Construction Industry Training Board

CITC Canadian Institute of Timber Construction; Construction Industry Training Centre

CITEL Committee for Inter-American Telecommunications

CITES Convention on International Trade in Endangered Species

CITI *Confédération internationale des travailleurs intellectuels* (French: International Confederation of Professional and Intellectual Workers)

cito disp. [medicine] *cito dispensatur* (Latin: let it be dispensed quickly) (in prescriptions)

CITV Children's Independent Television

CIU Club and Institute Union

CIUS *Conseil international des unions scientifiques* (French: International Council of Scientific Unions)

CIUSS Catholic International Union for Social Service

CIV City Imperial Volunteers; *Commission internationale du verre* (French: International Glass Commission)

civ. civil; civilian; civilization; civilize

CivE civil engineer

civvies [short form] civilian clothes

civvy [short form] civilian (as in **civvy street**)

CIW [USA] Carnegie Institute of Washington

CIWF Compassion in World Farming

CIX commercial Internet exchange

CJ Chief Justice; [vehicle registration] Gloucester

cj. conjectural

CJA Commonwealth Journalists' Association; Criminal Justice Act

CJCC Commonwealth Joint Communications Committee

CJD [medicine] Creutzfeld–Jakob disease

CJEC Court of Justice of the European Communities

CJM *Code de justice militaire* (French: Code of Military Justice); [Roman Catholic Church] Congregation of Jesus and Mary; *Congrès juif mondial* (French: World Jewish Congress)

CK [trademark] Calvin Klein; certified kosher; [fishing port] Colchester; [vehicle registration] Preston

ck cask; check; cook

CKD [computing] centre for key distribution; [commerce] completely knocked down (of goods sold in parts)

ckout checkout

ckpt cockpit

ckw. clockwise

CL calendar line; [fishing port] Carlisle; cathode luminescence; central locking (in car advertisement); civil law; Civil Lord; [Belgium] Commander of the Order of Leopold; common law; Communication Lieutenant; confidence limits; craft loss; critical list; [medicine] cruciate ligament; [vehicle registration] Norwich; [international vehicle registration] Sri Lanka (from former name Ceylon)

Cl [chemical element] chlorine

cl centilitre; council

c/l cash letter; craft loss

cl. claim; clarinet; class; classical; classics; classification; clause; clearance; clergy; clergyman; clerk; climb; close; closet; closure; cloth; clove

.cl Chile (in Internet address)

c.l. carload; central locking (in car advertisement); centre line; *cum laude* (Latin: with praise); cut lengths

CLA Canadian Library Association; Canadian Lumbermen's Association; Copyright Licensing Agency; Country Landowners' Association

Cla. Clackmannan(shire)

Clack. Clackmannan(shire)

CL(ADO) Contact Lens Diploma of the Association of Dispensing Opticians

CLAM chemical ramjet low-altitude missile

CLAN [computing] cordless local-area network

CLAP [USA] Citizens Lobbying Against Prostitution

CLAPA Cleft Lip and Palate Association

Clar. [heraldry] Clarenceux (King of Arms)

clar. [printing] clarendon (typeface); clarinet

Clarnico Clark, Nichols and Coombes (Limited) (confectionery manufacturers)

CLASS Computer-based Laboratory for Automated School Systems

class. classic; classical; classification; classified; classify

clav. [music] clavier

CLAW Consortium of Local Authorities in Wales

CLB [USA] Cape Lookout Bight (North Carolina); Church Lads' Brigade

CLC Canadian Labour Congress; Chartered Life Underwriter of Canada; Commonwealth Liaison Committee

CLCB Committee of London Clearing Banks

CLCr Communication Lieutenant-Commander

CLD [medicine] chronic liver disease; Doctor of Civil Law

cld [stock exchange] called; cancelled; cleared; coloured; cooled; could

CLE Council of Legal Education

CLEA Council of Local Education Authorities

CLEAPSE Consortium of Local Education Authorities for the Provision of Science Equipment

cler. clerical

cl. gt [bookbinding] cloth gilt

CLH *Croix de la Légion d'Honneur* (French: Cross of the Legion of Honour)

CLI [computing] command-line interface; cost-of-living index

CLIC Cancer and Leukaemia in Children

clim. climate; climatic

CLIMAP Climate: Long-range Interpretation, Mapping and Prediction (international project)

clin. clinic; clinical

CLit Companion of Literature

CLitt Companion of Literature

CLJ *Cambridge Law Journal*; Commander of the Order of St Lazarus of Jerusalem

clk clerk; clock

clkrm cloakroom (in property advertisement)

clks cloaks (= cloakroom)

clkw. clockwise

CLL [medicine] chronic lymphatic leukaemia

cl. L classical Latin

CLLR International Symposium on Computing in Literary and Linguistic Research

Cllr Councillor

CLM coal–liquid mixture; conservation and load management

clm column

CLML *Current List of Medical Literature*

CLNS [computing] connectionless network service

CLO chief liaison officer; cod liver oil

Clo. Close (in road name)

clo. closet; clothing

cloakrm cloakroom (in property advertisement)

c/lock. central locking (in car advertisement)

CLP China Light and Power (Company Limited); [computing] concurrent logic programming; Constituency Labour Party; [computing] constraint logic programming

CLPA Common Law Procedure Acts

CLR Central London Railway; City of London Rifles; computer-language recorder; [USA] Council on Library Resources

clr clear; colour; cooler

CLRAE Conference of Local and Regional Authorities of Europe

clrm classroom

CLRU Cambridge Language Research Unit

CLS Certificate in Library Science; Christian Literature Society; [statistics] classical least-squares; [statistics] constrained least-squares; Courts of London Sessions

cls. close

CLSB Committee of London and Scottish Bankers

CLT *Canadian Law Times; Compagnie Luxembourgeoise de Télédiffusion* (European media company); computer-language translator

CLU Chartered Life Underwriter

CLV [microbiology] carnation latent virus; [microbiology] cassava latent virus; [computing] constant linear velocity

clvd clavichord

CM Canadian Militia; Catholic Mission; [USA] Central Maine; central meridian; [physics] centre of mass; Certificated Master; Certificate of Merit; Certified Master; [UK postcode] Chelmsford; church mission; church missionary; circulation manager; [USA] Cleveland Museum (of Art); combustion modification; [astronautics] command module; Common Market; [music] common metre; complex mixture; composite material; condition monitoring; [computing] configuration management; [Roman Catholic Church] Congregation of the Mission; contrast medium (in radi-

ology); [nuclear technology] core meltdown; corporate membership; Corresponding Member; court martial; [microbiology] culture medium; [vehicle registration] Liverpool; Master of Surgery (from Latin *Chirurgiae Magister*); Member of the Order of Canada

Cm Command Paper (1987–); [chemical element] curium

cM [genetics] centimorgan

cm centimetre

.cm Cameroon (in Internet address)

c.m. *carat métrique* (French: metric carat); *causa mortis* (Latin: by reason of death); [physics] centre of mass; [music] common metre; [medicine] *cras mane* (Latin: tomorrow morning)

CMA Cable Makers' Association; [chemistry] calcium magnesium acetate; Canadian Medical Association; Catering Managers' Association; [USA] Certificate of Management Accounting; Chartered Management Accountant; Church Music Association; civil–military affairs; coal–mineral analysis; [USA] Colorado Mining Association; Commonwealth Medical Association; Communication Managers' Association; cost and management accountant; Country Music Association; Court of Military Appeals

CMa [astronomy] Canis Major

CMAC Catholic Marriage Advisory Council

CMACP *Conseil mondial pour l'assemblée constituante des peuples* (French: World Council for the People's World Convention)

CMAS Clergy Mutual Assurance Society; *Confédération mondiale des activités subaquatiques* (French: World Underwater Federation)

CMB Central Medical Board; Central Midwives Board; Chase Manhattan Bank; [chemistry] chemical mass balance; coastal motor boat; [astronomy] cosmic microwave background

CMBHI Craft Member of the British Horological Institute

CMBI Caribbean Marine Biological Institute

cmbt combat

CMC Canadian Marconi Company; Canadian Meteorological Centre; Canadian

Music Council; [chemistry] carboxyme-
thyl cellulose; Catholic Media Council;
Central Manpower Committee; ceramic-
matrix composite; [USA] certified management consultant; Collective
Measures Committee (of UN); Commandant of the Marine Corps; Conservation
Monitoring Centre

CMCW Calvinistic Methodist Church of
Wales

CMD [astronomy] colour-magnitude diagram; [music] common metre double;
conventional munitions disposal;
[physics] cryogenic magnetic detector

Cmd Command Paper (1919–56) (in parliamentary procedure)

cmdg commanding

Cmdr Commander

Cmdre Commodore

Cmdt Commandant

CME Chicago Mercantile Exchange; *Conférence mondiale de l'énergie* (French:
World Power Conference); [astronomy]
coronal mass ejection; [USA] cost and
manufacturability expert

CMEA Council for Mutual Economic
Assistance

CMF Cement Makers' Federation; Central
Mediterranean Force; [Australia] Citizen
Military Forces; Coal Merchants' Federa-
tion; [physics] coherent memory filter;
Commonwealth Military Forces;
[physics] compressed magnetic field;
[Roman Catholic Church] *Cordis Mariae
Filii* (Latin: Missionary Sons of the
Immaculate Heart of Mary)

CMG Commission on Marine Geology;
Companion of the Order of St Michael
and St George; Computer Management
Group

CMH Campaign for the Mentally Handicapped; combined military hospital;
[USA] Congressional Medal of Honor

CMHA Canadian Mental Health
Association

CMHC [Canada] Central Mortgage and
Housing Corporation

CMHR combustion modified highly
resilient

CMI [medicine] cell-mediated immunity;
Comité maritime international (French:
International Maritime Committee);
Commission mixte internationale pour la

*protection des lignes de télécommunication
et des canalisations* (French: Joint International Committee for the Protection
of Telecommunication Lines and Ducts);
Commonwealth Mycological Institute;
computer-managed instruction

CMi [astronomy] Canis Minor

CMIA Coal Mining Institute of America

CMIPS [computing] common management information protocol/service

CMIR [USA] Center for Medical Imaging
Research

CMJ Church's Ministry among the Jews

CML Central Music Library; [medicine]
chronic myeloid leukaemia; computer-
managed learning; Council of Mortgage
Lenders; [computing] current mode logic

cml commercial

CMLA Chief Martial Law Administrator

CMLJ Commander of Merit of the Order
of St Lazarus of Jerusalem

CMM [computing] capability and
maturity model; [Canada] Commander
of the Order of Military Merit

CMMA [USA] Coal Mining Management
College; Concrete Mixer Manufacturers'
Association

cmn commission

Cmnd Command Paper (1957–86) (in parliamentary procedure)

cmnr commissioner

CMO Central Merchandising Office (in
Zambia); chief medical officer; [USA] col-
lateralized mortgage-backed obligation;
[astronomy] compact massive object

CMOPE *Confédération mondiale des organisations de la profession enseignante*
(French: World Confederation of Organizations of the Teaching Profession)

CMOS [electronics] complementary metal
oxide semiconductor; [electronics] complementary metal oxide silicon

CMP [USA] Central Maine Power Company; Christian Movement for Peace;
[astronautics] command module pilot;
Commissioner of the Metropolitan
Police; cost of maintaining project

cmp. compromise

cmpd compound

CMPDI [USA] Central Mine Planning and
Design Institute

cm. pf. cumulative preference (shares);
cumulative preferred (shares)

Cmpn Companion

CMR Cape Mounted Rifles; central meter reading; cerebral metabolic rate; [electronics] common mode rejection

CMRA Chemical Marketing Research Association

CMRC [USA] Coal Mining Research Company

CMRO County Milk Regulations Officer

CMRR [electronics] common mode rejection ratio

CMRS [USA] Central Mining Research Station

CMS Catholic Missionary Society; [USA] Center for Measurement of Science; central materials supply; Certificate in Management Studies; Church Missionary Society; [computing] conversational monitor system

c.m.s. [medicine] *cras mane sumendus* (Latin: to be taken tomorrow morning) (in prescriptions)

CMSER [USA] Commission on Marine Science, Engineering and Resources

CM/SM [astronautics] command module service module

cmt cement

CMV [medicine] cerebral major vessel; [medicine] conventional mechanical ventilation; [microbiology] cucumber mosaic virus; [medicine] cytomegalovirus

CMY [computing] cyan, magenta, yellow

CMYK [computing] cyan, magenta, yellow, black

CMZS Corresponding Member of the Zoological Society

CN [fishing port] Campbeltown; Canadian National (Railway); [chemistry] cellulose nitrate; Chinese Nationalists; [chemistry] chloracetophenone; *Code Napoléon* (French: Napoleonic Code); common network; [physics] compound nucleus; [physics] condensation nucleus; Confederate Navy; [commerce] credit note; [civil aircraft marking] Morocco; [vehicle registration] Newcastle upon Tyne

C/N [ecology] carbon–nitrogen (as in **C/N ratio**); circular note; consignment note; contract note; [insurance] cover note; [commerce] credit note

Cn [ecclesiastical] Canon

.cn China (in Internet address)

c.n. [medicine] *cras nocte* (Latin: tomorrow night)

CNA Canadian Nuclear Association; [US navy] Center for Naval Analyses; Central News Agency (in Taiwan); [USA] Chemical Notation Association; [astronomy] cosmic noise absorption; Cyprus News Agency

CNAA Council for National Academic Awards

CNADS Conference of National Armaments Directors (in NATO)

CNAR Chief of Naval Air Services; [finance] compound net annual rate

CNC computerized numerical control

Cnc [astronomy] Cancer

CNCIEC China National Coal Import and Export Corporation

Cncl Council

Cnclr Councillor

CNCMH Canadian National Committee for Mental Hygiene

cncr. concurrent

CND Campaign for Nuclear Disarmament

CNDC Cherished Numbers Dealers Association; China Nuclear Data Centre

CNE *Comisión nacional de energía* (Spanish: National Energy Commission)

CNEAF coal, nuclear, electric and alternate fuels

CN(Eng)O Chief Naval Engineering Officer

CNES *Centre national d'études spatiales* (French: National Space Centre)

CNF Challis National Forest; Commonwealth Nurses' Federation

CNFD [USA] Commercial Nuclear Fuel Division

CNG compressed natural gas; consolidated natural gas

CNI Chief of Naval Information; Companion of the Nautical Institute

CNIP Ciskei National Independence Party

CNIPA Committee of National Institutes of Patent Agents

CNL Canadian National Library; [Australia] Commonwealth National Library; [USA] Crocker Nuclear Laboratory

cnl cancel

CNLA [USA] Council of National Library Associations

CNLS [statistics] complex nonlinear least-square

CNM [USA] Certified Nurse-Midwife

CNN Cable News Network; Certified Nursery Nurse

CNO chief nursing officer; Chief of Naval Operations

CNP Chief of Naval Personnel; Council for National Parks

CNR Canadian National Railway; Civil Nursing Reserve; *Conseil national de la révolution* (French: National Revolutionary Council) (in Burkina Faso); Council of National Representatives

cnr corner

CNRE [USA] cooperative networks on rural energy

CNRS *Centre national de la recherche scientifique* (French: National Centre for Scientific Research)

CNS [anatomy] central nervous system; [USA] Cherokee Nuclear Station; Chief of Naval Staff; China News Service (news agency); Community Nursing Services; Congress of Neurological Surgeons

c.n.s. [medicine] *cras nocte sumendus* (Latin: to be taken tomorrow night) (in prescriptions)

CNSI [USA] Chem-Nuclear Systems Incorporated

CNSLD chronic nonspecific lung disease

CNSSO Chief Naval Supply and Secretariat Officer

CNT Canadian National Telegraphs; celestial navigation trainer; [USA] Center for Neighborhood Technology; Commission for the New Towns; *Confederación nacional del trabajo* (Spanish: National Confederation of Labour)

cntn contain

cntr container

cntr. contribute; contribution

cnvt convict

CO Cabinet Office; [fishing port] Caernarvon; [medicine] cardiac output; careers officer; central office; chief officer; clerical officer; [UK postcode] Colchester; [international vehicle registration] Colombia; [US postcode] Colorado; [military] combined operations; commanding officer; command order; Commissioner of Oaths; Commonwealth Office (became part of FCO); [finance] *compte ouvert* (French: open account); conscientious objector;

criminal offence; Crown Office; [electronics] current oscillations; [vehicle registration] Exeter

C/O case oil; cash order; certificate of origin

Co [chemical element] cobalt

Co. Coalition; Colorado; Company; County

c/o care of (in postal addresses); [bookkeeping] carried over; change over

.co Colombia (in Internet address)

co. [navigation] course

c.o. [medicine] complains of; [bookkeeping] carried over

CO₂ carbon dioxide

COA change of address; College of Aeronautics; [medicine] condition on admission

coad. coadjutor

Coal. Coalition

COAS Council of the Organization of American States

coax [short form] coaxial cable

c.o.b. close of business

COBE [astronomy] Cosmic Background Explorer

Cobol [computing] common business-oriented language

c.o.b.q. *cum omnibus bonis quiescat* (Latin: may he/she rest with all good souls)

Cobra Cabinet Office Briefing Room

COC Chamber of Commerce; Clerk of the Chapel; [USA] combat operations center; [medicine] combined oral contraceptive; Corps of Commissionaires

coc. cocaine

COCA [USA] consent order and compliance agreement

COCAST Council for Overseas Colleges of Arts, Science and Technology

COCEMA *Comité des constructeurs européens de matériel alimentaire* (French: Committee of European Machinery Manufacturers for the Food Industries)

coch. [medicine] *cochleare* (Latin: spoonful)

coch. amp. [medicine] *cochleare amplum* (Latin: heaped spoonful)

cochl. [medicine] *cochleare* (Latin: spoonful)

coch. mag. [medicine] *cochleare magnum* (Latin: tablespoonful)

coch. med. [medicine] *cochleare medium* (Latin: dessertspoonful)

coch. parv. [medicine] *cochleare parvum* (Latin: teaspoonful)

COCI Consortium on Chemical Information

COCOM Coordinating Committee for Multinational Export Controls

COCOMO [computing] constructive cost model

COD cash on delivery; cause of death; Chamber of Deputies; chemical oxygen demand; [USA] collect on delivery; *Concise Oxford Dictionary*

Cod. Codex

cod. codex; codicil; codification

c.o.d. cargo on deck; cash on delivery; [USA] collect on delivery

CODAG [engineering] combined diesel and gas turbine

CODAN [telecommunications] carrier-operated device anti-noise

CODASYL [computing] Conference on Data Systems Languages

CODATA Confederation of Design and Technology Associations

codd. codices

codec [computing] coder-decoder

Codesh Convention for a Democratic South Africa

CODIPHASE [computing] coherent digital phased array system

CODOG [engineering] combined diesel or gas turbine

CODOT *Classification of Occupations and Directory of Occupational Titles*

COE Chamber Orchestra of Europe; *Conseil oecuménique des églises* (French: World Council of Churches); [USA] Corps of Engineers; cost of electricity; cost of energy

COED computer-operated electronic display; *Concise Oxford English Dictionary*

co-ed [short form] coeducational

coeff. coefficient

CoEnCo Committee for Environmental Conservation

COESA [USA] Committee on Extension to the Standard Atmosphere

COF *Comité olympique française* (French: French Olympic Committee)

C of A Certificate of Airworthiness; College of Arms

COFACE [commerce] *Compagnie française pour l'assurance du commerce extérieur* (French: French export credit guarantee company)

C of B confirmation of balance

C of C Chamber of Commerce

C of E Church of England; Council of Europe

C of ECS Church of England Children's Society

C of F Chaplain of the Fleet; chief of finance; [engineering] coefficient of friction

C of G centre of gravity

C of GH Cape of Good Hope

COFI Committee on Fisheries

C of I Church of Ireland

C of L City of London

C of M [aeronautics] Certificate of Maintenance

C of S Chief of Staff; Church of Scotland; conditions of service

COG Cleansing Officers' Guild

CoG centre of gravity

cog. cognate; cognizant; cognomen

c.o.g. centre of gravity

COGAG [engineering] combined gas and gas turbine

COGB certified official government business

COGECA *Comité général de la coopération agricole des pays de la CE* (French: General Committee for Agricultural Cooperation in the EU Countries)

Cogene Committee on Genetic Experimentation

COGLA Canada Oil and Gas Lands Administration

COGMA Concrete Garage Manufacturers' Association

COGS [astronautics] continual orbital guidance system; [accounting] cost of goods sold

coh. coheir

c.o.h. cash on hand

COHSE Confederation of Health Service Employees (became part of Unison)

COI Central Office of Information; certificate of origin and interest; *Commission océanographique intergouvernementale* (French: Intergovernmental Oceanographic Commission); [USA] cost of illness

COIC Canadian Oceanographic Identification Centre; Careers and Occupational Information Centre

COID Council on International Development

ColD Council of Industrial Design (former name of Design Council)

COIE Committee on Invisible Exports

COIF Control of Intensive Farming

COIL chemical oxygen–iodine laser

COIN [USA] counter-insurgency

COINS [USA] Committee on Improvement of National Statistics

COJO Conference of Jewish Organizations

COL centrally operated locking (in car advertisement); computer-oriented language; cost of living

Col [astronomy] Columba

Col. Colombia; Colombian; Colonel; Colorado; [Bible] Colossians

col. collect; collected; collection; collector; college; collegiate; colon; colonial; colony; colour; coloured; column

COLA Camping and Outdoor Leisure Association; [USA] cost-of-living adjustment (in employment contract)

Col. Comdt Colonel Commandant

COLD [medicine] chronic obstructive lung disease

Coling International Conference on Computational Linguistics

Coll. College

coll. collateral; colleague; collect; collected; collection; collective; collector; college; collegiate; colloquial; colloquialism; [medicine] collyrium (eyewash)

collab. collaborate; (in) collaboration (with); collaborator

collat. collateral; collaterally

collect. collective; collectively

colloq. colloquial; colloquialism; colloquially

coll'ott. [music] *coll'ottava* (Italian: in octaves)

collr collector

colly colliery

Colo. Colorado

colog. cologarithm

Coloss. [Bible] Colossians

Col. P [advertising] colour page

COLS [computing] communications for online systems

cols columns

Col-Sgt Colour-Sergeant

COM coal–oil mixture; [US navy] Commander; [chemistry] complex organic mixture; computerized operations management; computer output on microfiche (or microfilm)

Com [astronomy] Coma Berenices

Com. Commander; Commissary; Commissioner; Committee; Commodore; Commonwealth; Communist

com. comedy; comic; comma; commentary; commerce; commercial; commission; commissioner; committee; common; commoner; commonly; commune; communicate; communicated; communication(s); community

.com (US) commercial organization (in Internet address)

COMA Committee on Medical Aspects of Food Policy

COMAF *Comité des constructeurs de matériel frigorifique de la CE* (French: Committee of Refrigerating Plant Manufacturers of the EU)

COMAL [computing] common algorithmic language

COMAR [USA] Code of Maryland Air Regulations

COMARE [USA] Committee on Medical Aspects of Radiation in the Environment

COMART Commander, Marine Air Reserve Training

comb. combination; combine; combined; combining; combustible; combustion

Comd. Commander

comd command

comd. commanding

COMDEV Commonwealth Development Finance Company

Comdg [military] Commanding

Comdr Commander

Comdt Commandant

COME Chief Ordnance Mechanical Engineer

COMECON Council for Mutual Economic Assistance

Comet Committee for Middle East Trade; computer-operated management evaluation technique

COMEX [USA] Commodity Exchange (New York)

COMEXO Committee for Exploitation of the Oceans

comfy [short form] comfortable

Com-Gen Commissary-General
COMIBOL *Corporación Minera de Bolivia* (Bolivian state mining company)
Cominform Communist Information Bureau
COMINT communications intelligence
Comintern Communist International
coml commercial
COMLOGNET [US air force] combat logistics network
Comm. Commander; Commodore
comm. commentary; commerce; commercial; commercially; committee; commonwealth; communal; communication
Commd [military] Commissioned
commem. commemoration; commemorative
Commiss. Commissary
Commissr Commissioner
Commn Commission
commn commission
Commnd [military] Commissioned
Commr Commissioner
comms communications
commun. communication; community
Commy Commissary
COMO Committee of Marketing Organizations
Comp. Companion (of institute or institution)
comp. companion; comparative; compare; comparison; compass; compensation; compete; competition; competitive; competitor; compilation; compiled; compiler; complete; compose; composer; composite; composition; compositor; compound; compounded; comprehensive; compression; comprising
COMPAC Commonwealth Trans-Pacific Telephone Cable
compar. comparative; comparison
compd compound
Comp-Gen Comptroller-General
compl. complement; complete; compliment; complimentary
complt complainant; complaint
compo. composition
compr. compressive
Compsac International Computer Software and Applications Conference
compt compartment
Compt. Comptroller
Comptr Comptroller

Comr Commissioner
Com. Rom. Common Romance (language)
comsat communications satellite
ComSec Commonwealth Secretariat
COMSER Commission on Marine Science and Engineering Research (in UN)
Com. Teut. Common Teutonic (language)
Com. Ver. [Bible] Common Version
Com. W Ger. Common West Germanic (language)
Comy-Gen Commissary-General
Con. Conformist; Conservative; [finance] Consols; Constable; [military] Constructor; Consul; [music] contralto
con. concentration; concerning; concerto; conclusion; conditioning; confidence; conics; *conjunx* (Latin: wife); connection; conservation; consolidate; consolidated; [finance] consols; continue; continued; *contra* (Latin: against); convenience; conversation
CONAC [USA] Continental Air Command
CONAD [USA] Continental Air Defense Command
CONARC [USA] Continental Army Command
CONBA Council of National Beekeeping Associations of the United Kingdom
conbd contributed
Con. C Constructor Captain
conc. concentrate; concentrated; concentration; concerning; concerto; concise
concd concentrated
concg concentrating
conch. conchology
conchie [short form] conscientious objector
concn concentration
Con. Cr Constructor Commander
concr. concrete
con. cr. [book-keeping] contra credit
cond. condense; condensed; condenser; condition; conditional; conduct; conducted; conductivity; conductor
condr conductor
con esp. [music] *con espressione* (Italian: with expression)
con espr. [music] *con espressione* (Italian: with expression)
conf. confection; confectionery; *confer* (Latin: compare); conference; confession; confessor; confidential

confab [short form] confabulation

Confed. Confederacy; Confederate; Confederation

confed. confederate; confederated; confederation

Cong. Congregational; Congregationalist; Congress; Congressional

cong. [pharmacology] *congius* (Latin: gallon); congregation; congregational

Cong. R [USA] Congressional Records

Cong. Rec. [USA] Congressional Records

CONGU Council of National Golf Unions

CONI *Comitato Olimpico Nazionale Italiano* (Italian: Italian National Olympic Committee)

con. inv. consular invoice

conj. conjecture; [grammar] conjugation; [grammar] conjunction; conjunctive

Con. L Constructor Lieutenant

CONLAN [computing] consensus language

Con. LCr Constructor Lieutenant-Commander

Conn. Connecticut

conn. connect; connected; connection; connotation

conq. conquer; conquered; conqueror; conquest

CONS [computing] connection-oriented network service

Cons. Conservative; Conservatoire; Conservatorium; Conservatory; Constable; Constitution; Consul

cons. consecrate; consecrated; consecration; consecutive; consequence; conservation; conservative; conserve; consider; consigned; consignment; consolidated; consonant; constable; constitution; constitutional; construction; consul; consult; consulting

con. sec. conic section

Conserv. Conservatoire; Conservatorium; Conservatory

conserv. conservatory (in property advertisement)

cons. et prud. *consilio et prudentia* (Latin: by counsel and prudence)

consgt consignment

consid. consideration

Con. SL Constructor Sub-Lieutenant

consol. consolidated

consols [short form] consolidated annuities (or stock)

Const. Constable; Constitution

const. constable; constant; constituency; constitution; constitutional; construction

constit. constituent

constl constitutional

constr. construct; construction; construe

cont. container; containing; contents; continent; continental; continue; continued; [music] continuo; continuum; *contra* (Latin: against); contract; contraction; control; controller

contag. contagious

contbd contraband

contbg contributing

cont. bon. mor. *contra bonos mores* (Latin: contrary to good manners)

contd contained; continued

contemp. contemporary

contg containing

contn continuation

contr. contract(s); contracted; contraction; contralto; contrary; contrast; contrasted; control; controller

contr. bon. mor. *contra bonos mores* (Latin: contrary to good manners)

cont. rem. [medicine] *continuantur remedia* (Latin: let the medication be continued) (in prescriptions)

contrib. contributed; contributing; contribution; contributor

CONUS continental United States

Conv. Convocation

conv. convenience; convenient; convent; convention; conventional; conversation; conversion; converter; convertible

convce conveyance

COOC [insurance] contact with oil or other cargo

co-op [short form] cooperative (society or store)

COP [New Zealand] Certificate of Proficiency (university pass); coefficient of performance (in thermodynamics); [USA] community-oriented policing; custom of port

Cop. Copernican; Coptic

cop. copper; copulative; copyright; copyrighted

COPA *Comité des organisations professionnelles agricoles de la CE* (French: Committee of Agricultural Organizations in the EU)

COPAL Cocoa Producers' Alliance
COPD [medicine] chronic obstructive pulmonary disease
Copec Conference on Christian Politics, Economics and Citizenship
COPPSO Conference of Professional and Public Service Organizations
copr. copyright
COPS Council of Polytechnic Secretaries
Copt. Coptic
coptr copartner
COPUOS Committee on the Peaceful Uses of Outer Space
COPUS Committee on the Public Understanding of Science
COR Committee of the Regions (in EU)
Cor. [Bible] Corinthians; Coroner
cor. corner; cornet; [music] *corno* (Italian: horn); coroner; *corpus* (Latin: the body); correct; corrected; correction; correlative; correspondence; correspondent; corresponding; corrupt
Coral [computing] common real-time application language
Corat Christian Organizations Research and Advisory Trust
CORBA [computing] common object request broker architecture
CORD [medicine] chronic obstructive respiratory disease
Corda Coronary Artery Disease Research Association
CORE [USA] Congress of Racial Equality
CORES computer-aided (or -assisted) order routing and execution system (in Tokyo Stock Exchange)
CORGI Council for Registered Gas Installers
Cor. Mem. Corresponding Member
Corn. Cornish; Cornwall
Cornh. *Cornhill Magazine*
corol. corollary
coroll. corollary
Corp. Corporal; Corporation
Corpl Corporal
Corpn Corporation
corr. correct; corrected; correction; corrective; correlative; *corrente* (Italian: current); correspond; correspondence; correspondent; corresponding; corrigenda; corrugated; corrupt; corrupted; corruption
CORRA Combined Overseas Rehabilitation Relief Appeal

correl. correlative
corresp. correspondence; corresponding
Corresp. Mem. Corresponding Member
corrupt. corruption
CORS Chief of the Regulating Staff
Cors. Corsica; Corsican
Cor. Sec. corresponding secretary
CORSO [New Zealand] Council of Organizations for Relief Services Overseas
CORT Council of Regional Theatres; Council of Repertory Theatres
cort. cortex
COS [commerce] cash on shipment; Chamber of Shipping; Charity Organization Society; Chief of Staff; Cinema Organ Society
CoS Chief of Staff
Cos. Companies; Counties
cos [mathematics] cosine
c.o.s. [commerce] cash on shipment
COSA Colliery Officials and Staffs Association; [accounting] cost of sales adjustment
co. sa *come sopra* (Italian: as above)
COSAG [shipping] combined steam turbine and gas turbine
COSAR compression scanning array radar
COSATI Committee on Scientific and Technical Information
COSATU Congress of South African Trade Unions
COSBA Computer Services and Bureaux Association
COSE [computing] common open software environment
COSEC Coordinating Secretariat of the National Union of Students
cosec [mathematics] cosecant
cosech [mathematics] hyperbolic cosecant
COSFPS Commons, Open Spaces and Footpaths Preservation Society
cosh [mathematics] hyperbolic cosine
COSHEP Committee of Scottish Higher Education Principals
COSHH Control of Substances Hazardous to Health
CoSIRA Council for Small Industries in Rural Areas
COSLA Convention of Scottish Local Authorities
COSMD Combined Operations Signals Maintenance Division

cosmog. cosmogony; cosmographical; cosmography

COSMOS Coast Survey Marine Observation System

co. so. *come sopra* (Italian: as above)

COSPAR Committee on Space Research

Coss. *Consules* (Latin: Consuls)

COSSAC Chief of Staff to Supreme Allied Commander

COSSEC Cambridge, Oxford and Southern School Examinations Council

COST Committee for Overseas Science and Technology

COT [physics] change of temperature

CoT College of Technology

cot [mathematics] cotangent

cotan [mathematics] cotangent

COTC Canadian Officers' Training Corps

coth [mathematics] hyperbolic cotangent

COTR [USA] contracting officers' technical representative

Cots Childlessness Overcome Through Surrogacy

COTT [South Africa] Central Organization for Technical Training

couch. [heraldry] couchant

.co.uk UK commercial organization (in Internet address)

Coun. Council; Councillor; Counsellor

cour. *courant* (French: current, this month, inst.) (in correspondence)

COV [statistics] coefficient of variation; [chemistry] concentrated oil of vitriol; [electronics] corona onset voltage; [statistics] covariance; [genetics] crossover value

Cov. Coventry

cov. [statistics] covariance; covenant

covers [mathematics] coversed sine

cov. pt [cricket] cover point

COW character-oriented windows

COWAR Committee on Water Research

COWPS [USA] Council on Wages and Price Stability

Coy [military] company

COZI communications zone indicator

CP [civil aircraft marking] Bolivia; [medicine] Campylobacter pylori (bacterium causing gastric illness); Canadian Pacific (Railway); Canadian Press (news agency); Cape Province (former South African province); Captain of the Parish (in Isle of Man); [navigation] cardinal point; *casella postale* (Italian: post office box); [computing] central processor; [aeronautics] centre of pressure; centrifugal pump; [medicine] cerebral palsy; [surveying] change point; [physics] charge parity; charter party; chemically pure; Chief of Police; Chief Patriarch; [medicine] chronic pancreatitis; [medicine] cisplatin (used to treat cancer); civil power; civil procedure; Clarendon Press; Clerk of the Peace; code of procedure; *Codice Penale* (Italian: Penal Code); College of Preceptors; colour printing (as in **CP filter**); [military] Command Post; commercial paper; Common Pleas; Common Prayer; Communist Party; community physician; community programme; *Companhia dos Caminhos de Ferro Portugueses* (Portuguese railway company); [stock exchange] concert party; condensation product; conference paper; conference proceedings; [Roman Catholic Church] *Congregatio Passionis* (Latin: Congregation of the Passion); [India] Congress Party; [South Africa] Conservative Party; convict prison; corporal punishment; [Australia] Country Party (former name of National Party); county primary (school); Court of Probate; [biochemistry] creatine phosphate; [physics] cross polarization; current paper; [vehicle registration] Huddersfield

C/P charter party

Cp. [Roman Catholic Church] compline

cp. compare

c.p. candlepower; carriage paid; [aeronautics] centre of pressure; chemically pure; constant pressure

CPA Canadian Pharmaceutical Association; Canadian Psychological Association; central planning area; [USA] Certified Public Accountant; Chartered Patent Agent; Chick Producers' Association; [insurance] claims payable abroad; Clyde Port Authority; Commonwealth Parliamentary Association; Communist Party of Australia; Construction Plant Association; Contractors' Plant Association; contract price adjustment; cost planning and appraisal; Council of Provincial Associations; [computing] critical path analysis

CPAC Collaborative Pesticides Analytical Committee; Consumer Protection Advisory Committee

CPAG Child Poverty Action Group; [USA] Collision Prevention Advisory Group

CPAI Canvas Products Association International

C Pal. Crystal Palace

CPAM Committee of Purchasers of Aircraft Material

CPAS Catholic Prisoners' Aid Society; Church Pastoral Aid Society

CPB [medicine] cardiopulmonary bypass; [book-keeping] casual payments book; Central Planning Bureau; Communist Party of Britain

CPBF Campaign for Press and Broadcasting Freedom

CPC [USA] City Planning Commission; city police commissioner; Clerk of the Privy Council; [medicine] clinicopathological conference; Communist Party of China; Conservative Political Centre

CPCIZ *Comité permanent des congrès internationaux de zoologie* (French: Standing Committee of International Zoological Congresses)

CPCU [USA] Chartered Property and Casualty Underwriter

CPD [astronomy] Cape Photographic Durchmusterung (star catalogue); [medicine] chronic pulmonary disease; [electronics] contact potential difference; continuing professional development

cpd compound

c.p.d. [commerce] charterers pay dues

CPDL Canadian Patents and Developments Limited

CPDM Centre for Physical Distribution Management

CPE Certificate of Physical Education; [USA] Certified Property Exchanger; [medicine] chronic pulmonary emphysema; College of Physical Education; [law] Common Professional Examination; *Congrès du peuple européen* (French: Congress of European People); contractor performance evaluation; [microbiology] cytopathic effect

CPEA Catholic Parents' and Electors' Association; [USA] Cooperative Program for Educational Administration

c. pén. *code pénal* (French: penal code)

CPEQ Corporation of Professional Engineers of Quebec

CPF contributory pension fund

CPFF cost plus fixed fee

CPFS Council for the Promotion of Field Studies

CPG Coronary Prevention Group

CPGB Communist Party of Great Britain

CPH Certificate in Public Health

cph cycles per hour

CPHA Canadian Public Health Association

CPhys Chartered Physicist

CPI chief pilot instructor; Communist Party of India; consumer price index

cpi [printing] characters per inch

CPJI *Cour permanente de justice internationale* (French: Permanent Court of International Justice)

CPL Cats' Protection League; central public library; Colonial Products Laboratory; [computing] combined programming language; commercial pilot's licence

Cpl Corporal

cpl [printing] characters per line

CPM [USA] Certified Property Manager; Colonial Police Medal; [music] common particular metre; Communist Party of Malaya; computer program module; [computing] critical path method

CP/M [trademark] Control Program for Microcomputers

cpm [computing] characters per minute; cycles per minute

CPMEE&W Council for Postgraduate Medical Education in England and Wales

CPN *Communistische Partij van Nederland* (Dutch: Netherlands Communist Party); community psychiatric nurse

Cpn Copenhagen

cpn coupon

CPNA Council of Photographic News Agencies

Cpnhgn Copenhagen

CPNZ Communist Party of New Zealand

CPO cancel previous order; [chemistry] catalytic partial oxidation; Chief Petty Officer; command pay office; Commonwealth Producers' Organization; compulsory purchase order; county planning officer; crime prevention officer

CPP

CPP chemical processing plant; Convention People's Party (in Ghana); [computing] critical path plan(ning); current purchasing power (as in **CPP accounting**)

c.p.p. controllable pitch propeller

CPPA Canadian Pulp and Paper Association

CPPCC Chinese People's Political Consultative Conference

CPPS [computing] critical path planning and scheduling

CPR Canadian Pacific Railway; [medicine] cardiopulmonary resuscitation

CPRC Central Price Regulation Committee

CPRE Council for the Protection of Rural England

CPRS Central Policy Review Staff

CPRW Council for the Protection of Rural Wales

CPS Centre for Policy Studies; cents per share; [USA] Certified Professional Secretary; Church Patronage Society; Clerk of Petty Sessions; Commonwealth Public Service; Communist Party of Syria; Congregational Publishing Society; Crown Prosecution Service; *Custos Privati Sigilli* (Latin: Keeper of the Privy Seal)

cps [computing] characters per second; cycles per second

CPSA Civil and Public Services Association; Clay Pigeon Shooting Association

CPSC [USA] Consumer Product Safety Commission

CPSS Certificate in Public Service Studies

CPSU Communist Party of the Soviet Union

CPsychol Chartered Psychologist

CPT Canadian Pacific Telegraphs; [physics] charge parity–time; cost per thousand; [computing] critical path technique

Cpt. Captain

cpt cockpit; counterpoint

CPTB Clay Products Technical Bureau

CPU central packaging unit; [computing] central processing unit; collective protection unit; Commonwealth Press Union

CPUSA Communist Party of the United States of America

CPVE Certificate of Pre-vocational Education

CQ [military] charge of quarters; conditionally qualified

CQM Chief Quartermaster; Company Quartermaster

CQMS Company Quartermaster-Sergeant

CQR *Church Quarterly Review*

CQS Court of Quarter Sessions

CQSW Certificate of Qualification in Social Work

CR *Carolina Regina* (Latin: Queen Caroline); *Carolus Rex* (Latin: King Charles); carriage return; carrier's risk; cash receipts; central railway; central registry; Chief Ranger; [medicine] chronic rejection; *Civis Romanus* (Latin: Roman citizen); [USA] Commendation Ribbon; Community of the Resurrection (Anglican monastic order); company's risk; [medicine] complete regression; [medicine] complete remission; [engineering] compression ratio; [medicine] computed radiography; [chemistry] concentration ratio; [psychology] conditioned reflex; [psychology] conditioned response; conference report; Congo red (dye); consciousness raising; control relay; cosmic rays; [international vehicle registration] Costa Rica; crease-resistant; credit; credit rating; credit report; [statistics] critical ratio; [UK postcode] Croydon; current rate; *Custos Rotulorum* (Latin: Keeper of the Rolls); [vehicle registration] Portsmouth; [civil aircraft marking] Portugal

Cr [chemical element] chromium; Commander; Councillor; cruiser

c/r company's risk

cr. created; creation; credit; creditor; creek; [music] *crescendo* (Italian: with increasing loudness); crew; crimson; crown; cruise; *crux* (Latin: cross)

.cr Costa Rica (in Internet address)

c.r. *con riserva* (Italian: with reservations); [finance] cum rights (i.e. with rights)

CRA California Redwood Association; Canadian Rheumatism Association; [Northern Ireland] Civil Rights Association; Coal Research Association of New Zealand; Commander of the Royal Artillery; Commercial Rabbit Association; composite research aircraft; corrosion-resistant alloy

CrA [astronomy] Corona Australis

CrAA Commander-at-Arms

CRAC Careers Research and Advisory Centre; Central Religious Advisory Committee; Construction Research Advisory Council

CRAD Committee for Research into Apparatus for the Disabled

CRAE Committee for the Reform of Animal Experimentation

CRAeS Companion of the Royal Aeronautical Society

CRAF [USA] Civil Reserve Air Fleet

CRAMRA Convention on the Regulation of Antarctic Mineral Resource Activities

cran. craniology

craniol. craniology

craniom. craniometry

CRASC Commander of the Royal Army Service Corps

CRB Central Radio Bureau

CrB [astronomy] Corona Borealis

CRC [printing] camera-ready copy; Cancer Research Campaign; child-resistant closure; Civil Rights Commission; coal rank code; Community Relations Council; [printing] composing room chapel; [USA] Coordinating Research Council; cycle racing club; [computing] cyclic redundancy check

CRCC Canadian Red Cross Committee

CRCH central register and clearing house

CRCP Certificant of the Royal College of Physicians

CRCS Certificant of the Royal College of Surgeons (of England)

CRD [medicine] chronic respiratory disease; Crop Research Division

CRDEC [USA] Chemical Research, Development and Engineering Center

CRDF cathode-ray direction-finding

CRE [USA] Coal Research Establishment; Commander of the Royal Engineers; Commercial Relations and Exports; Commission for Racial Equality; cumulative radiation effect

CREFAL *Centro Regional de Educación Fundamental para la América Latina* (Spanish: Regional Centre of Fundamental Education for Latin America)

Cres. Crescent (in road name)

cres. [music] *crescendo* (Italian: with increasing loudness)

cresc. [music] *crescendo* (Italian: with increasing loudness)

CRF [finance] capital recovery factor; [medicine] chronic renal failure; [medicine] coagulase reacting factor; [biochemistry] corticotrophin-releasing factor

crg. carriage

CRH [biochemistry] corticotrophin-releasing hormone

CRI Caribbean Research Institute; Children's Relief International; [medicine] chronic renal insufficiency; [photography] colour reversal intermediate; [USA] Cray Research Incorporated; *Croce Rossa Italiana* (Italian: Italian Red Cross)

CRIB Current Research in Britain

CRIC [Roman Catholic Church] Canons Regular of the Immaculate Conception; Commercial Radio International Committee

crim. criminal

crim. con. [law] criminal conversation (i.e. adultery)

criminol. criminology

CRIS [medicine] clinical radiology imaging system; [computing] command retrieval information system; current research information system

crit. criterion; critic; critical; critically; criticism

Crk Cork (Ireland)

CRL [Roman Catholic Church] Canons Regular of the Lateran; Certified Record Librarian; Certified Reference Librarian; Chemical Research Laboratory

CRM [USA] Central Rocky Mountains; certified reference material; counter-radar missile; count-rate meter; cruise missile

CRMA Cotton and Rayon Merchants' Association

CRMF Cancer Relief Macmillan Fund

CRMP Corps of Royal Military Police

crn crown

crn. crane

CRNA Campaign for the Restoration of the National Anthem and Flag; Clinical Research Nurses' Association

CRNCM Companion of the Royal Northern College of Music

CRNSS Chief of the Royal Naval Scientific Service

CRO cathode-ray oscilloscope (or oscillograph); Cave Rescue Organization of Great Britain; chief recruiting officer; Commonwealth Relations Office (became part of FCO); community relations officer; Companies Registration Office; compulsory rights order; Criminal Records Office

Croat. Croatia; Croatian

CRP *Calendarium Rotulorum Patentium* (Latin: Calendar of the Patent Rolls); [Roman Catholic Church] Canons Regular of Prémontré; capacity requirement plan; [India] Central Reserve Police; coordinated research programme

CRPL [USA] Central Radio Propagation Laboratory

CRPPH [USA] Committee on Radiation Protection and Public Health

CRR constant ratio rule; Curia Regis Roll

CRS Catholic Record Society; Cereals Research Station; cold-rolled steel; Cooperative Retail Society; cosmic radio source

CRSI [USA] Concrete Reinforcing Steel Institute

CRT cathode-ray tube; [mathematics] Chinese remainder theorem; combat readiness training; composite rate tax

Crt Court; [astronomy] Crater

CRTC Canadian Radio-Television Commission

crtkr caretaker

CRTS Commonwealth Reconstruction Training Scheme

CRU civil resettlement unit; [computing] control register user

Cru [astronomy] Crux

Crv [astronomy] Corvus

crypto. cryptographic; cryptography

cryst. crystal; crystalline; crystallography

crystallog. crystallography

crystd crystallized

crystn crystallization

CRZZ *Centralna Rada Związków Zawadowych* (Polish: Central Council of Trade Unions)

CS [medicine] Caesarean section; [chemistry] calcium silicate; capital stock; carbon steel; (Ben) Carson and (Roger) Stoughton (as in **CS gas**); [biochemistry] casein; cast steel; Certificate in Statistics; Chartered Surveyor; Chemical Society; Chief of Staff; chief secretary; [computing] chip select; Christian Science; Christian Scientist; city surveyor; civil servant; Civil Service; Clerk of Session;

Clerk to the Signet; [medicine] clinical stage; close shot; close support; College of Science; [mining] colliery screened; [psychology] conditioned stimulus; [USA] Confederate States; [Roman Catholic Church] Congregation of Salesians; [physics] coolant system; Cooperative Society; cotton seed; county surveyor; Court of Session; [fishing port] Cowes; credit sales; cruiser squadron; *Custos Sigilli* (Latin: Keeper of the Seal); [vehicle registration] Glasgow; [civil aircraft marking] Portugal

C/S channel shank (buttons); cycles per second

Cs [chemical element] caesium

Cs [meteorology] cirrostratus

c/s cases; cycles per second

cs. case; census; consul

c.s. capital stock; *come sopra* (Italian: as above)

CSA Canadian Standards Association; Casualty Surgeons' Association; Channel Swimming Association; Child Support Agency; Common Services Agency; [USA] Community Services Administration; [Canada] Computer Science Association; Confederate States Army; Confederate States of America

CSAA Child Study Association of America

CSAB Civil Service Appeal Board

CSAE Canadian Society of Agricultural Engineering

CSAP Canadian Society of Animal Production

CSAR Communication Satellite Advanced Research

CSB Bachelor of Christian Science; [engineering] calcium silicate brick; Central Statistical Board; [medicine] chemical stimulation of the brain

CSBF Civil Service Benevolent Fund

CSBGM Committee of Scottish Bank General Managers

CSBM [military] confidence- and security-building measures

CSC Civil Service Commission; Commonwealth Science Council; Comprehensive Schools Committee; [Belgium] *Confédération des syndicats chrétiens* (French: Federation of Christian Trade Unions); Conspicuous Service Cross (replaced by DSC)

csc [mathematics] cosecant

CSCB Committee of Scottish Clearing Bankers

CSCBS Commodore Superintendent, Contract-Built Ships

CSCC Civil Service Commission of Canada; Council of Scottish Chambers of Commerce

CSCE Conference on Security and Cooperation in Europe (former name of OSCE)

CSCFE Civil Service Council for Further Education

CSCW computer-supported cooperative working

CSD Chartered Society of Designers (formerly SIAD); Civil Service Department; Commonwealth Society for the Deaf; [engineering] constant speed drive; Cooperative Secretaries Diploma; Doctor of Christian Science

CSDE Central Servicing Development Establishment (in RAF)

CSE Campaign for State Education; Central Signals Establishment; Certificate of Secondary Education (replaced by GCSE); [computing] cognitive systems engineering; Council of the Stock Exchange

cse course

CSEA [USA] Civil Service Employees Association

C-section [medicine] Caesarean section

CSED [US navy] coordinated ship electronics design

CSEU Confederation of Shipbuilding and Engineering Unions

CSF [medicine] cerebrospinal fluid; Coil Spring Federation; [medicine] colony-stimulating factor

CSFA Canadian Scientific Film Association

CSFE Canadian Society of Forest Engineers

CSG Catholic Social Guild; Companion of the Order of the Star of Ghana; [computing] constructive solid geometry

CSGA Canadian Seed Growers' Association

CS gas tear gas invented by (Ben) Carson and (Roger) Stoughton

CSH [chemistry] calcium silicate hydrate

csh cash

CSI Chartered Surveyors' Institution; Church of South India; *Commission sportive internationale* (French: International Sporting Commission); [image technology] compact source iodide (as in **CSI lamp**); Companion of the Order of the Star of India; [USA] Construction Specifications Institute

CSICC Canadian Steel Industries Construction Council

CSIP Committee for the Scientific Investigation of the Paranormal

CSIR Council for Scientific and Industrial Research

CSIRA Council for Small Industries in Rural Areas

CSIRO Commonwealth Scientific and Industrial Research Organization (Australia)

CSJ *Christian Science Journal*

csk cask; countersink

CSL [Australia] Commonwealth Serum Laboratories; Communication Sub-Lieutenant; computer simulation language; [computing] control and simulation language; Cub Scout leader

CSLATP Canadian Society of Landscape Architects and Town Planners

CSLO Canadian Scientific Liaison Office; Combined Services Liaison Officer

CSLT Canadian Society of Laboratory Technologists

CSM [medicine] cerebrospinal meningitis; *Christian Science Monitor*; Christian Socialist Movement; [astronautics] command service module; Commission for Synoptic Meteorology; Committee on Safety of Medicines; Company Sergeant-Major; [USA] corn, soya, milk (food supplement)

CSMA [computing] carrier sense multiple access; Chemical Specialities Manufacturers' Association; Civil Service Motoring Association

CSMA/CD [computing] carrier sense multiple access, collision detection (network protocol)

CSMMG Chartered Society of Massage and Medical Gymnastics

CSMTS Card Setting Machine Tenters' Society

CSN Confederate States Navy

CSNI [USA] Committee on the Safety of Nuclear Installations

CSO Caltech Submillimeter Observatory; Central Selling Organization; Central Statistical Office; chief scientific officer; Chief Signal Officer; Chief Staff Officer; Colonial Secretary's Office; [image technology] colour separation overlay; Command Signals Officer; Commonwealth Scientific Office; community service order

CSP Chartered Society of Physiotherapy; Civil Service of Pakistan; [computing] communicating sequential processes; Congregation of Saint Paul; Council for Scientific Policy

CSPAA *Conférence de solidarité des pays afro-asiatiques* (French: Afro-Asian People's Solidarity Conference)

CSPCA Canadian Society for the Prevention of Cruelty to Animals

CSPR [chemistry] chlorosulphonated polyethylene rubber

CSR [Australia] Colonial Sugar Refining Company; combat-stress reaction; Czechoslovak Socialist Republic

CSS [computing] centralized structure store; Certificate in Social Service; computer systems simulator; (member of the) Congregation of the Holy Ghost (from Latin *Sanctus Spiritus*); Council for Science and Society

CSSA Civil Service Supply Association

CSSB Civil Service Selection Board

CSSDA [USA] Council for Social Science Data Archives

CSSR [Roman Catholic Church] *Congregatio Sanctissimi Redemptoris* (Latin: Congregation of the Most Holy Redeemer, the Redemptorists)

CSSS Canadian Soil Science Society

CST [USA] Central Standard Time; College of Science and Technology; College of Speech Therapists; convulsive shock therapy

CSTA Canadian Society of Technical Agriculturists; [New Zealand] Canterbury Science Teachers' Association

CSTI Council of Science and Technology Institutes

CStJ Commander of the Most Venerable Order of the Hospital of St John of Jerusalem

CSU [medicine] catheter specimen of urine; Central Services Unit; Central Statistical Unit; *Christlich-Soziale Union* (German: Christian Social Union) (German political party); Civil Service Union; Colorado State University; [engineering] constant speed unit

CSV [computing] comma-separated variables; community service volunteer

CSW [USA] Certified Social Worker; continuous seismic wave

CSYS [Scotland] Certificate of Sixth Year Studies

CT cable transfer; Candidate in Theology; [UK postcode] Canterbury; Cape Town; [fishing port] Castletown; [medicine] cell therapy; [USA] Central Time; [medicine] cerebral thrombosis; [medicine] cerebral tumour; certifi(cat)ed teacher; Civic Trust; code telegrams; College of Technology; commercial traveller; *commissario tecnico* (Italian: sports coach); [medicine] compute(rize)d tomography (as in **CT scan**); [US postcode] Connecticut; [medicine] coronary thrombosis; corporation tax; counter trade; [electrical engineering] current transformer; cycle time; [vehicle registration] Lincoln

C/T Californian Terms (in grain trade)

Ct Count; Court

ct carat; caught; [currency] cent (hundredth of dollar etc.); [currency] centime (hundredth of franc etc.); circuit; *courant* (French: current, this month, inst.) (in formal correspondence); court; credit; current

Ct. Canton; Connecticut; [music] countertenor

ct. *centum* (Latin: hundred); certificate; crate

CTA Cable Television Association; Camping Trade Association; Canadian Tuberculosis Association; Caribbean Technical Assistance; Caribbean Tourist Association; Catering Teachers' Association; [chemistry] cellulose triacetate; Channel Tunnel Association; Chaplain Territorial Army; Chicago Transit Authority; Commercial Travellers' Association; [USA] commodities trading advisor; [medicine] compute(rize)d tomographic angiography; [medicine] compute(rize)d tomographic arteriography

c.t.a. [law] *cum testamento annexo* (Latin: with the will annexed)

CTAU Catholic Total Abstinence Union

CTB Commonwealth Telecommunications Board; comprehensive test ban

CTBT comprehensive test ban treaty

CTC Canadian Transport Commission; [chemistry] carbon tetrachloride; centralized traffic control; Central Training Council; [USA] Citizens' Training Corps; city technology college; Civil Technical Corps; Commando Training Centre; *Confederación de Trabajadores Cubanos* (Spanish: Confederation of Cuban Workers); *Congrès du travail du Canada* (French: Canadian Labour Congress); corn trade clauses; crushing, tearing and curling (machine); Cyclists' Touring Club

CTD central training depot; [electronics] charge-transfer device; classified telephone directory

ctd coated; continued; crated

CTE [physics] coefficient of thermal expansion

Cte *Comte* (French: Count)

CTEB Council of Technical Examining Bodies

Ctesse *Comtesse* (French: Countess)

CTETOC Council for Technical Education and Training for Overseas Countries

CText Chartered Textile Technologist

CTF Catholic Teachers' Federation; Chaplain to the Territorial Forces; coal-tar fuels

ctf. certificate; certify

ctge cartage; cartridge; cottage

CTH Corporation of Trinity House

CTI computer telephony integration

CTIO Cerro Tololo Inter-American Observatory (Chile)

CTL constant tensile load; [insurance] constructive total loss; [medicine] cytotoxic T-lymphocyte

ctl central

CTM [medicine] compute(rize)d tomographic myelography

CTMB Canal Transport Marketing Board

CTN confectioner, tobacconist and newsagent

ctn carton; [mathematics] cotangent

CTNC Committee on Transnational Corporations (in UN)

CTO [philately] cancelled to order; Central Telegraph Office; Central Treaty Organization; chief technical officer

CTOL [aeronautics] conventional take-off and landing

CTP *Confederación de Trabajadores del Peru* (Spanish: Peruvian Confederation of Labour)

ctpt [music] counterpoint

ctptal [music] contrapuntal

ctptst [music] contrapuntist

CTR certified test record; controlled thermonuclear reaction; controlled thermonuclear research

ctr. centre; contribution; contributor

CTRA Coal Tar Research Association

Ctrl [computing] control (key)

CTRP *Confederación de Trabajadores de la República de Panama* (Spanish: Confederation of Workers of the Republic of Panama)

CTS [medicine] carpal tunnel syndrome; Catholic Truth Society; characteristic time scale; [computing] clear to send; [medicine] compute(rize)d tomographic scanner; Consolidated Tin Smelters

cts cents; certificates; crates

CTSA Crucible and Tool Steel Association

CTT capital transfer tax

CTTB Central Trade Test Board (of RAF)

Cttee committee

CTTH Cathedrals Through Touch and Hearing

CTTSC Certificate in the Teaching and Training of Subnormal Children

CTU Conservative Trade Unionists

CTUC Commonwealth Trade Union Council

CTUS Carnegie Trust for the Universities of Scotland

CTV cable television; Canadian Television Network Limited; *Confederación de Trabajadores de Venezuela* (Spanish: Confederation of Venezuelan Workers)

CTVM Centre for Tropical Veterinary Medicine

CTZ control traffic zone (around airport)

CU Cambridge University; Christian Union; Church Union; [photography] close-up; Congregational Union (of England and Wales); [computing] control unit; Cooperative Union; [USA] Cornell University; [civil aircraft marking] Cuba;

Customs Union; [vehicle registration] Newcastle upon Tyne

Cu [chemical element] copper (from Latin *cuprum*)

Cu [meteorology] cumulus

cu. cubic

.cu Cuba (in Internet address)

CUA Canadian Underwriters' Association; Catholic University of America; Colour Users' Association; [computing] common user access; Conference of University Administrators

CUAC Cambridge University Athletic Club; Cambridge University Automobile Club

CUAFC Cambridge University Association Football Club

CUAS Cambridge University Agricultural Society; Cambridge University Air Squadron

cub. cubic

CUBC Cambridge University Boat Club; Cambridge University Boxing Club

CUC Canberra University College; Coal Utilization Council

CUCC Cambridge University Cricket Club

CUDAT Community Urban Development Assistance Team

CUDS Cambridge University Dramatic Society

CUEP Central Unit on Environmental Pollution

CUEW Congregational Union of England and Wales

CUF *Catholicarum Universitatum Foederatio* (Latin: Federation of Catholic Universities); common university fund

CUG closed user group

CUGC Cambridge University Golf Club

CUHC Cambridge University Hockey Club

cuis. cuisine

CUKT Carnegie United Kingdom Trust

CUL Cambridge University Library

cul. culinary

CULS [finance] convertible unsecured loan stock

CULTC Cambridge University Lawn Tennis Club

CUM Cambridge University Mission

cum. [finance] cumulative

Cumb. Cumberland

cum div. [finance] cum dividend (i.e. with dividend)

cum pref. [finance] cumulative preference (shares)

CUMS Cambridge University Musical Society

CUNA Credit Union National Association

CUNY City University of New York

CUOG Cambridge University Opera Group

CUP Cambridge University Press; [currency] Cuban peso

cur. currency; current

CURAC [Australia] Coal Utilization Research Advisory Committee

cur. adv. vult [law] *curia advisari vult* (Latin: the court wishes to consider it) (used in reports when judgment follows hearing)

CURE Care, Understanding and Research (drug addiction organization)

curt current (month)

CURUFC Cambridge University Rugby Union Football Club

CURV [US navy] cable-controlled undersea recovery vehicle

CUS Catholic University School

CUSO Canadian University Services Overseas

CUSRPG Canada–United States Regional Planning Group (in NATO)

cust. custard; custodian; custody

custod. custodian

CUTF Commonwealth Unit Trust Fund

CUTS [computing] cassette users' tape specification; [computing] computer users' tape system

CV calorific value; [medicine] cardiovascular; [astronomy] cataclysmic variable; *cavallo vapore* (Italian: horsepower); *cavalos vapor* (Portuguese: horsepower); [medicine] cerebrovascular; *cheval-vapeur* (French: horsepower); [statistics] coefficient of variation; [mathematics] collective vector; common valve; [Bible] Common Version; [medicine] contrast ventriculography; [finance] convertible; [UK postcode] Coventry; [Canada] Cross of Valour; [chemistry] crystal violet; curriculum vitae; [vehicle registration] Truro

cv. [botany] cultivar

.cv Cape Verde (in Internet address)

c.v. *cheval-vapeur* (French: horsepower); chief value; [medicine] *cras vespere* (Latin: tomorrow evening); curriculum vitae; *cursus vitae* (Latin: course of life)

CVA [medicine] cerebrovascular accident (i.e. stroke); [USA] Columbia Valley Authority

CVC capacitance-voltage characteristics; current-voltage characteristics

CVCP Committee of Vice-Chancellors and Principals (of UK universities)

CVD [medicine] cerebrovascular disease; [electronics] chemical vapour deposition; common valve development

c.v.d. [commerce] cash versus documents

CVE Certificate of Vocational Education; Council for Visual Education

CVEsc [currency] Cape Verde escudo

CVI chemical vapour infiltration; [medicine] common variable immunodeficiency

CVJ [engineering] constant velocity joint (in motor vehicles)

CVK centre vertical keel

CVL Central Veterinary Laboratory

CVM Company of Veteran Motorists

CVn [astronomy] Canes Venatici

CVO Commander of the Royal Victorian Order

CVP [medicine] central venous pressure; [Belgium] *Christelijk Volkspartif* (Flemish: Christian Social Party)

CVS [medicine] cardiovascular system; [medicine] chorionic villus sampling; Council of Voluntary Service

CVSNA Council of Voluntary Service National Association

CVT [mathematics] canonical variational theory; [chemistry] chemical vapour transport; [engineering] continuously variable transmission (in motor vehicles)

cvt. [finance] convertible

Cvt Gdn Covent Garden

CVWS combat vehicle weapons system

CVWW Council of Voluntary Welfare Work

CW Canada West; [physics] carrier wave; cavity wall (in property advertisement); chemical warfare; chemical weapons; child welfare; clerk of works; cold-worked (metals); commercial weight; Commissions and Warrants (department of Admiralty); complete with; continuous wave (as in **CW radar**); [UK

postcode] Crewe; [physics] Curie–Weiss (law); [vehicle registration] Preston

c/w [cycling] chainwheel

cw. clockwise

c.w. continuous weld

CWA Catering Wages Act; chemical warfare agent; [USA] Civil Works Administration; [USA] Clean Water Act; [Australia] Country Women's Association; Crime Writers' Association

CWB Canadian Wheat Board; Central Wages Board

CWBW chemical warfare/biological (or bacteriological) warfare

CWC Catering Wages Commission; Commonwealth of World Citizens

CWD civilian war dead

CWDE Centre for World Development Education

C'wealth Commonwealth

CWF coal–water fuel

CWG Cooperative Women's Guild

CWGC Commonwealth War Graves Commission (formerly IWGC)

CWINC [India] Central Waterways, Irrigation and Navigation Commission

CWIS [computing] campus-wide information service

CWL Catholic Women's League

Cwlth Commonwealth

CWM Council for World Mission

CWME Commission on World Mission and Evangelism

CWNA Canadian Weekly Newspapers Association

CWO Chief Warrant Officer

c.w.o. cash with order

CWOIH Conference of World Organizations Interested in the Handicapped

CWP Christian Workers' Party (in Malta); [USA] Communist Workers' Party

CWR continuous welded rail

CW radar continuous-wave radar

CWS coal–water slurry; Cooperative Wholesale Society; Court Welfare Service

CWT central war time

cwt hundredweight

CWU Chemical Workers' Union; Communication Workers' Union

CX [vehicle registration] Huddersfield; [civil aircraft marking] Uruguay

cx [medicine] cervix; convex

CXR chest X-ray
CXT Common External Tariff
CY calendar year; [fishing port] Castlebay; [international vehicle registration] Cyprus; [vehicle registration] Swansea
cy capacity; currency; cycle(s)
.cy Cyprus (in Internet address)
cyath. [medicine] *cyathus* (Latin: glassful)
cyath. vin. [medicine] *cyathus vinarius* (Latin: wineglassful)
cyber. cybernetics
cyc. cycle(s); cycling; cyclopedia; cyclopedic
CYCA Clyde Yacht Clubs Association
cyclo. cyclopedia
CYEE Central Youth Employment Executive
Cyg [astronomy] Cygnus

CYL Communist Youth League
cyl. cylinder; cylindrical
Cym. Cymric
CYMS Catholic Young Men's Society
CYO [USA] Catholic Youth Organization
Cyp. Cyprian; Cypriot; Cyprus
CYS Catholic Youth Services
CYSA Community Youth Services Association
CYWU Community Youth Workers' Union
CZ [vehicle registration] Belfast; Canal Zone; [international vehicle registration] Czech Republic
Cz [geology] Cenozoic
.cz Czech Republic (in Internet address)
CZMA [USA] Coastal Zone Management Act

D

D [currency] dalasi (used in Gambia); *Damen* (German: ladies); [geology] darcy (permeability coefficient of rock); December; defence (as in **D notice**); Democrat; Democratic; [paper size] demy; Department; destroyer; Detective; *Deus* (Latin: God); [chemistry] deuterium; [music] Deutsch (catalogue of Schubert's works); *Deutschland* (German: Germany); [geology] Devonian; [card games] diamonds; digital; dimension; dimensional (as in **3-D**); [currency] dinar; dioptre; director; *diretto* (Italian: through train); distinguished; doctor; *dogana* (Italian: customs); Dom (title of monks); *Dominus* (Latin: Lord, God, Christ); Don (Spanish title for men); [currency] dông (used in Vietnam); *douane* (French: customs); Dowager; [fishing port] Dublin; Duchess; Duke; Dutch; [Roman numeral] five hundred; [civil aircraft marking] Germany; [international vehicle registration] Germany (from German *Deutschland*); [music] note of scale; [medicine] rhesus antigen (as in **anti-D**); semiskilled or unskilled (occupational group)
D absorbed dose (of radiation); diameter; [chemistry] diffusion coefficient;

[physics] dispersion; [aeronautics] drag; [physics] electric flux density; [physics] electric flux displacement
d day; deci- (indicates one-tenth, as in **dl** = decilitre); [physics] deuteron; [music] do(h) (in tonic sol-fa); [physics] down (quark flavour); [meteorology] drizzle; [Roman numeral] five hundred; (old) pence (from Latin *denarii*); (old) penny (from Latin *denarius*)
d [chemistry] dextrorotatory; diameter; relative density
d. dam (in animal pedigree); damn; date; daughter; day; deacon; dead; deceased; [dentistry] deciduous; decision; decree; degree; delete; deliver; delivery; delta; density; depart(s); departure; depth; deputy; desert; deserted; deserter; *destro* (Italian: right); diameter; died; dime (= ten cents); [currency] dinar; discharge; distance; dividend; [currency] dollar; [medicine] dose; [currency] drachma; drama; *droite* (French: right); dump
D2 [civil aircraft marking] Angola
D2T2 [computing] dye diffusion thermal transfer
D4 [civil aircraft marking] Cape Verde
D6 [civil aircraft marking] Comoros Islands
3D [civil aircraft marking] Swaziland

3-D three-dimensional

DA [currency] Algerian dinar; [vehicle registration] Birmingham; [UK postcode] Dartford; Daughters of America; deed of arrangement; Defence Act; delayed action (bomb); [USA] Department of Agriculture; Depressives Anonymous; deputy advocate; deputy assistant; design automation; destructive analysis; developmental age; Diploma in Anaesthetics (or Anaesthesia); Diploma in Art; direct action; [chemistry] dissolved acetylene; [USA] District Attorney; Doctor of Arts; doesn't answer; [medicine] dopamine; [fishing port] Drogheda; duck's arse (hairstyle)

D/A [commerce] days after acceptance; [commerce] delivery on acceptance; deposit account; digital-to-analogue (converter); [commerce] documents against acceptance

D-A digital–analogue (converter)

Da dalton (unit of atomic mass)

Da. Danish

da deca- (indicates 10, as in **dal** = decalitre)

d/a [commerce] days after acceptance; deposit account; discharge afloat; [commerce] documents against acceptance

DAA *défense anti-aérienne* (French: anti-aircraft defence); [chemistry] diacetone acrylamide; [chemistry] diacetone alcohol; Diploma of the Advertising Association

DAA&QMG Deputy Assistant Adjutant and Quartermaster-General

DAAG Deputy Assistant Adjutant-General

DA&QMG Deputy Adjutant and Quartermaster-General

DAAS data acquisition and analysis system

DAB daily audience barometer; *Deutsches Apothekerbuch* (German: German Pharmacopoeia); *Dictionary of American Biography*; digital audio broadcasting

DABN [medicine] diffuse acute bacterial nephritis

DAC data analysis and control; Development Assistance Committee (of OECD); [computing] digital–analogue converter

DAc Doctor of Acupuncture

d.a.c. [insurance] deductible average clause; direct air cycle

DACC Dangerous Air Cargoes Committee

DACG Deputy Assistant Chaplain-General

dachs. dachshund

DACOR data correction

dact. dactyl

DAD deputy assistant director

DADG Deputy Assistant Director-General

DAdmin Doctor of Administration

DAE [USA] Department of Atomic Energy; *Dictionary of American English*; differential algebraic equation; Diploma in Advanced Engineering; Director of Army Education

DAEP Division of Atomic Energy Production

DAER Department of Aeronautical and Engineering Research

DAF [USA] Department of the Air Force; dissolved air flotation; *Doorne Automobielfabriek* (Dutch vehicle manufacturer); dry ash-free (coal)

d.a.f. described as follows

DAFS Department of Agriculture and Fisheries for Scotland

DAG Deputy Adjutant-General; *Deutsche Angestellten-Gewerkschaft* (German: German Salaried Employees' Union); development assistance group; [Ireland] Divorce Action Group

dag decagram

DAGMAR [commerce] defining advertising goals for measured advertising results

DAgr Doctor of Agriculture

DAgrSc Doctor of Agricultural Science

DAH [medicine] disordered action of the heart

DAI disease activity index; distributed artificial intelligence

d.a.i. death from accidental injuries

DAJAG Deputy Assistant Judge Advocate-General

Dak. Dakota

DAL direct acid leaching

dal decalitre

DALR [meteorology] dry adiabatic lapse rate

dal S [music] *dal segno* (Italian: (repeat) from the sign)

DAM Diploma in Ayurvedic Medicine

dam decametre

dam. damage

DAMS [USA] defense against missiles

system(s); deputy assistant military secretary

DAN (People's) Direct Action Network

Dan. [Bible] Daniel; Danish

D&AD Designers and Art Directors Association

D&B discipline and bondage; Dun and Bradstreet (financial reports)

D&C dean and chapter; [medicine] dil(at)ation and curettage (of cervix and uterus)

D&D death and dying; drunk and disorderly

D&G Dolce e Gabbana

D&HAA Dock and Harbour Authorities' Association

d&p developing and printing

d&s demand and supply

D&V [medicine] diarrhoea and vomiting

DAO district advisory officer

DAOT Director of Air Organization and Training

DAP Director of Administrative Planning; [computing] distributed array processor; [electronics] donor–acceptor pair; Draw a Person (psychological test)

d.a.p. do anything possible; documents against payment

DAP&E Diploma in Applied Parasitology and Entomology

DAPM Deputy Assistant Provost-Marshal

DAppSc Doctor of Applied Science

DAPS Director of Army Postal Services

DAQMG Deputy Assistant Quartermaster-General

DAR Daughters of the American Revolution; [USA] Defense Aid Reports; direct absorption receiver (of solar radiation); [Canada] Directorate of Atomic Research

DArch Doctor of Architecture

DARD Directorate of Aircraft Research and Development

DARE demand and resource evaluation

DARPA [USA] Defense Advanced Research Projects Agency (formerly ARPA)

DArt Doctor of Art

DAS [computing] data-acquisition system; development advisory service; Director of Armament Supply; double algebraic sum; Dramatic Authors' Society

d.a.s. [commerce] delivered alongside ship

DASA [USA] Defense Atomic Support Agency; Domestic Appliance Service Association

DASC [USA] Direct Air Support Centre

DASc Doctor of Agricultural Science

DASD [computing] direct-access storage device; Director of Army Staff Duties

DASH drone antisubmarine helicopter

dash [short form] dashboard

DASM delayed-action space missile

Dass Depressives Associated

DAT [medicine] dementia of the Alzheimer type; digital audio tape

dat. [grammar] dative

DATA Draughtsmen's and Allied Technician's Association

Datacom data communications

Datanet data network

Datastor data storage

Datran data transmission

Datrec data recording

DATV digitally assisted television

dau. daughter

DAV Disabled American Veterans

DAvMed Diploma in Aviation Medicine

DAW Drama Association of Wales; [nuclear technology] dry active waste

DAWS Director of Army Welfare Services

DAX [stock exchange] *Deutsche Aktienindex* (German: German share price index)

DAyM Doctor of Ayurvedic Medicine

DB Bachelor of Divinity (from Latin *Divinitatis Baccalaureus*); dark blue; database; [book-keeping] daybook; deals and battens (timber); delayed broadcast (in radio and television); *Deutsche Bundesbahn* (German: German Federal Railway); *Deutsche Bundesbank* (German: German Federal Bank); dock brief; Domesday Book; double-barrelled; [vehicle registration] Manchester

D/B [book-keeping] daybook

Db [currency] dobra (used in São Tomé and Príncipe)

dB decibel

d.b. [book-keeping] daybook; [music] double bass; double bed; double-breasted; drawbar (on tractors etc.)

DBA [computing] database administration; [computing] database administrator; [medicine] dihydrodimethylbenzopyranbutyric acid (used to treat sickle-cell anaemia); Doctor of Business Administration; doing business as (or at)

d.b.a. doing business as (or at)

DBB deals, battens and boards (timber); *Deutscher Beamtenbund* (German: German Civil Servants' Association) (trade union); dinner, bed and breakfast (in accommodation advertisement)

DBC Deaf Broadcasting Council

DBE Dame Commander of the Order of the British Empire; design-basis event

DBEATS dispatch payable both ends on all time saved

DBELTS dispatch payable both ends on lay time saved

DBH [forestry] diameter at breast height

DBib Douay Bible

DBIU [Canada] Dominion Board of Insurance Underwriters

dbk disembark; drawback

dbkn debarkation

dbl. double

dble double

DBM Diploma in Business Management

DBMC Danish Bacon and Meat Council

DBMS [computing] database management system

DBMT [medicine] displacement bone-marrow transplantation

Dbn Durban (South Africa)

DBO Diploma of the British Orthoptic Board

dbre *diciembre* (Spanish: December)

DBS direct broadcasting by satellite; direct-broadcast satellite

DBST Double British Summer Time

dbt debit

DBW desirable body weight

DC [music] *da capo* (Italian: from the head) (instruction to repeat from beginning); Daughters of Charity of St Vincent de Paul; death certificate; decimal currency; *Democrazia Cristiana* (Italian: Christian Democratic Party); [USA] Dental Corps; depth charge; deputy chief; deputy commissioner; deputy consul; deputy counsel; Detective Constable; [computing] device coordinates; diagnostic centre; diplomatic corps; [physics] direct current; Disarmament Conference; Disciples of Christ; district commissioner; district

council; district court; District of Columbia; [US postcode] District of Columbia; Doctor of Chiropractic; [commerce] documents against cash; Douglas Commercial (aircraft) (as in **DC10**); [theatre] down centre (of stage); [vehicle registration] Middlesbrough

D/C [insurance] deviation clause

dC *depois de Cristo* (Portuguese: after Christ, AD); *dopo Cristo* (Italian: after Christ, AD)

d.c. dead centre; [physics] direct current; [printing] double column; [music] double crotchet; [navigation] drift correction

DCA [USA] Defense Communications Agency; [Australia] Department of Civil Aviation; [computing] document content architecture

DCAe Diploma of the College of Aeronautics

DCAO deputy county advisor officer

DCAS Deputy Chief of Air Staff; Divorce Conciliation and Advisory Service

DCB Dame Commander of the Order of the Bath; double cantilever beam

DCBE [medicine] double-contrast barium enema

DCC Deputy Chief Constable; digital compact cassette; Diocesan Consistory Court; Diploma of Chelsea College

DCCC Domestic Coal Consumers Council

DCD [USA] Department of Community Development; Diploma in Chest Diseases; [electronics] drain-current drift

dcdr decoder

DCE [computing] data communications equipment; design and construction error; Diploma in Chemical Engineering; Doctor of Civil Engineering; domestic credit expansion

DCEP Diploma in Child and Educational Psychology

DCF [accounting] discounted cash flow

DCG Deputy Chaplain-General; direct coal gasification

dcg dancing

DCGS Deputy Chief of the General Staff

DCh Diploma in Child Health; Doctor of Surgery (from Latin *Doctor Chirurgiae*)

DChD Doctor of Dental Surgery

DChE Doctor of Chemical Engineering

DCI Detective Chief Inspector; direct com-

puter interviewing; [computing] display
control interface; [advertising] double
column inch; ductile cast iron

d.c.i. [advertising] double column inch

DCJ [USA] district court judge

DCL Distillers' Company Limited; Doctor
of Civil Law

dcl. [cricket] declaration; [cricket] declared

DCLI Duke of Cornwall's Light Infantry

DCLJ Dame Commander of the Order of
St Lazarus of Jerusalem

DClSc Doctor of Clinical Science

DCM Diploma in Community Medicine;
Distinguished Conduct Medal; district
court martial; Doctor of Comparative
Medicine

DCMG Dame Commander of the Order of
St Michael and St George

DCMS Department for Culture, Media
and Sport; Deputy Commissioner
Medical Services

DCnL Doctor of Canon Law

DCNS Deputy Chief of Naval Staff

DCO Duke of Cambridge's Own
(regiment)

DC of S Deputy Chief of Staff

d. col. [printing] double column

DComL Doctor of Commercial Law

DComm Doctor of Commerce

DCompL Doctor of Comparative Law

DCP Diploma in Clinical Pathology; Diploma in Clinical Psychology; Diploma in
Conservation of Paintings

DCPA [USA] Defense Civil Preparedness
Agency

DCPath Diploma of the College of Pathologists

DCR Diploma of the College of Radiographers

DCrim Doctor of Criminology

DCS Deputy Chief of Staff; Deputy Clerk
of Session(s); [physics] differential cross
section; digital camera system; Doctor of
Christian Science; Doctor of Commercial Sciences; [medicine] dorsal column
stimulator

DCSO deputy chief scientific officer

DCST Deputy Chief of Supplies and
Transport

DCT [computing] discrete cosine transform; Doctor of Christian Theology;
[medicine] dynamic compute(rize)d tomography

dct document

DCV [accounting] direct charge voucher

DCVO Dame Commander of the Royal
Victorian Order

DCW dead carcass weight; domestic cold
water

DD [insurance] damage done; dangerous
drug; [banking] demand draft; [USA]
Department of Defense; deputy director;
deputy directorate; Diploma in Dermatology; [banking] direct debit; *direttis-
simo* (Italian: fast train); discharged
dead; dishonourable discharge; Doctor
of Divinity (from Latin *Divinitatis
Doctor*); *dono dedit* (Latin: gave as a gift);
[paper size] double demy; [computing]
double density (disk); [medicine]
Duchenne dystrophy; [UK postcode]
Dundee; [vehicle registration] Gloucester

D/D [commerce] delivered at docks;
[banking] demand draft; dock dues

D/d days after date; [commerce] delivered

Dd. *Deo dedit* (Latin: gave to God)

dd dated; dedicated; delivered; drilled

d.d. days after date; *de dato* (Latin: today's
date); delayed delivery; [commerce]
delivered at docks; [banking] demand
draft; detergent dispersant; dry dock;
due date; due day

DDA Dangerous Drugs Act; Disabled
Drivers' Association

D-Day Day Day (i.e. specified day, esp.
date of Allied invasion of Europe)

DDBMS distributed database management system

DDC Dewey Decimal Classification (for library books); [medicine] dideoxycytidine
(used to treat Aids); [computing] direct
digital control; [computing] display data
channel

DDCMP [computing] digital data communication message protocol

DDD *dat, dicat, dedicat* (Latin: gives,
devotes and dedicates); deadline
delivery date; *dono dedit dedicavit* (Latin:
gave and dedicated as a gift)

DDDS Deputy Director of Dental Services

DDE [computing] direct data entry;
Dwight David Eisenhower (US president); dynamic data exchange

DDG Deputy Director-General

DDGAMS Deputy Director-General, Army
Medical Services

DDH Diploma in Dental Health

DDI [medicine] dideoxyinosine (used to treat Aids); Divisional Detective Inspector

d.d. in d. [medicine] *de die in diem* (Latin: from day to day)

DDL [computing] data definition language; [computing] data description language; Deputy Director of Labour; digital data link

DDM Diploma in Dermatological Medicine; Doctor of Dental Medicine

DDME Deputy Director of Mechanical Engineering

DDMI Deputy Director of Military Intelligence

DDMOI Deputy Director of Military Operations and Intelligence

DDMS Deputy Director of Medical Services

DDMT Deputy Director of Military Training

DDNI Deputy Director of Naval Intelligence

DDO Diploma in Dental Orthopaedics; district dental officer

DDOS Deputy Director of Ordnance Services

DDP [computing] distributed data processing

DDPH Diploma in Dental Public Health

DDPR Deputy Director of Personal Services; Deputy Director of Postal Services; Deputy Director of Public Relations

DDR *Deutsche Demokratische Republik* (German: German Democratic Republic, the former East Germany); Diploma in Diagnostic Radiology

DDRA Deputy Director, Royal Artillery

DDRB Doctors' and Dentists' Review Body

DDRD Deputy Directorate of Research and Development

DDS deep diving system; Deputy Directorate of Science; Dewey Decimal System (for classifying library books); [pharmacology] diaminodiphenyl sulphone (= dapsone, drug used to treat skin disease); digital data storage; Director of Dental Services; Doctor of Dental Science; Doctor of Dental Surgery

dd/s delivered sound

DDSc Doctor of Dental Science

DDSD Deputy Director of Staff Duties

DDSM [USA] Defense Distinguished Service Medal

DDSR Deputy Director of Scientific Research

DDST Deputy Director of Supplies and Transport

DDT dichlorodiphenyltrichloroethane (insecticide)

DDTL dreary desk-top lunch

DDVS Deputy Director of Veterinary Services

DDWE&M Deputy Director of Works, Electrical and Mechanical

DE *Dáil Éireann* (Gaelic: Assembly of Ireland) (lower chamber of Irish parliament); deflection error; [US postcode] Delaware; Department of Employment; [UK postcode] Derby; [military] destroyer escort; destruction efficiency; diesel engine; direct electrolysis; Doctor of Engineering; Doctor of Entomology; [paper size] double elephant; [fishing port] Dundee; [vehicle registration] Haverfordwest

.de Germany (in Internet address)

d.e. deckle edge; diesel-electric; [fencing] direct elimination; [book-keeping] double entry

DEA [computing] data encryption algorithm; Department of Economic Affairs (former government department); Department of External Affairs; [USA] Drug Enforcement Administration; [USA] Drug Enforcement Agency

Dea. Deacon; Dean

deb [short form] debutante

deb. debenture; debit; debut

debil. debilitating; debilitation

deb. stk debenture stock

DEC dental examination centre; [USA] Department of Environmental Conservation; Digital Equipment Corporation; Disasters Emergency Committee; Dollar Export Council

DEc Doctor of Economics

Dec. *Decani* (Latin: of the dean) (side of church choir); *Decanus* (Latin: dean); December; [architecture] Decorated

dec [astronomy] declination

dec. deceased; decimal; declaration; declare; declared; [grammar] declension; decorated; decoration; decorative;

decrease; [music] *decrescendo* (Italian: with decreasing loudness)

déc. *décembre* (French: December)

decaf [short form] decaffeinated (coffee)

decasyll. decasyllabic; decasyllable

decd deceased

decel. deceleration

decid. deciduous

decis. decision

decl. [grammar] declension

decn decontamination

decom. decommission

DEcon Doctor of Economics

DEconSc Doctor of Economic Science

DECR [meteorology] decrease

decr. decrease

decresc. [music] *decrescendo* (Italian: with decreasing loudness)

decrim. decriminalization

DED Department of Economic Development (Northern Ireland)

DEd Doctor of Education

ded. dedicate; dedicated; dedication; deduce; deduct; deduction

de d. in d. [medicine] *de die in diem* (Latin: from day to day)

deduct. deduction; deductive

DEE Diploma in Electrical Engineering

DEED [USA] Department of Energy and Economic Development

DEEP Directly Elected European Parliament

def. defecate; defecation; defect; defection; defective; defector; defence; defendant; deferred; deficit; define; definite; definition; definitive; deflagrate; deflect; deflection; defoliate; defrost; defunct; *defunctus* (Latin: deceased)

def. art. [grammar] definite article

DEFCON [military] defence readiness condition

defect. defective

defl. deflate; deflation; deflect; deflection

deft defendant

DEG [meteorology] degrees

deg. degree

degen. degeneration

degr. degradation; degree

dehyd. dehydration

DEI Dutch East Indies (former name of Indonesia)

Del [computing] delete (key); [astronomy] Delphinus

Del. Delaware; Delhi

del. delegate; delegation; delete; deletion; *delineavit* (Latin: (he/she) drew it); deliver; delivered; delivery

deld delivered

deleg. delegate; delegation

deli [short form] delicatessen

delib. deliberate; deliberation

deliq. deliquescent

DElo Doctor of Elocution

delv. deliver; delivered; delivery

dely delivery

Dem. Democrat; Democratic

dem. demand; demerara; democracy; democratic; demolish; demolition; [grammar] demonstrative; demurrage

DEME Directorate of Electrical and Mechanical Engineering

demo [short form] demonstration

demob [short form] demobilization; [short form] demobilize

demon. demonstrate; [grammar] demonstrative

demons. [grammar] demonstrative

demonstr. [grammar] demonstrative

DEMS defensively equipped merchant ships

DemU [Northern Ireland] Democratic Unionist

demur. demurrage

DEN District Enrolled Nurse

DEn Department of Energy; Doctor of English

Den. Denbighshire; Denmark; Denver

den. denier; denotation; denote; denoted; dental; dentist; dentistry

DenD *Docteur en droit* (French: Doctor of Law)

dend. dendrology

dendrochron. dendrochronology

dendrol. dendrological; dendrology

DEng Doctor of Engineering

DEngS Doctor of Engineering Science

DenM *Docteur en médecine* (French: Doctor of Medicine)

DenMed *Docteur en médecine* (French: Doctor of Medicine)

denom. denomination

DENR [USA] Department of Energy and Natural Resources

dens. density

DEnt Doctor of Entomology

dent. dental; dentist; dentistry; denture

DEOVR Duke of Edinburgh's Own Volunteer Rifles

DEP Department of Employment and Productivity; [USA] Department of Environmental Protection

dep. depart(s); department; departure; dependant; dependency; dependent; deponent; depose; deposed; deposit; deposition; depositor; depot; deputize; deputized; deputy

dép. *département* (French: department, administrative division); *député* (French: deputy, member of parliament)

Depca International Study Group for the Detection and Prevention of Cancer

dept department; deponent

dept. deputy

deptn deputation

DER [USA] Department of Environmental Resources

der. *derecha* (Spanish: right); derivation; derivative; derive; derived; *dernier* (French: last)

Derby. Derbyshire

Derbys Derbyshire

dereg. deregulation

deriv. derivation; derivative; derive; derived

DERL derived emergency reference level (of radiation)

derm. dermatitis; dermatology

dermat. dermatology

dermatol. dermatology

derog. derogatory

DERR Duke of Edinburgh's Royal Regiment

derv diesel-engined road vehicle (diesel oil used as transport fuel)

DES [computing] data encryption standard; Department of Education and Science (former government department); [pharmacology] diethylstilboestrol (synthetic hormone); Director of Educational Services

Des Deaconess

des. desert; design; designate; designated; designation; designer; desirable; desire; dessert

desc. descend; descendant; descent; describe; description

descr. description

desid. *desideratum* (Latin: something wanted)

desig. designate

DèsL *Docteur ès lettres* (French: Doctor of Letters)

desp. despatch; despatched

DesRCA Designer of the Royal College of Art

des res [short form] desirable residence

DèsS *Docteur ès sciences* (French: Doctor of Science)

DèsSc *Docteur ès sciences* (French: Doctor of Science)

DèsScPol *Docteur ès sciences politiques* (French: Doctor of Political Science)

dest. destination; destroyer

destn destination

DET [linguistics] determiner; [pharmacology] diethyltryptamine (hallucinogen); direct energy transfer

Det Detective

det. detach; detached (in property advertisement); detachment; detail; determine; [grammar] determiner; [medicine] *detur* (Latin: let it be given)

Det. Con. Detective Constable

Det. Insp. Detective Inspector

detn detention; determination

detox [short form] detoxification

DETR Department of the Environment, Transport and the Regions

Det. Sgt Detective Sergeant

Det. Supt Detective Superintendent

Deut. [Bible] Deuteronomy

Dev. Devon(shire)

dev. develop; developed; developer; development; deviate; [navigation] deviation

Devon. Devonshire

devp develop

devpt development

devs devotions

DEW directed-energy weapon; distant early warning

Dez. *Dezember* (German: December)

DF Dean of Faculty; [nuclear technology] decontamination factor; Defender of the Faith; [telecommunications] direction finder; [telecommunications] direction-finding; [currency] Djibouti franc; Doctor of Forestry; [paper size] double foolscap; [vehicle registration] Gloucester

d-f double-fronted (in property advertisement)

df. draft

d.f. [commerce] dead freight; drinking fountain

DFA [USA] Department of Foreign Affairs; Diploma in Foreign Affairs; Doctor of Fine Arts

DFC Distinguished Flying Cross

DFD [computing] dataflow diagram; data function diagram

DFDS *Det Forende Dampskibs-Selskab* (Danish shipping company)

DfEE Department for Education and Employment

DFHom Diploma of the Faculty of Homoeopathy

DFID Department for International Development

Dfl [currency] Dutch guilder (from alternative name florin)

DFLP Democratic Front for the Liberation of Palestine

DFLS Day Fighter Leaders' School

DFM Diploma in Forensic Medicine; Distinguished Flying Medal

dfndt defendant

DFR [nuclear technology] Dounreay fast reactor

d.f.r. decreasing failure rate

DFS disease-free survival; [computing] disk filing system

DFSc Doctor of Financial Science

DFT dual-flow turbine

dft defendant; draft

DFW Director of Fortifications and Works

DG *Dei gratia* (Latin: by the grace of God); *Deo gratias* (Latin: thanks be to God); dependence graph; *Deutsche Grammophon* (German record company); differential geometry; [navigation] directional gyro; Directorate-General; Director-General; double glazed (in property advertisement); double glazing (in property advertisement); Dragoon Guards; [UK postcode] Dumfries; [vehicle registration] Gloucester

dg decigram

DGA Director-General, Aircraft; Directors' Guild of America

DGAA Distressed Gentlefolk's Aid Association

DGAME Director-General, Army Medical Services

DGAS Double Glazing Advisory Service

DGB *Deutscher Gewerkschaftsbund* (German: German Trade Union Federation)

DGC Diploma in Guidance and Counselling

DGCA Director-General of Civil Aviation

DGCE Directorate-General of Communications Equipment

DGD Director, Gunnery Division

DGD&M Director-General, Dockyards and Maintenance

DGE Directorate-General of Equipment

DGEME Director-General, Electrical and Mechanical Engineering

DGI Director-General of Information; Director-General of Inspection

DGLP(A) Director-General, Logistic Policy (Army)

DGM Diploma in General Medicine; Director-General of Manpower

DGMS Director-General of Medical Services

DGMT Director-General of Military Training

DGMW Director-General of Military Works

Dgn Dragoon

DGO Diploma in Gynaecology and Obstetrics

DGP Director-General of Personnel; Director-General of Production

DGPS Director-General of Personal Services

DGR Dante Gabriel Rossetti (British poet and painter); Director of Graves Registration

DGS Diploma in General Studies; Diploma in General Surgery; Diploma in Graduate Studies; Directorate-General of Signals; Director-General, Ships

DGSRD Directorate-General of Scientific Research and Development

DGT Director-General of Training

DGW Director-General of Weapons; Director-General of Works

DH [fishing port] Dartmouth; [sports] dead heat; De Havilland (aircraft); Department of Health; [baseball] designated hitter; [currency] dirham (used in Morocco); district heating; Doctor of Humanities; [electronics] double heterostructure; [vehicle registration] Dudley; [UK postcode] Durham

Dh [currency] dirham (used in United Arab Emirates)

d.h. *das heisst* (German: that is, i.e.); [sports] dead heat

DHA Department of Humanitarian Affairs (of UN); district health authority

DHC Domestic Heating Council

Dhc *Doctor honoris causa* (Latin: Honorary Doctor)

DHDS Dolmetsch Historical Dance Society

DHHS [USA] Department of Health and Human Services

DHL Doctor of Hebrew Letters; Doctor of Hebrew Literature; Doctor of Humane Letters

DHMSA Diploma in the History of Medicine (Society of Apothecaries)

DHO damped harmonic oscillator; district headquarters; divisional headquarters

DHR [nuclear technology] decay heat removal

DHS Diploma in Horticultural Science; Doctor of Health Sciences

DHSA Diploma in Health Service Administration

DHSS Department of Health and Social Security (former government department)

DHumLit Doctor of Humane Letters

DHW domestic hot water

DHyg Doctor of Hygiene

DI Defence Intelligence; Department of the Interior; Detective Inspector; [medicine] diabetes insipidus; direct injection; Director of Infantry; district inspector; divisional inspector; [medicine] donor insemination; [paper size] double imperial; drill instructor

Di didymium

Di. [currency] dinar

di. diameter

d.i. daily inspection; *das ist* (German: that is, i.e.); de-ice; diplomatic immunity; document identifier

DIA [USA] Defense Intelligence Agency; Design and Industries Association; Diploma in International Affairs; Driving Instructors Association

dia. diagnose; diagram; dialect; diameter

diag. diagnose; diagnosis; diagonal; diagram

dial. dialect; dialectal; dialectic; dialectical; dialogue

diam. diameter

diamat dialectical materialism (in philosophy and economics)

DIANE Direct Information Access Network for Europe

diap. [music] diapason

diaph. diaphragm

DIAS Dublin Institute of Advanced Science

DIC Diamond Information Centre; Diploma of (Membership of the) Imperial College (of Science and Technology); [medicine] disseminated intravascular coagulation; [chemistry] dissolved inorganic carbon; drunk in charge

dic. *dicembre* (Italian: December)

DIChem Diploma in Industrial Chemistry

dicot. dicotyledon

dict. dictate; dictated; dictation; dictator; dictionary

DICTA Diploma of Imperial College of Tropical Agriculture

DIDS [electronics] donor-impurity density of states

DIE Designated Investment Exchange; Diploma in Industrial Engineering; Diploma of the Institute of Engineering

dieb. alt. [medicine] *diebus alternis* (Latin: on alternate days)

DIEL (Advisory Committee on Telecommunications for) Disabled and Elderly People

DIEME Directorate of Inspection of Electrical and Mechanical Equipment

diet. dietary; dietetics; dietician

DIF [computing] data interchange format; District Inspector of Fisheries

dif. differ; differential

diff. differ; difference; different; differential

diff. calc. differential calculus

diffr. diffraction

diffu. diffusion

DIG Deputy Inspector-General; disablement income group

dig. digest (compilation); digestion; digestive; digit; digital

DIH Diploma in Industrial Health

DIIR digital image-intensifier radiography

Dij. Dijon

DIL [electronics] dual in-line

dil. dilute; diluted; dilution

diln dilution

DIM Diploma in Industrial Management

dim. *dimanche* (French: Sunday); dimension; *dimidium* (Latin: half); diminish; [music] *diminuendo* (Italian: with diminishing loudness); diminutive

dimin. [music] *diminuendo* (Italian: with diminishing loudness); diminutive

Dimm [computing, electronics] dual in-line memory module

DIMS [computing] data and information management system

DIN *Deutsches Industrie Normen* (German: German Industry Standard); *Deutsches Institut für Normung* (German: German Standards Institute); [computing] digital imaging network

Din [currency] dinar

din. dining car; dining room (in property advertisement); dinner

DIng Doctor of Engineering (from Latin *Doctor Ingeniariae*)

dinky [informal] double (or dual) income, no kids (yet)

DInstPA Diploma of the Institute of Park Administration

DIO district intelligence officer

dio. diocese

dioc. diocesan; diocese

dioc. syn. diocesan synod

DIP [computing] document image processing; [electronics] dual in-line package; [electronics] dual in-line pin

Dip. Diploma

dip. diploma

DipAD Diploma in Art and Design

DipAe Diploma in Aeronautics

DipAgr Diploma in Agriculture

DipALing Diploma in Applied Linguistics

DipAM Diploma in Applied Mechanics

DipAppSc Diploma in Applied Science

DipArch Diploma in Architecture

DipArts Diploma in Arts

DipASE Diploma in Advanced Study of Education, College of Preceptors

DipAvMed Diploma in Aviation Medicine

DipBA Diploma in Business Administration

DipBac Diploma in Bacteriology

DipBMS Diploma in Basic Medical Sciences

DipBS Diploma in Fine Art, Byam Shaw School

DipCAM Diploma in Communication, Advertising and Marketing (of CAM Foundation)

DipCC Diploma of the Central College

DipCD Diploma in Child Development; Diploma in Civic Design

DipCE Diploma in Civil Engineering

DipChemEng Diploma in Chemical Engineering

DipCom Diploma in Commerce

DipDHus Diploma in Dairy Husbandry

DipDP Diploma in Drawing and Painting

DipDS Diploma in Dental Surgery

DipEcon Diploma in Economics

DipEd Diploma in Education

DipEl Diploma in Electronics

DipEng Diploma in Engineering

DipESL Diploma in English as a Second Language

DipEth Diploma in Ethnology

DipFA Diploma in Fine Arts

DipFD Diploma in Funeral Directing

DipFE Diploma in Further Education

DipFor Diploma in Forestry

DipGSM Diploma in Music, Guildhall School of Music (and Drama)

DipGT Diploma in Glass Technology

DipHA Diploma in Hospital Administration

DipHE Diploma in Higher Education; Diploma in Highway Engineering

DipHSc Diploma in Home Science

diphth. diphthong

DipHum Diploma in Humanities

DipJ Diploma in Journalism

DipL Diploma in Languages

dipl. diploma; diplomacy; diplomat; diplomatic

DipLA Diploma in Landscape Architecture

DipLib Diploma in Librarianship

DipLSc Diploma in Library Science

DipM Diploma in Marketing

DipMechE Diploma in Mechanical Engineering

DipMet Diploma in Metallurgy

DipMFOS Diploma in Maxillofacial and Oral Surgery

DipMusEd Diploma in Musical Education

DipN Diploma in Nursing

DipNEd Diploma in Nursery School Education

DipO&G Diploma in Obstetrics and Gynaecology

DipOL Diploma in Oriental Learning

DipOrth Diploma in Orthodontics

DipPA Diploma in Public Administration

DipP&OT Diploma in Physiotherapy and Occupational Therapy

DipPharmMed Diploma in Pharmaceutical Medicine

DipPhysEd Diploma in Physical Education

DipQS Diploma in Quantity Surveying

DipRADA Diploma of the Royal Academy of Dramatic Art

DipREM Diploma in Rural Estate Management

DIPS digital image-processing system

DipS&PA Diploma in Social and Public Administration

DipSMS Diploma in School Management Studies

DipSoc Diploma in Sociology

DipSpEd Diploma in Special Education

DipSS Diploma in Social Studies

DipSW Diploma in Social Work

DipT Diploma in Teaching

DipTA Diploma in Tropical Agriculture

DipT&CP Diploma in Town and Country Planning

DipTech Diploma in Technology

DipTEFL Diploma in the Teaching of English as a Foreign Language

DipTh Diploma in Theology

DipTP Diploma in Town Planning

DipTPT Diploma in Theory and Practice of Teaching

DIR [photography] developer inhibitor release

dir. direct; directed; direction; director; [currency] dirham

Dir-Gen Director-General

DIS [USA] Defense Intelligence School; Development Information System

dis. disabled; discharge; disciple; discipline; disconnect; discontinue; discontinued; discount; dispense; distance; distant; distribute

disab. disability

disabil. disability

disag. disagreeable

disb. disbursement

disc. disciple; discipline; discount; discover; discovered; discoverer; discovery

disch. discharge

disco [short form] discotheque

discont. discontinued

discr. discretion

disemb. disembark; disembarkation

DISH [medicine] diffuse idiopathic skeletal hyperostosis

dishon. dishonest; dishonourable; dishonourably

disloc. dislocation

dismac [military] digital scene-matching area correlation sensors

disp. dispensary; dispensation; dispense; disperse; dispersion; disputed

displ. displacement

diss. dissenter; dissertation; dissolve

dist. distance; distant; distilled; distinguish; distinguished; distribute; distributor; district

Dist. Atty [USA] District Attorney

distr. distribution; distributor

distrib. distributive

DistTP Distinction in Town Planning

DIT [medicine] desferrioxamine infusion test; Detroit Institute of Technology; double income tax (as in **DIT relief**)

DITB Distributive Industry Training Board

Div. Divine; Divinity

div [mathematics] divergence

div. diversion; divide; divided; dividend; divine; [music] *divisi* (Italian: divided) (referring to musical parts); division; divisor; divorce; divorced

div. in par. aeq. [medicine] *dividatur in partes aequales* (Latin: let it be divided into equal parts) (in prescriptions)

divn division

divnl divisional

DIY do-it-yourself

DJ dinner jacket; Diploma in Journalism; disc jockey; [USA] district judge; divorce judge; Doctor of Law (from Latin *Doctor Juris*); [finance] Dow Jones; dust jacket (of book); [vehicle registration] Liverpool

d.J *der Jüngere* (German: the Younger, Junior); *dieses Jahres* (German: of this year)

.dj Djibouti (in Internet address)

DJAG Deputy Judge Advocate-General

DJF Disc Jockeys Federation

DJI [finance] Dow Jones Index

DJIA [finance] Dow Jones Industrial Average

DJS Doctor of Juridical Science

DJT Doctor of Jewish Theology

DJTA [finance] Dow Jones Transportation Average

DJUA [finance] Dow Jones Utilities Average

DJur Doctor of Law (from Latin *Doctor Juris*)

DK [international vehicle registration] Denmark and Greenland; Dorling Kindersley (publishing company); [fishing port] Dundalk; [vehicle registration] Manchester

dk dark; deck; dock; duck

.dk Denmark (in Internet address)

DKB [computing] distributed knowledge base

dkhse deckhouse

DKNY [trademark] Donna Karan New York

Dkr [currency] Danish krone

DKS Deputy Keeper of the Signet

dkt docket

dkyd dockyard

DL [UK postcode] Darlington; [fishing port] Deal; Deputy Lieutenant; [physics] detection limit; diesel; [psychology] difference limen; [electronics] distribution line; Doctor of Laws (from Latin *Doctor Legum*); dog licence; [physics] dose level; [book-keeping] double ledger; [theatre] down left (of stage); [computing] download (on Internet); driving licence; [vehicle registration] Portsmouth

D/L data link; demand loan

dl decilitre

DLA diffusion limited aggregation

DLC Diploma of Loughborough College; divisional land commissioner; Doctor of Celtic Literature; [theatre] down left centre (of stage)

d.l.c. direct lift control

DLCO-EA Desert Locust Control Organization for Eastern Africa

dld delivered

d.l.d. deadline date

DLE [medicine] discoid lupus erythematosus

DLES Doctor of Letters in Economic Studies

DLett *Docteur ès lettres* (French: Doctor of Letters)

DLF Disabled Living Foundation

DLG David Lloyd George (British statesman)

DLI Durham Light Infantry

D-Lib [USA] Liberal Democrat

DLit Doctor of Literature

DLitt Doctor of Letters (from Latin *Doctor Litterarum*)

DLittS Doctor of Sacred Letters

DLJ Dame of Justice of the Order of St Lazarus of Jerusalem

DLL [computing] dynamic link library

DLM [genetics] dominant lethal mutation

DLO dead letter office (former name of RLO); Diploma in Laryngology and Otology; Diploma in Laryngology and Otorhinolaryngology; dispatch loading only

DLOY Duke of Lancaster's Own Yeomanry

DLP Democratic Labour Party

DLR Docklands Light Railway

dlr dealer

DLS debt liquidation schedule; Doctor of Library Science; Dominion Land Surveyor

DLSc Doctor of Library Science

DLT Dave Lee Travis (British disc jockey)

dlvd delivered

dlvr deliver

dlvy delivery

DLW Diploma in Labour Welfare

dly daily

DM [vehicle registration] Chester; *Daily Mail*; [astronomy] dark matter; deputy master; design manual; [currency] Deutschmark; [medicine] diabetes mellitus; [medicine] diastolic murmur; [physics] dipole moment; direct mail; Director of Music; dispersion measures; [computing] distributed memory; district manager; *Docteur en médecine* (French: Doctor of Medicine); Doctor of Mathematics; Doctor of Medicine; Doctor of Music

d.M *dieses Monats* (German: this month, inst.)

dm decimetre

.dm Dominica (in Internet address)

DMA Defence Manufacturers' Association; Diploma in Municipal Administration; [computing] direct memory access

DMAC [computing] direct memory access

control; [television] duobinary multiplexed analogue component

DM&CW Diploma in Maternity and Child Welfare

DMath Doctor of Mathematics

DMC direct manufacturing costs; district medical committee

DMD [computing] digital micromirror device; Doctor of Dental Medicine; Doctor of Mathematics and Didactics; Doctor of Medical Dentistry; [medicine] Duchenne muscular dystrophy

dmd demand

DME Diploma in Mechanical Engineering; [computing] direct machine environment; [aeronautics] distance-measuring equipment; [computing] distributed management environment; [electronics] dropping mercury electrode

DMed Doctor of Medicine

DMet Doctor of Metallurgy; Doctor of Meteorology

DMF decayed, missing and filled (teeth); Disabled Motorists Federation; [electronics] dose-modifying factor

DMFOS Diploma in Maxillofacial and Oral Surgery

dmg. damage

DMGO Divisional Machine-Gun Officer

DMGT [genetics] DNA-mediated gene transfer

DMHS Director of Medical and Health Services

DMI [computing] desktop management interface; Director of Military Intelligence

DMin Doctor of Ministry

DMJ Diploma in Medical Jurisprudence

DMJ(Path) Diploma in Medical Jurisprudence (Pathology)

DML [computing] data-manipulation language; Defence Medal for Leningrad (former Soviet decoration); Doctor of Modern Languages

dml. demolish

DMLJ Dame of Merit of the Order of St Lazarus of Jerusalem

DMLS Doppler microwave landing system

DMLT Diploma in Medical Laboratory Technology

DMM Defence Medal for Moscow (former Soviet decoration); [medicine] diffuse malignant mesothelioma

dmn dimension

dmnl dimensional

DMO Defence Medal for Odessa (former Soviet decoration); [astronomy] diffuse massive object; Director of Military Operations; district medical officer

DMO&I Director, Military Operations and Intelligence

DMP Diploma in Medical Psychology; Director of Manpower Planning

DMPB Diploma in Medical Pathology and Bacteriology

DMR Diploma in Medical Radiology; Director of Materials Research

DMRD Diploma in Medical Radiological Diagnosis; Directorate of Materials Research and Development

DMRE Diploma in Medical Radiology and Electrology

DMRT Diploma in Medical Radiotherapy

DMS [computing] database management system; [computing] data management system; [mining] dense-medium separation; Diploma in Management Studies; Directorate of Military Survey; Director of Medical Services; *Dis manibus sacrum* (Latin: consecrated to the souls of the departed); Doctor of Medical Science; Doctor of Medicine and Surgery

DMs Doc(tor) Martens (trademark for brand of lace-up boots)

DMSA [medicine] dimercaptosuccinic acid (used in diagnosis)

DMSO [medicine] dimethylsulphoxide (used in ointments)

DMSSB Direct Mail Services Standard Board

dmst. demonstration; demonstrator

dmstn demonstration

dmstr demonstrator

DMSV Defence Medal for Sevastopol (former Soviet decoration)

DMT [pharmacology] dimethyltryptamine (hallucinogen); Director of Military Training

DMTF [computing] desktop management task force

DMU [commerce] decision-making unit; directly managed unit (of hospital in NHS)

DMus Doctor of Music

DMV [USA] Department of Motor Vehicles; *Docteur en médecine vétérinaire*

(French: Doctor of Veterinary Medicine)

DMZ demilitarized zone

DN [commerce] debit note; *de novo* (Latin: from the beginning); Diploma in Nursing; *Dominus noster* (Latin: our Lord); [UK postcode] Doncaster; [vehicle registration] Leeds

D/N [commerce] debit note

Dn Deacon; *Don* (Spanish: Mr); Dragoon

dn down; dozen

DNA [USA] Defense Nuclear Agency; [genetics] deoxyribonucleic acid; *Det Norske Arbeiderpartiet* (Norwegian: Norwegian Labour Party); *Deutscher Normenausschuss* (German: German Standards Committee); [medicine] did not attend; Director of Naval Accounts; District Nursing Association

Dna *Doña* (Spanish: Mrs)

DNAase [biochemistry] deoxyribonuclease

DNAD Director of Naval Air Division

DNase [biochemistry] deoxyribonuclease

DNB *Dictionary of National Biography*

DNC [nuclear technology] delayed-neutron counting; Director of Naval Construction; [computing] distributed numerical control

DND Director of Navigation and Direction

DNE Diploma in Nursing Education; Director of Naval Equipment; Director of Nurse Education; Dounreay Nuclear Establishment

dne *douane* (French: customs)

DNES Director of Naval Education Service

DNF [sports] did not finish (in race)

DNH Department of National Heritage

DNHW [USA] Department of National Health and Welfare

DNI Director of Naval Intelligence

DNJC *Dominus noster Jesus Christus* (Latin: Our Lord Jesus Christ)

DNMS Director of Naval Medical Services

DNO Director of Naval Ordnance; district naval officer; district nursing officer; divisional nursing officer

DNP declared national programme; dynamic nuclear polarization

DNPDE Dounreay Nuclear Power Development Establishment

DNPP *Dominus Noster Papa Pontifex* (Latin: Our Lord the Pope)

DNR [USA] Department of Natural Resources; Director of Naval Recruitment; [medicine] do not resuscitate

Dnr [currency] dinar

DNS Department for National Savings; [computing] domain name system

dns downs (on map)

DNSA Diploma in Nursing Service Administration

DNT Director of Naval Training

DNWA Director of Naval Weather Service

DO defence order; [finance] deferred ordinary (shares); [commerce] delivery order; Diploma in Ophthalmology; Diploma in Osteopathy; [grammar] direct object; [commerce] direct order; dissolved oxygen; district office; district officer; divisional office; divisional officer; Doctor of Optometry; Doctor of Oratory; Doctor of Osteopathy; [fishing port] Douglas; drawing office; [vehicle registration] Lincoln

D/O [commerce] direct order

d/o [commerce] delivery order

Do. *Donnerstag* (German: Thursday)

do. ditto

.do Dominican Republic (in Internet address)

DOA date of availability; [medicine] dead on arrival; [USA] Department of the Army; dissolved-oxygen analyser

DOAE Defence Operational Analysis Establishment (of MOD)

DOB date of birth

d.o.b. date of birth

DObstRCOG Diploma in Obstetrics of the Royal College of Obstetricians and Gynaecologists

DOC *denominazione di origine controllata* (Italian: name of origin controlled) (wine classification); [USA] Department of Commerce; direct operating cost; [chemistry] dissolved organic carbon; District Officer Commanding

Doc. Doctor

doc [short form] doctor

doc. document(s)

d.o.c.a. date of current appointment

d.o.c.e. date of current enlistment

DocEng Doctor of Engineering

DOCG *denominazione di origine controllata garantita* (Italian: name of origin guaranteed controlled) (wine classification)

docu. document; documentary; documentation

DOD date of death; [USA] Department of Defense; died of disease

d.o.d. date of death

DOE [USA] Department of Energy; Department of the Environment; depends on experience (in job advertisement); Director of Education

d.o.e. depends on experience (in job advertisement)

DOF [science] degrees of freedom

D of Corn. LI Duke of Cornwall's Light Infantry

D of H degree of honour

D of L Duchy of Lancaster

D of S Director of Stores

DOG Directory of Opportunities for Graduates

DOH Department of Health

DOHC double overhead cam(shaft); dual overhead cam(shaft)

DOHS [USA] Department of Health Services

DOI Department of Industry; [USA] Department of the Interior; died of injuries; Director of Information

DOJ [USA] Department of Justice

DOL [USA] Department of Labor; Doctor of Oriental Learning

dol. [music] *dolce* (Italian: sweetly, gently); [currency] dollar

dolciss. [music] *dolcissimo* (Italian: very sweetly, very gently)

DOM date of marriage; *Deo Optimo Maximo* (Latin: to God, the best, the greatest); *département d'outre mer* (French: overseas department); [informal] dirty old man; dispersed organic material; dissolved organic material; [international vehicle registration] Dominican Republic; *Dominus omnium magister* (Latin: God the master of all)

Dom. Dominica; Dominical; [Roman Catholic Church] Dominican; *Dominus* (Latin: Lord)

dom. domain; *domenica* (Italian: Sunday); domestic; domicile; dominant; *domingo* (Spanish: Sunday); dominion

d.o.m. date of marriage

Dom. Bk Domesday Book

Dom. Proc. [law] *Domus Procerum* (Latin: House of Lords)

DOMS Diploma in Ophthalmic Medicine and Surgery

Domsat domestic communications satellite

DON [USA] Department of the Navy; Diploma in Orthopaedic Nursing; [chemistry] dissolved organic nitrogen

Don. Donegal

don. *donec* (Latin: until)

Doneg. Donegal

DOpt Diploma in Ophthalmic Optics

DOR Director of Operational Requirements

Dor [astronomy] Dorado

Dor. Dorian; Doric

DORA Defence of the Realm Act

dorm [short form] dormitory

Dors. Dorset

DOrth Diploma in Orthodontics; Diploma in Orthoptics

DOS date of sale; day of sale; [USA] Department of State; Diploma in Orthopaedic Surgery; Directorate of Overseas Surveys; Director of Ordnance Services; [computing] disk-operating system; Doctor of Ocular Science

dos. dosage

DOSV deep ocean survey vehicle

DOT Department of Overseas Trade; Department of Transport; [USA] Department of Transportation; designated order turnaround (in New York Stock Exchange); [computing] digital optical tape; Diploma in Occupational Therapy; [medicine] directly observed therapy; [physiology] dissolved oxygen tension

dot. [law] dotation (= endowment)

dott. *dottore* (Italian: doctor)

DOV double oil of vitriol (sulphuric acid)

DOW died of wounds

Dow. Dowager

dow. dowager

doz. dozen

DP data processing; decimal pitch; [chemistry] degree of polymerization; delivery point; Democratic Party; diametral pitch; Diploma in Psychiatry; (by) direction of the president; Director of Photography; disabled person; displaced person; Doctor of Philosophy; domestic prelate; [law] *Domus Procerum* (Latin: House of Lords); durable press; duty paid; [computing] dynamic programming; [vehicle registration] Reading

D/P delivery on payment; delivery papers; [commerce] documents against payment; [commerce] documents against presentation

dp deep

d.p. damp-proof; damp-proofed; damp-proofing; deep penetration; departure point; [finance] depreciation percentage; direct port; double paper; [baseball] double play; dry powder; dual purpose

DPA Data Protection Authority; *Deutsche Presse Agentur* (German news agency); Diploma in Public Administration; discharged prisoners' aid; [USA] Doctor of Public Administration

d.p.a. deferred payment account

DPAA Draught Proofing Advisory Association

DPAS Discharged Prisoners' Aid Society

DPath Diploma in Pathology

DPB [finance] deposit pass book

DPC Defence Planning Committee (in NATO)

d.p.c. damp-proof course

DPCM [telecommunications] differential pulse code modulation

DPCP Department of Prices and Consumer Protection

DPCS data personal communications service

DPD Data Protection Directive; Diploma in Public Dentistry; [statistics] discrete probability distributions

DPE Diploma in Physical Education

DPEc Doctor of Political Economy

DPed Doctor of Pedagogy

DPH Diploma in Public Health; Director of Public Health; [USA] Doctor of Public Health

DPh Doctor of Philosophy

DPharm Doctor of Pharmacy

DPHD Diploma in Public Health Dentistry

DPhil Doctor of Philosophy

DPHN Diploma in Public Health Nursing

DPhysMed Diploma in Physical Medicine

DPI Department of Public Information

dpi [computing] dots per inch

dpl. diploma; diplomat; duplex

DPM data processing manager; Deputy

Prime Minister; Deputy Provost-Marshal; Diploma in Psychological Medicine

DPMI [computing] DOS/Protected Mode Interface

DPMS [computing] display power management system

DPO distributing post office; district pay office

d.p.o.b. date and place of birth

DPolSc Doctor of Political Science

DPP [insurance] deferred payment plan; Diploma in Plant Pathology; Director of Public Prosecutions; [US finance] direct participation program

DPR Data Protection Register; Director of Public Relations

DPRK Democratic People's Republic of Korea (North Korea)

DPS Dales Pony Society; Director of Personal Services; Director of Postal Services; Doctor of Public Service

dps dividend per share

DPSA Diploma in Public and Social Administration

DPSK [computing] differential phase shift keying

DPSN Diploma in Professional Studies in Nursing

DPsSc Doctor of Psychological Science

DPsy *Docteur en psychologie* (French: Doctor of Psychology)

DPsych Diploma in Psychiatry; Doctor of Psychology

DPT [medicine] dental pantomogram; [medicine] diphtheria, pertussis (whooping cough), tetanus (vaccine)

dpt department; deponent; deposit; depot

dpty deputy

DPU data processing unit

DPW Department of Public Works

dpx duplex

DQ dispersion quotient; [sports] disqualified; [sports] disqualify; [civil aircraft marking] Fiji

d.q. direct question

DQDB [computing] distributed queue dual bus

DQMG Deputy Quartermaster-General

DQMS Deputy Quartermaster-Sergeant

DR [USA] Daughters of the Revolution; [navigation] dead reckoning; [physics] decay ratio; defence regulation; *Deutsches Reich* (German: German

Empire); dining room (in property advertisement); Diploma in Radiology; discount rate; dispatch rider; dispersion relation; district railway; district registry; [paper size] double royal; [fishing port] Dover; [theatre] down right (of stage); dry riser (for firefighter's hose); Dutch Reformed (Church); dynamic relaxation; [vehicle registration] Exeter

D/R deposit receipt

Dr Director; Doctor; [currency] drachma

Dr. Drive (in road name)

dr debtor; door; dram; [meteorology] drizzle and rain

dr. debit; drachm; [currency] drachma; drama; draw; drawer; drawn; dresser; driver; drum; drummer

d.r. deficiency report; design requirements; development report; document report

DRA de-rating appeals

Dra *Doctora* (Spanish: Doctor (female)); *Doutora* (Portuguese: Doctor (female)); [astronomy] Draco

DRAC Director, Royal Armoured Corps

DrAgr Doctor of Agriculture

DRAM [computing] dynamic random-access memory

dram. drama; dramatic; dramatist

dram. pers. *dramatis personae* (Latin: characters in the play)

DRAO Dominion Radio Astrophysical Observatory

Drav. Dravidian (language)

DRAW [computing] direct read after write

draw. drawing room (in property advertisement)

DrBusAdmin Doctor of Business Administration

DRC [theatre] down right centre (of stage); Dutch Reformed Church

DrChem Doctor of Chemistry

DRCOG Diploma of the Royal College of Obstetricians and Gynaecologists

DRCPath Diploma of the Royal College of Pathologists

DRCS [computing] dynamically redefinable character set

DRCST Diploma of the Royal College of Science and Technology (Glasgow)

DRD Diploma in Restorative Dentistry

DRDW [computing] direct read during write

DRE [medicine] digital rectal examination; Director of Religious Education; Doctor of Religious Education

DRelEd Doctor of Religious Education

DrEng Doctor of Engineering

DRG [medicine] diagnosis-related group

drg drawing

DRK *Deutsches Rotes Kreuz* (German: German Red Cross)

DRLS dispatch-rider letter service

DRM Diploma in Radiation Medicine; Diploma in Resource Management

DrMed Doctor of Medicine

drn drawn

DrNatSci Doctor of Natural Science

DRO daily routine order; disablement resettlement officer; divisional routine order

DrOecPol Doctor of Political Economics (from Latin *Doctor Oeconomiae Politicae*)

DRP dividend reinvestment plan

DrPH Doctor of Public Health

DrPhil Doctor of Philosophy

DrPolSci Doctor of Political Science

DRS Diploma in Religious Studies

DRSAMD Diploma of the Royal Scottish Academy of Music and Drama

DRSE [medicine] drug-related side effects

DRSN [meteorology] drifting snow

DRT [psychology] diagnostic rhyme test

DrTheol Doctor of Theology

Dr. und Vrl. *Druck und Verlag* (German: printed and published (by))

DRurSc Doctor of Rural Science

DRV dietary reference values

DRW [computing] draw format

drx. [currency] drachma

DS [music] *dal segno* (Italian: (repeat) from the sign); [finance] debenture stock; defect score; [physics] defect size; dental surgeon; Department of State; deputy secretary; Detective Sergeant; [physics] diffractive system; Directing Staff; [medicine] disseminated sclerosis; Doctor of Science; Doctor of Surgery; [computing] double-sided (disk); [medicine] Down's syndrome; driver seated (vehicle); [fishing port] Dumfries; [vehicle registration] Glasgow

D/S [medicine] dextrose saline

Ds *Deus* (Latin: God); *Dominus* (Latin: Lord, Master)

ds. *destro* (Italian: right)

d.s. date of service; daylight saving; days after sight; day's sight; document signed

DSA [medicine] digital subtraction angiography; Diploma in Social Administration; *Docteur ès sciences agricoles* (French: Doctor of Agricultural Science); Down's Syndrome Association; Driving Standards Agency

DSAC Defence Scientific Advisory Council

DSAO Diplomatic Service Administration Office

DSASO Deputy Senior Air Staff Officer

DSB *Dansk Statsbaner* (Danish: Danish State Railways); Drug Supervisory Body (of UN)

DSC Discovery Channel; Distinguished Service Cross (replacement for CSC); Doctor of Surgical Chiropody

DSc Doctor of Science

DScA *Docteur ès sciences agricoles* (French: Doctor of Agricultural Science); *Docteur ès sciences appliquées* (French: Doctor of Applied Sciences)

DSc(Agr) Doctor of Science in Agriculture

DSc(Eng) Doctor of Science in Engineering

DSc(For) Doctor of Science in Forestry

DSCHE Diploma of the Scottish Council for Health Education

DScMil Doctor of Military Science

DScTech Doctor of Technical Science

DSD Director of Signals Division; Director of Staff Duties

dsDNA [biochemistry] double-stranded deoxyribonucleic acid

DSDP deep-sea drilling project

DSE Doctor of Science in Economics

Dsf Düsseldorf

dsgn design

dsgn. designer

DSIR [New Zealand] Department of Scientific and Industrial Research

DSL district Scout leader; Doctor of Sacred Letters

DSM deputy stage manager; *Diagnostic and Statistical Manual* (of American Psychiatric Association); [computing] digital storage medium; Directorate of Servicing and Maintenance; Distinguished Service Medal; Doctor of Sacred Music

dsmd dismissed

DSN [astronautics] Deep-Space Network

DSO (Companion of the) Distinguished Service Order; District Staff Officer

DSocSC Doctor of Social Science(s)

DSP Democratic Socialist Party; [electronics] digital signal processing; [electronics] digital signal processor; *Docteur ès sciences politiques* (French: Doctor of Political Science); dye sublimation printing

d.s.p. *decessit sine prole* (Latin: died without issue)

dspl disposal

d.s.p.l. *decessit sine prole legitima* (Latin: died without legitimate issue)

d.s.p.m. *decessit sine prole mascula* (Latin: died without male issue)

d.s.p.m.s. *decessit sine prole mascula superstite* (Latin: died without surviving male issue)

dspn disposition

d.s.p.s. *decessit sine prole superstite* (Latin: died without surviving issue)

d.s.p.v. *decessit sine prole virile* (Latin: died without male issue)

d.s.q. discharged to sick quarters

DSR [commerce] debt service ratio; [medicine] digital subtraction radiography; Director of Scientific Research; [medicine] dynamic spatial reconstructor

DSRD Directorate of Signals Research and Development

DSS [computing] decision support system; Department of Social Security; Director of Social Services; Doctor of Holy (or Sacred) Scripture (from Latin *Doctor Sacrae Scripturae*); Doctor of Social Science

Dss Deaconess

DSSc Diploma in Sanitary Science; Doctor of Social Science

DST Daylight Saving Time; deep-sleep therapy; Director of Supplies and Transport; Doctor of Sacred Theology; Double Summer Time; [mining] drill-stem test

dstn destination

D Surg. Dental Surgeon

DSW [New Zealand] Department of Social Welfare; Doctor of Social Welfare; Doctor of Social Work

DT *Daily Telegraph*; damage-tolerant; data transmission; daylight time; [medicine] dead from tumour; delirium tremens; dental technician; [USA] Department of

Transportation; [USA] Department of Treasury; destructive testing; [US informal] detective; [nuclear technology] deuterium–tritium; Director of Transport; Doctor of Divinity (or Theology) (from Latin *Doctor Theologiae*); [UK postcode] Dorchester; [vehicle registration] Sheffield

d.t. delirium tremens; double throw

DTA [physics] differential thermal analysis; Diploma in Tropical Agriculture; Distributive Trades' Alliance

DTAM data transfer, access and manipulation

d.t.b.a. [commerce] date to be advised

DTC Department of Technical Cooperation; [USA] Depository Trust Company; Diamond Trading Company; [medicine] differentiated thyroid carcinoma; Diploma in Textile Chemistry; Docklands Transportation Consortium

DTCD [USA] Department of Technical Cooperation for Development; Diploma in Tuberculosis and Chest Diseases

DTD Diploma in Tuberculous Diseases; Director of Technical Development; document type definition

dtd dated

d.t.d. [medicine] *detur talis dosis* (Latin: let such a dose be given) (in prescriptions)

DTDP ditridecyl phthalate (PVC plasticizer)

DTE [computing] data terminal equipment

DTech Doctor of Technology

DTF Dairy Trade Federation; Domestic Textiles Federation

Dtg *Dienstag* (German: Tuesday)

DTH [immunology] delayed-type hypersensitivity; Diploma in Tropical Hygiene

DTh Doctor of Divinity (or Theology) (from Latin *Doctor Theologiae*)

DTheol Doctor of Divinity (or Theology) (from Latin *Doctor Theologiae*)

DThPT Diploma in Theory and Practice of Teaching

DTI Department of Trade and Industry

DTIC [medicine] dacarbazine (used to treat cancer)

DTL [electronics] diode-transistor logic; down the line (in shooting)

DTM Diploma in Tropical Medicine

Dtm. Dortmund

DTMH Diploma in Tropical Medicine and Hygiene

dto *direito* (Portuguese: right)

DTOD Director of Trade and Operations Division

DTP [computing] desktop publishing

DTPA [medicine] diethylenetriaminepentaacetic acid (used in diagnosis)

DTPH Diploma in Tropical Public Health

DTR [photography] diffusion-transfer reversal; Diploma in Therapeutic Radiology; double taxation relief

DTRP Diploma in Town and Regional Planning

DTRT [meteorology] deteriorating

DTS [medicine] dual tracer scintigraphy

DTs [informal] delirium tremens

DTV digital television

DTVM Diploma in Tropical Veterinary Medicine

DU [vehicle registration] Coventry; [physics] depleted uranium; died unmarried; Doctor of the University; [medicine] duodenal ulcer

Du. Ducal; Duchy; Duke; Dutch

DUART [computing, electronics] dual universal asynchronous receiver transmitter

Dub. Dublin

dub. dubious; *dubitans* (Latin: doubting)

Dubl. Dublin

DUC [meteorology] dense upper cloud

DUI [USA] driving under the influence (of alcohol or drugs)

Dumf. Dumfries and Galloway

Dun. Dundee

Dunelm. *Dunelmensis* (Latin: (Bishop) of Durham)

DUniv Doctor of the University

duo. [paper size] duodecimo

DUP [Northern Ireland] Democratic Unionist Party; *Docteur de l'Université de Paris* (French: Doctor of the University of Paris)

dup. duplicate

Dur. Durban; Durham

DUS Diploma of the University of Southampton

DUSC [US air force] deep underground support center

Dut. Dutch

DUV damaging ultraviolet (radiation)

DV defective vision; *Deo volente* (Latin: God willing); Diploma in Venereology;

direct vision; distinguished visitor; district valuer; [Bible] Douay Version; double vision; [vehicle registration] Exeter

DVA [medicine] digital video angiography; Diploma in Veterinary Anaesthesia; Dunkirk Veterans' Association

DV&D Diploma in Venereology and Dermatology

DVC [microbiology] direct viable count

DVD [computing] digital versatile disc; digital video disc

DVD-R [computing] digital versatile disc recordable

DVE Diploma in Vocational Education

DVH Diploma in Veterinary Hygiene

DVI [computing] digital video imaging; [computing] digital video interactive

DVLA Driver and Vehicle Licensing Agency

DVLC Driver and Vehicle Licensing Centre (Swansea)

DVM digital voltmeter; Doctor of Veterinary Medicine

d.v.m. *decessit vita matris* (Latin: died in the lifetime of the mother)

DVMS Doctor of Veterinary Medicine and Surgery

DVO district veterinary officer

d.v.p. *decessit vita patris* (Latin: died in the lifetime of the father)

DVPH Diploma in Veterinary Public Health

DVR Diploma in Veterinary Radiology; [computing] discrete-variable representation

DVS Doctor of Veterinary Surgery

DVSc Doctor of Veterinary Science

DVSci Doctor of Veterinary Science

DVT [medicine] deep-vein thrombosis

DW [vehicle registration] Cardiff; [chemistry] deionized water; [commerce] dock warrant

D/W [commerce] dock warrant

d/w dust wrapper

d.w. dead weight; delivered weight

DWA driving without awareness

DWAS Doctor Who Appreciation Society

d.w.c. deadweight capacity

dwel. dwelling

DWEM [USA] dead white European male

dwg drawing; dwelling

DWI [USA] driving while intoxicated; Dutch West Indies (former name of Netherlands Antilles)

DWR Duke of Wellington's Regiment

dwr drawer

dwt pennyweight

d.w.t. deadweight tonnage

DWU [USA] Distillery, Wine and Allied Workers International Union

DX [photography] daylight exposure; [vehicle registration] Ipswich; [telecommunications] long-distance

DXF data exchange format

DXR [medicine] deep X-ray

DXRT [medicine] deep X-ray therapy

DXS diagnostic X-ray spectrometry

DY [international vehicle registration] Benin (from former name Dahomey); [vehicle registration] Brighton; dockyard; [UK postcode] Dudley

Dy [chemical element] dysprosium

dy delivery; [paper size] demy

DYB do your best (Scout motto)

Dyd dockyard

dyn dyne

dyn. dynamic; dynamics; dynamite; dynamo; dynasty

DYS Duke of York's Royal Military School

DZ [international vehicle registration] Algeria (from Arabic *Djazïr*); [vehicle registration] Antrim; Doctor of Zoology; [meteorology] drizzle; [military] drop zone

dz. dozen

.dz Algeria (in Internet address)

DZool Doctor of Zoology

D-Zug *Durchgangszug* (German: express train)

E

E casual workers (occupational group); Earl; [astronomy] earth; [electrical engineering] earth; east; Easter; eastern; [UK postcode] east London; [slang] ecstasy (drug); Edinburgh; efficiency; Egypt; Egyptian; [chemistry] electromeric effect; electronic (as in **E-commerce**); [chemistry] elimination reaction; [astronomy] elliptical galaxy; elocution; [currency] emalangeni (used in Swaziland); eminence; enemy; engineer; engineering; England; English; [numismatics] English shilling; envoy; equator; *España* (Spanish: Spain); EU-recognized food additive (as in **E120** = cochineal); European; evening; evensong; exa- (indicates 10^{18}, as in **Em** = exametre); [fishing port] Exeter; [music] note of scale; [international vehicle registration] Spain (from Spanish *España*); [logic] universal negative categorical proposition

E [physics] electric field strength; [chemistry] electrode potential; [physics] electromotive force; [physics] energy; [physics] illuminance; [physics] irradiance

e [mathematics] base of natural logarithm; electromotive; [physics] electron; electronic (as in **e-text**); [physics] positron; [meteorology] wet air

e [mathematics] eccentricity (of ellipse); [physics] electron charge; [chemistry] equatorial conformation (of molecules); [physics] proton charge

e. edition; educated; elder; eldest; electric; electricity; electromotive; engineer; engineering; Erlang (unit of traffic intensity in telephony); [baseball] error; evening; excellence; excellent

EA [vehicle registration] Dudley; early antigen; East Anglia; economic adviser; educational age; effective action; effective agent (as in **EA content**); electrical artificer; *Ente Autonomo* (Italian: Autonomous Corporation); [Freemasonry] Entered Apprentice; enterprise allowance; environmental assessment; Evangelical Alliance; experimental area; exposure age

E/A enemy aircraft; experimental aircraft

ea. each

EAA Edinburgh Architectural Association; Electrical Appliance Association; [USA] Engineer in Aeronautics and Astronautics; [chemistry] eth(yl)ene acrylic acid

EAAA European Association of Advertising Agencies

EAAC European Agricultural Aviation Centre

EAAFRO East African Agriculture and Forestry Research Organization

EAAP European Association for Animal Production

EAB [medicine] extra-anatomic bypass

EAC East African Community; Educational Advisory Committee; Engineering Advisory Council; European Atomic Commission

EACA East Africa Court of Appeal; [medicine] epsilon aminocaproic acid

EACC East Asia Christian Conference

EACSO East African Common Services Organization

ead. *eadem* (Latin: the same (woman))

eaed. *eaedem* (Latin: the same (women))

EAEG European Association of Exploration Geophysicists

EAES European Atomic Energy Society

EAF electric-arc furnace

e.a.f. emergency action file

EAFFRO East African Freshwater Fisheries Research Organization

EAG Economists Advisory Group

EAGGF European Agricultural Guidance and Guarantee Fund (in EU)

EAHF [medicine] eczema, asthma, hay fever

EAK [international vehicle registration] (East Africa) Kenya

EAM *Ethniko Apelentherotiko Metopo* (Greek: National Liberation Front) (in World War II)

EAMF European Association of Music Festivals

EAMFRO East African Marine Fisheries Research Organization

EAMTC European Association of Management Training Centres

EAN [chemistry] effective atomic number; [computing] European Academic Network; European Article Number (computer coding for retail goods)

e&e each and every

E&O errors and omissions

E&OE errors and omissions excepted

e.a.o.n. except as otherwise noted

EAP East Africa Protectorate; Edgar Allan Poe (US writer); [USA] employee-assistance program; English for academic purposes

EAPC Euro-Atlantic Partnership Council (in NATO, replacement for NACC)

EAPR European Association for Potato Research

EAPROM [computing] electrically alterable programmable read-only memory

EAR employee advisory resource; employee attitude research; [engineering] energy-absorbing resin

EARCCUS East African Regional Committee for Conservation and Utilization of Soil

EARN [computing] European Academic and Research Network

EAROM [computing] electrically alterable read-only memory

EAROPH East Asia Regional Organization for Planning and Housing

EAS electronic article surveillance; [medicine] endotoxin-activated serum; [aeronautics] equivalent air speed; [aeronautics] estimated air speed

EASA Entertainment Arts Socialist Association

EASEP [astronautics] Early Apollo Scientific Experiments Package

EASHP European Association of Senior Hospital Physicians

east. eastern

EASTROPAC Eastern Tropical Pacific

EAT earliest arrival time; [medicine] Ehrlich ascites tumour; Employment Appeals Tribunal; estimated arrival time; [medicine] experimental autoimmune thyroiditis; [international vehicle registration] (East Africa) Tanzania

EATRO East African Trypanosomiasis Research Organization

EAU [international vehicle registration] (East Africa) Uganda

EAVRO East African Veterinary Research Organization

EAW Electrical Association for Women; equivalent average words

EAX [telecommunications] electronic automatic exchange

EAZ [international vehicle registration] (East Africa) Tanzania (formerly Zanzibar)

EB electricity board; electron beam; electronic book; *Encyclopaedia Britannica*; [medicine] epidermolysis bullosa (skin disease); Epstein–Barr (virus); [currency] Ethiopian birr; Evans blue (dye); [vehicle registration] Peterborough

Eb [computing] exabyte

e-b estate-bottled

EBA English Bowling Association

EB&RA Engineer Buyers' and Representatives' Association

e.b.a.r. edited beyond all recognition

EBC English Benedictine Congregation; European Billiards Confederation; European Brewery Convention

EBCDIC [computing] extended binary-coded decimal-interchange code

e-beam electron beam

EBICON [physics] electron-bombardment-induced conductivity

EBIT [accounting] earnings before interest and tax

EBL electron-beam lithography; European Bridge League

EBM electron-beam machining; [medicine] expressed breast milk

EBMC English Butter Marketing Company

EbN east by north

EBNF [computing] extended Backus normal form

Ebor. *Eboracensis* (Latin: (Archbishop) of York); *Eboracum* (Latin: York)

EBR electron-beam recording; [nuclear technology] experimental breeder reactor

EBRA Engineer Buyers' and Representatives' Association

EBRD European Bank for Reconstruction and Development

EBS emergency bed service; emergency

broadcast system; engineered barrier system; English Bookplate Society

EbS east by south

EBT [medicine] electron-beam therapy

EBU English Bridge Union; European Badminton Union; European Boxing Union; European Broadcasting Union

EBV [medicine] Epstein–Barr virus

EBWR [nuclear technology] experimental boiling-water reactor

EC East Caribbean; [UK postcode] east central London; east coast; Eastern Command; Ecclesiastical Commissioner; [international vehicle registration] Ecuador; [physics] eddy current; educational committee; education committee; [chemistry] effective concentration; electricity council; electrolytic corrosion; electronic computer; emergency commission; [medicine] endothelial cell; Engineering Corps; [biochemistry] Enzyme Commission (in enzyme code number); Episcopal Church; Established Church; [chemistry] eth(yl)ene carbonate; [Canada] *Étoile du Courage* (French: Star of Courage); European Commission; European Community; executive committee; [vehicle registration] Preston; [civil aircraft marking] Spain

Ec. Ecuador

.ec Ecuador (in Internet address)

ec. earth closet; enamel-coated; enamel-covered; error correction; *exempli causa* (Latin: for example); extended coverage; extension course

ECA Early Closing Association; Economic Commission for Africa; [USA] Economic Cooperation Administration; Educational Centres Association; Electrical Contractors' Association; European Congress of Accountants

ECAC Engineering College Administrative Council; European Civil Aviation Conference

ECAFE Economic Commission for Asia and the Far East (former name of ESCAP)

ECAS Electrical Contractors' Association of Scotland

ECAT [medicine] emission compute(rize)d axial tomography

ECB electronic codebook; electronic

components board; European Central Bank

ECBS engineering of computer-based systems

ECC [electrical engineering] earth continuity conductor; [physics] emergency core cooling (or coolant); energy-conscious construction; [computing] error-correction code; European Cultural Centre

Ecc. *Eccellenze* (Italian: Excellency)

ecc. *eccetera* (Italian: et cetera, etc.)

Ecc. Hom. *Ecce Homo* (Latin: behold the man)

ECCI European Confederation for Commerce and Industry plc

Eccl. [Bible] Ecclesiastes

eccl. ecclesiastic(al)

Eccles. [Bible] Ecclesiastes

eccles. ecclesiastic(al)

Ecclus. [Bible] Ecclesiasticus (book of Apocrypha)

ECCM [military] electronic counter-countermeasure(s)

ECCP European Committee on Crime Problems

ECCS [physics] emergency core cooling system

ECCU English Cross-Country Union

ECD early closing day; [electronics] electrostatic charge decay; [computing] enhanced colour display; estimated completion date

ECE Economic Commission for Europe

ECF [US medicine] extended-care facility; extracellular fluid

ECFA European Committee for Future Accelerators

ECFMG Educational Council for Foreign Medical Graduates

ECFMS Educational Council for Foreign Medical Students

ECG [medicine] electrocardiogram; [medicine] electrocardiograph; Export Credit Guarantee

ECGB East Coast of Great Britain

ECGC Empire Cotton Growing Corporation

ECGD Export Credits Guarantee Department

ech. echelon

ECHP [USA] Environmental Compliance and Health Protection

ECHR European Commission on Human Rights; European Court of Human Rights

ECI East Coast of Ireland; energy-cost indicator

ECIA European Committee of Interior Architects

ECITO European Central Inland Transport Organization

ECJ European Court of Justice

ECL [physics] emergency cooling limit; [electronics] emitter-coupled logic

ECLAC Economic Commission for Latin America and the Caribbean

eclec. eclectic; eclecticism

ecli. eclipse; ecliptic

ECLO [electronics] emitter-coupled logic operator

ECLOF Ecumenical Church Loan Fund

ECLSS environmental control and life-support system

ECM electric coding machine; electro-chemical machining; [military] electronic countermeasure(s); energy conservation measure; environmental corrosion monitor; extended core memory

ECMA [geology] East Coast Magnetic Anomaly; European Computer Manufacturers' Association

ECME Economic Commission for the Middle East

ECMF Electric Cable Makers' Federation

ECMO [medicine] extracorporeal membrane oxygenation

ECMRA European Chemical Market Research Association

ECMT European Conference of Ministers of Transport

ECMWF European Centre for Medium-range Weather Forecast

ECN epoxy–cresol–novolak (synthetic resin)

ECNSW Electricity Commission of New South Wales

ECO energy conservation opportunity; English Chamber Orchestra; European Coal Organization

eco. ecological; ecology

ECODU European Control Data Users

ECoG [medicine] electrocochleography; electrocorticogram

ecol. ecological; ecology

E coli *Escherichia coli* (Latin: name of bacterium)

Ecol. Soc. Am. Ecological Society of America

ECOM electronic computer-originated mail

ECOMOG ECOWAS Monitoring Group (peacekeeping force)

econ. economic(al); economics; economist; economy

Econ. J *Economic Journal*

Econ. R *Economic Review*

ECOR [USA] Engineering Committee on Ocean Resources

ECOSOC Economic and Social Council (of UN)

ECOVAST European Council for the Village and Small Town

ECOWAS Economic Community of West African States

ECP [finance] Euro-commercial paper; European Committee on Crop Protection; *Evangelii Christi Praedicator* (Latin: Preacher of the Gospel of Christ)

ECPA Electric Consumers Protection Act

ECPD [USA] Engineers' Council for Professional Development

ECPS European Centre for Population Studies

ECQAC Electronic Components Quality Assurance Committee

ECR electronic cash register

ECS emergency cooling (or coolant) system; environmental control system; European Communications Satellite; European Components Service

ECSC European Coal and Steel Community (predecessor of EU)

ECST European Convention on the Suppression of Terrorism

ECT [medicine] electroconvulsive therapy; [medicine] emission-compute(rize)d tomography

ECTA Electrical Contractors' Trading Association

ECTD [USA] Emission Control Technology Division

ECTF Enterprise Computer Telephony Forum

ECU English Church Union; environmental control unit; European Chiropractic Union; European Currency Unit;

European Customs Union; [photography] extreme close-up

ecu European Currency Unit

Ecua. Ecuador; Ecuadorian

ECUK East Coast of the United Kingdom

ECUSA Episcopal Church of the United States of America

ECV [obstetrics] external cephalic version

ECWA Economic Commission for Western Asia

ECWEC European Community Wind Energy Conference and Exhibition

ECWS English Civil War Society

ECY European Conservation Year

ECYO European Community Youth Orchestra

ED [USA] Doctor of Engineering; economic dispatch; Education Department; [pharmacology] effective dose; Efficiency Decoration; election district; [physics] electromagnetic dissociation; [electronics] electron device; [physics, chemistry] electron diffraction; [medicine] embryonic day; Employment Department; [medicine] end-diastole; [medicine] end-diastolic; entertainments duty; equilibrium dialysis; equivalent dose (of radiation); European Democrat; evening dinner (in accommodation advertisement); [finance] ex dividend; existence doubtful; experimental detector; [medicine] extensive disease; [finance] extra dividend; [vehicle registration] Liverpool

Ed. Edinburgh; Editor

ed. *edile* (Italian: building); *edilizia* (Italian: building); edited; edition; editor; educated; education

éd. *édition* (French: edition)

e.d. edge distance; enemy dead; error detecting; excused duty; extra duty

EDA [USA] Economic Development Administration; Electrical Development Association; electronic design automation; *Eniea Dimokratiki Aristera* (Greek: Union of the Democratic Left) (political party)

e.d.a. early departure authorized

ED&S *English Dance and Song* (publication of EFDSS)

EDAS [computing] enhanced data-acquisition system

EDB ethene dibromide (fuel additive)

EdB Bachelor of Education

EDBS [computing] expert database system

EDC Economic Development Committee; Engineering Design Centre; [computing] error-detection code; ethylene dichloride; European Defence Community; [obstetrics] expected date of confinement

e.d.c. error detection and correction; extra dark colour

EDD *English Dialect Dictionary*; exactly delayed detonator; [obstetrics] expected date of delivery

EdD Doctor of Education

edd. *ediderunt* (Latin: published by); *editiones* (Latin: editions)

EDE effective dose equivalent (of radiation)

EDF *Électricité de France* (French electricity corporation); [USA] Environmental Defense Fund; European Development Fund

EDG emergency diesel generator; European Democratic Group

EDHE experimental data handling equipment

EDI [computing] electronic data interchange

Edin. Edinburgh

Ed. in Ch. Editor in Chief

EDIP European Defence Improvement Programme (in NATO)

EDIS Engineering Data Information System

edit. edited; edition; editor; *editore* (Italian: publisher); editorial

EDL economic discard limits; [chemistry] electrical double layer; electrodeless discharge lamp

e.d.l. edition de luxe

EDM [chemistry] electrical-discharge machining; electric dipole moment; [surveying] electronic distance measurement; [physics] energy-density model

EdM Master of Education

EDMA European Direct Marketing Association

Edm. & Ips. (Bishop of) St Edmundsbury and Ipswich

Edmn Edmonton

edn edition

Ednbgh Edinburgh

EDNS expected demand not supplied

EDO [computing] extended data out

e.d.o.c. effective date of change

EDO DRAM [computing] extended data out dynamic random-access memory

EDP [physics] electron-diffraction pattern; [computing] electronic data processing; emergency defence plan; [medicine] end-diastolic pressure

EDPS [computing] electronic data-processing system

EDPT [computing] enhanced-drive parameter table

EDR electronic decoy rocket; Electronic Dictionary Research; European Depository Receipts; except during rain (following pollen count)

EDRF [medicine] endothelium-derived relaxing factor

EDRP European Demonstration Reprocessing Plant (for nuclear fuel)

EDS electrically adjusted driver's seat (in car advertisement); Electronic Data Systems Corporation; English Dialect Society; [computing] exchangeable disk store

EdS Education Specialist

EDSAC [computing] Electronic Delay Storage Automatic Calculator

EDSAT Educational Television Satellite

EDSP Exchange Delivery Settlement Price

EDSS expert decision-support system

ED/st electrically adjusted driver's seat (in car advertisement)

EDT [USA, Canada] Eastern Daylight Time; energy design technique

EDTA European Dialysis and Transplant Association

EDU European Democratic Union

.edu US educational institution (in Internet address)

educ. educated; education; educational

educn education

EDV [medicine] end-diastolic volume

EDVAC Electronic Discrete Variable Automatic Computer

Edw. Edward

EE Early English; Eastern Electricity; edge-to-edge; electrical engineer; electrical engineering; electron emission; electronic engineer; electronic engineering; employment exchange; environmental education; environmental engineering; Envoy Extraordinary; errors excepted; explosive emission; expressed emotion; [vehicle registration] Lincoln

e.e. errors excepted; eye and ear

.ee Estonia (in Internet address)

EEA Electronic Engineering Association; European Economic Area

EEAIE Electrical, Electronic and Allied Industries, Europe

EE&MP Envoy Extraordinary and Minister Plenipotentiary

EEB European Environmental Bureau

EEC [physics] energy–energy correlation; English Electric Company; European Economic Community (predecessor of EU); [electronics] explosive-emission cathode

EECA European Electronic Component Manufacturers' Association

EECS electrical-energy conversion system

EED effective equivalent dose (of radiation); electro-explosive device

EEDC Economic Development Committee for the Electronics Industry

EEF Egyptian Expeditionary Force; Engineering Employers' Federation; equivalent-energy function

EEG [medicine] electroencephalogram; [medicine] electroencephalograph; Essence Export Group

EEI [USA] Edison Electric Institute; [USA] Environmental Equipment Institute

EEIBA Electrical and Electronic Industries Benevolent Association

EEMJEB Electrical and Electronic Manufacturers' Joint Education Board

EEMS [computing] enhanced expanded memory specification

EEMUA Engineering Equipment and Materials Users Association

E Eng. Early English

EENT [medicine] eye, ear, nose and throat

EEO Energy Efficiency Office; equal employment opportunity

EEOC [USA] Equal Employment Opportunities Commission

EEPLD [computing] electrically erasable programmable logic device

EEPROM [computing] electrically erasable programmable read-only memory

EER energy–efficiency ratio

EERI [USA] Earthquake Engineering Research Institute

EEROM [computing] electrically erasable read-only memory

EES European Exchange System

EET Eastern European Time

EETPU Electrical, Electronic, Telecommunications and Plumbing Union (became part of AEEU)

EETS Early English Text Society

EEZ exclusive economic zone

EF edge-to-face; educational foundation; education foundation; [genetics] elongation factor; emergency fleet; [physics] enrichment factor; expectant father; expeditionary force; experimental flight; extra fine; [vehicle registration] Middlesbrough

EFA engine fault analysis; [biochemistry] essential fatty acid; Eton Fives Association; European Fighter Aircraft

EFB energy from biomass

EFC European Federation of Corrosion; European Forestry Commission

EFCE European Federation of Chemical Engineering

EFCT European Federation of Conference Towns

EFD [engineering] early fault detection

EFDSS English Folk Dance and Song Society

EFF Electronic Frontier Foundation; European Furniture Federation

eff. *effetto* (Italian: bill, promissory note); efficiency; effigy

EFG electric-field gradient

EFGF [electronics] epitaxial ferrite-garnet film

EFI electronic fuel injection

EFIS [aeronautics] electronic flight-information system

EFL English as a foreign language; external financial limit

EFM [medicine] electronic fetal monitor; European Federalist Movement

EFNS Educational Foundation for Nuclear Science

EFP [mathematics] Einstein–Fokker–Planck (differential equation); [photography] electronic field production; [commerce] exchange of futures for physicals; explosively formed penetrator; explosively formed projectile

EFPD effective full-power day

EFPH effective full-power hour

EFPW European Federation for the Protection of Waters

EFPY effective full-power year

EFR [astronomy] emerging flux region; [telecommunications] Enhanced Full Rate (for voice quality on mobile phone); [nuclear technology] European Fast Reactor; [nuclear technology] experimental fast reactor

EFRC [USA] Edwards Flight Research Center

EFSA European Federation of Sea Anglers

EFSC European Federation of Soroptimist Clubs

EFT electronic funds transfer

EFTA European Free Trade Association

EFTC Electrical Fair Trading Council

EFTPOS electronic funds transfer at point of sale

EFTS electronic funds transfer system; elementary flying training school

EFTU Engineering and Fastener Trade Union

EFU energetic feed unit; European Football Union

EFVA Educational Foundation for Visual Aids

EFW electric front windows (in car advertisement); energy from waste

EG Engineers Guild; equivalent grade; [chemistry] ethylene glycol; [vehicle registration] Peterborough

Eg. Egypt; Egyptian; Egyptologist; Egyptology

.eg Egypt (in Internet address)

e.g. *ejusdem generis* (Latin: of a like kind); *exempli gratia* (Latin: for example)

EGA Elizabeth Garrett Anderson (women's hospital); [computing] enhanced graphics adapter; European Golf Association

EGARD environmental gamma-ray and radon detector

EGAS Educational Grants Advisory Service

EGCI Export Group for the Construction Industries

EGCS English Guernsey Cattle Society

EGD epithermal gold deposit

EGEAS Electric Generating Expansion Analysis System

EGF [medicine] epidermal growth factor

EGFR [medicine] epidermal growth factor receptor

EGIFO Edward Grey Institute of Field Ornithology (Oxford)

EGL Engineers Guild Limited

EGM Empire Gallantry Medal (replaced by GC); European Glass Container Manufacturers' Committee; extraordinary general meeting

EGmbH [commerce] *Eingetragene Gesellschaft mit beschränkter Haftung* (German: registered limited company)

EGO eccentric (orbit) geophysical observatory

EGR [finance] earned growth rate; exhaust gas recirculation (as in **EGR valve**)

EGSP electronics glossary and symbol panel

EGT [physics] Einstein-invariant gauge theory (of gravitation)

e.g.t. exhaust gas temperature

EGU English Golf Union; [chemistry] external gelation of uranium

EGYPT eager to grab your pretty tits (on envelope of love letter)

Egypt. Egyptian

Egyptol. Egyptologist; Egyptology

EH [UK postcode] Edinburgh; [music] English horn (= cor anglais); [medicine] essential hypertension; [vehicle registration] Stoke-on-Trent

eh. *ehrenhalber* (German: honorary)

EHC effective heat capacity (of building); European Hotel Corporation; [medicine] external heart compression

EHF European Hockey Federation; experimental husbandry farm; [radio] extremely high frequency

EHG electro-hydraulic governor

EHL [physics] effective half-life

EHO environmental health officer

EHP electric and hybrid propulsion

ehp effective horsepower; electric horsepower

EHR Environmental Hazard Ranking; [USA] Environmental Health Services; European hybrid spectrometer; extra-high strength

EHT [electronics] extra-high tension

EHV electric and hybrid vehicle; extra-high voltage

EHWS extreme high water springs (level of tide)

EI earth (atmosphere) interface; East Indian; East Indies; electrical insulation; electromagnetic interaction; electron impact; electron ionization; [finance] endorsement irregular; energy intake; environmentally induced illness; [photography] exposure index; external irradiation; [civil aircraft marking] (Republic of) Ireland

EIA East Indian Association; economic impact assessment; [USA] Electrical Industries Association; [USA] Electronic Industries Association; Engineering Industries Association; environmental impact analysis; environmental impact assessment; Environmental Investigation Agency; [medicine] enzyme immunoassay; [medicine] exercise-induced asthma

EIB European Investment Bank; Export–Import Bank

EIC East India Company; Electrical Industries' Club; Engineering Institute of Canada

EICM employer's inventory of critical manpower

EICS East India Company's Service

EID East India Dock; [military] Electrical Inspection Directorate

EIDCT Educational Institute of Design, Craft and Technology

E-IDE enhanced integrated-drive electronics

EIEE [medicine] early infantile epileptic encephalopathy

EIEMA Electrical Installation Equipment Manufacturers' Association

EIF Elderly Invalids Fund

EIFAC European Inland Fisheries Advisory Committee

EIIR *Elizabetha Secunda Regina* (Latin: Queen Elizabeth the Second)

E-in-C Engineer-in-Chief

E Ind. East Indies

einschl. *einschliesslich* (German: including, inclusive)

Einw. *Einwohner* (German: inhabitant)

EIO extended interaction oscillator

EIPC European Institute of Printed Circuits

EIR [taxation] earned income relief; [computing] error-indicating recording

EIRMA European Industrial Research Management Association

EIS economic information system; Educational Institute of Scotland; effluent information system; energy information system; Enterprise Investment Scheme (replacement for BES); environmental impact statement; epidemic intelligence service

EISA [computing] enhanced industry standard architecture; [computing] extended industry standard architecture

EITB Engineering Industry Training Board

EITF [USA] Emerging Issues Task Force

EIU Economist Intelligence Unit

EIVT European Institute for Vocational Training

EJ elbow jerk; exajoule; [vehicle registration] Haverfordwest; [civil aircraft marking] (Republic of) Ireland

ej. *ejemplo* (Spanish: example)

EJC [USA] Engineers' Joint Council

EJMA English Joinery Manufacturers' Association

ejusd. *ejusdem* (Latin: of the same)

EK [civil aircraft marking] Armenia; East Kilbride; *Enosis Kentron* (Greek: Centre Union) (political party); [vehicle registration] Liverpool

eK *etter Kristi* (Norwegian: after Christ, AD)

Ekco E. K. Cole (manufacturer of electrical goods)

EKD *Evangelische Kirche in Deutschland* (German: Protestant Church in Germany)

EKG [USA] electrocardiogram; [USA] electrocardiograph; *Elektrokardiogramme* (German: electrocardiogram)

EL [vehicle registration] Bournemouth; [music] easy listening; electrical laboratory; electroluminescent; electronics laboratory; Engineer Lieutenant; epitaxial layer; Everyman's Library; explosive limit; [medicine] extracorporeal lithotripsy; [civil aircraft marking] Liberia

el. elect; elected; electric(al); electricity; element; elevated; elevated railway; elevation; elongation

ELA electronic learning aid; Eritrean Liberation Army

ELAS *Ethnikos Laikos Apeleutherotikos Stratos* (Greek: Hellenic People's Army of Liberation) (in World War II)

elas. elasticity

ELB Bachelor of English Literature

ELBS English Language Book Society

ELC Early Learning Centre (chain of educational toyshops); Environment Liaison Centre (Nairobi)

ELD economic load distribution

eld. elder; eldest

ELDC economic load dispatching centre; equivalent load duration curve

ELDO [astronautics] European Launcher Development Organization (became part of ESA)

ELEC European League for Economic Cooperation

elec. election; elector; electoral; electric(al); electrician; electricity; electron; electronic; [medicine] electuary

elect. election; elector; electoral; electric(al); electrician; electricity; electron; electronic; [medicine] electuary

electr. electrical; electrically

Electra Electrical, Electronics and Communications Trades Association

electron. electronic; electronically; electronics

elem. element(s); elementary

elev. elevation; elevator

ELF Eritrean Liberation Front; European Landworkers' Federation; [radio] extra-low frequency; [radio] extremely low frequency

e.l.f. early lunar flare

ELG [astronomy] emission-line galaxy

ELH [biochemistry] egg-laying hormone

ELI [sports] electronic line indicator

Eli. Elias; Elijah

Elien. *Eliensis* (Latin: (Bishop) of Ely)

Elint [military] electronic intelligence

ELISA [medicine] enzyme-linked immunosorbent assay

elix. [medicine] elixir

Eliz. Elizabethan

ELLA European Long Lines Agency

ellipt. elliptical

ELMA electromechanical aid

Elmint [military] electromagnetic intelligence

elo. elocution; eloquence

ELOISE European Large Orbiting Instrumentation for Solar Experiments

E Long. east longitude

elong. elongate; elongated; elongation

ELP equivalent local potential

ELR [meteorology] environment lapse rate; exceptional leave to remain (for asylum-seekers); export licensing regulations

ELS Electronic Lodgement Service

elsewh. elsewhere

ELSIE electronic speech information equipment

ELSS emergency life support system

ELT English language teaching (for foreign learners); European letter telegram

ELU English Lacrosse Union

ELV expendable launch vehicle; extra-low voltage

ELWS extreme low water springs (level of tide)

ely easterly

EM Earl Marshal; Edward Medal; [physics] effective mass; Efficiency Medal; electrical and mechanical; electromagnetic; electromotive; electronic mail; electron microscope (or microscopy); emission measure; engineering model; Engineer of Mines; [genetics] enhanced mutagenesis; enlisted man; environmental modelling; equipment module; European Movement; evaluation model; evening meal (in accommodation advertisement); expectation maximization; [vehicle registration] Liverpool; Master of the Horse (from Latin *Equitum Magister*)

Em. Eminence

em. emanation; embargo; eminent

e.m. electromagnetic; emergency maintenance; expanded metal; external memorandum

EMA effective medium approximation; [immunology] epithelial membrane antigen; European Marketing Association; European Monetary Agreement; Evangelical Missionary Alliance

EMAD engine maintenance and disassembly

e-mail electronic mail

EMAS [computing] Edinburgh multiaccess system; Employment Medical Advisory Service

EMB [USA] Energy Mobilization Board

Emb. Embankment (London); Embassy

emb. embargo; embossed

EMBL European Molecular Biology Laboratory

EMBO European Molecular Biology Organization

embr. embroider; embroidery

embryol. embryological; embryology

EMC [USA] Einstein Medical Center; [computing] electromagnetic compatibility; Energy Management Centre; Energy Management Company; [USA] Engineering Manpower Commission; environmental monitoring and compliance

EMCB earth-mounded concrete bunker

EMCC European Municipal Credit Community

EMCCC European Military Communications Coordinating Committee

EMCOF European Monetary Cooperation Fund

EMCS energy monitoring and control system

EME East Midlands Electricity

Emer. Emeritus

emer. emergency

EMet Engineer of Metallurgy

EMEU East Midlands Educational Union

EMF electromagnetic force; electromotive force; European Metalworkers' Federation; European Motel Federation

emf electromotive force

EMFI [USA] Energy and Mineral Field Institute

EMG [medicine] electromyogram; [medicine] electromyograph

EMI [USA] Earth Mechanics Institute; Electric and Musical Industries (Limited) (recording company); [computing] electromagnetic interference; European Monetary Institute

EMIC emergency maternity and infant care

EMK *elektromotorische Kraft* (German: electromotive force)

EML Environmental Measurement(s) Laboratory; Everyman's Library

EMLA [medicine] eutectic mixture of local anaesthetics (as in **EMLA cream**)

E Mn E Early Modern English

EMNRD Energy, Minerals and Natural Resources Department

e.m.o.s. earth's mean orbital speed

EMP ecological monitoring programme; electromagnetic pulse; electronic materials programme; environmental management (or monitoring) plan; environmental monitoring programme

Emp. Emperor; Empire; Empress

emp. [medicine] *emplastrum* (Latin: plaster); employed; employer; employment

emp. agcy employment agency

empld employed

EMR Eastern Mediterranean Region; electromagnetic radiation

EMRIC [USA] Educational Media Research Information Center

EMRS East Malling Research Station

EMS emergency management system; emergency medical service; energy management system; European Monetary System; [computing] expanded memory specification; [computing] expanded memory support

EMSA Electron Microscopy Society of America

EMSC [USA] Electrical Manufacturers' Standards Council

EMT [physics] effective-mass theory; emergency medical technician

EMTA Electro-Medical Trade Association

EMU electrical multiple unit; electromagnetic unit; European monetary union (in EU); [astronautics] extravehicular mobility unit

emu electromagnetic unit

EMV [accounting] expected monetary value

EMW energy from municipal waste

EN [meteorology] El Niño; *Emissora Nacional* (Portuguese: national broadcasting); [UK postcode] Enfield; English Nature (replacement for NCC); Enrolled Nurse; *Estrada Nacional* (Portuguese: national highway); Euro Norm (European standard); exceptions noted; extrapolation number; [vehicle registration] Manchester

En. Engineer; English

en. enemy

ENA Eastern News Agency (Bangladesh); Eastern North America; *École nationale d'administration* (French: national school of administration) (college for top civil servants); English Newspaper Association

ENAB Evening Newspaper Advertising Bureau

enam. enamel; enamelled

ENB English National Ballet; English National Board for Nursing, Midwifery and Health Visiting

ENC equivalent noise charge

enc. enclosed; enclosure

ENCA European Naval Communications Agency

Enc. Brit. Encyclopaedia Britannica

encl. enclosed; enclosure

ency. encyclopedia; encyclopedic; encyclopedism; encyclopedist

encyc. encyclopedia; encyclopedic

encycl. encyclopedia; encyclopedic

END European Nuclear Disarmament

ENDO Ethiopian National Democratic Organization

endow. endowment

endp. endpaper

ENDS Euratom Nuclear Documentation System

ENE east-northeast

ENEA European Nuclear Energy Agency

ENF European Nuclear Force

ENG [television] electronic news gathering; Enrolled Nurse (General) (formerly SEN)

Eng. England; English

eng. engine; engineer; engineering; engraved; engraver; engraving

EngD Doctor of Engineering

engg engineering

Eng. hn [music] English horn (= cor anglais)

engin. engineer; engineering

Engl. England; English

engr engineer; engraver

engr. engrave; engraved; engraving

EngScD Doctor of Engineering Science

EngTech Engineering Technician

ENIAC Electronic Numerical Integrator and Calculator (first electronic calculator)

ENIT *Ente Nazionale Industrie Turistiche* (Italian: National Tourist Authority)

enl. enlarge; enlarged; enlargement; enlisted

ENM Enrolled Nurse (Mental)

ENMH Enrolled Nurse (Mental Handicap)

ENO English National Opera

eno *enero* (Spanish: January)

ENP electronic number plate

ENR Energy and Natural Resources

ENS empty nest syndrome; European Nuclear Society

Ens. [music] Ensemble; Ensign

ens. [music] ensemble; en suite (in property or accommodation advertisement)

ENSA Entertainments National Service Association (in World War II)

ENSDF Evaluated Nuclear Structure Data File

ENSO [meteorology] El Niño southern oscillation

ENT [medicine] ear, nose and throat

Ent. [theatre] enter (stage direction)

ent. entertainment; entomological; entomology; entrance

entom. entomological; entomology

entomol. entomological; entomology

Ent. Sta. Hall entered at Stationers' Hall (registration of copyright pre-1924)

E-number code number of EU-recognized food additive

Env. Envoy

env. envelope; environment; environmental; environs

Env. Ext. Envoy Extraordinary

EO Eastern Orthodox (Church); education officer; [physics] electro-optic(al); emergency operation; employers' organization; Engineer Officer; entertainments officer; equal opportunities; executive officer; executive order; experimental officer; [vehicle registration] Preston

e.o. *ex officio* (Latin: by right of office)

EOA [USA] Essential Oil Association; examination, opinion and advice

EOARDC [USA] European Office of the Air Research and Development Command

EOB [computing] end of block; executive office building

EOC electron-optical camera; [USA] Emergency Operating Center; [USA] Emergency Operations Center; [physics] end of charge; end of cycle; Equal Opportunities Commission

Eoc [geology] Eocene

EOD [computing] end of data; [military] explosive ordnance demolition; [military] explosive ordnance disposal

e.o.d. entry on duty; every other day

EOE enemy-occupied Europe; equal opportunity employer; errors and omissions excepted; European Options Exchange

EOF [USA] Emergency Operating Facility; [USA] Emergency Operations Facility; [computing] end of file

EOG [medicine] electrooculogram

e.o.h.p. except otherwise herein provided

EOJ [computing] end of job

Eoka *Ethniki Organosis Kypriakou Agonos* (Greek: National Organization of the Cypriot Struggle)

EOL end of life

EOLM electro-optical light modulator

EOM Egyptian Order of Merit; [computing] end of message (on Internet); extractable organic material; extractable organic matter

e.o.m. [commerce] end of the month; every other month

EONR European Organization for Nuclear Research

e.o.o.e. [commerce] *erreur ou omission exceptée* (French: errors and omissions excepted)

EOP [microbiology] efficiency of plating; emergency operating procedure

EOPH Examined Officer of Public Health

EOQ [accounting] economic order quantity

EOQC European Organization for Quality Control

EOQL end of qualified life

EOR [astronautics] earth-orbit rendezvous; [computing] end of record; enhanced oil recovery

EORI [USA] Economic Opportunity Research Institute

EORTC European Organization for Research into the Treatment of Cancer

EOS [physics] equation of state; [computing] erasable optical storage; European Orthodontic Society

EOT [computing] end of tape; end of terrace (in property advertisement); [computing] end of transmission

e.o.t. enemy-occupied territory

EOTP European Organization for Trade Promotion

EP early picture; educational psychologist; [electronics] electrically conducting polymer; electroplate; electroplated; electrostatic precipitator; end point; environmental protection; [navigation] estimated position; European Parliament; expanded polystyrene; extended-play (record); extraction procedure; Extraordinary and Plenipotentiary; [civil aircraft marking] Iran; [vehicle registration] Swansea

Ep. *Episcopus* (Latin: Bishop); [Bible] Epistle

e.p. easy projection; *editio princeps* (Latin: first edition); electrically polarized; endpaper; engineering personnel; [chess] *en passant* (French: in passing); [navigation] estimated position; extreme pressure

EPA educational priority area; Emergency Powers Act; Employment Protection Act; energy-performance assessment; [USA] Environmental Protection Agency; European Productivity Agency

EPAA [USA] Emergency Petroleum Allocation Act

EPACCI Economic Planning and Advisory Council for the Construction Industries

EPAQ electronic parts of assessed quality

EPB equivalent pension benefit

EPC Economic and Planning Council; Educational Publishers' Council; evaporative pattern-casting (in foundry)

EPCA [USA] Energy Policy and Conservation Act; energy production and consumption account; European Petro-Chemical Association

EPCOT Experimental Prototype Community of Tomorrow (Florida)

EPD earliest practicable date

EPDA Emergency Powers Defence Act

EPDC [USA] Electric Power Development Company

EPEA Electrical Power Engineers' Association

EPF emulsified petroleum fuel; European Packaging Federation

EPFM elastic-plastic fracture mechanics

EPG [USA] Electronic Proving Ground; [medicine] electropalatogram; [medicine] electropalatology; Emergency Procedure Guideline(s); Eminent Persons Group

EPGS electric power generating system

Eph. [Bible] Ephesians

Ephes. [Bible] Ephesians

EPI echo planar imaging; electronic position indicator

EPIC Engineering and Production Information Council; European Prospective Investigation into Cancer

Epict. Epictetus (ancient Greek philosopher)

epid. epidemic

epil. epilogue

Epiph. Epiphany

EPIRB [navigation] emergency position indicator radio beacon

Epis. Episcopal; Episcopalian; [Bible] Epistle

Episc. Episcopal; Episcopalian

Epist. [Bible] Epistle

epit. epitaph; epitome

EPL exact power law

EPLD [computing] erasable programmable logic device

EPLF Eritrean People's Liberation Front

EPM electron-probe microanalysis; extract of particulate matter

EPMA electron-probe microanalysis

EPMI Esso Production Malaysia Incorporated

EPN elemental point number

EPNdB effective perceived noise decibels

EPNG El Paso Natural Gas Company

EPNS electroplated nickel silver; English Place-Name Society

EPO [medicine] erythropoietin

EPOC Eastern Pacific Oceanic Conference

Epoch End Physical Punishment of Children

EPOS [commerce] electronic point of sale (as in **EPOS system**)

EPP [physiology] endplate potential; [computing] enhanced parallel port; European People's Party; executive pension plan; [computing] extended parallel port

EPPO European and Mediterranean Plant Protection Organization

EPPT [computing] European printer performance test

EPPV electropneumatic proportional valve

EPR electron paramagnetic resonance; ethylene–propylene rubber

EPRDF Ethiopian People's Revolutionary Democratic Front

EPRI [USA] Electric Power Research Institute

EPROM [computing] erasable programmable read-only memory

EPS electrically positioned seats (in car

advertisement); electric(al) power system; [USA] Environmental Protection Service

eps earnings per share

EPSP [physiology] excitatory postsynaptic potential

EPSRC Engineering and Physical Sciences Research Council

EPSS electrical power supervision system

EPT [medicine] early pregnancy test; Environmental Protection Technology; ethylene–propylene terpolymer (synthetic rubber); excess profits tax

EPTA Expanded Programme of Technical Assistance (in UN)

Ep. tm [law] Epiphany term

EPU European Payments Union

Epus *Episcopus* (Latin: Bishop)

EPW earth-penetrator weapon; enemy prisoner of war

EQ educational quotient; [electronics] equalize; equipment qualification; [electronics] equivalence (as in **EQ gate**)

Eq. Equerry

eq. equal; equate; equation; equator; equatorial; equipment; equitable; equity; equivalent

EQA [commerce] European Quality Award

EQC external quality control

EQD Electrical Quality Assurance Directorate

EQDB equipment qualification data bank

EQI exhaust quality index

eqn equation

eqn. equine

eqpt equipment

Equ [astronomy] Equuleus

equil. equilibrium

EQUIP equipment usage information programme

equip. equipment

equiv. equivalent

ER [railways] Eastern Region; East Riding (of Yorkshire); *Eduardus Rex* (Latin: King Edward); efficiency report; *Elizabetha Regina* (Latin: Queen Elizabeth); [medicine] emergency room; engine room; [computing] entity relationship; evaporation residue; [civil aircraft marking] Moldova; [vehicle registration] Peterborough

Er [chemical element] erbium

er elder

.er Eritrea (in Internet address)

e.r. echo ranging; effectiveness report; electronic reconnaissance; emergency request; emergency rescue; established reliability; external resistance

ERA [baseball] earned run average; [USA] Economic Regulatory Administration; Education Reform Act; Electrical Research Association; electronic reading automation; Electronic Rentals Association; [USA] Emergency Relief Administration; engine-room artificer; [computing] entity relationship attribute; [USA] Equal Rights Amendment; European Ramblers' Association; Evangelical Radio Alliance

ERAB Energy Research Advisory Board

ERAMS Environmental Radiation Ambients Monitoring System

Eras. (Desiderius) Erasmus (Dutch humanist)

Erasmus European Community Action Scheme for the Mobility of University Students

ERB electric roller blind

ERBM extended-range ballistic missile

ERC Economic Research Council; Electronics Research Council; Employment Rehabilitation Centre; [medicine] endoscopic retrograde cholangiography; [USA] Energy Research Corporation

ERC&I Economic Reform Club and Institute

ERCB [USA] Energy Resources Conservation Board

ERCP [medicine] endoscopic retrograde cholangiopancreatography

ERCS emergency response computer system

ERD elastic recoil detection; Emergency Reserve Decoration; emergency return device; environmental radiation data; equivalent residual dose (of radiation); extrapolated response dose

ERDA [electronics] elastic recoil detection analysis; [Australia] Electrical and Radio Development Association; [USA] Energy Research and Development Administration

ERDAF [USA] Energy Research and Development in Agriculture and Food

ERDE Engineering Research and Development Establishment; Explosives

Research and Development Establishment

ERDF European Regional Development Fund

ERDIC Energy Research, Development and Information Centre

ERDL Engineering Research and Development Laboratory

ERDS emergency response data system

ERE *Ethniki Rizospastiki Enosis* (Greek: National Radical Union) (political party); extent of reaction effect

erec. erection

ERFA European Radio Frequency Agency

ERG electrical resistance gauge; [medicine] electroretinogram

ERGOM European Research Group on Management

ergon. ergonomic; ergonomics

ERI *Eduardus Rex et Imperator* (Latin: Edward King and Emperor)

Eri [astronomy] Eridanus

ERIC [USA] Educational Resources Information Center; energy rate input controller

ERIM Environmental Research Institute of Michigan

ERIS Emergency Response Information System; [astronautics] Exo-atmospheric Re-entry Vehicle Interceptor Subsystem

ERISA [USA] Employee Retirement Income Security Act

Erit. Eritrea

ERL Energy Research Laboratory

Erl. *Erläuterung* (German: explanatory note)

ERLL [computing] enhanced run length limited

ERM [finance] Exchange Rate Mechanism

erm. ermine

Ernie electronic random number indicator equipment (selecting winning premium bonds)

ERO European Regional Organization of the International Confederation of Free Trade Unions

EROM [computing] erasable read-only memory

EROPA Eastern Regional Organization for Public Administration

EROS earth resources observation satellite; [astronautics] experimental reflection orbital shot

ERP [medicine] endoscopic retrograde pancreatography; [commerce] enterprise resource planning; [biochemistry] enzyme-releasing peptide; European Recovery Programme

e.r.p. effective radiated power

ERPF [medicine] effective renal plasma flow

ERR energy release rate

erron. erroneous; erroneously

ERS earnings-related supplement; earth resources satellite; emergency radio service; emergency response system; engine repair section; Ergonomics Research Society; [USA] Experimental Research Society

ERT *Elliniki Radiophonia Tileorasis* (Greek: Hellenic National Radio and Television); excess retention tax

ERTA [USA] Economic Recovery and Tax Act

ERTS Earth Resources Technology Satellite; European Rapid Train System

ERU English Rugby Union

ERV [Bible] English Revised Version; [medicine] exercise radionuclide ventriculography

ERW enhanced radiation weapon

erw. *erweitert* (German: enlarged, extended)

erweit. *erweitert* (German: enlarged, extended)

ES [vehicle registration] Dundee; Econometric Society; Education Specialist; [chemistry] electronic structure; electrostatic; [international vehicle registration] El Salvador; [medicine] endoscopic sphincterotomy; [medicine] endsystole; [medicine] end-systolic; energy spectrum; engine-sized (paper); Entomological Society; [civil aircraft marking] Estonia; [mining] exploratory shaft

Es [chemical element] einsteinium

e/s en suite (in property or accommodation advertisement)

es. *esempio* (Italian: example)

.es Spain (in Internet address)

e.s. eldest son; electrical sounding; electric starting; [medicine] *enema saponis* (Latin: soap enema)

ESA Ecological Society of America; Educational Supply Association; electrostatic sector analyser; energy system analysis; Entomological Society of America; environmentally sensitive area; European Space Agency; Euthanasia Society of America

ESAAB [USA] Energy System Acquisition Advisory Board

ESAF enhanced structural adjustment facility (in IMF)

ESANZ Economic Society of Australia and New Zealand

ESAR electronically steerable array radar

ESB electrical stimulation of the brain; [USA] Electricity Supply Board; electric storage battery; Empire State Building; English Speaking Board; environmental specimen bank

ESBA English Schools' Badminton Association

ESBBA English Schools' Basket Ball Association

ESBTC [USA] European Space Battery Test Center

ESC Economic and Social Council (of UN); electric seat control (in car advertisement); electronic stills camera; electronic structural correlator; [USA] Energy Security Corporation; Energy Study Centre (Netherlands); English Stage Company; English Steel Corporation; Entomological Society of Canada; etched security code (in car advertisement); European Space Conference; [computing] extended core storage

Esc [computing] escape (key); [currency] escudo

esc. *escompte* (French: discount); escutcheon

ESCA [physical chemistry] electron spectroscopy for chemical analysis; English Schools' Cricket Association; English Schools' Cycling Association

ESCAP Economic and Social Commission for Asia and the Pacific (formerly ECAFE)

ESCB European System of Central Banks

ESCC [engineering] external stress corrosion cracking

ESCCD electrical short-circuit current decay

eschat. eschatology

ESCO Educational, Scientific and Cultural Organization (of UN)

ESCOM Electricity Supply Commission of South Africa

ESCR external standard channel ratio

ESD echo-sounding device; electromagnetic shower detector; [computing] electrostatic discharge; [USA] Environmental Sciences Division; Euratom Safeguards Directorate

Esd. [Bible] Esdras (books of Apocrypha)

Esda electrostatic deposition analysis; electrostatic document analysis

ESDAC European Space Data Centre

ESDI enhanced small-device interface

ESE east-southeast; engineers stores establishment

ESECA [USA] Energy Supply and Environmental Coordination Act

ESEF Electrotyping and Stereotyping Employers' Federation

ESES environmentally sound energy system

ESF European Science Foundation

ESG Education Support Grant; English Standard Gauge

ESH Environmental Safety and Health; equivalent standard hours; European Society of Haematology

ESI electricity supply industry; environment sensitivity index

ESITB Electricity Supply Industry Training Board

Esk. Eskimo

ESL English as a second language

e.s.l. expected significance level

ESLAB European Space Research Laboratory

ESMA Electrical Sign Manufacturers' Association

ESN educationally subnormal

esn. essential

ESNS educationally subnormal, serious

esntl essential

ESNZ Entomological Society of New Zealand

ESO Energy Services Operator; European Southern Observatory (Chile)

ESOC European Space Operations Centre

ESOL English for speakers of other languages

ESOMAR European Society for Opinion Surveys and Market Research

ESOP employee share-ownership plan; [USA] employee stock-option plan

ESOT employee share-ownership trust

ESP electric submersible pump(ing); [commerce] emotional selling proposition; English for special purposes; English for specific purposes; extrasensory perception

Esp. *Espagne* (French: Spain); *España* (Spanish: Spain); Esperanto

esp. especially; [music] *espressivo* (Italian: expressively)

espec. especially

espg. espionage

espr. [music] *espressivo* (Italian: expressively)

espress. [music] *espressivo* (Italian: expressively)

ESPRIT European strategic programme for research and development in information technology

Esq. Esquire

ESQA English Slate Quarries Association

esqo *esquerdo* (Portuguese: left)

Esqr. Esquire

ESR electric sunroof (in car advertisement); [physics] electron-spin resonance; [medicine] erythrocyte sedimentation rate

ESRC Economic and Social Research Council (formerly SSRC); Electricity Supply Research Council

ESRD [medicine] end-stage renal disease

ESRF [medicine] end-stage renal failure

ESRIN European Space Research Institute

ESRO European Space Research Organization (became part of ESA)

ESRS European Society for Rural Sociology

ESS energy storage system; evolutionarily stable strategy

Ess. Essex

ess. essence; [pharmacology] *essentia* (Latin: essence); essential

ESSA English Schools' Swimming Association; [USA] Environmental Science Services Administration

Esso Standard Oil (phonetic spelling of initials)

EST earliest start time; [USA, Canada] Eastern Standard Time; electric-shock treatment; electroshock therapy; [nuclear technology] ellipsoidal shell tokamak; [international vehicle registration] Estonia

Est. Established; Estonia; Estonian

est. establish; established; [law] estate; estimate; estimated; estimation; estimator; estuary

estab. establish; established; establishment

ESTEC European Space Technology Centre ·

estg estimating

Esth. [Bible] Esther

ESTI European Space Technology Institute

estn estimation

ESU electrostatic unit; English-Speaking Union

esu electrostatic unit

ESV [astronautics] earth satellite vehicle; [engineering] emergency shutdown valve; [medicine] end-systolic volume

ESWL [medicine] extracorporeal shockwave lithotripsy

ET [USA] Eastern Time; educational therapy; [international vehicle registration] (Arab Republic of) Egypt; [chemistry] electron transfer; [physics, chemistry] electron transition; [nuclear technology] elongated tokamak; [medicine] embryo transfer; emerging technology (in NATO); Employment Trainee; Employment Training (for unemployed); emptying time; English text; English translation; ephemeris time; [physics] equation of time; [civil aircraft marking] Ethiopia; [electronics] excitation transport; extraterrestrial; [vehicle registration] Sheffield

.et Ethiopia (in Internet address)

e.t. electric telegraph; engineering time; entertainment tax; exchange telegraph

ETA Entertainment Trades' Alliance; estimated time of arrival; European Teachers' Association; *Euzkadi ta Askatasuna* (Basque: Basque Nation and Liberty) (separatist organization)

Étab. *Établissement* (French: (business) establishment)

ETAC Education and Training Advisory Council

et al. *et alibi* (Latin: and elsewhere); *et alii* (Latin: and others)

ETB English Tourist Board

ETC Eastern Telegraph Company; European Translation Centre

etc. *et cetera* (Latin: and the other things)

ETCTA Electrical Trades Commercial Travellers' Association

ETD estimated time of departure; [telecommunications] extension trunk dialling

ETE estimated time en route; evacuation-time estimate; Experimental Tunnelling Establishment

ETF [banking] electronic transfer of funds

ETH [Switzerland] *Eidgenössische technische Hochschule* (German: Federal Institute of Technology); [international vehicle registration] Ethiopia

Eth. Ethiopia; Ethiopian; Ethiopic

eth. ether; ethical; ethics

ethnog. ethnographical; ethnography

ethnol. ethnological; ethnology

ETI estimated time of interception; extraterrestrial intelligence

e.t.i. elapsed time indicator

ETJC Engineering Trades Joint Council

e.t.k.m. every test known to man

ETMA English Timber Merchants' Association; European Television Magazine Association

ETO European Theatre of Operations (in World War II); European Transport Organization

e.t.o. estimated time off

ETOP [USA] Environmental Threat and Opportunity Profile

e.t.p. estimated turning (or turnaround) point

ETR [nuclear technology] engineering test reactor; estimated time of return; [nuclear technology] experimental test reactor; [nuclear technology] experimental thermonuclear reactor

Etr. Etruscan

ETS earth thermal storage; [USA] Educational Testing Service; [biochemistry] electron-transport system; estimated time of sailing; [US military] estimated time of separation (i.e. discharge); [medicine] exercise thallium scintigraphy; expiration of time of service

ETSA Electricity Trust of South Australia

et seq. *et sequens* (Latin: and the following); *et sequentia* (Latin: and those that follow)

et seqq. *et sequentia* (Latin: and those that follow)

ETSI European Telecommunications Standards Institute

e.t.s.p. entitled to severance pay

et sqq. *et sequentia* (Latin: and those that follow)

ETSU Energy Technology Support Unit

ETTA English Table Tennis Association

ETTU European Table Tennis Union

ETU Electrical Trades Union; experimental test unit

ETUC European Trade Union Confederation

ETUI European Trade Union Institute

et ux. *et uxor* (Latin: and wife)

ETV educational television; engine test vehicle

ety. etymological; etymologist; etymology

etym. etymological; etymologist; etymology

etymol. etymological; etymologist; etymology

EU [vehicle registration] Bristol; *Estados Unidos* (Portuguese or Spanish: United States); *États-Unis* (French: United States); European Union; Evangelical Union; [medicine] excretory urography; experimental unit

Eu [chemical element] europium

EUA *Estados Unidos da América* (Portuguese: United States of America); *Estados Unidos de América* (Spanish: United States of America); *États-Unis d'Amérique* (French: United States of America); [finance] European unit of account; [medicine] examination under anaesthesia

Euc. Euclid (ancient Greek mathematician)

Eucl. Euclid (ancient Greek mathematician)

EUCOM [US military] European Command

EUDISED European Documentation and Information Service for Education

EUFTT European Union of Film and Television Technicians

eugen. eugenics

EUI energy utilization index; energy utilization intensity

EUL Everyman's University Library

EUM *Estados Unidos Mexicanos* (Spanish: Mexico)

EUMETSAT European Meteorological Satellite System

EUP English Universities Press

euph. euphemism; euphemistic; euphemistically

EUR *Esposizione Universale di Roma* (Italian: Roman Universal Exhibition)

Eur. Europe; European

Euratom European Atomic Energy Authority (predecessor of EU)

Eureca [astronautics] European retrievable carrier

Eur. Ing. European Engineer (from the word for engineer in several European languages)

Eurip. Euripides (ancient Greek dramatist)

EURO European Regional Office

EUROCAE European Organization for Civil Aviation Electronics

EUROCEAN European Oceanographic Association

EUROCHEMIC European Company for the Chemical Processing of Irradiated Fuels

EUROCOM European Coal Merchants' Union

EUROM European Federation for Optics and Precision Mechanics

EURONET European data-transmission network

EUROP European Railway Wagon Pool

Europol European Police Office

EUROSPACE European Industrial Space Study Group

EUROTOX European Standing Committee for the Protection of Populations against the Risks of Chronic Toxicity

EUS Eastern United States

Eus. Eusebius of Caesarea (ecclesiastical historian)

Euseb. Eusebius of Caesarea (ecclesiastical historian)

EUV [physics] extreme ultraviolet

EUVE [astronomy] Extreme Ultraviolet Explorer

EUW European Union of Women

EV [vehicle registration] Chelmsford; electric vehicle; [Bible] English Version; [astronautics] entry vehicle; [medicine] equilibrium venography; [medicine] erythrocyte volume; [accounting] expected value; [image technology] exposure value

eV *eingetragener Verein* (German: registered society); electronvolt

ev. *evangelisch* (German: Protestant)

e.v. efficient vulcanization

EVA Electric Vehicle Association of Great Britain; Engineer Vice-Admiral; [chemistry] ethene and vinyl acetate; [astronautics] extravehicular activity

evac. evacuate; evacuated; evacuation

eval. evaluate; evaluated; evaluation

evan. evangelical; evangelist

evang. evangelical; evangelist

evap [short form] evaporated milk

evap. evaporate; evaporated; evaporation; evaporator

evce evidence

EVCS [astronautics] extravehicular communications system

EVFU [computing] electronic vertical format unit

evg evening

EVGA [computing] enhanced video graphics array

evid. evidence

evng evening

evol. evolution; evolutionary; evolutionist

EVR electronic video recording and reproduction

EVT Educational and Vocational Training

EVW European Voluntary Workers

evy every

EW [civil aircraft marking] Belarus; early warning; electric windows (in car advertisement); electronic warfare; [USA] enlisted woman; [vehicle registration] Peterborough

e.w. each way (in betting)

EWA [USA] Education Writers' Association

EWF Electrical Wholesalers' Federation; European Welding Federation

EWICS European Workshop for Industrial Computer Systems

EWL evaporative water loss

EWO educational welfare officer; essential work order; European Women's Orchestra

EWP emergency war plan

EWR early-warning radar

EWS emergency water supply; emergency welfare service

EWSF European Work Study Federation

EX [UK postcode] Exeter; [civil aircraft marking] Kyrgyzstan; [vehicle registration] Norwich

Ex. Exeter; [Bible] Exodus

ex. examination; examine; examined; examiner; example; excellent; except; excepted; exception; excess; exchange; exclude; excluding; exclusive; excursion; excursus (literary digression); execute; executed; executive; executor; exempt; exercise; export; express; extended; extension; extra; extract

exag. exaggerate; exaggerated; exaggeration

exam [short form] examination

exam. examine; examiner

examd examined

examg examining

examn examination

ex aq. [medicine] *ex aqua* (Latin: from water)

ex b. [finance] ex bonus (i.e. without bonus)

Exc. Excellency

exc. excellent; except; excepted; exception; exchange; excommunication; *excudit* (Latin: (he/she) engraved it); excursion

ex cap. [finance] ex capitalization (i.e. without capitalization)

excel. excellent

Exch. Exchequer

exch. exchange; exchequer

excl. exclamation; exclamatory; exclude; excluding; exclusive

exclam. exclamation; exclamatory

ex cp. [finance] ex coupon (i.e. without interest on coupon)

exd examined

ex div. [finance] ex dividend (i.e. without dividend)

exec. execute; execution; executive; executor

execx executrix

exempl. *exemplaire* (French: copy (of publication))

exes expenses

ex. g. *exempli gratia* (Latin: for example)

ex. gr. *exempli gratia* (Latin: for example)

exh. exhaust; exhibition

exhbn exhibition

exhib. exhibit; exhibition; exhibitioner; exhibitor

Ex-Im [USA] Export-Import Bank

Eximbank [USA] Export-Import Bank

ex int. [banking] ex interest (i.e. without interest)

ex lib. *ex libris* (Latin: from the books (of), from the library (of))

ex n. [stock exchange] ex new (of shares)

Exod. [Bible] Exodus

ex off. *ex officio* (Latin: by right of office)

Exon. *Exonia* (Latin: Exeter); *Exoniensis* (Latin: (Bishop) of Exeter)

exor executor

EXP Exchange of Persons Office (in UNESCO); [meteorology] expected

exp [mathematics] exponential

exp. expand; expansion; expedition; expense(s); experience; experiment; experimental; expiration; expire; expired; expiry; export; exportation; exported; exporter; exposed; express; expression; expurgated

ex p. [law] *ex parte* (Latin: on behalf of one party)

expdn expedition

exper. experimental

expl. explain; explanation; explanatory; explosion; explosive

exploit. exploitation

expn exposition

exp. o. experimental order

expr. express; expression

expt experiment

exptl experimental

exptr exporter

expurg. expurgate; expurgated

exr executor

exrx executrix

exs expenses

ext. extend; extension; extent; exterior; external; externally; extinct; extra; extract; extraction; [medicine] *extractum* (Latin: extract); extreme

EXTEL Exchange Telegraph (news agency)

exten. extension

EXTEND Exercise Training for the Elderly and/or Disabled

ext. liq. *extractum liquidum* (Latin: liquid extract)

extn extension

extr. extraordinary

extrad. extradition

EXW ex works (i.e. from the factory)

exx examples; executrix

EY [vehicle registration] Bangor; [civil aircraft marking] Tajikistan

EYC European Youth Campaign

EYR East Yorkshire Regiment

EZ [vehicle registration] Belfast; [US informal] easy; [civil aircraft marking] Turkmenistan

Ez. [Bible] Ezra
Ezek. [Bible] Ezekiel
Ezr. [Bible] Ezra

F

F Fahrenheit; fail; false; family; farad; fast (on clock or watch regulator); Father; fathom; [fishing port] Faversham; February; Federation; Fellow; female; [grammar] feminine; *ferrovia* (Italian: railway); [medicine] *fiat* (Latin: let it be made); fiction; [USA] fighter (aircraft) (as in **F-111**); [genetics] filial generation; [horseracing] filly; finance; fine; fleet; [chemical element] fluorine; [photography] f-number (as in **F16**); Fokker (aircraft); folio; foolscap; [sports] Formula (as in **F1**); [sports] foul; [currency] franc; [civil aircraft marking] France; [international vehicle registration] France; *Frauen* (German: women); *freddo* (Italian: cold); French; [ecclesiastical] *Frère* (French: Brother); Friday; *frio* (Portuguese or Spanish: cold); *froid* (French: cold); [music] note of scale

F [physics] Faraday constant; [physics] force

f [music] fa(h) (in tonic sol-fa); [numismatics] face value; femto- (indicates 10^{-15}, as in **fm** = femtometre); [photography] f-number (as in **f4**); [meteorology] fog; foreign

f [physics] focal length; [music] *forte* (Italian: loudly); [physics] frequency; [physical chemistry] fugacity; [mathematics] function; [biochemistry] furanose

f. facing; fair; farthing (quarter of old penny); father; fathom; feet; female; [grammar] feminine; [horseracing] filly; fine; [horseracing] firm; flat; fluid; folio; following (page); foot; for; forecastle; [botany] form (in classification of plants); formula; [sports] foul; founded; [currency] franc; freehold; from; front; fuck; furlong; furlough; furnished (in accommodation advertisement); [currency] guilder (from alternative name florin)

FA [statistics] factor analysis; Factory Act; Faculty of Actuaries; family allowance; [slang] Fanny Adams (i.e. nothing); farm adviser; [chemistry] fatty acid; field activities; field allowance; field ambulance; field artillery; filtered air; Finance Act; financial adviser; fine art; [immunology] fluorescent antibody; [building] fly ash; [biochemistry] folic acid; [biochemistry] folinic acid; Football Association; freight agent; [slang] fuck all (i.e. nothing); [building] fuel ash; [nuclear technology] fuel assembly; [metallurgy] furnace annealing; [vehicle registration] Stoke-on-Trent

Fa *Firma* (German: firm, business); Florida
Fa. Faeroes

fa *factura* (Spanish: invoice)

f.a. [slang] Fanny Adams (i.e. nothing); fire alarm; first aid; first attack; [commerce] free alongside; [optics] free aperture; freight agent; friendly aircraft; [slang] fuck all (i.e. nothing); fuel–air (ratio)

FAA [USA] Federal Aviation Administration; Fellow of the Australian Academy (of Science); Film Artistes' Association; Fleet Air Arm; [biochemistry] free amino acid; [insurance] free of all averages

FAAAS Fellow of the American Academy of Arts and Sciences; Fellow of the American Association for the Advancement of Science

FAAC Food Additives and Contaminants Committee

FAARM Fellow of the American Academy of Reproductive Medicine

FAAV Fellow of the Central Association of Agricultural Valuers

FAB [physics, electronics] fast-atom beam; [physics, electronics] fast-atom bombardment; Flour Advisory Bureau; French–American–British; fuel-air bomb

fab [short form] fabulous

fab. fabric; fabricate; [commerce] *fabrication* (French: make, manufacture)

f.a.b. first aid box

f. à b. [commerce] *franco à bord* (French: free on board)

fabbr. *fabbrica* (Italian: factory)

FABMDS [USA] field army ballistic missile defense system

fabr. fabricate; fabrication

Fab. Soc. Fabian Society

fabx fire alarm box

FAC Federation of Agricultural Cooperatives; [military] forward air controller

Fac. Faculty

fac. façade; facial; facility; facsimile; factor; factory; faculty

f.a.c. fast as can; [insurance] *franc d'avarie commune* (French: free of general average)

FACC [USA] Ford Aerospace and Communication Corporation

FACCP Fellow of the American College of Chest Physicians

FACD Fellow of the American College of Dentistry

FACE Fellow of the Australian College of Education; field artillery computer equipment; Fight Against Cuts in Education; [USA] Financial Advertising Code of Ethics

FACEM Federation of the Associations of Colliery Equipment Manufacturers

FACerS Fellow of the American Ceramic Society

facet. facetious

FACG Fellow of the American College of Gastroenterology

facil. facility

FACMTA [USA] Federal Advisory Council on Medical Training

FACOG Fellow of the American College of Obstetricians and Gynecologists

FACOM Fellow of the Australian College of Occupational Medicine

FACP Fellow of the American College of Physicians; Fellow of the American College of Radiology

FACRM Fellow of the Australian College of Reproductive Medicine

FACS Fellow of the American College of Surgeons; [immunology] fluorescence-activated cell sorter

facs. facsimile

facsim. facsimile

FACT Federation Against Copyright Theft; fully automatic compiler-translator

fact. *factura* (Spanish: invoice)

facta *factura* (Spanish: invoice)

FAD [biochemistry] flavin adenine dinucleotide

f.a.d. free air delivered

FADEC [computing] fully authorized digital engine control

FADO Fellow of the Association of Dispensing Opticians

FAE [military] fuel-air explosive(s)

Faer. Faeroes

FAGO Fellowship in Australia in Obstetrics and Gynaecology

FAGS Federation of Astronomical and Geophysical Services; Fellow of the American Geographical Society

Fah. Fahrenheit

Fahr. Fahrenheit

FAI *Fédération aéronautique internationale* (French: International Aeronautical Federation); Football Association of Ireland; fresh-air inlet

FAIA Fellow of the American Institute of Architects; Fellow of the Association of International Accountants; Fellow of the Australian Institute of Advertising

FAIAA Fellow of the American Institute of Aeronautics and Astronautics

FAIAS Fellow of the Australian Institute of Agricultural Science

FAIB Fellow of the Australian Institute of Builders

FAIC Fellow of the American Institute of Chemists

FAIE Fellow of the Australian Institute of Energy

FAII Fellow of the Australian Insurance Institute

FAIM Fellow of the Australian Institute of Management

FAK [shipping] freights all kinds

Fak. *Faktura* (German: invoice)

Falk. I Falkland Islands

Falk. Is. Falkland Islands

FALN *Fuerzas Armadas de Liberación Nacional* (Spanish: Armed Forces of National Liberation) (in Puerto Rico)

FAM Free and Accepted Masons

fam. familiar; family

FAMA Fellow of the American Medical Association; Fellow of the Australian Medical Association; Foundation for Mutual Assistance in Africa

FAMEME Fellow of the Association of Mining Electrical and Mechanical Engineers

FAmNucSoc Fellow of the American Nuclear Society

FAMS Fellow of the Ancient Monuments Society; Fellow of the Indian Academy of Medical Sciences

f&a fore and aft

F&AP [insurance] fire and allied perils

F&C full and change (tides)

F&D freight and demurrage

f&d fill and drain; freight and demurrage

f&f fixtures and fittings

F&Gs [bookbinding] folded and gathered pages

F&M [veterinary science] foot and mouth (disease)

F&T [insurance] fire and theft

FANY First Aid Nursing Yeomanry

FAO Fleet Accountant Officer; Food and Agriculture Organization (of the United Nations)

f.a.o. finish all over; for the attention of

FAP [USA] Family Assistance Program; fixed action pattern (in ethology); *Força Aérea Portuguesa* (Portuguese: Portuguese Air Force); [insurance] *franc d'avarie particulière* (French: free of particular average)

FAPA Fellow of the American Psychiatric Association; Fellow of the American Psychological Association

FAPHA Fellow of the American Public Health Association

FAQ [commerce] free alongside quay; [computing] frequently asked question (used on Internet)

f.a.q. [commerce] fair average quality; [commerce] free alongside quay

f.a.q.s. [commerce] fair average quality of season

FAR false alarm rate; [USA] Federal Aviation Regulation(s); [insurance] free (of claim) for accident reported; front arm rests (in car advertisement)

far. farriery; farthing (quarter of old penny)

FArborA Fellow of the Arboricultural Association

FARE Federation of Alcoholic Rehabilitation Establishments

FARELF Far East Land Forces

FAS Faculty of Architects and Surveyors; Federation of American Scientists; Fellow of the Anthropological Society; Fellow of the Antiquarian Society; [medicine] fetal alcohol syndrome; [commerce] free alongside ship

f.a.s. firsts and seconds; [commerce] free alongside ship

FASA Fellow of the Australian Society of Accountants

FASB [USA] Financial Accounting Standards Board

FASc Fellow of the Indian Academy of Sciences

fasc. [anatomy] fascicle (bundle of fibres); fascicule (instalment of printed work)

FASCE Fellow of the American Society of Civil Engineers

FASE Fellow of the Antiquarian Society, Edinburgh

FASEB Federation of American Societies for Experimental Biology

FASI Fellow of the Architects' and Surveyors' Institute

FASS Federation of the Associations of Specialists and Subcontractors

FAST factor analysis system; fast automatic shuttle transfer; Federation Against Software Theft; first atomic ship transport; forecasting and assessment in science and technology (in EU)

fastnr fastener

FAT [computing] file allocation table

fath. fathom

FATIS Food and Agriculture Technical Information Service (of OEEC)

FAU Friends' Ambulance Unit

FAusIMM Fellow of the Australasian Institute of Mining and Metallurgy

fav. favour; favourite

FAVO Fleet Aviation Officer

FAWA Federation of Asian Women's Associations

FAX fuel-air explosion

fax [short form] facsimile

FB [vehicle registration] Bristol; Fenian Brotherhood; film badge (for radiation protection); fire brigade; fisheries board; fishery board; [railways] flat bottom;

flying boat; [medicine] foreign body; Forth Bridge; Free Baptist; full board (in accommodation advertisement)

F-B full-bore

f.b. flat bar; fog bell; freight bill; full board (in accommodation advertisement); [sports] fullback

FBA Farm Buildings Association; [USA] Federal Bar Association; Federation of British Artists; Federation of British Astrologers; Fellow of the British Academy; fluorescent brightening agent (in detergent); Freshwater Biological Association

FBAA Fellow of the British Association of Accountants and Auditors

f'ball football

f.b.c. [insurance] fallen building clause

FBCM Federation of British Carpet Manufacturers

FBCO Fellow of the British College of Optometrists (or Ophthalmic Opticians)

FBCS Fellow of the British Computer Society

f.b.c.w. [insurance] fallen building clause waiver

fbd freeboard

FBEA Fellow of the British Esperanto Association

FBEC(S) Fellow of the Business Education Council (Scotland)

FBFM Federation of British Film Makers

FBH fire brigade hydrant

FBHI Fellow of the British Horological Institute

FBHS Fellow of the British Horse Society

FBHTM Federation of British Hand Tool Manufacturers

FBI [USA] Federal Bureau of Investigation; Federation of British Industries

FBIBA Fellow of the British Insurance Brokers' Association

FBIM Fellow of the British Institute of Management

FBINZ Fellow of the Bankers' Institute of New Zealand

FBIPP Fellow of the British Institute of Professional Photography

FBIS Fellow of the British Interplanetary Society

FBL [aeronautics] fly-by-light (aircraft control using optical fibres)

FBM fleet ballistic missile

FBMA Food and Beverage Managers' Association

f.b.o. for the benefit of

FBOA Fellow of the British Optical Association

FBOU Fellow of the British Ornithologists' Union

FBP [chemistry] final boiling point; [biochemistry] folate-binding protein

FBPS Fellow of the British Phrenological Society

FBPsS Fellow of the British Psychological Society

FBR [nuclear technology] fast breeder reactor

fbr. fibre

FBRAM Federation of British Rubber and Allied Manufacturers

fbro *febrero* (Spanish: February)

FBS Fellow of the Botanical Society; [medicine] fetal bovine serum; [military] forward-based system

FBSC Fellow of the British Society of Commerce

FBSE Fellow of the Botanical Society, Edinburgh

FBSM Fellow of the Birmingham School of Music

FBSS [medicine] failed back-surgery syndrome

FBT *Fédération des bourses du travail* (French: Federation of Labour Exchanges) (French trade union); fringe benefit tax

FBU Fire Brigades Union

FBu [currency] Burundi franc

FBW [aeronautics] fly-by-wire (aircraft control using electronic circuits)

f.b.y. future budget year

FC [Australia] Federal Cabinet; [Freemasonry] fellow craft; fencing club; *ferrocarril* (Spanish: railway); *fidei commissum* (Latin: bequeathed in trust); *fieri curavit* (Latin: the donor directed this to be done) (on monuments); fifth column; Fighter Command; fire cock; fire control; Fishmongers' Company; football club; Forestry Commission; [medicine] free cholesterol; Free Church; fuel cell; [medicine] full course (of treatment); [meteorology] funnel cloud; [vehicle registration] Oxford

f.c. [baseball] fielder's choice; filing

cabinet; *fin courant* (French: at the end of this month); fixed charge; [printing] follow copy; for cash

FCA [USA] Farm Credit Administration; Federation of Canadian Artists; Fellow of the Institute of Chartered Accountants

FCAATSI [Australia] Federal Council for the Advancement of Aborigines and Torres Strait Islanders

FC-AL [computing] fibre channel arbitrated loop

FCAnaes Fellow of the College of Anaesthetists

fcap.foolscap

FCAR [insurance] free of claim for accident reported

FCASI Fellow of the Canadian Aeronautics and Space Institute

FCB [computing] file control block

FCBA Federal Communications Bar Association; Fellow of the Canadian Bankers' Association

FCBSI Fellow of the Chartered Building Societies Institute

FCC [USA] Federal Communications Commission; Federal Council of Churches; first-class certificate

FCCA Fellow of the Chartered Association of Certified Accountants

FCCEA Fellow of the Commonwealth Council for Educational Administration

FCCEd Fellow of the College of Craft Education

FCCS Fellow of the Corporation of Secretaries (formerly Fellow of the Corporation of Certified Secretaries)

FCCSET [USA] Federal Coordinating Council on Science, Engineering and Technology

FCCT Fellow of the Canadian College of Teachers

FCD First Chief Directorate (of KGB)

FCDA [USA] Federal Civil Defense Administration

FCEC Federation of Civil Engineering Contractors

FCFC Free Church Federal Council

FCFI Fellow of the Clothing and Footwear Institute

fcg facing

FCGB Forestry Commission of Great Britain

FCGI Fellow of the City and Guilds (of London) Institute

FCH full central heating (in property advertisement)

FChS Fellow of the Society of Chiropodists

FCI *Fédération cynologique internationale* (French: International Federation of Kennel Clubs); Fellow of the Institute of Commerce

FCIA Fellow of the Corporation of Insurance Agents; Foreign Credit Insurance Association

FCIArb Fellow of the Chartered Institute of Arbitrators

FCIB Fellow of the Chartered Institute of Bankers; Fellow of the Corporation of Insurance Brokers

FCIBSE Fellow of the Chartered Institution of Building Services Engineers

FCIC [USA] Federal Crop Insurance Corporation; Fellow of the Chemical Institute of Canada

FCII Fellow of the Chartered Insurance Institute

FCILA Fellow of the Chartered Institute of Loss Adjusters

FCIM Fellow of the Chartered Institute of Marketing

FCIOB Fellow of the Chartered Institute of Building

FCIPA Fellow of the Chartered Institute of Patent Agents

FCIPS Fellow of the Chartered Institute of Purchasing and Supply

FCIS Fellow of the Institute of Chartered Secretaries and Administrators (formerly Fellow of the Chartered Institute of Secretaries)

FCIT Fellow of the Chartered Institute of Transport; Four Countries International Tournament (in basketball)

FCIV Fellow of the Commonwealth Institute of Valuers

FCMA Fellow of the Chartered Institute of Management Accountants

FCMS Fellow of the College of Medicine and Surgery

FCMSA Fellow of the College of Medicine of South Africa

FCNA Fellow of the College of Nursing, Australia

fcng facing

FCO Farmers' Central Organization; fire-control officer; Foreign and Commonwealth Office

fco [commerce] *franco* (French: free of charge)

f. co. [printing] fair copy

FCOG(SA) Fellow of the South African College of Obstetrics and Gynaecology

FCollP Fellow of the College of Preceptors

FCOphth Fellow of the College of Ophthalmologists

FCOT Fellow of the College of Occupational Therapists

FCP [engineering] fatigue-crack propagation; Fellow of the College of Clinical Pharmacology; Fellow of the College of Preceptors

fcp foolscap

FCPA Fellow of the Canadian Psychological Association; [USA] Foreign Corrupt Practices Act

FCPO Fleet Chief Petty Officer

FCPS Fellow of the College of Physicians and Surgeons

FCS Federation of Conservative Students; [medicine] fetal calf serum

fcs francs

f.c.s. [insurance] warranted free of capture, seizure, arrest, detainment and the consequences thereof

FCSA Fellow of the Institute of Chartered Secretaries and Administrators

FCSD Fellow of the Chartered Society of Designers

FCSP Fellow of the Chartered Society of Physiotherapy

f.c.s.r.c.c. [insurance] warranted free of capture, seizure, arrest, detainment and the consequences thereof, and damage caused by riots and civil commotions

FCST [USA] Federal Council for Science and Technology; Fellow of the College of Speech Therapists

FCT [Australia] Federal Capital Territory; Fellow of the Association of Corporate Treasurers

FCTB Fellow of the College of Teachers of the Blind

FCTU Federation of Associations of Catholic Trade Unionists

fcty factory

FCU fighter control unit

FD [vehicle registration] Dudley; *Fidei Defensor* (Latin: Defender of the Faith); financial director; [computing] finite difference; fire department; fleet duties; [fishing port] Fleetwood; [medicine] folate deficiency; free delivery; Free Democrat

fd field; fiord; ford; forward; found; founded; fund

f.d. flight deck; focal distance; free delivery; free discharge; free dispatch

FDA First Division Association (former name of AFDCS); [USA] Food and Drug Administration

FD&C [USA] Food, Drug and Color Regulations

FDC [USA] Fire Detection Center; [philately] first-day cover; [numismatics] *fleur de coin* (French: mint condition)

FDDI [computing] fibre distributed data interface

FDF Food and Drink Federation

fdg funding

FDHO Factory Department, Home Office

FDI *Fédération dentaire internationale* (French: International Dental Federation)

FDIC [USA] Federal Deposit Insurance Corporation; Food and Drink Industries Council

FDIF *Fédération démocratique internationale des femmes* (French: Women's International Democratic Federation)

FDM [computing] finite-difference method; [telecommunications] frequency-division multiplexing

FDO Fleet Dental Officer; [taxation] for declaration (purposes) only

FDP *Freie Demokratische Partei* (German: Free Democratic Party)

FDR Franklin Delano Roosevelt (US president); *Freie Demokratische Republik* (German: Free Democratic Republic, the former West Germany)

fdr founder

fdry foundry

FDS Fellow in Dental Surgery; [aeronautics] flight-director system

FDSRCPSGlas Fellow in Dental Surgery of the Royal College of Physicians and Surgeons of Glasgow

FDSRCS Fellow in Dental Surgery of the Royal College of Surgeons (of England)

FDSRCSE Fellow in Dental Surgery of the Royal College of Surgeons of Edinburgh

FE Far East; [fishing port] Folkestone; foreign editor; further education; [vehicle registration] Lincoln

Fe [chemical element] iron (from Latin *ferrum*)

f.e. first edition; for example

FEA [USA] Federal Energy Administration; [USA] Federal Executive Association; *Fédération internationale pour l'éducation artistique* (French: International Federation for Art Education); [mathematics] finite-element analysis

FEAF Far East Air Force

FEANI *Fédération européenne des associations nationales d'ingénieurs* (French: European Federation of National Associations of Engineers)

FEB [USA] Fair Employment Board; functional electronic block

Feb. February

febb. *febbraio* (Italian: February)

Febr. *Februar* (German: February)

FEBS Federation of European Biochemical Societies

Feby February

FEC [USA] Federal Election(s) Commission; First Edition Club; *Fondation européenne de la culture* (French: European Cultural Foundation)

fec. *fecit* (Latin: (he/she) made it)

FECB Foreign Exchange Control Board

FECDBA Foreign Exchange and Currency Deposit Brokers' Association

FECI Fellow of the Institute of Employment Consultants

FED Federal Reserve System

Fed. Federal; Federalist; Federated; Federation

fed. federal; federated

FEDC Federation of Engineering Design Consultants

FedEx [trademark] Federal Express

FEER [banking] fundamental equilibrium exchange rate

FEF Far East Fleet

FEI *Fédération équestre internationale* (French: International Equestrian Federation); [USA] Financial Executive Institute

FEIDCT Fellow of the Educational Institute of Design Craft and Technology

FEIS Fellow of the Educational Institute of Scotland

FEL free-electron laser

FELF Far East Land Forces

Fell. Fellow

FeLV [microbiology] feline leukaemia virus

FEM [physics] field-emission microscope (or microscopy); [mathematics] finite-element method

fem. female; [grammar] feminine

f. ém. *force électromotrice* (French: electromotive force, emf)

FEMA [USA] Federal Emergency Management Agency

fenc. fencing

FEng Fellow of the Fellowship of Engineering; Fellow of the Royal Academy of Engineering

FENSA Film Entertainments National Service Association

FEO Fleet Engineer Officer

FEOGA *Fonds européen d'orientation et de garantie agric019turel* (French: European Agricultural Guidance and Guarantee Fund) (in EU)

FEP fluorinated ethene propene (plastic)

FEPA [USA] Fair Employment Practices Act

FEPC [USA] Fair Employment Practices Committee

FEPEM Federation of European Petroleum Equipment Manufacturers

Fer. Fermanagh

FERA [USA] Federal Emergency Relief Administration

FERC [USA] Federal Energy Regulatory Commission

FERDU Further Education Review and Development Unit

Ferm. Fermanagh

ferr. *ferrovia* (Italian: railway)

ferv. [pharmacology] *fervens* (Latin: boiling)

FES Federation of Engineering Societies; Fellow of the Entomological Society; Fellow of the Ethnological Society; F(rederick) E(dwin) Smith, Earl of Birkenhead (British statesman); [fencing] foil, épée and sabre

Fest. Festival

FET [USA] federal estate tax; [USA] federal excise tax; field-effect transistor; fossil-energy technology

FEU Further Education Unit

feud. feudal; feudalism

FEV [medicine] forced expiratory volume

fév. *février* (French: February)

FEX [US navy] fleet exercise

FF [vehicle registration] Bangor; *Felicissimi Fratres* (Latin: Most Fortunate Brothers); Fellows; *Fianna Fáil* (Gaelic: Warriors of Ireland) (Irish political party); [military] field force; fixtures and fittings (in property advertisement); [USA] Ford Foundation; [currency] (French) franc; [military] frontier force; fully fitted (in property advertisement); fully furnished (in accommodation advertisement)

ff [music] *fortissimo* (Italian: very loudly)

f/f fully fitted (in property advertisement); fully furnished (in accommodation advertisement)

ff. *fecerunt* (Latin: (they) made it); folios; following (pages or lines); forms

f.f. factory fitted; fixed focus; fully fashioned

FFA Fellow of the Faculty of Actuaries; Fellow of the Institute of Financial Accountants; [biochemistry] free fatty acid; Future Farmers of America

f.f.a. free foreign agency; [commerce] free from alongside (ship)

FFARACS Fellow of the Faculty of Anaesthetists of the Royal Australasian College of Surgeons

FFARCS Fellow of the Faculty of Anaesthetists of the Royal College of Surgeons (of England)

FFARCSI Fellow of the Faculty of Anaesthetists of the Royal College of Surgeons in Ireland

FFAS Fellow of the Faculty of Architects and Surveyors

FFB Fellow of the Faculty of Building

FFC Foreign Funds Control

FFCM Fellow of the Faculty of Community Medicine

FFCMI Fellow of the Faculty of Community Medicine of Ireland

FFD Fellow of the Faculty of Dental Surgeons

FFDRCSI Fellow of the Faculty of Dentistry of the Royal College of Surgeons in Ireland

FFF Free French Forces

fff [music] *fortississimo* (Italian: as loudly as possible)

FFHC Freedom from Hunger Campaign

FFHom Fellow of the Faculty of Homoeopathy

FFI Fellow of the Faculty of Insurance; Finance for Industry; free from infection; French Forces of the Interior

FFJ Franciscan Familiar of Saint Joseph

FFL *Forces françaises libres* (French: Free French Forces)

ffly faithfully

FFOM Fellow of the Faculty of Occupational Medicine

FFPath Fellow of the Faculty of Pathologists

FFPHM Fellow of the Faculty of Public Health Medicine

FFPM Fellow of the Faculty of Pharmaceutical Medicine

FFPS Fauna and Flora Preservation Society; Fellow of the Faculty of Physicians and Surgeons

FFR Fellow of the Faculty of Radiologists

FFr [currency] French franc

Ffr [currency] French franc

FFRR full-frequency range recording

FFS [Algeria] *Front des Forces Socialistes* (French: Socialist Forces Front)

FFSS full-frequency stereophonic sound

FFT [computing] fast Fourier transform; [computing] final form text

f/furn fully furnished (in accommodation advertisement)

FFV [USA] First Families of Virginia

FFWM free-floating wave meter

FFY Fife and Forfar Yeomanry

ffy faithfully

FG [vehicle registration] Brighton; Federal Government; *Fine Gael* (Gaelic: Tribe of the Gaels) (Irish political party); fire guard; [engineering] flue gas; [meteorology] fog; foot guards; *frais généraux* (French: overheads); full gilt

fg fog

f.g. [sports] field goal; fine grain; [commerce] fully good

FGA Fellow of the Gemmological Association; [insurance] free of general average

FGCH full gas central heating (in property advertisement)

FGCM field general court martial

FGDS *Fédération de la gauche démocrate et*

socialiste (French: Federation of the Democratic and Socialist Left)

f.g.f. [commerce] fully good, fair

FGI *Fédération graphique internationale* (French: International Graphical Federation); Fellow of the Institute of Certificated Grocers

Fgn Foreign

FGO Fleet Gunnery Officer

Fg Off. Flying Officer

FGS Fellow of the Geological Society

FGSM Fellow of the Guildhall School of Music (and Drama)

FGT [USA] federal gift tax

fgt freight

FGTB *Fédération générale du travail de Belgique* (French: Belgian General Federation of Labour)

FH [fishing port] Falmouth; [medicine] family history; field hospital; fire hydrant; fly half (in rugby); [medicine] fetal heart; [vehicle registration] Gloucester

F/H freehold (in property advertisement)

f.h. [medicine] *fiat haustus* (Latin: let a draught be made); foghorn; forehatch; forward hatch

FHA [USA] Farmers' Home Administration; [USA] Federal Housing Administration; Finance Houses Association

FHAS Fellow of the Highland and Agricultural Society of Scotland

FHB [informal] family hold back

FHCIMA Fellow of the Hotel Catering and Institutional Management Association

FHH [medicine] fetal heart heard

FHI *Fédération haltérophile internationale* (French: International Weightlifting Federation)

FHLB [USA] Federal Home Loan Bank

FHLBA [USA] Federal Home Loan Bank Administration

FHLBB [USA] Federal Home Loan Bank Board

fhld freehold (in property advertisement)

FHLMC [USA] Federal Home Loan Mortgage Corporation

FHM *For Him Magazine*

FHNH [medicine] fetal heart not heard

f/hold freehold (in property advertisement)

fhp friction horsepower

FHR [Australia] Federal House of Representatives; [medicine] fetal heart rate

FHS Fellow of the Heraldry Society

FHSA Family Health Services Authority

FHSM Fellow of the Institute of Health Services Management

FHWA [USA] Federal Highway Administration

FI Faeroe Islands; Falkland Islands; Fiji Islands; fire insurance; [engineering] flow injection

.fi Finland (in Internet address)

f.i. for instance; [commerce] free in

FIA [USA] Federal Insurance Administration; *Fédération internationale de l'automobile* (French: International Automobile Federation); Fellow of the Institute of Actuaries; Fitness Industry Association; [commerce] full interest admitted

FIAA *Fédération internationale athlétique d'amateur* (French: International Amateur Athletic Federation)

FIAA&S Fellow of the Incorporated Association of Architects and Surveyors

FIAAS Fellow of the Institute of Australian Agricultural Science

FIAB *Fédération internationale des associations de bibliothécaires* (French: International Federation of Library Associations and Institutions); Fellow of the International Association of Bookkeepers

FIAF *Fédération internationale des archives du film* (French: International Federation of Film Archives)

FIAgrE Fellow of the Institution of Agricultural Engineers

FIAI *Fédération internationale des associations d'instituteurs* (French: International Federation of Teachers' Associations); Fellow of the Institute of Industrial and Commercial Accountants

FIAJ *Fédération internationale des auberges de la jeunesse* (French: International Youth Hostel Federation)

FIAL Fellow of the International Institute of Arts and Letters

FIAM Fellow of the Institute of Administrative Management; Fellow of the International Academy of Management

FIAP *Fédération internationale de l'art photographique* (French: International Federation of Photographic Art); Fellow of the Institution of Analysts and Programmers

FIAPF *Fédération internationale des associ-*

ations de producteurs de films (French: International Federation of Film Producers' Associations)

FIAS [USA] Fellow of the Institute of the Aerospace Sciences

FIASc Fellow of the Indian Academy of Sciences

Fiat *Fabbrica Italiana Automobili Torino* (Italian car manufacturer)

fib. [anatomy] fibula

f.i.b. free into barge; free into bond; free into bunker

FIBA *Fédération internationale de basketball amateur* (French: International Amateur Basketball Federation); Fellow of the Institute of Business Administration (Australia)

FIBD Fellow of the Institute of British Decorators

FIBiol Fellow of the Institute of Biology

FIBOR [finance] Frankfurt Inter-Bank Offered Rate

FIBOT Fair Isle Bird Observatory Trust

FIBP Fellow of the Institute of British Photographers

FIBScot Fellow of the Institute of Bankers in Scotland

FIBST Fellow of the Institute of British Surgical Technicians

FIC Falkland Islands Company; Fellow of Imperial College (London); Fellow of the Institute of Chemistry; frequency interference control

fic. fiction; fictional; fictitious

FICA [USA] Federal Insurance Contributions Act; Fellow of the Commonwealth Institute of Accountants; Food Industries Credit Association

FICAI Fellow of the Institute of Chartered Accountants in Ireland

FICC *Fédération internationale de camping et de caravanning* (French: International Federation of Camping and Caravanning); *Fédération internationale des ciné-clubs* (French: International Federation of Film Societies)

FICCI Federation of Indian Chambers of Commerce and Industry

FICD Fellow of the Indian College of Dentists; Fellow of the Institute of Civil Defence

FICE Fellow of the Institution of Civil Engineers

FICFor Fellow of the Institute of Chartered Foresters

FIChemE Fellow of the Institution of Chemical Engineers

FICI Fellow of the Institute of Chemistry in Ireland

FICM Fellow of the Institute of Credit Management

FICS Fellow of the Institute of Chartered Shipbrokers; Fellow of the International College of Surgeons

FICSA Federation of International Civil Servants' Associations

fict. *fictilis* (Latin: made of pottery); fiction; fictional; fictitious

FICW Fellow of the Institute of Clerks of Works of Great Britain

FID Falkland Islands Dependencies; *Fédération internationale de documentation* (French: International Federation for Documentation); *Fédération internationale du diabète* (French: International Diabetes Federation); Fellow of the Institute of Directors; field intelligence department

fid. fidelity; fiduciary

FIDA Fellow of the Institute of Directors, Australia

Fid. Def. *Fidei Defensor* (Latin: Defender of the Faith)

FIDDI [computing] fibre-distributed data interface

FIDE *Fédération internationale des échecs* (French: International Chess Federation); Fellow of the Institute of Design Engineers

FIDO Film Industry Defence Organization; [US astronautics] Flight Dynamics Officer; Fog Investigation Dispersal Operation (in World War II)

FIDP Fellow of the Institute of Data Processing

FIE *Fédération internationale d'escrime* (French: International Fencing Federation)

FIE(Aust) Fellow of the Institution of Engineers, Australia

FIED Fellow of the Institution of Engineering Designers

FIEE Fellow of the Institution of Electrical Engineers

FIEEE [USA] Fellow of the Institute of Electrical and Electronics Engineers

FIEI Fellow of the Institution of Engineers in Ireland

FIEJ *Fédération internationale des éditeurs de journaux* (French: International Federation of Newspaper Publishers)

FIET *Fédération internationale des employés, techniciens et cadres* (French: International Federation of Commercial, Clerical and Technical Employees)

FIEx Fellow of the Institute of Export

FIFA *Fédération internationale de football association* (French: International Federation of Association Football); *Fédération internationale du film d'art* (French: International Federation of Art Films); Fellow of the International Faculty of Arts

fi. fa. *fieri facias* (Latin: have it done) (writ of execution)

FIFCLC *Fédération internationale des femmes de carrières libérales et commerciales* (French: International Federation of Business and Professional Women)

FIFDU *Fédération internationale des femmes diplômées des universités* (French: International Federation of University Women)

FIFF Fellow of the Institute of Freight Forwarders

FIFireE Fellow of the Institution of Fire Engineers

FIFO first in, first out

FIFSP *Fédération internationale des fonctionnaires supérieurs de police* (French: International Federation of Senior Police Officers)

FIFST Fellow of the Institute of Food Science and Technology

FIG *Fédération internationale de gymnastique* (French: International Gymnastic Federation)

Fig. Figure (book illustration)

fig. figurative; figuratively; figure

FIGasE Fellow of the Institution of Gas Engineers

FIGC *Federazione Italiana Gioco Calcio* (Italian: Italian Football Association)

FIGCM Fellow of the Incorporated Guild of Church Musicians

FIGED *Fédération internationale des grandes entreprises de distribution* (French: International Federation of Distributors)

FIGO *Fédération internationale de gynécol-ogie et d'obstétrique* (French: International Federation of Gynaecology and Obstetrics)

FIGRS Fellow of the Irish Genealogical Research Society

FIH *Fédération internationale de hockey* (French: International Hockey Federation); *Fédération internationale des hôpitaux* (French: International Hospital Federation); Fellow of the Institute of Hygiene; [image technology] focused-image holography

FIHE Fellow of the Institution of Health Education

FIHort Fellow of the Institute of Horticulture

FIHospE Fellow of the Institute of Hospital Engineering

FIHT Fellow of the Institution of Highways and Transportation

FII franked investment income

FIIA Fellow of the Institute of Internal Auditors

FIIC Fellow of the International Institute for Conservation of Historic and Artistic Works

FIIE Fellow of the Institution of Incorporated Engineers

FIIM Fellow of the Institution of Industrial Managers

FIInfSc Fellow of the Institute of Information Scientists

FIInst Fellow of the Imperial Institute

FIISec Fellow of the International Institute of Security

FIITech Fellow of the Institute of Industrial Technicians

FIJ *Fédération internationale de judo* (French: International Judo Federation); *Fédération internationale des journalistes* (French: International Federation of Journalists)

FIL *Fédération internationale de laiterie* (French: International Dairy Federation); Fellow of the Institute of Linguists

fil. filament; fillet; filter; filtrate

FILA *Fédération internationale de lutte amateur* (French: International Amateur Wrestling Federation)

FILE Fellow of the Institute of Legal Executives

FILO first in, last out

FILT *Fédération internationale de lawn*

tennis (French: International Lawn Tennis Federation)

FIM *Fédération internationale des musiciens* (French: International Federation of Musicians); *Fédération internationale moto-cycliste* (French: International Motor-cycle Federation); Fellow of the Institute of Materials; field-ion microscope (or microscopy)

FIMA Fellow of the Institute of Mathematics and its Applications

FIMarE Fellow of the Institute of Marine Engineers

FIMBRA Financial Intermediaries, Managers and Brokers Regulatory Association

FIMC Fellow of the Institute of Management Consultants

FIMechE Fellow of the Institution of Mechanical Engineers

FIMGTechE Fellow of the Institution of Mechanical and General Technician Engineers

FIMH Fellow of the Institute of Military History

FIMI Fellow of the Institute of the Motor Industry

FIMIT Fellow of the Institute of Musical Instrument Technology

FIMM Fellow of the Institution of Mining and Metallurgy

FIMP *Fédération internationale de médecine physique* (French: International Federation of Physical Medicine)

FIMS *Fédération internationale de médecine sportive* (French: International Federation of Sporting Medicine); Fellow of the Institute of Mathematical Statistics

FIN [international vehicle registration] Finland

Fin. Finland; Finnish

fin. *ad finem* (Latin: at the end, towards the end); final; finance; financial; financier; *finis* (Latin: the end); finish

FINA *Fédération internationale de natation amateur* (French: International Amateur Swimming Federation)

f.i.n.a. following items not available

Findus Fruit Industries Limited

Finn. Finnish

Fin. Sec. financial secretary

FInstAM Fellow of the Institute of Administrative Management

FInstB Fellow of the Institution of Buyers

FInstCh Fellow of the Institute of Chiropodists

FInstD Fellow of the Institute of Directors

FInstE Fellow of the Institute of Energy

FInstF Fellow of the Institute of Fuel

FInstLEx Fellow of the Institute of Legal Executives

FInstMC Fellow of the Institute of Measurement and Control

FInstO Fellow of the Institute of Ophthalmology

FInstP Fellow of the Institute of Physics

FInstPet Fellow of the Institute of Petroleum

FInstPI Fellow of the Institute of Patentees and Inventors

FInstR Fellow of the Institute of Refrigeration

FInstSMM Fellow of the Institute Sales and Marketing Management

FINucE Fellow of the Institution of Nuclear Engineers

f.i.o. for information only; [commerce] free in and out

FIOA Fellow of the Institute of Acoustics

FIOP Fellow of the Institute of Printing

FIP *Fédération internationale de philatélie* (French: International Philatelic Federation); *Fédération internationale pharmaceutique* (French: International Pharmaceutical Federation); Fellow of the Institute of Plumbing

FIPA *Fédération internationale des producteurs agricoles* (French: International Federation of Agricultural Producers); Fellow of the Institute of Practitioners in Advertising

FIPENZ Fellow of the Institution of Professional Engineers, New Zealand

FIPG Fellow of the Institute of Professional Goldsmiths

FIPR Fellow of the Institute of Public Relations

FIPS [computing] Federal International Processing Standards

FIQ *Fédération internationale de quilleurs* (French: International Bowling Federation); Fellow of the Institute of Quarrying

FIQA Fellow of the Institute of Quality Assurance

FIQS Fellow of the Institute of Quantity Surveyors

FIR far-infrared radiation; fuel-indicator reading

fir. firkin

f.i.r. flight information region; floating-in rate; fuel-indicator reading

FIRA *Fédération internationale de rugby amateur* (French: International Amateur Rugby Federation); Furniture Industry Research Association

FIREE(Aust) Fellow of the Institute of Radio and Electronics Engineers (Australia)

FIRSE Fellow of the Institute of Railway Signalling Engineers

FIRST Far Infrared and Submillimetre Telescope; [computing] Forum of Incident and Response Teams

FIRTE Fellow of the Institute of Road Transport Engineers

FIS Family Income Supplement; farm improvement scheme; *Fédération internationale de sauvetage* (French: International Life Saving Federation); *Fédération internationale de ski* (French: International Ski Federation); Fellow of the Institute of Statisticians; [Algeria] *Front Islamique du Salut* (French: Islamic Salvation Front)

f.i.s. flight information service; free into store

FISA *Fédération internationale de sport automobile* (French: International Motor Sport Federation); *Fédération internationale des sociétés d'aviron* (French: International Rowing Federation); Fellow of the Incorporated Secretaries Association; Finance Industry Standards Association

FISE *Fédération internationale syndicale de l'enseignement* (French: International Federation of Teachers' Unions); Fellow of the Institution of Sales Engineers; *Fonds international de secours à l'enfance* (French: United Nations Children's Fund, UNICEF)

fish. fishery; fishes; fishing

FIST Fellow of the Institute of Science Technology

FISTC Fellow of the Institute of Scientific and Technical Communicators

FIStructE Fellow of the Institution of Structural Engineers

FISU *Fédération internationale du sport univ-ersitaire* (French: International University Sports Federation)

FISVA Fellow of the Incorporated Society of Valuers and Auctioneers

FISW Fellow of the Institute of Social Work

FIT [USA] federal income tax; *Fédération internationale des traducteurs* (French: International Federation of Translators)

f.i.t. [commerce] free in truck; free of income tax

FITA *Fédération internationale de tir à l'arc* (French: International Archery Federation)

FITCE *Fédération des ingénieurs des télécommunications de la CE* (French: Federation of Telecommunications Engineers in the EU)

FITD Fellow of the Institute of Training and Development

FITE Fellow of the Institution of Electrical and Electronics Technician Engineers

FITS [astronomy] flexible image transport system

FITT *Fédération internationale de tennis de table* (French: International Table Tennis Federation)

FITW [USA] federal income tax withholding

FIUO for internal use only

FIVB *Fédération internationale de volley-ball* (French: International Volleyball Federation)

f.i.w. [commerce] free in(to) wagon

FIWC Fiji Industrial Workers' Congress

FIWEM Fellow of the Institution of Water and Environmental Management

FIWSc Fellow of the Institute of Wood Science

fix. fixture(s)

fixt. fixture(s)

FJ [vehicle registration] Exeter

Fj. Fjord

.fj Fiji (in Internet address)

FJA Future Journalists of America

Fjd Fjord

FJI Fellow of the Institute of Journalists; [international vehicle registration] Fiji

FK [vehicle registration] Dudley; [UK postcode] Falkirk; [astronomy] *Fundamental Katalog* (German: Fundamental Catalogue)

fk fork

.fk Falkland Islands (in Internet address)

f.k. flat keel

FKC Fellow of King's College (London)

FKCHMS Fellow of King's College Hospital Medical School

Fkr [currency] Faeroese krone

FL Flag Lieutenant; Flight Lieutenant; [US postcode] Florida; football league; [international vehicle registration] Liechtenstein (from German *Fürstentum Liechtenstein*); [vehicle registration] Peterborough

Fl. Flanders; Flemish

fl. *fleuve* (French: river); floor; [medicine] *flores* (Latin: flowers) (powdered drug); [currency] florin; *floruit* (Latin: flourished) (of famous person whose dates (of birth and death) are not known); flourish; flourished; fluid; [music] flute; [currency] guilder (from alternative name florin)

f.l. *falsa lectio* (Latin: false reading)

FLA Fellow of the Library Association; *fiat lege artis* (Latin: let it be done by the rules of the art); Film Laboratory Association; Finance and Leasing Association; Future Large Aircraft (design project)

Fla Florida

flag. [music] flageolet

FLAI Fellow of the Library Association of Ireland

flak *Fliegerabwehrkanone* (German: aircraft defence gun)

FLCD [electronics] ferroelectric liquid-crystal display

FLCM Fellow of the London College of Music

FLCO Fellow of the London College of Osteopathy

fld failed; field; filed; fluid

fldg folding

fl. dr. fluid dram

Flem. Flemish

flex. flexible

flg flagging; flooring; flying; following

FLHS Fellow of the London Historical Society

FLI Fellow of the Landscape Institute

FLIA Fellow of the Life Insurance Association

Flint. Flintshire

FLIP [US navy] floating instrument platform

FLIR [military] forward-looking infrared

Flli *Fratelli* (Italian: Brothers)

FLN [Algeria] *Front de Libération Nationale* (French: National Liberation Front)

FLOOD [USA] fleet observation of oceanographic data

flops [computing] floating-point operations per second (measure of computer power)

Flor. Florence; Florentine; Florida

flor. [currency] florin; *floruit* (Latin: flourished) (of famous person whose dates (of birth and death) are not known)

fl. oz fluid ounce

f.l.p. [aeronautics] fault location panel

fl. pl. [botany] *flore pleno* (Latin: with double flowers)

FLQ [Canada] *Front de Libération du Québec* (French: Quebec Liberation Front) (French-speaking separatists)

flr floor

flr. failure; [currency] florin

FLRA [USA] Federal Labor Relations Authority

flrg flooring

fl. rt. flow rate

FLS Fellow of the Linnean Society

FLSA [USA] Fair Labor Standards Act

flst flautist

F/Lt Flight Lieutenant

Flt Flight (in air force rank)

flt flat; flight

Flt Cmdr Flight Commander

fltg floating

Flt Lt Flight Lieutenant

Flt Off. Flight Officer

Flt Sgt Flight Sergeant

flu [short form] influenza

fluc. fluctuant; fluctuate; fluctuated; fluctuating; fluctuation

fluor. fluorescent; fluoridation; fluoride; fluorspar

fly. [boxing] flyweight

FM [vehicle registration] Chester; [computing] facilities management; [electrical engineering] field magnet; Field Marshal; [aeronautics] figure of merit; Flight Mechanic; foreign mission; *Fraternitas Medicorum* (Latin: Fraternity of Physicians); *fraternité mondiale* (French: world brotherhood); freemason; [radio] frequency modulation; Friars Minor

Fm [chemical element] fermium
fm farm; fathom; femtometre; from
.fm Micronesia (in Internet address)
f.m. face measurement; facial measurement; [advertising] facing matter; *femmes mariées* (French: married women); [medicine] *fiat mistura* (Latin: let a mixture be made) (in prescriptions); fine measure; fine measurement; [radio] frequency modulation
FMA Farm Management Association; Fellow of the Museums Association; Food Machinery Association
fman foreman
FMANU *Fédération mondiale des associations pour les Nations Unies* (French: World Federation of United Nations Associations)
FMANZ Fellow of the Medical Association of New Zealand
FMAO farm machinery advisory officer
FMAS Foreign Marriage Advisory Service
FMB Farmers' Marketing Board (in Malawi); [USA] Federal Maritime Board; Federation of Master Builders
FMC [USA] Federal Maritime Commission; Fellow of the Medical Council; Forces Motoring Club; Ford Motor Company
FMCE Federation of Manufacturers of Construction Equipment
FMCG fast-moving consumer goods
FMCP Federation of Manufacturers of Contractors' Plant
FMCS [USA] Federal Mediation and Conciliation Service
FMCW [electronics] frequency modulated continuous wave
FMD [veterinary science] foot and mouth disease
fmd formed
FMDV [microbiology] foot and mouth disease virus
FMEA failure mode and effect analysis
FMES Fellow of the Minerals Engineering Society
FMF [medicine] Fiji Military Forces; Fleet Marine Force(s); fetal movements felt; Food Manufacturers' Federation
FMFPAC [USA] Fleet Marine Forces, Pacific
FMG Federal Military Government (in

Nigeria); [currency] franc malgache (used in Madagascar)
FMI Fellow of the Motor Industry; *Filii Mariae Immaculatae* (Latin: Sons of Mary Immaculate)
FMIG Food Manufacturers' Industrial Group
FMk [currency] Finnish markka
Fmk Finnmark
fml formal
FMLN *Farabundo Martí Liberación Nacional* (Spanish: Farabundo Martí National Liberation Front) (guerrilla movement in El Salvador)
FMN [biochemistry] flavin mononucleotide
fmn formation
FMO Fleet Medical Officer; Flight Medical Officer
FMPA *Fédération mondiale pour la protection des animaux* (French: World Federation for the Protection of Animals)
fmr farmer; former
fmrly formerly
FMRS Foreign Member of the Royal Society
FMS Federated Malay States; *Fédération mondiale des sourds* (French: World Federation of the Deaf); Fellow of the Institute of Management Studies; Fellow of the Medical Society; [computing] flexible manufacturing system; [aeronautics] flight management system(s)
FMSA Fellow of the Mineralogical Society of America
FMTS field maintenance test station
FMV [computing] full-motion video
FMVSS [USA] Federal Motor Vehicle Safety Standards
FN [vehicle registration] Maidstone
f.n. footnote
FNA Fellow of the Indian National Science Academy; French North Africa
f.n.a. for necessary action
FNAEA Fellow of the National Association of Estate Agents
FNAL Fermi National Accelerator Laboratory
FNB Federal Narcotics Bureau
FNCB [USA] First National City Bank
FNCO Fleet Naval Constructor Officer
fnd found; foundered
fnd. foundation

fndd founded
fndr founder
fndry foundry
FNECInst Fellow of the North East Coast Institution of Engineers and Shipbuilders
FNI *Fédération naturiste internationale* (French: International Naturist Federation); Fellow of the Nautical Institute
FNIF Florence Nightingale International Foundation
FNILP Fellow of the National Institute of Licensing Practitioners
FNL Friends of the National Libraries
FNLA *Frente Nacional de Libertação de Angola* (Portuguese: National Front for the Liberation of Angola)
FNMA [USA] Federal National Mortgage Association
FNO Fleet Navigation Officer
FNU *Forces des Nations Unies* (French: United Nations Forces)
f-number [photography] ratio of focal length to aperture
FNWC [USA] Fleet Numerical Weather Center
FNZIA Fellow of the New Zealand Institute of Architects
FO federal official; Field Officer; [commerce] firm offer; First Officer; Flag Officer (in Royal Navy); Flying Officer; Foreign Office (became part of FCO); [commerce] formal offer; [military] forward observer; [music] full organ; [vehicle registration] Gloucester
Fo [physics] Fourier number
fo *firmato* (Italian: signed)
f/o [commerce] for orders; full out
fo. folio
.fo Faeroe Islands (in Internet address)
f.o. fast operating; [commerce] free overside; fuel oil
FOAF friend of a friend (used on Internet)
FOB [medicine] faecal occult blood; [commerce] free on board
FOBFO Federation of British Fire Organizations
FOBS [military] fractional orbital bombardment system
FOBTSU [military] forward observer target survey unit
FOC [commerce] free of charge; free of claims

FoC father of the chapel (in printing or publishing trade union)
FOCL fibre-optic communications line
FOCOL Federation of Coin-Operated Launderettes
FOCUS Focus on Computing in the United States
FOD finger of death (in computer game); [aeronautics] foreign object damage (of aircraft engine); free of damage
FODA Fellow of the Overseas Doctors' Association
FOE [USA] Fraternal Order of Eagles
FoE Friends of the Earth
FOF [stock exchange] Futures and Options Fund
FOFA follow-on forces attack
FOFATUSA Federation of Free African Trade Unions of South Africa
F of F Firth of Forth
FOH [theatre] front of house
FOHCL falls off her/his chair laughing (in Internet chat)
FOI [USA] freedom of information
FOIA [USA] Freedom of Information Act
FOIC Flag Officer in Charge
f.o.k. [stock exchange] fill or kill (i.e. carry out or cancel)
FOL [New Zealand] Federation of Labour
fol. folio; follow; followed; following
folg following
foll. followed; following
FOM [statistics] figure of merit
FOMC [USA] Federal Open Market Committee
FONA Flag Officer, Naval Aviation
FONAC Flag Officer, Naval Air Command
FOP forward observation post
FOQ [commerce] free on quay
FOR Fellowship of Operational Research; flying objects research; [commerce] free on rail
For [astronomy] Fornax
For. [currency] forint (used in Hungary)
for. foreign; foreigner; forensic; forest; forester; forestry; [music] *forte* (Italian: loudly)
FORATOM *Forum atomique européen* (French: European Atomic Forum)
FORES floor order routing and execution system (in Tokyo Stock Exchange)
FOREST Freedom Organization for the Right to Enjoy Smoking Tobacco

FOREX foreign exchange
formn formation
form. wt [chemistry] formula weight
for. rts foreign rights
fort. fortification; fortified; fortify
f.o.r.t. [commerce] full out rye terms
Fortran formula translation (computer programming language)
Forts. *Fortsetzung* (German: continuation)
forz. [music] *forzando* (Italian: with force)
FOS Fisheries Organization Society; [finance] free of stamp; [commerce] free on ship; [commerce] free on station; [commerce] free on steamer
FOSDIC [computing] film optical sensing device
FOT [commerce] free of tax; [commerce] free on truck
Found. Foundation
found. foundry
FOV field of view
FOW [commerce] first open water; [commerce] free on wagon
FOX Futures and Options Exchange
FP Federal Parliament; field punishment; filter paper; fireplug; [insurance] fire policy; [nuclear technology] fission product; [insurance] floating policy; [optics] focal plane; [Australia] forensic pathologist; former pupil; [veterinary science] fowl pest; Free Presbyterian; freezing point; fresh paragraph; fully paid; [computing] functional programming; [vehicle registration] Leicester
Fp. frontispiece
fp foolscap
fp [music] *forte-piano* (Italian: loudly (then) softly)
fp. fireplace
f.p. [medicine] *fiat pilula* (Latin: let a pill be made) (in prescriptions); [medicine] *fiat potio* (Latin: let a drink be made) (in prescriptions); fine paper; [cricket] fine point; fixed price; flameproof; [chemistry] flash point; footpath; foot-pound; [sports] forward pass; freezing point; fresh paragraph; full point; fully paid (shares)
FPA Family Planning Association; Film Production Association of Great Britain; Fire Protection Association; [astronomy] first point of Aries; [computing] floating-point accelerator; Foreign Press Association; [insurance] free of particular average
f.p.b. fast patrol boat
f.p.b.g. fast patrol boat with guided missiles
FPC family planning clinic; Family Practitioner Committee; [USA] Federal Power Commission; Federation of Painting Contractors; fish protein concentrate; Flowers Publicity Council
f.p.c. for private circulation
FPEA Fellow of the Physical Education Association
FPF *Federação Portuguesa de Futebol* (Portuguese: Portuguese Football Federation)
FPGA [computing] field-programmable gate array
FPHA [USA] Federal Public Housing Authority
FPhyS Fellow of the Physical Society
FPI [USA] Federal Prison Industries
FPIA Fellow of the Plastics Institute of Australia
FPLA [computing, electronics] field-programmable logic array
fpm feet per minute
FPMI Fellow of the Pensions Management Institute
FPMR [USA] Federal Property Management Regulation
FPO field post office; fire prevention officer; [US navy] fleet post office
FPRC Flying Personnel Research Committee
FPROM [computing] field-programmable read-only memory; [computing] fusible-link programmable read-only memory
FPS Fellow of the Pharmaceutical Society; Fellow of the Philharmonic Society; Fellow of the Philological Society; Fellow of the Philosophical Society; Fellow of the Physical Society; [USA] Fluid Power Society
fps feet per second; foot-pound-second (as in **fps units**); [photography] frames per second
fpsps feet per second per second
FPT [commerce] fixed price tender; [nautical] forepeak tank
FPU [computing] floating point unit
f.q. [finance] fiscal quarter
FQDN [computing] fully qualified domain name

FQS [USA] Federal Quarantine Service

FR [international vehicle registration] Faeroe Islands; Federal Republic; Federal Reserve (System); fighter reconnaissance; [chemistry] fluorine rubber; *Forum Romanum* (Latin: Roman Forum); [fishing port] Fraserburgh; freight release; frequency rate; [nuclear technology] fusion reactor; [vehicle registration] Preston

F/R folio reference

Fr [ecclesiastical] Father; [chemical element] francium; [Roman Catholic Church] *Frater* (Latin: Brother)

Fr. France; *Fratelli* (Italian: Brothers); *Frau* (German: Mrs); French; Friar; Friday

fr. fragment; frame; [currency] franc; free; frequent; frequently; from; front; fruit; [botany] fruiting

.fr France (in Internet address)

f.r. *folio recto* (Latin: on the right-hand page)

FRA [finance] forward rate agreement

Fra [Roman Catholic Church] *Frate* (Italian: Brother)

f.r.a. flame retardant additive

FRACDS Fellow of the Royal Australian College of Dental Surgeons

FRACGP Fellow of the Royal Australian College of General Practitioners

FRACI Fellow of the Royal Australian Chemical Institute

FRACMA Fellow of the Royal Australian College of Medical Administrators

FRACO Fellow of the Royal Australian College of Ophthalmologists

FRACOG Fellow of the Royal Australian College of Obstetricians and Gynaecologists

FRACP Fellow of the Royal Australasian College of Physicians

FRACS Fellow of the Royal Australasian College of Surgeons

FRAD Fellow of the Royal Academy of Dancing

FRAeS Fellow of the Royal Aeronautical Society

FRAgSs Fellow of the Royal Agricultural Societies

FRAHS Fellow of the Royal Australian Historical Society

FRAI Fellow of the Royal Anthropological Institute

FRAIA Fellow of the Royal Australian Institute of Architects

FRAIC Fellow of the Royal Architectural Institute of Canada

FRAM Fellow of the Royal Academy of Music; [computing] ferroelectric random-access memory

FRAME Fund for the Replacement of Animals in Medical Experiments

Franc. Franciscan

f.r. & c.c. [insurance] free of riot and civil commotions

Frank. Frankish

FRAP *Frente de Acción Popular* (Spanish: Popular Action Front) (in Chile)

FRAPI Fellow of the Royal Australian Planning Institute

FRAS Fellow of the Royal Asiatic Society; Fellow of the Royal Astronomical Society

FRASE Fellow of the Royal Agricultural Society of England

frat. fraternity; fraternize

FRATE [railways] formulae for routes and technical equipment

fraud. fraudulent

FRB [USA] Federal Reserve Bank; [USA] Federal Reserve Board; Fisheries Research Board of Canada; *Frente de la Revolución Boliviana* (Spanish: Bolivian Revolutionary Front)

FRBS Fellow of the Royal Botanic Society; Fellow of the Royal Society of British Sculptors

FRC [USA] Federal Radiation Council; [USA] Federal Radio Commission; Financial Reporting Council; Flight Research Center (at NASA)

FRCA Fellow of the Royal College of Art

Fr-Can French-Canadian

FRCD Fellow of the Royal College of Dentists of Canada; [banking] floating-rate certificate of deposit

FRCGP Fellow of the Royal College of General Practitioners

FRCM Fellow of the Royal College of Music

FRCN Fellow of the Royal College of Nursing ·

FRCO Fellow of the Royal College of Organists

FRCO(CHM) Fellow of the Royal College

of Organists with Diploma in Choir Training

FRCOG Fellow of the Royal College of Obstetricians and Gynaecologists

FRCP Fellow of the Royal College of Physicians

FRCPA Fellow of the Royal College of Pathologists of Australasia

FRCPath Fellow of the Royal College of Pathologists

FRCPE Fellow of the Royal College of Physicians of Edinburgh

FRCPI Fellow of the Royal College of Physicians of Ireland

FRCPSGlas Fellow of the Royal College of Physicians and Surgeons of Glasgow

FRCPsych Fellow of the Royal College of Psychiatrists

FRCR Fellow of the Royal College of Radiologists

FRCS Fellow of the Royal College of Surgeons (of England)

FRCSE Fellow of the Royal College of Surgeons of Edinburgh

FRCSEd Fellow of the Royal College of Surgeons of Edinburgh

FRCSI Fellow of the Royal College of Surgeons in Ireland

FRCSoc Fellow of the Royal Commonwealth Society

FRCVS Fellow of the Royal College of Veterinary Surgeons

frd friend

FR Dist. [USA] Federal Reserve District

Fre. *Freitag* (German: Friday); French

fre *facture* (French: invoice)

FREconS Fellow of the Royal Economic Society

FRED Fast Reactor Experiment, Dounreay; figure reading electronic device; financial reporting exposure draft

Free. [USA] freeway

FREGG Free Range Egg Association

FREI Fellow of the Real Estate Institute (Australia)

Frelimo *Frente de Libertação de Moçambique* (Portuguese: Mozambique Liberation Front)

freq. frequency; frequent; [grammar] frequentative; frequently

FRES Federation of Recruitment and Employment Services; Fellow of the Royal Entomological Society

FRESH foil research hydrofoil

FRG Federal Republic of Germany

Fr. G French Guiana

FRGS Fellow of the Royal Geographical Society; Fellow of the Royal Geographical Society of Australasia

frgt freight

FRHB Federation of Registered House Builders

FRHistS Fellow of the Royal Historical Society

Frhr *Freiherr* (German: Baron)

FRHS Fellow of the Royal Horticultural Society

FRI Fellow of the Royal Institution; Food Research Institute

Fri. Fribourg; Friday

FRIA Fellow of the Royal Irish Academy

FRIAI Fellow of the Royal Institute of the Architects of Ireland

FRIAS Fellow of the Royal Incorporation of Architects in Scotland; Fellow of the Royal Institute for the Advancement of Science

FRIBA Fellow of the Royal Institute of British Architects

fric. friction; frictional

FRICS Fellow of the Royal Institution of Chartered Surveyors

frict. friction; frictional

fridge [short form] refrigerator

FRIH [New Zealand] Fellow of the Royal Institute of Horticulture

FRIIA Fellow of the Royal Institute of International Affairs

FRIN Fellow of the Royal Institute of Navigation

FRINA Fellow of the Royal Institution of Naval Architects

FRIPA Fellow of the Royal Institute of Public Administration

FRIPHH Fellow of the Royal Institute of Public Health and Hygiene

Fris. Friesland; Frisian

Frk. *Fröken* (Swedish: Miss); *Frøken* (Danish or Norwegian: Miss)

FRL full repairing lease

Frl. *Fräulein* (German: Miss)

frld foreland; freehold (in property advertisement)

frm from

FRMCM Fellow of the Royal Manchester College of Music

FRMCS Fellow of the Royal Medical and Chirurgical Society

FRMedSoc Fellow of the Royal Medical Society

FRMetS Fellow of the Royal Meteorological Society

FRMS Fellow of the Royal Microscopical Society

FRN [finance] floating-rate note

FRNCM Fellow of the Royal Northern College of Music

FRNS Fellow of the Royal Numismatic Society

FRNSA Fellow of the Royal Navy School of Architects

FRO Fellow of the Register of Osteopaths; Fire Research Organization; [insurance] fire risk only

f.r.o.f. [insurance] fire risk on freight

Frolinat *Front de Libération Nationale Tchadienne* (French: Chad National Liberation Front)

front. frontispiece

frontis. frontispiece

FRP fibreglass-reinforced plastic; fibre-reinforced plastic; fuel-reprocessing plant

frpf fireproof

FRPharmS Fellow of the Royal Pharmaceutical Society

FRPS Fellow of the Royal Photographic Society

FRPSL Fellow of the Royal Philatelic Society, London

FRQ [meteorology] frequent

frq. frequent

FRR Financial Reporting Release

FRRP Financial Reporting Review Panel

FRS [USA] Federal Reserve System; Fellow of the Royal Society; Ffestiniog Railway Society; Financial Reporting Standard; fuel research station

Frs. Frisian

FRSA Fellow of the Royal Society of Arts

FRSAI Fellow of the Royal Society of Antiquaries of Ireland

FRSAMD Fellow of the Royal Scottish Academy of Music and Drama

FRSC Fellow of the Royal Society of Canada; Fellow of the Royal Society of Chemistry

FRSCan Fellow of the Royal Society of Canada

FRSCM Fellow of the Royal School of Church Music

FRSE Fellow of the Royal Society of Edinburgh

FRSGS Fellow of the Royal Scottish Geographical Society

FRSH Fellow of the Royal Society of Health

FRSL Fellow of the Royal Society of Literature

FRSM Fellow of the Royal Society of Medicine

FRSNZ Fellow of the Royal Society of New Zealand

FRSS Fellow of the Royal Statistical Society

FRSSA Fellow of the Royal Scottish Society of Arts; Fellow of the Royal Society of South Africa

FRSSI Fellow of the Royal Statistical Society of Ireland

FRSSS Fellow of the Royal Statistical Society of Scotland

FRST Fellow of the Royal Society of Teachers

FRSTM&H Fellow of the Royal Society of Tropical Medicine and Hygiene

frt freight

frt fwd freight forward

FRTPI Fellow of the Royal Town Planning Institute

frt ppd freight prepaid

FRTS Fellow of the Royal Television Society

Fru [biochemistry] fructose

frum *fratrum* (Latin: of the brothers)

frust. [medicine] *frustillatim* (Latin: in small portions)

FRVA Fellow of the Rating and Valuation Association

FRVC Fellow of the Royal Veterinary College

frwk framework

frwy freeway

FRZSScot Fellow of the Royal Zoological Society of Scotland

FS [vehicle registration] Edinburgh; Fabian Society; Faraday Society; feasibility study; *Ferrovie dello Stato* (Italian: State Railways); field security; financial secretary; financial statement; Fleet Surgeon; Flight Sergeant; Foreign Service; [USA] Forest Service; Free State; Friendly Society

fs. facsimile

f.s. factor of safety; *faire suivre* (French: please forward); far side; film strip; fire station; flight service; flying saucer; flying status; foot-second

FSA [USA] Farm Security Agency; [USA] Federal Security Agency; [USA] Fellow of the Society of Actuaries; Fellow of the Society of Antiquaries; Field Survey Association; Financial Services Act; Financial Services Authority; [computing] finite-state automaton; foreign service allowance; Friendly Societies Act

f.s.a. fuel storage area

FSAA Fellow of the Society of Incorporated Accountants and Auditors

FSAE Fellow of the Society of Art Education; Fellow of the Society of Automotive Engineers

FSAI Fellow of the Society of Architectural Illustrators

FSAM Fellow of the Society of Art Masters

FSAScot Fellow of the Society of Antiquaries of Scotland

FSB Federation of Small Businesses

FSBI Fellow of the Savings Bank Institute

FSBR Financial Statement and Budget Report

FSC [USA] Federal Supreme Court; Field Studies Council; [Roman Catholic Church] *Fratres Scholarum Christianorum* (Latin: Brothers of the Christian Schools, Christian Brothers); Friends Service Council

FSCA Fellow of the Society of Company and Commercial Accountants

FSD full-scale deflection (of measuring instrument)

FSDC Fellow of the Society of Dyers and Colourists

FSE Fellow of the Society of Engineers; field support equipment

FSF Fellow of the Institute of Shipping and Forwarding Agents; Free Software Foundation

FSFMV [computing] full-screen, full-motion video

FSG Fellow of the Society of Genealogists

FSGT Fellow of the Society of Glass Technology

FSgt Flight Sergeant

FSH [biochemistry] follicle-stimulating hormone; full service history (in car advertisement)

FSHM Fellow of the Society of Housing Managers

FSI *Fédération spirite internationale* (French: International Spiritualist Federation); Free Sons of Israel

FSK [telecommunications] frequency shift keying

FSL First Sea Lord; Folger Shakespeare Library

FSLAET Fellow of the Society of Licensed Aircraft Engineers and Technologists

FSLIC [USA] Federal Savings and Loan Insurance Corporation

FSLN *Frente Sandinista de Liberación Nacional* (Spanish: Sandinista National Liberation Front) (in Nicaragua)

FSLTC Fellow of the Society of Leather Technologists and Chemists

FSM *Fédération syndicale mondiale* (French: World Federation of Trade Unions); [electronics] flying-spot microscope; [USA] Free Speech Movement

FSMC Freeman of the Spectacle-Makers' Company

FSME Fellow of the Society of Manufacturing Engineers

FSN federal stock number

FSO field security officer; Fleet Signals Officer; Foreign Service Officer

FSP field security police; foreign service pay

FSR Field Service Regulations; *Fleet Street Patent Law Reports*

FSRP Fellow of the Society for Radiological Protection

FSS Fellow of the Royal Statistical Society; [Algeria] *Front des forces socialistes* (French: Socialist Forces Front)

FSSI Fellow of the Statistical Society of Ireland

FSSU Federated Superannuation Scheme for Universities

FST flatter squarer tube (for computer or TV screen)

FSTD Fellow of the Society of Typographic Designers

FSU family service unit

FSUC Federal Statistics Unit Conference

FSVA Fellow of the Incorporated Society of Valuers and Auctioneers

FT *Financial Times*; [obstetrics] full term

(of pregnancy); [vehicle registration] Newcastle upon Tyne

Ft [currency] forint (used in Hungary); Fort

ft feet (unit of length); feint; [medicine] *fiat* (Latin: let there be made); foot (unit of length); fort

ft. fortification; fortify

f.t. formal training; full term(s)

FTA [medicine] fluorescent treponemal antibody; Free Trade Agreement; Free Trade Area; Freight Transport Association; Future Teachers of America

FTA Index Financial Times Actuaries Share Index

FTAM [computing] file transfer, access and management

FTASI Financial Times Actuaries All-Share Index

FTAT Furniture, Timber and Allied Trades Union

FTB first-time buyer (in property advertisement); fleet torpedo bomber

FTBD [obstetrics] full term, born dead

ftbrg. footbridge

FTC [USA] Federal Trade Commission; [USA] flight test center; flying training command; Full Technological Certificate (of City and Guilds Institute)

FTCD Fellow of Trinity College, Dublin

FTCL Fellow of Trinity College of Music, London

FTD foreign technology division

FTDA Fellow of the Theatrical Designers and Craftsmen's Association

f.t.e. full-time equivalent

FTESA Foundry Trades Equipment and Supplies Association

FTFL [computing] fixed-to-fixed-length (code)

FTG Fuji Texaco Gas

ftg fitting

fth. fathom

fthm fathom

FTI Fellow of the Textile Institute

FT Index Financial Times Ordinary Share Index

ft-lb foot-pound

Ft Lieut. Flight Lieutenant

FTM flying training manual; [medicine] fractional test meal

ft mist. [medicine] *fiat mistura* (Latin: let a mixture be made) (in prescriptions)

FTND [obstetrics] full term, normal delivery

FTO Fleet Torpedo Officer

FT Ord. Financial Times (Industrial) Ordinary Share Index

FTP [computing] file-transfer protocol (used on Internet)

FTPA Fellow of the Town and Country Planning Association

ft pulv. [medicine] *fiat pulvis* (Latin: let a powder be made) (in prescriptions)

FTS Fellow of the Tourism Society

FTS flying training school

ft/s feet per second

ft/s² feet per second per second

FTSC Fellow of the Tonic Sol-Fa College

FTSE 100 Financial Times Stock Exchange 100 Index (also called Footsie)

FTT [medicine] failure to thrive

fttgs fittings (in property advertisement)

fttr fitter

FTU Federation of Trade Unions (in Hong Kong); [photography] Freeman time-unit

FTVL [computing] fixed-to-variable-length (code)

FTW [commerce] tree-trade wharf

FTZ Free Trade Zone

FU Farmers' Union; [photography] Freeman time-unit; *Freie Universität* (German: Free University (of Berlin)); [vehicle registration] Lincoln

f.u. follow-up

FUACE *Fédération universelle des associations chrétiennes d'étudiants* (French: World Student Christian Federation)

FUEN Federal Union of European Nationalities

FUMIST Fellow of the University of Manchester Institute of Science and Technology

fund. fundamental

FUO [medicine] fever of uncertain origin

fur. furlong; furnished (in accommodation advertisement); further

furn. furnace; furnish; furnished (in accommodation advertisement); furniture

fus. fuselage; fusilier

fut. future; [finance] futures

FUW Farmers' Union of Wales

FV [vehicle registration] Preston

f.v. fire vent; fishing vessel; flush valve; *folio verso* (Latin: on the left-hand page)

FVC [medicine] forced vital capacity (in breathing tests)

FVRDE Fighting Vehicle Research and Development Establishment

FW [chemistry] formula weight; fresh water; [vehicle registration] Lincoln

FWA Factories and Workshops Act; Family Welfare Association; [USA] Federal Works Agency; Fellow of the World Academy of Arts and Sciences; Free Wales Army

FWAG Farming and Wildlife Advisory Group

FWB Free Will Baptists

f.w.b. four-wheel brake; four-wheel braking

FWCC Friends' World Committee for Consultation

fwd forward

f.w.d. four-wheel drive; fresh water damage; front-wheel drive

fwdg forwarding

FWeldI Fellow of the Welding Institute

FWFM Federation of Wholesale Fish Merchants

f.w.h. flexible working hours

FWI Federation of West Indies; French West Indies

FWIW for what it's worth (in Internet chat and e-mail)

FWL Foundation of World Literacy

FWO Federation of Wholesale Organizations; Fleet Wireless Officer

FWPCA [USA] Federal Water Pollution Control Administration

FWS fighter weapons school; fleet work study

FWSG farm water supply grant

fwt [boxing] featherweight

f.w.t. fair wear and tear

FX [vehicle registration] Bournemouth; foreign exchange; Francis Xavier (Spanish Jesuit missionary); [theatre] sound effects (phonetic spelling of 'effects'); [cinema] special effects (phonetic spelling of 'effects')

fxd fixed; foxed

fxg fixing

fxle [nautical] forecastle

FY [UK postcode] Blackpool; [USA, Canada] fiscal year; [fishing port] Fowey; [vehicle registration] Liverpool

f.y.a. first-year allowance

FYC Family and Youth Concern

FYI for your information

FYM farmyard manure

FYP [economics] Five-Year Plan

FYROM Former Yugoslav Republic of Macedonia

FZ [vehicle registration] Belfast; [meteorology] freezing; Free Zone; French Zone

fz. [music] *forzando* (Italian: accentuating strongly); [music] *forzato* (Italian: accentuated strongly)

FZA [USA] Fellow of the Zoological Academy

FZGB Federation of Zoological Gardens of Great Britain and Ireland

FZS Fellow of the Zoological Society

F-Zug *Fernschnellzug* (German: long-distance express train)

G

G [international vehicle registration] Gabon; [fishing port] Galway; gauss (unit of magnetic flux density); [cinema] general exhibition (film classification in Australia and USA); German; Germany; giga-(indicates 10^9, as in **GW** = gigawatt); [computing] giga- (indicates 2^{30}, as in **GB** = gigabyte); [UK postcode] Glasgow; [biochemistry] glycine; good; [currency] gourde (used in Haiti); [slang] grand (= 1,000 (pounds, dollars, etc.)); gravity (as in **G-force**); Great; green; Group; [biochemistry] guanine; [biochemistry] guanosine; [currency] guaraní (used in Paraguay); Guernsey; Gulf; [botany] gynoecium (in floral formula); [music] note of scale; [civil aircraft marking] United Kingdom

G [physics] conductance; [physics] gravitational constant

g [physics] acceleration of free fall; [meteorology] gale; gallon; gas; [chemistry] gaseous; [physics] gluon; [mathematics] grade; gram; grav (unit of acceleration); [physics] gravitational acceleration; gravity

g [physics] degeneracy

g. garage; *gauche* (French: left); gauge; gelding; gender; general; [grammar] genitive; geographical; gilt; goal; goalkeeper; gold; good; government; grand; great; green; grey; *gros(se)* (French: large); guardian; guide; [currency] guilder; [currency] guinea; gunnery

G3 [economics] Group of Three (most powerful western industrialized nations)

G³ [electronics] gadolinium gallium garnet

G5 [finance] Group of Five (nations stabilizing exchange rates)

G7 [economics] Group of Seven (leading industrialized nations)

G10 [finance] Group of Ten (nations lending money to IMF)

G24 [economics] Group of Twenty-Four (richest industrialized nations)

G77 [economics] Group of Seventy-Seven (developing nations)

9G [civil aircraft marking] Ghana

GA Gaelic Athletic (Club); Gamblers Anonymous; garrison artillery; General Accident (property and insurance company); general administrator; general agent; [linguistics] General American; [medicine] general anaesthesia; [medicine] general anaesthetic; General Assembly (of UN); general assignment; [insurance] general average; Geographical Association; Geologists' Association; [US postcode] Georgia; [obstetrics] gestational age; [vehicle registration] Glasgow; [netball] goal attack; government actuary; graphic arts

G/A [insurance] general average; ground-to-air

Ga [chemical element] gallium; Georgia

Ga. Gallic

g/a ground-to-air

.ga Gabon (in Internet address)

g.a. [insurance] general average

GAA [Ireland] Gaelic Athletic Association

GAAP generally accepted accounting principles

GAAR [taxation] general anti-avoidance rule

GAAS generally accepted auditing standards

GAB general arrangements to borrow (in IMF)

Gab. Gabon

GABA [biochemistry] gamma-aminobutyric acid (neurotransmitter)

Gae. Gaelic

Gael. Gaelic

GAFTA Grain and Free Trade Association

GAI General Assembly of International Sports Federations; [USA] guaranteed annual income; Guild of Architectural Ironmongers

Gal. [Bible] Galatians; Galicia; Galway

gal. gallon

gall. gallery; gallon

GALT [medicine] gut-associated lymphoid tissue

galv. galvanic; galvanize; galvanized; galvanometer

GAM guided aircraft missile

Gam. Gambia

G&AE [accounting] general and administrative expense(s)

G&O [medicine] gas and oxygen (in anaesthetic)

G&S (William Schwenck) Gilbert and (Arthur) Sullivan (British writers of comic operettas)

G&T gin and tonic

GAO [USA] General Accounting Office

GAP general assembly programme; great American public; [economics] gross agricultural product

GAPAN Guild of Air Pilots and Air Navigators

GAR Grand Army of the Republic (in American Civil War); guided aircraft rocket

gar. garage; garrison

gard. garden

GARIOA government aid and relief in occupied areas

GARP Global Atmospheric Research Programme

GASC German-American Securities Corporation

GASCO General Aviation Safety Committee

GASP Group Against Smokers' Pollution

gast. gastric

gastroent. gastroenterological; gastroenterology

GATB General Aptitude Test Battery

GATCO Guild of Air Traffic Control Officers

GATT General Agreement on Tariffs and Trade (replaced by WTO)

GAUFCC General Assembly of Unitarian and Free Christian Churches

GAV [accounting] gross annual value

GAW Global Atmosphere Watch; guaranteed annual wage

GAWF Greek Animal Welfare Fund

GAYE give as you earn

gaz. gazette; gazetteer

GB [medicine] gall bladder; gas board; [computing] gigabyte; Girls' Brigade; [vehicle registration] Glasgow; government and binding; Great Britain; [international vehicle registration] Great Britain; guide book; gunboat

Gb [computing] gigabyte; gilbert (unit of magnetomotive force)

GBA [international vehicle registration] Alderney; Governing Bodies Association

GB&I Great Britain and Ireland

GBCW Governing Body of the Church in Wales

GBDO Guild of British Dispensing Opticians

GBE (Dame or Knight) Grand Cross of the Order of the British Empire

g.b.e. gilt bevelled edge

GBF gay black female

GBG [international vehicle registration] Guernsey

GBGSA Governing Bodies of Girls' Schools Association

GBH grievous bodily harm

GBJ [international vehicle registration] Jersey

GBM gay black male; [international vehicle registration] Isle of Man

GBNE Guild of British Newspaper Editors

g.b.o. goods in bad order

g/box gearbox (in car advertisement)

GBP British pounds; [biochemistry] glutamate-binding protein; great British public

GBRE General Board of Religious Education

GBS George Bernard Shaw (Irish dramatist); [computing] Gragg–Burlisch–Stoer (method)

GBSM Graduate of Birmingham and Midland Institute School of Music

GBT Green Bank Telescope

GBTA Guild of Business Travel Agents

GBZ [international vehicle registration] Gibraltar

GC [astronomy] galactic centre; gas chromatography; gas council; [chemistry] gel chromatography; [astronomy] General Catalogue; George Cross (replacement for EGM); gliding club; Goldsmiths' College; golf club; good conduct; government chemist; Grand Chancellor; Grand Chaplain; Grand Chapter; Grand Conductor; Grand Cross; [vehicle registration] southwest London

g.c. going concern; good condition (in advertisement)

GCA Girls' Clubs of America; Global Commission on Aids; [aeronautics] ground-controlled approach; [international vehicle registration] Guatemala (Central America)

G Capt. Group Captain

GCB (Dame or Knight) Grand Cross of the Order of the Bath

GCBS General Council of British Shipping

GCC Game Conservancy Council; Gas Consumers' Council; Gulf Cooperation Council

GCD general and complete disarmament; [mathematics] greatest common divisor

GCE General Certificate of Education; [USA] General College Entrance

GCF [mathematics] greatest common factor

GCFR [nuclear technology] gas-cooled fast reactor

GCH gas central heating (in property advertisement); Guild Certificate of Hairdressing

GCHQ Government Communications Headquarters

GCI [aeronautics] ground-controlled interception

GCIE (Knight) Grand Commander of the Order of the Indian Empire

GCIU [USA] Graphic Communications International Union

GCL [aeronautics] ground-controlled

landing; Guild of Cleaners and Launderers

GCLH Grand Cross of the Legion of Honour

GCLJ (Knight) Grand Cross of the Order of St Lazarus of Jerusalem

GCM [meteorology] general circulation model; general court martial; Good Conduct Medal; [statistics] greatest common measure; [mathematics] greatest common multiple

GCMG (Dame or Knight) Grand Cross of the Order of St Michael and St George

GCO Gun Control Officer (in Royal Navy)

GCON Grand Cross of the Order of the Niger

GCR [nuclear technology] gas-cooled reactor; [computing] grey component replacement; ground-controlled radar; [computing] group code recording

GCRN General Council and Register of Naturopaths

GCRO General Council and Register of Osteopaths

GCSE General Certificate of Secondary Education (replacement for CSE and GCE O level)

GCSG (Knight) Grand Cross of the Order of St Gregory the Great

GCSI (Knight) Grand Commander of the Order of the Star of India

GCSJ (Knight) Grand Cross of the Order of St John of Jerusalem

GCStJ (Bailiff or Dame) Grand Cross of the Order of St John of Jerusalem

GCVO (Dame or Knight) Grand Cross of the Royal Victorian Order

GD [obstetrics] gestational day; [vehicle registration] Glasgow; [electronics] glow discharge; [netball] goal defence; Graduate in Divinity; Grand Duchess; Grand Duchy; Grand Duke; Gunnery Division

Gd [chemical element] gadolinium

gd good; granddaughter; ground

.gd Grenada (in Internet address)

g.d. general duties; gravimetric density

GDA Glasgow Development Agency

GDBA Guide Dogs for the Blind Association

GDC General Dental Council; General Dynamics Corporation

Gde [currency] gourde (used in Haiti)

GDI [computing] graphical device interface; [economics] gross domestic income

Gdk Gdansk

gdn garden; guardian

Gdns Gardens

GDP [economics] gross domestic product

GDPA General Dental Practitioners' Association

GDR German Democratic Republic (the former East Germany)

Gds Guards

gds goods

Gdsm. Guardsman

GDT graphic display terminal

GDU graphic display unit

GE garrison engineer; gastroenterology; general election; [USA] General Electric (Company); [international vehicle registration] Georgia; [vehicle registration] Glasgow; [fishing port] Goole; [astronomy] greatest elongation; gross energy

Ge [chemical element] germanium

.ge Georgia (in Internet address)

g.e. [bookbinding] gilt edges

GEA Garage Equipment Association

geb. *geboren* (German: born); *gebunden* (German: bound)

GEBCO general bathymetric chart of the oceans

Gebr. *Gebrüder* (German: brothers)

GEC General Electric Company

GED general educational development

Gedcom [computing] genealogical data communications

GEF Global Environment Facility

gegr. *gegründet* (German: founded)

gel. gelatin(e); gelatinous

GEM genetically engineered microorganism; [computing] graphics environment manager; ground effect machine; guidance evaluation missile; Guild of Experienced Motorists

Gem [astronomy] Gemini

GEMS Global Environmental Monitoring System (in UN)

Gen. General; [Bible] Genesis; Geneva; Genoa

gen [short form] (general) information

gen. gender; genealogy; general; generally; generator; generic; genetic; genetics; genital; [grammar] genitive; genuine; [biology] genus

gen. av. [insurance] general average

gend. *gendarme* (French: police officer)

geneal. genealogy

genit. genital; [grammar] genitive

Genl General

genn. *gennaio* (Italian: January)

gent [short form] gentleman

GEO geostationary earth orbit; geosynchronous earth orbit

Geo. George

geod. geodesy; geodetic

geog. geographer; geographic(al); geography

geol. geologic(al); geologist; geology

geom. geometer; geometric(al); geometry

GEON gyro-erected optical navigation

geophys. geophysical; geophysics

geopol. geopolitical; geopolitics

GEOREF World Geographic Reference System

GEOS geodetic orbiting satellite

GER gross energy requirement

Ger. German; Germany

ger. [grammar] gerund; [grammar] gerundive

Gerbil Great Education Reform Bill

GES Global Epidemiological Surveillance and Health Situation (of WHO)

Ges. [commerce] *Gesellschaft* (German: company, society)

GESP generalized extrasensory perception

GEST Grants for Education, Support and Training

gest. *gestorben* (German: deceased)

Gestapo *Geheime Staatspolizei* (German: secret state police) (in Nazi Germany)

GET [medicine] gastric emptying time

GETT [USA] Grants Equal To Tax

GeV gigaelectronvolt

GEW gram-equivalent weight

gez. *gezeichnet* (German: signed)

GF General Foods Limited; girlfriend; glass fibre; government form; gradient freezing; growth factor; Guggenheim Foundation; [currency] Guinea franc; [vehicle registration] southwest London

g/f ground floor (in property advertisement)

g.f.a. [commerce] good fair average; [commerce] good freight agent

GFCH gas-fired central heating (in property advertisement)

GFCM General Fisheries Council for the Mediterranean

GFD geophysical fluid dynamics

GFG *Good Food Guide*

GFH George Frederick Handel (German composer)

GFOF [stock exchange] Geared Futures and Options Fund

GFR German Federal Republic; [medicine] glomerular filtration rate

GFS Girls' Friendly Society

GFT Glasgow Film Theatre

GFTU [USA] General Federation of Trade Unions

GFWC General Federation of Women's Clubs

GG [medicine] gamma globulin; Girl Guides; [vehicle registration] Glasgow; Governor-General; great gross (= 144 dozen); Grenadier Guards

g.g. gas generator

GGA Girl Guides Association

GGC generalized genetic code

ggd great-granddaughter

gge garage (in property advertisement)

GGF Glass and Glazing Federation

GGG [electronics] gadolinium gallium garnet

g.gr. great gross (= 144 dozen)

ggs great-grandson

GGSM Graduate of the Guildhall School of Music (and Drama)

GH general hospital; [international vehicle registration] Ghana; [fishing port] Grangemouth; [military] Green Howards; Greenwich Hospital; [biochemistry] growth hormone; [vehicle registration] southwest London

.gh Ghana (in Internet address)

GHA [astronomy] Greenwich hour angle

GHB gamma hydroxybutyrate (bodybuilding drug)

GHCIMA Graduate of the Hotel Catering and Institutional Management Association

g.h.e. ground handling equipment

GHI Good Housekeeping Institute

GHMS Graduate in Homoeopathic Medicine and Surgery

GHOST global horizontal sounding technique (for collection of atmospheric data)

GHQ [military] General Headquarters

GHRH [biochemistry] growth-hormone-releasing hormone

GHS girls' high school

GHz gigahertz

GI galvanized iron; gastrointestinal; [USA] general issue; generic issue; Gideons International; (Royal) Glasgow Institute (of the Fine Arts); [USA] government issue; Government of India; [biochemistry] growth inhibitor; US soldier (from government (or general) issue)

Gi gilbert (unit of magnetomotive force)

gi. gill (unit of liquid measure)

.gi Gibraltar (in Internet address)

g.i. galvanized iron

GIA Garuda Indonesian Airways

GIB Gulf International Bank

Gib. Gibraltar

GIBiol Graduate of the Institute of Biology

GIC *Guilde internationale des coopératrices* (French: International Cooperative Women's Guild)

GIEE Graduate of the Institute of Electrical Engineers

GIF [computing] graphics interchange format; [biochemistry] growth-hormone inhibiting factor

GIFT [medicine] gamete intrafallopian transfer (infertility treatment)

gig [short form, computing] gigabyte

GIGO [computing] garbage in, garbage out

GIMechE Graduate of the Institution of Mechanical Engineers

GINO [computing] graphical input output

GInstAEA Graduate of the Institute of Automotive Engineer Assessors

GINucE Graduate of the Institution of Nuclear Engineers

gio. *giovedì* (Italian: Thursday)

GIP glazed imitation parchment (paper)

GIPME Global Investigation of Pollution in the Marine Environment

GIS [computing] geographical information system; [computing] geological information system; Global Information Solutions

GISS Goddard Institute for Space Studies

GITB Gas Industry Training Board

giu. *giugno* (Italian: June)

GIUK Greenland, Iceland, United Kingdom

GJ [vehicle registration] southwest London

GJD [Freemasonry] Grand Junior Deacon

GK goalkeeper; [fishing port] Greenock; [vehicle registration] southwest London

Gk Greek

GKA Garter King of Arms

GKC G(ilbert) K(eith) Chesterton (British writer)

GKN Guest, Keen and Nettlefold (engineering company)

GKS [computing] graphical kernel system

GL [shipping] *Germanischer Lloyd* (German shipping classification society); [UK postcode] Gloucester; good-looking (in personal advertisement); [printing] gothic letter; government laboratory; [Freemasonry] Grand Lodge; Grand Luxe (car); ground level; gun licence; [vehicle registration] Truro

Gl. Gloria (doxology)

gl gill (unit of liquid measure)

g/l grams per litre

gl. glass; gloss

.gl Greenland (in Internet address)

4GL [computing] fourth-generation language

GLAB Greater London Arts Board

glab. [botany] glabrous

Glam. Glamorgan

glam [informal] greying, leisured, affluent, married

gland. glandular

Glas. Glasgow; Glaswegian

glau. [botany] glaucous

glauc. [medicine] glaucoma

glaz. glazed; glazing

GLB gay, lesbian, bisexual; Girls' Life Brigade

GLC [chemistry] gas–liquid chromatography; Greater London Council (former local authority); ground-level concentration (of radioactive material); Guild of Lettering Craftsmen

GLCM Graduate of the London College of Music; ground-launched cruise missile

gld. [currency] guilder

GLDP Greater London Development Plan

GLM graduated length method (in skiing)

GLOBECOM [US air force] Global Communications System

GLOMEX Global Oceanographic and Meteorological Experiment

GLORIA Geological Long Range ASDIC

Glos Gloucestershire

gloss. glossary

Gloucestr. *Gloucestriensis* (Latin: (Bishop) of Gloucester)

GLS [Freemasonry] Grand Lodge of Scotland

GLT greetings letter telegram

glt [bookbinding] gilt

GM [physics] Geiger–Müller (as in **GM counter**); general manager; general merchandise; [computing] General Midi; general mortgage; General Motors Corporation; genetically modified; Geological Museum; geometric mean; George Medal; gold medal; gold medallist; Grand Marshal; Grand Master; [education] grant maintained; guided missile; [vehicle registration] Reading

gm gram

.gm Gambia (in Internet address)

gm² grams per square metre (unit of weight of paper)

GMAG Genetic Manipulation Advisory Group

G-man [USA] government man (FBI agent)

GMB General, Municipal, Boilermakers and Allied Trades Union; Grand Master Bowman (in archery); Grand Master of the Order of the Bath

g.m.b. good merchantable brand

GMBE Grand Master of the Order of the British Empire

GmbH [commerce] *Gesellschaft mit beschränkter Haftung* (German: limited company, Ltd)

GMC general management committee; General Medical Council; [astronomy] giant molecular cloud; Guild of Memorial Craftsmen

Gmc Germanic

GMF Glass Manufacturers' Federation

GMIE Grand Master of the Order of the Indian Empire

GMKP Grand Master of the Knights of St Patrick

GMMG Grand Master of the Order of St Michael and St George

GMO genetically modified organism

GMP [USA] Glass, Molders, Pottery, Plastics and Allied Workers International Union; Grand Master of the Order of St Patrick; [economics] gross material product; Gurkha Military Police

g.m.q. good merchantable quality

GMR ground-mapping radar

GMRT Giant Metre-wave Radio Telescope

GMS [education] grant-maintained status

GMSC General Medical Services Committee

GMSI Grand Master of the Order of the Star of India

GMST Grant-Maintained Schools Trust; [astronomy] Greenwich Mean Sidereal Time

GMT Greenwich Mean Time

GMTA great minds think alike (in Internet chat)

GMTV Good Morning Television

GMV [microbiology] golden mosaic virus

GMW gram-molecular weight

GN [USA] Graduate Nurse; [fishing port] Granton; [vehicle registration] southwest London

gn grandnephew; grandniece

gn. [currency] guinea

.gn Guinea (in Internet address)

GNA Ghana News Agency; Guinea News Agency; Guyana News Agency

GNAS Grand National Archery Society

GNC General Nursing Council (replaced by UKCC)

gnd ground

GNMA [USA] Government National Mortgage Association

GNP [economics] gross national product

GNR *Guarda Nacional Republicana* (Portuguese: National Republican Guard)

Gnr Gunner

GnRH [biochemistry] gonadotrophin-releasing hormone

gns guineas

GNTC Girls' Nautical Training Corps

GNVQ General National Vocational Qualification

GO gas operated; General Office; General Officer; [military] general order; [music] great organ; Group Officer; [vehicle registration] southwest London

g.o.a. gone on arrival

g.o.b. good ordinary brand

GOC General Officer Commanding; General Optical Council; Greek Orthodox Church

GOC-in-C General Officer Commanding-in-Chief

GOCO government-owned, contractor-operated

GOE General Ordination Examination

GOES [USA] Geostationary Operational Environmental Satellite

GOM Grand Old Man

GONG [astronomy] Global Oscillations Network Group

GOP *Girls' Own Paper*; [USA] Grand Old Party (i.e. the Republican Party)

Gopa Government Oil and Pipeline Agency

GORD [medicine] gastro-oesophageal reflux disease

Gos. *Gosudarstvo* (Russian: state) (in former USSR)

GOSIP [computing] government open systems interconnection profile

Gosplan *Gosudarstvennaya Planovaya Comissiya* (Russian: State Planning Commission) (in former USSR)

Gosud. *Gosudarstvo* (Russian: state) (in former USSR)

Goth. Gothic

gou. [currency] gourde (used in Haiti)

Gov. Government; Governor

gov. government; governor

.gov government (in Internet address)

Gov-Gen Governor-General

Govt Government

govt government

.gov.uk UK government (in Internet address)

GOX gaseous oxygen

GP Gallup Poll; gas-permeable (contact lenses); [medicine] general paralysis; [music] general pause; general practitioner; general purpose; general-purpose computer; *Gloria Patri* (Latin: Glory to the Father); government property; graduated pension; Graduate in Pharmacy; *grande passion* (French: great passion); grand passion; Grand Prix; gross profit; [vehicle registration] south-west London

gp group

g.p. [printing] galley proofs; [mathematics] geometrical progression; [printing] great primer

GPA General Practitioners' Association; [US education] grade point average

GPALS Global Protection Against Limited Strikes (reduced form of SDI)

GPC general purposes committee

g.p.c. good physical condition (in advertisement)

Gp Capt Group Captain

gpcd gallons per caput per day

Gp Comdr Group Commander

gpd gallons per day

GPDST Girls' Public Day School Trust

GPh Graduate in Pharmacy

gph gallons per hour

GPHI Guild of Public Health Inspectors

GPI [medicine] general paralysis of the insane

GPIB [computing] general-purpose interface bus

GPKT Grand Priory of the Knights of the Temple

GPM [USA] graduated payment mortgage; [Freemasonry] Grand Past Master

gpm gallons per minute

GPMU Graphical, Paper and Media Union (became part of NATSOPA)

GPO General Post Office; [USA] Government Printing Office

GPR *genio populi Romani* (Latin: to the genius of the Roman people); ground-penetrating radar

GPS Global Positioning System; Graduated Pension Scheme; [Australia] Great Public Schools

gps gallons per second

GPSS General Purpose System Simulator

GPT Guild of Professional Toastmasters

GPU General Postal Union (former name of UPU); [USA] General Public Utilities Corporation; *Gosudarstvennoye Politicheskoye Upravlenie* (Russian: State Political Administration) (former Soviet secret police)

GQ [military] general quarters

.gq Equatorial Guinea (in Internet address)

GQG *Grand Quartier Général* (French: General Headquarters)

GR gamma ray; general reconnaissance; [physics] general relativity; general reserve; *Georgius Rex* (Latin: King

George); [fishing port] Gloucester; grand recorder; [international vehicle registration] Greece; ground rent; *Gulielmus Rex* (Latin: King William); Gurkha Rifles; [vehicle registration] Newcastle upon Tyne

Gr Gunner

Gr. Great; Greater; Grecian; Greece; Greek; Grove (in road name)

gr. grade; grain (unit of weight); gram; grammar; grand; great; greater; grey; gross; ground; group

.gr Greece (in Internet address)

GRA Game Research Association; Greyhound Racing Association

GRACE group routing and charging equipment

grad. gradient; grading; gradual; graduate; graduated

GradIAE Graduate of the Institution of Automobile Engineers

GradInstBE Graduate of the Institution of British Engineers

GradInstP Graduate of the Institute of Physics

GradInstR Graduate of the Institute of Refrigeration

GradSE Graduate of the Society of Engineers

gram. grammar; grammarian; grammatical

GRAS [USA] generally regarded as safe

GRB [astronomy] gamma-ray burst; Gas Research Board

GRBI Gardeners' Royal Benevolent Institution

Gr. Br. Great Britain

Gr. Brit. Great Britain

GRBS Gardeners' Royal Benevolent Society

GRC General Research Corporation

Gr. Capt Group Captain

GRCM Graduate of the Royal College of Music

GRDF Gulf Rapid Deployment Force

GRE [USA] Graduate Record Examination; grant-related expenditure; Guardian Royal Exchange Assurance plc

GRF [biochemistry] growth-hormone releasing factor

gr.f. [horseracing] grey filly

GRI *Georgius Rex Imperator* (Latin: George

King and Emperor); [New Zealand] guaranteed retirement income

GRID gay-related immunodeficiency; Global Resource Information Database

Gr-L Graeco-Latin

grm gram

GRN goods received note

Grn Green (in road name)

grn green

GRO Gamma Ray Observatory; General Register Office; Greenwich Royal Observatory

Gro. Grove

gro. gross

GROBDM General Register Office for Births, Deaths and Marriages

gro. t. gross ton; gross tonnage

GRP glass(fibre)-reinforced plastic (or polyester)

grp group

GRS [astronomy] Great Red Spot (on Jupiter)

grs grains; gross

GRSC Graduate of the Royal Society of Chemistry

GRSE Guild of Radio Service Engineers

GRSM Graduate of the Royal Schools of Music

gr. t. gross ton

g.r.t. gross registered tonnage

GRU *Glavnoye Razvedyvatelnoye Upravleniye* (Russian: Central Intelligence Office) (in former USSR)

Gru [astronomy] Grus

gr. wt gross weight

g.r.y. [finance] gross redemption yield

GS General Schedule (in US civil service); general secretary; general service; [military] General Staff; geographical survey; geological survey; [netball] goal shooter; gold standard; grammar school; [aeronautics] ground speed; [vehicle registration] Luton

Gs gauss (unit of magnetic flux density); [currency] guaraní (used in Paraguay)

gs grandson; guineas

GSA [USA] General Services Administration; Girl Scouts of America; Girls' Schools Association; Glasgow School of Art

GS&WR [Ireland] Great Southern and Western Railway

GSB Government Savings Bank

GSC [chemistry] gas–solid chromatography; General Service Corps; [USA] General Staff Corps

GSD general supply depot; [astronomy] Greenwich sidereal gate

GSE ground service equipment; ground support equipment

GSEE *Geniki Synomospondia Ergaton Hellados* (Greek: Greek General Confederation of Labour)

GSGB Geological Survey of Great Britain; Golf Society of Great Britain

GSI [medicine] genuine stress incontinence

GSL Geological Society of London; group Scout leader; [USA] guaranteed student loan

GSM Garrison Sergeant-Major; general sales manager; General Service Medal; global system for mobile communications; (Member of the) Guildhall School of Music (and Drama)

gsm grams per square metre (unit of weight of paper)

g.s.m. [commerce] good sound merchantable (quality)

GSMD (Member of the) Guildhall School of Music and Drama

GSO General Staff Officer

GSOH good sense of humour (in personal advertisement)

GSP glass(fibre)-strengthened polyester; Good Service Pension; [economics] gross social product

G-spot Gräfenburg spot (erogenous zone)

GSR galvanic skin reflex; galvanic skin response

GSS geostationary satellite; global surveillance system; Government Statistical Service

GST [Canada, New Zealand] goods and services tax; [astronomy] Greenwich Sidereal Time

g. st. [knitting] garter stitch

GSVQ General Scottish Vocational Qualification

GSW gunshot wound

GT gas turbine; [physics] gauge theory; Good Templar; [Freemasonry] Grand Tiler; *Gran Turismo* (Italian: Grand Touring) (sports car); greetings telegram; [vehicle registration] southwest London

gt [bookbinding] gilt; great

gt. [medicine] *gutta* (Latin: a drop)

.gt Guatemala (in Internet address)

g.t. gas tight; [bookbinding] gilt top; gross tonnage

GTA gas–tungsten arc

Gt Br. Great Britain

Gt Brit. Great Britain

GTC [Scotland] General Teaching Council; Girls' Training Corps; [commerce] good till cancelled (or countermanded); Government Training Centre

GTCL Graduate of Trinity College of Music, London

gtd guaranteed

g.t.e. [bookbinding] gilt top edge

gtee guarantee

GTH [biochemistry] gonadotrophic hormone

GTI GT Injection (sports car)

gtm good this month

GTO *Gran Turismo Omologato* (Italian: homologated GT) (sports car)

GTR general theory of relativity

gtr greater

GTS gas turbine ship; [USA] General Theological Seminary

GTT [medicine] glucose tolerance test

gtt. [medicine] *guttae* (Latin: drops); [medicine] *guttatim* (Latin: drop by drop)

g.t.w. good this week

GU [medicine] gastric ulcer; [medicine] genitourinary; [fishing port] Guernsey; [UK postcode] Guildford; [vehicle registration] southeast London

Gu. Guinea

gu. [currency] guinea; [heraldry] gules (= red)

guar. guarantee; guaranteed

Guat. Guatemala

GUI Golfing Union of Ireland; [computing] graphical user interface

gui. guitar

GUIDO [US astronautics] Guidance Officer

guil. [currency] guilder

Guin. Guinea

Gulag *Glavnoye Upravleniye Lagerei* (Russian: Central Administration for Camps) (former Soviet labour camp system)

GUM [medicine] genitourinary medicine; *Gosudarstvenni Universalni Magazin* (Russian: Universal State Store)

gun. gunnery; gunpowder
GUR [medicine] glucose utilization rate
GUS Great Universal Stores
GUT [physics] grand unified theory
guttat. [medicine] *guttatim* (Latin: drop by drop)
guv [short form] governor
g.u.v. *gerecht und vollkommen* (German: correct and complete)
GUY [international vehicle registration] Guyana
GV *grande vitesse* (French: high speed (train)); [vehicle registration] Ipswich
g.v. gravimetric volume; gross valuation
GVH [medicine] graft versus host
GVHD [medicine] graft-versus-host disease
gvt government
GVW gross vehicle weight
GW George Washington (US president); gigawatt; [fishing port] Glasgow; gross weight; guided weapon(s); [vehicle registration] southeast London
.gw Guinea-Bissau (in Internet address)
GW-Basic [computing] gee whizz begin-

ners' all-purpose symbolic instruction code
GWF gay white female
GWH gigawatt-hour
GWM gay white male
GWP Government White Paper; [economics] gross world product
GWR Great Western Railway
Gwyn. Gwynedd
GX [vehicle registration] southeast London
GY [fishing port] Grimsby; [UK postcode] Guernsey; [vehicle registration] southeast London
Gy gray (unit of radiation dose)
.gy Guyana (in Internet address)
gym [short form] gymnasium; [short form] gymnastics
gyn. gynaecological; gynaecology
gynaecol. gynaecological; gynaecology
GZ [vehicle registration] Belfast; ground zero
G-Z [astronomy] Giacobini–Zinner (comet)

H

H [advertising] half page; harbour; hard (pencil lead); hardness; [card games] hearts; [immunology] heavy; height; henry (unit of electric inductance); herbaceous; [slang] heroin; [medicine] histamine receptor; [biochemistry] histidine; Holy; [music] horn; hospital; hour; [fishing port] Hull; [international vehicle registration] Hungary; hydrant; [chemical element] hydrogen
H [physics, medicine] dose equivalent; [physics] Hamiltonian; [physics, photography] light exposure; [physics] magnetic field strength
h [meteorology] hail; hecto- (indicates 100, as in **hg** = hectogram); hour
h [physics] heat transfer coefficient; height; [physics] Planck constant
h. hand; harbour; hard; hardness; heat; height; high; hip; [sports] hit; horizontal; [music] horn; horse; hot; hour; house; hundred; husband
H4 [civil aircraft marking] Solomon Islands

2H double hard (pencil lead)
3H treble hard (pencil lead)
5H [civil aircraft marking] Tanzania
9H [civil aircraft marking] Malta
HA [vehicle registration] Dudley; [medicine] haemagglutination; [horticulture] hardy annual; [UK postcode] Harrow; Hautes-Alpes (French department); health authority; heavy artillery; high altitude; Highway(s) Act; [biochemistry] histamine; Historical Association; Hockey Association; [astronomy] hour angle; [geology] humic acid; [civil aircraft marking] Hungary; Hydraulic Association of Great Britain
Ha [chemical element] hahnium
Ha. Haiti; Haitian; Hawaii; Hawaiian
ha hectare
h.a. heir apparent; high angle (in gunnery); *hoc anno* (Latin: in this year)
HAA heavy anti-aircraft; [immunology] hepatitis-associated antigen

HA&M *Hymns Ancient and Modern*

HAB high-altitude bombing

Hab. [Bible] Habakkuk

hab. habitat; habitation

hab. corp. [law] habeas corpus (type of writ)

habt *habeat* (Latin: let him have)

HAC high-alumina cement; Honourable Artillery Company

HACSG Hyperactive Children's Support Group

h.a.d. hereinafter described

haem. haemoglobin; haemorrhage

HAF Hellenic Air Force

Hag. [Bible] Haggai

hagiol. hagiology

HAI [medicine] haemagglutination inhibition; Health Action International; [medicine] hospital-acquired infection

HAIL Hague Academy of International Law

Hak. Soc. Hakluyt Society

Hal [computing] hard-array logic

hal. halogen

Hal. Orch. Hallé Orchestra

Ham. Hamburg

Han. Hanover; Hanoverian

H&C hot and cold (water)

H&E *Health and Efficiency*; heredity and environment

h&f heated and filtered (swimming pool)

h&j [printing] hyphenation and justification

h&t hardened and tempered; hospitalization and treatment

H&W Harland and Wolff (shipbuilding company); Hereford and Worcester

Hants Hampshire (from Old English name of county)

HAO hydrogenated anthracene oil

HAP hazardous air pollutant

HAPA Handicapped Adventure Playground Association

h. app. heir apparent

HAPPA Horses and Ponies Protection Association

HaPV [microbiology] hamster polyomavirus

har. harbour

HARCVS Honorary Associate of the Royal College of Veterinary Surgeons

HARM high-speed anti-radiation missile

harm. harmonic; harmony

harp. harpoon; harpsichord

HART [New Zealand] Halt All Racist Tours (sports organization)

Harv. [USA] Harvard University

HAS Headmasters' Association of Scotland; Health Advisory Service; Helicopter Air Service; Hospital Advisory Service

HASAWA Health and Safety at Work Act

HASTE Helicopter Ambulance Service to Emergencies

HAT housing action trust; housing association trust

haust. [medicine] *haustus* (Latin: draught)

HAV [medicine] hepatitis A virus

HAWT horizontal-axis wind turbine

haz. hazard; hazardous

HAZOP [computing] hazard and operability study

HB [vehicle registration] Cardiff; hard black (pencil lead softer than H); [horticulture] hardy biennial; His Beatitude; House of Bishops; [civil aircraft marking] Switzerland and Liechtenstein

Hb [biochemistry] haemoglobin

h.b. [sports] halfback; handbook; hard-back (of books); homing beacon; human being

HbA [biochemistry] adult haemoglobin

HBAB [medicine] hepatitis B antibody

h'back hatchback (in car advertisement)

HBAg [medicine] hepatitis B antigen

HBC [electrical engineering] high breaking capacity; Historic Buildings Council; Hudson's Bay Company

HBCU [USA] Historically Black Colleges and Universities

HBD had (or has) been drinking

hbd hardboard; headboard

h.b.d. hereinbefore described

HBF [medicine] hepatic blood flow; House-Builders' Federation

HbF [biochemistry] fetal haemoglobin

Hbf. *Hauptbahnhof* (German: central station)

HBIG [medicine] hepatitis B immunoglobulin

HBJ Harcourt Brace Jovanovich

hbk hardback (of books)

HBLV [medicine] human B-lymphotropic virus

HBM Her/His Britannic Majesty('s)

HBMC Historic Buildings and Monuments Commission for England
HBO hyperbaric oxygen
h/board hardboard; headboard
H-bomb hydrogen bomb
HBP [medicine] high blood pressure
HBPF High Blood Pressure Foundation
hbr harbour
HBS Harvard Business School
HbS [biochemistry] sickle-cell haemoglobin
HBT [electronics] heterojunction bipolar transistor
Hbt Hobart
HBV [medicine] hepatitis B virus
HBWTA Home Brewing and Winemaking Trade Association
hby hereby
HC [vehicle registration] Brighton; [civil aircraft marking] Ecuador; Hague Convention; Hairdressing Council; hard copy; Headmasters' Conference; Headteachers' Conference; health certificate; Heralds' College; High Church; High Commission; High Commissioner; High Court; higher certificate; highly commended; [computing] high-speed CMOS; *Highway Code*; hockey club; Holy Communion; home counties; *hors concours* (French: outside the competition); House of Clergy; House of Commons; house of correction; housing centre; housing corporation
H/C [insurance] held covered; hot and cold (water)
h.c. habitual criminal; hand control; heating cabinet; high capacity; *honoris causa* (Latin: for the sake of honour, honorary); hot and cold (water)
HCA Hospital Caterers' Association
HCAAS Homeless Children's Aid and Adoption Society
hcap handicap
HCB House of Commons Bill
HCBA Hotel and Catering Benevolent Association
HCC Housing Consultative Council for England
h.c.c. hydraulic cement concrete
h.c.d. high current density
h.c.e. human-caused error
HCEC Hospital Committee of the European Community

HCF high-calorific fuel; high carbohydrate and fibre; [mathematics] highest common factor; Honorary Chaplain to the Forces
h.c.f. hundred cubic feet
HCFC hydrochlorofluorocarbon
HCG [biochemistry] human chorionic gonadotrophin
HCH Herbert Clark Hoover (US president); hexachlorocyclohexane (insecticide)
HCI Hotel and Catering Institute; human–computer interaction (or interface)
HCIL Hague Conference on International Law
HCIMA Hotel Catering and Institutional Management Association
HCITB Hotel and Catering Industry Training Board
HCJ High Court of Justice; Holy Child Jesus
h.c.l. high cost of living
HCM Her Catholic Majesty; High Court Master; His Catholic Majesty
HCO Harvard College Observatory; higher clerical officer
HCOPIL Hague Conference on Private International Law
HCP House of Commons Paper
hcp handicap
HCPT Historic Churches Preservation Trust
hcptr helicopter
HCR High Chief Ranger; [USA] highway contract route
HCS Home Civil Service
h.c.s. high-carbon steel
HCSA Hospital Consultants and Specialists Association
HCT [computing] high-speed CMOS with TTL inputs
HCVC Historic Commercial Vehicle Club
HCVD [medicine] hypertensive cardiovascular disease
h.c.w. hot and cold water
HD heavy duty; [medicine] herniated disc; high density; high dose (of radiation); (51st) Highland Division; Hilda Doolittle (US poet); [medicine] Hodgkin's disease; home defence; honourable discharge; Hoover Dam; [UK postcode] Huddersfield; [vehicle registration] Huddersfield; [chemistry] hydrogen–deuterium

H/D [shipping] Havre–Dunkirk

hd hand; head

h.d. heavy duty; high density; [medicine] *hora decubitus* (Latin: at bedtime) (in prescriptions)

HDA [Australia] Hawkesbury Diploma in Agriculture; high-duty alloy; Hospital Doctors' Association

HDATZ high-density air traffic zone

hdbk handbook; hardback (of books)

HDC [medicine] high-dose chemotherapy; [law] holder in due course

HDCD high-density CD-ROM

HDCR Higher Diploma of the College of Radiographers

HDD [computing] hard disk drive; [aeronautics, computing] head-down display; heavy-duty diesel; Higher Dental Diploma

hdg heading

HDipEd Higher Diploma in Education

HDK husbands don't know

hdkf handkerchief

HDL [computing] hardware description language; [biochemistry] high-density lipoprotein

hdl. handle

HDLC [biochemistry] high-density lipoprotein cholesterol; [computing] high-level data link control

hdle handle; [horseracing] hurdle

hdlg handling

hdlr handler

HDM high-duty metal

HDN [medicine] haemolytic disease of the newborn

hdn harden

HDP heavy-duty petrol; [chemistry] high-density polyeth(yl)ene

HDPE [chemistry] high-density poly-eth(yl)ene

hdqrs headquarters

HDR high dose rate (of radiation); hot dry rock

HDRA Henry Doubleday Research Association

HDTV high-definition television

HDU haemodialysis unit

HDV heavy-duty vehicle; [medicine] hepatitis delta virus

hdw. [computing] hardware

hdwd hardwood; headword

HE [medicine] hepatic encephalopathy; Her Excellency; high energy; higher education; high explosive; His Eminence; His Excellency; home establishment; horizontal equivalent; hydraulic engineer; [vehicle registration] Sheffield

He [chemical element] helium

He. Hebrew

h.e. heat engine; *hic est* (Latin: this is); hub end

HEA Health Education Authority; Horticultural Education Association

HEAO High Energy Astronomy Observatory; High Energy Astrophysical Observatory

Heb. Hebraic; Hebrew; [Bible] Hebrews

Hebr. Hebrew; [Bible] Hebrews; Hebridean; Hebrides

HEC (*école des*) *hautes études commerciales* (French: (college of) higher commercial studies); Health Education Council; Higher Education Corporation; [chemistry] hydroxyethyl cellulose

HECTOR [nuclear technology] heated experimental carbon thermal oscillator reactor

HEDCOM [US air force] headquarters command

HEF high-energy fuel

HEFA Human Embryo and Fertilization Authority

HEFC Higher Education Funding Council

HEH Her/His Exalted Highness

h.e.i. high-explosive incendiary

HEIC Honourable East India Company

HEICS Honourable East India Company's Service

heir app. heir apparent

heir pres. heir presumptive

HEL high-energy laser

hel. helicopter

heli. helicopter

Hellen. Hellenic; Hellenism; Hellenistic

HELLP [medicine] haemolysis, elevated liver enzymes, low platelet count (as in **HELLP syndrome**)

helo [short form] helicopter; [short form] heliport

HELP helicopter electronic landing path; Help Establish Lasting Peace

HEMM heavy earth-moving machinery

HEMS helicopter-based emergency medical services

HEMT [electronics] high-electron-mobility transistor

HEO [astronautics] high earth orbit; higher executive officer

HEP [statistics] human error probability; hydroelectric power

HEPC [USA] hydroelectric power commission

HEPCAT helicopter pilot control and training

Her [astronomy] Hercules

Her. Hereford(shire)

her. heraldic; heraldry; [law] *heres* (Latin: heir)

HERA high-explosive rocket-assisted

HERALD [nuclear technology] Highly Enriched Reactor, Aldermaston

herb. herbaceous; herbalist; herbarium

hered. hereditary; heredity

HERI Higher Education Research Institute

herm. hermetic; hermetically

Herod. Herodotus (ancient Greek historian)

herp. herpetologist; herpetology

herpet. herpetologist; herpetology

herpetol. herpetologist; herpetology

Herts Hertfordshire

HERU Higher Education Research Unit

HET heavy-equipment transporter

heterocl. heteroclite

heterog. heterogeneous

HEU highly enriched uranium

heur. heuristic

HEW [USA] Department of Health, Education and Welfare (replaced by HHS)

hex [computing] hexadecimal (notation)

hex. hexachord; hexagon; hexagonal

hexa. hexamethylene tetramine (synthetic rubber)

hexag. hexagonal

HF hard firm (pencil lead); [radio] high frequency; Holy Father; home fleet; home forces; [vehicle registration] Liverpool

H/F [commerce] *Hlutafjelagid* (Icelandic: limited company, Ltd)

Hf [chemical element] hafnium

hf half

h.f. hold fire; [military] horse and foot

Hfa Haifa (Israel)

HFARA Honorary Foreign Associate of the Royal Academy

hf bd [bookbinding] half bound

HFC high-frequency current; [chemistry] hydrofluorocarbon

hf cf [bookbinding] half calf

hf cl. [bookbinding] half cloth

HFDF high-frequency direction-finder

HFEA Human Fertility and Embryology Authority

h.f.m. hold for money

hf mor. [bookbinding] half morocco

HFO heavy fuel oil; high-frequency oscillator

HFR [nuclear technology] high-flux reactor

hfr heifer

HFRA Honorary Foreign Member of the Royal Academy

HFRO Hill Farming Research Organization

HFS heated front seats (in car advertisement)

Hft *Heft* (German: part (of book))

HG [UK postcode] Harrogate; Haute-Garonne (French department); Her Grace; High German; high grade; His Grace; Holy Ghost; Home Guard; Horse Guards; [vehicle registration] Preston

Hg [chemical element] mercury (from Latin *hydrargyrum*)

hg hectogram

hgb. haemoglobin

HGC [computing] Hercules graphics card

HGCA Home Grown Cereals Authority

hgd hogshead

HGDH Her/His Grand Ducal Highness

HGG [biochemistry] human gamma-globulin; [medicine] hypogammaglobulinaemia

HGH [biochemistry] human growth hormone

HGHSC Home Grown Herbage Seeds Committee

HGMM Hereditary Grand Master Mason

hgr hangar; hanger

hgt height

HGTAC Home Grown Timber Advisory Committee

HGTMC Home Grown Timber Marketing Corporation

HGV heavy goods vehicle (replaced by LGV)

HGW heat-generating water; H(erbert) G(eorge) Wells (British writer)

hgwy highway

HH [vehicle registration] Carlisle; double hard (pencil lead); [civil aircraft marking]

Haiti; [fishing port] Harwich; [physics, chemistry] heavy hydrogen; Her Highness; Her Honour; (Member of the) Hesketh Hubbard Art Society; His Highness; His Holiness; His Honour

hh hands (unit of height of horses)

HHA [horticulture] half-hardy annual; Historic Houses Association

HHB [horticulture] half-hardy biennial

HHD [USA] Doctor of Humanities (from Latin *Humanitatum Doctor*); [medicine] hypertensive heart disease

hhd hogshead

HHDWS heavy handy deadweight scrap

HHFA [USA] Housing and Home Finance Agency

HHH treble hard (pencil lead)

HHI Highland Home Industries

hhld household

HHNK [medicine] hyperglycaemic hyperosmolar nonketoacidotic (diabetic coma)

H-Hour Hour Hour (i.e. specified time, esp. of commencement of operation)

HHP [horticulture] half-hardy perennial

HHS [USA] Department of Health and Human Services (replacement for HEW)

HHV [medicine] human herpes virus

HHW household hazardous waste

HI [civil aircraft marking] Dominican Republic; [US postcode] Hawaii; Hawaiian Islands; hearing impaired; [surveying] height of instrument; *hic iacet* (Latin: here lies) (on tombstone); high intensity

Hi. Hindi

HIA Housing Improvement Association

h.i.a. hold in abeyance

hi. ac. high accuracy

HIAS [USA] Hebrew Immigrant Aid Society

HIB Herring Industry Board

Hib [medicine] *Haemophilus influenzae* type B (as in **Hib vaccine**)

Hib. Hibernia; Hibernian

HICAT high-altitude clear air turbulence

Hi. Com. High Command; High Commission; High Commissioner

HIDB Highlands and Islands Development Board

HIE Highlands and Islands Enterprise

hier. hieroglyphics

hi-fi [short form] high fidelity (equipment)

HIH Her/His Imperial Highness

HIL [chemistry] hazardous immiscible liquid

HILAC [nuclear technology] heavy-ion linear accelerator

HILAT high-latitude (satellite)

HIM Her/His Imperial Majesty

Hind. Hindi; Hindu; Hindustan; Hindustani

HIP [USA] health-insurance plan; [accounting] human information processing

HIPAR high-power acquisition radar

hipot high potential

Hipp. Hippocrates (ancient Greek physician)

HIPPI [computing] high-performance parallel processor interface

HIPS high-impact polystyrene (synthetic plastic)

hi-rel high reliability

hi-res [physics] high resolution

HIS *hic iacet sepultus* (or *sepulta*) (Latin: here lies buried) (on tombstone)

hist. histology; historian; historic(al); history

histn historian

histol. histological; histologist; histology

hi-tech [short form] high technology

Hitt. Hittite

HIUS Hispanic Institute of the United States

HIV [medicine] human immunodeficiency virus (formerly LAV)

HIV-P [medicine] HIV-positive

HJ [vehicle registration] Chelmsford; *hic jacet* (Latin: here lies) (on tombstone); high jump; Hilal-e-Jurat (Pakistani honour); *Hitler Jugend* (German: Hitler Youth)

HJBT [electronics] heterojunction bipolar transistor

HJS *hic jacet sepultus* (or *sepulta*) (Latin: here lies buried) (on tombstone)

HJSC Hospital Junior Staff Council

HK [vehicle registration] Chelmsford; [civil aircraft marking] Colombia; Hong Kong; [international vehicle registration] Hong Kong; House of Keys (parliament of Isle of Man); [taxation] housekeeper allowance

.hk Hong Kong (in Internet address)

hkf handkerchief

HKI Helen Keller International

HKJ [international vehicle registration] (Hashemite Kingdom of) Jordan

HL hard labour; [fishing port] Hartlepool; Haute-Loire (French department); honours list; House of Laity; House of Lords; [civil aircraft marking] Republic of Korea; [vehicle registration] Sheffield

Hl. *Heilige(r)* (German: Saint)

hl hectolitre

h.l. *hoc loco* (Latin: in this place)

HLA [immunology] human lymphocyte antigen

HLBB [USA] Home Loan Bank Board

HLD Doctor of Humane Letters

HLE [physics] high-level exposure (to radiation)

HLG Historic Landscapes Group

HLHSR [computing] hidden-line/hidden-surface removal

HLI Highland Light Infantry

HLL [computing] high-level language

h/lmp headlamp

HLNW high-level nuclear waste

HLPR Howard League for Penal Reform

hlpr helper

HLRW high-level radioactive waste

HLS Harvard Law School

HLW headlamp wipers (in car advertisement); high-level waste

HLWN highest low water neaps (level of tide)

HLWW headlamp wash and wipe (in car advertisement)

HM [vehicle registration] central London; harbour master; [music] harmonic mean; Haute-Marne (French department); [chemistry] hazardous material; headmaster; headmistress; heavy metal; Her Majesty('s); His Majesty('s); home mission

hm hectometre

h.m. hallmark; *hoc mense* (Latin: in this month)

HMA Head Masters' Association; [computing] high-memory area

HMAC Her/His Majesty's Aircraft Carrier

HMAS Her/His Majesty's Australian Ship

HMBDV Her/His Majesty's Boom Defence Vessel

HMC Headmasters' and Headmistresses' Conference; Her/His Majesty's Customs; Historical Manuscripts Commission; Hor-ticultural Marketing Council; Hospital Management Committee; Household Mortgage Corporation

HMCA Hospital and Medical Care Association

HMCG Her/His Majesty's Coast Guard

HMCIC Her/His Majesty's Chief Inspector of Constabulary

HMCIF Her/His Majesty's Chief Inspector of Factories

HMCN Her/His Majesty's Canadian Navy

HMCS Her/His Majesty's Canadian Ship

HMCSC Her/His Majesty's Civil Service Commissioners

HMD [computing] head-mounted display; Her/His Majesty's Destroyer

hmd humid

HMF [chemistry] heavy-metal fluoride; Her/His Majesty's Forces

HMFI Her/His Majesty's Factory Inspec-torate

HMG heavy machine gun; Her/His Maj-esty's Government; [medicine] human menopausal gonadotrophin

HMHS Her/His Majesty's Hospital Ship

HMI Her/His Majesty's Inspector (of schools); Her/His Majesty's Inspectorate (of schools); [computing] human–machine interface

HMIC Her/His Majesty's Inspectorate of Constabulary

HMIED Honorary Member of the Insti-tution of Engineering Designers

HMIP Her/His Majesty's Inspectorate of Pollution

HMIT Her/His Majesty's Inspector of Taxes

HML Her/His Majesty's Lieutenant

HMLR Her/His Majesty's Land Registry

HMML Her/His Majesty's Motor Launch

HMMS Her/His Majesty's Mine Sweeper

HMNZS Her/His Majesty's New Zealand Ship

HMO [USA] health maintenance organ-ization

HMOCS Her/His Majesty's Overseas Civil Service

HMP Her/His Majesty's Prison; *hoc monu-mentum posuit* (Latin: (he/she) erected this monument)

h.m.p. handmade paper

HMRT Her/His Majesty's Rescue Tug

HMS [mining] heavy media separation;

Her/His Majesty's Service; Her/His Majesty's Ship

h.m.s. hours, minutes, seconds

HMSO Her/His Majesty's Stationery Office (replaced by The Stationery Office)

hmstd homestead

HMT Her/His Majesty's Trawler; Her/His Majesty's Treasury; Her/His Majesty's Tug

HMV His Master's Voice (music company)

HMW high molecular weight

HMWA Hairdressing Manufacturers' and Wholesalers' Association

HMXB [astronomy] high-mass X-ray binary

HN [vehicle registration] Middlesbrough

hn [music] horn

.hn Honduras (in Internet address)

h.n. [medicine] *hac nocte* (Latin: tonight)

HNC [education] Higher National Certificate

HND [education] Higher National Diploma

hndbk handbook

hndlg handling

hndlr handler

HNL [physics] helium–neon laser

hnRNA [biochemistry] heterogeneous nuclear ribonucleic acid

hnRNP [biochemistry] heterogeneous nuclear ribonucleoprotein

Hnrs Honours

HO [vehicle registration] Bournemouth; [law] habitual offender; head office; Home Office; hostilities only; Hydrographic Office

Ho [chemical element] holmium

ho. house

h.o. hold over

hobgoblin [informal] help, our budget's gone beyond the limits of our income

HOC heavy organic chemical

HoC House of Commons

h.o.c. held on charge

HOCRE Home Office Central Research Establishment

HoD head of department

H of C House of Commons

H of K House of Keys

H of L House of Lords

H of R [USA] House of Representatives

HoL House of Lords

Hol [geology] Holocene

Hol. Holland

hol. holiday

HOLC [USA] Home Owners' Loan Corporation

Holl. Holland

HOLLAND hope our love lasts and never dies (on envelope of love letter)

Holmes Home Office Large Major Enquiry System (crime-investigation computer)

hols [short form] holidays

Hom. Homer (ancient Greek poet)

homoeo. homoeopath; homoeopathic; homoeopathy

Hon. Honorary; Honorary Member; Honourable

hon. honorary; honour; honourable

Hond. Honduran; Honduras

Hono. Honolulu

Hons Honours

Hon. Sec. honorary secretary

HOOD [computing] hierarchical object-oriented design

hopeful [informal] hard-up old person expecting full useful life

Hor [astronomy] Horologium

Hor. Horace (Roman poet)

hor. horizon; horizontal; horology

hor. decub. [medicine] *hora decubitus* (Latin: at bedtime) (in prescriptions)

HoReCa (International Union of National Associations of) Hotel, Restaurant and Café Keepers

horol. horological; horologist; horology

hort. horticultural; horticulturalist; horticulture

hortic. horticultural; horticulture

HORU Home Office Research Unit

Hos. [Bible] Hosea

hosp. hospital

HOT Hawk and Owl Trust

HOTOL [astronautics] horizontal take-off and landing

HOV high-occupancy vehicle

how. howitzer

HP [vehicle registration] Coventry; Handley Page (aircraft); [horticulture] hardy perennial; Hautes-Pyrénées (French department); [UK postcode] Hemel Hempstead; [trademark] Hewlett-Packard (computer manufacturer); high performance; high power; high pressure; high priest; Himachal Pradesh; hire purchase; hot-pressed (paper); house phys-

ician; Houses of Parliament;
[horticulture] hybrid perpetual (rose);
[civil aircraft marking] Panama

hp horsepower

h.p. half pay; heir presumptive; high
power (electricity); hire purchase; hori-
zontally polarized

HPA Hospital Physicists' Association

HPC [medicine] history of present complaint

hpch. harpsichord

hpd harpsichord

HPF [computing] highest priority first

HPFS [computing] high-performance
filing system

HPGL [trademark, computing] Hewlett-
Packard graphics language

HPIB [trademark, computing] Hewlett-
Packard interface bus

HPk Hilal-e-Pakistan (Pakistani honour)

HPLC [chemistry] high-performance
liquid chromatography; [chemistry]
high-pressure liquid chromatography

HPPA Horses and Ponies Protection
Association

HPRU Handicapped Persons Research
Unit

HPS Highland Pony Society; high-
pressure steam; high-protein supplement

HPT high-pressure turbine

HPTA Hire Purchase Trade Association

HPV [medicine] human papilloma virus

HQ headquarters

h.q. headquarters; *hoc quaere* (Latin: look
for this)

HQA Hilal-i-Quaid-i-Azam (Pakistani
honour)

HQBA headquarters base area

HQMC [USA] Headquarters, Marine Corps

HR [international vehicle registration]
Croatia (from Croatian *Hrvatska*); [medi-
cine] heart rate; [UK postcode] Hereford;
Highland Regiment; [optics] high resolution; Home Rule; Home Ruler; [base-
ball] home run; [civil aircraft marking]
Honduras; [USA] House of Representatives; human resources; [vehicle regis-
tration] Swindon

H-R [astronomy] Hertzsprung–Russell
(diagram)

Hr *Herr* (German: Mr, Sir); Hussar

hr [meteorology] hail and rain; hour

.hr Croatia (in Internet address)

h.r. [baseball] home run

HRA [USA] Health Resources Administration

HRC [chemistry] high-resolution chromatography; Holy Roman Church

HRCA Honorary Royal Cambrian Academician

HRCT [medicine] high-resolution com-
pute(rize)d tomography

HRE Holy Roman Emperor; Holy Roman
Empire

HREM high-resolution electron microscope (or microscopy)

HRG high-resolution graphics

HRGC [chemistry] high-resolution gas
chromatography

HRGI Honorary Member of the Royal
Glasgow Institute of the Fine Arts

HRH Her/His Royal Highness

HRHA Honorary Member of the Royal
Hibernian Academy

HRI Honorary Member of the Royal Institute of Painters in Water Colours

HRIP *hic requiescit in pace* (Latin: here rests
in peace) (on tombstone)

HRM human resource management

Hrn *Herren* (German: Messrs, Sirs,
Gentlemen)

HROI Honorary Member of the Royal
Institute of Oil Painters

HRP Home Responsibilities Protection;
[military] human remains pouch

HRR [taxation] higher reduced rate

HRS Human Rights Society

hrs hours

HRSA Honorary Member of the Royal
Scottish Academy

hrsg. *herausgegeben* (German: edited, published)

HRSW Honorary Member of the Royal
Scottish Water Colour Society

HRT [medicine] hormone replacement
therapy

HRTEM high-resolution transmission electron microscope (or microscopy)

HRW heated rear window (in car advertisement)

HS [vehicle registration] Glasgow; Haute-
Saône (French department); Hawker Siddeley (aircraft); *hic sepultus* (or *sepulta*)
(Latin: here is buried) (on tombstone);
high school; Home Secretary; hospital

ship; house surgeon; [numismatics] ses-
terce (Roman coin); [civil aircraft
marking] Thailand

Hs [chemical element] hassium

Hs. *Handschrift* (German: manuscript)

hs [medicine] hail and snow

h.s. highest score; *hoc sensu* (Latin: in this
sense); [medicine] *hora somni* (Latin: at
bedtime) (in prescriptions)

HSA [USA] Health Systems Agency; [medi-
cine] human serum albumin; Humane
Slaughter Association

HSAB [chemistry] hard and soft acids and
bases

HSB [computing] hue, saturation,
brightness

HSBC Hongkong and Shanghai Banking
Corporation

HSC [medicine] haemopoietic stem cell;
Health and Safety Commission; [Aus-
tralia] Higher School Certificate

HSD heat-storage device; high-speed
diesel

HSDU hospital sterilization and disinfec-
tion unit

HSE Health and Safety Executive; *hic sepultus* (or *sepulta*) *est* (Latin: here is
buried) (on tombstone)

hse house

hsekpr housekeeper

hsg housing

HSH Her/His Serene Highness

HSI [computing] human–system interaction (or interface)

HSL [computing] hue, saturation, light-
ness; Huguenot Society of London

HSLA high strength, low alloy (steel)

HSM Her Serene Majesty; [computing]
hierarchical storage management; His
Serene Majesty

HSO Hamburg Symphony Orchestra

HSP [medicine] heat-shock protein

HSR [genetics] homogeneously staining
region

HSS high-speed steel; *Historicae Societatis
Socius* (Latin: Fellow of the Historical
Society)

Hss. *Handschriften* (German: manuscripts)

HSSU hospital sterile supply unit

HST Harry S Truman (US president);
Hawaii Standard Time; highest spring
tide; high-speed train; Hubble Space Telescope; hypersonic transport

HSV [medicine] herpes simplex virus

HSWA [USA] Hazardous and Solid Waste
Act; [USA] Hazardous and Solid Waste
Amendments

HT [vehicle registration] Bristol; [sports]
half time; Hawaii Time; heat-treated;
heat treatment; high temperature; [elec-
trical engineering] high tension; high
tide; high treason; [horticulture] hybrid
tea (rose)

ht heat; height

h/t [printing] half-title

.ht Haiti (in Internet address)

h.t. [sports] half time; halftone; heavy
tank; *hoc tempore* (Latin: at this time);
hoc titulo (Latin: under this title)

HTA Help the Aged; Horticultural Traders'
Association; Household Textile
Association

h.t.b. high-tension battery

HTC [physics] heat-transfer coefficient

htd heated

Hte *Haute* (French: high) (in place-names)

htg heating

HTGR [nuclear technology] high-
temperature gas-cooled reactor

HTLV [medicine] human T-cell lymph-
otropic virus

HTM heat-transfer medium

HTML [computing] hypertext markup language (used on Internet)

HTOL [astronautics] horizontal take-off
and landing

HTR [nuclear technology] high-
temperature reactor

htr heater

H Trin. Holy Trinity

HTS high-temperature superconductivity;
high-temperature superconductor; high-
tensile steel

Hts Heights (in place-names)

h.t.s. half-time survey; high-tensile steel

HTT heavy tactical transport

HTTP [computing] hypertext transfer protocol (used on Internet)

HTTR [nuclear technology] high-
temperature test reactor

HTV Harlech Television

ht wkt [cricket] hit wicket

HU [vehicle registration] Bristol;
Harvard University; [UK postcode]
Hull

.hu Hungary (in Internet address)

HUAC House (of Representatives) Un-American Activities Committee

HUD [aeronautics, computing] head-up display; [USA] (Department of) Housing and Urban Development

Hugo Human Genome Organization

HUJ Hebrew University of Jerusalem

HUKFORLANT [US navy] hunter-killer forces, Atlantic

HUKS [US navy] hunter-killer submarine

Hum. humanities (academic subject)

hum. human; humane; humanism; humanity; humble; humorous

HUMINT [military] human intelligence

HUMRRO Human Resources Research Office

HUMV [military] human light vehicle

hund. hundred

Hung. Hungarian; Hungary

Hunts Huntingdonshire

HUP Harvard University Press

hur. hurricane

Huridocs International Human Rights Information and Documentation System

hurr. hurricane

Husat Human Science and Advanced Technology Research Institute

husb. husband; husbandry

HV [vehicle registration] central London; health visitor; [anatomy] hepatic vein; high velocity; high voltage; *hoc verbum* (Latin: this word); [civil aircraft marking] Vatican City State

HVAC heating, ventilation and air conditioning; high-voltage alternating current

HVAR high-velocity aircraft rocket

HVCA Heating and Ventilating Contractors' Association

HVCert Health Visitor's Certificate

HVDC high-voltage direct current

HVEM high-voltage electron microscope (or microscopy)

HVP hydrolysed vegetable protein

HVT [physics] half-value thickness; health visitor teacher

hvy heavy

HW [vehicle registration] Bristol; hazardous waste; high water; hot water

h/w herewith; husband and wife

h.w. [cricket] hit wicket

HWL Henry Wadsworth Longfellow (US poet); high-water line

HWLB high water, London Bridge

HWM high-water mark

HWONT high water, ordinary neap tides

HWOST high water, ordinary spring tides

HWR [nuclear technology] heavy-water reactor

HWS hot water system; hurricane warning system

HWW headlamp wash and wipe (in car advertisement); [engineering] hot-and-warm worked

hwy highway

HX [vehicle registration] central London; [UK postcode] Halifax

HXR hard X-ray

HY [vehicle registration] Bristol

Hy. Henry

hy heavy; highway

Hya [astronomy] Hydra

hyb. hybrid

HyCoSy [medicine] hysterosalpingo-contrast sonography

hyd. hydrate; hydraulic; hydrographic

hydrog. hydrographic

hydt hydrant

hyg. hygiene; hygienic

Hyi [astronomy] Hydrus

hyp. hypodermic; [mathematics] hypotenuse; hypothesis; hypothetical

hyperb. hyperbole; hyperbolic

hypo [short form] hypodermic (syringe)

hypoth. hypothesis; hypothetical

HZ [civil aircraft marking] Saudi Arabia; [vehicle registration] Tyrone

Hz hertz

I

I *Iesus* (Latin: Jesus); *Imperator* (Latin: Emperor); *Imperatrix* (Latin: Empress); Imperial; *Imperium* (Latin: Empire); [advertising] (single column) inch; incumbent; Independence; Independent; India; Indian; [chemistry] inductive effect; *Infidelis* (Latin: infidel); information; inspector; Institute; instructor; intelligence; interceptor; International; interpreter; [chemical element] iodine; Ireland; Irish; Island; Isle; issue; Italian; [civil aircraft marking] Italy; [international vehicle registration] Italy; [Roman numeral] one

I [physics] electric current; [chemistry] ionic strength; [physics, chemistry] ionization potential; [physics] luminous intensity; [physics] moment of inertia (in mechanics); [physics] radiant intensity; [mathematics] unit matrix

i [mathematics] imaginary number (square root of −1); [Roman numeral] one

i [physics] instantaneous current

i. *id* (Latin: that); incisor (tooth); indicate; [banking] interest; [grammar] intransitive; island

3i Investors in Industry

IA [vehicle registration] Antrim; Incorporated Accountant; Indian Army; infected area; information anxiety; [taxation] initial allowance; Institute of Actuaries; Inter-American; [computing] International Alphabet (as in **IA5**); [medicine] intra-arterial; [US postcode] Iowa

I/A Isle of Anglesey

Ia Iowa

i.A. *im Auftrage* (German: by order of)

i.a. immediately available; *in absentia* (Latin: while absent); [aeronautics] indicated altitude; initial appearance

IAA indoleacetic acid (plant hormone); Institute of Industrial Administration; International Academy of Astronautics; International Actuarial Association; International Advertising Association

IAAA Irish Amateur Athletic Association; Irish Association of Advertising Agencies

IAAE [USA] Institution of Automotive and Aeronautical Engineers

IAAF International Amateur Athletic Federation

IAAP International Association of Applied Psychology

IAAS Incorporated Association of Architects and Surveyors

IAB Industrial Advisory Board; Industrial Arbitration Board; Inter-American Bank; Internet architecture board

IABA International Association of Aircraft Brokers and Agents

IABO International Association of Biological Oceanography

IAC [USA] Industrial Advisory Council; Institute of Amateur Cinematographers

i.a.c. integration, assembly and checkout

IACA Independent Air Carriers' Association

IACB International Advisory Committee on Bibliography (in UNESCO)

IACCP Inter-American Council of Commerce and Production

IACOMS International Advisory Committee on Marine Sciences

IACP International Association for Child Psychiatry and Allied Professions; International Association of Chiefs of Police; [USA] International Association of Computer Programmers

IACR Institute of Arable Crops Research

IACS International Annealed Copper Standard

IADB Inter-American Defense Board; Inter-American Development Bank

IADR International Association for Dental Research

IAE [USA] Institute of Atomic Energy; Institute of Automotive Engineers; Institution of Automobile Engineers

IAEA International Atomic Energy Agency

IAEC Israel Atomic Energy Commission

IAECOSOC Inter-American Economic and Social Council

IAEE International Association of Energy Economists

IAF Indian Air Force; Indian Auxiliary Force; International Archery Federation; International Astronautical Federation

i.a.f. [aeronautics] interview after flight

IAFD International Association on Food Distribution

IAG International Association of Geodesy; International Association of Geology; International Association of Gerontology

IAGB&I Ileostomy Association of Great Britain and Ireland

IAgrE Institution of Agricultural Engineers

IAH International Association of Hydrogeologists; International Association of Hydrology

IAHA Inter-American Hotel Association

IAHM Incorporated Association of Headmasters

IAHP International Association of Horticultural Producers

IAHR International Association for Hydraulic Research; International Association for the History of Religions

IAI International African Institute

IAL Imperial Airways Limited; Imperial Arts League; [computing] international algorithmic language; Irish Academy of Letters

IALA International African Law Association; International Association of Lighthouse Authorities

IALL International Association of Law Libraries

IALS International Association of Legal Science

IAM Institute of Administrative Management; Institute of Advanced Motorists; Institute of Aviation Medicine; [anatomy] internal auditory meatus; [USA] International Association of Machinists and Aerospace Workers; International Association of Meteorology; International Association of Microbiologists

IAMA Incorporated Advertising Managers' Association

IAMAP International Association of Meteorology and Atmospheric Physics

IAMC Indian Army Medical Corps

IAML International Association of Music Libraries

IAMS International Association of Microbiological Societies; International Association of Microbiological Studies

IANC International Airline Navigators' Council

I&D [medicine] incision and drainage

I&O intake and output

IANE Institute of Advanced Nursing Education

IANEC Inter-American Nuclear Energy Commission

IAO Incorporated Association of Organists

IAOC Indian Army Ordnance Corps

IAOS Irish Agricultural Organization Society

IAP International Academy of Pathology; Internet access provider

IAPA Inter-American Press Association

IAPB International Association for the Prevention of Blindness

IAPC International Auditing Practices Committee

IAPG International Association of Physical Geography

IAPH International Association of Ports and Harbours

IAPO International Association of Physical Oceanography

IAPS Incorporated Association of Preparatory Schools

IAPSO International Association for the Physical Sciences of the Oceans

IAPT International Association for Plant Taxonomy

IAR instruction address register

IARA Inter-Allied Reparations Agency

IARC Indian Agricultural Research Council; International Agency for Research on Cancer

IARD International Association for Rural Development

IARF International Association for Religious Freedom

IARI Indian Agricultural Research Institute

IARO Indian Army Reserve of Officers

IARU International Amateur Radio Union

IAS [computing] immediate access store; Indian Administrative Service (formerly ICS); [aeronautics] indicated air speed; [USA] Institute for Advanced Studies; [USA] Institute of the Aerospace Sciences; [aeronautics] instrument approach system; International Accounting Standard

IASA International Air Safety Association

IASC Indian Army Service Corps; International Accounting Standards Committee

IASH International Association of Scientific Hydrology

IASI Inter-American Statistical Institute

i.a.s.o.r. ice and snow on runway

IASS International Association for Scandinavian Studies; International Association of Soil Science

IAT International Atomic Time

i.a.t. inside air temperature

IATA International Air Transport Association; International Amateur Theatre Association

IATUL International Association of Technological University Libraries

IAU International Association of Universities; International Astronomical Union

IAUPL International Association of University Professors and Lecturers

IAV International Association of Vulcanology

IAVG International Association for Vocational Guidance

IAW International Alliance of Women

i.a.w. in accordance with

IAWPRC International Association on Water Pollution Research and Control

IB [vehicle registration] Armagh; in bond; incendiary bomb; industrial business; information bureau; instruction book; intelligence branch; International Baccalaureate; International Bank (for Reconstruction and Development); invoice book

ib. *ibidem* (Latin: in the same place) (indicating reference cited earlier)

IBA Independent Bankers' Association; Independent Broadcasting Authority (replacement for ITA); Industrial Bankers' Association; [taxation] industrial buildings allowances; International Bar Association; International Bowling Association; Investment Bankers' Association

IBAA Investment Bankers' Association of America

IBAE Institution of British Agricultural Engineers

IBB Institute of British Bakers; International Bowling Board; Invest in Britain Bureau

IBBR [finance] interbank bid rate

IBC International Broadcasting Corporation

IBD Incorporated Institute of British Decorators and Interior Designers; [medicine] inflammatory bowel disease; [electronics] ion-beam deposition

IBE Institution of British Engineers; International Bureau of Education (became part of UNESCO)

IBEL [finance] interest-bearing eligible liability

IBEW [USA] International Brotherhood of Electrical Workers

IBF Institute of British Foundrymen; International Badminton Federation; international banking facility; International Boxing Federation

IBG Incorporated Brewers Guild; Institute of British Geographers; [computing] interblock gap

IBI [book-keeping] invoice book inwards

IBID international bibliographical description

ibid. *ibidem* (Latin: in the same place) (indicating reference cited earlier)

IBiol Institute of Biology

IBK Institute of Book-keepers

IBM intercontinental ballistic missile; International Business Machines (Corporation) (computer manufacturer)

IBMBR [finance] interbank market bid rate

IBO [book-keeping] invoice book outwards

IBP initial boiling point; Institute of British Photographers; International Biological Programme

IBPAT [USA] International Brotherhood of Painters and Allied Trades

IBRC Insurance Brokers Registration Council

IBRD International Bank for Reconstruction and Development (World Bank)

IBRO International Bank Research Organization; International Brain Research Organization

IBS Institute of Bankers in Scotland; [medicine] irritable bowel syndrome

IBScot Institute of Bankers in Scotland

IBST Institute of British Surgical Technicians

IBT International Brotherhood of Teamsters, Chauffeurs, Warehousemen and Helpers of America

IBTE Institute of British Telecommunications Engineers

IBWM International Bureau of Weights and Measures

IC identity card; *Iesus Christus* (Latin: Jesus Christ); [grammar] immediate constituent; [immunology] immune complex; Imperial College (of Science and Technology, London); [astronomy] Index Catalogue; industrial court; information centre; [electronics] integrated circuit; Intelligence Corps; [engineering] internal-combustion (engine); [chemistry] ion chromatography; [physics] ionization chamber

I-C Indo-China

i/c in charge; in command

i.c. index correction; instrument correction; internal communication

ICA ignition control additive (for motor vehicles); Industrial Caterers' Association; Institute of Chartered Accountants (in England and Wales); Institute of Company Accountants; Institute of Contemporary Arts; [medicine] internal carotid artery; International Cartographic Association; International Chefs' Association; International Coffee Agreement; International Colour Authority; International Commercial Arbitration; International Commission on Acoustics; International Commodity Agreement; International Cooperation Administration; International Cooperative Alliance; International Council on Archives; International Court of Arbitration; International Cyclist Association; invalid care allowance

ICAA Invalid Children's Aid Association

ICAE International Commission on Agricultural Engineering

ICAEW Institute of Chartered Accountants in England and Wales

ICAI Institute of Chartered Accountants in Ireland; International Commission for Agricultural Industries

ICAM Institute of Corn and Agricultural Merchants

ICAN International Commission for Air Navigation

IC&CY Inns of Court and City Yeomanry

ICAO International Civil Aviation Organization

ICAP Institute of Certified Ambulance Personnel; International Congress of Applied Psychology

ICAR Indian Council of Agricultural Research

ICAS Institute of Chartered Accountants of Scotland; International Council of Aeronautical Sciences; International Council of Aerospace Sciences

ICB Institute of Comparative Biology

ICBA International Community of Booksellers' Associations

ICBD International Council of Ballroom Dancing

ICBHI Industrial Craft (Member) of the British Horological Institute

ICBM intercontinental ballistic missile

ICBN International Code of Botanical Nomenclature

ICBP International Council for Bird Preservation

ICC [USA] Indian Claims Commission; intercounty championship; International Chamber of Commerce; International Children's Centre; International Congregational Council; International Convention Centre (Birmingham); International Correspondence Colleges; International Cricket Conference (formerly Imperial Cricket Conference); [USA] Interstate Commerce Commission

ICCB Intergovernmental Consultation and Coordination Board

ICCC International Conference of Catholic Charities

ICCE International Council of Commerce Employers

ICCF International Correspondence Chess Federation

ICCH International Commodities Clearing House

ICCPR International Covenant on Civil and Political Rights (of UN)

ICCROM International Centre for Conservation at Rome

ICCS International Centre of Criminological Studies

ICD Institute of Cooperative Directors; International Classification of Diseases (published by WHO)

ICDO International Civil Defence Organization

ICE [medicine] ice, compress, elevation (treatment for bruised limbs); [computing] in-circuit emulator; Institute of Chartered Engineers; Institution of Civil Engineers; internal-combustion engine; International Cultural Exchange

Ice. Iceland; Icelander; Icelandic

ICED International Council for Educational Development

ICEF International Council for Educational Films

ICEI Institution of Civil Engineers of Ireland

Icel. Iceland; Icelander; Icelandic

ICeram Institute of Ceramics (became part of Institute of Materials)

ICES International Council for the Exploration of the Sea

ICETT Industrial Council for Educational and Training Technology

ICF Industrial and Commercial Finance Corporation; [nuclear technology] inertial-confinement fusion; International Canoe Federation; International Chess Federation

ICFTU International Confederation of Free Trade Unions

icg icing

ICGS interactive computer-graphics system; International Catholic Girls' Society

ich. ichthyology

ICHCA International Cargo Handling Coordination Association

IChemE Institution of Chemical Engineers

ICHEO Inter-University Council for Higher Education Overseas

ICHPER International Council for Health, Physical Education and Recreation

ichth. ichthyology

ichthyol. ichthyologist; ichthyology

ICI Imperial Chemical Industries; International Commission on Illumination; [USA] Investment Casting Institute

ICIA International Credit Insurance Association

ICIANZ Imperial Chemical Industries, Australia and New Zealand

ICID International Commission on Irrigation and Drainage

ICIDH International Classification of Impairments, Disabilities and Handicaps (published by WHO)

ICJ International Commission of Jurists; International Court of Justice

ICJW International Council of Jewish Women

ICL International Computers Limited; International Confederation of Labour

ICLA International Committee on Laboratory Animals

ICM Institute for Complementary Medicine; Institute of Credit Management; Intergovernmental Committee for Migrations (of UN); International Confederation of Midwives; [astronomy] intracluster medium; Irish Church Missions

ICMMP International Committee of Military Medicine and Pharmacy

ICMS International Centre for Mathematical Sciences (Edinburgh)

ICN *in Christi nomine* (Latin: in Christ's name); infection control nurse; International Council of Nurses

ICNA Infection Control Nurses' Association

ICNB International Code of Nomenclature of Bacteria

ICNCP International Code of Nomenclature of Cultivated Plants

ICNV International Code of Nomenclature of Viruses

ICO Institute of Careers Officers; International Coffee Organization; Islamic Conference Organization

ICOM International Council of Museums

ICOMOS International Council of Monuments and Sites

ICON indexed currency option note

icon. iconographical; iconography

ICOR Intergovernmental Conference on Oceanic Research (in UNESCO)

ICorrST Institution of Corrosion Science and Technology

ICP [medicine] intracranial pressure

ICPA International Commission for the Prevention of Alcoholism; International Cooperative Petroleum Association

ICPHS International Council for Philosophy and Humanistic Studies

ICPO International Criminal Police Organization (= Interpol)

ICPU International Catholic Press Union

ICQ [accounting] internal control questionnaire

ICR [computing] intelligent character recognition

ICRC International Committee of the Red Cross

ICRF Imperial Cancer Research Fund

ICRP International Commission on Radiological Protection

ICRU International Commission on Radiation Units (and Measurements)

ICRUM International Commission on Radiation Units and Measurements

ICS Imperial College of Science and Technology (London); Indian Civil Service (former name of IAS); instalment credit selling; Institute of Chartered Shipbrokers; International Chamber of Shipping; International College of Surgeons; international consultancy service; [finance] investors' compensation scheme

ICSA Institute of Chartered Secretaries and Administrators (formerly CIS)

ICSB International Congress of Small Businesses

ICSH [biochemistry] interstitial-cell-stimulating hormone

ICSI [medicine] intracytoplasmic sperm injection (infertility treatment)

ICSID International Council of Societies of Industrial Design

ICSLS International Convention for Safety of Life at Sea

ICSPE International Council of Sport and Physical Education

ICST Imperial College of Science and Technology (London)

ICSU International Council of Scientific Unions (in UNESCO)

ICTA International Council of Travel Agents

ICTP International Centre for Theoretical Physics

ICTU Irish Congress of Trade Unions

ICTV International Committee on Taxonomy of Viruses

ICU [medicine] intensive care unit; international code use (in signalling)

ICVA International Council of Voluntary Agencies

ICW Institute of Clerks of Works of Great Britain; International Congress of Women; [telecommunications] interrupted continuous wave

i.c.w. in connection with

ICWA Indian Council of World Affairs; Institute of Cost and Works Accountants

ICWG International Cooperative Women's Guild

ICWU [USA] International Chemical Workers Union

ICYF International Catholic Youth Federation

ICZN International Code of Zoological Nomenclature

ID [US postcode] Idaho; identification; identify; identity; infectious disease(s); information department; inside diameter; Institute of Directors; intelligence department; [medicine] intradermal; [currency] Iraqi dinar

Id. Idaho

id. *idem* (Latin: the same (man))

.id Indonesia (in Internet address)

i.d. inside diameter

IDA Industrial Diamond Association; International Development Association (affiliate of World Bank); Irish Dental Association; Islamic Democratic Association

IDB illicit diamond buyer; illicit diamond buying; Industrial Development Bank; [Northern Ireland] Industrial Development Board; Inter-American Development Bank; Internal Drainage Board

IDC industrial development certificate; insulation displacement connector

ID card identification card

IDD [medicine] insulin-dependent diabetes; [telecommunications] international direct dialling

IDDA Interior Decorators and Designers Association

IDDD [telecommunications] international direct distance dialling

IDDM [medicine] insulin-dependent diabetes mellitus

IDE [computing] integrated drive electronics; [computing] intelligent drive electronics; [computing] interactive development environment

iden. identification; identify; identity

ident. identification; identify; identity

IDF International Dairy Federation; International Democratic Fellowship; International Dental Federation; International Diabetes Federation

IDIB Industrial Diamond Information Bureau

IDL [biochemistry] intermediate-density lipoprotein; international date line; international driver's licence

IDLH immediately dangerous to life and health

IDMS [computing] integrated data-management system

IDN *in Dei nomine* (Latin: in God's name); [computing] integrated data network

IDP Institute of Data Processing; [computing] integrated data processing; International Driving Permit; [astronomy] interplanetary dust particle(s)

IDPM Institute of Data Processing Management

IDR [finance] International Depository Receipt

IDRC International Development Research Centre

IDS Income Data Services; Industry Department for Scotland; Institute of Development Studies

IDSM Indian Distinguished Service Medal

IDT industrial design technology

IDV International Distillers and Vintners

IE [medicine] immunoelectrophoresis; index error; Indian Empire; Indo-European (languages); Institute of Engineers and Technicians (became part of IIE); [chemistry] ion exchange; [chemistry] ionization energy; [fishing port] Irvine

.ie Ireland (in Internet address)

i.e. *id est* (Latin: that is); inside edge

IEA Institute of Economic Affairs; Institution of Engineers, Australia; International Economic Association; International Energy Agency; International Ergonomics Association

IE(Aust) Institution of Engineers, Australia

IEC industrial energy conservation; integrated environmental control; International Electrotechnical Commission

IED improvised explosive device; Information Engineering Directorate; Institution of Engineering Designers

IEDD improvised explosive device disposal

IEE [USA] Institute of Energy Economics; Institution of Electrical Engineers

IEEE Institute of Electrical and Electronics Engineers

IEEIE Institution of Electrical and Electronics Incorporated Engineers (became part of IIE)

IEF Indian Expeditionary Force

IEHO Institution of Environmental Health Officers

IEI Industrial Engineering Institute; Institution of Engineers of Ireland

IEM inborn error of metabolism

IEME Inspectorate of Electrical and Mechanical Engineering

IEng Incorporated Engineer

IER Institute of Environmental Research

IERE Institution of Electronic and Radio Engineers (became part of IEE)

IES Indian Educational Service; Institution of Engineers and Shipbuilders in Scotland

IET interest equalization tax

IETF Internet Engineering Task Force

IEW intelligence and electronic warfare

IExpE Institute of Explosives Engineers

IF [nuclear technology] inertial fusion; [baseball] infield; [biochemistry] inhibitory factor; [genetics] initiation factor; [sports] inside forward; Institute of Fuel; [medicine] interferon; [electronics] intermediate frequency

i-f in-flight

i.f. information feedback; *ipse fecit* (Latin: (he) did it himself)

IFA [medicine] immunofluorescence assay; Incorporated Faculty of Arts; independent financial adviser; instrumented fuel assembly; International Federation of Actors; International Fertility Association; International Fiscal Association; Irish Football Association

IFAA Independent Financial Advisers Association

IFAC International Federation of Automatic Control

IFAD International Fund for Agricultural Development

IFALPA International Federation of Air Line Pilots' Associations

IFAP International Federation of Agricultural Producers

IFATCA International Federation of Air Traffic Controllers' Associations

IFAW International Fund for Animal Welfare

IFB [finance] invitation for bid

IFBPW International Federation of Business and Professional Women

IFC International Finance Corporation

(affiliate of World Bank); [USA, Canada] International Fisheries Commission

IFCATI International Federation of Cotton and Allied Textile Industries

IFCC International Federation of Camping and Caravanning; International Federation of Children's Communities

IFCCPTE International Federation of Commercial, Clerical, Professional and Technical Employees

IFCO International Fisheries Cooperative Organization

IFCTU International Federation of Christian Trade Unions

IFE [computing] intelligent front end

IFF [radar] Identification, Friend or Foe; [computing] image file format; Institute of Freight Forwarders; [computing] interchange file format

iff [logic, mathematics] if and only if

IFFA International Federation of Film Archives

IFFPA International Federation of Film Producers' Associations

IFFS International Federation of Film Societies

IFFTU International Federation of Free Teachers' Unions

IFGA International Federation of Grocers' Associations

IFGO International Federation of Gynaecology and Obstetrics

IFHE International Federation of Home Economics

IFHP International Federation for Housing and Planning

IFIP International Federation for Information Processing

IFireE Institution of Fire Engineers

IFJ International Federation of Journalists

IFL International Friendship League

IFLA International Federation of Landscape Architects; International Federation of Library Associations

IFM International Falcon Movement

IFMC International Folk Music Council

IFMSA International Federation of Medical Students' Associations

IFOR Implementation Force (NATO-led peacekeeping force in Bosnia, replaced by SFOR); International Fellowship of Reconciliation

IFORS International Federation of Operational Research Societies

Ifox Irish Futures and Options Exchange

IFP [South Africa] Inkatha Freedom Party

IFPA Industrial Film Producers' Association

IFPAAW International Federation of Plantation, Agricultural and Allied Workers

IFPCS International Federation of Unions of Employees in Public and Civil Services

IFPM International Federation of Physical Medicine

IFPW International Federation of Petroleum (and Chemical) Workers

IFR [aeronautics] instrument flying regulations; [nuclear technology] integral fast reactor

IFRB International Frequency Registration Board

IFS Indian Forest Service; Institute for Fiscal Studies; International Federation of Surveyors; Irish Free State; [computing] iterated function system

IFSPO International Federation of Senior Police Officers

IFST Institute of Food Science and Technology

IFSW International Federation of Social Workers

IFTA International Federation of Teachers' Associations; International Federation of Travel Agencies

IFTC International Film and Television Council

IFTU International Federation of Trade Unions (replaced by WFTU)

IFUW International Federation of University Women

IFWEA International Federation of Workers' Educational Associations

IFWL International Federation of Women Lawyers

IG [UK postcode] Ilford; imperial gallon; Indo-Germanic (languages); industrial group; [astronomy] inertial guidance; inner guard; Inspector-General; Instructor in Gunnery; Irish Guards

Ig [immunology] immunoglobulin

ig. ignition

IGA International Geographical Association; International Golf Association

IGADD Intergovernmental Authority on Drought and Development

IGasE Institution of Gas Engineers

IGBT [computing] insulated-gate bipolar transistor

IGC Intergovernmental Conference

IGCM Incorporated Guild of Church Musicians

IGD illicit gold dealer

IGES [computing] initial graphics exchange specification

IGF Inspector-General of Fortifications; [medicine] insulin-like growth factor; International Gymnastic Federation

IGFA International Game Fish Association

IGFET [electronics] insulated-gate field-effect transistor

IGH Incorporated Guild of Hairdressers

IGM [chess] International Grandmaster

ign. ignite(s); ignition; *ignotus* (Latin: unknown)

IGO intergovernmental organization

IGPP Institute of Geophysics and Planetary Physics

IGRS Irish Genealogical Research Society

IGS Imperial General Staff; independent grammar school

IGU International Gas Union; International Geographical Union

IGWF International Garment Workers' Federation

IGY International Geophysical Year

IH *iacet hic* (Latin: here lies) (on tombstone); industrial hygiene; [computing] interrupt handler; [fishing port] Ipswich

IHA International Hotel Association

IHAB International Horticultural Advisory Bureau

IHB International Hydrographic Bureau

IHC [New Zealand] intellectually handicapped child; Intercontinental Hotels Corporation

IHCA International Hebrew Christian Alliance

IHD [medicine] ischaemic heart disease

IHEU International Humanist and Ethical Union

IHF Industrial Hygiene Foundation; International Hockey Federation; International Hospitals Federation

IHospE Institute of Hospital Engineering

ihp indicated horsepower

IHR Institute of Historical Research

IHRB International Hockey Rules Board

IHS *Iesous* (Greek: Jesus) (from first three letters of name in Greek alphabet); *Iesus Hominum Salvator* (Latin: Jesus Saviour of Mankind); *in hoc signo* (Latin: in this sign)

IHSM Institute of Health Services Management

IHT inheritance tax; Institution of Highways and Transportation

IHU Irish Hockey Union

IHVE Institute of Heating and Ventilation Engineers

II [electronics] image intensifier; [electronics] ion implantation

IIA International Institute of Agriculture

IIAC Industrial Injuries Advisory Council

IIAL International Institute of Arts and Letters

IIAS International Institute of Administrative Sciences

IIB *Institut international des brevets* (French: International Patent Institute)

IIBD&ID Incorporated Institute of British Decorators and Interior Designers

IID [medicine] insulin-independent diabetes; [electronics] ion-implantation doping

iid. *iidem* (Latin: the same (men))

i.i.d. [statistics] independent identically distributed (random variables)

IIE Institute for International Education; Institution of Incorporated Engineers (in Electronic, Electrical and Mechanical Engineering); International Institute of Embryology

IIEP International Institute of Educational Planning

IIExE Institution of Incorporated Executive Engineers

IIF [computing] image interchange facility

IIHF International Ice Hockey Federation

III International Institute of Interpreters

IIL [electronics] integrated injection logic

IIM Institution of Industrial Managers

IInfSc Institute of Information Scientists

IIP *Institut international de la presse* (French: International Press Institute); International Ice Patrol; International Institute of Philosophy

IIR [chemistry] isobutylene-isoprene rubber

IIRS [Ireland] Institute for Industrial Research and Standards

IIS Institute of Information Scientists; International Institute of Sociology

IISO Institution of Industrial Safety Officers

IISS International Institute of Strategic Studies

IIT Indian Institute of Technology

IIW International Institute of Welding

IJ [vehicle registration] Down

i.J *im Jahre* (German: in the year)

IKBS [computing] intelligent knowledge-based system

IL [vehicle registration] Fermanagh; [US postcode] Illinois; Ilyushin (aircraft); [sports] inside left; Institute of Linguists; [aeronautics] instrument landing; [immunology] interleukin; [international vehicle registration] Israel

I/L import licence

.il Israel (in Internet address)

i.l. inside leg

ILA Individual Learning Account (for vocational training); [physics] induction linear accelerator; Institute of Landscape Architects; [aeronautics] instrument landing approach; International Law Association; International Longshoremen's Association

ILAA International Legal Aid Association

ILAB International League of Antiquarian Booksellers

ILAE International League Against Epilepsy

ILBM [computing] interleaved bit map

ILC International Law Commission (of UN)

ILD [medicine] interstitial lung disease

ILE Institution of Locomotive Engineers

ILEA Inner London Education Authority

ILEC Inner London Education Committee

ILF International Landworkers' Federation

ILGA Institute of Local Government Administration

ILGWU [USA] International Ladies' Garment Workers' Union

Ill. Illinois

ill. illustrate; illustrated; illustration; illustrator; *illustrissimus* (Latin: most distinguished)

illegit. illegitimate

illit. illiterate

illum. illuminate; illuminated; illumination

illus. illustrate; illustrated; illustration; illustrator

illust. illustrate; illustrated; illustration; illustrator

ILN *Illustrated London News*

ILO industrial liaison officer; International Labour Office (of UN); International Labour Organization

i.l.o. in lieu of

ILocoE Institution of Locomotive Engineers

ILP Independent Labour Party

ILR Independent Law Reports; independent local radio

ILRM International League for the Rights of Man

ILS Incorporated Law Society; [aeronautics] instrument landing system; [statistics] inverse least-squares

i.l.t. in lieu thereof

ILTF International Lawn Tennis Federation

ILU Institute of London Underwriters

ILW [nuclear technology] intermediate-level waste

ILY I love you

IM Indian Marines; Institute of Materials; Institute of Metals (became part of Institute of Materials); interceptor missile; [chess] International Master; [medicine] intramuscular; [UK postcode] Isle of Man

Im. Imperial

IMA Indian Military Academy; Institute of Mathematics and its Applications; International Music Association; Irish Medical Association

imag. imaginary; imagination; imagine

IM&AWU [USA] International Molders' and Allied Workers' Union

IMarE Institute of Marine Engineers

IMAS International Marine and Shipping Conference

IMB Institute of Marine Biology

IMC [photography] image motion compensation; Institute of Management Consultants; Institute of Measurement and Control; [aeronautics] instrument meteorological conditions; International Maritime Committee; International Missionary Council; International Music Council

IMCO Intergovernmental Maritime Consultative Organization (former name of IMO)

IME Institute of Medical Ethics

IMEA Incorporated Municipal Electrical Association

IMechE Institution of Mechanical Engineers

I Meth. Independent Methodist

IMF International Monetary Fund; International Motorcycle Federation; interplanetary magnetic field (in astrophysics)

IMG [computing] image file format

IMGTechE Institution of Mechanical and General Technician Engineers

IMHO in my humble opinion (in Internet chat and e-mail)

IMinE Institution of Mining Engineers (became part of IMM)

IMINT [military] image intelligence (from aerial photographs)

imit. imitate; imitation; imitative

IMM Institution of Mining and Metallurgy; International Mercantile Marine; International Monetary Market

imm. immediately

immac. immaculate (in advertisement)

immed. immediate

IMMTS Indian Mercantile Marine Training Ship

immun. immunity; immunization; immunology

IMO in my opinion (in Internet chat and e-mail); International Maritime Organization (formerly IMCO); International Meteorological Organization; International Miners' Organization

IMP [computing] interface message processor (in network); [card games] International Match Point (in bridge); interplanetary measurement probe

Imp. *Imperator* (Latin: Emperor); *Imperatrix* (Latin: Empress); Imperial

imp. imperative; imperfect; imperial; impersonal; implement; import; important; imported; importer; impression; imprimatur; *imprimeur* (French: printer); *imprimé* (French: printed); imprint; improved; improvement

IMPA International Master Printers' Association

IMPACT implementation, planning and control technique

impce importance

imper. imperative

imperf. imperfect; [philately] imperforate (of stamps)

impers. impersonal

impf. imperfect

impft imperfect

imp. gal. imperial gallon

imposs. impossible

IMPR [meteorology] improving

impreg. impregnate; impregnated; impregnation

improp. improper; improperly

impt important

imptd imported

imptr importer

IMR individual medical report; infant mortality rate; Institute of Medical Research

IMRA Industrial Marketing Research Association

IMRAN international marine radio aids to navigation

IMRO Investment Management Regulatory Organization

IMS Indian Medical Service; industrial methylated spirit; [trademark, computing] Information Management System; Institute of Management Services; International Musicological Society

IMT International Military Tribunal

IMU International Mathematical Union

IMunE Institution of Municipal Engineers (became part of Institution of Civil Engineers)

IMVS [Australia] Institute of Medical and Veterinary Science

IMW Institute of Masters of Wine; intermediate molecular weight

IN [US postcode] Indiana; Indian Navy

In [chemical element] indium

In. India; Indian; Instructor

in. inch

.in India (in Internet address)

INA Indian National Army; Institution of Naval Architects; International Newsreel Association; Iraqi News Agency

INAO *Institut national des appellations d'origine des vins et eaux-de-vie* (French authority controlling wine production)

inaud. inaudible

inaug. inaugural; inaugurate; inaugurated; inauguration
inbd inboard
Inbucon International Business Consultants
INC *in nomine Christi* (Latin: in the name of Christ); Indian National Congress; International Numismatic Commission
Inc. Incorporated (after US company name)
inc. include; included; including; inclusive; income; incomplete; incorporate; incorporated; increase; increment; incumbent
INCA International Newspaper Colour Association
incalz. [music] *incalzando* (Italian: hastening)
INCB International Narcotics Control Board (of UN)
incho. [law] inchoate
incid. incidental
incl. inclination; incline; include(s); included; including; inclusive
incldg including
incls. inclusive
incog. incognito
incomp. incomplete
incompat. incompatibility; incompatible
incorp. incorporated; incorporation
incorr. incorrect
INCPEN Industry Committee for Packaging and the Environment
INCR [meteorology] increase
incr. increase; increased; increasing; increment
incumb. incumbent
incun. incunabula
IND [international vehicle registration] India; *in nomine Dei* (Latin: in the name of God); [US pharmacology] investigational (or investigative) new drug
Ind [astronomy] Indus
Ind. Independent; India; Indian; Indiana; Indies
ind. independence; independent; index; indicate; indication; indicative; indigenous; indigo; indirect; indirectly; industrial; industry
in d. [medicine] *in dies* (Latin: daily)
indecl. [grammar] indeclinable
indef. indefinite
indep. independence; independent

indic. indicating; indicative; indicator
Ind. Imp. *Indiae Imperator* (Latin: Emperor of India); *Indiae Imperatrix* (Latin: Empress of India)
indiv. individual
individ. individual
Ind. Meth. Independent Methodist
Indo-Eur. Indo-European
Indo-Ger. Indo-Germanic
Indon. Indonesia; Indonesian
indre indenture
induc. inductance; induction
indust. industrial; industrialized; industrious; industry
ined. *ineditus* (Latin: unpublished)
INER Institute of Nuclear Energy Research
INET Institute of Nuclear Energy Technology
in ex. *in extenso* (Latin: in full)
INF intermediate-range nuclear forces; International Naturist Federation; International Nuclear Force
Inf. Infantry
inf. infant; infectious; inferior; [grammar] infinitive; influence; informal; information; *infra* (Latin: below); [medicine] *infusum* (Latin: infusion)
infin. [grammar] infinitive
infirm. infirmary
infl. inflammable; inflated; inflect; inflection; [botany] inflorescence; influence; influenced
infm. information
info [short form] information
infra dig [short form] *infra dignitatem* (Latin: beneath one's dignity, undignified)
Ing. *Ingenieur* (German: engineer)
Ingl. *Inghilterra* (Italian: England)
INGO international nongovernmental organization
INH [pharmacology] isonicotinic acid hydrazide (= isoniazid, drug used to treat tuberculosis)
inh. *Inhaber* (German: proprietor); *Inhalt* (German: contents)
inhab. inhabitant
INI *in nomine Iesu* (Latin: in the name of Jesus)
init. initial; initially; *initio* (Latin: in the beginning)
INJ *in nomine Jesu* (Latin: in the name of Jesus)

inj. injection; injury

INLA International Nuclear Law Association; Irish National Liberation Army

in lim. *in limine* (Latin: at the outset)

in loc. *in loco* (Latin: in the place (of))

in loc. cit. *in loco citato* (Latin: in the place cited)

Inmarsat International Maritime Satellite Organization

in mem. *in memoriam* (Latin: to the memory (of))

inn. [cricket] innings

INO Inspectorate of Naval Ordnance

inorg. inorganic

INP Institute of Nuclear Physics

in pr. *in principio* (Latin: in the beginning)

in pro. in proportion

inq. inquest; inquiry; inquisition

INR independent national radio (as in **INR licence**); Index of Nursing Research

INRI *Iesus Nazarenus Rex Iudaeorum* (Latin: Jesus of Nazareth King of the Jews)

INS [USA] Immigration and Naturalization Service; Indian Naval Ship; inertial navigation system; International News Service; [fishing port] Inverness

Ins [computing] insert (key)

ins. inches; inscribe; inscription; insert; inspection; inspector; insular; insulate; insulated; insulation; insurance

in s. in situ

INSA Indian National Science Academy

INSAG International Nuclear Safety Advisory Group

insce insurance

inscr. inscribe; inscription

INSEA International Society for Education through Art

INSEAD *Institut européen d'administration des affaires* (French: European Institute of Administrative Affairs)

insep. inseparable

INSET [education] in-service (education and) training

insol. insoluble

insolv. insolvent

Insp. Inspector; Inspectorate

insp. inspect; inspected; inspection; inspector

Insp-Gen Inspector-General

INST *in nomine Sanctae Trinitatis* (Latin: in the name of the Holy Trinity)

Inst. Institute; Institution

inst. instance; instant; instant (= this month, used in formal correspondence); instantaneous; institute; institution; instruct; instruction; instructor; instrument; instrumental

INSTAB Information Service on Toxicity and Biodegradability (relating to water pollution)

InstAct Institute of Actuaries

InstBE Institution of British Engineers

InstCE Institution of Civil Engineers

InstD Institute of Directors

InstE Institute of Energy

InstEE Institution of Electrical Engineers

InstF Institute of Fuel

instl. installation

InstMM Institution of Mining and Metallurgy

Instn Institution

instn institution

InstP Institute of Physics

InstPet Institute of Petroleum

InstPI Institute of Patentees and Inventors

InstR Institute of Refrigeration

instr. instruction; instructor; instrument; instrumental

INSTRAW United Nations International Research and Training Institute for the Advancement of Women

InstSMM Institute of Sales and Marketing Management

InstT Institute of Transport

INT Isaac Newton Telescope (La Palma)

int. intelligence; intercept; interest; interim; interior; [grammar] interjection; intermediate; internal; international; interpret; interpretation; interpreter; interval; [grammar] intransitive; [music] introit

.int international (in Internet address)

INTAL Institute for Latin American Integration (Buenos Aires)

int. al. *inter alia* (Latin: among other things)

int. comb. internal combustion

Intelsat International Telecommunications Satellite Organization

intens. intensifier; intensify; intensive

inter. intermediate

intercom [short form] intercommunication (system)

interj. [grammar] interjection

internat. international

interp. interpreter

Interpol International Criminal Police Organization

interrog. interrogate; interrogation; [grammar] interrogative; interrogatively

intl international

INTO Irish National (Primary) Teachers' Organization

intr. [grammar] intransitive

intrans. [grammar] intransitive

in trans. in transit

intro [short form] introduction

intro. introduce; introduction; introductory

introd. introduce; introduction; introductory

INTUC Indian National Trade Union Congress

INucE Institution of Nuclear Engineers

Inv. Inverness

inv. *invenit* (Latin: (he/she) designed it); invent; invented; invention; inventor; inventory; inverse; inversion; invert; investment; invoice

inv. et del. *invenit et delineavit* (Latin: (he/she) designed and drew it)

invty inventory

IO India Office; [grammar] indirect object; inspecting officer; integrated optics; intelligence officer

I/O [computing] input/output; inspecting order

Io. Iowa

IOA Institute of Acoustics

IOB Institute of Bankers (former name of CIB); Institute of Biology; Institute of Book-keepers; Institute of Brewing; Institute of Building (former name of CIOB)

IOC Intergovernmental Oceanographic Commission; International Olympic Committee

IOCU International Organization of Consumers' Unions

IOD injured on duty; Institute of Directors

IODE [Canada] Imperial Order of Daughters of the Empire

IOE International Organization of Employers

IOF Independent Order of Foresters; Institute of Fuel; International Oceano-

graphic Foundation; International Orienteering Federation

IOFB [medicine] intraocular foreign body

I of E Institute of Export

I of M Isle of Man

I of W Isle of Wight

IOGT International Order of Good Templars

IOJ Institute of Journalists; International Organization of Journalists

IOM Indian Order of Merit; Institute of Materials; Institute of Medicine; Isle of Man

IOMTR International Office for Motor Trades and Repairs

Ion. Ionic

IONARC Indian Ocean National Association for Regional Cooperation

IOO Inspecting Ordnance Officer

IOOF Independent Order of Oddfellows

IOP [computing] input/output processor; Institute of Painters in Oil Colours; Institute of Petroleum; Institute of Physics; Institute of Plumbing; Institute of Printing; [medicine] intraocular pressure

IOPAB International Organization for Pure and Applied Biophysics

IOPCW International Organization for the Prohibition of Chemical Weapons

IOR Independent Order of Rechabites

IOS [computing] integrated office system

IoS *Independent on Sunday*

IOSCO International Organization of Securities Commissions

IOSM Independent Order of the Sons of Malta

IOT Institute of Transport

IOU Industrial Operations Unit; I owe you

IOW in other words (in Internet chat and e-mail); Isle of Wight

IP [electronics] image processing; Imperial Preference; India Paper; [baseball] innings pitched; [medicine] in-patient; [electrical engineering] input primary; instalment plan; Institute of Petroleum; Institute of Plumbing; International Pharmacopoeia; [computing] Internet protocol; [chemistry] ionization potential; [UK postcode] Ipswich

i.p. identification point; incentive pay; indexed and paged; initial phase; [electrical engineering] input primary

IPA India Pale Ale; Insolvency Practitioners' Association; Institute of Park Administration; Institute of Practitioners in Advertising; International Phonetic Alphabet; International Phonetic Association; International Poetry Archives (Manchester); International Police Academy; International Police Association; International Publishers' Association

IPAA International Petroleum Association of America; International Prisoners' Aid Association

IPARS International Programmed Airline Reservation System

IPBM interplanetary ballistic missile (in computer game)

IPC [astronomy] imaging proportional counter; International Petroleum Company; International Polar Commission; International Publishing Corporation; [computing] interprocess communication; Iraq Petroleum Company

IPCA International Pest Control Association

IPCC Intergovernmental Panel on Climatic Change (of UN)

IPCS Institution of Professional Civil Servants; [computing] intelligent process-control system

IPD individual package delivery; [law] *in praesentia dominorum* (Latin: in the presence of the Lords (of Session)) (Scotland); Institute of Personnel and Development; [medicine] intermittent peritoneal dialysis

IPE Institution of Plant Engineers; International Petroleum Exchange

IPF [medicine] interstitial pulmonary fibrosis; Irish Printing Federation

IPFC Indo-Pacific Fisheries Council

IPG Independent Publishers' Guild; Industrial Painters' Group

IPH [medicine] idiopathic portal hypertension; industrial process heat(ing)

iph impressions per hour

IPHE Institution of Public Health Engineers

IPI [computing] image processing and interchange; Institute of Patentees and Inventors; Institute of Professional Investigators; International Press Institute

i.p.i. *in partibus infidelium* (Latin: in the regions of unbelievers)

IPL [computing] information processing language; [computing] initial program load

IPlantE Institution of Plant Engineers

IPLO Irish People's Liberation Organization

IPM [Freemasonry] immediate past master; Institute of Personnel Management

ipm inches per minute; inches per month

IPMS Institute of Professionals, Managers and Specialists

IPO [US stock exchange] initial public offering (flotation on market); [computing] input-process-output; Israel Philharmonic Orchestra

IPP Institute for Plasma Physics; [medicine] intermittent positive pressure (in ventilation)

IPPF International Planned Parenthood Federation

IPPR Institute for Public Policy Research

IPPS Institute of Physics and the Physical Society

IPPV [medicine] intermittent positive-pressure ventilation

IPR Institute of Public Relations

IPRA International Public Relations Association

IPRE Incorporated Practitioners in Radio and Electronics

IProdE Institution of Production Engineers (became part of IEE)

IPS Indian Police Service; Indian Political Service; International Confederation for Plastic Surgery; [astronomy] interplanetary scintillations; Inter Press Service (Italian news agency); [computing] interpretative programming system

Ips. Ipswich

ips inches per second; [computing] instructions per second

IPSA International Political Science Association

IPSE [computing] integrated project support environment

IPSP [physiology] inhibitory post-synaptic potential

IPT Institute of Petroleum Technologies; interpersonal therapy

IPTO [astronautics] independent power take-off

IPTPA International Professional Tennis Players' Association

IPTS [physics] International Practical Temperature Scale

IPU Inter-Parliamentary Union

IPX Internet package exchange

ipy inches per year

IQ Institute of Quarrying; intelligence quota; international quota

.iq Iraq (in Internet address)

i.q. *idem quod* (Latin: the same as)

IQA Institute of Quality Assurance

IQS Institute of Quantity Surveyors

IR [meteorology] ice on runway; incidence rate; index register; industrial relations; informal report; information retrieval; infrared (radiation); Inland Revenue; [sports] inside right; inspector's report; Institute of Refrigeration; instrument reading; international registration; [international vehicle registration] Iran; [currency] Iranian rial; [chemistry] isoprene rubber

Ir [chemical element] iridium

Ir. Ireland; Irish

i.R *im Ruhestand* (German: retired, emeritus)

.ir Iran (in Internet address)

i.r. inside radius

IRA [USA] individual retirement account; Institute of Registered Architects; Irish Republican Army

IRAD Institute for Research on Animal Diseases

IRAF [astronomy] image reduction and analysis facility

IRAM *Institut de radioastronomie millimétrique* (French: Institute of Millimetre Radioastronomy)

Iran. Iranian

i.r.a.n. inspect and repair as necessary

IRAS Infrared Astronomical Satellite

IRB industrial revenue bond; Irish Republican Brotherhood

IRBM intermediate-range ballistic missile

IRC Industrial Reorganization Corporation; Infantry Reserve Corps; interdisciplinary research centre (of EPSRC); International Red Cross; international reply coupon; International Research Council; Internet relay chat

IRCert Industrial Relations Certificate

IRD International Research and Development Company

IRDA Industrial Research and Development Authority; Infra-Red Data Association

IRE [USA] Institute of Radio Engineers

Ire. Ireland

IREE(Aust) Institution of Radio and Electronics Engineers (Australia)

Irel. Ireland

IRF International Road Federation; International Rowing Federation

IRFB International Rugby Football Board

IRFU Irish Rugby Football Union

IRI Institution of the Rubber Industry (became part of Institute of Materials); *Istituto per la Ricostruzione Industriale* (Italian: Industrial Reconstruction Institute)

irid. iridescent

IRIS International Research and Information Service

Iris infrared intruder system

IRL in real life (in Internet chat); infrared (remote) locking (in car advertisement); [international vehicle registration] Ireland

IRLS [navigation] interrogation recording location system

IRM Islamic Republic of Mauritania; [geology] isothermal remanent magnetization

IRN Independent Radio News

IRO industrial relations officer; Inland Revenue Office; International Refugee Organization; International Relief Organization

iron. ironic(al)

IRPA International Radiation Protection Association

IRQ [computing] interrupt request; [international vehicle registration] Iraq

IRR infrared radiation; Institute of Race Relations; [finance] internal rate of return

irr. [finance] irredeemable; irregular

irreg. irregular; irregularly

IRRI International Rice Research Institute

IRRV Institute of Revenues, Rating and Valuation

IRS [computing] information retrieval system; [USA] Internal Revenue Service

IRSF Inland Revenue Staff Federation (became part of PTC)

IRTE Institute of Road Transport Engineers

IRTF Infrared Telescope Facility (Mauna Kea, Hawaii)

IRU industrial rehabilitation unit; International Relief Union; International Road Transport Union

IRWC International Registry of World Citizens

IS [international vehicle registration] Iceland (from Icelandic *Ísland*); independent suspension (in car advertisement); Industrial Society; information science; information system; [electrical engineering] input secondary; [genetics] insertion sequence; internal security; International Society of Sculptors, Painters and Gravers; Irish Society

Is. [Bible] Isaiah; Islam; Islamic; Island(s); Isle(s); Israel; Israeli

.is Iceland (in Internet address)

i.s. [electrical engineering] input secondary

ISA Independent Schools' Association; Individual Savings Account (replacement for TESSA); [computing] Industry Standard Architecture; International Sociological Association; [aeronautics] International Standard Atmosphere (formerly Interim Standard Atmosphere); International Standards in Auditing

Isa. [Bible] Isaiah

ISAB Institute for the Study of Animal Behaviour

ISAC Industrial Safety Advisory Council

ISAM [computing] indexed sequential access method

ISAS [Japan] Institute of Space and Astronautical Science

ISBA Incorporated Society of British Advertisers

ISBN International Standard Book Number (replacement for SBN)

ISC Imperial Service College (Haileybury); Imperial Staff College; Indian Staff Corps; [medicine] intermittent self-catheterization; International Seismological Centre; International Student Conference; International Sugar Council; [Freemasonry] International Supreme Council

ISCE International Society of Christian Endeavour

ISCM International Society for Contemporary Music

ISCO Independent Schools Careers Organization; International Standard Classification of Occupations

ISD international standard depth; international subscriber dialling

ISDA International Swaps and Derivatives Association

ISDN [computing, telecommunications] Integrated Services Digital Network

ISE Indian Service of Engineers; Institution of Structural Engineers; International Stock Exchange

ISEE [astronomy] International Sun–Earth Explorer

ISF [computing] integrated systems factory; International Shipping Federation; International Spiritualist Federation

ISGE International Society of Gastroenterology

ISH International Society of Haematology

ISHS International Society for Horticultural Science

ISI Indian Standards Institution; International Statistical Institute; Iron and Steel Institute (became part of Institute of Materials)

ISIS Independent Schools Information Service; International Shipping Information Services

ISJC Independent Schools Joint Council

ISK [currency] Icelandic króna

isl. island; isle

ISM *Iesus Salvator Mundi* (Latin: Jesus Saviour of the World); Imperial Service Medal; Incorporated Society of Musicians; [astronomy] interstellar medium

ISMA International Securities Market Association

ISME International Society for Musical Education

ISMRC Inter-Services Metallurgical Research Council

ISO Imperial Service Order; Infrared Space Observatory; International Organization for Standardization (from Greek *iso*-meaning 'equal', chosen as a multilingual abbreviation); International Sugar Organization

ISOL [meteorology] isolated

isol. isolate; isolated; isolation

ISP Institute of Sales Promotion; [computing] instruction set processor; International Study Programme; Internet service provider

ISPA International Society for the Protection of Animals; International Sporting Press Association

ISPEMA Industrial Safety (Personal Equipment) Manufacturers' Association

ISQ *in statu quo* (Latin: in the same state)

ISR information storage and retrieval; Institute of Social Research; International Society for Radiology; [computing] interrupt service routine

ISRB Inter-Services Research Bureau

ISRD International Society for Rehabilitation of the Disabled

ISRO International Securities Regulatory Organization

ISS Institute for Strategic Studies; Institute of Space Sciences; Institute of Space Studies; International Social Service(s); interstellar scintillations

iss. issue; issued

ISSA International Social Security Association

ISSC International Social Science Council

ISSN International Standard Serial Number

ISSS International Society of Soil Science

IST Indian Standard Time; information sciences technology; Institute of Science Technology; [medicine] insulin shock therapy

ISTC Institute of Scientific and Technical Communicators; Iron and Steel Trades Confederation

ISTD Imperial Society of Teachers of Dancing

ISTEA Iron and Steel Trades Employers' Association

isth. isthmus

IStructE Institution of Structural Engineers

ISU International Seamen's Union; International Shooting Union; International Skating Union

ISV independent software vendor; International Scientific Vocabulary

ISVA Incorporated Society of Valuers and Auctioneers

ISWG Imperial Standard Wire Gauge

IT ignition temperature; income tax; [USA] Indian Territory; industrial tribunal; infantry training; information technology; [law] Inner Temple; [physics] International Table (as in **IT calorie**); Investment Trust

It [short form] Italian vermouth

It. Italian; Italy

it. italic (type)

.it Italy (in Internet address)

i.t. in transit; inspection tag; internal thread (of tool)

ITA Independent Television Authority (replaced by IBA); industrial and technical assistance; Industrial Transport Association; Information Technology Agreement; Initial Teaching Alphabet; Institute of Air Transport; Institute of Travel Agents

ITAI Institution of Technical Authors and Illustrators

Ital. Italian; Italy

ital. italic (type)

ITALY I trust and love you (on envelope of love letter)

ITAR Information Telegraph Agency of Russia

ITB Industry Training Board; International Time Bureau; Irish Tourist Board

ITC Imperial Tobacco Company; Independent Television Commission; Industrial Training Council; International Tin Council; International Trade Centre; [meteorology] intertropical confluence; [USA] investment tax credit

i.t.c. installation time and cost

ITCA Independent Television Contractors' Association

ITCZ [meteorology] intertropical convergence zone

ITDA [military] indirect target damage assessment

ITE Institute of Terrestrial Ecology

ITEME Institution of Technician Engineers in Mechanical Engineering

ITER [nuclear technology] international thermonuclear engineering reactor; [nuclear technology] international tokamak engineering reactor

ITF [accounting] integrated test facility; International Tennis Federation; International Trade Federations; International Transport Workers' Federation

ITGWF International Textile and Garment Workers' Federation

itin. itinerary

ITMA Institute of Trade Mark Agents; *It's That Man Again* (former radio comedy series)

ITN Independent Television News

ITO [electronics] indium–tin oxide; International Trade Organization

ITS Industrial Training Service; [USA] Intermarket Trading System; International Trade Secretariat

ITT [medicine] insulin tolerance test; International Telephone and Telegraph Corporation

ITTF International Table Tennis Federation

ITU [computing] intelligent thermal update; [medicine] intensive therapy unit; International Telecommunication Union; International Temperance Union; International Typographical Union

ITV Independent Television; [USA] instructional television

ITVA International Television Association

ITWF International Transport Workers' Federation

IU immunizing unit; [pharmacology] international unit(s); *Izquierda Unida* (Spanish: United Left) (political party)

IUA International Union against Alcoholism; International Union of Architects

IUAA International Union of Advertisers' Associations

IUAES International Union of Anthropological and Ethnological Sciences

IUAI International Union of Aviation Insurers

IUAO International Union for Applied Ornithology

IUAPPA International Union of Air Pollution Prevention Associations

IUB International Union of Biochemistry; International Universities Bureau

IUBS International Union of Biological Sciences

IUCD [medicine] intrauterine contraceptive device

IUCN International Union for the Conservation of Nature and Natural Resources

IUCr International Union of Crystallography

IUCW International Union for Child Welfare

IUD [medicine] intrauterine death; [medicine] intrauterine (contraceptive) device

IUE [astronomy] International Ultraviolet Explorer; [USA] International Union of Electronic, Electrical, Salaried, Machine and Furniture Workers

IUF International Union of Food and Allied Workers' Associations

IUFO International Union of Family Organizations

IUFRO International Union of Forest Research Organizations

IUGG International Union of Geodesy and Geophysics

IUGR [medicine] intrauterine growth retardation

IUGS International Union of Geological Sciences

IUHPS International Union of the History and Philosophy of Science

IUI [medicine] intrauterine insemination

IULA International Union of Local Authorities

IUMF *institut universitaire de formation des maîtres* (French: university institute for advanced teacher education)

IUMI International Union of Marine Insurance

IUMSWA Industrial Union of Marine and Shipbuilding Workers of America

IUNS International Union of Nutritional Sciences

IUOE [USA] International Union of Operating Engineers

IUP *institut universitaire professionnel* (French: vocational university institute); [medicine] intrauterine pressure

IUPAB International Union of Pure and Applied Biophysics

IUPAC International Union of Pure and Applied Chemistry

IUPAP International Union of Pure and Applied Physics

IUPS International Union of Physiological Sciences

IUS [astronautics] inertial upper stage; International Union of Students; [medicine] intrauterine system (contraceptive device)

IUSP International Union of Scientific Psychology

IUSY International Union of Socialist Youth

IUT *institut universitaire de technologie* (French: university institute of technology); [medicine] intrauterine transfusion

IUTAM International Union of Theoretical and Applied Mechanics

IV interactive video; [chemistry] intermediate valency; [medicine] intravenous; [medicine] intravenously; [UK postcode] Inverness; invoice value

i.V *in Vertretung* (German: by proxy)

i.v. increased value; initial velocity; [medicine] intravenous; [medicine] intravenously; invoice value

IVA individual voluntary arrangement (in bankruptcy proceedings); invalidity allowance

IVB invalidity benefit

IVBF International Volleyball Federation

IVC [medicine] inferior vena cava; inter-varsity club

IVF [medicine] in vitro fertilization

IVL in virtual life (in Internet chat)

IVM illuminated vanity mirror

IVP [medicine] intravenous pyelogram

IVR international vehicle registration

IVS International Voluntary Service

IVT [astronautics] intravehicular transfer; [medicine] intravenous transfusion

IVU International Vegetarian Union

IW inspector of works; Isle of Wight; [vehicle registration] Londonderry

i.w. indirect waste; inside width

IWA Inland Waterways Association; Institute of World Affairs

IWC International Whaling Commission; International Wheat Council

IWD Inland Waterways and Docks

IWEM Institution of Water and Environmental Management (replacement for IWPC)

IWGC Imperial War Graves Commission (former name of CWGC)

IWM Imperial War Museum

IWO Institute of Welfare Officers; Institution of Water Officers

IWPC Institute of Water Pollution Control (replaced by IWEM)

IWS International Wool Secretariat

IWTA Inland Water Transport Association

IWW Industrial Workers of the World; International Workers of the World

IX *Iesous Christos* (Greek: Jesus Christ) (from initial letters in Greek alphabet)

IY Imperial Yeomanry

IYHF International Youth Hostels Federation

IYRU International Yacht Racing Union

iyswim if you see what I mean

IZ I Zingari (cricket club)

IZS [medicine] insulin zinc suspension (used to treat diabetes)

J

J [engineering] advance ratio; [vehicle registration] Durham; [card games] jack; Jacobean; [mathematics] Jacobian determinant; *Jahr* (German: year); January; [international vehicle registration] Japan; [fishing port] Jersey; Jesus; jet; Jew; Jewish; [immunology] joining region (of immunoglobulin chain); [slang] joint (of cannabis); joule; Journal; Judaic; Judaism; *judex* (Latin: judge); Judge; July; June; [geology] Jurassic; Justice

J [physics] angular momentum; [physics] magnetic polarization; [physics] sound intensity

j imaginary number (square root of −1)

j. *jour* (French: day); *juris* (Latin: of law); *jus* (Latin: law)

J2 [civil aircraft marking] Djibouti

J3 [civil aircraft marking] Grenada

J5 [civil aircraft marking] Guinea-Bissau

J6 [civil aircraft marking] St Lucia

J7 [civil aircraft marking] Dominica

9J [civil aircraft marking] Zambia

JA [international vehicle registration]
Jamaica; [civil aircraft marking] Japan;
joint account; Judge Advocate; Justice of
Appeal; [vehicle registration] Manchester

J/A joint account

Ja. January

JAA Japan Aeronautic Association; Jewish
Athletic Association

Jaat [military] joint air attack team

JAC Joint Advisory Committee (of UN);
[USA] Joint Apprenticeship Committee;
[USA] Junior Association of Commerce

Jac. Jacobean

JACARI Joint Action Commission Against
Racial Interference

JACNE Joint Advisory Committee on
Nutritional Education

JACT Joint Association of Classical
Teachers

JAD Julian Astronomical Day

JADB [USA] Joint Air Defense Board

JAEC Japan Atomic Energy Commission;
Joint Atomic Energy Committee (of US
Congress)

JAF Judge Advocate of the Fleet

JAFC Japan Atomic Fuel Corporation

Jafo [military slang] just another fucking
observer

JAG Judge Advocate-General

Jag [short form] Jaguar (car)

JAIEG Joint Atomic Information
Exchange Group

JAL jet approach and landing (chart)

Jam. Jamaica; Jamaican; [Bible] James

JAMA *Journal of the American Medical
Association*

Jan. *Januar* (German: January); January

jan. janitor

J&K Jammu and Kashmir

j. & w.o. [insurance] jettisoning and
washing overboard

JANET [computing] Joint Academic
Network

janv. *janvier* (French: January)

Jap. Japan; Japanese

jap. japanned

jar. jargon

JARE Japanese Antarctic Research
Expedition

JAS Jamaica Agricultural Society; Junior
Astronomical Society

Jas. [Bible] James

jastop [aeronautics] jet-assisted stop

JAT *Jugoslovenski Aero-Transport* (Yugoslav
airline company)

JATCC Joint Aviation Telecommunications Coordination Committee

JATCRU joint air traffic control radar unit

JATO [aeronautics] jet-assisted take-off

JATS joint air transportation service

jaund. jaundice

Jav. Java; Javanese

jav. [athletics] javelin

JB Bachelor of Laws (from Latin *Juris Baccalaureus*); junior beadle; [vehicle regis-
tration] Reading

Jb. *Jahrbuch* (German: yearbook, annual)

j.b. jet bomb; joint board; junction box

JBAA *Journal of the British Archaeological
Association*

JBC Jamaica Broadcasting Corporation;
Japan Broadcasting Corporation

JBCNS Joint Board of Clinical Nursing
Studies

Jber. *Jahresbericht* (German: annual
report)

JBES Jodrell Bank Experimental Station

JBL *Journal of Business Law*

JBS [USA] John Birch Society

JC [vehicle registration] Bangor; Jesus
Christ; *Jewish Chronicle*; Jockey Club;
Julius Caesar (Roman emperor); [USA]
Junior Chamber (of Commerce) (applied
to members); [USA] junior college; [law]
jurisconsult (legal adviser); Justice Clerk;
justiciary case; juvenile court

J-C *Jésus-Christ* (French: Jesus Christ)

j.c. joint compound

JCAC [USA] Joint Civil Affairs Committee

JCAR Joint Commission on Applied Radioactivity

JCB Bachelor of Canon Law (from Latin
Juris Canonici Baccalaureus); Bachelor of
Civil Law (from Latin *Juris Civilis Baccalaureus*); Joseph Cyril Bamford (manufacturer of excavating machines)

JCC Joint Consultants' Committee; Joint
Consultative Committee; Junior
Chamber of Commerce

JCD Doctor of Canon Law (from Latin
Juris Canonici Doctor); Doctor of Civil
Law (from Latin *Juris Civilis Doctor*)

JCHMT Joint Committee on Higher
Medical Training

JCHST Joint Committee on Higher Surgical Training

JCI Junior Chamber International

JCL [computing] job-control language; Licentiate in Canon Law (from Latin *Juris Canonici Licentiatus*); Licentiate in Civil Law (from Latin *Juris Civilis Licentiatus*)

JCMC Joint Conference on Medical Conventions

JCMD Joint Committee on Mobility for the Disabled

JCMT James Clerk Maxwell Telescope

JCNAAF Joint Canadian Navy-Army-Air Force

JC of C Junior Chamber of Commerce

JCP Japan Communist Party

JCR junior combination room (in university or college); junior common room (in university or college)

JCS Jersey Cattle Society of the United Kingdom; Joint Chiefs of Staff; Joint Commonwealth Societies; *Journal of the Chemical Society*

jct. junction

jctn junction

JCWI Joint Council for the Welfare of Immigrants

JD [vehicle registration] central London; Diploma in Journalism; Doctor of Jurisprudence (or Laws) (from Latin *Jurum Doctor*); [currency] Jordanian dinar; [astronomy] Julian date; junior deacon; junior dean; jury duty; [USA] Justice Department; juvenile delinquent

jd joined

JDA Japan Defence Agency

JDB Japan Development Bank

JDipMA Joint Diploma in Management Accounting Services

JDL [USA] Jewish Defense League

JDM [medicine] juvenile diabetes mellitus

JDS [accounting] Joint Disciplinary Scheme

j.d.s. job data sheet

JE [UK postcode] Jersey; [vehicle registration] Peterborough

JEA Jesuit Educational Association; Joint Engineering Association

j.e.a. joint export agent

JEB Joint Examining Board

JEC Joint Economic Committee (of US Congress)

JECFI Joint Expert Committee on Food Irradiation

JECI *Jeunesse étudiante catholique internationale* (French: International Young Catholic Students)

JEDEC Joint Electronic Devices Engineering Council

JEIDA Japanese Electronic Industry Development Association

Jer. [Bible] Jeremiah; Jersey; Jerusalem

JERC Joint Electronic Research Committee

JERI Japan Economic Research Institute

jerob. jeroboam (large wine bottle)

Jes. Jesus

JESA Japanese Engineering Standards Association

JESSI Joint European Submicron Silicon Initiative

JET [nuclear technology] Joint European Torus (Culham, Oxfordshire); Joint European Transport

jet. jetsam; jettison

JETCO Jamaican Export Trading Company; Japan Export Trading Company

JETP *Journal of Experimental and Theoretical Physics*

JETRO Japan External Trade Organization

jett. jettison

jeu. *jeudi* (French: Thursday)

JF [vehicle registration] Leicester

J/F [book-keeping] journal folio

JFET [electronics] junction field-effect transistor

JFK John Fitzgerald Kennedy (US president)

JFM *Jeunesse fédéraliste mondiale* (French: Young World Federalists)

JFTC Joint Fur Trade Committee

JFU Jersey Farmers' Union

JG [vehicle registration] Maidstone

Jg. *Jahrgang* (German: year's issues (of magazine))

j.g. junior grade

JGTC Junior Girls' Training Corps

JGW [Freemasonry] Junior Grand Warden

JH [numismatics] Jubilee head (of Queen Victoria); [biochemistry] juvenile hormone; [vehicle registration] Reading

Jh. *Jahresheft* (German: annual volume); *Jahrhundert* (German: century)

j.h.a. job hazard analysis

JHDA Junior Hospital Doctors' Association

JHMO junior hospital medical officer

JHS *Jesus Hominum Salvator* (Latin: Jesus

Saviour of Men); [USA] junior high school

JHU [USA] Johns Hopkins University

JI Journalists' Institute; [vehicle registration] Tyrone

JIB joint intelligence bureau

JIC joint industrial council; [USA] joint intelligence center; [USA] joint intelligence committee; just in case

JICNARS Joint Industry Committee for National Readership Surveys

JICRAR Joint Industry Committee for Radio Audience Research

JICTAR Joint Industry Committee for Television Advertising Research

JIE Junior Institute of Engineers

JIM Japan Institute of Metals

JINS [USA] juvenile(s) in need of supervision

JINucE Junior Member of the Institution of Nuclear Engineers

JIOA joint intelligence objectives agency

JIS Jamaica Information Service; Japan Industrial Standard; Jewish Information Society; joint intelligence staff

JIT [commerce] just-in-time (manufacturing system)

JIU joint inspection unit

JJ jaw jerk; (Sir) Joseph John Thomson (British physicist); [electronics] Josephson junction; Judges; Justices; [vehicle registration] Maidstone

JK [vehicle registration] Brighton

JKG John Kenneth Galbraith (US economist)

jkt jacket

j.k.t. job knowledge test

JL [vehicle registration] Lincoln

Jl. July

jl journal

JLA Jewish Lads' Brigade; Jewish Librarians' Association

JLC [USA] Jewish Labor Committee

JLP Jamaica Labour Party

JM [vehicle registration] Reading

.jm Jamaica (in Internet address)

JMA Japanese Meteorological Agency

JMB J(ames) M(atthew) Barrie (Scottish writer); Joint Matriculation Board

JMBA *Journal of the Marine Biological Association*

JMC Joint Mathematical Council of the United Kingdom

JMCS Junior Mountaineering Club of Scotland

JMJ [Roman Catholic Church] Jesus, Mary and Joseph

JMPR Joint Meeting on Pesticide Residues (of WHO)

JMSAC Joint Meteorological Satellite Advisory Committee

JN [vehicle registration] Chelmsford

Jn Junction

jn join; junction

jn. junior

JNA Jordan News Agency

JNC joint negotiating committee

jnc. junction

JND just noticeable difference

JNEC Jamaican National Export Corporation

JNF Jewish National Fund

Jnl Journal

jnl journal

jnlst journalist

JNR Japanese National Railways

Jnr Junior

jnr junior

j.n.s. just noticeable shift

jnt joint

JNTO Japan National Tourist Organization

jnt stk joint stock

JO job order; *Journal Officiel* (French: Official Gazette); junior officer; [vehicle registration] Oxford

.jo Jordan (in Internet address)

Jo. Bapt. John the Baptist

Joburg [short form] Johannesburg

JOC *Jeunesse ouvrière chrétienne* (French: Young Christian Workers); [USA] joint operations center

joc. jocose; jocular

JOD [medicine] juvenile onset diabetes

j.o.d. joint occupancy date

J of E *Journal of Education*

JOG junior offshore group (in yachting)

Johan. Johannesburg

join. joinery

Jon. [Bible] Jonah

Jos. Joseph

Josh. [Bible] Joshua

JOT joint observer team

jour. journal; journalist; journey; journeyman

JOVIAL [computing] Jules' own version of

JP jet-propelled; jet propulsion; Justice of the Peace; [vehicle registration] Liverpool

.jp Japan (in Internet address)

JPA Jamaica Press Association

JPC joint planning council; joint production council; Judge of the Prize Court

JPCAC Joint Production, Consultative and Advisory Committee

JPEG Joint Photographic Expert Group

JPL Jet Propulsion Laboratory (California); *Journal of Planning Law*

JPMO Jersey Potato Marketing Organization

Jpn Japan

JPRS [USA] Joint Publications Research Service

JPS jet-propulsion system; [USA] Jewish Publications Society; Joint Parliamentary Secretary; joint planning staff; Junior Philatelic Society

JPTO [astronautics] jet-propelled take-off

JR *Jacobus Rex* (Latin: King James); joint resolution; Judges' Rules; Jurist Reports; [vehicle registration] Newcastle upon Tyne

Jr Junior; juror

jr *jour* (French: day); junior

jr. journal

JRA [medicine] juvenile rheumatoid arthritis

JRAI *Journal of the Royal Anthropological Institute*

JRC Junior Red Cross

JS [vehicle registration] Inverness; [USA] Japan Society; [law] judgment summons; [law] judicial separation

JSA jobseekers' allowance

JSAWC Joint Services Amphibious Warfare Centre

JSB joint-stock bank

JSC Johnson Space Center (Texas)

JSD Doctor of Juristic Science; [computing] Jackson system development

JSDC Joint Service Defence College

JSE Johannesburg Stock Exchange

Jsey Jersey

JSLS Joint Services Liaison Staff

JSP [trademark, computing] Jackson Structured Programming; Japan Socialist Party

JSPS Japan Society for the Promotion of Science

JSS Jacob Sheep Society; joint services standard

JSSC Joint Services Staff College; joint shop stewards' committee

J-stars joint surveillance and targeting acquisition radar system

JT [vehicle registration] Bournemouth

jt joint

j.t. [law] joint tenancy

JTC Junior Training Corps

Jt Ed. joint editor

JTIDS Joint Tactical Information Distribution Systems

jtly jointly

JTMP [computing] job transfer and manipulation protocol

JTO [aeronautics] jump take-off

JTS job training standards

JTUAC Joint Trade Union Advisory Committee

JU [vehicle registration] Leicester

Ju. June

j.u. joint use

JUD Doctor of Canon and Civil Law (from Latin *Juris Utriusque Doctor*)

Jud. Judaea; [Bible] Judah; Judaism; Judge; [Bible] Judges; [Bible] Judith (book of Apocrypha)

jud. judgment; judicial; judo

Judg. [Bible] Judges

judgt judgment

juev. *jueves* (Spanish: Thursday)

JUGFET [electronics] junction-gate field-effect transistor

juil. *juillet* (French: July)

Jul. July

jul. *julio* (Spanish: July)

Jun. June; Junior

jun. *junio* (Spanish: June); junior

junc. junction

jun. part. junior partner

Junr Junior

JurD Doctor of Law (from Latin *Juris Doctor*)

jurisd. jurisdiction

jurisp. jurisprudence

jus. justice

JUSMAG Joint United States Military Advisory Group

juss. [grammar] jussive

Just. Justinian (Byzantine emperor)

just. justice

Juv. (Decimus Junius) Juvenal(is) (Roman poet)

juv. juvenile

JUWTFA Joint Unconventional Warfare Task Force, Atlantic

jux. juxtaposed; juxtaposition

JV [commerce] joint venture; [anatomy] jugular vein; [USA] junior varsity; [vehicle registration] Lincoln

Jv. Java; Javanese

JVS Jewish Vegetarian and Natural Health Society

JW [vehicle registration] Birmingham; Jehovah's Witness(es); junior warden

JWB Jewish Welfare Board; joint wages board

JWEF Joinery and Woodwork Employers' Federation

JWG joint working group

jwlr jeweller

j.w.o. [insurance] jettisoning and washing overboard

JWPAC Joint Waste Paper Advisory Council

JWS Joint Warfare Staff

JWV Jewish War Veterans

JX [vehicle registration] Huddersfield; Jesus Christ

JY [vehicle registration] Exeter; [civil aircraft marking] Jordan

Jy jansky (unit used in astronomy); July; jury

JZ [vehicle registration] Down

K

K [botany] calyx (in floral formula); [international vehicle registration] Cambodia (from former name Kampuchea); [geology] Cretaceous; *Kalt* (German: cold); [physics] kaon; kelvin (unit of thermodynamic temperature); [immunology] killer (as in **K-cell**); [computing] kilo- (indicates 1,024, as in **KB** = kilobyte); [currency] kina (used in Papua New Guinea); King('s); [chess, card games] king; [currency] kip (used in Laos); [music] Kirkpatrick (catalogue of Domenico Scarlatti's works); [fishing port] Kirkwall; kitchen (in property advertisement); Knight; knighthood; [music] Köchel (catalogue of Mozart's works); *koel* (Dutch: cold); [currency] krona (used in Sweden); [currency] króna (used in Iceland); [currency] krone (used in Denmark and Norway); [currency] kwacha (used in Zambia); [currency] kyat (used in Myanmar); [vehicle registration] Liverpool; [chemical element] potassium (from Latin *kalium*); [astronomy] solar constant; [baseball] strikeout; thousand (from prefix kilo-)

K [physics] bulk modulus; [ecology] carrying capacity; [chemistry] equilibrium constant; [physics] kinetic energy; [physics] luminous efficacy

k [mathematics] constant; [mathematics] curvature; kilo- (indicates 1,000, as in **kg** = kilogram); [computing] kilo- (indicates 1,024, as in **kbyte** = kilobyte)

k radius of gyration (in mechanics); [chemistry] rate coefficient; [chemistry] rate constant; [physics] thermal conductivity

k. [USA] karat; keel; killed; king; kingdom; knight; [knitting] knit; knot; [currency] kopek (hundredth of rouble); kosher

K9 [military] canine (referring to army dogs)

9K [civil aircraft marking] Kuwait

KA [UK postcode] Kilmarnock; King of Arms; Knight of St Andrew, Order of Barbados; [vehicle registration] Liverpool

KADU Kenya African Democratic Union (became part of KANU)

KAI Keep America Independent

KAK *Kungliga Automobil Klubben* (Swedish: Royal Automobile Club)

Kal. *Kalendae* (Latin: calends, first day of month)

Kan. Kansas

k&b kitchen and bathroom (in property advertisement)

Kans. Kansas

KANTAFU Kenya African National Traders' and Farmers' Union

KANU Kenya African National Union

KANUPP Karachi Nuclear Power Plant

KAO Kuiper Airborne Observatory

kao. kaolin

Kap. [finance] *Kapital* (German: capital); *Kapitel* (German: chapter)

KAR King's African Rifles

Kar. Karachi

Karel. Karelia; Karelian

Kash. Kashmir

KB [computing] kilobyte; King's Bench; [chess] kings' bishop; Knight Bachelor; [knitting] knit into back of stitch; [computing] knowledge base; *Koninkrijk België* (Flemish: Kingdom of Belgium); [vehicle registration] Liverpool

kb kilobar (unit of pressure)

KBC [law] King's Bench Court

KBD [law] King's Bench Division

kbd keyboard

KBE Knight Commander of the Order of the British Empire

KBES [computing] knowledge-based expert system

Kbhvn *København* (Danish: Copenhagen)

Kbl Kabul

KBP [chess] king's bishop's pawn

KBS Knight of the Blessed Sacrament; [computing] knowledge-based system

KBW King's Bench Walk (Temple, London)

kbyte [computing] kilobyte

KC Kansas City; Kennel Club; King's College; King's Counsel; King's Cross (London); Knight Commander; Knight of the Crescent (in Turkey); Knights of Columbus; [vehicle registration] Liverpool

kc kilocycle(s per second) (unit of frequency)

KCA *Keesing's Contemporary Archives*

kcal kilocalorie

KCB Knight Commander of the Order of the Bath

KCC (Knight) Commander of the Order of the Crown (Belgium and the Congo Free State)

K-cell [immunology] killer cell

KCH King's College Hospital (London); Knight Commander of the Hanoverian Order

KCHS Knight Commander of the Order of the Holy Sepulchre

KCIE Knight Commander of the Order of the Indian Empire

KCL King's College, London

KCLJ Knight Commander of the Order of St Lazarus of Jerusalem

KCMG Knight Commander of the Order of St Michael and St George

KCMS [trademark] Kodak colour management system

KCNA Korean Central News Agency

Kcs [currency] koruna (used in Czech Republic)

kc/s kilocycles per second (unit of frequency)

KCSA Knight Commander of the Military Order of the Collar of St Agatha of Paterna

KCSG Knight Commander of the Order of St Gregory the Great

KCSI Knight Commander of the Order of the Star of India

KCSJ Knight Commander of the Order of St John of Jerusalem (Knights Hospitallers)

KCSS Knight Commander of the Order of St Silvester

KCVO Knight Commander of the Royal Victorian Order

KD kiln dried; knock down (at auction); [commerce] knocked down (of goods sold in parts); *Kongeriget Danmark* (Danish: Kingdom of Denmark); [currency] Kuwaiti dinar; [vehicle registration] Liverpool

kd killed

KDC [computing] key distribution centre; [commerce] knocked-down condition (of goods sold in parts)

KDD [computing] knowledge discovery in databases

KDF *Kraft durch Freude* (German: Strength through Joy) (Nazi holiday scheme)

KDG King's Dragoon Guards

KDM *Kongelige Danske Marine* (Danish: Royal Danish Navy)

KE kinetic energy; kinetic equation; [vehicle registration] Maidstone

.ke Kenya (in Internet address)

KEAS [aeronautics] knots equivalent air speed

Kef. Keflavik (Iceland)

KEH King Edward's Horse
Ken. Kensington; Kentucky; Kenya
Kent. Kentucky
KEO King Edward's Own
Ker. Kerry
keV kiloelectronvolt
KEY keep extending yourself
KF [vehicle registration] Liverpool
KFA Keep-Fit Association; Kenya Farmers' Association
KFAED Kuwait Fund for Arab Economic Development
KFAT National Union of Knitwear, Footwear and Apparel Trades
KFC [trademark] Kentucky Fried Chicken
KFL Kenya Federation of Labour
Kfm. *Kaufmann* (German: merchant)
kfm. *kaufmännisch* (German: commercial)
KFOR Kosovo Force (NATO-led peacekeeping force)
Kfz. *Kraftfahrzeug* (German: motor vehicle)
KG [vehicle registration] Cardiff; Knight of the Order of the Garter; [commerce] *Kommanditgesellschaft* (German: limited partnership)
kg keg; kilogram
.kg Kyrgyzstan (in Internet address)
KGB *Komitet Gosudarstvennoi Bezopasnosti* (Russian: Committee of State Security) (former Soviet secret police)
KGC Knights of the Golden Circle (US antifederal organization)
Kgf. *Kriegsgefangener* (German: prisoner-of-war)
kgf [physics] kilogram-force
KGFR [medicine] kidney glomerular filtration rate
Kgl. *Königlich* (German: Royal)
Kgn Kingston (Jamaica)
KGS known geological structure
Kgs [Bible] Kings
KGV Knight of Gustavus Vasa (Swedish decoration)
KH [vehicle registration] Hull; kennel huntsman; [astronautics] keyhole (as in **KH-11**, name of NASA satellite); King's Hussars; Knight of the Hanoverian Order
.kh Cambodia (in Internet address)
KHC King's Honorary Chaplain
KHDS King's Honorary Dental Surgeon
KHM King's Harbour Master

KHNS King's Honorary Nursing Sister
KHP King's Honorary Physician
KHS King's Honorary Surgeon; Knight of the Order of the Holy Sepulchre
kHz kilohertz
.ki Kiribati (in Internet address)
KIA killed in action
KIAS [aeronautics] knots indicated air speed
kid. kidney
kil. kilderkin (brewing cask size)
Kild. Kildare
kild. kilderkin (brewing cask size)
Kilk. Kilkenny
Kinc. Kincardineshire
kind. kindergarten
kingd. kingdom
Kinr. Kinross
KIO Kuwait Investment Office
Kirk. Kirkcudbrightshire
KISS keep it short and simple; [informal] keep it simple, stupid; [stock exchange] Kurs Information Service System
kit. kitchen (in property advertisement)
kitch. kitchen (in property advertisement)
KJ [medicine] knee jerk; Knight of St Joachim; [vehicle registration] Maidstone
kJ kilojoule
KJV [Bible] King James Version
KK [commerce] *Kabushiki Kaisha* (Japanese: joint-stock company); [vehicle registration] Maidstone
KKK Ku Klux Klan
KKt [chess] king's knight
KKtP [chess] king's knight's pawn
KL [astronomy] Kleinmann–Low (as in **KL nebula**); Kuala Lumpur; [vehicle registration] Maidstone
kl kilolitre
KLA Kosovo Liberation Army
klax. klaxon
KLH Knight of the Legion of Honour
KLJ Knight of the Order of St Lazarus of Jerusalem
KLM *Koninklijke Luchtvaart Maatschappij* (Dutch airline company)
KLS [medicine] kidney, liver, spleen
KLSE Kuala Lumpur Stock Exchange
KM King's Medal; Knight of Malta; [vehicle registration] Maidstone
km kilometre
.km Comoros (in Internet address)

KMF [currency] Comorian franc
km/h kilometres per hour
KMO Kobe Marine Observatory (Japan)
KMP [computing] Knuth–Morris–Pratt (algorithm)
kmph kilometres per hour
KMT Kuomintang (Chinese Nationalist Party)
KN [chess] king's knight; [numismatics] King's Norton (Birmingham mint mark); *Kongeriket Norge* (Norwegian: Kingdom of Norway); [vehicle registration] Maidstone
kn knot (unit of speed); [currency] krona (used in Sweden); [currency] krone (used in Denmark and Norway)
KNA Kenya News Agency; *Kongelig Norsk Automobil-klubb* (Norwegian: Royal Norwegian Automobile Club)
KNM *Kongelige Norske Marine* (Norwegian: Royal Norwegian Navy)
KNP [chess] king's knight's pawn; Kruger National Park (South Africa)
KNPC Kuwait National Petroleum Company
Knt Knight
KO [informal] knock out; [informal] knockout; [vehicle registration] Maidstone
k.o. keep off; keep out; kick-off (in football); [informal] knock out; [informal] knockout
KOC Kuwait Oil Company
KOD [navigation] kick-off drift
K of C Knights of Columbus
K of K (Lord) Kitchener of Khartoum (British field marshal)
K of P [USA] Knights of Pythias
KOM Knight of the Order of Malta
Komintern *Kommunisticheskii Internatsionál* (Russian: Communist International)
Komp. [commerce] *Kompanie* (German: company)
Komsomol *Kommunisticheskii Soyuz Molodezhi* (Russian: Communist Union of Youth)
kop. [currency] kopek (hundredth of rouble)
Kor. Koran; Korea; Korean
KORR King's Own Royal Regiment
KOSB King's Own Scottish Borderers

KOYLI King's Own Yorkshire Light Infantry
KP King's Parade; [chess] king's pawn; [US military] kitchen police; Knight of the Order of St Patrick; [vehicle registration] Maidstone
.kp North Korea (in Internet address)
k.p. key personnel
kpc kiloparsec (unit of astronomical distance)
KPD *Kommunistische Partei Deutschlands* (German: German Communist Party)
KPDR Korean People's Democratic Party
KPFSM King's Police and Fire Service Medal
kpg kilometres per gallon
kph kilometres per hour
KPM King's Police Medal
KPMG (Piet) Klynveld, (William Barclay) Peat, (James) Marwick, (Reinhard) Goerdeler (founding members of international accounting group)
Kpmtr [music] *Kapellmeister* (German: conductor)
KPNLF Khmer People's National Liberation Front
KPNO Kitt Peak National Observatory (Arizona)
KPP Keeper of the Privy Purse
kpr keeper
KPTT [medicine] kaolin partial thromboplastin time
KPU Kenya People's Union
KR King's Regiment; [military] King's Regulations; [chess] king's rook; [vehicle registration] Maidstone
Kr [currency] króna (used in Iceland); [chemical element] krypton
kr. [currency] krona (used in Sweden); [currency] krone (used in Denmark and Norway)
.kr Republic of Korea (in Internet address)
KRC Knight of the Red Cross
KRE Knight of the Order of the Red Eagle
KRL [computing] knowledge representation language
KRP [chess] king's rook's pawn
KRR King's Royal Rifles
KRRC King's Royal Rifle Corps
KS [vehicle registration] Edinburgh; [US postcode] Kansas; [medicine] Kaposi's sarcoma; King's Scholar; King's School; Kipling Society; Kitchener Scholar;

Konungariket Sverige (Swedish: Kingdom of Sweden); [international vehicle registration] Kyrgyzstan

KSA Kitchen Specialists Association

KSC Kennedy Space Center (Florida); King's School, Canterbury; Knight of St Columba

KSF key success factor

KSG Knight of the Order of St Gregory the Great

Ksh [currency] Kenya shilling

KSI Knight of the Order of the Star of India

KSJ Knight of the Order of St John of Jerusalem (Knights Hospitallers)

KSL [medicine] kidney, spleen, liver

KSLI King's Shropshire Light Infantry

KSM Korean Service Medal; *Kungliga Svenska Marinen* (Swedish: Royal Swedish Navy)

KSS Knight of the Order of St Silvester

KSSU KLM, SAS, Swissair, UTA (international airline organization)

KStJ Knight of the Order of St John of Jerusalem (Knights Hospitallers)

KSU Kansas State University

KT [UK postcode] Kingston-upon-Thames; Knight of the Order of the Thistle; Knight Templar; [meteorology] knot; [vehicle registration] Maidstone

Kt knight

kt [USA] karat; kilotonne; knot (unit of speed)

Kt Bach. Knight Bachelor

Kto [banking] *Konto* (German: account)

KU [vehicle registration] Sheffield

Ku [chemical element] kurchatovium (alternative name for rutherfordium)

KUB [medicine] kidney, ureter, bladder

KUTD keep up to date

Kuw. Kuwait

KV [vehicle registration] Coventry; [music] *Köchel Verzeichnis* (German: Köchel catalogue) (catalogue of Mozart's works)

kV kilovolt

KW [UK postcode] Kirkwall (Orkney); [vehicle registration] Sheffield

kW kilowatt

.kw Kuwait (in Internet address)

KWAC key word and context

kWh kilowatt hour

KWIC key word in context

KWOC key word out of context

KWP Korean Workers' Party

KWT [international vehicle registration] Kuwait

KX [vehicle registration] Luton

KY [US postcode] Kentucky; [fishing port] Kirkcaldy; [UK postcode] Kirkcaldy; *Kol Yisrael* (Israeli broadcasting station); [vehicle registration] Sheffield

Ky Kentucky

ky. [currency] kyat (used in Myanmar)

kybd keyboard

Kyr. *Kyrie eleison* (Greek: Lord have mercy) (ecclesiastical invocation)

KZ [vehicle registration] Antrim; [international vehicle registration] Kazakhstan; [military] killing zone

.kz Kazakhstan (in Internet address)

Kzrl [currency] kwanza (used in Angola)

L

L [Roman numeral] fifty; [electrical engineering] inductor; [politics] Labour; Lady; Lake; lambert (former unit of luminance); [military] Lancers; [linguistics] language; large; Latin; law; League; learner (driver) (as in **L-plate**); lecturer; left; [currency] lempira (used in Honduras); lethal; *liber* (Latin: book); [politics] Liberal; Licentiate; Lieutenant; [aeronautics] lift; [immunology] light; [fishing port] Limerick; line (of text); linear; link; [currency] lira; litre; [electrical engineering] live; [UK postcode] Liverpool; Loch; *locus* (Latin: place); Lodge (of fraternal organization); London; Lord; [sports] lost; Lough; low; [international vehicle registration] Luxembourg; [currency] pound sterling (from Latin *libra*); [theatre] stage left

L [physics] angular momentum; [chemistry] Avogadro constant; [physics] Lagrangian function; [physics] latent heat;

length; [biochemistry] linking number; longitude; [physics] luminance; [astronomy] luminosity; [physics] radiance; [electrical engineering] self-inductance; [physics] sound intensity

l [Roman numeral] fifty; [music] la(h) (in tonic sol-fa); [meteorology] lightning; [chemistry] liquid; [currency] lira; litre; [currency] pound sterling (from Latin *libra*)

l [chemistry] laevorotatory; length; [physics] lepton number

l. lake; land; large; late; lateral; latitude; law; leaf; league; leasehold; left; legitimate; length; light; line (of text); link; literate; little; loch; long; lost; lough; low

4L [civil aircraft marking] Georgia

9L [civil aircraft marking] Sierra Leone

LA [UK postcode] Lancaster; [photography] large aperture; Latin America; Latin American; law agent; leave allowance; [medicine] left atrial; [medicine] left atrium; legal adviser; Legislative Assembly; letter of authority; Library Association; Licensing Act; licensing authority; Lieutenant-at-Arms; [physics] linear accelerator; [computing] linear arithmetic; Literate in Arts; Liverpool Academy; [fishing port] Llanelly; Lloyd's agent; local agent; local anaesthetic; local association; local authority; long acting; Los Angeles; [US postcode] Louisiana; low altitude; [vehicle registration] northwest London

La [chemical element] lanthanum; Louisiana

La. Lancastrian; Lane

la. last

.la Laos (in Internet address)

l.a. landing account; leading article; [medicine] *lege artis* (Latin: as directed) (in prescriptions); lighter than air

LAA [USA] League of Advertising Agencies; Library Association of Australia; Libyan Arab Airlines; Lieutenant-at-Arms; [USA] Life Assurance Advertisers; light anti-aircraft

LAADS [USA] Los Angeles Air Defense Sector

LAAOH Ladies' Auxiliary, Ancient Order of Hibernians

LAAR liquid-air accumulator rocket

LAB Legal Aid Board; [chemistry] linear alkyl benzene; load aboard barge; low-altitude bombing

Lab. [USA] Laborite; [politics] Labour; Labrador

lab [short form] laboratory; [short form] labrador (dog)

lab. label; laboratory; labour; labourer

LABA [USA] Laboratory Animal Breeders' Association

LABBS Ladies' Association of British Barbershop Singers

LAC Laboratory Animals Centre; Landscape Advisory Committee; leading aircraftman; Licentiate of the Apothecaries' Company; London Athletic Club; [finance] long-run average cost

Lac [astronomy] Lacerta

lac. lacquer; lactation

LACES London Airport cargo electronic processing scheme; [USA] Los Angeles Council of Engineering Societies

LACONIQ [computing] laboratory computer online inquiry

LACS League Against Cruel Sports

LACSA *Lineas Aéreas Costarricenses* (Costa Rican airline company)

LACSAB Local Authorities' Conditions of Service Advisory Board

LACW leading aircraftwoman

LAD [linguistics] language acquisition device; light aid detachment

ladar laser detection and ranging

Ladp Ladyship

L Adv. Lord Advocate

LAE [mathematics] linear algebraic equation

laev. [medicine] *laevus* (Latin: left)

LAF *L'Académie française* (French: the French Academy)

LaF Louisiana French

LAFC Latin American Forestry Commission

La Font. (Jean de) La Fontaine (French writer)

LAFTA Latin American Free Trade Association (former name of LAIA)

lag. lagoon

LAH Licentiate of the Apothecaries' Hall (Dublin)

Lah. Lahore

LAHS low altitude, high speed

LAI [botany] leaf area index; Library

Association of Ireland; *Logos Agencia de Información* (Spanish news agency)

LAIA Latin American Integration Association (formerly LAFTA)

LAK [medicine] lymphokine-activated killer (cell) (used to treat cancer)

LAL *Laboratoire de l'accélérateur linéaire* (French: Linear Accelerator Laboratory)

lali [informal] lonely aged low income

LAM London Academy of Music (and Dramatic Art); Master of the Liberal Arts (from Latin *Liberalium Artium Magister*)

Lam. Lamarck (French naturalist); [Bible] Lamentations

lam. laminate; laminated; lamination

LAMA Locomotive and Allied Manufacturers' Association of Great Britain

Lamb. Lambeth

LAMC Livestock Auctioneers' Market Committee of England and Wales

LAMCO Liberian-American-Swedish Mineral Corporation

LAMDA London Academy of Music and Dramatic Art

LAMIDA Lancashire and Merseyside Industrial Development Association

LAMP low-altitude manned penetration; [USA] Lunar Analysis and Mapping Program

LAMS launch acoustic measuring system

LAMSAC Local Authorities' Management Services and Computer Committee

LAN *Linea Aérea Nacional (de Chile)* (Chilean airline company); local apparent noon; [computing] local area network

LANBY large automatic navigation buoy

Lanc. Lancaster; [military] Lancers

Lancs Lancashire

L&D loans and discounts; loss and damage

L&ID London and India Docks

L&NRR [USA] Louisville and Nashville Railroad

L&NWR London and North-Western Railway

L&SWR London and South-Western Railway

l&w living and well

L&YR Lancashire and Yorkshire Railway

Lan. Fus. Lancashire Fusiliers

Lang. Languedoc

lang. language

LANICA *Lineas Aéreas de Nicaragua* (Nicaraguan airline company)

LANL [USA] Los Alamos National Laboratory

LANRAC Land Army Reunion Association Committee

LanR(PWV) Lancashire Regiment (Prince of Wales' Volunteers)

LANSA *Lineas Aéreas Nacionales SA* (Peruvian airline company)

Lantirn [military] low-altitude navigation and targeting infrared system

LAO [international vehicle registration] Laos; Licentiate in the Art of Obstetrics

LAOAR [US air force] Latin American Office of Aerospace Research

LAP [USA] Laboratory of Aviation Psychology; *Lineas Aéreas Paraguayas* (Paraguayan airline company); [computing] link access protocol

Lap. Lapland; Lappish

LAPD Los Angeles Police Department

LAPES low-altitude parachute extraction system

LAPO Los Angeles Philharmonic Orchestra

LAPT London Association for the Protection of Trade

LAR [botany] leaf area ratio; [international vehicle registration] Libya (Arab Republic); [taxation] life assurance relief; [computing] limit address register

LARA light armed reconnaissance aircraft

larg. [music] *largamente* (Italian: broadly); *largeur* (French: width); [music] *largo* (Italian: broad, slow)

LARO Latin American Regional Office

LARSP Language Assessment, Remediation and Screening Procedure

laryngol. laryngologist; laryngology

LAS Land Agents' Society; large astronomical satellite; League of Arab States; Legal Aid Society; London Archaeological Service; Lord Advocate of Scotland; low-altitude satellite; lower airspace

LASER London and South Eastern Library Region

laser light amplification by stimulated emission of radiation

LASH [commerce] lighter aboard ship

LASL [USA] Los Alamos Scientific Laboratory

LASMO London and Scottish Marine Oil
LASP low-altitude space platform
LASS lighter-than-air submarine simulator
LAT local apparent time; *Los Angeles Times*
Lat. Latin; Latvia; Latvian
lat. latent; lateral; latitude; *latus* (Latin: wide)
LATCC London air traffic control centre
LATCRS London air traffic control radar station
lat. ht latent heat
LATS [medicine] long-acting thyroid stimulator
Latv. Latvia
Latvn Latvian
lau. laundry
LAUK Library Association of the United Kingdom
laun. launched
LAUTRO Life Assurance and Unit Trust Regulatory Organization
LAV light armoured vehicle; *Lineas Aéreas Venezolanas* (Venezuelan airline company); [medicine] lymphadenopathy-associated virus (former name of HIV)
lav [short form] lavatory
LAW League of American Writers; light anti-tank weapon
law. lawyer
Lawn [computing] local area wireless network
LAWRS limited airport weather reporting system
lax. laxative
LB Bachelor of Letters (or Literature) (from Latin *Litterarum Baccalaureus*); late bottled (wine); [international vehicle registration] Liberia; light bomber; local board; [vehicle registration] northwest London
L.b. *Lectori benevolo* (Latin: to the kind reader)
lb binary logarithm; pound (unit of weight, from Latin *libra*)
.lb Lebanon (in Internet address)
l.b. landing barge; [sports] left back; [cricket] leg bye; letter box; link belt
LBA late booking agent (= ticket tout); linear-bounded automaton; [computing] logical block address

LB&SCR London, Brighton and South Coast Railway
LBB [engineering] leak before break
LBBB [medicine] left bundle branch block
LBC Land Bank Commission; London Broadcasting Company
Lbc. Lübeck
LBCH London Bankers' Clearing House
LBCM Licentiate of the Bandsmen's College of Music; London Board of Congregational Ministers
LBD League of British Dramatists
L/Bdr Lance-Bombardier
LBF [medicine] liver blood flow
lbf pound-force
lb-ft pound-foot
LBH length, breadth, height
LBI [astronomy] long baseline interferometry
LBJ Lyndon Baines Johnson (US president)
LBL [medicine] lymphoblastic lymphoma
LBO [commerce] leveraged buyout
LBP length between perpendiculars
lbr labour; lumber
LBS Libyan Broadcasting Service; lifeboat station; London Business School
L.b.s. *Lectori benevolo salutem* (Latin: to the kind reader, greeting)
LBSM Licentiate of Birmingham and Midland Institute School of Music
LBV landing barge vehicle; late bottled vintage (port); [astronomy] luminous blue variable
LBW live body weight
lbw [cricket] leg before wicket
LC Cross of Leo; landing craft; [medicine] Langerhans cells; Leander Club; Legislative Council; letter of credit; level crossing (on map); [USA] Library of Congress; Lieutenant-Commander; [chemistry] linear chain; [electronics] linear contact; [military slang] line crosser (i.e. defector); [chemistry] liquid chromatography; [electronics] liquid crystal; livestock commissioner; Lord Chamberlain; Lord Chancellor; Lower Canada; Lutheran Council of Great Britain; [vehicle registration] northwest London
L/C letter of credit
l/c letter of credit
.lc St Lucia (in Internet address)
l.c. label clause; law courts; lead covered;

leading cases; left centre; legal currency; letter card; letter of credit; *loco citato* (Latin: in the place (already) cited); low-calorie; low-carbon; [printing] lower case

LCA Library Club of America; Licensed Company Auditor; [computing] logic cell array; low-cost automation

LCAD London Certificate in Art and Design

LCAP [computing] loosely coupled array of processors

LCB [theatre] left centre back (of stage); [USA] Liquor Control Board; London Convention Bureau; Lord Chief Baron

l.c.b. longitudinal centre of buoyancy

LCC [electronics] leadless chip carrier; Legalize Cannabis Campaign; [accounting] life-cycle cost(ing); load-carrying capability; London Chamber of Commerce; London County Council (former local authority)

LCCC [USA] Library of Congress Catalog Card

LCD [electronics] liquid-crystal display; Lord Chamberlain's Department; Lord Chancellor's Department; lower court decisions; [mathematics] lowest common denominator

LCDT London Contemporary Dance Theatre

LCE Licentiate in Civil Engineering; London Commodity Exchange

lce lance

LCF Law Centres Federation; [mathematics] lowest common factor

l.c.f. longitudinal centre of flotation

l.c.g. longitudinal centre of gravity

LCGB Locomotive Club of Great Britain

LCH London Clearing House

LCh Licentiate in Surgery (from Latin *Licentiatus Chirurgiae*); Lord Chancellor

LChir Licentiate in Surgery (from Latin *Licentiatus Chirurgiae*)

LCIGB Locomotive and Carriage Institution of Great Britain and Ireland

LCIOB Licentiate of the Chartered Institute of Building

LCJ Lord Chief Justice

LCL [US commerce] less-than-carload lot; [commerce] less-than-container load; Licentiate in Canon Law

l.c.l. lower control limit

LCLS Livestock Commission Levy Scheme

LCM landing craft mechanized; [mathematics] least common multiple; [computing] life-cycle management; London College of Music; [mathematics] lowest common multiple

LCN [aeronautics] load classification number; local civil noon

Lcn Lincoln

LCO landing craft officer; launch control officer

L/Corp. Lance-Corporal

LCP last complete programme; least-cost planning; Licentiate of the College of Preceptors; [chemistry] liquid-crystal polymer; London College of Printing; low-cost production

LCP&SA Licentiate of the College of Physicians and Surgeons of America

LCP&SO Licentiate of the College of Physicians and Surgeons of Ontario

L/Cpl Lance-Corporal

LCPS Licentiate of the College of Physicians and Surgeons

l/cr. *lettre de crédit* (French: letter of credit)

LCS London Cooperative Society

LCSAJ [computing] linear code sequence and jump

LCSP London and Counties Society of Physiologists

LCST Licentiate of the College of Speech Therapists

LCT landing craft tank; local civil time

LCU [photography] large close-up

LCV Licentiate of the College of Violinists

LD Doctor of Letters (or Literature) (from Latin *Litterarum Doctor*); Lady Day; *laus Deo* (Latin: praise be to God); [education, psychology] learning difficulties; [education, psychology] learning-disabled; legal dose (or dosage); *lepide dictum* (Latin: wittily said); [pharmacology] lethal dose (as in LD_{50}, dose killing 50% of test group); Liberal and Democratic; Liberal Democrat(s); [currency] Libyan dinar; Licentiate in Divinity; Light Dragoons; *Litera Dominicalis* (Latin: Dominical letter); [UK postcode] Llandrindod Wells; London Docks; low density; Low Dutch; [vehicle registration] northwest London

L/D letter of deposit

Ld Limited (company); Lord (in titles)

ld land; [printing] lead; load

l.d. light difference; line of departure; line of duty

LDA Lead Development Association

Lda [commerce] *Sociedade de responsabilidade limitada* (Portuguese: limited company, Ltd)

l.d.b. light distribution box

LDC less developed country; local distribution company

l.d.c. long-distance call; lower dead centre

LDDC London Docklands' Development Corporation

LDEF [astronomy] long duration exposure facility

LDEG *laus Deo et gloria* (Latin: praise and glory be to God)

LDentSc Licentiate in Dental Science

L'derry Londonderry

Ldg Leading (in military rank)

ldg landing; leading; loading; lodging

Ldge Lodge

Ld'H *Légion d'Honneur* (French: Legion of Honour)

LDiv Licentiate in Divinity

ldk lower deck

LDL [biochemistry] low-density lipoprotein

ldmk landmark

LDN less developed nation

Ldn London

LDOS Lord's Day Observance Society

LDP Liberal Democratic Party; [finance] London daily price; long-distance path

Ldp Ladyship; Lordship

LDPE low-density polyethylene (packaging material)

LDR Liberal, Democratic and Reform Goup (in European Parliament); low dose rate

ldr leader; ledger; lodger

ldry laundry

LDS Latter-Day Saints; *laus Deo semper* (Latin: praise be to God for ever); Licentiate in Dental Surgery

lds loads

LDSc Licentiate in Dental Science

LDT [finance] licensed deposit taker

LDV Local Defence Volunteers (i.e. Home Guard)

LDWA Long Distance Walkers' Association

LDX long-distance xerography

LDY Leicestershire and Derbyshire Yeomanry

LE labour exchange (former name for jobcentre); [UK postcode] Leicester; London Electricity; low energy; [medicine] lupus erythematosus; [vehicle registration] northwest London

Le [currency] leone (used in Sierra Leone)

Le. Lebanese; Lebanon

l.e. leading edge; left eye; library edition; light equipment; limited edition; low explosive

LEA local education authority

lea. league; leather; leave

LEAJ [USA] Law Enforcement and Administration of Justice

LEAP Life Education for the Autistic Person; lift-off elevation and azimuth programmer; Loan and Educational Aid Programme

LEB London Electricity Board; [astronautics] low-energy booster

Leb. Lebanese; Lebanon

LEC Local Employment Committee; Local Enterprise Company

lect. *lectio* (Latin: lesson); lecture; lecturer

lectr lecturer

LED [electronics] light-emitting diode

led. ledger

LEDC Lighting Equipment Development Council

LEFM linear elastic fracture mechanics

leg. legal; legate; legation; [music] *legato* (Italian: bound, smoothly); legion; legislation; legislative; legislature; legitimate

legg. [music] *legg(i)ero* (Italian: light, rapid)

legis. legislation; legislative; legislature

legit [short form] legitimate

Leics Leicestershire

Leip. Leipzig

Leit. Leitrim

LEL Laureate in English Literature; [physics] linear energy loss

LEM [astronautics] lunar excursion module

LEMA Lifting Equipment Manufacturers' Association

LENTA London Enterprise Agency

LEO [astronautics] low earth orbit; Lyons Electronic Office (early computer)

LEP [physics] large electron-positron (collider) (at CERN)

Lep [astronomy] Lepus
LEPMA [USA] Lithographic Engravers' and Plate Makers' Association
LEPORE [USA] long-term and expanded program of oceanic research and exploration
LEPRA Leprosy Relief Association
LEPT long-endurance patrolling torpedo
LES launch escape system; Liverpool Engineering Society
Lès L *Licencié ès lettres* (French: Bachelor of Arts)
LESS least-cost estimating and scheduling
Lès S *Licencié ès sciences* (French: Bachelor of Science)
LEST large earth-based solar telescope
LET [physics] linear energy transfer
let. letter
LETS Local Employment and Trade System; Local Exchange and Trading System (community bartering system)
LEU [physics] low-enriched uranium
LEV [astronautics] lunar excursion vehicle
Lev. Levant; [Bible] Leviticus
Levit. [Bible] Leviticus
LEX land exercise
lex. lexicon
lexicog. lexicographer; lexicographical; lexicography
LEY Liberal European Youth
LF Lancashire Fusiliers; line feed; [radio] low frequency; [astronomy] luminosity function; [currency] Luxembourg franc; [vehicle registration] northwest London
Lf limit of flocculation (in toxicology)
lf leaf
l.f. ledger folio; life float; [printing] light face
LFA less favoured area; local freight agent
LFB London Fire Brigade
LFBC London Federation of Boys' Clubs
LFC low-frequency current; Lutheran Free Church
LFCDA London Fire and Civil Defence Authority
LFD least fatal dose; low-fat diet
LFE laboratory for electronics
Lfg *Lieferung* (German: delivery)
LFO low-frequency oscillator
lft leaflet
LFTU landing force training unit
LG [vehicle registration] Chester; Lady

Companion of the Order of the Garter; landing ground; Lewis gun; Lieutenant-General; Life Guards; (David) Lloyd George (British statesman); *London Gazette*; Low German
lg common logarithm; long
lg. lagoon; large
LGAR [USA] Ladies of the Grand Army of the Republic
LGB Local Government Board
LGBC Local Government Boundary Commission for England
LGC lunar (module) guidance computer
lge large; league; lounge (in property advertisement)
LGEB Local Government Examination Board
L-Gen Lieutenant-General
LGer Low German
LGIO Local Government Information Office
LGk Late Greek
LGM little green men; Lloyd's Gold Medal
LGO [USA] Lamont Geological Observatory
LGPRA Local Government Public Relations Association
LGR leasehold ground rent; local government reports
LGr Late Greek
LGSM Licentiate of the Guildhall School of Music (and Drama)
LGTB Local Government Training Board
lgth length
lg tn long ton
LGU Ladies' Golf Union
LGV large goods vehicle (replacement for HGV)
LH left hand; left handed; [fishing port] Leith; licensing hours; Licentiate in Hygiene; [military] Light Horse; [biochemistry] luteinizing hormone; [vehicle registration] northwest London
L/H leasehold (in property advertisement)
l.h. [sports] left half; left hand; left handed
LHA landing helicopter assault; local health authority; local hour angle; Lord High Admiral; lower hour angle
l.h.b. [sports] left halfback
LHC [physics] Large Hadron Collider (at CERN); Lord High Chancellor

LHCIMA Licentiate of the Hotel Catering and Institutional Management Association

LHD Doctor of Humanities (or Literature) (from Latin *Litterarum Humaniorum Doctor*)

l.h.d. left-hand drive (in car advertisement)

LHDC lateral homing depth charge

LHeb Late Hebrew

lhld leasehold (in property advertisement)

LHMC London Hospital Medical College

LHO livestock husbandry officer

lhr lumen-hour

LHRC Light and Health Research Council

LH-RH [biochemistry] luteinizing-hormone-releasing hormone

LHS left hand side

LHSM Licentiate of the Institute of Health Services Management

LHT Lord High Treasurer

LHWN lowest high water neaps (level of tide)

LI Leeward Islands; Liberal International; [USA] Licentiate in Instruction; Light Infantry; [law] Lincoln's Inn; [fishing port] Littlehampton; Long Island (New York)

Li [chemical element] lithium

li. link; [currency] lira

.li Liechtenstein (in Internet address)

l.i. letter of introduction; longitudinal interval

LIA [USA] Laser Industry Association; [USA] Lead Industries Association; Leather Industries of America; Lebanese International Airways; Life Insurance Association

LIAB Licentiate of the International Association of Book-keepers

LIAT London International Arbitration Trust

Lib [astronomy] Libra

Lib. [politics] Liberal; Liberia; Liberian; Libya; Libyan

lib. *liber* (Latin: book); liberation; liberty; librarian; library; libretto

LIBA Lloyd's Insurance Brokers' Association

lib. cat. library catalogue

Lib. Cong. [USA] Library of Congress

Lib Dem [short form] Liberal Democrat

LIBER *Ligue des bibliothèques européennes*

de recherche (French: League of European Research Libraries)

LIBID [finance] London Inter-Bank Bid Rate

LIBOR [finance] London Inter-Bank Offered Rate

libst librettist

LIC Lands Improvement Company; [electronics] linear integrated circuit

Lic. *Licenciado* (Spanish: Bachelor) (in academic degrees); Licentiate (in academic degrees)

lic. licence; licensed

LicAc Licentiate of Acupuncture

LicMed Licentiate in Medicine

LicTheol Licentiate in Theology

LICW Licentiate of the Institute of Clerks of Works of Great Britain

lidar light detection and ranging

LIDC Lead Industries Development Council

LIE loss of independent existence

Lieut. Lieutenant

Lieut-Cdr Lieutenant-Commander

Lieut-Col Lieutenant-Colonel

Lieut-Com Lieutenant-Commander

Lieut-Gen Lieutenant-General

Lieut-Gov Lieutenant-Governor

LIF [medicine] left iliac fossa; [computing] low insertion force

LIFFE London International Financial Futures (and Options) Exchange

LIFireE Licentiate of the Institution of Fire Engineers

LIFO last in, first out

Lig. Liguria; Limoges

LIHG *Ligue internationale de hockey sur glace* (French: International Ice Hockey Federation)

LILO last in, last out

LIM linear-induction motor; [computing] Lotus, Intel, Microsoft

Lim. Limerick

lim. limit; limited

LIMEAN [finance] London Inter-Bank Mean Rate

limo [short form] limousine

lin. lineal; linear; liniment

linac [physics] linear accelerator

Lincs Lincolnshire

ling. linguistic; linguistics

Linn. (Carolus) Linnaeus (Swedish botanist); Linnean

lino [short form] linoleum

LInstP Licentiate of the Institute of Physics

LIOB Licentiate of the Institute of Building

LIP life insurance policy; [medicine] lymphocytic interstitial pneumonitis

LIPA Liverpool Institute for the Performing Arts

LIPM Lister Institute of Preventive Medicine

lips [computing] logical inferences per second

liq. liquid; liquor

LIRA Linen Industry Research Association

LIRMA London International Insurance and Reinsurance Market Association

LIS laser isotope separation

Lis. Lisbon

LISA *Library and Information Science Abstracts*

LISC Library and Information Services Council

LISM Licentiate of the Incorporated Society of Musicians

LISP list processing (computer programming language)

Lit [currency] Italian lira

lit. literal; literally; literary; literature; litre; litter; little; liturgy

LitB Bachelor of Letters (or Literature) (from Latin *Litterarum Baccalaureus*)

lit crit [short form] literary criticism

LitD Doctor of Letters (or Literature) (from Latin *Litterarum Doctor*)

Lith. Lithuania; Lithuanian

lith. lithograph; lithography

litho. lithograph; lithographic; lithography

lithog. lithograph; lithographic; lithography

lithol. lithology

Lit. Hum. *Literae Humaniores* (Latin: Humane Letters) (classics degree at Oxford University)

LitM Master of Letters (or Literature) (from Latin *Litterarum Magister*)

Lit. Sup. *(Times) Literary Supplement*

LittB Bachelor of Letters (or Literature) (from Latin *Litterarum Baccalaureus*)

LittD Doctor of Letters (or Literature) (from Latin *Litterarum Doctor*)

LittM Master of Letters (or Literature) (from Latin *Litterarum Magister*)

liturg. liturgical; liturgy

LIUNA Laborers' International Union of North America

Liv. Liverpool; Livy (Roman historian)

liv. [commerce] *livraison* (French: delivery)

liv. st. *livre sterling* (French: pound sterling)

Lix [computing] legal information exchange

LJ [vehicle registration] Bournemouth; *Library Journal*; [athletics] long jump; Lord Justice

l.j. life jacket

LJA Lady Jockeys' Association

LJC London Juvenile Courts

LJJ Lords Justices

LK [fishing port] Lerwick; [vehicle registration] northwest London

Lk [currency] lek (used in Albania)

.lk Sri Lanka (in Internet address)

lkd locked

lkg locking

lkge leakage

lkr locker

LL Late Latin; Law Latin; *Law List*; laws; lending library; lend-lease; limited liability; [mathematics, physics] linear-linear; lines (of text); [fishing port] Liverpool; [UK postcode] Llandudno; London Library; Lord Lieutenant; Lords; [medicine] lower limb; Low Latin; [vehicle registration] northwest London

L/L [commerce] *Lutlang* (Norwegian: limited company, Ltd)

ll. leaves; *leges* (Latin: laws); lines (of text)

l.l. live load; *loco laudato* (Latin: in the place cited with approval); lower left; lower limit

LLA Lady Literate in Arts

LL.AA.II. *Leurs Altesses Impériales* (French: Their Imperial Highnesses)

LL.AA.RR. *Leurs Altesses Royales* (French: Their Royal Highnesses)

LLB Bachelor of Laws (from Latin *Legum Baccalaureus*)

l.l.c. lower left centre

LLCM Licentiate of the London College of Music

LLCO Licentiate of the London College of Osteopathy

LLD Doctor of Laws (from Latin *Legum Doctor*)

Llds [insurance] Lloyd's

LLE low-level exposure (to radiation)

LL.EE. *Leurs Éminences* (French: Their Eminences); *Leurs Excellences* (French: Their Excellencies)

LLett Licentiate of Letters

LLI Lord Lieutenant of Ireland

l.l.i. latitude and longitude indicator

LLL Licentiate in Laws; loose leaf ledger; [computing] low-level language; [computing] low-level logic

LLLW [nuclear technology] liquid low-level waste

LLM Master of Laws (from Latin *Legum Magister*)

LLMCom Master of Laws in Commercial Law

LL.MM. *Leurs Majestés* (French: Their Majesties)

LLN [USA] League for Less Noise

LLNL [USA] Lawrence Livermore National Laboratory

LLNW low-level nuclear waste

LLRW low-level radioactive waste

LLS [astronautics] lunar logistics system

LLSV [astronautics] lunar logistics system vehicle

LLU lending library unit

LLV [astronautics] lunar logistics vehicle

LLW [nuclear technology] low-level waste

LM Legion of Merit; Licentiate in Medicine; Licentiate in Midwifery; Licentiate in Music; light microscopy; liquid metal; [electrical engineering] load management; London Museum; [music, prosody] long metre; [Scotland] Lord Marquis; Lord Mayor; [astronautics] lunar module; [currency] Maltese lira; [vehicle registration] northwest London

l.M *laufenden Monats* (German: of the current month)

lm lumen (unit of luminous flux)

l.m. land mine; light metal; *locus monumenti* (Latin: place of the monument)

LMA Linoleum Manufacturers' Association; low moisture avidity

LMBC Liverpool Marine Biological Committee

LMC [astronomy] Large Magellanic Cloud; [nuclear technology] liquid-metal coolant; Lloyd's Machinery Certificate; local medical committee

LMCC Licentiate of the Medical Council of Canada

LMD local medical doctor; [music, prosody] long metre double

lmd leafmould

LME London Metal Exchange

LMed Licentiate in Medicine

LMFBR [nuclear technology] liquid-metal-cooled fast breeder reactor

LMG light machine gun

LMI [USA] Logistics Management Institute

LMi [astronomy] Leo Minor

LMO lens-modulated oscillator; light machine oil

LMP [medicine] last menstrual period; [astronautics] lunar module pilot

LMR [nuclear technology] liquid-metal reactor; [railways] London Midland Region

LMRCP Licentiate in Midwifery of the Royal College of Physicians

LMRSH Licentiate Member of the Royal Society of Health

LMRTPI Legal Member of the Royal Town Planning Institute

LMS Latin Mass Society; Licentiate in Medicine and Surgery; [education] local management of schools; London Mathematical Society; London Medical Schools; London Missionary Society; London, Midland and Scottish (Railway); [medicine] loss of memory syndrome

LMSR London, Midland and Scottish Railway

LMSSA Licentiate in Medicine and Surgery of the Society of Apothecaries

LMT [physics] length, mass, time; [astronomy] local mean time

LMus Licentiate in Music

LMVD [New Zealand] Licensed Motor Vehicle Dealer

LMW low molecular weight

LMX [insurance] London Market Excess of Loss (at Lloyd's)

LMXB [astronomy] low-mass X-ray binary

LN [fishing port] King's Lynn; [UK postcode] Lincoln; liquid nitrogen; [medicine] lymph node; [vehicle registration]

northwest London; [civil aircraft marking]
Norway

Ln. Lane

ln natural logarithm (from Latin *logar-ithmus naturalis*)

LNat Liberal National

LNB low noise blocker (on satellite dish)

LNC League of Nations Covenant

LNER London and North Eastern Railway

LNG liquefied natural gas

lnge lounge (in property advertisement)

LNLC Ladies' Naval Luncheon Club

Lnrk Lanark

LNS land navigation system

LNT liquid-nitrogen temperature

LNU League of Nations Union

LNWR London and North Western Railway

LO *Landsorganisationen i Sverige* (Swedish: General Federation of Swedish Trade Unions); launch operator; liaison officer; [fishing port] London; London office; [vehicle registration] northwest London

Lo. Lord

l/o [commerce] *leur ordre* (French: their order)

lo. loam; local

l.o. lubricating oil

LOA leave of absence; length over all; light observation aircraft

l.o.a. length over all

LOB [baseball] left on base; line of balance; Location of Offices Bureau

LOBAL long-base-line buoy

LOBAR long-base-line radar

LOC launch operations centre; [USA] Library of Congress; [meteorology] locally

loc. local; location; [grammar] locative

l.o.c. letter of credit; line(s) of communication

LOCA [nuclear technology] loss-of-coolant accident

loc. cit. *loco citato* (Latin: in the place (already) cited)

loc. laud. *loco laudato* (Latin: in the place cited with approval)

locn location

loco. locomotion; locomotive

loc. primo cit. *loco primo citato* (Latin: in the place first cited)

LOD limit(s) of detection

LOF loss of flow; loss of fluid; loss of function

L of C [USA] Library of Congress; line(s) of communication

L of N League of Nations

LOFT low-frequency radio telescope

log [short form] logarithm

log. logic; logical; logistic

LOH light observation helicopter

LOI [Northern Ireland] Loyal Orange Institution; lunar orbit insertion

LOL laughs out loud (in Internet chat); [Northern Ireland] Loyal Orange Lodge

LOLA library on-line acquisition; lunar orbit landing approach

LOM [USA] Loyal Order of Moose

LOMA [USA] Life Office Management Association

Lomb. Lombard; Lombardy

lombard [informal] loads of money but a right dickhead

Lon. London; Londonderry

lon. longitude

Lond. London; Londonderry

Londin. *Londiniensis* (Latin: (Bishop) of London)

Long. Longford

long. longitude

longl longitudinal

Lonrho [finance] London Rhodesian

LOOM [USA] Loyal Order of Moose

l.o.p. [navigation] line of position

LOPAR low-power acquisition radar

loq. *loquitur* (Latin: (he/she) speaks)

LOR light output ratio; lunar orbit rendezvous

LORAC long-range accuracy

LORAD long-range active detection

LORAN long-range navigation

LORAPH long-range passive homing system

LORCS League of Red Cross and Red Crescent Societies

LORV low observable re-entry vehicle

LOS Latin Old Style; Law of the Seas; line of sight; loss of signal

LOSS large-object salvage system

LOT large orbital telescope; *Polskie Linie Lotnicze* (Polish airline company)

lot. lotion

LOTC [finance] London over-the-counter market

Lou. Louisiana

LOX liquid oxygen

loy. loyal; loyalty

LOYA League of Young Adventurers
LP Labour Party; Lady Provost; large paper (edition of book); [paper size] large post; last post; legal procurator; Liberal Party; life policy; limited partnership; [computing] linear programming; liquid petroleum; liquid propellant; long play (on video recorder); long-playing (record); Lord Provost; low pressure; [medicine] lumbar puncture; [vehicle registration] northwest London
Lp Ladyship; Lordship
L/P letterpress; life policy
lp limp
l.p. last paid; latent period; launch platform; [printing] long primer (type size); low pressure
LPA Leather Producers' Association for England; Local Productivity Association
LPC leaf protein concentrate (in nutrition); Legal Practice Course; Lord President of the Council
l.p.c. low pressure chamber
LPE [electronics] liquid-phase epitaxy; London Press Exchange
LPEA Licentiate of the Physical Education Association
LPed Licentiate in Pedagogy
LPF [computing] League for Programming Freedom
LPG liquefied petroleum gas
LPGA Ladies' Professional Golf Association
LPh Licentiate in Philosophy
lpi lines per inch
LPLC low-pressure liquid chromatography
lpm lines per millimetre; lines per minute
LPN [USA] Licensed Practical Nurse
LPNA [USA] Lithographers' and Printers' National Association
LPO local post office; local purchasing officer; London Philharmonic Orchestra
L'pool Liverpool
LPRP Laotian People's Revolutionary Party
LPS London Philharmonic Society; Lord Privy Seal
LPSO Lloyd's Policy Signing Office
LPU low pay unit
lpw lumens per watt
Lpz. Leipzig

LQ [civil aircraft marking] Argentina; [computing] letter quality (of printing); [mathematics] linear-quadratic
l.q. *lege quaeso* (Latin: please read)
lqdr liquidator
LQR *Law Quarterly Review*
LQT [commerce] Liverpool quay terms
LR [fishing port] Lancaster; Land Registry; Law Report; left-(to-)right; Lloyd's Register (of Shipping); Lowland Regiment; Loyal Regiment; [vehicle registration] northwest London
Lr Lancer; [chemical element] lawrencium; ledger; [currency] lira
l.R *laufen der Rechnung* (German: current account)
lr ledger; [currency] lira; lower
.lr Liberia (in Internet address)
l.r. landing report; log run; long range; long run
LRA Local Radio Association
LRAC Law Reports, Appeal Cases; [finance] long-run average cost
LRAD Licentiate of the Royal Academy of Dancing
LRAM Licentiate of the Royal Academy of Music
LRB London Residuary Body; London Rifle Brigade
LRC Labour Representation Committee; Langley Research Center (in NASA); Leander Rowing Club; London Rowing Club; [computing] longitudinal redundancy check
LRCh Law Reports, Chancery Division
LRCM Licentiate of the Royal College of Music
LRCP Licentiate of the Royal College of Physicians
LRCPE Licentiate of the Royal College of Physicians of Edinburgh
LRCPI Licentiate of the Royal College of Physicians of Ireland
LRCPSGlas Licentiate of the Royal College of Physicians and Surgeons of Glasgow
LRCS League of Red Cross Societies; Licentiate of the Royal College of Surgeons (of England)
LRCSE Licentiate of the Royal College of Surgeons of Edinburgh
LRCSI Licentiate of the Royal College of Surgeons in Ireland

LRCVS Licentiate of the Royal College of Veterinary Surgeons

LREC [medicine] Local Research Ethics Committee

LRHL Law Reports, House of Lords

LRIBA Licentiate of the Royal Institute of British Architects

LRKB Law Reports, King's Bench

LRM language reference manual

LRP Law Reports, Probate Division; long-range planning

LRPS Licentiate of the Royal Photographic Society

LRQB Law Reports, Queen's Bench

LRR [taxation] lower reduced rate

LRS Land Registry Stamp; Lloyd's Register of Shipping

Lrs Lancers

LRSC Licentiate of the Royal Society of Chemistry

LRSM Licentiate of the Royal Schools of Music

LRT light rail transit; London Regional Transport; long-range transport

LRTF long-range theatre nuclear forces

LRTI [medicine] lower respiratory tract infection

LRU least recently used; line replaceable unit

LRV light rail vehicle; lunar roving vehicle

LRWES long-range weapons experimental station

LS [vehicle registration] Edinburgh; Law Society; leading seaman; [UK postcode] Leeds; legal seal; [international vehicle registration] Lesotho; letter service; Licensed Surveyor; Licentiate in Surgery; [psychology] liminal sensitivity; Linnean Society; [law] *locus sigilli* (Latin: the place of the seal); London Scottish; London Sinfonietta; [cinema] long shot; loudspeaker

ls litres per second

.ls Lesotho (in Internet address)

l.s. landing ship; left side; letter signed; local sunset; [law] *locus sigilli* (Latin: the place of the seal); long sight; low speed; lump sum

LSA Land Settlement Association; leading supply assistant; learning support assistant; Licence in Agricultural Sciences; Licentiate of the Society of Apothecaries

LSAA Linen Supply Association of America

LS&GCM Long Service and Good Conduct Medal

LSB [computing] least significant bit; London School Board

LSC Licentiate in Sciences; [chemistry] liquid–solid chromatography; London Salvage Corps; Lower School Certificate

l.s.c. *loco supra citato* (Latin: in the place cited above)

LScAct Licentiate in Actuarial Science

LSCF [statistics] least squares curve fitting

LSCS [obstetrics] lower segment Caesarean section

LSD League of Safe Drivers; [computing] least significant digit; *librae, solidi, denarii* (Latin: pounds, shillings, pence); Lightermen, Stevedores and Dockers; [pharmacology] lysergic acid diethylamide (hallucinogen, from German *Lysergsäure-Diäthylamid*)

l.s.d. *librae, solidi, denarii* (Latin: pounds, shillings, pence)

lsd li. leased line

LSE [chemistry] liquid–solid extraction; [chemistry] liquid–solvent extraction; London School of Economics and Political Science; London Stock Exchange

lse lease

l.s.e. limited signed edition

L/Sgt Lance-Sergeant

LSHTM London School of Hygiene and Tropical Medicine

LSI Labour and Socialist International; [electronics] large-scale integration

LSJ London School of Journalism

LSJM *laus sit Jesu et Mariae* (Latin: praise be to Jesus and Mary)

LSL landing ship logistic; low-speed logic

LSM laser scanning microscope; [mathematics, physics] least-squares method; [electrical engineering] linear synchronous motor

l.s.m. *litera scripta manet* (Latin: the written word remains)

LSO London Symphony Orchestra

LSS large-scale structure; large-scale system; Licentiate in Sacred Scripture; life-saving station (or service); life-support system

LSSc Licentiate in Sanitary Science

LST landing ship (for) tanks; landing ship (for) transport; Licentiate in Sacred Theology; [astronomy] local sidereal time; local standard time

l.s.t. local standard time

LSU Louisiana State University

LSW lights spray and wipe (in car advertisement)

LSZ [New Zealand] limited speed zone

LT lawn tennis; leading telegraphist; letter telegram; [medicine] leukotriene; Licentiate in Teaching; Licentiate in Theology; [international vehicle registration] Lithuania; London Transport; [fishing port] Lowestoft; low temperature; [electrical engineering] low tension; [vehicle registration] northwest London; [currency] Turkish lira

Lt Lieutenant; [military] Light

lt light

.lt Lithuania (in Internet address)

l.t. landed terms; landing team; large tug; local time; locum tenens (person standing in for another); long ton; loop test

LTA Lawn Tennis Association; lighter than air (of aircraft); London Teachers' Association

LTAA Lawn Tennis Association of Australia

LT&SR London, Tilbury and Southend Railway

LTB London Tourist Board; London Transport Board

l.t.b. low-tension battery

LTBT Limited Test Ban Treaty

LTC lawn tennis club

Lt-Cdr Lieutenant-Commander

LTCL Licentiate of Trinity College of Music, London

Lt-Col Lieutenant-Colonel

Lt-Com Lieutenant-Commander

Ltd Limited (after company name)

LTDP long-term defence programme

LTE [astronomy] local thermodynamic equilibrium; London Transport Executive

LTF Lithographic Technical Foundation

ltg lettering; lighting

ltge [commerce] lighterage

Lt-Gen Lieutenant-General

Lt-Gov Lieutenant-Governor

LTH light training helicopter; [biochemistry] luteotrophic hormone

LTh Licentiate in Theology

LTheol Licentiate in Theology

lthr leather

LTI Licentiate of the Textile Institute

LTIB Lead Technical Information Bureau

Lt Inf. Light Infantry

LTL [US commerce] less-than-truckload lot

LTM Licentiate in Tropical Medicine; London Terminal Market; long-term memory

ltn. lightning

LTO leading torpedo operator

LTOM London Traded Options Market

LTP [biochemistry] lipid-transfer protein; [science] long-term potentiation

LTR [genetics] long terminal repeat

ltr letter; lighter; litre

LTRA Lands Tribunal Rating Appeals

LtRN Lieutenant, Royal Navy

LTRS Low Temperature Research Station

LTSC Licentiate of Tonic Sol-Fa College

LTTE Liberation Tigers of Tamil Eelam (in Sri Lanka)

LTU *Lufttransport-Unternehmen GmbH* (German airline company)

LU Liberal Unionist; lock-up (in property advertisement); loudness unit; [UK postcode] Luton; [vehicle registration] northwest London

Lu [chemical element] lutetium

Lu. Lucerne

l/u [shipping] laid up; [shipping] lying up

lu. *luglio* (Italian: July)

.lu Luxembourg (in Internet address)

LUA Liverpool Underwriting Association

lub. lubricant; lubricate; lubrication

lubr. lubricant; lubricate; lubrication

LUC London Underwriting Centre

LUCOM lunar communication system

LUD leather-upholstered dashboard (in car advertisement)

LUG light utility glider; [computing] local users group

lug. luggage; lugger

LUHF [electronics] lowest useful high frequency

LULOP *London Union List of Periodicals*

LUM lunar excursion module

lum. lumbago; lumber; luminous

LUMAS lunar mapping system

lun. *lundi* (French: Monday); *lunedì*

(Italian: Monday); *lunes* (Spanish: Monday)

LUNCO Lloyd's Underwriters Non-Marine Claims Office

LUOTC London University Officers' Training Corps

Lup [astronomy] Lupus

l/up lock-up

LUS Land Utilization Survey

LUSCS [obstetrics] lower uterine segment Caesarean section

LUSI lunar surface inspection

lusing. [music] *lusingando* (Italian: coaxing, caressing)

LUT [computing] look-up table

Luth. Lutheran

Lux. Luxembourg; Luxembourger

lux. luxurious; luxury

LV [civil aircraft marking] Argentina; [international vehicle registration] Latvia; [medicine] left ventricle; [medicine] left ventricular; licensed victualler; [meteorology] light and variable; [vehicle registration] Liverpool; luncheon voucher

Lv [currency] lev (used in Bulgaria)

lv. leave (of absence); *livre* (French: book)

.lv Latvia (in Internet address)

l.v. low voltage

LVA Licensed Victuallers' Association

LVF [medicine] left ventricular function

LVI *laus Verbo Incarnato* (Latin: praise to the Incarnate Word); low viscosity index

LVLO Local Vehicle Licensing Office

LVN [USA] Licensed Vocational Nurse

LVO Lieutenant of the Royal Victorian Order

LVS Licentiate in Veterinary Science

lvs leaves

LVT landing vehicle, tracked

LW light weight; [radio] long wave; low water; [vehicle registration] northwest London

Lw [chemical element] lawrencium (former symbol, replaced by Lr)

lw lumens per watt

l.w. [sports] left wing

LWA London Weighting Allowance; London Welsh Association

LW&S lights wipe and spray (in car advertisement)

l.w.b. long wheelbase (in car advertisement)

LWEST low water equinoctial spring tide

LWF Lutheran World Federation

LWL length at waterline (of boat or ship); [shipping] load waterline

LWM low water mark

LWONT low water ordinary neap tides

LWOST low water ordinary spring tides

LWR [nuclear technology] light-water reactor

LWRA London Waste Regulation Authority

LWT London Weekend Television

LWV [USA] League of Women Voters

LX electricians (phonetic spelling of 'elecs'); electrics (phonetic spelling of 'elecs'); [civil aircraft marking] Luxembourg; [vehicle registration] northwest London

lx lux (unit of light)

Lxmbrg Luxembourg

LXX [Bible] Septuagint (Roman numeral for 70)

LY [civil aircraft marking] Lithuania; [fishing port] Londonderry; [vehicle registration] northwest London

Ly. Lyon

.ly Libya (in Internet address)

l.y. light year

Lyn [astronomy] Lynx

Lyr [astronomy] Lyra

lyr. lyric; lyrical; lyrics

LZ [vehicle registration] Armagh; [civil aircraft marking] Bulgaria

M

M [printing] em; [currency] (ma)loti (used in Lesotho); [aeronautics] Mach (followed by number); *Magister* (Latin: Master); magistrate; Majesty; [international vehicle registration] Malta; [UK postcode] Manchester; Manitoba; March; [currency] mark; Marquess; Marquis; martyr; [grammar] masculine;

Master; [cinema] mature audience (film classification in Australia); May; medal; medieval; medium (size); mega- (indicates one million, as in **MHz** = megahertz); [computing] mega- (indicates 2^{20}, as in **MB** = megabyte); Member; [chemistry] mesomeric effect; [astronomy] Messier Catalogue; [chemistry] metal (in chemical formula); Methodist; [music] metronome; metropolitan; *mezzo* (Italian: half); Middle; [fishing port] Milford; militia; million; minesweeper; minim (unit of liquid measure); Monday; [economics] monetary aggregate (in measures of money supply); *Monsieur* (French: Mr, Sir); *Monte* (Italian: Mount); mother; motorway (as in **M6**); mountain; mud (on chart); [Roman numeral] thousand

M [astronomy] absolute magnitude; [physics] magnetic quantum number; [physics] magnetization; mass; molar mass; [physics] moment (of a force); [electrical engineering] mutual inductance

m [printing] em; [music] me (in tonic sol-fa); metre; milli- (indicates one-thousandth, as in **mm** = millimetre); million; [meteorology] mist; [Roman numeral] thousand

m [astronomy] apparent magnitude; [physics] magnetic moment; [physics] magnetic quantum number; [chemistry] mass; [chemistry] molality

m. [cricket] maiden (over); male; *manipulus* (Latin: handful); mare; [currency] mark; married; [grammar] masculine; master; mate; measure; medical; medicine; medium; memorandum; meridian; *meridies* (Latin: noon); meridional; midday; middle; mile; [currency] mill (thousandth of dollar); *mille* (French: thousand); minim (unit of liquid measure); minor; minute; [medicine] *misce* (Latin: mix); mixture; moderate; *mois* (French: month); molar (tooth); month; moon; morning; *mort(e)* (French: dead); *morto* (Italian: dead); mountain

3M Minnesota Mining and Manufacturing Company

9M [civil aircraft marking] Malaysia

MA [vehicle registration] Chester; Magistrates' Association; [USA] Manpower Administration; [USA] Maritime Administration; [US postcode] Massachusetts; Master of Arts; Mathematical Association; medieval archaeology; [psychology] mental age; Middle Ages; Military Academy; military assistant; military attaché; *Missionarius Apostolicus* (Latin: Apostolic Missionary); mobility allowance; [international vehicle registration] Morocco; Mountaineering Association; Museums Association

Ma [aeronautics] Mach number

Ma. *Mater* (Latin: Mother)

mA milliampere

m/a [book-keeping] my account

.ma Morocco (in Internet address)

m.a. manufacturing assembly; map analysis; menstrual age

MAA Manufacturers' Agents Association of Great Britain; Master-at-Arms; Mathematical Association of America; Member of the Architectural Association; Motor Agents' Association; [USA] Mutual Aid Association; [USA] Mutual Assurance Association

MAAAS Member of the American Academy of Arts and Sciences

MAAF Mediterranean Allied Air Forces

ma'am madam

MAAT Member of the Association of Accounting Technicians

MAB monoclonal antibody

MABP [medicine] mean arterial blood pressure

MABS [USA] marine air base squadron

MAC maximum allowable concentration; [computing] media access control; [television] multiplexed analogue component(s); [USA] Municipal Assistance Corporation

MAc Master of Accountancy

Mac. Macao; [Bible] Maccabees (books of Apocrypha)

mac [short form] mackintosh

MACA Mental After Care Association

MACC military aid to the civilian community

Macc. [Bible] Maccabees (books of Apocrypha)

MACE Member of the Association of Conference Executives; Member of the Australian College of Education

Maced. Macedonia; Macedonian

mach. machine; machinery; machinist
MACHO [astronomy] massive astrophysical compact halo object
MACM Member of the Association of Computing Machines
macroecon. macroeconomics
MACS Member of the American Chemical Society
MAD magnetic anomaly detection; maintenance, assembly and disassembly; [psychology] major affective disorder; [commerce] mean absolute deviation; [military] mutual assured destruction
Mad. Madeira
Madag. Madagascar
MADD Mothers Against Drunk Driving
MADO Member of the Association of Dispensing Opticians
Madr. Madras; Madrid
MAE Master of Aeronautical Engineering; Master of Art Education; Master of Arts in Education
m.a.e. mean absolute error
MA(Econ) Master of Arts in Economics
MA(Ed) Master of Arts in Education
MAEE Marine Aircraft Experimental Establishment
maesto. [music] *maestoso* (Italian: majestic)
MAFA Manchester Academy of Fine Arts
MAFF Ministry of Agriculture, Fisheries and Food
MAG Motorcycle Action Group
MAg Master of Agriculture
Mag. Magnificat (canticle); Magyar
mag [short form] magazine
mag. magazine; magnesium; magnet; magnetic; magnetism; magneto; magnitude; magnum
MAgEc Master of Agricultural Economics
magg. *maggio* (Italian: May); [music] *maggiore* (Italian: major) (key or scale)
maglev magnetic levitation (for high-speed train)
magn. magnetic; magnetism
magnif. magnificent (in property advertisement)
MAGPI [medicine] meatal advancement and glanuloplasty (surgical operation)
MAgr Master of Agriculture
MAgrSc Master of Agricultural Science
mah. mahogany
mahog. mahogany

MAI Master of Engineering (from Latin *Magister in Arte Ingeniaria*); [forestry] mean annual increment; Member of the Anthropological Institute
MAIAA Member of the American Institute of Aeronautics and Astronautics
MAIB Marine Accidents Investigation Branch
MAICE Master of the American Institute of Consulting Engineers
MAIChE Master of the American Institute of Chemical Engineers
maint. maintenance
mais. maisonette (in property advertisement)
MAISE Member of the Association of Iron and Steel Engineers
Maj. [military] Major
maj. major; majority
Maj-Gen Major-General
MAL [international vehicle registration] Malaysia
Mal *Maréchal* (French: Field Marshal)
Mal. [Bible] Malachi; Malay; Malaya; Malayan; Malaysia; Malaysian; Malta; Maltese
MALD Master of Arts in Law and Diplomacy
mall. malleable
MAM [computing] multiple allocation memory
MAMBO Mediterranean Association for Marine Biology and Oceanography
MAMEME Member of the Association of Mining Electrical and Mechanical Engineers
MAN [computing] metropolitan area network
Man. Manchester; Manila; Manitoba
man. management; manager; managing; manual; manually; manufacture; manufacturer; manufacturing
MAnaes Master of Anaesthesiology
Manch. Manchester; Manchuria
mand. [law] mandamus (High Court order); mandatory; mandolin
M&A [finance] mergers and acquisitions
M&B May and Baker (pharmaceutical company); mild and bitter (beer); Mills and Boon (publishing company)
M&E music and effects
M&G Mercantile and General (insurance company)

Man. Dir. managing director
m&r maintenance and repairs
M&S Marks and Spencer plc (chain store)
m&s maintenance and supply
Man. Ed. managing editor
MANF May, August, November, February (end of financial quarters)
manf. manufacture; manufactured; manufacturer
mang. B manganese bronze
Manit. Manitoba
man. op. manually operated
man. pr. [medicine] *mane primo* (Latin: first thing in the morning)
Mans. Mansion(s)
manuf. manufacture; manufactured; manufacturer; manufacturing
manufac. manufacture; manufactured; manufacturer; manufacturing
Manweb Merseyside and North Wales Electricity Board
MAO Master of Arts in Obstetrics; [biochemistry] monoamine oxidase
MAOI [pharmacology] monoamine oxidase inhibitor (antidepressant)
MAOT Member of the Association of Occupational Therapists
MAOU Member of the American Ornithologists' Union
MAP major air pollutant; [computing] manufacturing automation protocol; maximum average price; [medicine] mean arterial (blood) pressure; medical aid post; Member of the Association of Project Managers; Ministry of Aircraft Production; [USA] modified American plan (for payment of hotel bills)
MAPI [computing] messaging application program interface
MAppArts Master of Applied Arts
MAppSc Master of Applied Science
MAPsS Member of the Australian Psychological Society
MAR [taxation] marginal age relief; Master of Arts in Religion; [computing] memory address register
Mar. March
mar. *mardi* (French: Tuesday); [music] marimba; marine; maritime; marriage; married; *martedì* (Italian: Tuesday); *martes* (Spanish: Tuesday); *marzo* (Italian: March); *marzo* (Spanish: March)

MARAC Member of the Australasian Register of Agricultural Consultants
MARC [bibliography] machine-readable cataloguing
marc. [music] *marcato* (Italian: marked, emphasizing each note)
MArch Master of Architecture
March. Marchioness
MArchE Master of Architectural Engineering
marg [short form] margarine
marg. margin; marginal
marit. maritime
mar. lic. marriage licence
MARMAP [USA] Marine Resources Monitoring Assessment and Prediction
Marq. Marquess; Marquis
MARS meteorological automatic reporting station (or system)
mart market
mart. martyr
MARV [military] manœuvrable re-entry vehicle
MAS Malaysian Airline System; Master of Agricultural Science; Master of Applied Science; Medical Advisory Service; Military Agency for Standardization
mas. [grammar] masculine
MASC Member of the Australian Society of Calligraphers
MASc Master of Applied Science
masc. [grammar] masculine
MASCE Member of the American Society of Civil Engineers
mascon [astronomy] mass concentration
maser microwave amplification by stimulated emission of radiation
MASH [USA] mobile army surgical hospital
MASI Member of the Architects' and Surveyors' Institute
MASME Member of the American Society of Mechanical Engineers
MA(SS) Master of Arts in Social Sciences
Mass. Massachusetts
MASTA Medical Advisory Service for Travellers Abroad
MAT [insurance] marine, aviation and transport; Master of Arts in Teaching
mat. maternity; matinée; matins; [printing] matrix; mature; [finance] maturity
MATA multiple answering teaching aid

MATh Master of Arts in Theology

math [US and Canadian short form] mathematics

math. mathematical; mathematically; mathematician; mathematics

maths [short form] mathematics

MATIF *marché à terme des instruments financiers* (French: financial futures market)

matr. matrimonial; *matrimonium* (Latin: marriage)

matric [short form] matriculation (former school examination)

MATS [US air force] Military Air Transport Service

MATSA Managerial Administrative Technical Staff Association

Matt. [Bible] Matthew

MATTS [military] multiple airborne target trajectory system

MATV master antenna television

MAU [computing] multi-station access unit

Maur. Mauritian; Mauritius

Mau Rs [currency] Mauritian rupee

MAusIMM Member of the Australasian Institute of Mining and Metallurgy

MAW [USA] marine air wing; [military] medium assault weapon

MAX maximum

max. maxim; maximum

MAYC Methodist Association of Youth Clubs

MB Bachelor of Medicine (from Latin *Medicinae Baccalaureus*); Bachelor of Music (from Latin *Musicae Baccalaureus*); [vehicle registration] Chester; Manitoba; maritime board; marketing board; mark of the Beast; maternity benefit; [Canada] Medal of Bravery; medical board; [computing] megabit; [computing] megabyte; metropolitan borough; millibar (unit of atmospheric pressure); motor barge; motorboat; municipal borough

mb millibar (unit of atmospheric pressure)

m.b. magnetic bearing; main battery; medium bomber; [medicine] *misce bene* (Latin: mix well); motor barge; motorboat

MBA Master of Business Administration

Mba Mombasa

MBAC Member of the British Association of Chemists

MBAcC Member of the British Acupuncture Council

mbar millibar (unit of atmospheric pressure)

MBASW Member of the British Association of Social Workers

MBC metropolitan borough council; mountain bike club; municipal borough council

m.b.c. [medicine] maximum breathing capacity

MBCO Member of the British College of Optometrists (or Ophthalmic Opticians)

MBCPE Member of the British College of Physical Education

MBCS Member of the British Computer Society

MBD [medicine] minimal brain dysfunction

MBdgSc Master of Building Science

MBE Member of the Order of the British Empire; [electronics] molecular-beam epitaxy

MBF Musicians Benevolent Fund

MBG microemulsion-based gel

MBH [astronomy] massive black hole

mbH [commerce] *mit beschränkter Haftung* (German: with limited liability) (of company)

MBHI Member of the British Horological Institute

MBI [finance] management buy-in

MBIAT Member of the British Institute of Architectural Technologists

MBIFD Member of the British Institute of Funeral Directors

MBIM Member of the British Institute of Management

MBK [military] missing, believed killed

MBKSTS Member of the British Kinematograph, Sound and Television Society

MBL [medicine] menstrual blood loss

MBM Master of Business Management

MBNOA Member of the British Naturopathic and Osteopathic Association

MBNQA [commerce] Malcolm Baldridge National Quality Award

MBO [finance] management buyout; [commerce] management by objectives

MBOU Member of the British Ornithologists' Union

MBP [medicine] mean blood pressure

MBPICS Member of the British

Production and Inventory Control Society

MBPsS Member of the British Psychological Society

MBR [astronomy] microwave background radiation

mbr member

MBRF [military] mutual and balanced force reduction

MBS Manchester Business School

MBSc Master of Business Science

MBT [military] main battle tank; [medicine] mean body temperature

MBuild Master of Building

MBWA [commerce] management by wandering around

Mbyte [computing] megabyte

MC machinery certificate; magistrates' court; [navigation] magnetic course; marginal cost; [USA] Marine Corps; [USA] Maritime Commission; marriage certificate; Master of Ceremonies; Master of Surgery (from Latin *Magister Chirurgiae*); medical certificate; [USA] Medical Corps; [astrology] *Medium Caeli* (Latin: Midheaven); [USA] Member of Congress; Member of Council; mess committee; Methodist Church; military college; Military Cross; Missionaries of Charity; [astronomy] molecular cloud; [chemistry] molecular cluster; [international vehicle registration] Monaco; [politics] Monday Club; Monte Carlo; Morse code; motor contact; [vehicle registration] northeast London

M/C Manchester; [finance] marginal credit

Mc megacycle

m/c machine; motorcycle

.mc Monaco (in Internet address)

m.c. *mois courant* (French: current month); motorcycle

MCA Management Consultants' Association; Manufacturing Chemists' Association; Maritime and Coastguard Agency; Master of Commerce and Administration; Matrimonial Causes Act; [trademark, computing] micro channel architecture; monetary compensatory amount(s); Motor Cycle Association; [electronics] multichannel analyser; multicriteria analysis; [electronics] multiple channel analyser; multiple classification analysis

MCAB [USA] Marine Corps air base

MCAM Member of the CAM Foundation

MC&G mapping, charting and geodesy

MCANW Medical Campaign Against Nuclear Weapons

MCAV [computing] modified constant angular velocity

MCB [USA] Marine Corps Base; Master of Clinical Biochemistry; [computing] memory control block; Metric Conversion Board; miniature circuit breaker; [military] multiple-cratering bomblets

MCBSI Member of the Chartered Building Societies Institute

MCC Manchester Computer Centre; Marylebone Cricket Club; Maxwell Communications Corporation; Melbourne Cricket Club; member of the county council; metropolitan county council; [navigation] mid-course correction; Motor Caravanners' Club

MCCA Minor Counties Cricket Association

MCCC Middlesex County Cricket Club

MCCD RCS Member in Clinical Community Dentistry of the Royal College of Surgeons (of England)

MCCU [medicine] mobile coronary care unit

MCD Master of Civic Design; [medicine] mean cell diameter; [medicine] mean corpuscular diameter; Movement for Christian Democracy

MCDS management control data system

MCE Master of Chemical Engineering; Master of Civil Engineering

MCFP [Canada] Member of the College of Family Physicians

MCG Melbourne Cricket Ground

MCGA [computing] multicolour graphics array

MCGB Master Chef of Great Britain

McGU McGill University (Canada)

MCH [medicine] mean cell haemoglobin; [medicine] mean corpuscular haemoglobin; [biochemistry] melanin-concentrating hormone

MCh Master of Surgery (from Latin *Magister Chirurgiae*)

Mch. Manchester

MCHC [medicine] mean cell haemoglobin concentration; [medicine] mean corpuscular haemoglobin concentration

MChD Master of Dental Surgery (from Latin *Magister Chirurgiae Dentalis*)

MChE Master of Chemical Engineering

MChemA Master in Chemical Analysis

MChemEng Master of Chemical Engineering

MChir Master of Surgery (from Latin *Magister Chirurgiae*)

MChOrth Master of Orthopaedic Surgery (from Latin *Magister Chirurgiae Orthopaedicae*)

MChS Member of the Society of Chiropodists

mcht merchant

mchy machinery

mCi millicurie (unit of radioactivity)

m.c.i. malleable cast iron

MCIBSE Member of the Chartered Institution of Building Services Engineers

MCIM Member of the Chartered Institute of Marketing

MCIOB Member of the Chartered Institute of Building

MCIS Member of the Institute of Chartered Secretaries and Administrators (formerly Member of the Chartered Institute of Secretaries)

MCIT Member of the Chartered Institute of Transport

MCL Master of Civil Law; maximum contamination levels

MClinPsychol Master of Clinical Psychology

MClSc Master of Clinical Science

MCLV [computing] modified constant linear velocity

MCM [mathematics] Monte Carlo method; [computing] multichip module; multistage conventional munitions

MCMES Member of the Civil and Mechanical Engineers' Society

MCO Managed Care Organization

Mco Morocco

mcol. musicological; musicologist; musicology

MCollH Member of the College of Handicrafts

MCom Master of Commerce

MCommH Master of Community Health

MConsE Member of the Association of Consulting Engineers

MCOphth Member of the College of Ophthalmologists

MCP male chauvinist pig; [USA] Master of City Planning; Member of Colonial Parliament; Member of the College of Preceptors

MCPO Master Chief Petty Officer

MCPP Member of the College of Pharmacy Practice

MCPS Mechanical Copyright Protection Society; Member of the College of Physicians and Surgeons

m.c.q. multiple-choice question

MCR mass communications research; [engineering] maximum continuous rating; [medicine] metabolic clearance rate; middle common room (in university or college); mobile control room

MCS Madras Civil Service; Malayan Civil Service; Marine Conservation Society; Master of Commercial Science; Military College of Science; monitoring and control system; [electronics] multichannel scaler

Mc/s megacycles per second

MCSD [computing] Microsoft Certified Solutions Developer

MCSE Microsoft Certified Systems Engineer

MCSP Member of the Chartered Society of Physiotherapy

MCST Member of the College of Speech Therapists

MCT mainstream corporation tax; Member of the Association of Corporate Treasurers

MCU main control unit; [photography] medium close-up

MCV [medicine] mean cell volume; [medicine] mean corpuscular volume

MCW [telecommunications] modulated continuous wave

MD Doctor of Medicine (from Latin *Medicinae Doctor*); [music] *main droite* (French: right hand); malicious damage; managing director; [music] *mano destra* (Italian: right hand); map distance; market day; [US postcode] Maryland; medical department; [banking] memorandum of deposit; mentally deficient; mess deck; Middle Dutch; military district; minidisc (audio recording); [international vehicle registration] Moldova; molecular dynamics; Monroe Doctrine; [medicine] muscular dystrophy; musical

director; [vehicle registration] northeast London

Md Maryland; [chemical element] mendelevium

M/d [commerce] months after date

.md Moldova (in Internet address)

MDA [pharmacology] methylenedioxyamphetamine (= ice, hallucinogenic drug); minimum detectable activity; minimum detectable amount; [computing] monochrome display adapter; [finance] multiple discriminant analysis; Muscular Dystrophy Association

MDAM [computing] multidimensional access memory

MD&A [commerce] management discussion and analysis

MDAP [USA] Mutual Defense Assistance Program

M-day [USA] mobilization day

MDB *Movimento Democrático Brasileiro* (Portuguese: Brazilian Democratic Movement)

MdB *Mitglied des Bundestages* (German: Member of the Bundestag)

MDC metropolitan district council; minimum detectable concentration; modification and design control; more developed country

MDD minimum detectable dose

Mddx Middlesex

MDentSc Master of Dental Science

MDes Master of Design

MDF Manic Depression Fellowship; medium-density fibreboard

MDG Medical Director-General

MDHB Mersey Docks and Harbour Board

m. dict. [medicine] *more dicto* (Latin: in the manner directed) (in prescriptions)

MDip Master of Diplomacy

mdise merchandise

MDiv Master of Divinity

MDL minimum detectable level

mdl model

Mdlle *Mademoiselle* (French: Miss)

Mdm Madam

MDMA [pharmacology] methylenedioxymethamphetamine (= ecstasy, hallucinogenic drug)

Mdme *Madame* (French: Mrs)

mdn median

MDNS [computing] managed data network service

mdnt midnight

MDP Mongolian Democratic Party

MDQ minimum detectable quantity

MDR [computing] memory data register; minimum daily requirement

MDRAM [computing] multibank dynamic random-access memory

MDS main dressing station; Master of Dental Surgery; memory-adjusted driver's seat (in car advertisement); microprocessor development system

MDSc Master of Dental Science

mdse merchandise

MD/st memory-adjusted driver's seat (in car advertisement)

MDT [computing] mean downtime; [USA] Mountain Daylight Time

MDU Medical Defence Union

MDu Middle Dutch

MDV Doctor of Veterinary Medicine

MDW Military Defence Works

Mdx Middlesex

ME [US postcode] Maine; managing editor; marine engineer; marine engineering; [USA] marriage encounter; Master of Education; Master of Engineering; mechanical engineer; mechanical engineering; [USA] Medical Examiner; [UK postcode] Medway; [medicine] metabolizable energy; Methodist Episcopal; Middle East; Middle Eastern; Middle English; military engineer; milled edge; mining engineer; mining engineering; [fishing port] Montrose; [physics] Mössbauer effect; Most Excellent; [medicine] myalgic encephalomyelitis; [vehicle registration] northeast London

Me Maine; *Maître* (French: Master) (title of lawyer); Messerschmitt (German aircraft); [chemistry] methyl (used in formulae)

m.e. [bookbinding] marbled edges; maximum effort; mobility equipment; [bookbinding] mottled edges

MEA Member of the European Assembly; Middle East Airlines

MEAF Middle East Air Force

meas. measurable; measure; measurement

MEB Midlands Electricity Board

MEC [finance] marginal efficiency of capital; Master of Engineering Chemistry; Member of the Executive Council;

Methodist Episcopal Church; Middle East Command; minimum effective concentration

MEc Master of Economics

MECAS Middle East Centre for Arab Studies

mech. mechanic; mechanical; mechanically; mechanics; mechanism; mechanize; mechanized

MechE mechanical engineer

ME(Chem) Master of Chemical Engineering

MECI Member of the Institute of Employment Consultants

MECO [astronautics] main engine cut off

MEcon Master of Economics

MED maximum equivalent dose; [pharmacology] minimum effective dose; [chemistry] molecular electronic device; [New Zealand] Municipal Electricity Department

MEd Master of Education

Med [short form] Mediterranean

Med. Mediterranean

med. medal; medallist; median; medical; medicine; medieval; medium

Medit. Mediterranean

med. jur. medical jurisprudence

MEDLARS [USA] Medical Literature Analysis and Retrieval System

Med. Lat. Medieval Latin

MedRC Medical Reserve Corps

MedScD Doctor of Medical Science

med. tech. medical technician; medical technology

MEE Master of Electrical Engineering

ME(Elec) Master of Electrical Engineering

MEF Mediterranean Expeditionary Force; Middle East Force

meg [short form, computing] megabyte

MEIC Member of the Engineering Institute of Canada

Mej. *Mejuffrouw* (Dutch: Miss)

MEK methyl ethyl ketone (solvent)

Melan. Melanesia; Melanesian

Melb. Melbourne

MELF Middle East Land Forces

Mem. Member

mem. member; *memento* (Latin: remember); memoir(s); memorandum; memorial; memory

ME(Mech) Master of Mechanical Engineering

memo [short form] memorandum

MEN [medicine] multiple endocrine neoplasia

Men [astronomy] Mensa

MENA Middle East News Agency

Mencap Royal Society for Mentally Handicapped Children and Adults

MEng Master of Engineering

MENS [medicine] multiple endocrine neoplasia syndromes

menst. menstrual; menstruation

mensur. mensuration

ment. mental; mention; mentioned

mentd mentioned

MEO Marine Engineering Officer

MEP *Mahajana Eksath Peramuna* (Sinhalese: People's United Front) (in Sri Lanka); Master of Engineering Physics; mean effective pressure; Member of the European Parliament

MEPA Master of Engineering and Public Administration

Mer. Merionethshire

mer. mercantile; merchandise; *mercoledì* (Italian: Wednesday); *mercredi* (French: Wednesday); mercury; meridian; meridional

Merc [short form] Mercedes (car)

merc. mercantile; mercury

MERCOSUR *Mercado Común del Sur* (Spanish: Southern (American) Common Market)

MERLIN [astronomy] Multi-Element Radio-linked Interferometer Network

MERU Maharishi European Research University

MèsA *Maître ès arts* (French: Master of Arts)

MESc Master of Engineering Science

MESFET [electronics] metal-semiconductor field-effect transistor

Messrs *Messieurs* (French: gentlemen, sirs) (plural of Mr in English)

Met [short form] Metropolitan Opera House (New York); [short form] Metropolitan Police

Met. Meteorological (as in **Met. Office**)

met. metallurgical; metallurgist; metallurgy; metaphor; metaphoric(al); metaphysical; metaphysics; meteorological; meteorology; metronome; metropolitan

metall. metallurgical; metallurgist; metallurgy

metaph. metaphor; metaphoric(al); metaphysical; metaphysics
METAR Meteorological Airfield Report
met. bor. metropolitan borough
MetE metallurgical engineer
meteor. meteorological; meteorology
meteorol. meteorological; meteorology
Meth. Methodist
meths [short form] methylated spirits
M-et-L Maine-et-Loire (French department)
M-et-M Meurthe-et-Moselle (French department)
m. et n. [medicine] *mane et nocte* (Latin: morning and night) (in prescriptions)
MetR Metropolitan Railway (London)
metro [short form] metropolitan railway
metrol. metrological; metrology
metrop. metropolis; metropolitan
metropol. metropolis; metropolitan
metsat meteorological satellite
MeV megaelectronvolt
Mev. *Mevrouw* (Dutch: Mrs)
MEW [finance] measure of economic welfare; [military] microwave early warning (system)
MEX [international vehicle registration] Mexico
Mex. Mexican; Mexico
MEXE Military Engineering Experimental Establishment
Mex. Sp. Mexican Spanish
MEZ *Mitteleuropäische Zeit* (German: Central European Time)
mez. [music] *mezza* (Italian: half, medium); [music] *mezzo* (Italian: half, medium)
mezzo. mezzotint
MF machine finish (on paper); machine finished (paper); magnetic field; Master of Forestry; [radio] medium frequency; melamine-formaldehyde (as in **MF resin**); Middle French; mill finish; [US slang] motherfucker; [telecommunications] multifrequency; [vehicle registration] northeast London
M/F male or female
mF millifarad
mf [music] *mezzo forte* (Italian: moderately loudly)
MFA Master of Fine Arts; Multi-Fibre Arrangement

MFAMus Master of Fine Arts in Music
MFARCS Member of the Faculty of Anaesthetists of the Royal College of Surgeons (of England)
MFB Metropolitan Fire Brigade
MFC Mastership in Food Control; motorfuel consumption
MFCM Member of the Faculty of Community Medicine
MFD minimum fatal dose
mfd manufactured
mfg manufacturing
MFH Master of Foxhounds; mobile field hospital
MFHom Member of the Faculty of Homoeopathy
MFlem Middle Flemish
mflops [computing] millions of floating-point operations per second (measure of computer power)
MFM [computing] modified frequency modulation
MFN most favoured nation (in trade agreement)
MFOM Member of the Faculty of Occupational Medicine
MFP [physics] mean free path
MFPA Mouth and Foot Painting Artists
MFr Middle French
mfr manufacturer
mfr. manufacture
mfre manufacture
MFS Master of Food Science; Master of Foreign Study
mfst manifest
MFT [computing] master file table
m. ft [medicine] *mistura fiat* (Latin: let a mixture be made) (in prescriptions)
m.f.t. motor freight tariff
MFV motor fleet vehicle; motor fleet vessel
MG machine glazed (paper); machine gun; [music] *main gauche* (French: left hand); Major-General; [building] make good; Morris Garages (sports car manufacturer); motor generator; [medicine] myasthenia gravis; [vehicle registration] northeast London
Mg [chemical element] magnesium
mg milligram
.mg Madagascar (in Internet address)
MGA Major-General in charge of Administration

m.g.a.w.d. make good all works disturbed (in commercial contract)

MGB metropolitan green belt; *Ministerstvo Gosudarstvennoi Bezopasnosti* (Russian: Ministry of State Security) (former Soviet secret police); motor gunboat

MGC Machine Gun Corps; Marriage Guidance Council (former name of Relate)

mgd million gallons per day

MGDS RCS Member in General Dental Surgery of the Royal College of Surgeons (of England)

mge message

MGGS Major-General, General Staff

MGI Member of the Institute of Certificated Grocers

MGk Medieval Greek; Modern Greek

M Glam. Mid Glamorgan

MGM Metro-Goldwyn-Mayer (film studio); mobile guided missile

mgmt management

MGN Mirror Group Newspapers

MGO Master General of the Ordnance; Master of Gynaecology and Obstetrics

MGP manufactured-gas plant

MGR [nuclear technology] modular gas-cooled reactor

MGr Medieval Greek; Modern Greek

Mgr Manager; *Monseigneur* (French: my lord); [Roman Catholic Church] Monsignor

mgr manager

Mgrs Managers; *Monseigneurs* (French: my lords); [Roman Catholic Church] Monsignors

mgs metre-gram-second

mgt management

MH [navigation] magnetic heading; [nautical] main hatch; marital history; Master of Horse; Master of Horticulture; Master of Hounds; Master of Hygiene; [USA] Medal of Honor; medical history; mental health; [fishing port] Middlesbrough; military hospital; Ministry of Health; [vehicle registration] northeast London

mH millihenry (unit of electric inductance)

.mh Marshall Islands (in Internet address)

MHA [USA] Master of Hospital Administration; [Australia, Canada] Member of the House of Assembly; [USA] Mental Health Administration; Methodist Homes for the Aged

MHC [immunology] major histocompatibility complex

MHCIMA Member of the Hotel Catering and Institutional Management Association

MHD [physics] magnetohydrodynamics

MHE Master of Home Economics

MHeb Middle Hebrew

MHF massive hydraulic fracture (or fracturing); [radio] medium high frequency

MHG Middle High German

MHK Member of the House of Keys (in Isle of Man)

MHLG Ministry of Housing and Local Government

M Hon. Most Honourable

MHortSc Master of Horticultural Science

MHR [USA, Australia] Member of the House of Representatives

MHRA Modern Humanities Research Association

MHRF Mental Health Research Fund

MHS medical history sheet; Member of the Historical Society; [computing] message-handling service (or system)

MHTGR [nuclear technology] modular high-temperature gas-cooled reactor

MHum Master of Humanities

MHW mean high water (level of tide)

MHWN mean high water neaps (level of tide)

MHWS mean high water springs (level of tide)

MHy Master of Hygiene

MHz megahertz

MI malleable iron; [civil aircraft marking] Marshall Islands; medical inspection; [US postcode] Michigan; Military Intelligence (as in **MI5**); Ministry of Information; [biology] mitotic index; moment of inertia; mounted infantry; [medicine] myocardial infarction

Mi. Minor; Mississippi

mi. mile; [currency] mill (thousandth of dollar); minute

MI5 Military Intelligence, section five (popular name for UK counterintelligence agency)

MI6 Military Intelligence, section six (popular name for UK intelligence and espionage agency)

MIA Master of International Affairs; [military] missing in action; [Australia] Murrumbidgee Irrigation Area

MIAA&S Member of the Incorporated Association of Architects and Surveyors

MIAgrE Member of the Institution of Agricultural Engineers

MIAM Member of the Institute of Administrative Management

MIAP Member of the Institution of Analysts and Programmers

MIAS Member of the Institute of Accounting Staff

MIB [computing] management information base

MIBE Member of the Institution of British Engineers

MIBF Member of the Institute of British Foundrymen

MIBiol Member of the Institute of Biology

MIBK methyl isobutyl ketone (solvent)

MIBritE Member of the Institution of British Engineers

MIBScot Member of the Institute of Bankers in Scotland

Mic [astronomy] Microscopium

Mic. [Bible] Micah

MICE Member of the Institution of Civil Engineers

MICEI Member of the Institution of Civil Engineers of Ireland

MICFor Member of the Institute of Chartered Foresters

Mich. Michaelmas; Michigan

MIChemE Member of the Institution of Chemical Engineers

MICorrST Member of the Institution of Corrosion Science and Technology

MICR [computing] magnetic ink character recognition

Micro Micronesia; Micronesian; Multinational Initiative for the Use of Computers in Research Organizations

micro. microscope; microscopic; microscopist; microscopy

microbiol. microbiology

micros. microscope; microscopic; microscopist; microscopy

MICS Member of the Institute of Chartered Shipbrokers

MICU [medicine] mobile intensive care unit

MICV [military] mechanized infantry combat vehicle

MID minimum infective dose

Mid. Midlands; Midshipman

mid. middle; midnight

MIDAS [computing] measurement information and data analysis system; missile defence alarm system

Middx Middlesex

MIDELEC Midlands Electricity Board

Midi musical instrument digital interface

Midl. Midlands; Midlothian

Mid. Lat. Middle Latin

MIDPM Member of the Institute of Data Processing Management

midw. midwest; midwestern

MIE(Aust) Member of the Institution of Engineers, Australia

MIED Member of the Institution of Engineering Designers

MIEE Member of the Institution of Electrical Engineers

MIEEE [USA] Member of the Institute of Electrical and Electronics Engineers

MIEI Member of the Institution of Engineering Inspection

MIE(Ind) Member of the Institution of Engineers, India

miér. *miércoles* (Spanish: Wednesday)

MIES Member of the Institution of Engineers and Shipbuilders, Scotland

MIEx Member of the Institute of Export

MIExpE Member of the Institute of Explosives Engineers

MIF [computing] management information format; [immunology] migration inhibition factor; milk in first (in pouring tea); Miners' International Federation

MIFA Member of the Institute of Field Archaeologists

MIFF Member of the Institute of Freight Forwarders

MIFireE Member of the Institute of Fire Engineers

MIG metal-inert gas (as in **MIG welding**); mortgage indemnity guarantee

MiG Mikoyan and Gurevich (designers of Soviet fighter aircraft)

MIGA Multilateral Investment Guarantee Agency (affiliate of World Bank)

MIGasE Member of the Institution of Gas Engineers

MIGeol Member of the Institution of Geologists

MIH Master of Industrial Health

MIHort Member of the Institute of Horticulture

MIHT Member of the Institution of Highways and Transportation

MIIE Member of the Institution of Industrial Engineers

MIIM Member of the Institution of Industrial Managers

MIInfSc Member of the Institute of Information Sciences

MIISec Member of the International Institute of Security

MIL Member of the Institute of Linguists; [USA] one million

Mil. Milan

mil. mileage; military; militia

.mil US military (in Internet address)

Mil. Att. Military Attaché

MILGA Member of the Institute of Local Government Administrators

milit. military

mill. million

MILocoE Member of the Institution of Locomotive Engineers

Milw. Milwaukee

MIM Member of the Institute of Materials

MIMarE Member of the Institute of Marine Engineers

MIMC Member of the Institute of Management Consultants

MIMD [computing] multiple instruction, multiple data

MIME multipurpose Internet mail extension

MIMechE Member of the Institution of Mechanical Engineers

MIMGTechE Member of the Institution of Mechanical and General Technician Engineers

MIMI Member of the Institute of the Motor Industry

MIMM Member of the Institution of Mining and Metallurgy

MIMS *Monthly Index of Medical Specialities*

MIN minimum

Min. Minister; Ministry

min. mineralogical; mineralogy; minim (unit of liquid measure); minimum; mining; ministerial; minor; minute

mineral. mineralogical; mineralogy

Minn. Minnesota

Min. Plen. Minister Plenipotentiary

Min. Res. Minister Resident(iary)

MINS [USA] minor(s) in need of supervision

MInstAM Member of the Institute of Administrative Management

MInstBE Member of the Institution of British Engineers

MInstD Member of the Institute of Directors

MInstE Member of the Institute of Energy

MInstEnvSci Member of the Institute of Environmental Sciences

MInstMC Member of the Institute of Measurement and Control

MInstMM Member of the Institution of Mining and Metallurgy

MInstP Member of the Institute of Physics

MInstPet Member of the Institute of Petroleum

MInstPI Member of the Institute of Patentees and Inventors

MInstPkg Member of the Institute of Packaging

MInstR Member of the Institute of Refrigeration

MInstRA Member of the Institute of Registered Architects

MInstTM Member of the Institute of Travel Managers in Industry and Commerce

MInstWM Member of the Institute of Wastes Management

MINucE Member of the Institution of Nuclear Engineers

Mio [geology] Miocene

MIOSH Member of the Institution of Occupational Safety and Health

MIP marine insurance policy; maximum investment plan; Member of the Institute of Plumbing; monthly investment plan

m.i.p. mean indicated pressure

MIPA Member of the Institute of Practitioners in Advertising

MIPD Member of the Institute of Personnel and Development

MIPR Member of the Institute of Public Relations

mips [computing] millions of instructions per second

MIQ Member of the Institute of Quarrying

MIQA Member of the Institute of Quality Assurance

MIR [taxation] mortgage interest relief

MIr Middle Irish

MIRA Member of the Institute of Registered Architects; Motor Industry Research Association

MIRAS [taxation] mortgage interest relief at source

MIRD medical internal radiation dose

MIRT Member of the Institute of Reprographic Technicians

MIRTE Member of the Institute of Road Transport Engineers

MIRV [military] multiple independently targeted re-entry vehicle

MIS management information system; manufacturing information system; marketing information system; Member of the Institute of Statisticians; meteorological information system; Mining Institute of Scotland

Mis [geology] Mississippian

misc. miscellaneous; miscellany

MISD [computing] multiple instruction, single data

MISFET [electronics] metal-insulator-semiconductor field-effect transistor

Miss. Mission; Missionary; Mississippi

mist. *mistura* (Latin: mixture)

mistrans. mistranslation

MIStructE Member of the Institution of Structural Engineers

MIT Massachusetts Institute of Technology

Mit. *Mittwoch* (German: Wednesday)

MITA Member of the Industrial Transport Association

MITD Member of the Institute of Training and Development

MITE Member of the Institution of Electrical and Electronics Technician Engineers

MITI [Japan] Ministry of International Trade and Industry

MITL magnetically insulated transmission line

MITT Member of the Institute of Travel and Tourism

mitts minutes of telecommunications traffic

MIU Maharishi International University

MIWEM Member of the Institution of Water and Environmental Management

mixt. mixture

MJ [vehicle registration] Luton; megajoule; Ministry of Justice

MJA Medical Journalists' Association

MJD management job description

MJI Member of the Institute of Journalists

MJQ Modern Jazz Quartet

MJS Member of the Japan Society

MJSD March, June, September, December (end of financial quarters)

MJur Master of Law (from Latin *Magister Juris*)

MK [international vehicle registration] Macedonia; [currency] Malawi kwacha; [UK postcode] Milton Keynes; [vehicle registration] northeast London

Mk mark (model of car etc.); Mark; [currency] markka (used in Finland)

mk [currency] mark

.mk Macedonia (in Internet address)

mkd marked

MKO Mauna Kea Observatory (Hawaii)

mks [currency] marks; metre-kilogram-second (as in **mks units**)

mksA metre-kilogram-second-ampere (as in **mksA system**)

mkt market

ML Licentiate in Medicine (from Latin *Medicinae Licentiatus*); Licentiate in Midwifery; Master of Law(s); Master of Letters; [statistics] maximum likelihood; Medieval Latin; [fishing port] Methil (Scotland); [UK postcode] Motherwell; motor launch; muzzle-loading (gun); [vehicle registration] northeast London

ml mail; millilitre

.ml Mali (in Internet address)

m.l. machine language; mean level; minelayer

MLA [accounting] mandatory liquid assets; Master Locksmiths Association; Master of Landscape Architecture; Master of the Liberal Arts; Medical Library Association; Member of the Legislative Assembly; [USA] Modern Language Association

MLArch Master of Landscape Architecture

MLC Meat and Livestock Commission; [Australia, India] Member of the Legisla-

tive Council; [medicine] mixed lymphocyte culture

MLCOM Member of the London College
of Osteopathic Medicine

MLD Master of Landscape Design; [phar-
macology] mean lethal dose; [pharma-
cology] minimum lethal dose

mld mould; moulded

mldg moulding

m.l.e. maximum loss expectancy

MLF *Mouvement de libération des femmes*
(French: Women's Liberation Movement); [military] multilateral (nuclear)
force

MLG Middle Low German

mlg. mileage (in car advertisement)

MLib Master of Library Science

MLibSc Master of Library Science

MLitt Master of Letters (from Latin
Magister Litterarum)

MLK Martin Luther King (US civil-rights
leader)

Mlle *Mademoiselle* (French: Miss)

MLNS [medicine] mucocutaneous lymph
node syndrome

MLO military liaison officer; [micro-
biology] mycoplasma-like organism(s)

MLR [banking] minimum lending rate;
[medicine] mixed lymphocyte reaction;
Modern Language Review; [statistics] multiple linear regression

MLRS multiple-launch rocket system

MLS main-line station; Master of Library
Science; [cinema] medium long shot;
Member of the Linnean Society; [aero-
nautics] microwave landing system;
mixed language system; multi-language
system

MLSO medical laboratory scientific officer

MLV [microbiology] murine leukaemia
virus

MLW mean low water (level of tide)

MLWN mean low water neaps (level of
tide)

MLWS mean low water springs (level of
tide)

MM [music] Maelzel's metronome (indication of tempo); maintenance manual;
Majesties; [medicine] malignant mela-
noma; Martyrs; [Freemasonry] Master
Mason; Master Mechanic; Master of
Music; Medal of Merit; mercantile
marine; *Messieurs* (French: gentlemen,

sirs) (plural of M (Monsieur) in French);
Military Medal; [medicine] mucus membrane; music master; [vehicle regis-
tration] northeast London

mm millimetre

.mm Myanmar (in Internet address)

m.m. made merchantable; *mutatis mut-
andis* (Latin: with the necessary changes)

MMA Metropolitan Museum of Art;
[astronomy] Millimeter Array; Music
Masters' Association

MMath Master of Mathematics

MMB Milk Marketing Board (replaced by
Milk Marque)

MMC metal-matrix composite; Mon-
opolies and Mergers Commission

MMD Movement for Multiparty Democracy (in Zambia)

MMDA [USA] money market deposit
account

MMDS [radio] multipoint microwave distribution system

MME Master of Mechanical Engineering;
Master of Mining Engineering; Master of
Music Education

Mme *Madame* (French: Mrs)

MMechE Master of Mechanical Engineering

MMed Master of Medicine

MMedSci Master of Medical Science

Mmes *Mesdames* (French: plural of Mme)

MMet Master of Metallurgy

MMetE Master of Metallurgical Engineering

mmf [physics] magnetomotive force

MMG [military] medium machine gun

MMGI Member of the Mining, Geological
and Metallurgical Institute of India

mmHg millimetre(s) of mercury (unit of
pressure)

MMI [computing] man–machine
interface; Municipal Mutual Insurance

MMin Master of Ministry

MMM [Canada] Member of the Order of
Military Merit

mmol millimole

MMP [biochemistry] matrix metalloprotei-
nase (enzyme); Military Mounted Police;
mixed member proportional (system of
proportional representation)

m.m.p. [chemistry] mixture melting point

MMPI [psychology] Minnesota Multi-
phasic Personality Inventory

MMQ minimum manufacturing quantity

MMR [medicine] mass miniature radiography; [medicine] measles, mumps and rubella (vaccine)

MMRBM mobile medium-range ballistic missile

MMS Marine Meteorological Services; Member of the Institute of Management Services; Methodist Missionary Society; Moravian Missionary Society; multimission modular spacecraft

MMSA Master of Midwifery of the Society of Apothecaries

MMSc Master of Medical Science

MMT methylcyclopentadienyl manganese tricarbonyl (fuel additive); Multiple Mirror Telescope (Arizona)

MMU [computing] memory management unit; [finance] million monetary units

MMus Master of Music

MMusEd Master of Musical Education

MMX multimedia extension

MN magnetic north; [fishing port] Maldon; Master of Nursing; Merchant Navy; [US postcode] Minnesota

Mn [chemical element] manganese; Modern (language)

mn *maison* (French: house); million

mn. midnight

.mn Mongolia (in Internet address)

m.n. *mutato nomine* (Latin: with the name changed)

MNA Master of Nursing Administration; Member of the National Assembly (of Quebec)

MNAD Multinational Airmobile Division (of NATO)

MNAEA Member of the National Association of Estate Agents

MNAS [USA] Member of the National Academy of Sciences

MNC major NATO command; multinational company

MND Ministry of National Defence; [medicine] motor neurone disease

MNE multinational enterprise

MnE Modern English

MNECInst Member of the North East Coast Institution of Engineers and Shipbuilders

mng managing

MnGk Modern Greek

mngmt management

MnGr Modern Greek

mngr manager

MNI Member of the Nautical Institute

MNIMH Member of the National Institute of Medical Herbalists

Mnl. Manila

mnm minimum

MNOS [electronics] metal-nitride-oxide semiconductor

MNP microcomputer networking protocol

MNR marine nature reserve; mean neap rise (of tide); Mozambique National Resistance

Mnr *Mijnheer* (Dutch: Mr, Sir)

MNSc Master of Nursing Science

MNT mean neap tide

MNurs Master of Nursing

MO mail order; manually operated; mass observation; Master of Obstetrics; Master of Oratory; medical officer; medical orderly; Meteorological Office; military operations; [US postcode] Missouri; *modus operandi* (Latin: method of operating); [chemistry] molecular orbital; money order; monthly order; motor-operated; municipal officer; [vehicle registration] Reading

Mo [computing] magneto-optical; [chemical element] molybdenum

Mo. Missouri; Monday

m-o months old

mo. moment; month; mouth

m.o. mail order; *modus operandi* (Latin: method of operating); money order

MOA memorandum of agreement; Ministry of Aviation

MO&G Master of Obstetrics and Gynaecology

MOB movable object block

mob. mobile; mobilization; mobilize

MOBS multiple orbit bombardment system (nuclear weapons)

MOC management and operating contractor; [international vehicle registration] Mozambique (from Portuguese *Moçambique*)

MoC mother of the chapel (in printing or publishing trade union)

MOD mail-order department; Ministry of Defence; Ministry of Overseas Development

mod [computing, mathematics] modulo

mod. model; moderate; [music] *moderato* (Italian: at a moderate tempo); modern; modernization; modernized (in property advertisement); modification; modified; [mathematics] modulus

mod cons [short form] modern conveniences

mod. dict. [medicine] *modo dicto* (Latin: as directed) (in prescriptions)

modem [computing] modulator demodulator

MODFET [electronics] modulation-doped field-effect transistor

modif. modification; modified

mod. praes. [medicine] *modo praescripto* (Latin: as directed) (in prescriptions)

Mods [short form] Honour Moderations (at Oxford University)

modto [music] *moderato* (Italian: at a moderate tempo)

MODU mobile offshore drilling unit

.mod.uk Ministry of Defence (in Internet address)

MOEH Medical Officer for Environmental Health

MOF [medicine] multiple organ failure

M of A Ministry of Agriculture, Fisheries and Food

M of W Ministry of Works

MOH Master of Otter Hounds; Medical Officer of Health; Ministry of Housing (and Local Government)

MOHLG Ministry of Housing and Local Government

MOHLL [computing] machine-oriented high-level language

MOI military operations and intelligence; Ministry of Information; Ministry of the Interior

MOL [astronautics] manned orbital laboratory; Ministry of Labour

mol mole (unit of amount of substance)

mol. molecular; molecule

Mold. Moldavia; Moldavian; Moldova

Moldv. Moldavia; Moldavian; Moldova

mol. wt molecular weight

MOM milk of magnesia

m.o.m. middle of month

MOMA Museum of Modern Art

MOMI Museum of the Moving Image

MOMIMTS Military and Orchestral Instrument Makers' Trade Society

moms *mervaerdiomsaetningsskat* (Danish:

value-added tax); *mervardesomsattningsskatt* (Swedish: value-added tax)

Mon [astronomy] Monoceros

Mon. Monaco; Monaghan; Monday; Monegasque; Monmouth(shire); *Montag* (German: Monday); Montana

mon. monastery; monastic; monetary; monitor; monsoon; month

Monag. Monaghan

MONEP *Marché des options négotiables de Paris* (French: Paris traded option market)

Mong. Mongolia; Mongolian

Mongol. Mongolia; Mongolian

Monm. Monmouth(shire)

monog. monogram; monograph

Mons. *Monsieur* (French: Mr)

Mont. Montana; Montgomeryshire

Montgom. Montgomeryshire

Montr. Montreal

MOO [computing] multiuser object-oriented

m.o.p. mother-of-pearl

MOPA [electronics] master oscillator power amplifier

MOPH [USA] Military Order of the Purple Heart

MOPS Mail Order Protection Scheme

MOR middle-of-the-road; [engineering] modulus of rupture

Mor. Moroccan; Morocco

mor. [music] *morendo* (Italian: dying away); [bookbinding] morocco

MORC Medical Officer Reserve Corps

mor. dict. [medicine] *more dicto* (Latin: as directed) (in prescriptions)

Mori Market and Opinion Research Institute (as in **Mori poll**)

morn. morning

morph. morphological; morphology

morphol. morphological; morphology

mor. sol. [medicine] *more solito* (Latin: in the usual way) (in prescriptions)

mort. mortal; mortality; mortar; mortgage; mortuary

MOS magneto-optical system; [electronics] metal oxide semiconductor; [electronics] metal oxide silicon; Ministry of Supply

Mos. Moscow; Moselle

mos. months

MOSFET [electronics] metal-oxide-silicon field-effect transistor

MOST [electronics] metal-oxide-silicon transistor

MOT Ministry of Transport (as in **MOT test**)

mot. motor; motorized

MOTNE meteorological operational tele-communications network

MOU memorandum of understanding

MOUS [medicine] multiple occurrence of unexplained symptoms

MOUSE [military] minimum orbital unmanned satellite of the earth (used to gather information)

MOV [engineering] motor-operated valve

mov. [music] *movimento* (Italian: movement, motion)

MOVE Men Over Violence (organization counselling wife-batterers)

movt movement

MOW [New Zealand] Ministry of Works; Movement for the Ordination of Women

MOX mixed oxide (as in **MOX fuel**)

Moz. Mozambique

MP Madhya Pradesh; [metallurgy] martensitic phase; medium pressure; melting point; Member of Parliament; [physiology] membrane potential; [cartography] Mercator's projection; metal pollutant; Methodist Protestant; Metropolitan Police; mile post (on map); Military Police; Military Policeman; *mille passuum* (Latin: 1,000 paces) (Roman mile); Minister Plenipotentiary; miscellaneous papers; miscellaneous publications; Mounted Police; Mounted Policeman; [vehicle registration] north-east London

M/P memorandum of partnership

mp [music] *mezzo piano* (Italian: moderately softly)

m.p. meeting point; melting point; mile post (on map); months after payment; mooring post

MPA Master of Professional Accounting; Master of Public Administration; Master Printers Association; Member of the Parliamentary Assembly of Northern Ireland; Music Publishers' Association

MPAA Motion Picture Association of America

MPAGB Modern Pentathlon Association of Great Britain

MPB male pattern baldness; [USA] Missing Persons Bureau

MPC mathematics, physics, chemistry; maximum permissible concentration; Metropolitan Police College; Metropolitan Police Commissioner; multimedia personal computer

MPD maximum permissible dose

MPE Master of Physical Education; maximum permissible exposure (to radiation); maximum possible error

MPEA Member of the Physical Education Association

MPEG [computing] Moving Picture Expert Group

MPer Middle Persian

MPF [medicine] maturation-promoting factor

MPG [education] main professional grade (basic salary); *Max-Planck-Gesellschaft zur Förderung der Wissenschaften* (German: Max Planck Society for the Advancement of Science)

mpg miles per gallon

MPH Master of Public Health

MPh Master of Philosophy

mph miles per hour

MPharm Master of Pharmacy

MPhil Master of Philosophy

MPI Max Planck Institute; maximum permissible intake

m.p.i. mean point of impact

MPIA Master of Public and International Affairs

MPIR Max Planck Institute for Radio Astronomy

MPL maximum permissible level

MPLA *Movimento Popular de Libertação de Angola* (Portuguese: Popular Movement for the Liberation of Angola)

mpm metres per minute

MPO management and personnel office; Metropolitan Police Office; military post office; mobile printing office; mobile publishing office

MPP [computing] massively parallel processor; Member of the Provincial Parliament (of Ontario)

m.p.p. most probable position

MPR *Majelis Permusyawaratan Rakyat* (Bahasa Indonesian: People's Consultative Assembly); maximum permitted radiation; Mongolian People's Republic

MPRISA Member of the Public Relations Institute of South Africa

MPRP Mongolian People's Revolutionary Party

MPS manufacturer's part specification; marginal propensity to save; master production schedule; Medical Protection Society; Member of the Pharmaceutical Society; Member of the Philological Society; Member of the Physical Society; [medicine] mucopolysaccharide (as in **MPS disease**)

MPs Master of Psychology

mps metres per second

MPsSc Master of Psychological Science

MPsych Master of Psychology

MPsyMed Master of Psychological Medicine

MPTA Municipal Passenger Transport Association

MPU Medical Practitioners Union; [computing] microprocessor unit

MPV multipurpose vehicle

Mpy [commerce] *Maatschappij* (Dutch: company, Co.)

MQ [photography] metol-quinol (developing fluid)

mq. mosque

Mqe Martinique

MR magnetic resonance (as in **MR scan**); [computing] magneto-resistive; [fishing port] Manchester; map reference; [law] Master of the Rolls; match rifle; [commerce] mate's receipt; mental retardation; metabolic rate; Middlesex Regiment; Minister Resident(iary); motivation(al) research; motorways regulations; municipal reform; [vehicle registration] Swindon

Mr Master; Mister

.mr Mauritania (in Internet address)

m.r. memorandum receipt

MRA Maritime Royal Artillery; Moral Rearmament

MRAC Member of the Royal Agricultural College

MRACP Member of the Royal Australasian College of Physicians

MRACS Member of the Royal Australasian College of Surgeons

MRadA Member of the Radionic Association

MRAeS Member of the Royal Aeronautical Society

MRAF Marshal of the Royal Air Force

MRAIC Member of the Royal Architectural Institute of Canada

MRAO Mullard Radio Astronomy Observatory

MRAS Member of the Royal Academy of Science; Member of the Royal Asiatic Society; Member of the Royal Astronomical Society

MRB Mersey River Board

MRBM medium-range ballistic missile

MRBS Member of the Royal Botanic Society

MRC Medical Registration Council; Medical Research Council; Medical Reserve Corps; Model Railway Club

MRCA multirole combat aircraft

MRCGP Member of the Royal College of General Practitioners

MRC-LMB Medical Research Council Laboratory of Molecular Biology

MRCO Member of the Royal College of Organists

MRCOG Member of the Royal College of Obstetricians and Gynaecologists

MRCP Member of the Royal College of Physicians

MRCPA Member of the Royal College of Pathologists of Australia

MRCPath Member of the Royal College of Pathologists

MRCPE Member of the Royal College of Physicians of Edinburgh

MRCPI Member of the Royal College of Physicians of Ireland

MRCPSGlas Member of the Royal College of Physicians and Surgeons of Glasgow

MRCPsych Member of the Royal College of Psychiatrists

MRCS Member of the Royal College of Surgeons (of England)

MRCSE Member of the Royal College of Surgeons of Edinburgh

MRCSI Member of the Royal College of Surgeons in Ireland

MRCVS Member of the Royal College of Veterinary Surgeons

MRD machine-readable dictionary; minimal residual disease

MRE Master of Religious Education; [military] meal(s) ready to eat; Member of the Royal Society of Painter-Printmakers (formerly Member of the Royal Society of Painter-Etchers and Engravers); Microbiological Research Establishment; Mining Research Establishment

MRes Master of Research

MRG Minority Rights Group

MRGS Member of the Royal Geographical Society

MRH Member of the Royal Household

MRHS Member of the Royal Horticultural Society

MRI [medicine] magnetic resonance image; [medicine] magnetic resonance imaging; Member of the Royal Institution

MRIA Member of the Royal Irish Academy

MRIAI Member of the Royal Institute of the Architects of Ireland

MRICS Member of the Royal Institution of Chartered Surveyors

MRIN Member of the Royal Institute of Navigation

MRINA Member of the Royal Institution of Naval Architects

MRIPHH Member of the Royal Institute of Public Health and Hygiene

mrkr marker

MRM mechanically recovered meat (in food processing)

MRMetS Member of the Royal Meteorological Society

MRN materials return note

mRNA [biochemistry] messenger ribonucleic acid

mrng morning

MRO Member of the Register of Osteopaths

MRP manufacturer's recommended price; Master of Regional Planning; [commerce] material requirements planning

MRPharmS Member of the Royal Pharmaceutical Society

MRRP manufacturer's recommended retail price

MRS Market Research Society; [computing] monitored retrievable storage

MRs [currency] Mauritian rupee

Mrs Mistress

MRSC Member of the Royal Society of Chemistry

MRSH Member of the Royal Society of Health

MRSL Member of the Royal Society of Literature

MRSM Member of the Royal Society of Medicine; Member of the Royal Society of Musicians of Great Britain

MRSPP Member of the Royal Society of Portrait Painters

MRST Member of the Royal Society of Teachers

MRT [medicine] magnetic resonance tomography; mass rapid transit

MRTPI Member of the Royal Town Planning Institute

MRU manpower research unit; mobile repair unit

MRUSI Member of the Royal United Service Institution

MRV [military] multiple re-entry vehicle

MRVA Member of the Rating and Valuation Association

MS [vehicle registration] Edinburgh; [physics] magnetic susceptibility; mail steamer; [astronomy] main sequence; [music] *mano sinistra* (Italian: left hand); manuscript; [physics, chemistry] mass spectrometer; [physics, chemistry] mass spectrometry; [USA] Master of Science; Master of Surgery; [international vehicle registration] Mauritius; media studies; medical staff; [photography] medium shot; *memoriae sacrum* (Latin: sacred to the memory of) (on tombstone); Mess Sergeant; [photography] mid-shot; milestone (on map); minesweeper; Ministry of Supply; [US postcode] Mississippi; [medicine] mitral stenosis; [USA] motor ship; [medicine] multiple sclerosis; municipal surveyor

Ms Miss or Mrs

ms millisecond

m/s metres per second; [finance] months after sight

ms. manuscript

m.s. mail steamer; margin of safety; maximum stress; mild steel

m/s² metres per second per second (unit of acceleration)

MSA Malaysia-Singapore Airways; Master of Science and Arts; Master of Science in Agriculture; Media Studies Association; Member of the Society of Apothecaries;

Merchant Shipping Act; metropolitan statistical area; Mineralogical Society of America; Motor Schools Association of Great Britain Limited; motorway service area; [USA] Mutual Security Agency

MSAE [USA] Master of Science in Aeronautical Engineering; [USA] Member of the Society of Automotive Engineers

MSAgr Master of Science in Agriculture

MS&R Merchant Shipbuilding and Repairs

MSArch Master of Science in Architecture

MSB Maritime Safety Board; Metropolitan Society for the Blind; [computing] most significant bit

MSBA Master of Science in Business Administration

MSBus Master of Science in Business

MSByte [computing] most significant byte

MSC major subordinate command (in NATO); Manchester Ship Canal; Manpower Services Commission; medical staff corps; Metropolitan Special Constabulary

MSc Master of Science

msc. miscellaneous

m.s.c. moved, seconded and carried

MSc(Ag) Master of Science in Agriculture

MScApp Master of Applied Science

MSc(Arch) Master of Science in Architecture

MSc(ChemE) Master of Science in Chemical Engineering

MScD [USA] Doctor of Medical Science; Master of Dental Science

MSCE Master of Science in Civil Engineering

MSc(Econ) Master of Science in Economics

MSc(Ed) Master of Science in Education

MSChE Master of Science in Chemical Engineering

MSc(Hort) Master of Science in Horticulture

MSCI Index [finance] Morgan Stanley Capital International World Index

MScMed Master of Medical Science

MSc(Nutr) Master of Science in Nutrition

MSCP Master of Science in Community Planning

MScTech Master of Technical Science

MSD Doctor of Medical Science; Master of

Science in Dentistry; Master Surgeon Dentist; [computing] most significant digit

MSDent Master of Science in Dentistry

MS-DOS [trademark, computing] Microsoft Disk Operating System

MSE Master of Science in Education; Master of Science in Engineering; Member of the Society of Engineers

MSEd Master of Science in Education

MSEE Master of Science in Electrical Engineering

MSEM Master of Science in Engineering Mechanics; Master of Science in Engineering of Mines

MSF Manufacturing, Science and Finance (Union); Master of Science in Forestry; *Médecins sans frontières* (French: Doctors Without Frontiers) (charity); minesweeping flotilla

MSFC [USA] Marshall Space Flight Center

MSG monosodium glutamate (food additive)

msg. message

Msgr *Monseigneur* (French: my lord); [Roman Catholic Church] Monsignor

msgr messenger

MSgt [US military] Master Sergeant

MSH Master of Staghounds; [biochemistry] melanocyte-stimulating hormone

MSHE Master of Science in Home Economics

MSHEc Master of Science in Home Economics

Mshl Marshal

MSHyg Master of Science in Hygiene

MSI [electronics] medium-scale integration; Member of the Securities Institute; *Movimento Sociale Italiano* (Italian: Italian Social Movement)

MSIE Master of Science in Industrial Engineering

MSJ Master of Science in Journalism

MSL Master of Science in Linguistics; mean sea level

MSLS Master of Science in Library Science

MSM Master of Sacred Music; Master of Science in Music; Meritorious Service Medal

MSME Master of Science in Mechanical Engineering

MSMed Master of Medical Science

MSMetE Master of Science in Metallurgical Engineering

MSMus Master of Science in Music

MSN Master of Science in Nursing; [trademark, computing] Microsoft Network

MSO Member of the Society of Osteopaths

MSocIS *Membre de la société des ingénieurs et scientifiques de France* (French: Member of the Society of Engineers and Scientists of France)

MSocSc Master of Social Science(s)

MSP matched sale–purchase agreement; [trademark, computing] Microsoft Paint

MSPE Master of Science in Physical Education

MSPH Master of Science in Public Health

MSPhar Master of Science in Pharmacy

MSPharm Master of Science in Pharmacy

MSPHE Master of Science in Public Health Engineering

MSQ managing service quality

MSR [computing] magnetic stripe reader; main supply route; manual sunroof (in car advertisement); mean spring rise (of tide); Member of the Society of Radiographers; [military] missile-site radar

MSRP [USA] manufacturer's suggested retail price

MSS manuscripts; [computing] mass storage system; Master of Social Science; Master of Social Service; Member of the Royal Statistical Society; [medicine] midstream specimen (of urine)

mss manuscripts

MSSc Master of Social Science

MSSE [USA] Master of Science in Sanitary Engineering

MST Master of Sacred Theology; Master of Science in Teaching; mean spring tide; mean survival time; [USA] Mountain Standard Time

MSt Master of Studies

mst measurement

MStat Master of Statistics

MSTD Member of the Society of Typographic Designers

Mstr Master

MSTS [US navy] Military Sea Transportation Service

MSU [medicine] midstream specimen of urine

MSUL Medical Schools of the University of London

MSurv Master of Surveying

MSurvSc Master of Surveying Science

MSW magnetic surface wave(s); Master of Social Welfare; Master of Social Work; medical social worker; municipal solid waste

MSw Middle Swedish

MSX [trademark, computing] Microsoft extended Basic

MSY maximum sustainable yield (of natural resource)

MT machine translation; magnetic tape; mail transfer; [medicine] malignant tumour; mandated territory; [fishing port] Maryport; mass transport; mean time; mechanical transport; megaton (unit of explosive power); [currency] metical (used in Mozambique); [law] Middle Temple; [US postcode] Montana; motor tanker; motor transport; [USA] Mountain Time; [vehicle registration] northeast London

M/T empty; mail transfer

Mt [chemical element] meitnerium; Mount

Mt. Mountain

mt. megaton (unit of explosive power); mountain

.mt Malta (in Internet address)

m.t. metric ton; missile test

MTA [computing] message transfer agent; minimum terms agreement; Music Teachers' Association; Music Trades' Association

MTB motor torpedo boat; mountain bike

MTBE methyl tertiary-butyl ether (fuel additive)

MTBF [computing] mean time between failures

MTBI [computing] mean time between incidents

MTC Mechanized Transport Corps; Music Teacher's Certificate

MTCA Ministry of Transport and Civil Aviation

MTD maximum tolerated dose; mean temperature difference; Midwife Teacher's Diploma; moving target detector

mtd mounted

mtDNA [biochemistry] mitochondrial deoxyribonucleic acid

MTech Master of Technology
MTEFL Master in the Teaching of English as a Foreign Language
MTFA medium-term financial assistance
MTG [USA] methanol to gasoline
mtg meeting; mounting
mtg. mortgage
mtgd mortgaged
mtge mortgage
mtgee mortgagee
mtgor mortgagor
MTh Master of Theology
mth month
MTI [radar] moving target indicator (or indication)
MTL mean tide level
mtl material
mtl. *monatlich* (German: monthly)
MTM methods-time measurement
MTN [finance] medium-term note; multilateral trade negotiations
mtn motion; mountain
MTNA Music Teachers' National Association
MTO made to order; mechanical transport officer
MTP Master of Town Planning
MTR minimum time rate
mtr meter
Mt Rev. Most Reverend (title of archbishop)
MTS Master of Theological Studies; Merchant Taylors' School; [computing] Michigan terminal system; motor transport service; [USA] multichannel television sound
Mts Mountains; Mounts
MTT [electronics] mean transit time
MTTR mean time to repair; mean time to restore
MTU [computing] magnetic tape unit; [computing] maximum transfer unit; [US air force] missile training unit
MTV motor torpedo vessel; [USA] music television
MU maintenance unit; marginal utility; monetary unit; Mothers' Union; Musicians' Union; [vehicle registration] northeast London
m/u make-up
.mu Mauritius (in Internet address)
MUC Missionary Union of the Clergy
MU car [US railways] multiple-unit car

MUD [computing] multi-user dungeon (or dimension) (in game)
MUF [telecommunications] maximum usable frequency
MUFTI [military] minimum use of force tactical intervention
MUG [computing] multi-user game
MUGA [medicine] multiple-gated arteriography (as in **MUGA scan**)
Multics [trademark] Multiplexed Information and Computing Service
mun. municipal; municipality; munitions
munic. municipal; municipality
MUniv Master of the University
Mus [astronomy] Musca
mus. museum; music; musical; musician
musa multiple unit steerable aerial (or antenna)
MusB Bachelor of Music (from Latin *Musicae Baccalaureus*)
MusD Doctor of Music (from Latin *Musicae Doctor*)
MusM Master of Music (from Latin *Musicae Magister*)
musn musician
mut. mutilate; mutilated; mutual
MUX multiplexer
MV market value; megavolt; merchant vessel; [chemistry] mixed valence; motor vessel; muzzle velocity (of gun); [vehicle registration] southeast London
mV millivolt
.mv [music] *mezza voce* (Italian: half voice, softly)
.mv Maldives (in Internet address)
m.v. market value; mean variation; merchant vessel; motor vessel
MVB Bachelor of Veterinary Medicine
MVD Doctor of Veterinary Medicine; *Ministerstvo Vnutrennikh Del* (Russian: Ministry of Internal Affairs) (former Soviet police organization); [medicine] mitral valve disease
MVEE Military Vehicles and Engineering Establishment
MVetMed Master of Veterinary Medicine
MVetSc Master of Veterinary Science
MVL motor-vehicle licence
mvmt movement
MVO Member of the Royal Victorian Order
MVP most valuable player; most valued player

MVRA Motor Vehicle Repairers Association

MVS Master of Veterinary Science

MVSc Master of Veterinary Science

mvt movement

MW [international vehicle registration] Malawi; Master of Wine; [radio] medium wave; megawatt; Middle Welsh; [nuclear technology] mixed waste; molecular weight; Most Worshipful; Most Worthy; [vehicle registration] Swindon

mW milliwatt

.mw Malawi (in Internet address)

MWA Mystery Writers of America

MWC municipal waste combustion

MWeldI Member of the Welding Institute

MWF Medical Women's Federation

MWG music wire gauge

MWGM [Freemasonry] Most Worshipful Grand Master; [Freemasonry] Most Worthy Grand Master

MWh megawatt hour

MWI municipal waste incineration; municipal waste incinerator

MWIA Medical Women's International Association

MWO Meteorological Watch Office

MWP mechanical wood pulp

MWPA Married Women's Property Act

MX missile-experimental; [vehicle registration] southeast London

Mx maxwell (unit of magnetic flux); Middlesex

.mx Mexico (in Internet address)

mxd mixed

mxm maximum

MY motor yacht; [vehicle registration] southeast London

my. myopia; myopic

.my Malaysia (in Internet address)

m.y. million years

myc. mycological; mycology

mycol. mycological; mycology

MYOB [informal] mind your own business

MYRA [finance] multiyear rescheduling agreement

myst. mysteries; mystery

myth. mythical; mythological; mythology

mythol. mythological; mythology

MZ [vehicle registration] Belfast

Mz [geology] Mesozoic

.mz Mozambique (in Internet address)

N

N [printing] en; [chess] knight; [currency] naira (used in Nigeria); National; Nationalist; navigation; Navy; neap (tide); near; [electrical engineering] neutral; New; [fishing port] Newry; newton (unit of force); [currency] ngultrum (used in Bhutan); [chemical element] nitrogen; Norse; north; northern; [UK postcode] north London; [international vehicle registration] Norway; November; nuclear; [physics] nucleon; [law] nullity; nurse; nursing; [civil aircraft marking] United States of America

N [physics] neutron number; [physics, chemistry] number (of molecules etc.)

n [printing] en; nano- (indicates 10^{-9}, as in **nm** = nanometre); [physics] neutron

n [genetics] haploid chromosome number; [mathematics] indefinite number; [chemistry] normal; [physics, chemistry] number density (of atoms etc.); [physics] principal quantum number; [optics] refractive index; [physics] rotational frequency

n. nail (former unit of length); name; nasal; *natus* (Latin: born); nautical; naval; near; negative; nephew; nerve; [commerce] net; [grammar] neuter; neutral; new; night; [grammar] nominative; noon; norm; normal; *nostro* (Italian: our); note; *notre* (French: our); [grammar] noun; *nous* (French: we, us); number

'n' and (as in **fish 'n' chips**)

5N [civil aircraft marking] Nigeria

9N [civil aircraft marking] Nepal

NA [vehicle registration] Manchester; Narcotics Anonymous; [USA] National Academician; National Academy; National Airlines; National Archives; National Army; National Assembly; nautical almanac; naval architect; naval attaché;

naval auxiliary; [international vehicle registration] Netherlands Antilles; [engineering] neutral axis; [banking] new account; [medicine] *Nomina Anatomica* (Latin: Anatomical Names) (official terminology); [biochemistry] noradrenaline; North America; North American; [optics] numerical aperture; nursing auxiliary

N/A [banking] new account; no account; [banking] no advice; [banking] non-acceptance; not applicable; not available

Na Nebraska; [chemical element] sodium (from Latin *natrium*)

n/a not applicable; not available

.na Namibia (in Internet address)

NAA [USA] National Aeronautic Association; National Association of Accountants; [USA] National Automobile Association; Nursing Auxiliaries' Association

n.a.a. [shipping] not always afloat

NAAA National Alliance of Athletic Associations

NAACP [USA] National Association for the Advancement of Colored People

NAAFA National Association to Aid Fat Americans

NAAFI Navy, Army and Air Force Institutes

NAAQS [USA] National Ambient Air Quality Standard

NAAS National Agricultural Advisory Service

NAB National Advisory Body for Public Sector Higher Education; National Alliance of Businessmen; National Assistance Board (former government department); [USA] National Association of Broadcasters; National Australia Bank; naval air base; naval amphibious base; New American Bible; News Agency of Burma

NABC National Association of Boys' Clubs

NABS National Advertising Benevolent Society

NAC National Advisory Council; National Agricultural Centre; [USA] National Airways Corporation; National Anglers' Council; National Archives Council; National Association for the Childless; [geology] North American craton; North Atlantic Council (in NATO)

NACA [USA] National Advisory Committee for Aeronautics

NACAB National Association of Citizens' Advice Bureaux

NACC North Atlantic Cooperation Council (in NATO, replaced by EAPC)

NACCAM National Coordinating Committee for Aviation Meteorology

NACCB National Accreditation Council for Certification Bodies

NACEIC National Advisory Council on Education for Industry and Commerce

NACF National Art Collections Fund

NACM National Association of Colliery Managers

NACNE National Advisory Committee on Nutrition Education

NACO National Association of Cooperative Officials

NACODS National Association of Colliery Overmen, Deputies and Shotfirers

NACOSS National Approval Council for Security Systems

NACRO National Association for the Care and Resettlement of Offenders

NACS National Association of Chimney Sweeps

NACST National Advisory Council on the Training and Supply of Teachers

NAD [USA] National Academy of Design; naval aircraft department; naval air division; [medicine] no abnormality detected; no appreciable difference; not on active duty

nad. nadir

NADC naval aide-de-camp

NADEC National Association of Development Education Centres

NADFAS National Association of Decorative and Fine Arts Societies

NADGE NATO Air Defence Ground Environment

NADOP [USA] North American Defense Operational Plan

NADW North Atlantic deep water

NADWARN [USA] Natural Disaster Warning System

NAE [USA] National Academy of Engineering; naval aircraft establishment

NAEA National Association of Estate Agents

NAEP [USA] National Assessment of Educational Progress

NAEW NATO Airborne Early Warning

NAf [currency] Netherlands Antilles guilder (from alternative name florin)

NAFD National Association of Funeral Directors

NAFO National Association of Fire Officers; Northwest Atlantic Fisheries Organization

NAFTA New Zealand and Australia Free Trade Agreement; North American Free Trade Agreement; North Atlantic Free Trade Area

NAG National Association of Goldsmiths

Nag. Nagasaki

n.a.g. net annual gain

NAGC National Association for Gifted Children

NAGS National Allotments and Gardens Society

Nah. [Bible] Nahum

NAHA National Association of Health Authorities

Nahal *No'ar Halutzi Lohem* (Hebrew: Pioneer and Military Youth) (in Israel)

NAHAT National Association of Health Authorities and Trusts

NAHB [USA] National Association of Home Builders

NAHT National Association of Head Teachers

NAI nonaccidental injury

NAIR [USA] national arrangements for incidents involving radioactivity

NAIRU [economics] nonaccelerating inflation rate of unemployment

NAITA National Association of Independent Travel Agents

NAK [telecommunications] negative acknowledgment

NAL [USA] National Aerospace Laboratory

NALC [USA] National Association of Letter Carriers

NALGO National and Local Government Officers' Association (became part of Unison)

NALHM National Association of Licensed House Managers

NAM [international vehicle registration] Namibia; [USA] National Association of Manufacturers

N Am. North America; North American

NAMAS National Measurement and Accreditation Service

NAMB National Association of Master Bakers

NAMCW National Association of Maternal and Child Welfare

NAMH National Association for Mental Health (former name of MIND)

NAMMA NATO MRCA Management Agency

NAMS [USA] national air-monitoring sites

NAN News Agency of Nigeria

NANC non-adrenergic non-cholinergic

N&Q notes and queries

n&v [medicine] nausea and vomiting

NAO National Audit Office

NAP National Association for the Paralysed

Nap. Naples; Napoleon (Bonaparte) (French emperor); Napoleonic

NAPA [USA] National Association of Performing Artists

NAPF National Association of Pension Funds

naph. [chemistry] naphtha

NAPLPS [computing] North American presentation level protocol syntax

NAPO National Association of Probation Officers; National Association of Property Owners

NAPT National Association for the Prevention of Tuberculosis

NAPV National Association of Prison Visitors

NAR [botany] net assimilation rate

nar. narrow

narc. narcotic; narcotics

NARM natural and accelerator-produced radioactive material

NAS [USA] National Academy of Sciences; National Adoption Society; National Association of Schoolmasters (became part of NAS/UWT); naval air station; Noise Abatement Society; nursing auxiliary service

NASA [USA] National Aeronautics and Space Administration

NASCAR [USA] National Association for Stock Car Auto Racing

NASD National Amalgamated Stevedores and Dockers; [USA] National Association of Securities Dealers

NASDA [Japan] National Space Development Agency

NASDAQ [USA] National Association of Securities Dealers Automated Quotations (system)

Nash. Nashville

NASL North American Soccer League

Nass. Nassau

NAS/UWT National Association of Schoolmasters/Union of Women Teachers

NASW [USA] National Association of Social Workers

NAT National Arbitration Tribunal

Nat. Natal; National; Nationalist

nat. national; nationalist; native; natural; naturalize; naturalized; nature; naturist; *natus* (Latin: born)

N At. North Atlantic

n.a.t. normal allowed time

NATCS National Air Traffic Control Service

NATE National Association for the Teaching of English

NATFHE National Association of Teachers in Further and Higher Education

nat. hist. natural history

Nativ. Nativity

natl national

NATLAS National Testing Laboratory Accreditation Scheme

NATM New Austrian Tunnelling Method

NATO North Atlantic Treaty Organization

nat. phil. natural philosophy

NATS National Air Traffic Services; [USA] Naval Air Transport Service

NatScD Doctor of Natural Science

nat. sci. natural science(s)

NATSOPA National Society of Operative Printers, Graphical and Media Personnel (formerly National Society of Operative Printers and Assistants)

N Att. naval attaché

NATTKE National Association of Theatrical, Television and Kinematographic Employees

NATTS National Association of Trade and Technical Schools

natur. naturalist

NatWest National Westminster Bank plc

NAU [international vehicle registration] Nauru

naut. nautical

NAV [finance] net asset value (of organization)

nav. naval; navigable; navigation; navigator

NAVAIR [USA] Naval Air Systems Command

Nav. E naval engineer

navig. navigable; navigation; navigator

NAVS National Anti-Vivisection Society

NAVSAT navigational satellite

NAWB National Association of Workshops for the Blind

NAWC National Association of Women's Clubs

NAWO National Alliance of Women's Organizations

NAYC Youth Clubs UK (formerly National Association of Youth Clubs)

NAYPIC National Association of Young People in Care

NAYT National Association of Youth Theatres

naz. *nazionale* (Italian: national)

Nazi *Nationalsozialisten* (German: National Socialist)

NB [vehicle registration] Manchester; narrow bore; naval base; Nebraska; [medicine] needle biopsy; [physics] neutral beam; New Brunswick; North Britain (i.e. Scotland); *nota bene* (Latin: note well)

Nb [chemical element] niobium

Nb [meteorology] nimbus

n.b. [cricket] no ball; *nota bene* (Latin: note well)

NBA [USA] National Basketball Association; [USA] National Book Award; [USA] National Boxing Association; National Building Agency; Net Book Agreement; North British Academy

NBC [USA] National Basketball Committee; National Book Council (former name of NBL); National Boys' Club; [USA] National Broadcasting Company; National Bus Company; nuclear, biological and chemical (weapons or warfare)

NBCD [computing] natural binary-coded decimal

NBD [statistics] negative binomial distribution

NbE north by east

NBER [USA] National Bureau of Economic Research

n.b.g. [informal] no bloody good

NBI National Benevolent Institution; [medicine] no bone injury

NBK National Bank of Kuwait

NBL National Book League (formerly NBC)

n.b.l. [informal] not bloody likely

NBP [chemistry] normal boiling point

NBPI National Board for Prices and Incomes (replacement for PIB)

NBR National Buildings Record; [chemistry] nitrile-butadiene rubber

nbre *noviembre* (Spanish: November)

NBRI National Building Research Institute

NBS [USA] National Bureau of Standards; Newcastle Business School

NBTS National Blood Transfusion Service

NBV [accounting] net book value (of asset)

NbW north by west

NC [vehicle registration] Manchester; National Certificate; National Congress; National Council; [education] National Curriculum; Nature Conservancy; New Caledonia; New Church; nickel–cadmium (battery); nitrocellulose; [chemistry] nitrogen compound; [meteorology] no change; no charge; normally closed; North Carolina; [US postcode] North Carolina; Northern Command; numerical control; numerically controlled; [USA] Nurse Corps

N/C new charter; nitrocellulose; no charge

NCA National Certificate of Agriculture; National Childminding Association; National Cricket Association; no copies available

NCAA [USA] National Collegiate Athletic Association; Northern Counties Athletic Association

NCACC National Civil Aviation Consultative Committee

NCAR [USA] National Center for Atmospheric Research (Colorado)

NCARB [USA] National Council of Architectural Registration Boards

NCB National Children's Bureau; National Coal Board (replaced by BCC); Nippon Credit Bank; [insurance] no-claim(s) bonus

NCBA National Cattle Breeders' Association

NCBAE [insurance] no-claim(s) bonus as earned

NCBW nuclear, chemical and biological warfare

NCC [USA] National Climatic Center; National Computing Centre; National Consumer Council; [USA] National Council of Churches; [education] National Curriculum Council; Nature Conservancy Council (replaced by EN)

NCCA National Carpet Cleaners Association

NCCI National Committee for Commonwealth Immigrants

NCCJ National Conference of Christians and Jews

NCCL National Council for Civil Liberties (former name of Liberty)

NCCS national command and control system; National Council for Civic Responsibility

NCCVD National Council for Combating Venereal Diseases

NCD naval construction department

n.c.d. [informal] no can do

NCDAD National Council for Diplomas in Art and Design

NCDL National Canine Defence League

NCERT National Council for Educational Research and Training

NCET National Council for Educational Technology

NCFT National College of Food Technology

NCH National Children's Home; National Clearing House

n.Chr. *nach Christus* (German: after Christ, AD)

NCI [USA] National Cancer Institute; [finance] New Community Instrument

n.c.i. no common interest

NCIC National Cancer Institute of Canada; [USA] National Crime Information Center

NCIS National Criminal Intelligence Service

NCL National Carriers Limited; National Central Library; National Chemical Laboratory; National Church League

NCLC National Council of Labour Colleges

NCN National Council of Nurses

NCNA New China News Agency

NCNC National Convention of Nigeria and the Cameroons; National Convention of Nigerian Citizens (political party)

NCO noncommissioned officer

NCP National Car Parks (Limited); [Australia] National Country Party (former name of National Party); national cycling proficiency; [computing] network control protocol

n.c.p. [engineering] normal circular pitch

NCPL National Centre for Programmed Learning

NCPS noncontributory pension scheme

NCPT [USA] National Congress of Parents and Teachers

NCR National Cash Register (Company Limited); no carbon required (of paper)

NCRE Naval Construction Research Establishment

NCRL National Chemical Research Laboratory

NCRP [USA] National Council on Radiation Protection and Measurement

NCS [USA] National Communications System

NCSC [Australia] National Companies and Securities Commission; [USA] National Computer Security Center

NCSE National Council for Special Education

NCSS National Council of Social Service

NCT National Chamber of Trade; National Childbirth Trust; [medicine] neutron-capture therapy; [medicine] neutron compute(rize)d tomography

NCTA [USA] National Community Television Association

NCTE [USA] National Council of Teachers of English

NCU National Communications Union (became part of CWU); National Cyclists' Union

n.c.u.p. no commission until paid

NCV no commercial value

NCVCCO National Council of Voluntary Child Care Organizations

NCVO National Council of Voluntary Organizations

NCVQ National Council for Vocational Qualifications

NCW National Council of Women (of Great Britain)

ND [vehicle registration] Manchester; national debt; National Diploma; Naturopathic Diploma; [photography] neutral density; no date; nondelivery; North Dakota; [US postcode] North Dakota

N-D *Notre-Dame* (French: Our Lady) (in church names)

Nd [chemical element] neodymium

n.d. [photography] neutral density; next day (delivery); no date; no decision; no deed; no delay; no demand; nondelivery; not dated; not deeded; [banking] not drawn; [informal] nothing doing

NDA National Dairymen's Association; National Diploma in Agriculture; [engineering] nondestructive analysis; [engineering] nondestructive assay

NDAC [USA] National Defense Advisory Commission

N Dak. North Dakota

NDB [aeronautics] nondirectional beacon

NDC National Dairy Council; NATO Defence College; [computing] normalized device coordinates

NDCS National Deaf Children's Society

NDD National Diploma in Dairying; National Diploma in Design

NDE near-death experience; [engineering] nondestructive evaluation; [engineering] nondestructive examination

NDF National Diploma in Forestry

NDH National Diploma in Horticulture

NDIC National Defence Industries Council

Ndl. Netherlands

NDN National District Nurse Certificate

NDP National Democratic Party; [economics] net domestic product; [Canada] New Democratic Party

n.d.p. [engineering] normal diametric pitch

NDPB nondepartmental public body

NDPS National Data Processing Service

NDR [electronics] negative differential resistance; [electronics] negative differential resistivity; nondomestic rates; *Norddeutscher Rundfunk* (German: North German Radio)

NDRC National Defence Research Committee

NDSB Narcotic Drugs Supervisory Body (of UN)

NDT [engineering] nondestructive testing; [commerce] nondistributive trade

NDTA [USA] National Defense Transportation Association

NDU Nursing Development Unit

NDV [microbiology] Newcastle disease virus

NE [vehicle registration] Manchester; national emergency; National Executive; naval engineer; [US postcode] Nebraska; [fishing port] Newcastle upon Tyne; [UK postcode] Newcastle upon Tyne; new edition; New England; news editor; [banking] no effects (= no funds); northeast; northeastern; nuclear energy; nuclear explosion; nuclear explosive

Ne [chemical element] neon

Ne. Nepal; Nepalese; Nepali; Netherlands

n/e new edition; [banking] no effects (= no funds); [accounting] not entered

.ne Niger (in Internet address)

n.e. not essential; not exceeding

NEA [USA] National Education Association; [USA] National Endowment for the Arts; North East Airlines

NEAC New English Art Club

NEACP [USA] National Emergency Airborne Command Post (pronounced 'kneecap')

NEAF Near East Air Force

NEAFC North-East Atlantic Fisheries Commission

Neapol. Neapolitan

NEARELF Near East Land Forces

NEB [USA] National Electricity Board; [USA] National Energy Board; National Enterprise Board; New English Bible

Neb. Nebraska

NEBOSH National Examination Board in Occupational Safety and Health

Nebr. Nebraska

NEBSS National Examinations Board for Supervisory Studies

NEC [USA] National Economic Council; [USA] National Electric Code; National Electronics Council; National Equestrian Centre; National Executive Committee; National Exhibition Centre (Birmingham); National Extension College (Cambridge); [medicine] necrotizing enterocolitis; [Japan] Nippon Electric Company

nec. necessary

n.e.c. not elsewhere classified

NECCTA National Educational Closed Circuit Television Association

NECInst North East Coast Institution of Engineers and Shipbuilders

necr. necrosis

necrol. necrology

NED [medicine] no evidence of disease

NEDC National Economic Development Council (also called Neddy); North East Development Council

NEDO National Economic Development Office

NEEB North Eastern Electricity Board

NEF National Energy Foundation; [acoustics] noise exposure forecast (value)

neg. negation; negative; negatively; negligence; negotiable (in job advertisement); negotiate; negotiation

NEH National Endowment for the Humanities

Neh. [Bible] Nehemiah

NEI Netherlands East Indies

n.e.i. *non est inventa* (Latin: (she) has not been found); *non est inventum* (Latin: (it) has not been found); *non est inventus* (Latin: (he) has not been found); not elsewhere indicated

NEL [USA] National Electronics Laboratory; National Engineering Laboratory

nem. con. *nemine contradicente* (Latin: nobody opposing, unanimously)

nem. dis. *nemine dissentiente* (Latin: nobody opposing, unanimously)

NE/n.d. [bibliography] new edition, no date given

N Eng. New England; northern England

neol. neologism

NEP [international vehicle registration] Nepal; New Economic Policy (in USSR in 1920s)

Nep. Nepal; Nepalese; Nepali; Neptune

n.e.p. new edition pending

NEPA [USA] National Environmental Policy Act

NEPP [USA] National Energy Policy Plan

NEQ [computing] nonequivalence (as in **NEQ gate**)

NERA [USA] National Emergency Relief Administration

NERC National English Rabbit Club; Natural Environment Research Council

NERIS National Educational Resources Information Service

NES National Eczema Society

n.e.s. not elsewhere specified

NESC [USA] National Electric Safety Code

NESTOR [nuclear technology] neutron source thermal reactor

NET [USA] National Educational Television; [nuclear technology] Next European Torus

.net network (in Internet address)

n.e.t. not earlier than

Neth. Netherlands

Neth. Ant. Netherlands Antilles

n. et m. [medicine] *nocte et mane* (Latin: night and morning) (in prescriptions)

neurol. neurological; neurology

neut. [grammar] neuter; neutral; neutralize; neutralized; neutralizer

Nev. Nevada

NEW [US economics] net economic welfare

Newf. Newfoundland

New M New Mexico

news. newsagency; newsagent

New Test. New Testament

NF [vehicle registration] Manchester; *Nationale Front* (German: National Front); [US pharmacology] National Formulary; National Front; [medicine] neurofibromatosis; New Forest; Newfoundland; New French; [banking] no funds; [telecommunications] noise factor; [telecommunications] noise figure; Norman French (language)

N/F [banking] no funds

n.f. [engineering] near face; [informal] no fool; [grammar] noun feminine

NFA National Farmers' Association; National Federation of Anglers; [USA] National Food Administration; [USA] National Futures Association; no fixed abode; no fixed address

n.f.a. no further action

NFAL National Foundation of Arts and Letters

NFB National Film Board (of Canada)

NFBPM National Federation of Builders' and Plumbers' Merchants

NFBTE National Federation of Building Trades Employers

NFC [USA] National Football Conference; National Freight Consortium

n.f.c. not favourably considered

NFCO National Federation of Community Organizations

NFD Newfoundland; no fixed date

Nfd Newfoundland

NFDM nonfat dry milk

NFER National Foundation for Educational Research

NFFC National Film Finance Corporation

NFFE [USA] National Federation of Federal Employees

NFFO non-fossil-fuel obligation (for electricity companies)

NFFPT National Federation of Fruit and Potato Trades

NFHA National Federation of Housing Associations

NFI National Federation of Ironmongers

NFL [USA, Canada] National Football League

Nfld Newfoundland

n.f.m. nearest full moon; next full moon

NFMPS National Federation of Master Printers in Scotland

NFMS National Federation of Music Societies

NFO National Freight Organization

NFPW National Federation of Professional Workers

n.f.r. no further requirements

NFRC National Federation of Roofing Contractors

NFRN National Federation of Retail Newsagents

NFS National Fire Service; National Flying Services; National Forest Service; [computing] network filing service; [computing] network filing system; not for sale

NFSE National Federation of the Self-Employed

NFT National Film Theatre

NFTS National Film and Television School

NFU National Farmers' Union

NFUW National Farmers' Union of Wales

NFWI National Federation of Women's Institutes

NFYFC National Federation of Young Farmers' Clubs

NG [railways] narrow gauge; National Gallery; National Government; [USA] National Guard; National Guardsman; New Granada; [medicine] new growth; New Guinea; nitroglycerine; [Freemasonry] Noble Grand; [Freemasonry] Noble Guard; no go; no good; North Germanic; [vehicle registration] Norwich; [UK postcode] Nottingham

Ng [geology] Neogene

Ng. Norwegian

.ng Nigeria (in Internet address)

n.g. no good; not given

NGA National Glider Association; National Graphical Association (became part of GPMU)

NGC [USA] National Grid Company; [astronomy] New General Catalogue

NGF [biochemistry] nerve growth factor

NGk New Greek

NGL [chemistry] natural-gas liquid(s)

NGNP [economics] nominal gross national product

NGO [USA] National Gas Outlet; [India] nongazetted officer; nongovernmental organization

NGR [international vehicle registration] Nigeria

NGr New Greek

NGRC National Greyhound Racing Club

NGRS Narrow Gauge Railway Society

NGS National Galleries of Scotland; National Geographic Society; nuclear generating station

NGT National Guild of Telephonists

ngt *négociant* (French: merchant)

NGTE National Gas Turbine Establishment

NGU [medicine] nongonococcal urethritis

NGV natural-gas vehicle

NH National Hunt; naval hospital; New Hampshire; [US postcode] New Hampshire; [vehicle registration] Northampton; northern hemisphere; Northumberland Hussars

NHA National Horse Association of Great Britain; [USA] National Housing Agency

NHBC National Housebuilding Council

NHBRC National House-Builders' Registration Certificate

NHC National Hunt Committee

NHD Doctor of Natural History

NHeb New Hebrew

N Heb. New Hebrides

NHF National Hairdressers' Federation

NHG New High German

NHI National Health Insurance

NHK *Nippon Hoso Kyokai* (Japanese: Japanese Broadcasting Corporation)

NHL [USA] National Hockey League; [medicine] non-Hodgkin lymphoma

NHLBI [USA] National Heart, Lung and Blood Institute

NHMF National Heritage Memorial Fund

NHMRCA National Health and Medical Research Council of Australia

NHO Navy Hydrographic Office

nhp nominal horsepower

NHR National Housewives Register; National Hunt Rules

NHS National Health Service

NHSTA National Health Service Training Authority

NHTPC National Housing and Town Planning Council

NI National Insurance; Native Infantry; naval instructor; Naval Intelligence; new impression; News International; [computing] noninterfaced; Northern Ireland; North Island (New Zealand)

Ni [chemical element] nickel

.ni Nicaragua (in Internet address)

NIA [USA] National Intelligence Authority; Newspaper Institute of America

NIAAA Northern Ireland Amateur Athletic Association

NIAB National Institute of Agricultural Botany

NIACRO Northern Ireland Association for the Care and Resettlement of Offenders

NIAE National Institute of Agricultural Engineering

NIAID National Institute of Allergy and Infectious Diseases

Nibmar no independence before majority African rule

NIBSC National Institute for Biological Standards Control

NIC National Incomes Commission; National Insurance contribution(s); network interface card; newly industrialized country; [international vehicle registration] Nicaragua

Nic. Nicaragua; Nicaraguan

n.i.c. not in contract

Nica. Nicaragua; Nicaraguan

NiCad nickel–cadmium (battery)

NICAM [electronics] near-instantaneous companded audio multiplex (for coding sound signals digitally)

Nicar. Nicaragua; Nicaraguan

NiCd nickel–cadmium (battery)

NICEC National Institute for Careers Education and Counselling

NICEIC National Inspection Council for Electrical Installation Contracting

NICF Northern Ireland Cycling Federation

NICG Nationalized Industries Chairmen's Group

NICRA Northern Ireland Civil Rights Association

NICS Northern Ireland Civil Service

NICU [medicine] neonatal intensive care unit

NID National Institute for the Deaf; [India] National Institute of Design; Naval Intelligence Division; Northern Ireland District

NIDC Northern Ireland Development Council

NIDD [medicine] non-insulin-dependent diabetes

NIES Northern Ireland Electricity Service

NIESR National Institute of Economic and Social Research

NIF [finance] note issuance facility

NIFES National Industrial Fuel Efficiency Service

NIFO next in, first out

NIFTP [computing] network independent file transfer protocol

Nig. Nigeria; Nigerian

NIH [USA] National Institutes of Health; North Irish Horse (former regiment)

NIHCA Northern Ireland Hotels and Caterers Association

NIHE [Ireland] National Institute for Higher Education

NII Nuclear Installations Inspectorate

NIIP National Institute of Industrial Psychology

NILP Northern Ireland Labour Party

NIMA National Infomercial Marketing Association

nimby [informal] not in my back yard

NIMH National Institute of Medical Herbalists; [USA] National Institute of Mental Health

n. imp. new impression

NIMR National Institute for Medical Research

NIN national information network

NINO no inspector, no operator (system)

NIO National Institute of Oceanography

NIOSH [USA] National Institute for Occupational Safety and Health

Nip. Nippon; Nipponese

nip. [engineering] nipple

ni. pri. *nisi prius* (Latin: unless previously)

NIR non-ionizing radiation; Northern Ireland Railways

N Ir. Northern Ireland

NIRA [USA] National Industrial Recovery Act

NIRC National Industrial Relations Court

N Ire. Northern Ireland

NIREX Nuclear Industry Radioactive Waste Executive

NIRS [USA] National Institute of Radiological Sciences

NIS [currency] (new) Israeli shekel

n.i.s. not in stock

NISA National Independent Supermarkets' Association

NISC National Industrial Safety Committee

NIST [USA] National Institute of Standards and Technology

NISTRO Northern Ireland Science and Technology Regional Organization

NISW National Institute for Social Workers

NIT national intelligence test; negative income tax

NITB Northern Ireland Tourist Board

NIV New International Version (of Bible)

NIWAAA Northern Ireland Women's Amateur Athletic Association

NJ [vehicle registration] Brighton; New Jersey; [US postcode] New Jersey; [informal] nose job

n.J *nächsten Jahres* (German: next year)

NJA National Jewellers' Association

NJAC National Joint Advisory Council

NJC National Joint Council

NJCC National Joint Consultative Committee

NJNC National Joint Negotiating Committee

NK [vehicle registration] Luton; [immunology] natural killer (as in **NK-cell**); not known

NKC [immunology] natural killer cell

NKGB *Narodny Komissariat Gosudarstvennoi Bezopasnosti* (Russian: People's

Commissariat of State Security) (former Soviet secret police)

NKr [currency] Norwegian krone

NKVD *Narodny Komissariat Vnutrennikh Del* (Russian: People's Commissariat of Internal Affairs) (former Soviet police organization)

NL National Labour; [USA] National League (baseball); National Liberal; Navy League; Navy List; [international vehicle registration] Netherlands; [vehicle registration] Newcastle upon Tyne; New Latin; no liability (after Australian company name); north latitude

Nl National

.nl Netherlands (in Internet address)

n.l. [printing] new line; *non licet* (Latin: it is not permitted); *non liquet* (Latin: it is not clear)

N Lat. north latitude

NLB National Library for the Blind

NLBD National League for the Blind and Disabled

NLC National Liberal Club; National Library of Canada

NLCB National Lottery Charities Board

NLCS North London Collegiate School

NLD National League for Democracy (in Myanmar)

NLF National Labour Federation; National Liberal Federation; National Liberation Front; National Loans Fund

n.l.f. nearest landing field

NLI National Library of Ireland

NLLST National Lending Library for Science and Technology

NLM National Library of Medicine

NLMC National Labour Management Council

NLN National League for Nursing

n.l.n. no longer needed

NLO naval liaison officer

NLP [computing] natural language processing; Natural Law Party; [USA] neighborhood loan program; [computing] neurolinguistic programming

NLQ [computing] near letter quality (of printing)

NLR [astronomy] narrow-line region

NLRB [USA] National Labor Relations Board

NLS National Library of Scotland

n.l.t. not later than; not less than

NLW National Library of Wales

nly northerly

NLYL National League of Young Liberals

NM [vehicle registration] Luton; national marketing; nautical mile; New Mexico; [US postcode] New Mexico; nuclear medicine

N/m [commerce] no mark(s) (on bill of lading)

Nm. *Nachmittag* (German: afternoon); [advertising] next matter

n.M *nächsten Monats* (German: next month)

nm nanometre

n/m not married (in personal advertisement)

nm. nutmeg

n.m. nautical mile; new moon; [medicine] *nocte et mane* (Latin: night and morning) (in prescriptions); nonmetallic; [grammar] noun masculine

NMA National Management Association; National Medical Association

NMB National Maritime Board

NMC National Marketing Council; [USA] National Meteorological Center

n.m.c. no more credit

N Mex. New Mexico

NMFS [USA] National Marine Fisheries Service

NMHA National Mental Health Association

NMHF [USA] National Mental Health Foundation

NMI [computing] non-maskable interrupt

n mile nautical mile

NMP [economics] net material product

NMR nuclear magnetic resonance

NMRI [medicine] nuclear magnetic resonance imaging

NMS [USA] National Market System; National Museums of Scotland; [stock exchange] Normal Market Size

NMSQT [USA] National Merit Scholarship Qualifying Test

NMSS [USA] National Multiple Sclerosis Society

n.m.t. not more than

NMTF National Market Traders' Federation

NMU National Maritime Union

NMW national minimum wage

NN [fishing port] Newhaven; no name;

N/N [UK postcode] Northampton; [vehicle registration] Nottingham

N/N [banking] not to be noted

nn. names; notes; nouns

NND [medicine] neonatal death

NNE north-northeast

NNEB National Nursery Examination Board

NNF Northern Nurses' Federation

NNHT Nuffield Nursing Homes Trust

NNI noise and number index (for aircraft noise); noise nuisance index

NNMA Nigerian National Merit Award

NNOM Nigerian National Order of Merit

NNP [economics] net national product

NNR national nature reserve

NNSA [USA] National Nuclear Safety Administration

NNT nuclear nonproliferation treaty

NNTP [computing] net(work) news transfer protocol

NNTR no need to return

NNW north-northwest

NO [vehicle registration] Chelmsford; natural order; naval officer; naval operations; navigation officer; New Orleans; Nuffield Observatory (Jodrell Bank, Cheshire); nursing officer

N/O [banking] no orders

No [chemical element] nobelium

No. north; northern; Norway; Norwegian; number (from Latin *numero*, ablative of *numerus*, or French *numéro*)

no. north; northern; number (from Latin *numero*, ablative of *numerus*, or French *numéro*)

.no Norway (in Internet address)

n.o. normally open; [cricket] not out

NOA National Opera Association; National Orchestral Association; not otherwise authorized

NOAA [USA] National Oceanic and Atmospheric Administration

NOAO [USA] National Optical Astronomy Observatories

NOB naval operating base

nob. *nobis* (Latin: for our part, on our part); noble

NOC National Olympic Committee; not otherwise classified

n.o.c. notation of content; not otherwise classified

NOCD [informal] not our class, dear

No. Co. northern counties

noct. [medicine] *nocte* (Latin: at night) (in prescriptions)

NOD Naval Ordnance Department; night observation device

NODA National Operatic and Dramatic Association

NODC non-OPEC developing country

NOE nuclear Overhauser effect

n.o.e. notice of exception; not otherwise enumerated

NOERC North of England Regional Consortium

n.o.h.p. not otherwise herein provided

n.o.i.b.n. not otherwise indexed by name

NOIC Naval Officer in Charge

NOISE [USA] National Organization to Insure a Sound-controlled Environment

n.o.k. next of kin

NOL [USA] Naval Ordnance Laboratory

nol. con. [law] *nolo contendere* (Latin: I do not wish to contend)

nol. pros. [law] *nolle prosequi* (Latin: to be unwilling to prosecute)

nom. nomenclature; nominal; nominated; nomination; [grammar] nominative

nom. cap. [finance] nominal capital

nomen. nomenclature

nomin. nominal; nominated; nomination; [grammar] nominative

nom. nov. *nomen novum* (Latin: new name)

NOMSS [USA] National Operational Meteorological Satellite System

noncom. noncommissioned

Noncon. Nonconformist

non cul. *non culpabilis* (Latin: not guilty)

non obst. *non obstante* (Latin: notwithstanding)

non pros. [law] *non prosequitur* (Latin: he does not prosecute)

non rep. [medicine] *non repetatur* (Latin: do not repeat) (in prescriptions)

non seq. *non sequitur* (Latin: it does not follow (logically))

nonstand. nonstandard

nonstd nonstandard

non-U not upper-class

NOP National Opinion Poll; not our publication

n.o.p. not otherwise provided (for)

NOPWC National Old People's Welfare Council

NOR [biology] nucleolar-organizing region

Nor [astronomy] Norma

Nor. Norman; Normandy; north; northern; Norway; Norwegian; Norwich

nor. normal; north; northern

NORAD North American Air Defense Command

Norf. Norfolk

NORM not operationally ready maintenance

Norm. Norman; Normandy

norm. normal; normalized

NORML [USA] National Organization for the Reform of Marijuana Laws

NORS not operationally ready supply (or supplies)

Northants Northamptonshire

Northd Northumberland

Northumb. Northumberland

Norvic. *Norvicensis* (Latin: (Bishop) of Norwich)

Norw. Norway; Norwegian

Norweb North Western Electricity Board

NORWICH knickers off ready when I come home (on envelope of love letter)

NOS *Nederlandse Omroep Stichting* (Dutch: Netherlands Broadcasting Corporation); [computing] network operating system

Nos. numbers

nos. numbers

n.o.s. not otherwise specified

NOSC [US navy] Naval Ordnance Systems Command

Not. Notary

not. notice

NOTAR no-tail rotor (of aircraft)

NOTB National Ophthalmic Treatment Board

Nottm Nottingham

Notts Nottinghamshire

notwg notwithstanding

nouv. *nouveau* (French: new); *nouvelle* (French: new)

Nov. November; *November* (German: November)

nov. novel; novelist; *novembre* (Italian: November); *novembre* (French: November); novice; novitiate

NOW [USA] National Organization for Women; [US banking] negotiable order of withdrawal; New Opportunities for Women

NoW *News of the World*

NOX nitrogen oxide(s)

n.o.y. not out yet

noz. nozzle

NP Nationalist Party; national park; National Party; National Power plc; net profit; neuropsychiatric; neuropsychiatry; [UK postcode] Newport; New Providence (Bahamas); nitro proof (in firearms); Nobel Prize; [chemistry] nonpolar; Notary Public; [grammar] noun phrase; nurse practitioner; [vehicle registration] Worcester

Np napalm; neap (tide); neper (unit used in telecommunications); [chemical element] neptunium

np neap (tide); new pence (used in 1970s, after decimalization)

n/p net proceeds

.np Nepal (in Internet address)

n.p. near point; [law] net personalty; net proceeds; [printing] new paragraph; new pattern; nickel-plated; *nisi prius* (Latin: unless previously); [medicine] *nomen proprium* (Latin: its own name) (in prescriptions); nonparticipating; [bibliography] no place of publication (given); no printer; no publisher; normal pitch; not paginated; nursing procedure

NPA National Park Authority; National Pigeon Association; New People's Army (in Philippines); Newspaper Publishers' Association

NPACI National Production Advisory Council on Industry

NPBA National Pig Breeders' Association

NPC [China] National People's Congress; [USA] National Petroleum Council; National Ports Council; [USA] National Press Club; no-player character (in computer game); [computing] normalized projection coordinates; Northern People's Congress (in Nigeria)

NPCS Narrowband Personal Communications Service

NPD *Nationaldemokratische Partei Deutschlands* (German: National Democratic Party of Germany); [marketing] new product development; [astronomy] north polar distance

NPF National Progressive Front (in Syria); Newspaper Press Fund

n.p.f. not provided for

NPFA National Playing Fields Association

NPG National Portrait Gallery; Nuclear Planning Group (in NATO)

NPGH [education] National Professional Qualification for Headship

NPH [chemistry] normal paraffin hydrocarbon

NPh nuclear physics

NPHT Nuffield Provincial Hospitals Trust

NPK nitrogen, phosphorus and potassium (in fertilizers, from chemical symbols)

NPL National Physical Laboratory (Teddington, Middlesex)

n. pl. [grammar] noun plural

NPN [medicine] nonprotein nitrogen

n.p.n.a. [commerce] no protest for non-acceptance

NPO New Philharmonia Orchestra

n.p.o. [medicine] *ne per oris* (Latin: not by mouth)

n.p. or d. no place or date

NPP nuclear power plant

n.p.p. no passed proof

NPR [USA] National Public Radio; noise power ratio

NPRA National Petroleum Refiners Association

NPS National Portrait Society; nuclear power source; nuclear power station

n.p.s. nominal pipe size; no prior service

NPT (Nuclear) Non-Proliferation Treaty

NPTA National Pest Technicians' Association

NPU National Pharmaceutical Union; National Postal Union; [medicine] not passed urine

n.p.u. *ne plus ultra* (Latin: not more beyond) (i.e. extremity, culmination or perfection)

NPV [finance] net present value; [finance] no par value (of shares)

NPW nuclear-powered warship

n.q.a. [finance] net quick assets

NQOC [informal] not quite our class

NR [vehicle registration] Leicester; National Register; natural rubber; naval rating; Navy Regulations; [insurance] no risk; North Riding (former division of Yorkshire); [UK postcode] Norwich

Nr *Nummer* (German: number)

nr near; number

.nr Nauru (in Internet address)

n.r. net register; [insurance] no risk

NRA National Reclamation Association; [USA] National Recovery Administration; National Recreation Area; [USA] National Rehabilitation Association; National Rifle Association; National Rivers Authority; nuclear-reaction analysis

n.r.a. never refuse anything

NRAA National Rifle Association of America

NRAO [USA] National Radio Astronomy Observatory

NRC National Redemption Council (in Ghana); National Research Council; [USA] Nuclear Regulatory Commission

NRCA National Retail Credit Association

NRCC National Research Council of Canada

NRD National Registered Designer; National Register of Designers

NRDC National Research Development Corporation; [USA] Natural Resources Defense Council

NRDS [medicine] neonatal respiratory distress syndrome

NREM [physiology] non-rapid eye movement (as in **NREM sleep**)

NREN [computing] National Research and Education Network

NRF National Relief Fund

NRFL Northern Rugby Football League

NRI National Resources Institute

NRK *Norsk Rikskringkasting* (Norwegian broadcasting company)

NRL National Reference Library; [USA] Naval Research Laboratory

NRM National Resistance Movement (in Uganda)

NRMA [Australia] National Roads and Motorists Association

nrml normal

NROR [finance] normal rate of return

NROTC Naval Reserve Officer Training Corps

NRP nuclear reprocessing plant

NRPB National Radiological Protection Board

NRR net reproduction rate (of populations); Northern Rhodesia Regiment

NRS National Readership Survey; National Rose Society

NRs [currency] Nepalese rupee

n.r.t. net registered tonnage

NRTA [USA] National Retired Teachers Association

NRV [finance] net realizable value; non-return valve

Nrw. Norwegian

NRZ [computing] nonreturn to zero

NS [vehicle registration] Glasgow; *Nachschrift* (German: postscript, PS); [computing] Nassi–Schneidermann (as in **NS chart**); National Service; National Society; natural science; naval service; [fishing port] New Ross; new series; Newspaper Society; New Style (in dates); non-smoker (in personal advertisement); Nova Scotia; nuclear science; nuclear ship; Numismatic Society

N/S nonsmoker (in personal advertisement)

N-S *Notre-Seigneur* (French: Our Lord)

Ns [meteorology] nimbostratus

ns nanosecond

n/s news-sheet; nonsmoker (in personal advertisement); [banking] not sufficient (funds)

n.s. near side; new series; nickel steel; not satisfactory; not significant; not specified; [banking] not sufficient (funds)

NSA [USA] National Security Agency; [USA] National Shipping Authority; National Skating Association; [USA] National Standards Association; [USA] National Student Association; New Society of Artists; non-sterling area

NSACS National Society for the Abolition of Cruel Sports

NSAE National Society of Art Education

NSAFA National Service Armed Forces Act

NSAID [pharmacology] nonsteroidal anti-inflammatory drug

NSB National Savings Bank; [USA] National Science Board

NSBA National Sheep Breeders' Association

NSC National Safety Council; National Savings Certificate(s); [USA] National Security Council; National Sporting Club; National Steel Corporation

NSCA National Society for Clean Air

NSCC [USA] National Securities Clearing Corporation

NSCR National Society for Cancer Relief

NSD naval supply depot; nominal standard dose; normal spontaneous delivery

NSDAP *Nationalsozialistische Deutsche Arbeiterpartei* (German: National Socialist German Workers' Party, Nazis)

NSERC [USA] Natural Sciences and Engineering Research Council

NSF [USA] National Science Foundation; [banking] not sufficient funds; Nuclear Structure Facility (Daresbury, Cheshire)

n.s.f. [banking] not sufficient funds

NSFGB National Ski Federation of Great Britain

NSG [education] nonstatutory guidelines (relating to National Curriculum)

NSGT non-self-governing territory (or territories)

NSHEB North of Scotland Hydroelectric Board

NSI [USA] National Security Information

n. sing. [grammar] noun singular

NSL National Sporting League

NSM new smoking material; non-stipendiary minister

NSO National Solar Observatory; Naval Staff Officer

NSP nonsmoker preferred (in personal advertisement)

NSPCC National Society for the Prevention of Cruelty to Children

NSPE [USA] National Society of Professional Engineers

n.s.p.f. not specifically (or specially) provided for

NSRA National Small-Bore Rifle Association

NSS national sample survey; National Secular Society; New Shakespeare Society; [medicine] normal saline solution

NSSA National School Sailing Association

NSSU National Sunday School Union

NST Newfoundland Standard Time

NSTC Nova Scotia Technical College

NSTP Nuffield Science Teaching Project

NSU [medicine] nonspecific urethritis

NSW New South Wales

NSY New Scotland Yard

NT [Ireland] National Teacher; National Theatre; National Trust; neap tide(s);

[fishing port] Newport; new technology; New Testament; New Translation; Northern Territory (Australia); not titled; [card games] no-trump(s) (in bridge); Nurse Teacher; [vehicle registration] Shrewsbury

n.t. net terms; net tonnage; normal temperature

NTA [USA] National Technical Association; National Training Award; net tangible assets

NTB [economics] non-tariff barrier

NTC [physics] negative temperature coefficient

NTD [informal] not top drawer

NTDA National Trade Development Association

NTEU [USA] National Treasury Employees Union

NTFS new technology filing system

ntfy notify

NTG North Thames Gas

NTGB North Thames Gas Board

NTGk New Testament Greek

Nth North

Nthb. Northumberland

nthn northern

NTI noise transmission impairment

NTIA [USA] National Telecommunications and Information Administration

NTL [electronics] non-threshold logic

n.t.l. no time lost

NTM [economics] non-tariff measure

NTO naval transport officer

n.t.o. not taken out

NTP normal temperature and pressure

n.t.p. normal temperature and pressure; no title page

NTS National Trust for Scotland; Nevada Test Site; not to scale

NTSB [USA] National Transportation Safety Board

NTSC [USA] National Television System Committee (US broadcasting system)

NTT New Technology Telescope

NTUC National Trades Union Congress (in Singapore)

NTV Nippon Television

NTVLRO National Television Licence Records Office

NTW no time wasters (in personal advertisement)

nt wt net weight

NU name unknown; National Union; *Nations Unies* (French: United Nations, UN); natural uranium; Northern Union; [vehicle registration] Nottingham; number unobtainable

Nu [currency] ngultrum (used in Bhutan)

n.u. name unknown; number unobtainable

NUAAW National Union of Agricultural and Allied Workers

NUBE National Union of Bank Employees

nuc. nuclear

nucl. nuclear

NUCPS National Union of Civil and Public Servants (became part of PTC)

NUCUA National Union of Conservative and Unionist Associations

nud. nudism; nudist

NUDAGO National Union of Domestic Appliances and General Operatives

NUDETS nuclear detection system

NUI National University of Ireland

NUIW National Union of Insurance Workers

NUJ National Union of Journalists

NUJMB Northern Universities Joint Matriculation Board

NUKFAT National Union of Knitwear, Footwear and Apparel Trades

NUL [USA] National Urban League

NULMW National Union of Lock and Metal Workers

NUM National Union of Mineworkers; New Ulster Movement

Num. [Bible] Numbers

num. number; numeral(s); numerical; numerological; numerologist; numerology; numerous

NUMAST National Union of Marine, Aviation and Shipping Transport Officers

Numb. [Bible] Numbers

numis. numismatic; numismatics; numismatist

numism. numismatic; numismatics; numismatist

NUOS Naval Underwater Ordnance Station

NUPE National Union of Public Employees (became part of Unison)

NUR National Union of Railwaymen (became part of RMT)

NURBS [computing] nonuniform rational B-splines

NUS National Union of Seamen (became part of RMT); National Union of Students

NUT National Union of Teachers

N-u-T Newcastle-upon-Tyne

NUTG National Union of Townswomen's Guilds

NUTN National Union of Trained Nurses

nutr. nutrition

NUU New University of Ulster

NV [commerce] *Naamloze Vennootschap* (Dutch: public limited company, plc); needle valve; [US postcode] Nevada; New Version; nonvintage (wine); [finance] nonvoting (shares); [shipping] *Norske Veritas* (Norwegian shipping classification society); [vehicle registration] Northampton

N/V nonvintage (wine); [banking] no value

n.v. nonvoting

NVALA National Viewers' and Listeners' Association

NVB National Volunteer Brigade

NVC nonverbal communication

n.v.d. no value declared

NVG [military] night-vision goggles

NVGA [USA] National Vocational Guidance Association

NVI nonvalue indicator (postage stamp)

NVM Nativity of the Virgin Mary; [chemistry] nonvolatile matter

NVQ National Vocational Qualification

NVRAM [computing] nonvolatile random-access memory

NVRS National Vegetable Research Station

NW [vehicle registration] Leeds; net worth; North Wales; northwest; northwestern; [UK postcode] northwest London

n.w. net weight; no wind

NWC National War College

NWEB North Western Electricity Board

Nwfld Newfoundland

NWFP North-West Frontier Province (Pakistan)

NWG national wire gauge

NWGA National Wool Growers' Association

NWI Netherlands West Indies (former name of Netherlands Antilles)

NWIDA North West Industrial Development Association

NWS [USA] National Weather Service; normal water surface

NWT Northwest Territories (Canada)

nwt nonwatertight

n. wt net weight

NWTV North West Television

NX [vehicle registration] Dudley

NY [vehicle registration] Cardiff; new year; New York; [US postcode] New York

NYA [USA] National Youth Administration

NYC New York City

NYCSCE New York Coffee, Sugar and Cocoa Exchange

NYD [medicine] not yet diagnosed

NYFE New York Futures Exchange

nyl. nylon

NYMEX New York Mercantile Exchange

NYMT National Youth Music Theatre

NYO National Youth Orchestra

NYOS National Youth Orchestra of Scotland

NYP not yet published

NYPD New York Police Department

NYR not yet returned

NYS New York State

NYSE New York Stock Exchange

NYT National Youth Theatre; *New York Times*

NYU New York University

NZ [vehicle registration] Londonderry; neutral(ity) zone; New Zealand; [international vehicle registration] New Zealand

.nz New Zealand (in Internet address)

NZBC New Zealand Broadcasting Corporation

NZDSIR New Zealand Department of Scientific and Industrial Research

N Zeal. New Zealand

NZEF New Zealand Employers' Federation; New Zealand Expeditionary Force (in both world wars)

NZEFIP New Zealand Expeditionary Force in the Pacific (in World War II)

NZEI New Zealand Educational Institute

NZFL New Zealand Federation of Labour

NZIA New Zealand Institute of Architects

NZLR New Zealand Law Reports

NZMA New Zealand Medical Association

NZPA New Zealand Press Association

NZRFU New Zealand Rugby Football Union

NZRN New Zealand Registered Nurse

O

O [medicine] blood group; observe; observer; [obstetrics] occiput; occupation; Ocean; [pharmacology] *octarius* (Latin: pint); [printing] octavo; October; [medicine] *oculus* (Latin: eye); Oddfellows; *oeste* (Portuguese or Spanish: west); office; officer; Ohio; old; operation; [genetics] operator; [slang] opium; orange; [computing, mathematics] order; Order (of monks, knights, etc.); ordinary; [geology] Ordovician; Orient; *Osten* (German: east); [music] *ottava* (Italian: octave); *ouest* (French: west); [cricket] over; *ovest* (Italian: west); owner; [chemical element] oxygen

o [computing, mathematics] order; [meteorology] overcast

o' of

o. occasional; [printing] octavo; off; old; only; *optimus* (Latin: best); order; organ; [music] *ottava* (Italian: octave); [baseball] out; over; overseer; owner

6O [civil aircraft marking] Somalia

7O [civil aircraft marking] Yemen

OA [vehicle registration] Birmingham; objective analysis; office address; office automation; Officers' Association; *Officier d'Académie* (French: Officer of the Academy); [banking] old account; [chemistry] oleic acid; operational analysis; [medicine] osteoarthritis; overall

O/A [banking] old account

o/a on account (of); on or about

o.a. overall

OAA *Organisation pour l'alimentation et l'agriculture* (French: Food and Agriculture Organization, FAO); Outdoor Advertising Association of Great Britain

OACI *Organisation de l'aviation civile internationale* (French: International Civil Aviation Organization, ICAO)

OAD [medicine] obstructive airways disease

o.a.d. overall depth

OAG [USA] Official Airline Guide

o.a.h. overall height

o. alt. hor. [medicine] *omnibus alternis horis* (Latin: every other hour)

OAMDV *omnia ad majorem Dei gloriam* (Latin: all to the greater glory of God)

OANA Organization of Asian News Agencies

O&A October and April (on bills)

O&C Oxford and Cambridge (Schools Examination Board)

o&c onset and course

O&E [USA] Operations and Engineers (or Engineering)

O&G obstetrics and gynaecology

O&M Ogilvie and Mather (advertising agency); organization and method(s)

O&O Oriental and Occidental Steamship Company; owned and operated

OAO one and only; Orbiting Astronomical Observatory

o.a.o. off and on

OAP old age pension; old age pensioner

OAPC [USA] Office of Alien Property Custodian

OAPEC Organization of Arab Petroleum Exporting Countries

OAR [Roman Catholic Church] Order of Augustinian Recollects

OAr Old Arabic

OAS [military] offensive air support; on active service; *Organisation de l'armée secrète* (French: Secret Army Organization); Organization of American States

OASIS optimal aircraft sequencing using intelligent systems

OAT outside air temperature

OATC Oceanic Air Traffic Control

OATG outside air temperature gauge

OATUU Organization of African Trade Union Unity (replacement for AATUF)

OAU Organization of African Unity

OB [vehicle registration] Birmingham; [fishing port] Oban; observed bearing; [USA] obstetric; [USA] obstetrician; [USA] obstetrics; [theatre] off-Broadway; official board; Old Bailey; old bonded (whisky); old boy; Order of Barbados; order of battle; Order of the Bath;

[insurance] ordinary business (in life assurance); ordnance board; outside broadcast; [civil aircraft marking] Peru

Ob. [Bible] Obadiah

o/b on or before

ob. *obiit* (Latin: (he/she) died); *obiter* (Latin: incidentally); obligation; oboe; observation; obsolete; obstetric; obstetrics

o.b. ordinary building (grade of timber)

OBA optical bleaching agent (in detergent)

Obad. [Bible] Obadiah

ÖBB *Österreichische Bundesbahnen* (German: Federal Railways of Austria)

obb. [music] *obbligato* (Italian: essential (part))

obbl. [music] *obbligato* (Italian: essential (part))

OBC old boys' club; on-board computer (in car advertisement)

OBD [medicine] organic brain disease

ob. dk observation deck

obdt obedient

OBE (Officer of the) Order of the British Empire; out-of-the-body experience

OBEV *Oxford Book of English Verse*

ob-gyn obstetrics-gynaecology

OBI Order of British India

obit [short form] obituary

obj. object; objection; objective

objn objection

obl. obligation; oblige; oblique; oblong

OBLI Oxford and Buckinghamshire Light Infantry

OBM [surveying] Ordnance benchmark

OBO ore-bulk-oil (ship)

o.b.o. or best offer (in advertisement)

Obogs [military] on-board oxygen-generating system

ob. ph. [surveying] oblique photograph (or photography)

obre *octobre* (French: October)

OBS [medicine] organic brain syndrome

Obs. Observatory

Obs. *The Observer*

obs. obscure; observation; observatory; observe; observed; observer; obsolete; obstacle; obstetric; obstetrician; obstetrics; obstruction

obsc. obscure

obscd obscured

OBSF [accounting] off balance sheet finance

obsol. obsolescent; obsolete

ob.s.p. *obiit sine prole* (Latin: died without issue)

obst oboist

obstet. obstetric; obstetrician; obstetrics

obstn obstruction

obt obedient

obtd obtained

OBU offshore banking unit; One Big Union

OBV ocean boarding vessel

obv. obverse

OC [vehicle registration] Birmingham; Observer Corps; [USA] Office of Censorship; officer commanding; Officer in Charge; [electrical engineering] operating characteristic; operations centre; [pharmacology] oral contraceptive; Order in Council; (Officer of the) Order of Canada; orienteering club; [philately] original cover; Oslo Convention; Ottawa Convention; overseas command; overseas country

Oc. Ocean

o/c officer commanding; overcharge

o.c. office copy; official classification; [architecture] on centre; only child; [shipping] open charter; open cover; *opere citato* (Latin: in the work cited); over-the-counter

OCA Old Comrades Association

oca. [music] ocarina

OCAM *Organisation commune africaine et malgache* (French: African and Malagasy Common Organization)

OCarm. Order of Carmelites

OCart. Order of Carthusians

OCAS Organization of Central American States

OCAW [USA] Oil, Chemical and Atomic Workers International Union

occ. occasion; occasional; occasionally; occident; occidental; occupation; occupied; occurrence

occas. occasional; occasionally

occn occasion

OCD [medicine] obsessive compulsive disorder; [USA] Office of Civil Defense; [computing] on-line communications driver; *Ordinis Carmelitarum Discalceatorum* (Latin: of the Order of Discalced

Carmelites); *Ordo Carmelitarum Discalcea-torum* (Latin: Order of Discalced Carmelites)

OCDE *Organisation de coopération et de développement economiques* (French: Organization for Economic Cooperation and Development, OECD)

OCDM [USA] Office of Civil Defense Mobilization

OCDS [Canada] Overseas College of Defence Studies

O/Cdt Officer-Cadet

oceanog. oceanography

OCelt Old Celtic

OCF Officiating Chaplain to the Forces

OCH oil central heating (in property advertisement)

och. ochre

OCNL [meteorology] occasional

OCorn Old Cornish

OCPSF organic chemicals, plastics and synthetic fibres

OCR [computing] optical character reader; [computing] optical character recognition; *Ordinis Cisterciensium Reformatorum* (Latin: of the Order of Reformed Cistercians); *Ordo Cisterciensium Reformatorum* (Latin: Order of Reformed Cistercians, Trappists)

OCS [USA] Officer Candidate School; Old Church Slavonic; outer continental shelf

OCSC Office of the Civil Service Commissioners

OCSO Order of Cistercians of the Strict Observance (= Trappists)

ocst [meteorology] overcast

Oct [astronomy] Octans

Oct. October

oct. [music] octave; [printing] octavo; *octubre* (Spanish: October)

OCTU Officer Cadet Training Unit

OCTV open-circuit television

OCU Operational Conversion Unit

OCUC Oxford and Cambridge University Club

OCV open-circuit voltage

OD Doctor of Ophthalmology; Doctor of Optometry; Doctor of Osteopathy; [vehicle registration] Exeter; [civil aircraft marking] Lebanon; [medicine] *oculus dexter* (Latin: right eye); officer of the day; Old Dutch; [military] olive drab; operations division; [Jamaica] (Officer of

the) Order of Distinction; ordinary seaman; ordnance datum (standard sea level); ordnance department; ordnance depot; organization development; other denominations; outside diameter; overdose

O/D on deck; [banking] on demand; [banking] overdraft; [banking] overdrawn

o/d on deck; overdose

od. *oder* (German: or)

o.d. [medicine] *oculus dexter* (Latin: right eye); [military] olive drab; optical density; outside diameter

ODA [computing] office document architecture; [computing] open (or office) document architecture; [medicine] operating department assistant; Overseas Development Administration (former government department)

ODan Old Danish

ODAS Ocean Data Station

ODC Order of Discalced Carmelites

ODCh Chaplain for Other Denominations

ODE [mathematics] ordinary differential equation

ODECA *Organización de estados centroamericanos* (Spanish: Organization of Central American States, OCAS)

ODESSA Ocean Data Environmental Sciences Services Acquisition; *Organisation der SS-Angehörigen* (German: Organization of SS Members)

ODETTE Organization for Data Exchange through Tele-Transmission in Europe

ODI [computing] open datalink interface; Overseas Development Institute

ODLQC Open and Distance Learning Quality Council (formerly CACC)

ODO outdoor officer (at customs)

ODP official development planning; [computing] open distributed processing; open-door policy; overall development planning

ODV [informal] brandy (phonetic spelling of French name *eau de vie*)

OE [civil aircraft marking] Austria; [vehicle registration] Birmingham; [USA] Office of Education; Old English; Old Etonian; [medicine] on examination; Order of Excellence (in Guyana); original error; outboard engine

Oe oersted (unit of magnetic field strength)

o.e. omissions excepted; open end

OEA Overseas Education Association; oxygen-enriched air

OEC oxygen-enriched combustion

OECD Organization for Economic Cooperation and Development (replacement for OEEC)

OECS Organization of Eastern Caribbean States

OED *Oxford English Dictionary*

OEEC Organization for European Economic Cooperation (replaced by OECD)

OEF Organization of Employers' Federations and Employers in Developing Countries

OEIC open-ended investment company

OEL occupational exposure limit (of radiation)

OEM [computing] original equipment manufacturer

OEO [USA] Office of Economic Opportunity

OEP [USA] Office of Economic Preparedness

OER Officers' Emergency Reserve; Organization for European Research

OES ocean energy system(s); [USA] Office of Economic Stabilization; Order of the Eastern Star; Organization of European States

OET Office of Education and Training

OF [vehicle registration] Birmingham; Oddfellows; oil-filled; oil-fired; [printing] old face (type); Old French; operating forces; operational forces; Order of the Founder (of Salvation Army); oxidizing flame

o.f. optional form; outside face

OFA [medicine] oncofetal antigen

O factor [psychology] oscillation factor

OFB [computing] output feedback

OFEMA *Office français d'exportation de matériel aéronautique* (French: French Office for the Export of Aeronautical Material)

Off. Offaly

off. offer; offered; offering; office; officer; official; officinal

Offer Office of Electricity Regulation

offg offering; officiating

offic. official; officially

offl official

offr officer

Ofgas Office of Gas Supply

OFHC [engineering] oxygen-free high-conductivity copper

Oflag *Offizierslager* (German: officers' (prisoner-of-war) camp)

OFlem Old Flemish

Oflot Office of the National Lottery

OFM Order of Friars Minor (= Franciscans); *Ordo Fratrum Minorum* (Latin: Order of Friars Minor)

OFMCap. Order of Friars Minor Capuchin

OFMConv. Order of Friars Minor Conventual

OFR Order of the Federal Republic of Nigeria

OFr Old French

OFris Old Frisian

OFS Orange Free State

Ofsted Office for Standards in Education

OFT Office of Fair Trading

Oftel Office of Telecommunications

Ofwat Office of Water Services

OG [vehicle registration] Birmingham; [astronomy] object glass; officer of the guard; [architecture] ogee; Olympic Games; [US slang] original gangster (criminals' term of respect); original gravity (in brewing); [philately] original gum; outside guard

o.g. [philately] original gum; [sports] own goal

OGael Old Gaelic

ÖGB *Österreichischer Gewerkschaftsbund* (German: Austrian Federation of Trade Unions)

OGCM [meteorology] ocean general circulation model

OGD [medicine] oesophagogastroduodenoscopy

OGL [commerce] open general licence

OGM ordinary general meeting

OGO Orbiting Geophysical Observatory

OGPU *Obyedinyonnoye Gosudarstvennoye Politicheskoye Upravleniye* (Russian: United State Political Administration) (former Soviet police organization)

OGS Oratory of the Good Shepherd; [electronics] oxide glassy (or glasslike) semiconductor

OH [vehicle registration] Birmingham; [civil aircraft marking] Finland; [US postcode] Ohio; [numismatics] old head (of Queen Victoria)

o.h. observation helicopter; office hours; [medicine] *omni hora* (Latin: hourly); on hand; open hearth; overhead

OHAC own house and car (in personal advertisement)

OHBMS On Her/His Britannic Majesty's Service

OHC overhead cam(shaft) (in car advertisement)

OHD [medicine] organic heart disease

OHDETS over-horizon detection system

OHG [commerce] *Offene Handelsgesellschaft* (German: partnership); Old High German

OHMS On Her/His Majesty's Service

OHN occupational health nurse

OHNC occupational health nursing certificate

OHP overhead projector

OHS occupational health service; [metallurgy] open-hearth steel

OHV overhead valve

OI [vehicle registration] Belfast; office instruction; Old Irish; operating instructions; [medicine] osteogenesis imperfecta

OIC Officer in Charge; *Organisation internationale du commerce* (French: International Trade Organization, ITO); Organization of the Islamic Conference

OIcel Old Icelandic

OIEO offers in excess of (in advertisement)

OIG *organisation intergouvernementale* (French: intergovernmental organization)

OII [physics] optical imaging instrument

OILC Offshore Industry Liaison Committee

OIPC *Organisation internationale de police criminelle* (French: International Criminal Police Organization, Interpol)

OIr Old Irish

OIRO offers in the region of (in advertisement)

OIRT *Organisation internationale de radiodiffusion et télévision* (French: International Radio and Television Organization)

OIS organizer industrial safety; overnight indexed swap

OIT *Organisation internationale du travail*

(French: International Labour Organization, ILO)

OIt Old Italian

OJ [vehicle registration] Birmingham; *Official Journal* (of EU); orange juice; Order of Jamaica

o.j. open joint; open joist

OJAJ October, January, April, July (end of financial quarters)

OJCS Office of the Joint Chiefs of Staff

Ojocs [horseracing] overnight declaration of jockeys

OJR old Jamaica rum

OJT on-the-job training

OK all correct (perhaps from facetious misspelling 'oll korrekt'); [vehicle registration] Birmingham; [civil aircraft marking] Czech Republic; [US postcode] Oklahoma

o.k.a. otherwise known as

OKH *Oberkommando der Heeres* (German: Army High Command) (in World War II)

Okla Oklahoma

Okt. *Oktober* (German: October)

OL [vehicle registration] Birmingham; [medicine] *oculus laevus* (Latin: left eye); [UK postcode] Oldham; Old Latin; [computing] on-line; operating licence; (Officer of the) Order of Leopold; Ordnance Lieutenant; [sports] outside left; overflow level; overhead line

Ol. Olympiad; Olympic

ol. [medicine] *oleum* (Latin: oil)

o.l. [medicine] *oculus laevus* (Latin: left eye)

OLC oak-leaf cluster (US military decoration)

Old Test. Old Testament

OLE [computing] object linking and embedding

O level [education] Ordinary level (replaced by GCSE)

OLG Old Low German

Oli [geology] Oligocene

o'lkng overlooking (in property advertisement)

OLQ officer-like qualities

OLR off-line reader

OLRT [computing] on-line real time

OLS [statistics] ordinary least squares

OM [vehicle registration] Birmingham; old man; optical microscopy; *Optimus*

Maximus (Latin: greatest and best) (Roman title for Jupiter); Order of Merit; ordnance map; organic matter; [civil aircraft marking] Slovakia

Om. Oman

.om Oman (in Internet address)

o.m. old measurement; [medicine] *omni mane* (Latin: every morning)

OMA [US finance] orderly marketing agreement

OMB [USA] Office of Management and Budget

OMC operation and maintenance costs

OMCS Office of the Minister for the Civil Service

OMI Oblate(s) of Mary Immaculate

OMM [Canada] (Officer of the) Order of Military Merit

omn. hor. [medicine] *omni hora* (Latin: every hour)

omn. noct. [medicine] *omni nocte* (Latin: every night)

OMO one-man operation (or operator) (of bus)

OMR [computing] optical mark reading (or reader)

OMRS Orders and Medals Research Society

OMS [computing] object management system; [astronautics] orbital manoeuvring system; *Organisation mondiale de la santé* (French: World Health Organization, WHO)

o.m.s. output per man shift

OMT [computing] object modelling technique

OMV open-market value

ON [vehicle registration] Birmingham; octane number; Old Norse; Ontario; [Jamaica] Order of the Nation; orthopaedic nurse

o.n. [medicine] *omni nocte* (Latin: every night)

ONC Ordinary National Certificate; Orthopaedic Nursing Certificate

OND Ophthalmic Nursing Diploma; Ordinary National Diploma; [medicine] other neurological disorders

ONERA *Office national d'études et de recherches aérospatiales* (French: National Office of Aerospace Study and Research)

ONF Old Norman French; Old Northern French

ONG *organisation non-gouvernementale* (French: nongovernmental organization)

ONGC [USA] Oil and Natural Gas Commission

ONI Office of Naval Intelligence

o.n.o. or near(est) offer (in advertisement)

onomat. onomatopoeia; onomatopoeic

ONorw Old Norwegian

ONR [USA] Office of Naval Research

ONS Office for National Statistics

ONT ordinary neap tide

Ont. Ontario

ONZ Order of New Zealand

OO [civil aircraft marking] Belgium; [vehicle registration] Chelmsford; observation officer; [informal] once-over; operation order; orderly officer

o/o offers over (in advertisement); on order; order of

OOBE out-of-the-body experience

OOD [computing] object-oriented design; officer of the day; officer of the deck

OODBMS [computing] object-oriented database management system

OOG officer of the guard

OOL [computing] object-oriented language

OON Officer of the Order of the Niger

o/o/o out of order

o.o.o. of obscure origin

OOP [computing] object-oriented programming; out-of-pocket (expenses)

OOT out of town

OOW officer of the watch

OP [vehicle registration] Birmingham; observation point; observation post; old people; Old Persian; old prices; [insurance] open policy; [theatre] opposite prompt (side); *Ordinis Praedicatorum* (Latin: of the Order of Preachers); *Ordo Praedictatorum* (Latin: Order of Preachers, Dominicans); organophosphate; osmotic pressure; [informal] other people('s); out of print; [medicine] outpatient; over proof (of alcohol)

Op. [music] Opus (piece by composer)

op [short form] operation

op. opaque; opera; *opera* (Latin: works); operation; operational; operator; opinion; opposite; optical; *optimus* (Latin: best, excellent); *opus* (Latin: work)

o.p. old pattern; open pattern; open-plan (in property advertisement); [theatre] opposite prompt (side); out of print; over proof (of alcohol)

OPA [USA] Office of Price Administration (in World War II); Orbis Press Agency (Czech news agency)

op art [short form] optical art

OPAS Occupational Pensions Advisory Board

OPB Occupational Pensions Board

OPC [computing] optical photoconductor; ordinary Portland cement; [medicine] outpatient(s') clinic; Overseas Press Club of America

op. cit. *opere citato* (Latin: in the work cited)

OPCON operational control

OPCS Office of Population Censuses and Surveys

OPD [medicine] outpatient(s') department

OPDAR optical detection and ranging

OPE out-of-pocket expenses

OPEC Organization of (the) Petroleum Exporting Countries

Op-Ed [USA] opposite editorial (page) (in newspaper)

OPEIU [USA] Office and Professional Employees International Union

OPEP *Organisation des pays exportateurs de pétrole* (French: Organization of Petroleum Exporting Countries, OPEC)

OPers Old Persian

OPEX operational, executive and administrative personnel (in UN)

OPG [dentistry] orthopantomogram

OPg Old Portuguese

opg opening

Oph [astronomy] Ophiuchus

oph. ophthalmic

ophthal. ophthalmic; ophthalmologist; ophthalmology

ophthalmol. ophthalmologist; ophthalmology

OPIC [USA] Overseas Private Investment Corporation

opl operational

OPM [USA] Office of Personnel Management; [informal] other people's money; output per man

opm operations per minute

OPMA Overseas Press and Media Association

opn operation; opinion; option

o.p.n. *ora pro nobis* (Latin: pray for us)

OPO one-person operation (of bus); one-person operator (of bus)

OPol Old Polish

OPP oriented polypropene (film); out of print at present

Opp. [music] Opuses (pieces by composer)

opp. *opera* (Latin: works); opportunity; oppose; opposed; opposite; opposition

oppy opportunity

OPQ occupational personality questionnaire

OPr Old Provençal

opr operator

opr. operate

OPRAF Office of Passenger Rail Franchising

OProv Old Provençal

OPruss Old Prussian

OPS Office of Public Service

ops [short form] operations

OPT optimized production technology

opt. [grammar] optative; optic(al); optician; optics; optimal; *optime* (Latin: best, excellently); optimum; option; optional

OptD Doctor of Optometry

OPV [medicine] oral poliomyelitis vaccine

OQ (Officer of the) National Order of Quebec

OR [statistics] odds ratio; official receiver; official referee; Old Roman; [currency] Omani rial; [US medicine] operating room; operational (or operations) requirement; operational (or operations) research; orderly room; [US postcode] Oregon; [military] other ranks; [sports] outside right; [insurance] owner's risk; [vehicle registration] Portsmouth

ÖR *Österreichischer Rundfunk* (German: Austrian Radio) (broadcasting service)

or other

or. orange; oratorio; orient; oriental; orientalist; original

o.r. operationally risky; operational (or operations) requirement; operations room; out of range; overhaul and repair; [insurance] owner's risk

Oracle [trademark] optional reception of announcements by coded line electronics (teletext service)

orat. oration; orator; oratorical; oratorically; oratorio; oratory

ORB oceanographic research buoy; omni-directional radio beacon

o.r.b. [insurance] owner's risk of breakage

ORBIS orbiting radio beacon ionospheric satellite

ORBIT on-line retrieval of bibliographical information

ORC [USA] Officers' Reserve Corps; Overseas Research Council

ORCA Ocean Resources Conservation Association

orch. orchestra; orchestral; orchestrated (by); orchestration

orchd orchestrated (by)

orchid [informal] one recent child, heavily in debt

ord. ordain; ordained; order; ordinal; ordinance; ordinary; ordnance

o.r.d. [insurance] owner's risk of damage

ordn. ordnance

ORE occupational radiation exposure

Ore. Oregon

Oreg. Oregon

ORELA Oak Ridge Electron Linear Accelerator

ORESCO Overseas Research Council

ORF [genetics] open reading frame

o.r.f. [insurance] owner's risk of fire

org. organ; organic; organism; organist; organization; organize; organized; organizer

.org noncommercial organization (in Internet address)

ORGALIME *Organisme de liaison des industries métalliques européennes* (French: Liaison Group for the European Metal Industries)

organ. organic; organization

orgst organist

orgzn organization

Ori [astronomy] Orion

orient. oriental; orientalist

orig. origami; origin; original; originally; originate; originated

ORIT *Organización regional interamericana de trabajadores* (Spanish: Inter-American Regional Organization of Workers)

Ork. Orkney (Islands)

Orkn. Orkney (Islands)

ORL [medicine] otorhinolaryngology (= ear, nose and throat (ENT))

o.r.l. [insurance] owner's risk of leakage

orn. ornament; ornamental; ornithology

ornith. ornithological; ornithology

ornithol. ornithological; ornithology

ORNL Oak Ridge National Laboratory

OROM [computing] optical read-only memory

ORP off-road parking (in property advertisement)

orph. orphan; orphanage

ORR Office of the Rail Regulator

o.r.r. owner's risk rates

ORS [geology] Old Red Sandstone; Operational Research Society

ors others

ORSL Order of the Republic of Sierra Leone

ORSORT Oak Ridge School of Reactor Technology

ORT [medicine] oral rehydration therapy; [USA] Organization for Rehabilitation by Training

ORTF *Office de radiodiffusion-télévision française* (French: French Radio and Television Organization) (former state broadcasting service)

Orth. Orthodox

orth. orthographic(al); orthography; orthopaedic; orthopaedics

ORuss Old Russian

ORV off-road vehicle

OS [vehicle registration] Glasgow; [medicine] *oculus sinister* (Latin: left eye); Old Saxon; Old School; old series; Old Side; Old Style (in dates); [computing] operating system; Ordinary Seaman; Ordnance Survey; out of stock; outsize (clothing)

Os [chemical element] osmium

o/s on sale; out of service; out of stock; outsize (clothing); [banking] outstanding

o.s. ocean station; [medicine] *oculus sinister* (Latin: left eye); oil switch; old series; only son; on station; outside

OSA [USA] Office of the Secretary of the Army; Official Secrets Act; [printing] old style antique (type); Order of St Augustine (= Augustinians); *Ordinis Sancti Augustini* (Latin: of the Order of St Augustine); *Ordo Sancti Augustini* (Latin: Order of St Augustine, Augustinians); Overseas Sterling Area

OSAF [USA] Office of the Secretary of the Air Force

OS&W [building] oak, sunk and weathered

OSax Old Saxon

OSB Order of St Benedict (= Benedictines); *Ordinis Sancti Benedicti* (Latin: of the Order of St Benedict); *Ordo Sancti Benedicti* (Latin: Order of St Benedict, Benedictines)

OSC on-site cover; Order of St Clare (= Poor Clares)

osc. oscillator

OScan Old Scandinavian

OScand Old Scandinavian

OSCAR Orbital Satellites Carrying Amateur Radio; Organization for Sickle Cell Anaemia Research

OSCE Organization for Security and Cooperation in Europe (formerly CSCE)

OSCH off-peak (or overnight) storage central heating (in property advertisement)

OSD [USA] Office of the Secretary of Defense; Order of St Dominic (= Dominicans)

OSE operational support equipment

OSerb Old Serbian

OSF [computing] Open Software Federation; Order of St Francis (= Franciscans); *Ordinis Sancti Francisci* (Latin: of the Order of St Francis); *Ordo Sancti Francisci* (Latin: Order of St Francis, Franciscans)

OSFC Order of St Francis, Capuchin

OSHA [USA] Occupational Safety and Health Administration

OSI [USA] Office of Scientific Integrity; on-site inspection; [computing] open systems interconnection

O/Sig Ordinary Signalman

OSJ on a secret journey

OSL Old Style Latin

OSl Old Slavonic

Osl. Oslo

OSlav Old Slavonic

OSM Order of the Servants of Mary (= Servites)

OSN [USA] Office of the Secretary of the Navy

OSNC Orient Steam Navigation Company

OSO orbiting solar observatory

OSP off-street parking (in property advertisement)

OSp Old Spanish

o.s.p. *obiit sine prole* (Latin: died without issue)

OSR [USA] Office of Science and Research

OSRB Overseas Service Resettlement Bureau

OSRD [USA] Office of Scientific Research and Development

OSRO Office for Special Relief Operations

OSS Office for the Supervision of Solicitors; [USA] Office of Space Sciences (in NASA); [USA] Office of Strategic Services (in World War II)

O.SS.S. *Ordinis Sanctissimi Salvatoris* (Latin: of the Order of the Most Holy Saviour); *Ordo Sanctissimi Salvatoris* (Latin: Order of the Most Holy Saviour, Bridgettines)

O.SS.T. *Ordinis Sanctissimae Trinitatis Redemptionis Captivorum* (Latin: of the Order of the Most Holy Trinity for the Redemption of Captives); *Ordo Sanctissimae Trinitatis Redemptionis Captivorum* (Latin: Order of the Most Holy Trinity for the Redemption of Captives, Trinitarians)

OST [USA] Office of Science and Technology; ordinary spring tide

osteo. osteopath; osteopathic; osteopathy

OSTI [USA] Office of Scientific and Technical Information; [USA] Organization for Social and Technological Innovation

OStJ (Officer of the) Order of St John of Jerusalem

OSU Order of St Ursula (= Ursulines)

OSUK Ophthalmological Society of the United Kingdom

OSV ocean station vessel

OSw Old Swedish

OT occupational therapist; occupational therapy; off time; Old Testament; Old Teutonic; [medicine] operating theatre; [Australia] Overland Telegraph (from Adelaide to Darwin); overseas trade; overtime; [vehicle registration] Portsmouth

OTA Office of Technology Assessment

OTAN *Organisation du traité de l'Atlantique nord* (French: North Atlantic Treaty Organization, NATO)

OTASE *Organisation du traité de défense collective pour l'Asie du sud-est* (French: South-East Asia Treaty Organization, SEATO)

OTB [USA] off-track betting; oxide titanium bronze

otbd outboard

OTC [USA] officer in tactical command; Officers' Training Corps; Officers' Transit Camp; one-stop-inclusive tour charter; Organization for Trade Cooperation; over-the-counter (as in **OTC medicines**); [pharmacology] oxy-tetracycline (antibiotic)

OTE on-target earnings (in job advertisement); or the equivalent

OTEC ocean thermal-energy conversion

OTeut Old Teutonic

OTF [photography] off the film

OTG outside temperature gauge (in car advertisement)

OTH [telecommunications] over the horizon

OTOH on the other hand (in Internet chat and e-mail)

otol. otological; otology

OTP [computing] one-time programmable (EPROM)

OTS Office of Technical Services; Officers' Training School; [advertising] opportunities to see

OTT [medicine] oesophageal transit test; [informal] over the top

Ott. Ottawa

ott. [music] *ottava* (Italian: octave); *ottobre* (Italian: October)

OTU [biology] operational taxonomic unit; operation training unit

OTurk Old Turkish

OU [vehicle registration] Bristol; official use; Open University; Oxford University

OUAC Oxford University Appointments Committee; Oxford University Athletic Club

OUAFC Oxford University Association Football Club

OUBC Oxford University Boat Club

OUCC Oxford University Cricket Club

OUDS Oxford University Dramatic Society

OUP [Northern Ireland] Official Unionist Party; Oxford University Press

OURC Oxford University Rifle Club

OURFC Oxford University Rugby Football Club

OURT Order of the United Republic of Tanzania

out. outlet

outbd outboard

OV [vehicle registration] Birmingham

Ov. Ovid (Roman poet)

ov. ovary; over; overture

ovbd overboard

o.v.c. [law] other valuable consideration

overlkg overlooking (in property advertisement)

ovfl. overflow

OVH overhead projector

ovhd overhead

ovld overload

OVNI *objet volant non identifié* (French: unidentified flying object, UFO)

o.v.n.o. or very near offer (in advertisement)

ÖVP *Österreichische Volkspartei* (German: Austrian People's Party)

ovpd overpaid

ovrd. override

OW Office of Works; Old Welsh; old woman; [vehicle registration] Portsmouth

O/W oil in water (emulsion)

o.w. one way; out of wedlock

OWC Ordnance Weapons Command

OWF optimum working frequency

OWI [USA] Office of War Information (in World War II); [USA] operating (a motor vehicle) while intoxicated

own. owner

OWRS [USA] Office of Water Regulations and Standards

OWS ocean weather service; ocean weather ship; ocean weather station

OX [vehicle registration] Birmingham; [UK postcode] Oxford

Ox. Oxford

Oxf. Oxford(shire)

Oxfam Oxford Committee for Famine Relief

Oxon. Oxfordshire (from Latin *Oxonia*); *Oxoniensis* (Latin: of Oxford)

OY [civil aircraft marking] Denmark; [vehicle registration] northwest London

oys. oysters

OZ [vehicle registration] Belfast

oz ounce (from Italian *onza*)

oz ap apothecaries' ounce

oz av avoirdupois ounce

oz avdp avoirdupois ounce

oz T troy ounce

P

P [civil aircraft marking] North Korea; [Roman Catholic Church] *Papa* (Latin: Pope); [genetics] parental generation; park; parking; parson; pass; passed; [US education] passing; pastor; *pater* (Latin: father); [chess] pawn; [music] pedal; pedestrian; pedestrian crossing; [horticulture] perennial; [ecclesiastical] *Père* (French: Father); [botany] perianth (in floral formula); period; [geology] Permian; personnel; peta- (indicates 10^{15}, as in **Pm** = petametre); pharmacy (on non-prescription medicine); [currency] Philippine peso; [biochemistry] phosphate; [chemical element] phosphorus; [botany] phytochrome; pitch; [physics] poise; [computing] polynomial; [Roman Catholic Church] Pope; *populus* (Latin: people); port; [fishing port] Portsmouth; [international vehicle registration] Portugal; positive; post; postage; posterior; post office (on map); Presbyterian; President; priest; Prince; probate; pro-consul; [politics] Progressive; [theatre] prompt (side); proprietary (product); Protestant; public; [currency] pula (used in Botswana); pupil

P [physics] dielectric polarization; [physics] parity; [physics] power; [physics] pressure; [genetics] promoter

p page; [currency] pence; [currency] penny; per; pico- (indicates 10^{-12}, as in **ps** = picosecond); [physics] proton; [meteorology] shower

p [physics] electric dipole moment; [physics] momentum (in vector equations); [chemistry] permanent dipole moment (of molecule); [music] *piano* (Italian: softly); [physics] pressure; [biochemistry] pyranose

p. page; pamphlet; paragraph; part; [grammar] participle; particle; *partim* (Latin: in part); pass; passed; [grammar] passive; [grammar] past; peak; pectoral (fin); per; *per* (Latin: by, for); perch (unit of measure for stone); [music] percussion; perennial; [grammar] person;

[currency] peseta; [currency] peso; [currency] piastre; *pied* (French: foot); pint; pipe; *pius* (Latin: holy); plaster; polar; pole; *pondere* (Latin: by weight); population; port; positive; *post* (Latin: after); *pouce* (French: inch); *pour* (French: for, per); power; [grammar] present; *primus* (Latin: first); *pro* (Latin: for, in favour of); professional; [knitting] purl

P2 [civil aircraft marking] Papua New Guinea

P4 [civil aircraft marking] Aruba

7P [civil aircraft marking] Lesotho

8P [civil aircraft marking] Barbados

PA [vehicle registration] Guildford; [UK postcode] Paisley; Pakistan Army; [international vehicle registration] Panama; [chemistry] parent atom; Parents' Association; [insurance] particular average; Patients' Association; Pedestrians' Association; [US postcode] Pennsylvania; performance assessment; [medicine] pernicious anaemia; [insurance] personal accident; personal account; [taxation] personal allowance; personal appearance; personal assistant; [chemistry] phosphoric acid; photograph appreciated (in personal advertisement); [USA] physician assistant; Pierre Allain (brand of climbing boot); Piper Aircraft; [engineering] pitch angle; [medicine] plasminogen activator; political agent; *por autorización* (Spanish: by authority of); [astronomy] position angle; power amplifier; power of attorney; [Roman Catholic Church] Prefect Apostolic; press agent; Press Association; press attaché; private account; product analysis; programme assistant; [USA] prosecuting attorney; Protestant Alliance; [medicine] psoriatic arthritis; [USA] public accountant; public address (system); publicity agent; Publishers Association; [medicine] pulmonary artery; [engineering] pulsed annealing; purchasing agent

P/A [insurance] particular average; personal account; power of attorney; private account

Pa pascal (unit of pressure); Pennsylvania; [chemical element] protactinium

p.A *per Adresse* (German: care of, c/o) (in postal addresses)

pa. past

.pa Panama (in Internet address)

p.a. [grammar] participial adjective; *per annum* (Latin: yearly); permanent address; personal appearance

PAA Pan American Airways; [chemistry] peracetic acid; [chemistry] polyacrylic acid

PAADC Principal Air Aide-de-camp

PABIAC Paper and Board Industry Advisory Committee

PABLA problem analysis by logical approach

PABX [telecommunications] private automatic branch exchange

PAC [US air force] Pacific Air Command; Pan-African(ist) Congress; Pan-American Congress; [building] passive air cycle; Permanent Agricultural Committee (of ILO); [USA] political action committee; polymer–asphalt composite; [chemistry] powdered activated carbon; Public Accounts Committee; Public Assistance Committee; [stock exchange] put-and-call (option)

P-A-C [psychology] parent, adult, child

Pac. Pacific

PACA Public Art Commissions Agency

PACAF [US air force] Pacific Air Forces

PACE Parental Alliance for Choice in Education; performance and cost evaluation; Police and Criminal Evidence Act; precision analogue computing equipment; Protestant and Catholic Encounter

Pacif. Pacific

PACOM [USA] Pacific Command

PACS Pacific area communications system; [medicine] picture archiving and communication system

PACT Producers' Alliance for Cinema and Television

PAD [computing] packet assembler/disassembler; passive air defence; payable after death

PaD Pennsylvania Dutch

pad. padding; paddock; padlock

PADAR [military] passive detection and ranging

PADLOC [military] passive detection and location of countermeasures

p. Adr. *per Adresse* (German: care of, c/o) (in postal addresses)

PADT Public Art Development Trust

p. ae. [pharmacology] *partes aequales* (Latin: equal parts)

paediat. paediatrician; paediatrics

PAF [computing] peripheral address field; [medicine] platelet-activating factor; [Northern Ireland] Protestant Action Force

p.a.f. *puissance au frein* (French: brake horsepower)

PAFC phosphoric acid fuel cell

PAg Professional Agronomist

PaG Pennsylvania German

PAGB Poultry and Egg Producers' Association of Great Britain; Proprietary Association of Great Britain

PAHO Pan-American Health Organization

PAI [medicine] platelet accumulation index

PAICV *Partido Africano da Independencia de Cabo Verde* (Portuguese: African Party for the Independence of Cape Verde)

PAIN Parents Against Injustice

paint. painter; painting

PAIS [USA] Public Affairs Information Service

PAISLEY pants away if sexual liaison expected – yes! (on envelope of love letter)

Pak. Pakistan; Pakistani

PakRs [currency] Pakistan rupee

PAL [USA] Parcel Air Lift; [computing] peripheral availability list; [television] phase alternation line (European broadcasting system); Philippine Airlines; [USA] Police Athletic League; present atmospheric level; [computing, electronics] programmable array logic

Pal [geology] Palaeocene

Pal. Palace; Palestine; Palestinian

pal. palace; palaeography; palaeontology

palaeob. palaeobotanical; palaeobotany

palaeobot. palaeobotanical; palaeobotany

palaeog. palaeographic(al); palaeography

palaeontol. palaeontological; palaeontology

PALS [computing] permissive action link systems

PAM [telecommunications] pulse-amplitude modulation

pam. pamphlet

PAMA Pan-American Medical Association; Press Advertisement Managers' Association

pamph. pamphlet

PAMR Public Access Mobile Radio

PAN [Mexico] *Partido Acción Nacional* (Spanish: National Action Party); peroxyacetyl nitrate (pollutant of atmosphere); Pesticides Action Network; polyacrylonitrile (polymer)

Pan. Panama; Panamanian

pan. panchromatic; panoramic; pantomime; pantry

PANA Pan-African News Agency

PANAFTEL Pan-African Telecommunications Network

Pan. Can. Panama Canal

P&E plant and equipment

P&F chart point-and-figure chart

P&G Procter and Gamble

P&L profit and loss

P&O Peninsular and Oriental (shipping company)

p&p postage and packing

P&RT physical and recreational training

P&S [US stock exchange] purchase and sales

PANN Professional Association of Nursery Nurses

PANS procedures for air navigation services

panto [short form] pantomime

PAO [medicine] peak acid output; Prince Albert's Own (regiment); public affairs officer

PAP People's Action Party (in Singapore); *Polska Agencja Prasowa* (Polish news agency); [medicine] pulmonary arterial pressure

Pap. Papua; Papuan

PAPS periodic armaments planning system

PAR [military] perimeter acquisition radar; phased-array radar; [botany] photosynthetically active radiation; [computing] positive acknowledgment and retransmission; [aeronautics] precision approach radar; programme analysis review; [electronics] pulse acquisition radar

Par. Paraguay; Paraguayan

par. paragraph; parallax; parallel; paraphrase; parenthesis; parish; parochial

p.a.r. planed all round (in woodworking)

Para. Paraguay; Paraguayan

para [short form] paratrooper

para. parachute; paragraph

parab. parabola

par. aff. [pharmacology] *pars affecta* (Latin: to the affected part)

Par. Ch. parish church

parch. parchment

paren. parenthesis

parens. parentheses

park. parking

Parl. Parliament; Parliamentary

parl. parliament; parliamentary

parl. agt parliamentary agent

parl. proc. parliamentary procedure

Parly Sec. Parliamentary Secretary

PARM programme analysis for resource management

part. partial; participate; participation; [grammar] participial; [grammar] participle; particle; particular; partition; [grammar] partitive; partner; partnership

part. aeq. [pharmacology] *partes aequales* (Latin: in equal parts)

PARU [medicine] post-anaesthetic recovery unit

PAS public address system

pas. [grammar] passive

p.a.s. power-assisted steering (in car advertisement)

PASCAL *programme appliqué à la sélection et la compilation automatique de la littérature* (French: program applied to the selection and automatic compilation of literature)

Pasok *Panellenion Sozialistikon Kinema* (Greek: Panhellenic Socialist Movement)

Pass. Passover

pass. passage; passenger; *passim* (Latin: here and there throughout); [grammar] passive

PASSIM [USA] Presidential Advisory Staff on Scientific Management

PAT planned activities time; [banking] pre-authorized automatic transfer; Professional Association of Teachers

pat. patent; patented; pattern

p.a.t. *poids atomique* (French: atomic weight)

PATA Pacific Air Travel Association

Pata. Patagonia; Patagonian

patd patented

path. pathological; pathology

pathol. pathological; pathology

Pat. Off. Patent Office

pat. pend. patent pending

PAU Pan American Union; programmes analysis unit

Pav [astronomy] Pavo

pav. pavilion

PAW plasma-arc welding; powered all the way

PAWA Pan American World Airways

PAWC Pan-African Workers' Congress

PAWR [USA] Public Authority for Water Resources

PAX [telecommunications] private automatic exchange

p.a.x. per annum, exclusive (in accommodation advertisement)

PAYE [taxation] pay as you earn; pay as you enter

paymr paymaster

PAYP pay as you play (at golf club)

payt payment

PAYV pay as you view

PB Bachelor of Philosophy (from Latin *Philosophiae Baccalaureus*); [vehicle registration] Guildford; passbook; permanent base; [athletics] personal best; *Pharmacopoeia Britannica* (Latin: British Pharmacopoeia); [pharmacology] phenobarbitone; plastic-bonded; Plymouth Brethren; pocket book; power brakes; Prayer Book; premium bond; Primitive Baptists; [USA] Publications Board; [knitting] purl into back of stitch

Pb [chemical element] lead (from Latin *plumbum*); [computing] petabyte

p/b purpose-built (in property advertisement); push-button

p.b. paperback (of books); [baseball] passed ball(s)

PBA [informal] poor bloody assistant; [USA] Professional Bowlers Association; [USA] Public Buildings Administration

PBAB please bring a bottle

PBB [chemistry] polybrominated biphenyl (constituent of plastics)

PBC powerboat club

PBI Peace Brigades International; [informal] poor bloody infantry; [medicine] protein-bound iodine

pbk paperback (of books)

PBM [surveying] permanent benchmark; play by mail (of games)

PBMA Plastic Bath Manufacturers' Association

PBR payment by results

PBS [medicine] phosphate-buffered saline; Public Broadcasting Service

PBT [accounting] pay-back time

p.b.t. [finance] profit before tax

p.b.u.h. peace be upon him

PBX [telecommunications] private branch exchange

PC [vehicle registration] Guildford; Panama Canal; [chemistry] paper chromatography; [chemistry] paraffin concentration; parish council; parish councillor; Parliamentary Commissioner (= ombudsman); *Partie Communiste* (French: Communist Party); Past Commander; Paymaster Captain; [Ireland] Peace Commissioner; [USA] Peace Corps; perpetual curate; personal computer; [military] pioneer corps; [engineering] pitch circle; *Plaid Cymru* (Welsh: Party of Wales); Police Constable; politically correct; political correctness; polo club; [chemistry] polycarbonate; polymer concrete; polyprop(yl)ene carbonate (plastic); Poor Clares (religious order); Portland cement; port of call; postcard; Post Commander; potentially correct; preparatory commission; Press Council; prestressed concrete; Prince Consort; [electronics] printed circuit; Prison Commission; Privy Council; Privy Counsellor; process control; [USA] professional corporation; [Canada] Progressive Conservative; [chemistry] prop(yl)ene carbonate; propositional calculus; public convenience (on map); pulverized coal; [microbiology] pure culture

P/C petty cash; photocopy; price(s) current

pc parsec (unit of astronomical distance)

pc. percentage; [printing] pica; piece; price

p.c. per cent; postcard; [medicine] *post*

cibum (Latin: after meals) (in prescriptions)

PCA Parliamentary Commissioner for Administration (= ombudsman); Parochial Clergy Association; [medicine] patient-controlled analgesia; Permanent Court of Arbitration; Police Complaints Authority; [statistics] principal component analysis; Professional Cycling Association

PCAS Polytechnics Central Admissions System (became part of UCAS)

PC-AT personal computer, advanced technologies

PCB petty cash book; [chemistry] polychlorinated biphenyl (constituent of plastics); [medicine] post-coital bleeding; [electronics] printed-circuit board; [insurance] private car benefits

PCC parochial church council; *Partido Comunista de Cuba* (Spanish: Communist Party of Cuba); political consultative committee; Press Complaints Commission; Privy Council cases; Professional Conduct Committee (disciplinary body of BMA)

PCCS Primate Captive Care Society

PCD [electronics] photo compact disc

PC-DOS [trademark, computing] Personal Computer Disk Operating System

PCE *Partido Comunista de España* (Spanish: Communist Party of Spain); Postgraduate Certificate of Education; [engineering] pyrometric cone equivalent

pce piece

PCF *Parti Communiste Français* (French: French Communist Party); pistol, centre fire (gun calibre)

pcf pounds per cubic foot

PCFRE Professional Council for Religious Education

PCGC pulverized coal gasification and combustion

PCGG Primary Care Group in Gynaecology

PCGN Permanent Committee on Geographical Names

P Ch. parish church

PCI *Partito Comunista Italiano* (Italian: Italian Communist Party) (former name of PDS); Pax Christi International; [computing] peripheral component interconnect; [computing] personal computer interface

p.c.i. pounds per cubic inch

PCID Pontifical Council for Inter-Religious Dialogue

PCIFC Permanent Commission of the International Fisheries Convention

PCIJ Permanent Court of International Justice

PCIS Period Cottage Improvement Society

PCIUG personal computer independent user group

PCL [computing] printer control language

pcl parcel

PCM photochemical machinery; [USA] plug-compatible manufacturer; polyatomic ceramic material; protein-calorie malnutrition; [telecommunications] pulse-code modulation

pcm per calendar month

PCMA Plastic Crate Manufacturers' Association; Potato Chip Manufacturers' Association

PCMCIA Personal Computer Memory Card International Association

PCMI photochromic microimage

PCMO Principal Colonial Medical Officer

PCN *Partido de Conciliación Nacional* (Spanish: National Conciliation Party) (in El Salvador); [computing] personal communications network

PCOB Permanent Central Opium Board (in UN)

PCOD [medicine] polycystic ovary disease

PCP Past Chief Patriarch; pentachlorophenol (wood preservative); [finance] permissible capital payment; [trademark, pharmacology] phencycl(ohexylpiper)idine (= angel dust, hallucinogenic drug); [medicine] *Pneumocystis carinii* pneumonia; polychloroprene (rubber); prime commercial paper

PCPCU Pontifical Council for Promoting Christian Unity

PCPI Parent Cooperative Preschools International; Permanent Committee on Patent Information (of WIPO)

PCR Pedestrian Crossings Regulations; [medicine] plasma clearance rate; politically correct retailing; [biochemistry] polymerase chain reaction

PCRS Poor Clergy Relief Society

PCS [electronics] plasma-current switch; [Scotland] Principal Clerk of Session

pcs. pieces; prices

PCSP Permanent Commission for the South Pacific

PCT [medicine] positron compute(rize)d tomography; product consistency test

pct per cent

PCTCT [accounting] profit chargeable to corporation tax

PCTE [computing] portable common tool environment

PCTFE polychlorotrifluoroeth(yl)ene (plastic coating)

PCU plant control unit; power control unit; power conversion unit; pressurization control unit

p.c.u. passenger car unit

PCV [medicine] packed cell volume; passenger-carrying vehicle; passenger-controlled vehicle; [USA] Peace Corps Volunteers; positive crankcase ventilation (in car); pressure containment vessel

PCWPC Permanent Committee of the World Petroleum Congress

PCX [computing] picture exchange format

PC-XT personal computer extended

PCZ Panama Canal Zone

PCZST Panama Canal Zone Standard Time

PD Doctor of Pharmacy (from Latin *Pharmaciae Doctor*); [vehicle registration] Guildford; [fishing port] Peterhead; *Pharmacopoeia Dublinensis* (Latin: Dublin Pharmacopoeia); polar distance; [USA] Police Department; port dues; *posdata* (Spanish: postscript, PS); postal district; preventive detainee; preventive detention; *Privatdozent* (German: unsalaried university teacher); probability of detection; production department; [Ireland] Progressive Democrat(s); progressive disease; [insurance] property damage; [USA] Public Defender; [computing] public domain (software)

P/D price–dividend (ratio)

Pd [chemical element] palladium

pd paid; passed

p/d postdated

p.d. *per diem* (Latin: daily); [engineering] pitch diameter; poop deck; postage due; postdated; [physics] potential difference;

preliminary design; printer's devil

PDA [medicine] patent ductus arteriosus; [computing] personal digital assistant; *pour dire adieu* (French: to say goodbye); [navigation] predicted drift angle

PDAD Probate, Divorce and Admiralty Division (former High Court division)

PdB [USA] Bachelor of Pedagogy (from Latin *Pedagogiae Baccalaureus*)

PDC *Partido Demócrata Cristiano* (Spanish: Christian Democratic Party) (in El Salvador); personnel dispatch centre; personnel dispersal centre; Programme Delivery Control (for video recording); [engineering] pulse-discharge cleaning

PDCI *Parti Démocratique de la Côte d'Ivoire* (French: Democratic Party of Côte d'Ivoire)

PDD precise delay detonator

PdD [USA] Doctor of Pedagogy (from Latin *Pedagogiae Doctor*)

PDE [mathematics] partial differential equation; Projectile Development Establishment

P-de-C Pas-de-Calais (French department)

P-de-D Puy-de-Dôme (French department)

PDF [statistics] probability density function

PDFLP Popular Democratic Front for the Liberation of Palestine

PDG *Parti Démocratique de Guinée* (French: Democratic Party of Guinea); Paymaster Director-General; *président directeur général* (French: chairman and managing director)

PDGF [medicine] platelet-derived growth factor

PDH [computing] plesiochronous digital hierarchy

PDI [astronautics] powered descent initiation; product data interchange

p.d.i. predelivery inspection

PDL [computing] page definition language; [computing] page description language; poverty datum line; [computing] program design language

pdl poundal (unit of force)

PDM physical distribution management; [telecommunications] pulse-duration modulation

PdM [USA] Master of Pedagogy (from Latin *Pedagogiae Magister*)

PDN public data network
pdn production
PDP [computing] parallel distributed processing; program development plan (in NASA); programmed data processor (or processing)
PDPA People's Democratic Party of Afghanistan
PDQ [informal] pretty damn quick
PDR People's Democratic Republic; [astronomy] photodissociation region; [engineering] pitch-to-diameter ratio; precision depth recorder; price–dividend ratio
PDRA postdoctoral research assistant
P/D ratio price–dividend ratio
PDRE People's Democratic Republic of Ethiopia
PDRY People's Democratic Republic of Yemen
PDS Parkinson's Disease Society; *Partei Demokratischen Sozialismus* (German: Party of Democratic Socialism); *Partito Democratico della Sinistra* (Italian: Democratic Party of the Left) (formerly PCI); previously digested sludge; [computing] programming documentation standards
PDSA People's Dispensary for Sick Animals
PDSR Principal Director of Scientific Research
PDT Pacific Daylight Time; personal development technology; [medicine] photodynamic therapy
PDTC Professional Dancer's Training Course (Diploma)
PDU process-development unit
PE [vehicle registration] Guildford; peat extract; permissible error; [insurance] personal effects; [international vehicle registration] Peru; [UK postcode] Peterborough; [USA] petroleum engineer; *Pharmacopoeia Edinburgensis* (Latin: Edinburgh Pharmacopoeia); [computing] phase-encoded (tape format); physical education; plastic explosive; pocket edition; polyeth(yl)ene; [fishing port] Poole; Port Elizabeth (South Africa); [physics] potential energy; Presiding Elder; printer's error; [statistics] probable error; [computing] processing element; procurement executive;

[USA] Professional Engineer; Protestant Episcopal; [medicine] pulmonary embolism
P/E part exchange (in advertisement); port of embarkation; price–earnings (ratio)
.pe Peru (in Internet address)
p.e. [law] personal estate; printer's error
PEA Physical Education Association of Great Britain and Northern Ireland
PEAB Professional Engineers' Appointments Bureau
PEC photoelectric cell; photoelectrochemical cell; Protestant Episcopal Church
pec [short form] pectoral (muscle)
PECD [electronics] photoelectric conversion device
ped. pedal; pedestal; pedestrian
PedD [USA] Doctor of Pedagogy (from Latin *Pedagogiae Doctor*)
PEDir Director of Physical Education
Peeb. Peebles(shire)
PEEP pilot's electronic eye-level presentation
PEF Palestine Exploration Fund; [US insurance] personal effects floater; [electronics] pulsed electric field
PEFCO Private Export Funding Corporation
Peg [astronomy] Pegasus
PEI [Canada] Prince Edward Island
pej. pejorative
p.ej. *por ejemplo* (Spanish: for example)
Pek. Peking
PEL permissible exposure level; permissible exposure limit
Pembs Pembrokeshire
Pemex *Petróleos Mexicanos* (Mexican oil company)
PEN International Association of Poets, Playwrights, Editors, Essayists and Novelists
Pen [geology] Pennsylvanian
Pen. Peninsula; Penitentiary
pen. penal; penetrate; penetration; peninsula; peninsular
PEng Member of the Society of Professional Engineers; [Canada] (Registered) Professional Engineer
Penn. Pennsylvania
penol. penology
Pent. [Bible] Pentateuch; Pentecost

pent. pentagon

penthse penthouse (in accommodation advertisement)

PEO [USA] Philanthropic Educational Organization

PEP [radio] peak envelope power; personal equity plan (savings scheme); political and economic planning

PEPP [USA] Professional Engineers in Private Practice

PER price–earnings ratio; Professional and Executive Recruitment; Professional Employment Register

Per [astronomy] Perseus

Per. Persia; Persian

per. percentile; period; person

PERA Production Engineering Research Association of Great Britain

per an. *per annum* (Latin: yearly)

per ann. *per annum* (Latin: yearly)

P/E ratio price–earnings ratio

perc. [music] percussion

per con. [book-keeping] *per contra* (Latin: on the other side)

perd. [music] *perdendosi* (Italian: dying away)

perf. perfect; perfection; perforate; perforated; perforation; performance; performed (by); performer

perh. perhaps

peri. perigee

perig. perigee

perjy perjury

perk [short form] percolate; [short form] perquisite

PERL [computing] practical extraction and report language; [medicine] pupils equal and react(ive) to light

Perm pre-embossed rigid magnetic technology

perm [short form] permanent wave; [short form] permutation

perm. permanent; permission

PERME Propellants, Explosives and Rocket Motor Establishment

perp. perpendicular; perpetual

per pro. *per procurationem* (Latin: through the agency of)

Pers. Persia; Persian

pers. person; personal; personally; perspective

persp. perspective

PERT [commerce] performance evaluation and review technique; [computing] program evaluation and review technique; programme evaluation and review technique; project evaluation and review technique

pert. pertaining

Peruv. Peruvian

PES [computing] programmable electronic system

Pes. [currency] peseta

PESA [medicine] percutaneous epididymal sperm aspiration

PESC Public Expenditure Survey Committee

PESGB Petroleum Exploration Society of Great Britain

Pesh. Peshawar (Pakistan)

PEST political, environmental, social and technological; Pressure for Economic and Social Toryism

PET polyeth(yl)ene terephthalate (packaging plastic); [medicine] positron emission tomography (as in **PET scanner**); [taxation] potentially exempt transfer; [medicine] pre-eclamptic toxaemia

Pet. [Bible] Peter; (Gaius) Petronius (Roman satirist)

pet. petrol; petroleum; petrological; petrologist; petrology

PETA People for Ethical Treatment of Animals

Pet.E [USA] petroleum engineer

PETN pentaerythritol tetranitrate (explosive)

petn petition

PETP [chemistry] polyeth(yl)ene terephthalate (polyester)

petr. petrification; petrify; petrology

Petriburg. *Petriburgensis* (Latin: (Bishop) of Peterborough)

petro. petrochemical

petrochem. petrochemical

petrog. petrography

petrol. petrological; petrology

PETS [computing] posting and enquiry terminal system

P/Ex part exchange (in advertisement)

p.ex. *par exemple* (French: for example, e.g.)

PF [vehicle registration] Guildford; Pagan Federation; panchromatic film; Patriotic Front; phenol–formaldehyde (as in **PF resin**); [building] plain face; power factor; Procurator Fiscal; [finance] public funding; pulverized fuel

Pf [currency] Pfennig (hundredth of Deutschmark)

pF picofarad (unit of electrical capacitance)

pf [music] piano(forte); proof

pf [music] *piano e forte* (Italian: softly and (then) loudly); [music] *più forte* (Italian: louder)

pf. perfect; [finance] preferred (stock)

p.f. pneumatic float; pro forma (invoice)

PFA Popular Flying Association; [USA] Private Fliers' Association; Professional Footballers' Association; pulverized fuel ash

P factor [psychology] preservation factor

PFB [building] preformed beam(s)

PFBR [nuclear technology] prototype fast breeder reactor

PFC polychlorinated fluorocarbon (synthetic resin); [US informal] poor foolish (or forlorn) civilian

Pfc [US military] Private first class

pfce performance

PFD personal flotation device; position fixing device

Pfd *Pfund* (German: pound)

pfd preferred

pfd sp. preferred spelling

PFF pathfinder force

pfg [currency] Pfennig (hundredth of Deutschmark)

PFLO Popular Front for the Liberation of Oman

PFLP Popular Front for the Liberation of Palestine

PFLT People's Front of Liberation Tigers (Sri Lankan separatist group)

PFM [telecommunications] pulse-frequency modulation

PFMA Pet Food Manufacturers Association

PFP Partnership for Peace (in NATO); personal financial planning; [South Africa] Progressive Federal Party

PFPUT Pension Fund Property Unit Trust

PFR [nuclear technology] prototype fast reactor

PFRT preliminary flight rating test

PFSA *pour faire ses adieux* (French: to say goodbye)

PFSF Parents for Safe Food

PFT [medicine] pulmonary function test

PFV *pour faire visite* (French: to make a call)

pfx [grammar] prefix

PG [vehicle registration] Guildford; [cinema] parental guidance (film classification); [Freemasonry] Past Grand; paying guest; postgraduate; Preacher-General; [US informal] pregnant; *prisonnier de guerre* (French: prisoner of war); Procurator-General; [pharmacology] prostaglandin

Pg [geology] Palaeocene

Pg. Portugal; Portuguese

pg. page

.pg Papua New Guinea (in Internet address)

p.g. pay group; paying guest; *persona grata* (Latin: acceptable person); proof gallon (of alcohol); proving ground

PGA [electronics] pin grid array; Power Generation Association; Prison Governors' Association; Professional Golfers' Association; [computing] programmable gate array; [biochemistry] pteroylglutamic acid (folic acid)

p.g.c. [navigation] per gyrocompass

PGCE Postgraduate Certificate of Education

PGCert Postgraduate Certificate

PGD [Freemasonry] Past Grand Deacon

PGDip Postgraduate Diploma

PgDn [computing] page down (key)

PGDRS psychogeriatric dependency rating scale

PGF [medicine] polypeptide growth factor

PGG Professional Gardeners' Guild

PGJD [Freemasonry] Past Grand Junior Deacon

PGL [medicine] persistent generalized lymphadenopathy (stage of Aids); [Freemasonry] Provincial Grand Lodge

PGM [Freemasonry] Past Grand Master; precision-guided missile (or munition)

pgn pigeon

PGP [computing] pretty good privacy

PGR [cinema] parental guidance recommended (film classification in Australia); population growth rate; [psychology] psychogalvanic response

PGSD [Freemasonry] Past Grand Senior Deacon

p.g.t. per gross ton

PgUp [computing] page up (key)

PH [vehicle registration] Guildford; [civil aircraft marking] Netherlands; [UK postcode] Perth; petroleum hydrocarbon; [fishing port] Plymouth; previous (medical) history; public health; public house (on map); [medicine] pulmonary hypertension; Purple Heart (US military decoration)

Ph [geology] Phanerozoic

Ph. Philosophy (in academic degrees)

pH [chemistry] potential of hydrogen ions (measure of acidity or alkalinity)

ph phot (unit of illumination)

ph. phase; philosopher; philosophy; phone

.ph Philippines (in Internet address)

p.h. [engineering] precipitation hardening

PHA [immunology] phytohaemagglutinin; Public Health Act; [USA] Public Housing Administration; [USA] public housing authority

PHAB Physically Handicapped and Able Bodied

phal. phalanx

phar. pharmaceutical; pharmacist; pharmacology; pharmacopoeia; pharmacy

PharB Bachelor of Pharmacy (from Latin *Pharmaciae Baccalaureus*)

PharD Doctor of Pharmacy (from Latin *Pharmaciae Doctor*)

PharM Master of Pharmacy (from Latin *Pharmaciae Magister*)

pharm. pharmaceutical; pharmacist; pharmacology; pharmacopoeia; pharmacy

pharmacol. pharmacological; pharmacology

PharmB Bachelor of Pharmacy (from Latin *Pharmaciae Baccalaureus*)

pharm. chem. pharmaceutical chemistry

PharmD Doctor of Pharmacy (from Latin *Pharmaciae Doctor*)

PharmM Master of Pharmacy (from Latin *Pharmaciae Magister*)

PhB Bachelor of Philosophy (from Latin *Philosophiae Baccalaureus*)

ph. brz. phosphor bronze

PHC pharmaceutical chemist; primary health care

PHCA Private Hire Car Association

PHD Doctor of Public Health

PhD Doctor of Philosophy (from Latin *Philosophiae Doctor*)

PhDEd Doctor of Philosophy in Education

PHE public health engineer

Phe [astronomy] Phoenix

PhG [USA] Graduate in Pharmacy

PHI permanent health insurance; public health inspector

PHIBLANT [US navy] Amphibious Forces, Atlantic

PHIBPAC [US navy] Amphibious Forces, Pacific

PHIGS [computing] programmers' hierarchical interactive graphics standard

Phil. Philadelphia; Philharmonic; [Bible] Philippians; Philippines

phil. philological; philology; philosopher; philosophical; philosophy

Phila. Philadelphia

Philem. [Bible] Philemon

Phil. I Philippine Islands

Phil. Is. Philippine Islands

philol. philological; philology

philos. philosopher; philosophical; philosophy

Phil. Soc. Philharmonic Society

Phil. Trans. *Philosophical Transactions of the Royal Society of London*

PhL Licentiate in Philosophy (from Latin *Philosophiae Licentiatus*)

PHLS Public Health Laboratory Service

PHLSB Public Health Laboratory Service Board

PhM Master of Philosophy (from Latin *Philosophiae Magister*)

PHN public health nurse

Phoen. Phoenician; Phoenix

phon. phonetic; phonetically; phonetics; phonological; phonology

phone [short form] telephone

phonet. phonetic; phonetically; phonetics

phonog. phonography

phonol. phonological; phonology

phot. photograph; photographer; photographic; photography

photog. photograph; photographer; photographic; photography

photom. photometric(al); photometry

php pounds per horsepower; pump horsepower

PHR [engineering] power-to-heat ratio

phr. phrase; phraseology

phren. phrenological; phrenology

phrenol. phrenological; phrenology
PHRG Parliamentary Human Rights Group
PHS [USA] Public Health Service
PHSA Provincial Hospital Services Association
PHTS [USA] Psychiatric Home Treatment Service
PHWR [nuclear technology] pressurized heavy-water reactor
phys. physical; physically; physician; physicist; physics; physiological; physiology
phys. ed. physical education
physio [short form] physiotherapy
physiog. physiognomy; physiography
physiol. physiological; physiologist; physiology
phys. sc. physical science
PI [medicine] parainfluenza virus; Pasteur Institute; [mathematics] path integral; per inquiry; [US law] personal injury; petrol-injected; *Pharmacopoeia Internationalis* (Latin: International Pharmacopoeia); Philippine Islands; [civil aircraft marking] (Republic of the) Philippines; photographic interpretation; photographic interpreter; [US informal] pimp; [USA] principal investigator; Privacy International; private investigator; [accounting] profitability index; [computing] programmed instruction
p.i. [insurance] professional indemnity
PIA Pakistan International Airlines Corporation; [computing] peripheral interface adapter; Personal Investment Authority
PIAC Petroleum Industry Advisory Council
piang. [music] *piangendo* (Italian: plaintively)
pianiss. [music] *pianissimo* (Italian: very softly)
piano [short form] pianoforte
PIARC Permanent International Association of Road Congresses
PIAT [military] projector infantry antitank (weapon)
PIB Petroleum Information Bureau; Prices and Incomes Board (replaced by NBPI)
PIBOR [finance] Paris Inter-Bank Offered Rate
PIBS permanent interest-bearing share

PIC [computing] picture format; Poultry Industry Conference; [computing] problem isolation code; product of incomplete combustion; [computing] programmable interrupt controller
Pic [astronomy] Pictor
pic [short form] picture
pic. [music] piccolo; pictorial; picture
PICC Provisional International Computation Centre
PICS [computing] platform for Internet content selection
pict. pictorial; picture
PICUTPC Permanent and International Committee of Underground Town Planning and Construction
PICV Permanent International Commission of Viticulture
PID [medicine] pelvic inflammatory disease; [computing] personal identification device; [medicine] prolapsed intervertebral disc (= slipped disc)
PIDE *Polícia Internacional e de Defesa do Estado* (Portuguese: International Police for the Defence of the State) (former state security system)
PIDS [medicine] primary immune deficiency syndrome
PIE Proto-Indo-European
PIF [computing] program information file
PIFA Packaging and Industrial Films Association
pigmt pigment
pigmtn pigmentation
PIH Paintings in Hospitals; [medicine] pregnancy-induced hypertension
PIK payment in kind
PIL [computing] paper interchange language; payment in lieu; Pest Infestation Laboratory
pil. [medicine] *pilula* (Latin: pill) (in prescriptions)
PILL [computing] programmed instruction language learning
PILOT [computing] programmed inquiry, learning or teaching
PIM [computing] personal information manager; [telecommunications] pulse-interval modulation
PIME *Pontificium Institutum pro Missionibus Externis* (Latin: Pontifical Institute for Foreign Missions)
PIMS profit impact of market strategy

PIN personal identification number

PINC property income certificate

P-in-C Priest-in-Charge

Pind. Pindar (ancient Greek poet)

PING [computing] Packet Internet Groper

PINS [USA] person(s) in need of supervision

pinx. *pinxit* (Latin: (he/she) painted it)

PIO [computing] parallel input/output; photographic interpretation officer; [US military] public information office; [US military] public information officer

PIPO [computing] parallel in, parallel out

pippy [informal] person inheriting parent's property

PIR passive infrared

PIRA Paper Industries Research Association; Provisional Irish Republican Army

PISO [computing] parallel in, serial out

PITB Petroleum Industry Training Board

PITCOM Parliamentary Information Technology Committee

PIX [computing] picture exchange format

pix [short form] pictures

pixel [computing] picture element

pizz. [music] *pizzicato* (Italian: plucked)

PJ [vehicle registration] Guildford; [civil aircraft marking] Netherlands Antilles; petajoule; Presiding Judge; Probate Judge; [informal] pyjama(s)

p.j. physical jerks; [informal] pyjama(s)

PK [vehicle registration] Guildford; [civil aircraft marking] Indonesia and West Irian; [international vehicle registration] Pakistan; personal knowledge; psychokinesis

pk pack; park; peak; peck (unit of dry measure)

pk. package

.pk Pakistan (in Internet address)

pkg packing; parking

pkg. package

pkge package

PKI *Partai Komunis Indonésia* (Bahasa Indonesian: Indonesian Communist Party)

PKP *Polskie Koleje Państwowe* (Polish: Polish State Railways)

pkt packet; pocket

PKTF Printing and Kindred Trades Federation

PKU [medicine] phenylketonuria

pkwy [USA] parkway

PL [vehicle registration] Guildford; [insurance] partial loss; [insurance] passenger liability; patrol leader (in Scouts or Guides); Paymaster Lieutenant; [fishing port] Peel; *Pharmacopoeia Londiniensis* (Latin: Pharmacopoeia of London); [shipping] Plimsoll line; [UK postcode] Plymouth; Poet Laureate; [international vehicle registration] Poland; position line; Primrose League; [law] product liability; product licence (on medicinal product); programmed learning; [computing] programming language; public law; public library

P/L [insurance] partial loss; [law] product liability

P-L [astronomy] period–luminosity

Pl. Place (in road name); Plate(s) (book illustration); *Platz* (German: Square) (in road name)

p/l profit and loss

pl. place; plain; plate; platoon; [grammar] plural; pole (unit of length)

.pl Poland (in Internet address)

PLA [China] People's Liberation Army; Port of London Authority; Private Libraries Association; [computing, electronics] programmable logic array; [computing, electronics] programmed logic array

Pla. Plaza

p.l.a. passengers' luggage in advance

PLAN People's Liberation Army of Namibia

plan. planet; planetarium

plas. plaster; plastic

plat. plateau; platform; platinum; platonic; platoon

platf. platform

PLATO [computing] programmed logic for automatic teaching operation

Plaut. (Titus Maccius) Plautus (Roman dramatist)

PLC Poor Law Commissioners; [marketing] product life cycle; [computing] programmable logic controller; public limited company

plc public limited company

PLCC [computing] plastic leadless chip carrier

PLCWTWU Power Loom Carpet Weavers' and Textile Workers' Union

plcy policy

PLD potentially lethal damage; [computing] programmable logic device

pld payload
Ple [geology] Pleistocene
pleb [short form] plebeian
Plen. Plenipotentiary
PLF Palestine Liberation Front; [medicine] (serum) placental fementin
plf plaintiff
plff plaintiff
PLG private/light goods (vehicle)
PLI *Partito Liberale Italiano* (Italian: Italian Liberal Party); President of the Landscape Institute
Pli [geology] Pliocene
PLJ [trademark] pure lemon juice
PLL [computing] phase-locked loop
PLM Paris–Lyons–Mediterranean (railway); [telecommunications] pulse-length modulation
PL/M [computing] Programming Language for Microcomputers
plmb. plumber; plumbing
plng planning
PLO Palestine Liberation Organization
PLP Parliamentary Labour Party; Progressive Labour Party (in Bermuda); Progressive Liberal Party (in Bahamas)
PLR public lending right
PLS [statistics] partial least-squares; [computing] programmable logic sequencer
Pls. Plates (book illustrations)
Pl. Sgt Platoon Sergeant
plsnt pleasant
PLSS [astronautics] personal life-support system; [astronautics] portable life-support system
plstc plastic
plstr plasterer
PLT Princeton Large Torus (nuclear reactor)
plt pilot
pltc. political
pltf plaintiff
PLU [informal] people like us
plu. [grammar] plural
PLUNA *Primeras Lineas Uruguayas de Navegación Aérea* (Uruguayan airline company)
plup. [grammar] pluperfect
plupf. [grammar] pluperfect
plur. [grammar] plural; plurality
Pluto pipe line under the ocean (for fuel in World War II)
Ply. Plymouth

plywd plywood
PL/Z [computing] Programming Language Zilog
PM [vehicle registration] Guildford; Pacific mail; parachute mine; [music] particular metre; Past Master (of fraternity); Paymaster; [music] peculiar metre; [telecommunications] phase modulation; *piae memoriae* (Latin: of pious memory); Pipe Major; police magistrate; *polícia militar* (Portuguese: military police); *polizia militare* (Italian: military police); Pope and Martyr; Postmaster; *post meridiem* (Latin: after noon); postmortem (examination); powder metallurgy; predictive maintenance; preventive maintenance; Prime Minister; product manager; [music] proper metre; Provost Marshal
Pm [chemical element] promethium
pm. premium
p.m. permanent magnet; *post meridiem* (Latin: after noon); postmortem (examination); premolar (tooth)
PMA Pakistan Medical Association; [dentistry] papillary, marginal, attached (gingivitis); [pharmacology] paramethoxyamphetamine (hallucinogen); personal military assistant; [chemistry] phenylmercuric acetate; [chemistry] polymethyl acrylate; [USA] Purchasing Management Association
PMAF [USA] Pharmaceutical Manufacturers' Association Foundation
PM&ATA Paint Manufacturers' and Allied Trades Association
PM&R physical medicine and rehabilitation
PMB Potato Marketing Board
PMBX [telecommunications] private manual branch exchange
PMC Personnel Management Centre; [building] plaster-moulded cornice
PMD [USA] Program for Management Development
PMDA Pianoforte Manufacturers' and Distributors' Association
PME [electronics] protective multiple earthing
PMF probable maximum flood; [physics] pulsating magnetic field
PMG *Pall Mall Gazette*; Paymaster-General; [electrical engineering] permanent-magnet generator;

Postmaster-General; Provost Marshal-General

PMH previous medical history

p.m.h. per man-hour

PMI Pensions Management Institute

pmk postmark

PML Prime Minister's list; [insurance] probable maximum loss

PMM platinum-metal minerals; [telecommunications] pulse-mode multiplex

PMMA polymethylmethacrylate (synthetic resin)

PMMS Plainsong and Medieval Music Society

PMN [medicine] polymorphonuclear

PMO principal medical officer

PMR Pacific missile range; [medicine] polymyalgia rheumatica

pmr paymaster

PMRAFNS Princess Mary's Royal Air Force Nursing Service

PMS [printing] Pantone Matching System; [medicine] pregnant mare's serum; [medicine] premenstrual syndrome; President of the Miniature Society; [computing] processor-memory-switch (notation); project management system

PMSG [medicine] pregnant mare's serum gonadotrophin

PMT [photography] photomechanical transfer; [US finance] post-market trading; [medicine] premenstrual tension; project management team

pmt payment

PMTS [commerce] predetermined motion-time standards

PMU Pontifical Missionary Unit

PMV predicted mean vote

PMX [telecommunications] private manual exchange

PN [vehicle registration] Brighton; Pakistan Navy; [medicine] parenteral nutrition; [engineering] performance number; [astronomy] planetary nebula; [medicine] postnatal; [physics] post-Newtonian; [fishing port] Preston; [commerce] promissory note; [computing] pseudonoise; psychoneurotic

P/N part number; [commerce] promissory note

p.n. percussion note; percussive note; please note; [commerce] promissory note; [physics] proton number

PNA Pakistan National Alliance; paranitroaniline (dye); Philippines News Agency; Psychiatric Nurses Association

Pna Panama

PNB Philippine National Bank

PNC Palestinian National Council; People's National Congress (in Guyana)

PND [medicine] postnatal depression

PNdB perceived noise decibel

pndg pending

PNEU Parents' National Education Union

pneu. pneumatic

pneum. pneumatic

PNG Papua New Guinea; [international vehicle registration] Papua New Guinea

p.n.g. *persona non grata* (Latin: unacceptable person)

PNI [medicine] psychoneuroimmunology

PNL Pacific Northwest Laboratory

pnl panel

PNLA Palestine National Liberation Army

PNLM Palestine National Liberation Movement

PNM People's National Movement (in Trinidad and Tobago)

PNO principal nursing officer

PNP *Partido Nuevo Progresista* (Spanish: New Progressive Party) (in Puerto Rico); [Jamaica] People's National Party

PnP [computing] plug and play

PNR [physics] prompt nuclear reaction

pnr pioneer

p.n.r. prior notice required

PNS [anatomy] parasympathetic nervous system

PNSB [microbiology] purple nonsulphur bacteria

Pnt. [USA] Pentagon

PNTO principal naval transport officer

pntr painter

PNV *Partido Nacional Vasco* (Spanish: Basque National Party)

pnxt *pinxit* (Latin: (he/she) painted it)

PNYA Port of New York Authority

Pnz. Penzance

PO parcels office; parole officer; *par ordre* (French: by order); Passport Office; Patent Office; personnel officer; petty officer; philharmonic orchestra; pilot officer; [UK postcode] Portsmouth; [vehicle registration] Portsmouth; postal order; post office; power-operated; power oscillator; Province of Ontario;

public office; public officer; Pyrénées-Orientales (French department)

Po [chemical element] polonium

p/o printout

p.o. part of; [medicine] *per os* (Latin: by mouth) (in prescriptions); postal order; previous order(s)

POA price on application (in advertisement); primary optical area (in graphic design); Prison Officers' Association

POAC Post Office Advisory Council

POB Post Office Box

PO Box Post Office Box

POC port of call; [chemistry] product of combustion

POD payment on delivery; pay on death; pay on delivery; *Pocket Oxford Dictionary*; port of debarkation; [USA] Post Office Department

POE port of embarkation; port of entry

POED Post Office Engineering Department

poet. poetic(al); poetry

POETS day [slang] piss off early tomorrow's Saturday (facetious name for Friday)

POEU Post Office Engineering Union

P of W Prince of Wales

POG passion fruit, orange and guava (juice)

POGO Polar Orbiting Geophysical Observatory

poi. poison; poisonous

POL Patent Office Library; petrol(eum), oil and lubricants; [computing] problem-oriented language

Pol. Poland; Polish

pol. polar; polarize; polarized; police; political; politician; politics

pol. ad. political adviser

pol. econ. political economy

pol. ind. pollen index

Polis Parliamentary On-Line Information Service

polit. political; politics

poll. pollution

pol. sci. political science

poly [short form] polytechnic

Poly. Polynesia; Polynesian; Polytechnic

Polyb. Polybius (ancient Greek historian)

Polyn. Polynesia; Polynesian

POM particulate organic matter; prescription-only medicine (or medication)

POMEF Political Office Middle East Force

PON [computing] passive optical network

PONI product of Northern Ireland

Ponsi [military slang] person of no strategical importance

pont. br. pontoon bridge

Ponti [military slang] person of no tactical importance

POO Post Office order

POOF [computing] peripheral on-line oriented function

POP plaster of Paris; [computing] point of presence; point of purchase; Post Office preferred (size of stationery); [computing] post office protocol; [photography] printing-out paper; [pharmacology] progestogen-only pill; proof of purchase

pop. popular; popularly; population

p.o.p. point of purchase

POPA Property Owners Protection Association

POPIN Population Information Network

POPL [computing] principles of programming languages

por. porosity; porous; portion; portrait

p.o.r. pay(able) on receipt; pay(able) on return; port of refuge

PORIS Post Office Radio Interference Station

porn [short form] pornography

Port. Portugal; Portuguese

port. portable; portrait; portraiture

POS [grammar] part of speech; point of sale; [medicine] polycystic ovary syndrome; Port of Spain (Trinidad); [computing] product of sums

pos. position; positive; possession; [grammar] possessive

POSAS Patent Office Search and Advisory Service

posn position

POSS Palomar Observatory Sky Survey; passive optical surveillance system; prototype optical surveillance system

poss. possession; [grammar] possessive; possible; possibly

POSSLQ [US informal] person of the opposite sex sharing living quarters

Possum patient-operated selector mechanism (phonetic spelling of initials)

POST Parliamentary Office of Science and

Technology; point-of-sale terminal;
[computing] power-on self test
postgrad [short form] postgraduate
posth. posthumous; posthumously
posthum. posthumous; posthumously
pot. potash; potassium; potential; poten-
tiometer
poul. poultry
POUM *Partido Obrero de Unificación Marx-
ista* (Spanish: Workers' Party of Marxist
Unity)
POUNC Post Ofice Users' National
Council
POV point of view
p.o.v. point of view; privately owned
vehicle
POW please oblige with; Prince of Wales;
prisoner of war
POWAGOD Prince of Wales' Advisory
Group on Disability
powd. powder
POY [textiles] partially oriented yarn
PP [civil aircraft marking] Brazil; [vehicle
registration] Luton; [geology] Pacific
plate; parcel post; parish priest; parliamentary papers; *Partido Popular*
(Spanish: Popular Party); *Pastor Pastorum*
(Latin: Shepherd of the Shepherds); Past
President; *Pater Patriae* (Latin: Father of
his Country); *Patres* (Latin: Fathers);
[medicine] pellagra-preventive; permanent pass; petrol point; [chemistry]
phenolphthalein (alkalinity test); pilot
plant; [chemistry] polyprop(yl)ene;
[grammar] prepositional phrase; present
pupil
pp [music] *pianissimo* (Italian: very softly)
pp. pages
p.p. parcel post; [grammar] past participle; per person; *per procurationem*
(Latin: through the agency of); planning permission (in property advertisement); play or pay; post(age) paid;
[medicine] *post prandium* (Latin: after
meals) (in prescriptions); prepaid; present position; privately printed
PPA Pakistan Press Association; *Parti Populaire Algérien* (French: Popular Party of
Algeria); Periodical Publishers' Association; Pools Proprietors' Association;
Pre-School Playgroups Association
PPARC Particle Physics and Astronomy
Research Council

PPB paper, printing and binding; party
political broadcast; planning-
programming-budgeting (system); private posting box
ppb parts per billion
PPBAS planning-programming-
budgeting-accounting system
PPBS planning-programming-budgeting
system
PPC *Patres Conscripti* (Latin: Conscript
Fathers) (members of Roman Senate);
pour prendre congé (French: to take
leave); Professional Purposes Committee; [medicine] progressive patient
care; prospective parliamentary
candidate; [USA] Public Power
Corporation
PPCLI Princess Patricia's Canadian Light
Infantry
PPCS [New Zealand] Primary Producers'
Cooperation Society
PPD *Partido Popular Democrático* (Spanish:
Popular Democratic Party) (in Puerto
Rico); [medicine] purified protein deriva-
tive (of tuberculin)
ppd post(age) paid; prepaid
PPE personal protective equipment; philosophy, politics and economics (academic course)
PPF [US insurance] personal property
floater
PPFA Planned Parenthood Federation of
America
PPG Pacific proving grounds
PPH [USA] paid personal holidays; [medi-
cine] postpartum haemorrhage
pph. pamphlet
PPI Pakistan Press International; [USA]
patient package insert (instructions with
prescribed medication); [radar] plan-
position indicator; [insurance] policy
proof of interest; [economics] producer
price index
p.p.i. parcel post insured
PPITB Printing and Publishing Industry
Training Board
PPK *Polizei Pistole Kriminal* (German:
police criminal pistol)
PPL private pilot's licence
pple [grammar] participle
PPLO [microbiology] pleuropneumonia-
like organism(s)
PPM [electronics] peak programme meter;

[telecommunications] pulse-position modulation

ppm pages per minute; parts per million

PPMA Produce Packaging and Marketing Association

PPN [computing] public packet network

PPO [US medicine] preferred-provider organization

PPP Pakistan People's Party; People's Progressive Party (in Gambia and Guyana); personal pension plan; [computing] point-to-point protocol; Private Patients Plan; psychology, philosophy and physiology (academic course); [economics] purchasing power parity

ppp [music] *pianississimo* (Italian: as softly as possible)

pppm per person per month

pppn per person per night

PPPS *post post postscriptum* (Latin: third postscript)

PPR printed paper rate (of postage)

ppr paper; proper

p.pr. [grammar] participle present

PPRA Past President of the Royal Academy

PPRBA Past President of the Royal Society of British Artists

PPRBS Past President of the Royal Society of British Sculptors

p.pro. *per procurationem* (Latin: through the agency of)

PPS Parliamentary Private Secretary; [medicine] pelvic pain syndrome; *post postscriptum* (Latin: second postscript); [Australia] prescribed payments system; Principal Private Secretary; *Proceedings of the Prehistoric Society*; purchasing power standard

PPT *Parti Progressiste Tchadien* (French: Chad Progressive Party); [electrical engineering] peak power transfer

ppt. [chemistry] precipitate

pptd [chemistry] precipitated

pptg [chemistry] precipitating

pptn [chemistry] precipitation

ppty property

PPU Peace Pledge Union; Primary Producers' Union

PQ parliamentary question; [Canada] *Parti Québecois* (French: Quebec Party); personality quotient; Province of Quebec

p.q. preceding question; previous question

PR [vehicle registration] Bournemouth; parliamentary report; [medicine] partial remission; partial response; *Partido Radical* (Spanish: Radical Party) (in Chile); *Parti Républicain* (French: Republican Party); [computing] pattern recognition; payroll; percentile rank; performance ratio; [law] personal representative; photographic reconnaissance; Pipe Rolls (former public records); plotting and radar; *Populus Romanus* (Latin: the Roman people); postal regulations; preliminary report; Pre-Raphaelite; press release; press representative; [UK postcode] Preston; [boxing] prize ring; production rate; profit rate; progress report; project report; [politics] proportional representation; public relations; Puerto Rican; Puerto Rico; purchase request

P/R payroll

Pr [chemical element] praseodymium

Pr. *Praça* (Portuguese: Square) (in road name); Prince; Protestant; Provençal

pr painter; pair; paper; per; power

pr. prayer; [US finance] preferred (stock); [grammar] present; pressure; price; priest; print; printed; printer; printing; [grammar] pronoun; proof; proper; prove; provincial

p.r. parcel receipt; [medicine] *per rectum* (Latin: by the rectum) (in prescriptions)

PRA [medicine] plasma renin activity; President of the Royal Academy; probabilistic risk analysis; probabilistic risk assessment; [USA] Public Roads Administration

prag. pragmatic; pragmatism

pram [short form] perambulator

PRB People's Republic of Bulgaria; Pre-Raphaelite Brotherhood

PRBS President of the Royal Society of British Sculptors

PRC People's Republic of China; [medicine] plasma renin concentration; [USA] Postal Rate Commission; *post Romam conditam* (Latin: after the foundation of Rome); [USA] Price Regulation Committee

PRCA President of the Royal Cambrian Academy; Public Relations Consultants' Association

prchst parachutist

PRCP President of the Royal College of Physicians

PRCS President of the Royal College of Surgeons (of England)

prcs process

prcst precast

PRE petroleum refining engineer; President of the Royal Society of Painter-Printmakers (formerly President of the Royal Society of Painter-Etchers and Engravers)

Preb. Prebend(ary)

Prec. Precentor

prec. preceding; precision

PRECIS preserved context index system

pred. [grammar] predicate; predicative; predicatively

predic. [grammar] predicate; predicative; predicatively

Pref. Prefect

pref. preface; prefatory; preferably; preference; preferred; [grammar] prefix

prefab [short form] prefabricated (building)

prehist. prehistoric(al); prehistory

prej. prejudice

prel. prelude

Prela *Prensa Latina* (Cuban news agency)

prelim. preliminary

prem. premature; premium

premed [short form] premedical (student); [short form] premedication

prems premises

PrEng [USA] Professional Engineer

prep [short form] preparation (for schoolwork); [short form] preparatory (school); [short form] prepare

prep. preparation; preparatory; [grammar] preposition

prepd prepared

prepg preparing

prepn preparation

PREPP Post-Registration Education and Practice Project (in nursing)

Pres. Presbyterian; President

pres. present; presentation; presidency; presidential; presumed; presumptive

Presb. Presbyterian

press. pressure

PRESTO [USA] program reporting and evaluation system for total operation

presv. preservation; preservative; preserve

pret. [grammar] preterite

prev. previous; previously

PRF Petroleum Research Fund; [electronics] pulse recurrence frequency; [electronics] pulse repetition frequency

prf proof

prfnl professional

prfr proofreader

PRHA President of the Royal Hibernian Academy

PRI [Mexico] *Partido Revolucionario Institucional* (Spanish: Institutional Revolutionary Party); *Partito Repubblicano Italiano* (Italian: Italian Republican Party); Penal Reform International; Plastics and Rubber Institute (became part of Institute of Materials); President of the Royal Institute of Painters in Water Colours; [computing] primary-rate ISDN

pri. primary; primate; primer; priority; private

PRIA President of the Royal Irish Academy

PRIAS President of the Royal Incorporation of Architects in Scotland

PRIBA President of the Royal Institute of British Architects

PRII Public Relations Institute of Ireland

prim. primary; primate; primer; primitive

primip. [obstetrics] primipara (woman who has given birth once)

Prin. Principal; Principality

prin. principal; principle

Princ. Principal; Principality

princ. principal; principle

print. printed; printer; printing

PRISA Public Relations Institute of South Africa

PRISM [USA] program reliability information system for management

prism. prismatic

priv. private; privative

PRM personal radiation monitor

prm premium

PRML [computing] partial-response maximum-likelihood

prn [medicine] *pro re nata* (Latin: when required) (in prescriptions)

PRO Public Record Office; public relations officer

Pr. O press officer

Pro. Provost

pro [short form] professional; [short form] prostitute

pro. procedure; proceed; procure; profession; professional; [finance] promissory (note)

pro-am [sports] professional–amateur

prob. probability; probable; probably; probate; probation; problem

prob. off. probation

Proc. Proceedings; Proctor

proc. procedure; proceedings; process; processed; processing

Proc. Roy. Soc. *Proceedings of the Royal Society*

prod. produce; produced; producer; product; production

Prof. Professor

prof. profession; professional

Prof. Eng. [USA] Professional Engineer

Pr. of Man. [Bible] Prayer of Manasseh (book of Apocrypha)

Prog. [politics] Progressive

prog [short form] programme

prog. prognosis; [computing] program; programme; progress; progressive

PROI President of the Royal Institute of Oil Painters

proj. project; projectile; projection; projector

prol. prologue

prole [short form] proletarian

PROLOG programming in logic (computer programming language)

PROM [computing] programmable read-only memory

prom [short form] promenade

prom. prominent; promontory; promote; promoter; promotion

pron. [grammar] pronominal; [grammar] pronoun; pronounce; pronounceable; pronounced; pronouncement; pronouncing; pronunciation

PRONED Promotion of Non-Executive Directors

pronunc. pronunciation

PROP Preservation of the Rights of Prisoners

prop [short form] propeller; [short form] property (in theatre)

prop. proper; properly; property; proportion; proportional; proposition; proprietary; proprietor

propl proportional

propn proportion

propr proprietor

props [short form] properties (in theatre)

PRORM Pay and Records Office, Royal Marines

PROS preventive maintenance, repair and operational services

pros. prosecution; prosodical; prosody; [advertising] prospectus rate

Pros. Atty [USA] prosecuting attorney

prosc. proscenium

prost. [medicine] prostate; prostitution

Prot. Protectorate; Protestant

pro tem. *pro tempore* (Latin: for the time being)

Prov. Provençal; Provence; [Bible] Proverbs; Province; Provost

prov. proverb; proverbial; proverbially; province; provincial; provision; provisional

Prov. GM [Freemasonry] Provincial Grand Master

prox. *proximo* (Latin: in the next (month)) (used in formal correspondence)

prox. acc. *proxime accessit* (Latin: (he/she) came nearest (to the winner)) (referring to runner-up in competition)

prox. luc. *proxima luce* (Latin: on the day before)

PRP performance-related pay; petrol refilling point; profit-related pay

pr.p. [grammar] present participle

pr. pr. *praeter propter* (Latin: about, nearly)

PRR [electronics] pulse repetition rate

PRS Performing Right Society Limited; President of the Royal Society; Protestant Reformation Society

PRs [currency] Pakistan rupee

prs pairs

PRSA President of the Royal Scottish Academy; Public Relations Society of America

prsd pressed

PRSE President of the Royal Society of Edinburgh

PRSH President of the Royal Society of Health

PRST please return some time

Pr.ST [USA] Prairie Standard Time

PRSW President of the Royal Scottish Water Colour Society

PRT [USA] personal rapid transit; petroleum revenue tax

PRTC Princess Royal Trust for Carers

prtg printing

PRU photographic reconnaissance unit(s) (in RAF)

PRUAA President of the Royal Ulster Academy of Arts

Prus. Prussia; Prussian

PRV *pour rendre visite* (French: to return a call); pressure-reducing valve

PRWA President of the Royal West of England Academy

PRWS President of the Royal Watercolour Society

PS [vehicle registration] Aberdeen; paddle steamer; Parliamentary Secretary; *Partido Socialista* (Portuguese: Socialist Party); *Parti Socialiste* (French: Socialist Party); passenger steamer; Pastel Society; penal servitude; Permanent Secretary; [computing] personal system; Pharmaceutical Society; Philological Society; [linguistics] phrase structure; Physical Society; [electronics] plasma switch; Police Sergeant; [chemistry] polystyrene; postscript; power steering (in car advertisement); press secretary; private secretary; Privy Seal; [theatre] prompt side; [biochemistry] protein synthesis; Provost Sergeant; *Pubblica Sicurezza* (Italian: police); [USA] public school; [Australia] public service

Ps. Psalm; [Bible] Psalms

ps picosecond

ps. pieces; pseudonym

p.s. particle size; pull switch

PSA Passenger Shipping Association; Petty Sessions Area; Photographic Society of America; pleasant Sunday afternoon; Political Studies Association of the United Kingdom; President of the Society of Antiquaries; [Australia] Prices Surveillance Authority; probabilistic safety analysis; probabilistic safety assessment; Property Services Agency; [medicine] prostatic specific antigen; [New Zealand] Public Service Association; Public Services Authority

PsA [astronomy] Piscis Austrinus

Psa. Psalm; [Bible] Psalms

PSAB Public Schools Appointments Bureau

PSAC [USA] President's Science Advisory Committee; Production Statistics Advisory Committee

PSAT [USA] Preliminary Scholastic Aptitude Test

PSB pistol, small-bore; [Japan] Postal Savings Bureau; Prayer Book Society; Premium Savings Bond

PSBA Public School Bursars' Association

PSBR public sector borrowing requirement

PSC [Belgium] *Parti Social Chrétien* (French: Christian Social Party); Pipe Smokers' Council; [meteorology] polar stratospheric clouds; Professional Services Committee; [USA] Public Service Commission

Psc [astronomy] Pisces

PSCD patrol service central depot

PSD *Partido Social Democrata* (Portuguese: Social Democratic Party); *Parti Social Démocrate* (French: Social Democratic Party) (in Madagascar); pay supply depot; [law] Petty Sessional Division; [physics] position-sensitive detector; [USA] prevention of significant deterioration

PSDI *Partito Socialista Democratico Italiano* (Italian: Italian Democratic Socialist Party)

PSDR public sector debt requirement

PSE Pacific Stock Exchange; pale soft exudate (in meat processing); Pidgin Sign English; [computing] programming support environment; [computing] project support environment; psychological stress evaluator (lie detector)

pseud. pseudonym

PSF [image technology] point spread function

psf pounds per square foot

PSG [linguistics] phrase-structure grammar

PSGB Pharmaceutical Society of Great Britain

PSHFA Public Servants Housing Finance Association

PSI *Partito Socialista Italiano* (Italian: Italian Socialist Party); [education] personalized system of instruction; Pharmaceutical Society of Ireland; Policy Studies Institute

psi pounds per square inch

psia pounds per square inch, absolute

psid pounds per square inch, differential

PSIF Prison Service Industries and Farms

psig pounds per square inch, gauge

PSIS Permanent Secretaries Commission on the Intelligence Services

PSIUP *Partito Socialista Italiano di Unità Proletaria* (Italian: Italian Socialist Party of Proletarian Unity)

PSK [telecommunications] phase shift keying

PSL Paymaster Sublieutenant; [USA] Primary Standards Laboratory; [economics] private-sector liquidity; public-sector loan(s)

PSL/PSA [computing] problem statement language/problem statement analyser

PSM product sales manager

PSMA President of the Society of Marine Artists

PSN [computing] packet-switching network; [computing] packet switch node; [computing] public switched network

PSNC Pacific Steam Navigation Company

PSO Personal Staff Officer; principal scientific officer

PSOE *Partido Socialista Obrero Español* (Spanish: Spanish Workers Socialist Party)

PSP *Pacifistisch Socialistische Partij* (Dutch: Pacifist Socialist Party); [medicine] phenolsulphonphthalein (in kidney function test)

PSPS Paddle Steamer Preservation Society

PSR [commerce] profit-sharing ratio

PSRAM [computing] pseudo static random-access memory

PSRO [USA] Professional Standards Review Organization

PSS [computing] packet switching service; Palomar Sky Survey; Partially Sighted Society; [medicine] physiological saline solution; postscripts; power-system stabilizer; Printing and Stationery Service; professional services section

Pss. Psalms

PSSC Personal Social Services Council

p.s.s.o. [knitting] pass slipped stitch(es) over

PST [USA, Canada] Pacific Standard Time

pstl postal

PSTN [telecommunications] public switched telephone network

PSU *Partito Socialista Unitario* (Italian: Unitary Socialist Party); police support unit; [computing] power supply unit; process support unit

p. surg. plastic surgery

PSV public service vehicle

PSW [computing] processor status word; [computing] program status word; psychiatric social worker

psych. psychiatric; psychiatry; psychic(al); psychological; psychologist; psychology

psychiat. psychiatric; psychiatry

psychoanal. psychoanalysis; psychoanalytic(al)

psychol. psychological; psychologist; psychology

PT [civil aircraft marking] Brazil; [vehicle registration] Newcastle upon Tyne; [USA] Pacific Time; [USA] patrol torpedo (as in **PT boat**); [insurance] *perte totale* (French: total loss); [physics] perturbation theory; [physics] phase transition; physical therapist; physical therapy; physical training; physiotherapist; physiotherapy; [fishing port] Port Talbot; postal telegraph; post town; preferential treatment; [medicine] previously treated; Public Trustee; pupil teacher; purchase tax

Pt [chemical element] platinum; Point (in place-names); Port (in place-names)

pt part; patient; payment; pint; point; port

pt. [grammar] preterite

.pt Portugal (in Internet address)

p.t. part time; [grammar] past tense; point of turn(ing); primary target; *pro tempore* (Latin: for the time being)

PTA Parent–Teacher Association; Passenger Transport Authority; [medicine] percutaneous transluminal angioplasty; Pet Traders' Association; Piano Tuners' Association; [medicine] plasma thromboplastin antecedent; [medicine] post-traumatic amnesia; preferential trade area; Printing Trades Alliance; [medicine] prior to admission

Pta [currency] peseta; Pretoria

ptbl. portable; potable (= drinkable)

PT boat [USA] patrol torpedo boat

PTBT partial test-ban treaty

PTC [medicine] percutaneous transhepatic

cholangiography; personnel transfer capsule (in diving); photographic type composition; [medicine] plasma thromboplastin component; primary training centre; Public Services, Tax and Commerce Union

Ptc [geology] Pleistocene

PTCA [medicine] percutaneous transluminal coronary angioplasty

PTD permanent total disability

ptd painted; printed

PTE Passenger Transport Executive; posttest examination

Pte Plate (book illustration); [military] Private; [commerce] private (equivalent of Ltd after company name in India and elsewhere)

pt ex. part exchange (in advertisement)

pt exch. part exchange (in advertisement)

PTFE polytetrafluoroeth(yl)ene

Ptg. Portugal; Portuguese

ptg painting; printing

PTH [biochemistry] parathyroid hormone; [USA] public teaching hospital

PTI physical training instructor; Press Trust of India; [computing] public tool interface

PTIA Pet Trade and Industry Association

PTM [telecommunications] pulse-time modulation

PTMA phosphotungstomolybdic acid (used in pigments)

PTN [informal] pay through the nose; public telephone network; public transport(ation) network

ptn partition; portion

ptnr partner

PTO [USA] Patent and Trademark Office; please turn over; [astronautics] power take-off; public telecommunications operator; Public Trustee Office

p.t.o. please turn over

ptp. [grammar] past participle

ptpg participating

pt/pt [horseracing] point-to-point

ptr porter (in property advertisement); printer

PTS Philatelic Traders' Society; pressurized thermal shock; printing technical school

Pts. Portsmouth

pts parts; payments; pints; points; ports

PTSD [medicine] post-traumatic stress disorder

pts/hr parts per hour

Ptsmth Portsmouth

PTT [medicine] partial thromboplastin time; Postal, Telegraph and Telephone Administration; *Postes, télécommunications et télédiffusion* (French post office and telephone service)

pt-tm part-time

PTU Plumbing Trades Union

PTUF Professional Tennis Umpires' Federation

PTV [USA] public television

p.t.w. per thousand words

Pty [commerce] proprietary (equivalent of Ltd after company name in Australia, South Africa and elsewhere)

pty party

PU [vehicle registration] Chelmsford; [medicine] passed urine; [medicine] peptic ulcer; pick-up; [chemistry] polyurethane; [computing] processing unit; public utility

Pu [chemical element] plutonium

p.u. paid up

pub [short form] public house

pub. public; publican; publication; publicity; publish; published; publisher; publishing

pubd published

pub. doc. public document

publ. public; publican; publication; publicity; publish; published; publisher; publishing

pubn publication

pubr publisher

pub. wks public works

PUC papers under consideration; pick-up car; [USA] Public Utilities Commission

PUD pick-up and deliver; pick-up and delivery; [USA] planned unit development (large condominium)

pud [short form] pudding

PUFA polyunsaturated fatty acids

pug. pugilist

PUHCA [USA] Public Utility Holding Company Act

pulv. [pharmacology] *pulvis* (Latin: powder)

p.u.m.s. permanently unfit for military service

pun. punish; punishment

punc. punctuation
punct. punctuation
Punj. Punjab
PUO [medicine] pyrexia (fever) of unknown origin
PUP People's United Party; [USA] Princeton University Press; [Northern Ireland] Progressive Unionist Party
Pup [astronomy] Puppis
pur. purchase; purchased; purchaser; purification; purified; purify; purity; purple; pursuit
purch. purchase; purchased; purchaser
purp. purple
PURV powered underwater research vehicle
PUS Parliamentary Undersecretary; Permanent Undersecretary
p.u.s. permanently unfit for service
PUVA [medicine] psoralen ultraviolet A (used to treat psoriasis)
PUWP Polish United Workers' Party
PV [vehicle registration] Ipswich; patrol vessel; *petite vitesse* (French: low speed (train)); [sports] pole vault; positive vetting; [microbiology] potato virus; power voltage; pressure vessel; pressure–volume; profit–volume
pv. [microbiology] pathovar
p.v. [medicine] *per vaginam* (Latin: by the vagina) (in prescriptions)
PVA polyvinyl acetate (synthetic resin)
PVC [computing] permanent virtual circuit; polyvinyl chloride
p.v.c. pigment volume concentration (in paint)
PVCu polyvinyl chloride unplasticized
PVD [medicine] peripheral vascular disease; physical vapour deposition
PVDA *Partij van de Arbeid* (Dutch: Labour Party)
PVF polyvinyl fluoride (synthetic resin)
PVFS [medicine] postviral fatigue syndrome
PVO principal veterinary officer
PVOA Passenger Vehicle Operators' Association
PVP polyvinyl pyrrolidone (synthetic resin)
PVR premature voluntary retirement
PVS [medicine] persistent vegetative state; [USA] post-Vietnam syndrome; [medicine] postviral (fatigue) syndrome

PVSM [India] Param Vishisht Seva Medal
PVT pressure, volume, temperature
Pvt. [military] Private
p.v.t. *par voie télégraphique* (French: by telegraph)
pvte private
PW [vehicle registration] Norwich; [fishing port] Padstow; policewoman; power windows (in car advertisement); prisoner of war; public works; [electronics] pulse width
p.w. per week
PWA [medicine] person with Aids; [USA] Public Works Administration
PWC [USA] personal watercraft; postwar credits
PWD Public Works Department
pwd powered
PWE Political Welfare Executive
PWG Permanent Working Group (of European Junior Hospital Doctors)
PWLB Public Works Loan Board
PWM [telecommunications] pulse-width modulation
PWO Prince of Wales's Own (regiment)
p.w.p. price when perfect
PWPS Pure Water Preservation Society
PWR [nuclear technology] pressurized-water reactor
pwr power
pwr sup. power supply
pwt pennyweight
PWV Pretoria-Witwatersrand-Vereeniging (former name of Gauteng province)
PX part exchange (in advertisement); physical examination; please exchange; [vehicle registration] Portsmouth; [USA] Post Exchange (army or navy retail store); [telecommunications] private exchange
pxt *pinxit* (Latin: (he/she) painted it)
PY [vehicle registration] Middlesbrough; [international vehicle registration] Paraguay
.py Paraguay (in Internet address)
PYB [accounting] preceding-year basis
PYO pick your own (fresh produce)
pyro. pyrotechnics
pyrotech. pyrotechnical; pyrotechnics
Pyx [astronomy] Pyxis
PZ [vehicle registration] Belfast; [fishing port] Penzance; [civil aircraft marking] Suriname

Pz [geology] Palaeozoic
PZI [medicine] protamine zinc insulin (used to treat diabetes)

PZS President of the Zoological Society
PZT [astronomy] photographic zenith tube

Q

Q [international vehicle registration] Qatar; quality; quantity; [nautical] quarantine; quarterly; Quartermaster; [advertising] quarter-page; Quarto (early Shakespearean text); [geology] Quaternary; Quebec; Queen('s); [chess] queen; Queensland; query; question; [currency] quetzal (used in Guatemala); queue; (Sir Arthur Thomas) Quiller-Couch (British writer)

Q [electrical engineering] quality factor; [physics] quantity of electricity (i.e. electric charge); [physics] quantity of heat; [physics] quantity of light; [electrical engineering] reactive power; [chemical engineering] throughput

q [physics] quark; quintal (= 100 lb or 100 kg); [meteorology] squall

q [physics] density of heat flow rate; [physics] electric charge

q. *quaere* (Latin: inquire); *quaque* (Latin: every); quart; quarter; quarterly; quarto; *quasi* (Latin: almost); queen; quench; query; question; quick; quire

8Q [civil aircraft marking] Maldives
9Q [civil aircraft marking] Democratic Republic of Congo (formerly Zaïre)

QA qualification approval; quality assurance; quarters allowance
Q/A qualification approval
.qa Qatar (in Internet address)
q.a. quick assembly
QAB Queen Anne's Bounty (in Church of England)
QADS quality-assurance data system
QAIMNS Queen Alexandra's Imperial Military Nursing Service
QALY quality-adjusted life year (used in assessment of treatment)
QAM [telecommunications] quadrature amplitude modulation
Q&A question and answer
Qantas Queensland and Northern Territory Aerial Service (Australian airline company)
QARANC Queen Alexandra's Royal Army Nursing Corps
QARNNS Queen Alexandra's Royal Naval Nursing Service
QB [USA, Canada] quarterback (in American and Canadian football); [law] Queen's Bench; [chess] queen's bishop
Qbc Quebec
QBD Queen's Bench Division
QBE [computing] query by example
QBI [informal] quite bloody impossible
QBO [meteorology] quasi-biennial oscillation
Q-boat query-boat (vessel of uncertain status, with concealed guns)
QBP [chess] queen's bishop's pawn
QC quality control; Quartermaster Corps; Queen's College; Queen's Consort; Queen's Counsel; [law] quit claim
QCD [physics] quantum chromodynamics
QCE quality-control engineering
QCH Queen Charlotte's Hospital
QC Is. Queen Charlotte Islands (Canada)
qck quick
QCR quality-control reliability
QCT quality-control technology; [medicine] quantitative compute(rize)d tomography
QCVSA Queen's Commendation for Valuable Service in the Air
q.d. [medicine] *quaque die* (Latin: every day) (in prescriptions); *quasi dicat* (Latin: as if one should say); *quasi dictum* (Latin: as if said); [medicine] *quater (in) die* (Latin: four times a day) (in prescriptions)
QDRI [USA] qualitative development requirement information
q.d.s. [medicine] *quater (in) die sumendus* (Latin: to be taken four times a day) (in prescriptions)
QE quantum electronics

q.e. *quod est* (Latin: which is)

QE2 Queen Elizabeth II (passenger ship)

QED [physics] quantum electrodynamics; *quod erat demonstrandum* (Latin: which was to be proved)

QEF *quod erat faciendum* (Latin: which was to be done)

QEH Queen Elizabeth Hall (London)

QEI *quod erat inveniendum* (Latin: which was to be found out)

QEO Queen Elizabeth's Own (regiment)

QER *Quarterly Economic Review*

QF [electronics] quality factor; quick-firing

QFA [computing] quick file access

QFD [commerce] quality function deployment; [physics] quantum flavour-dynamics

QFSM Queen's Fire Service Medal

QFT [physics] quantum field theory

QG Quartermaster-General; *quartiere generale* (Italian: headquarters); *quartier-général* (French: headquarters)

QGM Queen's Gallantry Medal

q.h. [medicine] *quaque hora* (Latin: every hour) (in prescriptions)

QHC Queen's Honorary Chaplain

QHDS Queen's Honorary Dental Surgeon

QHM Queen's Harbour Master

QHNS Queen's Honorary Nursing Sister

QHP Queen's Honorary Physician

QHS Queen's Honorary Surgeon

QI quartz–iodine (as in **QI lamp**)

QIC [computing] Quarter Inch (Cartridge Standards) Committee; [computing] quarter inch cartridge

q.i.d. [medicine] *quater in die* (Latin: four times a day) (in prescriptions)

QIP *quiescat in pace* (Latin: may he/she rest in peace)

QISAM [computing] queued indexed sequential access method

qk quick

QKt [chess] queen's knight

QKtP [chess] queen's knight's pawn

QL Queen's Lancers; [computing] query language

ql quarrel; quintal (= 100 lb or 100 kg)

q.l. [medicine] *quantum libet* (Latin: as much as you please) (in prescriptions)

Qld Queensland

QLF [commerce] quality loss function

q.lib. [medicine] *quantum libet* (Latin: as much as you please) (in prescriptions)

qlty quality

qly quarterly

QM [physics] quantum mechanics; [physics] quark model; Quartermaster; Queen's Messenger

qm. *quomodo* (Latin: by what means)

q.m. [medicine] *quaque mane* (Latin: every morning) (in prescriptions)

QMAAC Queen Mary's Army Auxiliary Corps

QMC Quartermaster Corps; Queen Mary College (London) (became part of QMW)

Q Mess. Queen's Messenger

QMG Quartermaster-General

QMGF Quartermaster-General to the Forces

QMR qualitative material requirement

Qmr Quartermaster

QMS Quartermaster-Sergeant

QMW Queen Mary and Westfield College (London)

QN [chess] queen's knight

Qn Queen

qn question; quotation

q.n. [medicine] *quaque nocte* (Latin: every night) (in prescriptions)

QNI Queen's Nursing Institute

QNP [chess] queen's knight's pawn

QNS quantity not sufficient

qnt quintet

qnty quantity

QO qualified in ordnance (in Royal Navy); qualified officer

QOCH Queen's Own Cameron Highlanders

QOOH Queen's Own Oxfordshire Hussars

QOR qualitative operational requirement

QP qualification pay; [chess] queen's pawn; [computing] query processing

q.p. [medicine] *quantum placet* (Latin: as much as seems good) (in prescriptions)

QPC Qatar Petroleum Company

q.pl. [medicine] *quantum placet* (Latin: as much as seems good) (in prescriptions)

QPM Queen's Police Medal

QPO [astronomy] quasi-periodic oscillation

QPR Queen's Park Rangers (football club)

QPS Quaker Peace and Service

Qq. Quartos (early Shakespearian texts)

qq. questions

qq.v. *quae vide* (Latin: which (items) see) (multiple cross-reference)

QR [currency] Qatari riyal; *Quarterly Review*; [chess] queen's rook; [marketing] quick response

qr quarter

qr. quarterly; quire

QRA [military] quick reaction alert (of aircraft)

QRIH Queen's Royal Irish Hussars

QRP [chess] queen's rook's pawn

QRR Queen's Royal Rifles

qrs quarters

QS quadraphonic-stereophonic (audio equipment); quantity surveyor; quarantine station; quarter sessions; Queen's Scholar; [building] quick sweep

q.s. [medicine] *quantum sufficit* (Latin: as much as will suffice) (in prescriptions); quarter section (of land)

QSAR quantitative structure–activity relationship

QSE qualified scientist and engineer

Q-ship query-ship (vessel of uncertain status, with concealed guns)

QSM [New Zealand] Queen's Service Medal

QSMR quantitative structure–metabolism relationship

QSO [astronomy] quasi-stellar object; [New Zealand] Queen's Service Order

QSS [astronomy] quasi-stellar source

QSTOL [aeronautics] quiet short take-off and landing

QSTS quadruple screw turbine ship

qt quart; quartet

qt. quantity

q.t. [informal] quiet (as in **on the q.t.**)

qtly quarterly

qto quarto

QTOL [aeronautics] quiet take-off and landing

qtr quarter

QTS Qualified Teacher Status

qty quantity

Qu. Queen

qu. quart; quarter; quarterly; queen; query; question

quad [short form] quadrangle; [short form] quadraphonic; [short form] quadruplet

quad. quadrant; quadrilateral; quadruple; quadruplicate

quadr. quadruplicate

quadrupl. quadruplicate

qual. qualification; qualified; qualitative; quality

qualgo quasi-autonomous local government organization

qualn qualification

quango quasi-autonomous national government organization; quasi-autonomous nongovernmental organization

quant. quantitative; quantity

quant. suff. [medicine] *quantum sufficit* (Latin: as much as will suffice) (in prescriptions)

quar. quarter; quarterly

quart. quarter; quarterly

quasar [astronomy] quasi-stellar object

quat. quaternary; [medicine] *quattuor* (Latin: four) (in prescriptions)

QUB Queen's University, Belfast

Que. Quebec

ques. question

questn. questionnaire

quin [short form] quintuplet

quint. quintuplicate

QUIP [computing] query interactive processor

quor. quorum

quot. quotation; quoted

quotid. [medicine] *quotidie* (Latin: daily)

q.v. [medicine] *quantum vis* (Latin: as much as you wish) (in prescriptions); *quod vide* (Latin: which see) (cross-reference)

QVR Queen Victoria Rifles

QWERTY standard keyboard layout (from first six letters on upper row)

QWL quality of working life

qy quay; query

qz quartz

R

R rabbi; [politics] Radical; [chemistry] radical (in formulae); radiology; radius; [USA] railroad; railway; [fishing port] Ramsgate; [currency] rand (used in South Africa); *rapido* (Italian: express train); [mathematics] ratio; [physics] Réaumur (temperature scale); *Recht* (German: law); [medicine] *recipe* (Latin: take) (in prescriptions); recommendation; rector; red; redactor; Regiment; *Regina* (Latin: Queen); registered; Regius (Professor); regular (clothing size); [navigation] relative; reliability; reply; report; Republic; Republican; reserve; [electrical engineering] resistance; [genetics] resistance; [chemistry] resonance effect; response (in liturgy); *Respublica* (Latin: Republic); [cinema] restricted (film classification in Australia and USA); *retarder* (French: slow down) (on clock or watch regulator); return (fare or ticket); reverse (in car); reward; *Rex* (Latin: King); [military] Rifles; right; river; road; roentgen (unit of electromagnetic radiation dose); Roman; Romania; Romanian; Rome; [chess] rook; rosary; [currency] rouble; route; Royal; *Rue* (French: Street); [sports] run(s); [currency] rupee; [theatre] stage right

® registered trademark

r [meteorology] rain; [music] ray (or re) (in tonic sol-fa); [biochemistry] ribonucleoside

r internal resistance (in electricity); [mathematics, physics] position vector; radius; [mathematics] radius vector; [ecology] rate of increase

r. radius; [USA] railroad; railway; rain; range; rare; ratio; rear; [commerce] received; [medicine] *recipe* (Latin: take) (in prescriptions); [printing] recto (right-hand page); red; replacing; reply; reserve; residence; resides; response; retired; right; rises (referring to the sun); river; road; rod (unit of length); [currency] rouble; [card games] rubber; ruled; [sports] run(s); [currency] rupee

4R [civil aircraft marking] Sri Lanka

5R [civil aircraft marking] Madagascar

8R [civil aircraft marking] Guyana

RA [international vehicle registration] (Republic of) Argentina; [vehicle registration] Nottingham; Racecourse Association; [meteorology] rain; Ramblers' Association; Rear-Admiral; reduction of area; Referees' Association (in football); [USA] Regular Army; *República Argentina* (Spanish: Argentine Republic); [USA] Resettlement Administration; [medicine] rheumatoid arthritis; [astronomy] right ascension; [medicine] right atrium; Road Association; Royal Academician; Royal Academy; Royal Artillery; Rural Action; [civil aircraft marking] Russia

R/A [finance] refer to acceptor (on bill of exchange); return to author

Ra [chemical element] radium

ra. radio

RAA Rabbinical Alliance of America; Regional Arts Association; Royal Academy of Arts; Royal Artillery Association; Royal Australian Artillery

RAAF Royal Australian Air Force; Royal Auxiliary Air Force

RAAFNS Royal Australian Air Force Nursing Service

RAAMC Royal Australian Army Medical Corps

RAANC Royal Australian Army Nursing Corps

Rab. Rabat (Morocco)

Rabb. Rabbinate; Rabbinic(al)

RABDF Royal Association of British Dairy Farmers

RABI Royal Agricultural Benevolent Institution

RAC Railway Association of Canada; Regional Advisory Committee (of TUC); Regional Advisory Council; Royal Aero Club (of the United Kingdom); Royal Agricultural College; Royal Armoured Corps; Royal Automobile Club

RACA Royal Automobile Club of Australia

RACE rapid automatic checkout equipment; Research and Development in

Advanced Communication Technologies for Europe

RACGP Royal Australian College of General Practitioners

RAChD Royal Army Chaplains' Department

RACI Royal Australian Chemical Institute

RACO Royal Australian College of Ophthalmologists

RACOG Royal Australian College of Obstetricians and Gynaecologists

RACP Royal Australasian College of Physicians

RACS Royal Arsenal Cooperative Society; Royal Australasian College of Surgeons

RAD radiation absorbed dose; [medicine] reflex anal dilation; Royal Academy of Dancing; Royal Albert Docks

Rad. [politics] Radical; Radnor(shire)

rad radian (unit of angle)

rad. radar; radiator; radical; radio; radiologist; radiology; radiotherapist; radiotherapy; radius; [mathematics, anatomy] radix

r.a.d. rapid automatic drill

RADA Royal Academy of Dramatic Art

RADAR Royal Association for Disability and Rehabilitation

radar radio detection and ranging

RADAS random access discrete address system

RADC Royal Army Dental Corps

RADCM radar countermeasure

raddol. [music] *raddolcendo* (Italian: becoming calmer)

RAdm Rear-Admiral

radmon radiological monitor(ing)

radn radiation

RAE Royal Aerospace Establishment (formerly Royal Aircraft Establishment); Royal Australian Engineers

r.a.e. radio astronomy explorer

RAEC Royal Army Educational Corps

RAeroC Royal Aero Club (of the United Kingdom)

RAeS Royal Aeronautical Society

RAF *Rote Armee Faktion* (German: Red Army Faction) (terrorist group); Royal Aircraft Factory; Royal Air Force

RAFA Royal Air Forces Association; Royal Australian Field Artillery

RAFBF Royal Air Force Benevolent Fund

RAFES Royal Air Force Educational Service

RAFG Royal Air Force Germany

RAFMS Royal Air Force Medical Services

RAFR Royal Air Force Regiment

RAFRO Royal Air Force Reserve of Officers

RAFSAA Royal Air Force Small Arms Association

RAFSC Royal Air Force Staff College; Royal Air Force Strike Command

RAFT [banking] revolving acceptance facility by transfer

RAFTC Royal Air Force Transport Command

RAFVR Royal Air Force Volunteer Reserve

r.a.g. river assault group

RAGA Royal Australian Garrison Artillery

RAH Royal Albert Hall

RAHS Royal Australian Historical Society

RAI *Radiotelevisione Italiana* (Italian broadcasting company, formerly *Radio Audizioni Italiane*); Royal Anthropological Institute; Royal Archaeological Institute

RAIA Royal Australian Institute of Architects

RAIC Royal Architectural Institute of Canada

RAID [computing] redundant array of independent (or inexpensive) disks

Raj. Rajasthan

RAJAR Radio Joint Audience Research

RAK random act of kindness

RAL Rutherford Appleton Laboratory (Harwell, Oxfordshire)

rall. [music] *rallentando* (Italian: slowing down)

RALS [aeronautics] remote augmented lift system

RAM [aeronautics] radar absorbing material; [computing] random-access memory; [USA] reverse-annuity mortgage; rocket-assisted motor; Royal Academy of Music; Royal Air Maroc (Moroccan airline company); [Freemasonry] Royal Arch Masons

r.a.m. relative atomic mass

RAMAC Radio Marine Associated Companies

ramb. rambler (rose)

RAMC Royal Army Medical Corps

RAN request for authority to negotiate; Royal Australian Navy

RANC Royal Australian Naval College

RANCOM random communication satellite

R&A Royal and Ancient (Golf Club) (St Andrews)

R&B rhythm and blues; ring and ball (game)

R&CC [insurance] riot and civil commotion

R&D research and development

R&E research and engineering

R&I *Regina et Imperatrix* (Latin: Queen and Empress); *Rex et Imperator* (Latin: King and Emperor)

R&M reliability and marketing

r&m reports and memoranda

R&R [medicine] rescue and resuscitation; rest and recreation; rock and roll

R&T research and technology

RANN [USA] Research Applied to National Needs

RANR Royal Australian Naval Reserve

RANVR Royal Australian Naval Volunteer Reserve

RAOB Royal Antediluvian Order of Buffaloes

RAOC Royal Army Ordnance Corps

RAOU Royal Australian Ornithologists' Union

RAP ready-assembled price; Regimental Aid Post; remedial action plan (or programme); [medicine] right atrial pressure

rap. rapid

RAPC Royal Army Pay Corps

RAPID Register for the Ascertainment and Prevention of Inherited Diseases

RAPRA Rubber and Plastics Research Association of Great Britain

RAR Royal Australian Regiment

RARDE Royal Armament Research and Development Establishment

RARE [computing] *Réseaux associés pour la recherche européenne* (French: Associated Networks for European Research)

RARO Regular Army Reserve of Officers

RAS [aeronautics] rectified air speed; Royal Agricultural Society; Royal Asiatic Society; Royal Astronomical Society

RASC Royal Army Service Corps (former name of RCT)

RASE Royal Agricultural Society of England

raser radio-frequency amplification by stimulated emission of radiation

RAT rocket-assisted torpedo

rat. rateable; rating; ration

RATAN radar and television aid to navigation

RATO rocket-assisted take-off

RATP *Régie autonome des transports parisiens* (French: Paris transport authority)

RAuxAF Royal Auxiliary Air Force

RAVC Royal Army Veterinary Corps

RAWC Radioactive Waste Coordinating Committee

RAX [telecommunications] rural automatic exchange

RB [international vehicle registration] (Republic of) Botswana; [vehicle registration] Nottingham; [astronomy] radiation belt; radiation burn; reconnaissance bomber (aircraft); representative body; *República Boliviana* (Spanish: Republic of Bolivia); review body; Rifle Brigade; *Ritzaus Bureau* (Danish news agency); Royal Ballet (formerly SWRB)

Rb [chemical element] rubidium

r.b. [sports] right back; rubber band

RBA Retail Book, Stationery and Allied Trades Employees Association; Royal Society of British Artists

RBAF Royal Belgian Air Force

RBC [medicine] red blood cell; [medicine] red blood (cell) count; Royal British Colonial Society of Artists

RBE relative biological effectiveness (of radiation)

r/belt rear seat belt (in car advertisement)

RBerks Royal Berkshire Regiment

RBG Royal Botanic Gardens (Kew)

RBI resource-based industry; right back inside (of skate); [baseball] run(s) batted in

r.b.i. require better information; [baseball] run(s) batted in

RBK&C Royal Borough of Kensington and Chelsea

RBL Royal British Legion

rbl. [currency] rouble

RBN Registry of Business Names

RBn radio beacon

RBNA Royal British Nurses' Association

RBO right back outside (of skate)

RBP [biochemistry] retinol-binding protein

RBS [medicine] radionuclide bone scintigraphy; Rare Breeds Society; Royal Botanical Society; Royal Society of British Sculptors

RBSA Royal Birmingham Society of Artists

RBT random breath-testing; [computing] remote batch terminal

rbt roundabout

RBY Royal Bucks Yeomanry

RC [vehicle registration] Nottingham; [cycling] racing club; radio/cassette (player); [medicine] red (blood) cell; [medicine] red corpuscle; Red Cross; Reformed Church; reinforced concrete; remote control; reproductive capacity; [USA] Republican Convention; research centre; reserve corps; [photography] resin-coated; [electronics] resistance-capacitance; [electronics] resistor-capacitor; [telecommunications] reversed charge; rifle club; [cycling] road club; Roman Catholic; [building] rough cutting; Royal College; Royal Commission; [international vehicle registration] Taiwan (Republic of China)

R/C recredited

r.c. radio code; radio coding; reinforced concrete; release clause; reverse course; right centre; rotary combustion; rubber-cushioned

RCA [international vehicle registration] Central African Republic (from French *République Centrafricaine*); Rabbinical Council of America; Racecourse Association; Radio Corporation of America; [medicine] right coronary artery; Royal Cambrian Academy; Royal Canadian Academy of Arts; Royal College of Art; Royal Company of Archers; Rural Crafts Association

RCAC Royal Canadian Armoured Corps

RCAF Royal Canadian Air Force

RCamA Royal Cambrian Academy

RCAMC Royal Canadian Army Medical Corps

RCASC Royal Canadian Army Service Corps

RCB [international vehicle registration] (Republic of) Congo (from former name Congo-Brazzaville); [theatre] right centre back (of stage)

RCC recovery control centre; [medicine] renal cell carcinoma; rescue coordination centre; Roman Catholic Chaplain; Roman Catholic Church; Rural Community Council

RCCh Roman Catholic Church

RCD *Rassemblement Constitutionnel Démocratique* (French: Democratic Constitutional Rally) (Tunisian political party); Regional Cooperation for Development (association of Asian countries); [electronics] residual current device

rcd received

RCDC Royal Canadian Dental Corps

RCDS Royal College of Defence Studies

RCE [engineering] rotary combustion engine

RCF Redundant Churches Fund

r.c.f. relative centrifugal force

RCFCA Royal Canadian Flying Clubs' Association

RCGA Royal Canadian Golf Association

RCGP Royal College of General Practitioners

RCGS Royal Canadian Geographical Society

RCH [international vehicle registration] (Republic of) Chile; railway clearing house

RCHA Royal Canadian Horse Artillery

RCHM Royal Commission on Historical Manuscripts; Royal Commission on Historical Monuments

RCI Radiochemical Inspectorate; Royal Canadian Institute

r.c.i. radar coverage indicator

RCJ Royal Courts of Justice

RCL Royal Canadian Legion; ruling case law

RCM radar countermeasures; radio countermeasures; [medicine] radiological contrast medium; regimental court martial; Royal College of Midwives; Royal College of Music

RCMP Royal Canadian Mounted Police (formerly RNWMP)

RCN Royal Canadian Navy; Royal College of Nursing

RCNC Royal Corps of Naval Constructors

RCNR Royal Canadian Naval Reserve

RCNT Registered Clinical Nurse Teacher

RCNVR Royal Canadian Naval Volunteer Reserve

RCO Royal College of Organists

RCOG Royal College of Obstetricians and Gynaecologists

RCP Revolutionary Communist Party; Royal College of Physicians; Royal College of Preceptors

RCPath Royal College of Pathologists

RCPB Revolutionary Communist Party of Great Britain

RCPE Royal College of Physicians of Edinburgh

RCPEd Royal College of Physicians of Edinburgh

RCPI Royal College of Physicians of Ireland

RCPSG Royal College of Physicians and Surgeons of Glasgow

RCPsych Royal College of Psychiatrists

rcpt receipt

RCR Royal College of Radiologists

RCRP Rape Counselling and Research Project

RCS reaction control system (in spacecraft); [nuclear technology] reactor cooling system; remote control system; Royal Choral Society; Royal College of Science; Royal College of Surgeons (of England); Royal Commonwealth Society; Royal Corps of Signals; Royal Counties Show

RCSB Royal Commonwealth Society for the Blind

RCSC Radio Components Standardization Committee

RCSE Royal College of Surgeons of Edinburgh

RCSEd Royal College of Surgeons of Edinburgh

RCSI Royal College of Surgeons in Ireland

RCSLT Royal College of Speech and Language Therapists

RCSS random communications satellite system

RCT randomized clinical trial; regimental combat team; Registered Clinical Teacher; remote control transmitter; Royal Corps of Transport (formerly RASC)

rct receipt; recruit

RCU remote control unit; road-construction unit; rocket-countermeasure unit

rcvr receiver

RCVS Royal College of Veterinary Surgeons

RD radiation dose; [metallurgy] radiation-induced defect; [vehicle registration] Reading; *récemment dégorgé* (French: recently disgorged) (in winemaking); [banking] refer to drawer (on cheque); [USA] Registered Dietician; *República Dominicana* (Spanish: Dominican Republic); research department; (Royal Naval and Royal Marine Forces) Reserve Decoration; Royal Dragoons; Rural Dean; [New Zealand] Rural Delivery

R/D [banking] refer to drawer (on cheque)

Rd Road

rd rendered; road; rod (unit of length); round; rutherford (unit of radioactivity)

r.d. [physics] relative density; *rive droite* (French: right bank); [shipping] running days

RDA *Rassemblement Démocratique Africain* (French: African Democratic Rally) (political party); recommended daily allowance (of nutrients etc.); recommended dietary allowance; Retail Distributors' Association; Riding for the Disabled Association; Royal Defence Academy; Royal Docks Association

RD&D research, development and demonstration

RD&E research, development and engineering

RDAT rotary-head digital audio tape

RDB [military] Research and Development Board; Royal Danish Ballet; Rural Development Board

RDBMS [computing] relational database management system

RDC Royal Defence Corps; [insurance] running-down clause; Rural Development Commission; rural district council

RDCA Rural District Councils' Association

RDD [US marketing] random digital dialing

r.d.d. required delivery date

RDE Research and Development Establishment; [chemistry] rotating-disc electrode

RDF radio direction finder (or finding); [US military] Rapid Deployment Force; refuse-derived fuel; Royal Dublin Fusiliers

RDI Royal Designer for Industry

RDP [South Africa] Reconstruction and Development Programme

RDPL [civil aircraft marking] Laos

rdr radar

RDS radio data system (for automatic tuning); Research Defence Society; [medicine] respiratory distress syndrome; Royal Drawing Society; Royal Dublin Society

rds. [shipping] roadstead

RDT&E research, development, testing and engineering

RDV rendezvous

RDX Research Department Explosive (= cyclonite)

RDY Royal Dockyard

rdy ready

RDZ radiation danger zone

RE [chemistry] rare earth; [USA] real estate; Reformed Episcopal; religious education; renewable energy; revised edition; Right Excellent; Royal Engineers; Royal Exchange; Royal Society of Painter-Printmakers (formerly Royal Society of Painter-Etchers and Engravers); [vehicle registration] Stoke-on-Trent

R/E [USA] real estate

Re [chemical element] rhenium; [currency] rupee

r.e. right eye

REA Radar and Electronics Association; request for engineer's authorization; Rubber Export Association; [USA] Rural Electrification Administration

REAC Regional Education Advisory Committee (of TUC)

reac. reactor

REACH Retired Executives' Action Clearing House

REACT research education and aid for children with potentially terminal illness

Rear-Adm Rear-Admiral

reasm. reassemble

Réau. Réaumur (temperature scale)

REB regional examining body

REC Railway Executive Committee; regional electricity company

rec [short form] recreation ground

rec. receipt; receive; received; [medicine] *recens* (Latin: fresh) (in prescriptions); recent; reception; reception room (in property advertisement); recipe; recognized; recommended; record; recorded; recorder; recording; recreation

recap [short form] recapitulate; [short form] recapitulation

recce [short form] reconnaissance; [short form] reconnoitre

recd received

recep. reception; reception room (in property advertisement)

recept. reception; reception room (in property advertisement)

RECHAR *Reconversion de bassins charbonniers* (French: Reconversion of Coal Fields) (EU funding programme)

recip. reciprocal; reciprocity

recirc. recirculate

recit. recitation; [music] recitative

reclam. reclamation

recm. recommend

recmd recommended

RECMF Radio and Electronic Component Manufacturers' Federation

recog. recognition; recognize

recom. recommend

recon. reconciliation; recondition; reconditioned; reconnaissance; reconnoitre; reconsign; reconsignment; reconstruct; reconstruction

recond. recondition; reconditioned

REconS Royal Economic Society

reconst. reconstruct; reconstruction

recpt receipt; reception; reception room (in property advertisement)

recr receiver

rec. sec. recording secretary

Rect. Rector; Rectory

rect receipt

rect. rectangle; rectangular; [medicine] *rectificatus* (Latin: rectified) (in prescriptions); rectify

red. [finance] redeemable; reduce; reduced; reduction

redox [chemistry] reduction–oxidation

redup. reduplicate; reduplication; reduplicative

redupl. reduplicate; reduplication; reduplicative

REE [chemistry] rare-earth element

Ref. Reformation; Reformatory; Reformed

ref [short form] referee

ref. refer; referee; reference; referred; refined; refining; reform; reformation; reformed; reformer; refrigerated ship; refund; refunding; refuse

refash. refashion; refashioned

Ref. Ch. Reformed Church
refd referred; refund
refl. reflect; reflection; reflective; reflex; [grammar] reflexive
Reform. Reformatory
Ref. Pres. Reformed Presbyterian
refrig. refrigerate; refrigerated; refrigeration; refrigerator
Ref. Sp. Reformed Spelling
refurb. refurbished
Reg. Regent; *Regina* (Latin: Queen); Regius (Professor)
reg. regiment; region; regional; register; registered; registrar; registration; registry; regular; regularly; regulation; regulator
REGAL [aeronautics] range and elevation guidance for approach and landing
regd registered
Reg-Gen Registrar-General
Reg. Prof. Regius Professor
regr registrar
Regt Regent; Regiment
regtl regimental
Reg. TM registered trademark
REHAB [medicine] Rehabilitation Evaluation of Hall and Baker
rehab [short form] rehabilitation
reinf. reinforce; reinforced
reinfmt reinforcement
REIT [USA] real-estate investment trust
reit. [printing] reiteration
rej. reject
REL recommended exposure limit (to radiation)
rel. relate; related; relating; relation; relative; relatively; release; released; relic; [bibliography] *relié* (French: bound); religion; religious; *reliquiae* (Latin: relics)
relig. religion; religious
rel. pron. [grammar] relative pronoun
REM [physiology] rapid eye movement (as in **REM sleep**); [chemistry] rare-earth metal
rem roentgen equivalent man (former unit of radioactivity)
rem. remainder; remains; remark(s); remission; remit; remittance
REMC Radio and Electronics Measurements Committee
REME Royal Electrical and Mechanical Engineers

remitt. remittance
Ren. Renaissance
Renf. Renfrew(shire)
RENFE *Red Nacional de Ferrocarriles Españoles* (Spanish: Spanish National Railway Network)
REngDes Registered Engineering Designer
renv. renovate; renovation
REO regional education officer
REP [USA] Recovery and Evacuation Program
Rep. Repertory (Theatre); [USA] Representative; Republic; Republican
rep [short form] repertory (theatre); [short form] representative
rep. repair; repeat; [theatre] repertory (company); [medicine] *repetatur* (Latin: let it be repeated) (in prescriptions); repetition; report; reported; reporter; represent; representative; representing; reprint
REPC Regional Economic Planning Council
repl. replace; replaced; replacement; replica; replicate
repo. repossess; repossession
repr. represent; representative; represented; representing; reprint; reprinted; reprinting
repres. represent; representative; represented; representing
repro. reproduced; reproduction
rept receipt; report
Repub. Republic; Republican
repub. republish; republished
req. request; require; required; requirement; requisition
reqd required
reqn requisition
reqs requires
RER renewable energy resource(s)
RERO Royal Engineers Reserve of Officers
RES renewable energy source; renewable energy system; [physiology] reticuloendothelial system; Royal Entomological Society of London
res. rescue; research; researcher; reservation; reserve; reserved; reservoir; reside; residence; resident; residential; resides; resigned; resolution
resgnd resigned
resid. residential; residual
resig. resignation

resp. respective; respectively; respiration; respondent; response; responsibility

res. phys. resident physician

res. sec. resident secretary

Rest. Restoration (historical period)

rest. restaurant; restoration; restored (in property advertisement); restraint; restrict; restricted; restriction

RET [computing] resolution enhancement technology

Ret [astronomy] Reticulum

ret. retain; retained; retainer; retire; retired; return; returned

retd retained; retired; returned

R et I *Regina et Imperatrix* (Latin: Queen and Empress); *Rex et Imperator* (Latin: King and Emperor)

retnr retainer

RETRA Radio, Electrical and Television Retailers' Association

REV [astronautics] re-entry vehicle

Rev. [Bible] Revelation; Revenue; Reverend; Review; Revised; Revolution

rev [short form] revolution

rev. revenue; reverse; reversed; review; reviewed; reviewer; revise; revised; revision; revolution; revolve; revolver; revolving

rev. ac. revenue account(s)

Revd Reverend

rev. ed. revised edition

Rev. Stat. Revised Statutes

Rev. Ver. Revised Version (of Bible)

rew. reward; rewind; rewired; rewiring

REXX [computing] restructured extended executor

RF radio frequency; reconnaissance fighter (aircraft); [military] regular forces; [genetics] release factor; [cartography] representative fraction; *République française* (French: French Republic); research foundation; [military] reserve force; Rockefeller Foundation; Royal Fusiliers; rugby football; [currency] Rwanda franc; [vehicle registration] Stoke-on-Trent

Rf [currency] rufiyaa (used in Maldives); [chemical element] rutherfordium

rf reef; [music] *rinforzando* (Italian: reinforcing)

r.f. radio frequency; range finder; rapid fire; [telecommunications] reception fair; relative flow; [medicine] rheumatic fever; [baseball] right field; [baseball] right fielder; rough finish (of paper)

RFA Royal Field Artillery; Royal Fleet Auxiliary; Rugby Fives Association

RFAC Royal Fine Art Commission

RFC [USA] Reconstruction Finance Corporation; [computing] request for comments; Royal Flying Corps; rugby football club

RFD radio-frequency device; reporting for duty; [USA] rural free delivery (postal service)

RFDS [Australia] Royal Flying Doctor Service

RFE Radio Free Europe

RFH Royal Festival Hall (London)

RFI radio-frequency interference; request for information; right forward inside (of skate)

RFL Rugby Football League

RFN Registered Fever Nurse

Rfn Rifleman

RFO right forward outside (of skate)

RFP [nuclear technology] reversed-field pinch

r.f.p. retired on full pay

RFPC [electronics] radio-frequency pulse compression

RFQ [commerce] request for quotation

RFR Royal Fleet Reserve

rfrd referred

RFS rear-facing seat; Registry of Friendly Societies; Royal Forestry Society

RFSU Rugby Football Schools' Union

RFT [computing] revisable form text; [astronomy] richest-field telescope

RFTF Retail Fruit Trade Federation

RFU Rugby Football Union

rfz. [music] *rinforzando* (Italian: reinforcing)

RG [international vehicle registration] (Republic of) Guinea; [vehicle registration] Newcastle upon Tyne; [UK postcode] Reading; reserve guard

r.g. *rive gauche* (French: left bank)

RGA remote geological analysis; residual-gas analyser; Royal Garrison Artillery; Royal Guernsey Artillery

RGB red, green, blue (in colour transmission etc.)

RGBI red, green, blue intensity

rgd registered; reigned

rge range

R-Gen Registrar-General
RGG Royal Grenadier Guards
RGH Royal Gloucestershire Hussars
RGI Royal Glasgow Institute of the Fine Arts
RGJ Royal Green Jackets
RGN Registered General Nurse (formerly SRN)
Rgn Rangoon
rgn region
RGNP [economics] real gross national product
RGO Royal Greenwich Observatory
RGS Royal Geographical Society
RGSA Royal Geographical Society of Australasia
RGT [physics] relativistic gravitational theory
Rgt Regiment
rgtl regimental
RH [international vehicle registration] (Republic of) Haiti; [vehicle registration] Hull; [UK postcode] Redhill; [meteorology] relative humidity; remote handling; right hand; right handed; [fishing port] Rochester; Royal Highlanders; Royal Highness; Royal Hospital
Rh [medicine] rhesus (factor) (as in **Rh negative**); [chemical element] rhodium
r.h. [sports] right half; right hand; right handed
RHA regional health authority; Road Haulage Association; Royal Hibernian Academy; Royal Horse Artillery
RHAF Royal Hellenic Air Force
RHamps Royal Hampshire Regiment
rhap. rhapsody
RHAS Royal Highland and Agricultural Society of Scotland
RHB regional hospital board
r.h.b. [sports] right halfback
RHBNC Royal Holloway and Bedford New College (London)
r.h.d. right-hand drive (in car advertisement)
RHEL Rutherford High Energy Laboratory
rheo. rheostat
rheol. rheological; rheology
rhet. rhetoric; rhetorical
RHF Royal Highland Fusiliers
RHG Royal Horse Guards
RHHI Royal Hospital and Home for Incurables

RHistS Royal Historical Society
RHM Ranks Hovis McDougall
RHMS Royal Hibernian Military School
rhomb. rhombic; rhomboid; rhombus
rhp rated horsepower
RHQ regimental headquarters
RHR rear head restraints (in car advertisement); Royal Highland Regiment
r/h/r rear head restraints (in car advertisement)
RHS Robin Hood Society; Royal Highland Show; Royal Historical Society; Royal Horticultural Society; Royal Humane Society
r.h.s. right-hand side; round-headed screw
RHSI Royal Horticultural Society of Ireland
RHT Railway Heritage Trust
RHV Registered Health Visitor
RI [international vehicle registration] (Republic of) Indonesia; radio interference; radioisotope; Railway Inspectorate; refractive index; Regimental Institute; *Regina et Imperatrix* (Latin: Queen and Empress); reinsurance; religious instruction; report of investigation; *Rex et Imperator* (Latin: King and Emperor); Rhode Island; [US postcode] Rhode Island; Rockwell International Corporation; Rotary International; Royal Institute of Painters in Water Colours; Royal Institution
R/I reinsurance
r.i. reflective insulation; rubber insulation
RIA [medicine] radioimmunoassay; Royal Irish Academy
RIAA Recording Industry Association of America
RIAC Royal Irish Automobile Club
RIAF Royal Indian Air Force
RIAI Royal Institute of the Architects of Ireland
RIAM Royal Irish Academy of Music
RIAS Royal Incorporation of Architects in Scotland
RIASC Royal Indian Army Service Corps
RIB Racing Information Bureau; rigid-hull inflatable boat; Rural Industries Bureau
RIBA Royal Institute of British Architects
RIBI Rotary International in Great Britain and Ireland
RIC [chemistry] radiation-induced change;

[physics] radiation-induced conductivity; Radio Industry Council; Royal Institute of Chemistry (former name of RSC); Royal Irish Constabulary

RICA Research Institute for Consumer Affairs

RICE rest, ice, compression, elevation (treatment for sports injuries)

RICO [USA] Racketeer Influenced and Corrupt Organizations Act

RICS Royal Institution of Chartered Surveyors

RID [physics] radiation-induced defect; [physics] radiation-induced diffusion

RIE [commerce] recognized investment exchange; Royal Indian Engineering College

RIF [military] reduction in force; Royal Inniskilling Fusiliers

Rif. Brig. Rifle Brigade

RIFF [computing] raster image file format

RIGS regionally important geological site

RIIA Royal Institute of International Affairs

RILC Racing Industry Liaison Committee

RILKO Research into Lost Knowledge Organization

RIM [international vehicle registration] (Islamic Republic of) Mauritania (from French *République Islamique de Mauritanie*); Royal Indian Marines

RIMB [South Africa] Research Institute for Medical Biophysics

RIMNET Radioactive Incident Monitoring Network

RIN [aeronautics] reference indicator number; Royal Indian Navy

RINA Royal Institution of Naval Architects

rinf. [music] *rinforzando* (Italian: reinforcing)

RINVR Royal Indian Naval Volunteer Reserve

RIO reporting in and out

RIOP Royal Institute of Oil Painters

RIP [computing] raster input processor; *requiescant in pace* (Latin: may they rest in peace); *requiescat in pace* (Latin: may he/she rest in peace); rest in peace

rip. [music] *ripieno* (Italian: filled, for all players)

RIPA Royal Institute of Public Administration

RIPHH Royal Institute of Public Health and Hygiene

RIR Royal Irish Regiment

RIrF Royal Irish Fusiliers

RIS Research Information Service

RISC reduced-instruction-set computer

RIT [psychology] Rorschach inkblot test

rit. [music] *ritardando* (Italian: slowing down); [music] *ritenuto* (Italian: held back)

RITA reusable interplanetary transport approach (vehicle)

ritard. [music] *ritardando* (Italian: slowing down)

riten. [music] *ritenuto* (Italian: held back)

riv. river

RJ [vehicle registration] Manchester; ramjet; road junction

RJA Royal Jersey Artillery

RJE [computing] remote job entry

RJET [computing] remote job entry terminal

RJF Reformed Jokers' Federation

RJLI Royal Jersey Light Infantry

RJM Royal Jersey Militia

RK [vehicle registration] northwest London; [medicine] radical keratotomy (used to treat myopia); religious knowledge

RKKA *Rabochekrest'yanshi Krasny* (Russian: Red Army of Workers and Peasants)

RKO Radio-Keith-Orpheum (US broadcasting and former film company)

rky rocky

RL [international vehicle registration] (Republic of) Lebanon; reference library; research laboratory; rocket launcher; Rugby League; [vehicle registration] Truro

Rl [currency] rouble; Royal

RLC Royal Logistic Corps

RLD [USA] retail liquor dealer

RLF Royal Literary Fund

RLL [computing] run length limited

RLO railway liaison officer; returned letter office (formerly DLO)

RLPAS Royal London Prisoners' Aid Society

RLPO Royal Liverpool Philharmonic Orchestra

RLPS Royal Liverpool Philharmonic Society

RLS Robert Louis Stevenson (Scottish writer)

Rls [currency] rial (used in Iran)

RLSS Royal Life Saving Society

rlwy railway

rly railway; relay

RM [vehicle registration] Carlisle; [international vehicle registration] (Republic of) Madagascar; radiation monitoring; radio monitoring; [computing] Reed-Muller (code); Registered Midwife (replacement for SCM); [currency] Reichsmark (formerly used in Germany); remote monitoring; resident magistrate; riding master; [UK postcode] Romford; Royal Mail; Royal Marines

rm ream; room

RMA Royal Marine Artillery; Royal Marines Association; Royal Military Academy (formerly RMC); Royal Musical Association

RMC regional meteorological centre; Royal Military College (former name of RMA)

RMCC Royal Military College of Canada

RMCM Royal Manchester College of Music

RMCS Royal Military College of Science

r.m.d. ready money down

RMedSoc Royal Medical Society (Edinburgh)

RMetS Royal Meteorological Society

RMFVR Royal Marine Forces Volunteer Reserves

RMH Royal Marsden Hospital (London)

RMI Resource Management Initiative (for NHS)

RMIT Royal Melbourne Institute of Technology

RMLI Royal Marine Light Infantry

RMM [international vehicle registration] (Republic of) Mali

r.m.m. [chemistry] relative molecular mass

RMN Registered Mental Nurse

RMO Regimental Medical Officer; regional medical officer; resident medical officer; Royal Marine Office

RMP Royal Marine Police; Royal Military Police

RMPA Royal Medico-Psychological Association

RMR Royal Marines Reserve

RMRA Royal Marines Rifle Association

RMS radiation-monitoring system; remote monitoring system; [mathematics] root mean square; Royal Mail Service; Royal Mail Ship; Royal Mail Steamer; Royal Medical Society; Royal Microscopical Society; Royal Society of Miniature Painters

rms [mathematics] root mean square; rooms (in property advertisement)

RMSchMus Royal Marines School of Music

RMSM Royal Military School of Music

RMT National Union of Rail, Maritime and Transport Workers

RN [international vehicle registration] (Republic of) Niger; [vehicle registration] Preston; Registered Nurse; *route nationale* (French: trunk road); Royal Naval; Royal Navy; [fishing port] Runcorn

Rn [chemical element] radon

r.n. [telecommunications] reception nil

RNA [biochemistry] ribonucleic acid; Romantic Novelists' Association; Royal Naval Association

RNAS Royal Naval Air Service; Royal Naval Air Station

RNase [biochemistry] ribonuclease

RNAW Royal Naval Aircraft Workshop

RNAY Royal Naval Aircraft Yard

RNB Royal Naval Barracks

R 'n' B rhythm and blues

RNBS Royal Naval Benevolent Society

RNBT Royal Naval Benevolent Trust

RNC [USA] Republican National Committee

RNC Royal Naval College

RNCM Royal Northern College of Music

RND Royal Naval Division

rnd round

RNEC Royal Naval Engineering College

RNF Royal Northumberland Fusiliers

RNHA Registered Nursing Home Association

RNIB Royal National Institute for the Blind

RNID Royal National Institute for the Deaf

RNLAF Royal Netherlands Air Force

RNLI Royal National Lifeboat Institution

RNLO Royal Naval Liaison Officer

RNMDSF Royal National Mission to Deep Sea Fishermen

RNMH Registered Nurse for the Mentally Handicapped

RNMS Royal Naval Medical School

RNoN Royal Norwegian Navy

RNP [biochemistry] ribonucleoprotein

RNPFN Royal National Pension Fund for Nurses

RNR Royal Naval Reserve

R 'n' R rock and roll

RNRA Royal Naval Rifle Association

RNRS Royal National Rose Society

RNS [stock exchange] Regulatory News Service; [mathematics] residue number system; Royal Numismatic Society

rns runs

RNSA Royal Naval Sailing Association

RNSC Royal Naval Staff College

RNSR Royal Naval Special Reserve

RNSS Royal Naval Scientific Service

RNT Registered Nurse Tutor; Royal National Theatre

RNTE Royal Naval Training Establishment

RNTNEH Royal National Throat, Nose and Ear Hospital

RNTU Royal Naval Training Unit

RNVR Royal Naval Volunteer Reserve

RNVSR Royal Naval Volunteer Supplementary Reserve

RNWMP [Canada] Royal Northwest Mounted Police (former name of RCMP)

rnwy runway

RNXS Royal Naval Auxiliary Service

RNZAC Royal New Zealand Armoured Corps

RNZAF Royal New Zealand Air Force

RNZIR Royal New Zealand Infantry Regiment

RNZN Royal New Zealand Navy

RNZNVR Royal New Zealand Naval Volunteer Reserve

RO [vehicle registration] Luton; radar observer; radar operator; radio operator; Radio Orchestra; [psychology] reality orientation; receiving office; receiving officer; receiving order; record(s) office; recruiting officer; regimental order; registered office; relieving officer; reserved occupation; returning officer; [chemistry] reverse osmosis; [currency] rial Omani; [international vehicle registration] Romania; [fishing port] Rothesay; Royal Observatory

ro. [printing] recto (right-hand page); roan

.ro Romania (in Internet address)

r.o. [rowing] rowed over; [cricket] run out

ROA Racehorse Owners' Association; [education] record of achievement; Reserve Officers' Association; [finance] return on assets

ROAM [finance] return on assets managed

ROAR right of admission reserved

ROB remaining on board

ROC [finance] return on capital; Royal Observer Corps

ROCE [finance] return on capital employed

ROE [finance] return on equity; Royal Observatory, Edinburgh

ROF Royal Ordnance Factory

Roffen. *Roffensis* (Latin: (Bishop) of Rochester)

R of O Reserve of Officers

ROG receipt of goods

ROH Royal Opera House (Covent Garden)

ROI region of interest; [finance] return on investment; Royal Institute of Oil Painters

ROK [international vehicle registration] (Republic of) Korea

Rolls [short form] Rolls-Royce (car)

ROM [computing] read-only memory; [medicine] rupture of membranes

Rom. Roman; Romance (language); Romania; Romanian; Romanic (language); [Bible] Romans

rom. roman (type)

Rom. Cath. Roman Catholic

RONA [finance] return on net assets

ROP [advertising] run of paper

RORC Royal Ocean Racing Club

ro-ro roll on, roll off (ferry)

ROS [computing] remote operations service

Ros. Roscommon

Rosa [computing] recognition of open systems achievement

ROSAT [astronomy] *Röntgenstrahlen Satellit* (German: X-ray satellite)

Rosco Road Operators' Safety Council

ROSE [computing] Research Open Systems in Europe

ROSL Royal Overseas League

ROSLA raising of school-leaving age

RoSPA Royal Society for the Prevention of Accidents

ROT Registered Occupational Therapist; remedial occupational therapy; rule of thumb

Rot. Rotterdam

rot. rotary; rotating; rotation; rotor

ROTC [USA] Reserve Officers' Training Corps

ROTFL rolls on the floor laughing (in Internet chat)

ROU [international vehicle registration] (Republic of) Uruguay

rout. routine

ROV remotely operated vehicle

ROW right of way; Rights of Women

ROWPU reverse osmosis water purification unit

Rox. Roxburghshire

Roy. Royal

RP [vehicle registration] Northampton; [civil aircraft marking] (Republic of the) Philippines; [international vehicle registration] (Republic of the) Philippines; radiation protection; [chemistry] reaction product; Received Pronunciation; recommended practice; recommended price; recovery phase; redundancy payment; Reformed Presbyterian; regimental police; regimental policeman; Registered Plumber; Regius Professor; reinforced plastic; reply paid; reprint; reprinting; *República Portuguesa* (Portuguese: Republic of Portugal); [US finance] repurchase agreement; research paper; [medicine] retinitis pigmentosa; [insurance] return (of) premium; *Révérend Père* (French: Reverend Father); rocket projectile; Royal Society of Portrait Painters; rules of procedure

R/P reprint; reprinting

Rp [currency] rupiah (used in Indonesia)

r.p. [telecommunications] reception poor; regimental policeman; reply paid

RPA radiation protection adviser; Rationalist Press Association; [education] record of personal achievement; Registered Plumbers' Association

RPB recognized professional body

RPC rapid Portland cement; [computing] remote procedure call; [USA] Republican Party Conference; request the pleasure of your company; Royal Pioneer Corps

RPD Doctor of Political Science (from Latin *Rerum Politicarum Doctor*); regional port director

RPE radio production executive; Reformed Protestant Episcopal; [medi-

cine] retinal pigment epithelium (of eye)

RPF [medicine] renal plasma flow; [medicine] retroperitoneal fibrosis; Rwanda Patriotic Front

RPG [computing] report program generator; [military] rocket-propelled grenade; role-playing game

rpg rounds per gun

rph revolutions per hour

RPhilS Royal Philharmonic Society

RPI retail price index

rplca replica

RPM reliability performance measure; resale price maintenance; retail price maintenance

rpm revolutions per minute

RPMS Royal Postgraduate Medical School

RPN Registered Psychiatric Nurse; [computing, mathematics] reverse Polish notation

RP/ND reprinting, no date

RPO railway post office; regional personnel officer; Royal Philharmonic Orchestra

RPQ [commerce] request for price quotation

RPR *Rassemblement pour la République* (French: Rally for the Republic) (= Gaullists, formerly UDR)

RPRA Royal Pigeon Racing Association

RPS radiological protection service; rapid processing system; Royal Philharmonic Society; Royal Photographic Society

rps revolutions per second

RPSGB Royal Pharmaceutical Society of Great Britain

RPSL Royal Philatelic Society, London

RPT Registered Physiotherapist

rpt repeat; report; reprint

RPV [nuclear technology] reactor pressure vessel; [military] remotely piloted vehicle

RQ regraded quality (of tyre); remoulded quality (of tyre); [commerce] request for quotation; [medicine] respiratory quotient

R/Q [commerce] request for quotation

RQL reference quality level

RQMS Regimental Quartermaster-Sergeant

rqmt requirement

rqr. require; requirement

RR [vehicle registration] Nottingham; radiation resistance; [USA] railroad; Remington Rand (manufacturing company); research report; return rate; Right Reverend; [cycling] road race; [fishing port] Rochester; Rolls-Royce; [USA] rural route

rr. rare

r.r. ready reckoner

RRA Royal Regiment of Artillery

RRB Race Relations Board

RRC [cycling] Road Racing Club; Road Runners' Club; Royal Red Cross

RRE Royal Radar Establishment (former name of RSRE)

RRF [military] Rapid Reaction Force; Royal Regiment of Fusiliers

RRI Rowett Research Institute (Aberdeen)

RRL Registered Record Librarian; Road Research Laboratory

RRM [USA] renegotiable-rate mortgage

rRNA [biochemistry] ribosomal ribonucleic acid

RRP recommended retail price

RR.PP. *Révérends Pères* (French: Reverend Fathers)

RRR [USA] return receipt requested (of registered mail)

RRS Royal Research Ship

RRT rail rapid transit

RS [vehicle registration] Aberdeen; Rallye Sport; Received Standard (English); reconnaissance squadron; reconnaissance strike; recording secretary; recruiting service; [computing] Reed–Solomon (as in **RS code**); Reformed Spelling; remote sensing; research station; [medicine] respiratory system; [law] Revised Statutes; Royal Scots (regiment); Royal Society

R/S rejection slip

Rs [currency] rupee

rs [meteorology] rain and snow (i.e. sleet)

r.s. right side

3Rs reading, (w)riting and (a)rithmetic

RSA Republic of South Africa; [New Zealand] Returned Services Association; [computing] Rivest, Shamir and Adelman (as in **RSA cipher**); Road Safety Act; Royal Scottish Academician; Royal Scottish Academy; Royal Society for the Encouragement of Arts, Manufactures and Commerce; Royal Society of Arts; Royal Society of Australia

RSAA Royal Society for Asian Affairs

RSAD Royal Surgical Aid Society

RSAF Royal Small Arms Factory

RSAI Royal Society of Antiquaries of Ireland

RSAMD Royal Scottish Academy of Music and Drama

RSAS Royal Surgical Aid Society

r.s.b. range safety beacon

RSC Royal Shakespeare Company; Royal Society of Canada; Royal Society of Chemistry (formerly RIC); Rules of the Supreme Court

RSCDS Royal Scottish Country Dance Society

rsch research

RSCJ *Religiosae Sacratissimi Cordis Jesus* (Latin: Nuns of the Most Sacred Heart of Jesus, Sacred Heart Society)

RSCM Royal School of Church Music

RSCN Registered Sick Children's Nurse (formerly SRCN)

RSD recovery, salvage and disposal; Royal Society of Dublin

rsdntl residential

RSE Received Standard English; Royal Society of Edinburgh

RSF [building] rough sunk face; Royal Scots Fusiliers

RSFS Royal Scottish Forestry Society

RSFSR Russian Soviet Federative Socialist Republic (former official Soviet name of Russia)

RSG rate-support grant; recirculating steam generator; regional seat of government (in civil defence); Royal Scots Greys

RSGB Radio Society of Great Britain

RSGS Royal Scottish Geographical Society

RSH Royal Society of Health

RSHA *Reichssicherheitshauptamt* (German: Reich Security Central Office) (in Nazi Germany)

RSI regional staff inspector; [medicine] repetitive strain (or stress) injury; Royal Sanitary Institute

RSJ [building] rolled-steel joist

RSL [Australia] Returned Services League; Royal Society of Literature

RSLA raising of school-leaving age

RSM Regimental Sergeant-Major; regional sales manager; Royal School of Mines; Royal Society of Medicine; Royal Society of Musicians of Great Britain; [international vehicle registration] (Republic of) San Marino

RSMA Royal Society of Marine Artists

RSME Royal School of Military Engineering

rsn reason

RSNA Radiological Society of North America

RSNC Royal Society for Nature Conservation

RSNO Royal Scottish National Orchestra

RSNT Railway Staffs National Tribunal

RSNZ Royal Society of New Zealand

RSO Radio Symphony Orchestra; radiological safety officer; railway sorting office; railway suboffice; [military] range safety officer; Recruiting Staff Officer; resident surgical officer; Royal Scottish Orchestra (formerly SNO); rural suboffice

RSocMed Royal Society of Medicine

r.s.p. [cricket] rain stopped play

RSPB Royal Society for the Protection of Birds

RSPBA Royal Scottish Pipe Band Association

RSPCA Royal Society for the Prevention of Cruelty to Animals

RSPE Royal Society of Painter-Printmakers (formerly Royal Society of Painter-Etchers and Engravers)

RSPP Royal Society of Portrait Painters

RSPS Royal Scottish Pipers' Society

rsq. rescue

RSRE Royal Signals and Radar Establishment (formerly RRE)

RSS *Regiae Societatis Socius* (Latin: Fellow of the Royal Society); Royal Statistical Society

RSSA Royal Scottish Society of Arts

RSSPCC Royal Scottish Society for the Prevention of Cruelty to Children

RSTM&H Royal Society of Tropical Medicine and Hygiene

rstr. restricted

RSU road safety unit

RSUA Royal Society of Ulster Architects

RSV [medicine] respiratory syncytial virus; Revised Standard Version (of Bible); [microbiology] Rous sarcoma virus

RSVP *répondez s'il vous plaît* (French: please reply)

rsvr reservoir

RSW Royal Scottish Water Colour Society

RSWC right side up with care

RSwN Royal Swedish Navy

RT [vehicle registration] Ipswich; [medicine] radiation therapy; radio telegraph; radio telegraphy; radio telephone; radio telephony; reaction time; reading test; received text; return ticket; room temperature; round table; round trip

R/T radio telegraph; radio telegraphy; radio telephone; radio telephony

rt right

RTA reciprocal trade agreement(s); road traffic accident; Road Traffic Act

RTB return to base (as in **RTB warranty**)

RTBA rate to be agreed

RTBF *Radio-Télévision Belge de la Communauté Française* (Belgian broadcasting company)

RTC [computing] real-time clock; [India] Road Transport Corporation; Round Table Conference

rtc. ratchet

rtd retired; returned

rtd ht [cricket] retired hurt

RTDS [computing] real-time data system

RTE *Radio Telefís Éireann* (Irish broadcasting company); [computing] real-time execution

rte route

RTECS Registry of Toxic Effects of Chemical Substances

RTF *Radiodiffusion-Télévision Française* (European broadcasting company); [computing] rich text format

RTFM [slang, computing] read the fucking manual

RTG [astronomy] radioisotope thermoelectric generator; [physics] relativistic theory of gravitation

rtg rating

Rt Hon. Right Honourable

RTI [medicine] respiratory tract infection; Round Table International

RTITB Road Transport Industry Training Board

RTK right to know

RTL *Radio-Télé Luxembourg* (European broadcasting company); [computing] real-time language; [electronics] resistor-transistor logic

RTM [computing] read the manual; registered trademark
rtn retain; return
rtng returning
RTO [USA] railroad transportation officer; railway transport officer
RTOL [aeronautics] reduced take-off and landing
RTP [engineering] rated thermal power; [physics] room temperature and pressure
RTPI Royal Town Planning Institute
RTR Royal Tank Regiment
RTRA Road Traffic Regulation Act
Rt Rev. Right Reverend
Rt Revd Right Reverend
RTS Religious Tract Society; [computing] request to send; reserve tug service; Royal Television Society; Royal Toxophilite Society
RTSA Retail Trading Standards Association
RTT radioteletype
RTTC [cycling] Road Time Trials Council
RTU [military] return(ed) to unit
RTV real-time video
RTW ready to wear
Rt W Right Worshipful
rty rarity
RTYC Royal Thames Yacht Club
RTZ Rio Tinto Zinc Corporation Limited
RU [vehicle registration] Bournemouth; [international vehicle registration] (Republic of) Burundi (from former name Urundi); Readers' Union; [computing] registered user; reprocessed uranium; Rugby Union
Ru [chemical element] ruthenium
Ru. Russia; Russian
.ru Russia (in Internet address)
RUA Royal Ulster Academy of Painting, Sculpture and Architecture
RUAS Royal Ulster Agricultural Society
rub. rubber
RUC Royal Ulster Constabulary
RUCR Royal Ulster Constabulary Reserve
rud. rudder
RUF [banking] revolving underwriting facility
RUG [computing] restricted users group
RUI Royal University of Ireland
RUKBA Royal United Kingdom Beneficent Association

rumpie [informal] rural upwardly mobile professional
RUPP road used as public path
RUR Royal Ulster Regiment
RURAL Society for the Responsible Use of Resources in Agriculture and on the Land
RUS [international vehicle registration] Russia
Rus. Russia; Russian
RUSI Royal United Services Institute for Defence Studies (formerly Royal United Service Institution)
RUSM Royal United Service Museum
Russ. Russia; Russian
Rut. Rutland
Rutd Rutland
RV [vehicle registration] Portsmouth; rateable value; [USA] recreational vehicle; [astronautics] re-entry vehicle; rendezvous; research vessel; [medicine] residual volume; Revised Version (of Bible); Rifle Volunteers; [medicine] right ventricle; [medicine] right ventricular
r.v. [statistics] random variable; rendezvous
RVA Rating and Valuation Association
RVC Rifle Volunteer Corps; Royal Veterinary College
RVCI Royal Veterinary College of Ireland
RVLR Road Vehicles Lighting Regulations
RVM Royal Victorian Medal
RVO Royal Victorian Order
RVR runway visual range
RVSVP *répondez vite, s'il vous plaît* (French: please reply quickly)
RVU research vessel unit
RW [vehicle registration] Coventry; rainwater; right of way; Right Worshipful; Right Worthy; Royal Warrant; runway
R/W right of way
Rw. Rwanda; Rwandan
r/w read/write
.rw Rwanda (in Internet address)
r.w. [sports] right wing
RWA Race Walking Association; Royal West of England Academy; [international vehicle registration] Rwanda
RWAFF Royal West African Frontier Force
R War. R Royal Warwickshire Regiment
RWAS Royal Welsh Agricultural Society
RWD radioactive waste disposal
r.w.d. rear-wheel drive

RWEA Royal West of England Academy

RWF Radio Wholesalers' Federation; Royal Welch Fusiliers

RWFCS Red and White Friesian Cattle Society

RwFr [currency] Rwanda franc

RWGM [Freemasonry] Right Worshipful Grand Master

RWGR [Freemasonry] Right Worthy Grand Representative

RWGS [Freemasonry] Right Worthy Grand Secretary

RWGT [Freemasonry] Right Worthy Grand Templar; [Freemasonry] Right Worthy Grand Treasurer

RWGW [Freemasonry] Right Worthy Grand Warden

RWIC Rioja Wine Information Centre

RWK Queen's Own Royal West Kent Regiment

RWM radioactive waste management; [computing] read–write memory

RWMAC Radioactive Waste Management Advisory Committee

RWP rainwater pipe

RWS Royal Watercolour Society

rwy railway

RX [vehicle registration] Reading; [fishing port] Rye

Rx recording (in broadcasting)

RY [vehicle registration] Leicester; [fishing port] Ramsey

ry railway

RYA Royal Yachting Association

RYC in reply to your cable

RYS Royal Yacht Squadron

RZ [vehicle registration] Antrim

r.z. return to zero

RZS Royal Zoological Society

RZSI Royal Zoological Society of Ireland

RZSS Royal Zoological Society of Scotland

RZSScot Royal Zoological Society of Scotland

S

S Sabbath; [heraldry] sable; [anatomy] sacral (of vertebrae); Saint; *San* (Italian: Saint); *Sankt* (German: Saint); *Santa* (Italian: Saint); *Santo* (Italian: Saint); *São* (Portuguese: Saint); satisfactory; Saturday; Saxon; [currency] Schilling; School; Scotland; Scottish; Sea; secondary; secret; secretary; section; *Seite* (German: page); Senate; *Señor* (Spanish: Mr); sentence; September; *sepultus* (Latin: buried); series; [UK postcode] Sheffield; ship; siemens (unit of electric conductance); signaller; signature; *Signor* (Italian: Mr); *Signora* (Italian: Mrs); [geology] Silurian; silver; [fishing port] Skibbereen; slow (on clock or watch regulator); small; [microbiology] smooth; Socialist; Society; *Socius* (Latin: Fellow) (used in titles); solar; [astronomy] solar mass; [music] soprano; south; southern; [card games] spades; [astronomy] spiral galaxy; square; staff; [law] statute; [microbiology] strain; submarine; [chemistry] substitution reaction; [currency] sucre (used in Ecuador); [chemical element] sulphur; summer; [shipping] summer (load line); sun; Sunday; Sweden; [international vehicle registration] Sweden

S [electrical engineering] apparent power; [physics] entropy; [music] *segno* (Italian: sign); [chemistry] sinister; [physics] spin quantum number (of system); [physics] strangeness quantum number

s second; shilling(s) (from Latin *solidus*); [meteorology] snow; [music] soh (in tonic sol-fa); [chemistry] solid; [physics] strange (quark flavour)

s [chemistry] secondary (isomer); [chemistry] sedimentation coefficient; [physics] specific entropy; [physics] spin quantum number; [chemistry] symmetric

s/ *sur* (French: on) (in place-names)

s. school; sea; seaman; section; see; semi-; series; sermon; set; sets (referring to the sun); *siècle* (French: century); *siehe* (German: see); sign; signed; *sine* (Latin: without); single; [grammar] singular; *sinister* (Latin: left); *sinistra* (Italian: left); sire; sister; small; snow; society; solo; son; [music] soprano; spherical; steamer;

steel; stem; stock; [grammar] substantive; succeeded; suit; summer; sun; sunny; surplus

S2 [civil aircraft marking] Bangladesh

S4C *Sianel 4 Cymru* (Welsh: Channel 4 Wales)

S5 [civil aircraft marking] Slovenia

S7 [civil aircraft marking] Seychelles

SA [vehicle registration] Aberdeen; Salvation Army; Saudi Arabia; [international vehicle registration] Saudi Arabia; Saudi Arabian; seaman apprentice; secret agent; [USA] Secretary of the Army; [horticulture] semiannual; senior administrator; sex appeal; [microbiology] simian agent; [medicine] sinoatrial (as in **SA node**); small arms; [commerce] *sociedad anónima* (Spanish: (public) limited company, plc or Ltd); [commerce] *sociedade anónima* (Portuguese: (public) limited company, plc or Ltd); [commerce] *società anonima* (Italian: (public) limited company, plc or Ltd); [commerce] *société anonyme* (French: (public) limited company, plc or Ltd); Society of Antiquaries; Society of Arts; Society of Authors; Soil Association; *Son Altesse* (French: Her/His Highness); South Africa; South African; South America; South American; South Australia; South Australian; special agent; spherical aberration; [computing] structured systems analysis; *Sturmabteilung* (German: storm troopers) (Nazi militia); subsistence allowance; surface area; surface-to-air (missile); [fishing port] Swansea; [UK postcode] Swansea; systems analysis; systems analyst

S/A subject to acceptance; subject to approval; [US banking] survivorship agreement

Sa. Saturday

sa. [heraldry] sable

.sa Saudi Arabia (in Internet address)

s.a. safe arrival; *secundum artem* (Latin: by skill, scientifically, in the standard way); see also; [horticulture] semiannual; sex appeal; *siehe auch* (German: see also); *sine anno* (Latin: without year, undated); [chemistry] soluble in alkali; storage area; subject to acceptance; subject to approval; subsistence allowance

SAA Scottish Archery Association; small arms ammunition; South African Air-

ways; Speech Association of America; Standards Association of Australia; [chemistry] surface-active agent; [computing] systems application architecture

SAAA Scottish Amateur Athletic Association

SAAAU South African Amateur Athletic Union

Saab *Svensk Aeroplan Aktiebolag* (Swedish car and aircraft manufacturer)

SAABS Scottish Action Against Blood Sports

SAAD small arms ammunition depot

SAAF South African Air Force

SAAFA Special Arab Assistance Fund for Africa

SAAO South African Astronomical Observatory

SAARC South Asian Association for Regional Cooperation

SAAU South African Agricultural Union

SAB Science Advisory Board; Scientific Advisory Board; Society of American Bacteriologists; [music] soprano, alto, bass; South Atlantic Bight

Sab. Sabbath

sab. *sabato* (Italian: Saturday); sabbatical

sáb. *sábado* (Spanish: Saturday)

SABA Scottish Amateur Boxing Association

Sabbat. Sabbatical

SABC Scottish Association of Boys' Clubs; South African Broadcasting Corporation

Sabena *Société anonyme belge d'exploitation de la navigation aérienne* (Belgian airline company)

SABIC Society for the Advancement of Brain-Injured Children

SABMIS seaborne antiballistic missile intercept system

sabo. sabotage

SABRA South African Bureau of Racial Affairs

SABS South African Bureau of Standards

SAC Scientific Advisory Committee; Scottish Arts Council; Scottish Automobile Club; Senior Aircraftman; [finance] short-run average cost; small-arms club; South Atlantic Coast; (Post Office) Stamp Advisory Committee; [USA] State Athletic Commission; [USA] Strategic Air Command

SACAB Scottish Association of Citizens' Advice Bureaux

SACEUR Supreme Allied Commander Europe

SACHR Standing Advisory Commission on Human Rights

SACL South African Confederation of Labour

SACLANT Supreme Allied Commander Atlantic

SACO *Sveriges Akademikers Centralorganisation* (Swedish: Swedish Confederation of Professional Associations)

SACP South African Communist Party

Sacr. Sacramento; Sacrist

SACRO Scottish Association for the Care and Resettlement of Offenders

SACSEA Supreme Allied Command, Southeast Asia

SACSIR South African Council for Scientific and Industrial Research

SACU single-application computer user; Society for the Promotion of Anglo-Chinese Understanding; Southern African Customs Union

SACW Senior Aircraftwoman

SAD Scottish Action on Dementia; Scottish Association for the Deaf; [psychology] seasonal affective disorder; systems analysis and design

SADC Southern African Development Community

SADCC Southern African Development Coordination Conference

SADF South African Defence Force

SADG *Société des architectes diplômés par le gouvernement* (French: Society of Government-Certified Architects)

SADI Society of Approved Driving Instructors

SADIE scanning analogue to digital input equipment

SADT [trademark, computing] structured analysis and design technique

SAE self-addressed envelope; [USA] Society of Automotive Engineers (motor-oil viscosity scale); stamped addressed envelope

s.a.e. self-addressed envelope; stamped addressed envelope

SAEF Stock Exchange Automatic Execution Facility

SAF Scottish Athletic Federation; [USA] Secretary of the Air Force; Society of American Foresters; [USA] Strategic Air Force; structural adjustment facility (in IMF)

SAFA Scottish Amateur Football Association; South Africa Freedom Association

s.a.f.e. stamped addressed foolscap envelope

S Afr. South Africa; South African

SAfrD South African Dutch

SAFU Scottish Amateur Fencing Union

SAG [USA] Screen Actors' Guild

SAGA Scottish Amateur Gymnastics Association; Society of American Graphic Artists

SAGB Schizophrenia Association of Great Britain; Spiritualist Association of Great Britain

SAGE [military] semiautomatic ground environment

SAGGA Scout and Guide Graduate Association

SAH [medicine] subarachnoid haemorrhage; Supreme Allied Headquarters

SAHC Scottish Association of Health Councils

SAHGB Society of Architectural Historians of Great Britain

SAHR Society of Army Historical Research

Sai. Saigon

SAIC Scottish Agricultural Improvement Council

SAID sexual allegations in divorce

SAIDS simian acquired immune deficiency syndrome

SAIF South African Industrial Federation

SAIMR South African Institute of Medical Research

SAIRR South African Institute of Race Relations

SAISSA Scottish Amateur Ice Speed Skating Association

SAL South Arabian League; surface airlifted (mail)

sal. salary

SALA South African Library Association

SALC symmetry-adapted linear combinations

Salop Shropshire (from old name of county)

SALP South African Labour Party

SALR [meteorology] saturated adiabatic lapse rate; South African Law Reports

SALT Scottish Association for Language Teaching; Strategic Arms Limitation Talks; Strategic Arms Limitation Treaty

Salv. Salvador; Salvadorian

salv. salvage

SAM Scottish Aids Monitor; [USA] shared-appreciation mortgage; [USA] Space Available Mail; surface-to-air missile

S Am. South America; South American

Sam. Samaria; Samaritan; Samoa; Samoan; *Samstag* (German: Saturday); [Bible] Samuel

sam. *samedi* (French: Saturday)

SAMA Saudi Arabian Monetary Agency; Scottish Amateur Music Association

Samar. Samaritan

SAMC South African Medical Corps

S Amer. South America; South American

SAMH Scottish Association for Mental Health

SAMU *Service d'assistance médicale d'urgence* (French: emergency medical assistance service)

SAN styrene–acrylonitrile (polymer)

san. sanitary

SANA Scottish Anglers' National Association

sanat. sanatorium

SANCAD Scottish Association for National Certificates and Diplomas

SAND Scotland Against Nuclear Dumping

sand. sandwich

s&d search and destroy; song and dance

S&F [insurance] stock and fixtures

s&f [informal] shopping and fucking (popular fiction genre)

S&FA shipping and forwarding agents

S&H shipping and handling (charges)

S&L [USA] savings and loan association

S&M sadism and masochism; [insurance] stock and machinery

s&m sausages and mash

S&P 500 [USA] Standard and Poors 500 Stock Index

Sands Stillbirth and Neonatal Death Society

s&s [informal] sex and shopping (popular fiction genre)

s&sc sized and supercalendered (paper)

S&T signalling and telecommunications; supply and transport

S&TA Salmon and Trout Association

Sane Schizophrenia – A National Emergency

SANFP Scottish Association for Natural Family Planning

sanit. sanitary; sanitation

s.a.n.r. subject to approval, no risk

Sans. Sanskrit

sans. [printing] sanserif

Sansk. Sanskrit

SANZ Standards Association of New Zealand

SAO Scottish Association of Opticians

SAOS Scottish Agricultural Organization Society

SAP South African Police

s.a.p. soon as possible

SAPA South African Press Association; South African Publishers' Association

SAPC Scottish Accident Prevention Council

sapfu [slang] surpassing all previous foul-ups

sapl [shipping] sailed as per list (referring to Lloyd's List)

SAPT Scottish Association for Public Transport

SAR search and rescue; *Son Altesse Royale* (French: Her/His Royal Highness); Sons of the American Revolution; South African Republic; [China] Special Administrative Region; [physics] specific absorption rate; synthetic aperture radar

Sar. Sarawak; Sardinia; Sardinian

SARA Scottish Amateur Rowing Association; Scottish Anti-Racist Alliance

SARAH search and rescue homing (radar system); [medicine] surgery assistant robot acting on the head (in brain surgery)

SARBE search and rescue beacon equipment

Sarl [commerce] *société à responsabilité limitée* (French: limited company, Ltd)

SARM Scottish Anti-Racist Movement

SARs Substantial Acquisition Rules (for mergers and takeovers)

SARSAT search and rescue satellite(-aided tracking)

SA/RT [computing] structured systems analysis for real time

Sarum. *Sarumensis* (Latin: (Bishop) of Salisbury)

SAS Scandinavian Airlines System; Small

Astronomical Satellite; *Societatis Antiquariorum Socius* (Latin: Fellow of the Society of Antiquaries); *Son Altesse Sérénissime* (French: Her/His Most Serene Highness); [military] Special Air Service; Statement of Auditing Standards

Sas [commerce] *società in accomàndita semplice* (Italian: limited partnership)

SASA Scottish Amateur Snooker Association; Scottish Amateur Swimming Association

SASC Small Arms School Corps

SASE [USA] self-addressed stamped envelope

SASF Salvation Army Students' Fellowship

Sask. Saskatchewan

SASO Senior Air Staff Officer; South African Students' Organization

SASR Special Air Service Regiment

SASV Scottish Association for the Speaking of Verse

SAT [USA] scholastic aptitude test; Senior Member of the Association of Accounting Technicians; ship's apparent time; South Australian Time; [education] standard assessment task

S At. South Atlantic

Sat. Saturday

sat. satellite; saturate; saturated

SATB [music] soprano, alto, tenor, bass

SATCO signal automatic air traffic control system

SATEX semiautomatic telegraph exchange

SATIPS Society of Assistant Teachers in Preparatory Schools

satn saturation

SATRA Shoe and Allied Trades Research Association

SATRO Science and Technology Regional Organization

SATS South African Transport Services

S Aus. South Australia; South Australian

S Austral. South Australia; South Australian

SAV [microbiology] simian adenovirus

s.a.v. sale at valuation; stock at valuation

SAVS Scottish Anti-Vivisection Society

SAW Scottish Association of Writers; [advertising] space at will; submerged arc welding; [telecommunications] surface acoustic wave

SAWA Scottish Amateur Wrestling Association

SAWS synoptic automatic weather station

Sax. Saxon; Saxony

sax [short form] saxophone

sax. saxophone

SAYC Scottish Association of Youth Clubs

SAYE save as you earn

SB Bachelor of Science (from Latin *Scientiae Baccalaureus*); [astronomy] barred spiral galaxy; [vehicle registration] Glasgow; sales book; [military] Sam Browne (officer's belt with diagonal strap); savings bank; selection board; Serving Brother (of order); [commerce] short bill (of exchange); sick bay; Signal Boatswain; signal book; simultaneous broadcast(ing); [chemical engineering] slurry bed; small business; [chemistry] sodium borate; South Britain (i.e. England and Wales); Special Branch; statute book; [medicine] stillborn; stretcher bearer; sub-branch

Sb [chemical element] antimony (from Latin *stibium*)

sb stilb (unit of luminance)

sb. [grammar] substantive

.sb Solomon Islands (in Internet address)

s.b. single-breasted; small bore (rifle); smooth bore; [baseball] stolen base(s)

SBA School of Business Administration; Scottish Basketball Association; sick-bay (or -berth) attendant; [USA] Small Business Administration; [aeronautics] standard beam approach

SBAA Sovereign Base Areas Administration

SBAC Society of British Aerospace Companies (formerly Society of British Aircraft Constructors)

SBB *Schweizerische Bundesbahnen* (German: Swiss Federal Railways)

SBBNF Ship and Boat Builders' National Federation

SBC School Broadcasting Council; single-board computer; [electrical engineering] small bayonet cap

SBD [slang] silent but deadly (breaking of wind); Soviet Block Division (of CIA); [electronics] surface-barrier diode

SBE Southern British English

SbE south by east

SBGI Society of British Gas Industries

SBH Scottish Board of Health

SBIC [USA] small business investment company

SBL Society of Biblical Literature; [electronics] surface boundary layer

SBLI [USA] savings bank life insurance

SBM single buoy mooring

SBN Standard Book Number (replaced by ISBN)

SBNO Senior British Naval Officer

s'board starboard

SBOT Sacred Books of the Old Testament

SBP [medicine] systolic blood pressure

SBPR Society for Back Pain Research

SBR [medicine] strict bed rest; styrene–butadiene rubber

sbre *septiembre* (Spanish: September)

SBS [medicine] sick building syndrome; [military] Special Boat Service

SBSA Scottish Board Sailing Association

SBStJ Serving Brother of the Order of St John of Jerusalem

SBT [shipping] segregated ballast tanks

SBTD Society of British Theatre Designers

SBU Scottish Badminton Union; strategic business unit

SBV seabed vehicle

SbW south by west

SC [vehicle registration] Edinburgh; safe custody; sailing club; Salvage Corps; [law] same case; [US military] Sanitary Corps; [Australia, New Zealand] School Certificate; Schools Council; [fishing port] Scilly; Security Council (of UN); self-contained (in accommodation advertisement); *Senatus Consultum* (Latin: decree of the Senate); Senior Counsel; service certificate; [law] Sessions Cases; shooting club; short course; Signal Corps; [printing] single column; [chemistry] single crystal; skating club; skiing club; small craft; social club; solar cell; South Carolina; [US postcode] South Carolina; [military] Southern Command; special case; Special Constable; Special Constabulary; sports club; Staff Captain; staff college; Staff Corps; standing committee; standing conference; [Canada] Star of Courage; statutory committee; [engineering] stress corrosion; [grammar] structural change; [medicine] subcutaneous; Suffolk and Cambridgeshire

(regiment); supercalendered (paper); Supreme Court; surface contamination; swimming club

Sc [chemical element] scandium

Sc [meteorology] stratocumulus

Sc. Scandinavia; Scandinavian; Science; Scotch; Scotland; Scots; Scottish; sculptor

s/c self-catering (in accommodation advertisement); self-contained (in accommodation advertisement); [commerce] *son compte* (French: (on) her/his account)

sc. scale; scene; science; scientific; *scilicet* (= namely, that is, from Latin *scire licet*); screw; scruple (unit of weight); *sculpsit* (Latin: (he/she) carved it); sculptor

.sc Seychelles (in Internet address)

s.c. salvage charges; self-contained (in property or accommodation advertisement); [printing] single column; [printing] small capital(s); steel casting; supercalendered (paper)

SCA Scottish Canoe Association; Scottish Chess Association; Scottish Council on Alcohol; Scottish Croquet Association; [medicine] sickle-cell anaemia; Suez Canal Authority; [computing] synchronous concurrent algorithm

SCAAA Southern Counties Amateur Athletic Association

SCAARF Scottish Combined Action Against Racism and Fascism

Scada system control and data acquisition

SCAFA Scottish Child and Family Alliance

SCAHT Scottish Churches Architectural Heritage Trust

SCAN suspected child abuse and neglect

Scan. Scandinavia; Scandinavian

Scand. Scandinavia; Scandinavian

SCAO Senior Civil Affairs Officer

SCAP Supreme Command Allied Powers; Supreme Commander Allied Powers

SCAPA Society for Checking the Abuses of Public Advertising

s. caps [printing] small capitals

SCAR Scientific Committee on Antarctic Research; Special Committee on Antarctic Research

SCARA selective compliance assembly robot arm

Scarab submerged craft assisting repair and burial

SCARF Sickle Cell Anaemia Research Foundation; [accounting] systems control and review file

SCART *Syndicat des constructeurs des appareils radio récepteurs et téléviseurs* (French: Syndicate of Radio and Television Manufacturers) (designers of plug-and-socket system used in home entertainment equipment)

SCAT [medicine] sheep-cell agglutination test

SCB Solicitors Complaints Bureau; [medicine] special-care baby; Speedway Control Board (in motorcycle racing)

ScB Bachelor of Science (from Latin *Scientiae Baccalaureus*)

ScBC Bachelor of Science in Chemistry

ScBE Bachelor of Science in Engineering

SCBU [medicine] special-care baby unit

SCC Scottish Churches Council; Scottish Consumer Council; Sea Cadet Corps; Society of Church Craftsmen; [medicine] squamous-cell carcinoma; [engineering] stress-corrosion cracking

s.c.c. [printing] single column centimetre; [electrical engineering] single cotton-covered (wire)

SCCA Scottish Consumer Credit Association; Society of Company and Commercial Accountants; Sports Car Club of America

SCCAPE Scottish Council for Commercial, Administrative and Professional Education

SCCL Scottish Council for Civil Liberties

SCD Scottish Council on Disability; [medicine] sickle-cell disease

ScD Doctor of Science (from Latin *Scientiae Doctor*)

scd scheduled

SCDA Scottish Community Drama Association

SCDC Schools Curriculum Development Committee

ScDHyg Doctor of Science in Hygiene

ScDMed Doctor of Science in Medicine

SCE schedule compliance evaluation; Scottish Certificate of Education; [genetics] sister-chromatid exchange

sce. scenario

SCEC Scottish Community Education Council

SCET Scottish Council for Educational Technology

SCF Save the Children Fund; Senior Chaplain to the Forces

scf standard cubic feet

scfd standard cubic feet per day

scfh standard cubic feet per hour

scfm standard cubic feet per minute

SCG Sydney Cricket Ground

scg scoring

SCGB Ski Club of Great Britain

Sch. [taxation] schedule; [currency] Schilling; School

sch. schedule; scholar; scholarship; scholastic; scholiast; *scholium* (Latin: note); school; schooner

sched. schedule

schem. schematic

scherz. [music] *scherzando* (Italian: joking, playfully)

SchMusB Bachelor of School Music

schol. scholar; scholarship; scholastic; scholiast; *scholium* (Latin: note)

schr schooner

SCI Scottish Central Institutions; Society of the Chemical Industry

sci. science; scientific

s.c.i. [printing] single-column inch

SCIAF Scottish Catholic International Aid Fund

SCID Scotland's Campaign against Irresponsible Drivers; [medicine] severe combined immune deficiency

sci. fa. *scire facias* (Latin: cause it to be known) (judicial writ)

sci-fi [short form] science fiction

scil. *scilicet* (= namely, that is, from Latin *scire licet*)

SCIT Special Commissioners of Income Tax

SCK Servants of Christ the King

SCL Scottish Central Library; Student of Civil Law

Scl [astronomy] Sculptor

SCLC Scottish Child Law Centre; [medicine] small-cell lung cancer (or carcinoma); Southern Christian Leadership Conference

SCLI Somerset and Cornwall Light Infantry

SCM [stock exchange] smaller companies market; State Certified Midwife (replaced

by RM); Student Christian Movement;
summary court martial

ScM Master of Science (from Latin *Scientiae Magister*)

SCMA Society of Cinema Managers of
Great Britain and Ireland (Amalgamated); Stilton Cheese Manufacturers'
Association

SCMAC Scottish Catholic Marriage
Advisory Council

SCMES Society of Consulting Marine
Engineers and Ship Surveyors

ScMHyg Master of Science in Hygiene

SCNE Select Committee on National
Expenditure

SCNI Sports Council for Northern Ireland

SCNO Senior Canadian Naval Officer

Sco [astronomy] Scorpius

SCOBEC Scottish Business Education
Council

SCODL [computing] scan conversion
object description language

SCOFF Society for the Conquest of Flight
Fear

Scolag Scottish Legal Action Group

S Con. Res. [USA] Senate concurrent resolution

SCONUL Standing Conference of
National and University Libraries

SCOR Scientific Committee on Oceanic
Research; Standing Committee on
Refugees

Scot. Scotch; Scotland; Scottish

ScotBIC Scottish Business in the Community

SCOTEC Scottish Technical Education
Council

SCOTUS Supreme Court of the United
States

SCOTVEC Scottish Vocational Educational Council (became part of SQA)

SCOUT [commerce] shared currency
option under tender

SCP single-cell protein (in food technology); [Canada] Social Credit Party

SCPC [telecommunications] single channel
per carrier

SCPR Scottish Council of Physical Recreation

SCPS Society of Civil and Public Servants

SCR [chemical engineering] selective catalytic reactor; senior combination room
(in university or college); senior

common room (in university or college);
sequence control register; [electronics]
silicon-controlled rectifier; small companies rate (of corporation tax)

scr. [finance] scrip; script; scruple (unit of
weight)

SCRAM Scottish Campaign to Resist the
Atomic Menace

SCRE Scottish Council for Racial Equality;
Scottish Council for Research in Education

SCREAM Society for the Control and
Registration of Estate Agents and Mortgage Brokers

Script. Scriptural; Scripture(s)

SCS Scottish Crime Squad; [USA] Soil Conservation Service; space communications system

SCSA signal computing system achitecture; Soil Conservation Society of
America

SCSI small computer systems interface
(pronounced 'scuzzy')

SCSS Scottish Council of Social Service

Sct [astronomy] Scutum

SCTR Standing Conference on Telecommunications Research

SCU Scottish Cricket Union; Scottish Cyclists' Union; [medicine] special care unit

SCUA Scottish Conservative and Unionist
Association; Suez Canal Users'
Association

scuba self-contained underwater
breathing apparatus

sculp. *sculpsit* (Latin: (he/she) carved it);
sculptor; sculptural; sculpture

sculps. *sculpsit* (Latin: (he/she) carved it)

sculpt *sculpsit* (Latin: (he/she) carved it)

sculpt. sculptor; sculptural; sculpture

SCV *Stato della Città del Vaticano* (Italian:
Vatican City State)

SCWS Scottish Cooperative Wholesale
Society

SCY [vehicle registration] Truro (Isles of
Scilly)

SCYA Scottish Christian Youth Assembly

SD Diploma in Statistics; Doctor of Science (from Latin *Scientiae Doctor*);
[vehicle registration] Glasgow; *salutem
dicit* (Latin: (he/she) sends greeting); sea-damaged; [USA] Secretary of Defense;
semi-detached (in property advertisement); *Senatus Decreto* (Latin: by decree

of the Senate); send direct; [medicine] senile dementia; senior deacon; sequence date; [military] service dress; [commerce] short delivery; *Sicherheitsdienst* (German: Security Service) (in Nazi Germany); [finance] sight draft; Signal Department; Signal Division; [computing] single density (disk); South Dakota; [US postcode] South Dakota; special delivery; special duty; spin dryer (in accommodation advertisement); staff duties; stage door; [statistics] standard deviation; [USA] State Department; [grammar] structural description; submarine detector; [currency] Sudanese dinar; [fishing port] Sunderland; supply depot; [international vehicle registration] Swaziland

S/D [USA] school district; [finance] sight draft

sd said; sailed; [bookbinding] sewed; signed; sound

.sd Sudan (in Internet address)

s.d. safe deposit; same date; *sans date* (French: no date); semi-detached (in property advertisement); sense datum (in philosophy); several dates; [commerce] short delivery; *siehe dies* (German: see this); *sine die* (Latin: without a day (being fixed)); [statistics] standard deviation

SDA Scottish Darts Association; Scottish Development Agency; Scottish Dinghy Association; Scottish Diploma in Agriculture; Seventh Day Adventist(s); Social Democratic Alliance; spray-drying absorption (or absorber)

S Dak. South Dakota

SD&T staff duties and training

SDAT [medicine] senile dementia of the Alzheimer type

S-DAT stationary digital audio tape

SDC Society of Dyers and Colourists; submersible decompression chamber

SDCGB Square Dance Callers of Great Britain

SDD Scottish Development Department; [telecommunications] subscriber direct dialling

SDECE *Service de documentation étrangère et de contre-espionnage* (French counterintelligence agency)

SDF Social Democratic Federation

SDG *Soli Deo Gloria* (Latin: Glory to God Alone)

SDH [computing] synchronous digital hierarchy

SDHE spacecraft data-handling equipment

SDI selective dissemination of information; Strategic Defense Initiative (US Star Wars programme)

SDIO [USA] Strategic Defense Initiative Office

SDL special duties list

sdl. saddle

SDLC [computing] synchronous data link control

SDLP [Northern Ireland] Social Democratic and Labour Party

SDMJ September, December, March, June (end of financial quarters)

SDO senior dental officer; senior duty officer; station duty officer; subdivisional officer

S Doc. [USA] Senate document

SDP Social Democratic Party (former political party); [insurance] social, domestic and pleasure

SDPM [computing] software development process model

SDR special dispatch rider; *Suddeutscher Rundfunk* (German: South German Radio)

SDRAM [computing] synchronous dynamic random-access memory

SDRs [finance] special drawing rights (in IMF)

SDRT stamp duty reserve tax

SDS scientific data system; Sisters of the Divine Saviour; sodium dodecyl sulphate (detergent); *Sozialistischer Deutscher Studentenbund* (German: Federation of Socialist Students); [USA] strategic defense system; [USA] Students for a Democratic Society

SDT Society of Dairy Technology

SDTU Sign and Display Trades Union

SDUK Society for the Diffusion of Useful Knowledge

SE [vehicle registration] Aberdeen; [fishing port] Salcombe; sanitary engineering; Scottish Enterprise; Society of Engineers; [computing] software engineering; *Son Éminence* (French: His Eminence); *Son Excellence* (French: Her/His Excellency);

southeast; southeastern; [UK postcode] southeast London; Staff Engineer; Standard English; Stirling engine; stock exchange; [building] stopped end; [civil aircraft marking] Sweden

S/E stock exchange

Se [chemical element] selenium

.se Sweden (in Internet address)

s.e. single end; single ended; single engine; [book-keeping] single entry; special equipment; [statistics] standard error; straight edge

SEA Southeast Asia

SEAAC Southeast Asia Air Command

SEAC School Examination and Assessment Council; Southeast Asia Command; Standard Eastern Automatic Computer

SEAL [US navy] sea-air-land

SEALF Southeast Asia Land Forces

SE&CR South Eastern and Chatham Railway

SEAQ Stock Exchange Automated Quotations (System)

SEAT *Sociedad Española de Automoviles de Tourismo* (Spanish vehicle manufacturer)

SEATO Southeast Asia Treaty Organization

SEATS Stock Exchange Alternative Trading Service

SEB Scottish Education Board (became part of SQA); Southern Electricity Board

SEC Scottish Evangelistic Crusade; Secondary Examinations Council; [USA] Securities and Exchange Commission; [military] Southeastern Command

Sec. Secretary

sec [mathematics] secant; [short form] second

sec. second; secondary; seconded; secretary; section; sector; *secundum* (Latin: according to); security

SECAM [television] *séquentiel couleur à mémoire* (French: colour sequence by memory) (broadcasting system)

SECC Scottish Exhibition and Conference Centre

Sec-Gen Secretary-General

sech [mathematics] hyperbolic secant

Sec. Leg. Secretary of the Legation

sec. leg. *secundum legem* (Latin: according to law)

sec. nat. *secundum naturam* (Latin: according to nature, naturally)

sec. reg. *secundum regulam* (Latin: according to rule)

sect. section

secy secretary

SED Scottish Education Department; shipper's export declaration; *Sozialistische Einheitspartei Deutschlands* (German: Socialist Unity Party) (former East German Communist Party)

sed. sedative; sediment

SEDAR [navigation] submerged electrode detection and ranging

sedt sediment

sedtn sedimentation

SEE senior electrical engineer; Society of Environment Engineers

Seeboard Southeastern Electricity Board

SEF Shipbuilding Employers' Federation

SEG [taxation] Self Employment Group; socioeconomic grade

seg. segment; segregate; [music] *segue* (Italian: follows, comes after)

SEIF *Secretaria de Estado da Informação e Turismo* (Portuguese: State Information and Tourist Board)

SEIS submarine escape immersion suit

seismol. seismological; seismology

SEIU [USA] Service Employees International Union

sel. select; selected; selection; *selig* (German: deceased)

Selk. Selkirk

SELNEC Southeast Lancashire, Northeast Cheshire

SEM scanning electron microscope (or microscopy)

Sem. Seminary; Semitic

sem. semester; semicolon; seminary

s.e.m. [statistics] standard error of the mean

semi [short form] semi-detached house

semp. [music] *sempre* (Italian: always, still)

s/empl. self-employed

SEN special educational needs; State Enrolled Nurse (former name of ENG)

Sen. Senate; Senator; (Marcus Annaeus) Seneca (Roman writer); Senior

sen. senior; [music] *senza* (Italian: without)

S en C [commerce] *sociedad en comandita* (Spanish: limited partnership); [commerce] *société en commandite* (French: limited partnership)

Sennac Special Educational Needs National Advisory Council

S en NC [commerce] *société en nom collectif* (French: partnership)

Senr Senior

sent. sentence

SEO senior executive officer; senior experimental officer; Society of Educational Officers

s.e.o.o. *sauf erreur ou omission* (French: errors or omissions excepted)

SEP [USA] simplified employee pension

Sep. September; Septuagint

sep. [botany] sepal; separable; separate; separated; separation

SEPA Scottish Environment Protection Agency

SEPM Society of Economic Palaeontologists and Mineralogists

sepn separation

SEPON Stock Exchange Pool Nominees Limited

Sept. *September* (German: September); September; Septuagint

sept. *septem* (Latin: seven); *septembre* (French: September)

seq. sequel; sequence; *sequens* (Latin: the following (one)); *sequente* (Latin: and in what follows); *sequitur* (Latin: it follows)

seq. luce [medicine] *sequenti luce* (Latin: on the following day) (in prescriptions)

seqq. *sequentia* (Latin: the following (ones)); *sequentibus* (Latin: in the following (places))

Ser [astronomy] Serpens

ser. serial; series; sermon; servant; service

SERA Socialist Environment and Resources Association

Serb. Serbia; Serbian

SERC Science and Engineering Research Council (formerly SRC)

Serg. Sergeant

Sergt Sergeant

Serj. Serjeant

Serjt Serjeant

SERL Services Electronics Research Laboratory

SERLANT [US navy] Service Forces, Atlantic

SERPAC [US navy] Service Forces, Pacific

Serps State Earnings-Related Pension Scheme

SERT Society of Electronic and Radio Technicians

serv. servant; service

SES Scientific Exploration Society; [USA] socioeconomic status; Stock Exchange of Singapore

SESCO secure submarine communications

SESDAQ Stock Exchange of Singapore Dealing and Automated Quotation System

SESI Stock Exchange of Singapore Index

SESO Senior Equipment Staff Officer

sess. session

SET Securities Exchange of Thailand; selective employment tax (former tax)

SETI [astronomy] search for extraterrestrial intelligence

S-et-L Saône-et-Loire (French department)

S-et-M Seine-et-Marne (French department)

S-et-O Seine-et-Oise (French department)

Sets Stock Exchange electronic trading system

sett. *settembre* (Italian: September)

sev. sever; several; severe

sevl several

SEW safety-equipment worker

sew. sewage; sewer; sewerage

Sex [astronomy] Sextans

sex. sextet; sexual

Sexag. Sexagesima

sext. sextant

SF [vehicle registration] Edinburgh; San Francisco; science fiction; Senior Fellow; [military] Sherwood Foresters; shipping federation; [telecommunications] signal frequency; [finance] sinking fund; Sinn Féin; Society of Friends; special facilities; special forces; [electrical engineering] standard frequency

Sf [currency] Suriname guilder (from alternative name florin)

sf. [music] *sforzando* (Italian: strengthening, strongly accented)

s.f. [baseball] sacrifice fly; [commerce] *sans frais* (French: no expenses); science fiction; [telecommunications] signal frequency; [finance] sinking fund; *sub finem* (Latin: towards the end)

SFA Scottish Football Association; Securities and Futures Authority; Small Farmers' Association; sulphated fatty alcohol (in detergent); [slang] sweet Fanny Adams (i.e. nothing); [slang] sweet fuck all (i.e. nothing)

SFAC Statement of Financial Accounting Concepts

SFAS Statement of Financial Accounting Standards

SFB *Sender Freies Berlin* (German: Broadcasting Station of Free Berlin)

SFBMS Small Farm Business Management Scheme

SFC specific fuel consumption (of jet engine)

Sfc [USA] Sergeant first class

SFD [obstetrics] small for dates (of baby)

SFEP Society of Freelance Editors and Proofreaders

SFEU Scottish Further Education Unit

SFF [computing] small form factor

sfgd safeguard

SFHEA Scottish Further and Higher Education Association

SFI *Société financière internationale* (French: International Finance Corporation)

SFInstE Senior Fellow, Institute of Energy

SFL Scottish Football League; [aeronautics] sequenced flashing lights (on runway)

sfm surface feet per minute

SFO Senior Flag Officer; Serious Fraud Office; Superannuation Funds Office

SFOF spaceflight operations facility (in NASA)

SFOR Sustaining (or Stabilization) Force (NATO-led peacekeeping force in Bosnia, replacement for IFOR)

sfp [music] *sforzato-piano* (Italian: strongly accented (then) soft)

SFR [finance] sinking fund rate of return

SFr [currency] Swiss franc

SFSR Socialist Federation of Soviet Republics

SFT supercritical fluid technology

SFTCD Senior Fellow of Trinity College, Dublin

SFU signals flying unit; suitable for upgrade (on airline ticket)

sfz. [music] *sforzando* (Italian: strengthening, strongly accented)

SG [vehicle registration] Edinburgh; *Sa Grâce* (French: Her/His Grace); *Sa Grandeur* (French: Her/His Highness); Scots

Guards; Seaman Gunner; Secretary-General; *selon grandeur* (French: according to size) (on menus etc.); [US education] senior grade; [astronomy] Seyfert galaxy; ship and goods; Showmen's Guild of Great Britain; Society of Genealogists; Solicitor-General; spin-glass (type of crystal); [UK postcode] Stevenage; Surgeon-General

Sg [chemical element] seaborgium

Sg. Surgeon

sg. [grammar] singular

.sg Singapore (in Internet address)

s.g. specific gravity; steel girder

SGA Scottish Games Association; [obstetrics] small for gestational age; Society of Graphic Art

SGB *Schweizerischer Gewerkschaftsbund* (German: Swiss Federation of Trade Unions)

SGBI Schoolmistresses' and Governesses' Benevolent Institution

SgC Surgeon Captain

SgCr Surgeon Commander

SGD [Freemasonry] Senior Grand Deacon

sgd signed

sgdg *sans garantie du gouvernement* (French: without government guarantee) (of patent)

Sge [astronomy] Sagitta

SGF Scottish Grocers' Federation

SGHWR [nuclear technology] steam-generating heavy-water reactor

sgl. single

S Glam. South Glamorgan

SgLCr Surgeon Lieutenant-Commander

sgle single

SGM Sea Gallantry Medal

SGML [computing] standard generalized markup language

SGO Squadron Gunnery Officer

SGOT [medicine] serum glutamic oxaloacetic transaminase

SGP [international vehicle registration] Singapore

SGPT [medicine] serum glutamic pyruvic transaminase

Sgr [astronomy] Sagittarius

SgRA Surgeon Rear-Admiral

SGRAM [computing] synchronous graphics random-access memory

SGT Society of Glass Technology

Sgt Sergeant

Sgt-Maj Sergeant-Major

SGTS Scottish Gaelic Texts Society

SGU Scottish Gliding Union; Scottish Golf Union

SgVA Surgeon Vice-Admiral

SGW [Freemasonry] Senior Grand Warden

SH [vehicle registration] Edinburgh; [fishing port] Scarborough; Schleswig-Holstein; school house; scrum half (in rugby); sexual harassment; [meteorology] showers; [numismatics] small head; southern hemisphere

Sh. [military] Shipwright

s/h shorthand

sh. shall; [stock exchange] share; sheep; [bookbinding] sheet; shilling; shower (in property or accommodation advertisement)

s.h. [baseball] sacrifice hit; second-hand; shit-house; slant height; slope height

SHA Scottish Hockey Association; Secondary Heads Association; [astronomy, navigation] sidereal hour angle; special health authority; [mathematics] spherical harmonic analysis

SHAC Shelter Housing Aid Centre

SHACT Scottish Housing Associations Charitable Trust

SHAEF Supreme Headquarters Allied Expeditionary Forces (in World War II)

Shak. (William) Shakespeare (English writer)

Shakes. (William) Shakespeare (English writer)

SH&MA Scottish Horse and Motormen's Association

SHAPE Supreme Headquarters Allied Powers Europe (of NATO)

SHC [physics] specific heat capacity

SHCJ Society of the Holy Child Jesus

shd should

SHE safety, health and ergonomics

S/HE [shipping] Sundays and holidays excepted

Shef. Sheffield

SHEFC Scottish Higher Education Funding Council

Sheff. Sheffield

Shet. Shetland Islands

Shetl. Shetland Islands

SHEX [shipping] Sundays and holidays excepted

SHF [radio] superhigh frequency

Sh.F shareholders' funds

SHGF Scottish Hang-Gliding Federation

SHHD Scottish Home and Health Department

shipmt shipment

shipt shipment

s/hist. service history (in car advertisement)

SHM [physics] simple harmonic motion; Society of Housing Managers

SHMIS Society of Headmasters and Headmistresses of Independent Schools

SHMO senior hospital medical officer

SHO senior house officer

SHORAN short-range navigation

SHP [chemical engineering] selective hydrogenation process; [horticulture] single-flowered hardy perennial (rose); [horticulture] single-flowered hybrid perpetual (rose)

shp shaft horsepower

shpg shipping

shpt shipment

SHQ station headquarters; supreme headquarters

shr. share(s)

shrap. shrapnel

SHRG Scottish Homosexual Rights Group

Shrops Shropshire

SHS Shire Horse Society; Social History Society of the United Kingdom; *Societatis Historicae Socius* (Latin: Fellow of the Historical Society)

SHT [horticulture] single-flowered hybrid tea (rose)

sht [bookbinding] sheet

shtg. shortage

SHU Scottish Hockey Union

s.h.v. *sub hac voce* (Latin: under this word) (in reference book); *sub hoc verbo* (Latin: under this word) (in reference book)

SHW safety, health, and welfare

shwr shower (in property or accommodation advertisement)

SI Sandwich Islands (former name of Hawaii); seriously ill; Shetland Islands; Smithsonian Institution (Washington, DC); Socialist International; [USA] Society of Illustrators; South Island (New Zealand); Staff Inspector; (Order of the) Star of India; Staten Island (New York); statutory instrument (of government); styrene–isoprene (polymer); *Système*

International (*d'Unités*) (French: International System (of Units), as in **SI unit**)

Si [chemical element] silicon

.si Slovenia (in Internet address)

s.i. sum insured

SIA Securities Industry Association; Society of Investment Analysts; Spinal Injuries Association

SIAC [USA] Securities Industry Automation Corporation

SIAD Society of Industrial Artists and Designers (former name of CSD)

SIAM [USA] Society of Industrial and Applied Mathematics

SIAS Statement on Internal Auditing Standards

SIB Savings and Investment Bank; Securities and Investments Board; [medicine] self-injurious behaviour; Shipbuilding Industry Board; Special Investigation Branch (of police)

Sib. Siberia; Siberian

SIBH Society for the Interpretation of Britain's Heritage

SIBOR [finance] Singapore Inter-Bank Offered Rate

SIC [USA] Scientific Information Center; Standard Industrial Classification

Sic. Sicilian; Sicily

sic. [pharmacology] *siccus* (Latin: dry)

SICAV *société d'investissement à capital variable* (French: unit trust)

SICOT *Société internationale de chirurgie orthopédique et de traumatologie* (French: International Society of Orthopaedic Surgery and Traumatology)

SID Society for International Development; *Spiritus in Deo* (Latin: her/his spirit is with God); [radio] sudden ionospheric disturbance

SIDA Swedish International Development Authority; [medicine] *syndrome immunodéficitaire acquis* (French: acquired immune deficiency syndrome, Aids)

SIDF system independent data format

SIDS [medicine] sudden infant death syndrome (= cot death)

SIEC Scottish Industrial Estates Corporation

SIESO Society of Industrial and Emergency Service Officers

SIF selective identification feature; [engineering] stress-intensity factor

SIFS special instructors' flying school

SIG [numismatics] signature of engraver present; special interest group

Sig. *Signor* (Italian: Mr); *Signore* (Italian: Sir)

sig. signal; signature; *signetur* (Latin: let it be written, let it be labelled); significant; signification; signifies

SIGAC Scottish Industrial Groups Advisory Council

SIGBI Soroptimist International of Great Britain and Ireland

sig. fig. [mathematics] significant figures

sigill. *sigillum* (Latin: seal)

SIGINT signals intelligence (gathering network)

SIGMA Science in General Management

Sigmn Signalman

sign. signature

signif. significant; signifier

sig. n. pro. [medicine] *signa nomine proprio* (Latin: label with the proper name) (in prescriptions)

Sig. O Signal Officer

SIH Society for Italic Handwriting

SIL [electronics] single in-line; *Société internationale de la lèpre* (French: International Leprosy Association)

Sil. Silesia; Silesian

SIM self-inflicted mutilation; *Société internationale de musicologie* (French: International Musicological Society); survey information on microfilm

sim. similar; similarly; simile

SIMA Scientific Instrument Manufacturers' Association of Great Britain; Steel Industry Management Association; [psychology] system for identifying motivated abilities

SIMC *Société internationale pour la musique contemporaine* (French: International Society for Contemporary Music)

Simca *Société industrielle de mécanique et carrosserie automobiles* (French car manufacturer)

SIMD [computing] single instruction, multiple data

SIME Security Intelligence Middle East

SIMEX Singapore International Monetary Exchange

SIMG *Societas Internationalis Medicinae Gen-*

eralis (Latin: International Society of General Medicine)

SIMM [computing, electronics] single in-line memory module

SIMPL Scientific, Industrial and Medical Photographic Laboratories

SIN [accounting] stores issue note

sin [mathematics] sine

sin. sinecure; *sinistra* (Italian: left)

sinbad [informal] single income, no boyfriend, absolutely desperate

Sing. Singapore; Singaporean

sing. [grammar] singular; [medicine] *singulorum* (Latin: of each) (in prescriptions)

Sinh. Sinhalese

sinh [mathematics] hyperbolic sine

SINS ship's inertial navigation system

SIO senior intelligence officer; [computing] serial input/output

SIOP [USA] single integrated operations plan (for nuclear war)

SIP [computing] single in-line package; [USA] supplemental income plan

SIPC [USA] Securities Investor Protection Corporation

SIPO [computing] serial in, parallel out

SIPRC Society of Independent Public Relations Consultants

SIPRI Stockholm International Peace Research Institute

SIPS side impact protection system (in car bodywork)

SIR [taxation] small income relief

Sir [computing] serial infrared

SIRA Scientific Instrument Research Association

SIRS [medicine] systemic inflammatory response syndrome

SIRTF Space Infrared Telescope Facility

SIS Satellite Information Services; Secret Intelligence Service (= MI6); [New Zealand] Security Intelligence Service

sis [short form] sister

sis. sister

SISD Scottish Information Service for the Disabled; [computing] single instruction, single data

SISO [computing] serial in, serial out; [electronics] single input, single output

SISS submarine integrated sonar system

SISTER Special Institutions for Scientific and Technological Education and Research

SIT Society of Industrial Technology; Society of Instrument Technology; [engineering] spontaneous ignition temperature; [currency] tolar (used in Slovenia)

sit. sitting room (in property advertisement); situated; situation

s.i.t. stopping in transit; storing in transit

SITA *Société internationale de télécommunications aéronautiques* (French: International Society of Aeronautical Telecommunications); Students' International Travel Association

SITC Standard International Trade Classification

sitcom [short form] situation comedy

SITC(R) Standard International Trade Classification (Revised)

SITPRO Simpler Trade Procedures Board (formerly Simplification of International Trade Procedures)

sits vac. situations vacant

sitt. sitting room (in property advertisement)

sit. vac. situation(s) vacant

SIUNA Seafarers International Union of North America

SI unit *Système international* unit

SIV [microbiology] simian immunodeficiency virus

SIW self-inflicted wound

SIWA Scottish Inland Waterways Association

SJ [vehicle registration] Glasgow; Society of Jesus (= Jesuits); supersonic jet

s.j. [law] sub judice

SJA St John Ambulance

SJAA St John Ambulance Association

SJAB St John Ambulance Brigade

SJC standing joint committee; [USA] Supreme Judicial Court

SJCRE Scottish Joint Committee on Religious Education

SJD Doctor of Juridical (or Juristic) Science (from Latin *Scientiae Juridicae Doctor*)

SJF Scottish Judo Federation

SK [vehicle registration] Inverness; Saskatchewan; Sealed Knot (historical re-enactment society); [international vehicle registration] Slovakia; [UK postcode] Stockport

Sk [currency] Slovakian koruna

sk sack; sick

sk. sketch

.sk Slovakia (in Internet address)

SKAMP station keeping and mobile platform (unmanned boat)

SKC Scottish Kennel Club

SKFA Scottish Keep Fit Association

Skm Stockholm

s.k.p.o. [knitting] slip one, knit one, pass slipped stitch over

Skr Skipper; [currency] Swedish krona

Skr. Sanskrit

Skt Sanskrit

SKU [commerce] stock-keeping unit

SL [vehicle registration] Dundee; [insurance] salvage loss; Scout leader; sea level; Second Lieutenant; security list; Sergeant-at-Law; [building] short lengths; Sierra Leone; [UK postcode] Slough; Solicitor-at-Law; source language; southern league; south latitude; [commerce] specification limits; Squadron Leader; supplementary list

Sl. Slovak; Slovakian

sl. sleet; slightly; slip

.sl Sierra Leone (in Internet address)

s.l. [insurance] salvage loss; *secundum legem* (Latin: according to law); seditious libel; [bibliography] *sine loco* (Latin: without place (of publication)); support line

SLA School Libraries Association; Scottish Library Association; special landscape area (in conservation); [USA] Special Libraries Association; Symbionese Liberation Army

SLAC Stanford Linear Accelerator Center

SLADE Society of Lithographic Artists, Designers, Engravers and Process Workers

SLAET Society of Licensed Aircraft Engineers and Technologists

Slam standoff land-attack missile

s.l.a.n. [bibliography] *sine loco, anno vel nomine* (Latin: without place, year or name (of publisher))

Slar [military] side-looking airborne radar

SLAS Society for Latin American Studies

SLASH Scottish Local Authorities Special Housing Group

S Lat. south latitude

Slav. Slavic; Slavonian; Slavonic

SLBM submarine-launched ballistic missile

SLC Scottish Land Court; Scottish Law Commission; Scottish Leaving Certificate; Statute Law Committee; Surgeon Lieutenant-Commander

SLCM sea-launched cruise missile; ship-launched cruise missile; submarine-launched cruise missile

SLD self-locking device; Social and Liberal Democrats (former name of Liberal Democrats)

sld sailed; sealed; sold; solid

S Ldr Squadron Leader

SLE [medicine] systemic lupus erythematosus

s.l. et a. [bibliography] *sine loco et anno* (Latin: without place and year (of publication))

S level [education] Special level (formerly Scholarship level)

SLF Scottish Landowners' Federation

s.l.f. [telecommunications] straight-line frequency

SLFP Sri Lanka Freedom Party

SLGA Scottish Ladies' Golfing Association

SLIC [USA] (Federal) Savings and Loan Insurance Corporation

SLIM South London Industrial Mission

SLIP [computing] serial line Internet protocol

Slipar [military] short light pulse alerting receiver (in aircraft)

SLLA Scottish Ladies' Lacrosse Association

SLLW solid low-level (radioactive) waste

SLM ship-launched missile

SLMA [USA] Student Loan Marketing Association

SLMC Scottish Ladies' Mountaineering Club

s.l.n.d. [bibliography] *sine loco nec data* (Latin: without date or place (of publication))

SLO senior liaison officer; [international vehicle registration] Slovenia

SLOA Steam Locomotive Operators' Association

SLOC [computing] source lines of code

SLP Scottish Labour Party; [USA] Socialist Labor Party

slp slip

s.l.p. *sine legitime prole* (Latin: without lawful issue)

SLR satellite laser ranging; self-loading rifle; single-lens reflex (camera)

SLRS Sexual Law Reform Society

SL Rs [currency] Sri Lankan rupee

SLS sodium lauryl sulphate (detergent); Stephenson Locomotive Society

SLSC surf life-saving club

SLSI [electronics] super large-scale integration

SLTA Scottish Lawn Tennis Association; Scottish Licensed Trade Association

Slud [military slang] salivate, lachrymate, urinate, defecate (effects of chemical weapons)

SLV Society of Licensed Victuallers; space launch vehicle; standard launch vehicle

SLW solid low-level (radioactive) waste

sly slowly; southerly

SM [vehicle registration] Carlisle; Master of Science (from Latin *Scientiae Magister*); sadomasochism; sadomasochist; sales manager; *Sa Majesté* (French: Her/His Majesty); *sanctae memoriae* (Latin: of holy memory); *Seine Majestät* (German: Her/His Majesty); senior magistrate; Sergeant-Major; [USA] service mark (registered proprietary name); [astronautics] service module; shipment memorandum; [fishing port] Shoreham; [music] short metre; silver medal; silver medallist; Sisters of Mercy; Society of Miniaturists; Sons of Malta; Staff Major; stage manager; [astronomy] standard model; [USA] state militia; station master; stipendiary magistrate; strategic missile; *Sua Maestà* (Italian: Her/His Majesty); (officer qualified for) Submarine Duties; *Su Magestad* (Spanish: Her/His Majesty); Surgeon Major; [UK postcode] Sutton (Surrey); [medicine] systolic murmur

Sm [chemical element] samarium

s/m sadomasochism; sadomasochist

sm. small

.sm San Marino (in Internet address)

SMA [medicine] spinal muscular atrophy; [USA] Surplus Marketing Administration

SMAC Standing Medical Advisory Committee (of NHS)

SMATV satellite (or small) master antenna television

SMAW shielded metal-arc welding

SMB Bachelor of Sacred Music; *Sa Majesté Britannique* (French: Her/His Britannic Majesty)

SMBA Scottish Marine Biological Association

SMBF Scottish Musicians' Benevolent Fund

SMBG [medicine] self-monitoring of blood glucose (in diabetes)

SMC *Sa Majesté Catholique* (French: Her/His Catholic Majesty); School Meals Campaign; Scottish Mountaineering Club; Scottish Museums Council; [astronomy] Small Magellanic Cloud; [aeronautics] standard mean chord

sm. caps [printing] small capitals

SMC(Disp) Dispensing Certificate of the Worshipful Company of Spectacle Makers

SMD Doctor of Sacred Music; [medicine] senile macular degeneration; [music] short metre double; submarine mine depot; [electronics] surface-mounted device (on printed circuit board)

SMDS [computing] switched multi-megabit data service

SME *Sancta Mater Ecclesia* (Latin: Holy Mother Church); seismic-margin earthquake; [international vehicle registration] Suriname

SMERSH *Smert Shpionam* (Russian: death to spies) (section of KGB)

SMEs small and medium enterprises

SMEX [astronomy] Small Explorer

SMG Scottish Media Group; submachine gun

SMGC Scottish Marriage Guidance Council

SMH [fishing port] St Margaret's Hope (Orkney)

SMHD Higher Diploma in Ophthalmic Optics of the Worshipful Company of Spectacle Makers

SMHI Swedish Meteorological and Hydrological Institute

SMHO Sovereign Military Hospitaller Order (in Malta)

SMI *Sa Majesté Impériale* (French: Her/His Imperial Majesty); Swiss Market Index

SMIA Sheet Metal Industries Association

SMIEEE [USA] Senior Member of the Institute of Electrical and Electronics Engineers

SMIRE [USA] Senior Member of the Institute of Radio Engineers

Smith. Inst. Smithsonian Institution (Washington, DC)

SMJ Sisters of Mary and Joseph

smk. smoke

SML Science Museum Library

sml small; small, medium, large

sml. simulate; simulation; simulator

SMLE short magazine Lee-Enfield (rifle)

SMM Master of Sacred Music; *Sancta Mater Maria* (Latin: Holy Mother Mary)

SMMB Scottish Milk Marketing Board

SMMT Society of Motor Manufacturers and Traders Limited

SMO senior medical officer; Sovereign Military Order

SMON [medicine] subacute myelo-opticoneuropathy

smorz. [music] *smorzando* (Italian: becoming slower and softer)

SMP Society of Mural Painters; statutory maternity pay; [computing] symmetric multiprocessing

s.m.p. *sine mascula prole* (Latin: without male issue)

SMPS Society of Master Printers of Scotland; switched-mode power supply

SMPTE [USA] Society of Motion Picture and Television Engineers

SMR *Sa Majesté Royale* (French: Her/His Royal Majesty); standardized mortality ratio; standard Malaysian rubber; [medicine] standard metabolic rate; standard mortality rate

SMRC Scottish Motor Racing Club

SMRE Safety in Mines Research Establishment

SMRTB Ship and Marine Requirements Technology Board

SMS secondary modern school; Shipwrecked Mariners' Society; synchronous meteorological satellite

SMSA [USA] Standard Metropolitan Statistical Area

SMSO Senior Maintenance Staff Officer

SMT ship's mean time; [computing] surface mount technology

SMTA Scottish Motor Trade Association

SMTF Scottish Milk Trade Federation

SMTO senior mechanical transport officer

SMTP [computing] simple mail transfer protocol

SMTWTFS Sunday, Monday, Tuesday, Wednesday, Thursday, Friday, Saturday

SMV submentovertical (in radiology)

SMW standard metal window

SMWIA [USA] Sheet Metal Workers' International Association

SMWS Scottish Malt Whisky Society

SN [vehicle registration] Dundee; [fishing port] North Shields; [USA] Secretary of the Navy; [international vehicle registration] Senegal; Sergeant Navigator; shipping note; [meteorology] snow; [astronomy] supernova; [UK postcode] Swindon

S/N shipping note; [electronics] signal-to-noise (as in **S/N ratio**)

Sn [chemical element] tin (from Latin *stannum*)

s/n serial number; series number; service number

sn. senior; snow

.sn Senegal (in Internet address)

s.n. *secundum naturam* (Latin: according to nature, naturally); serial number; series number; service number; *sine nomine* (Latin: without name); *sub nomine* (Latin: under the (specified) name)

SNA Scottish Netball Association; [computing] systems network architecture

snafu [slang] situation normal, all fouled (or fucked) up

SNAME [USA] Society of Naval Architects and Marine Engineers

SNAP Shelter Neighbourhood Action Project; systems for nuclear auxiliary power

SNB [stock exchange] sellers no buyers

SNBTS Scottish National Blood Transfusion Service

SNCB *Société nationale des chemins de fer belges* (French: Belgian National Railways)

SNCF *Société nationale des chemins de fer français* (French: French National Railways)

SND Sisters of Notre Dame

Snd Sound (in place-names)

SNECMA *Société nationale d'étude et de construction de moteurs d'aviation* (French: national aeroengine research and construction company)

SNF solids, nonfat (in nutrition); spent nuclear fuel; [USA] strategic nuclear forces

SNFA Standing Naval Force, Atlantic

SNFU Scottish National Farmers' Union

SNG substitute natural gas; synthetic natural gas

Sng. Singapore

SNH Scottish National Heritage

SNIF [finance] short-term note issuance facility

SNIG sustainable noninflationary growth

SNIPEF Scottish and Northern Ireland Plumbing Employers' Federation

SNL Sandia National Laboratories (Albuquerque); standard nomenclature list

SNLA Scottish National Liberation Army

SNLR services no longer required

SNLV strategic nuclear launch vehicle

SNM [USA] Society of Nuclear Medicine; Somali National Movement

SNMP [computing] simple network management protocol

SNO Scottish National Orchestra (former name of RSO); senior naval officer; senior navigation officer; senior nursing officer

SNOBOL string oriented symbolic language (computer programming language)

SNP Scottish National Party

SNPA Scottish National Newspaper Proprietors' Association

SNR [electronics] signal-to-noise ratio; Society for Nautical Research; [astronomy] supernova remnant

Snr Senior

Sñr *Señor* (Spanish: Mr)

snr senior

Snra *Senhora* (Portuguese: Mrs)

Sñra *Señora* (Spanish: Mrs)

Sñrta *Señorita* (Spanish: Miss)

SNSC Scottish National Ski Council

SNSS School Natural Science Society

SNTPC Scottish National Town Planning Council

SNTS Society for New Testament Studies

SNU [astronomy] solar neutrino unit; Spiritualists' National Union

Snug Scottish Network Users' Group

SO [vehicle registration] Aberdeen; scientific officer; Scottish Office; section officer; senior officer; shale oil (residue); Signal Officer; [fishing port] Sligo; [computing] small outline; [international vehicle registration] Somalia; sorting office; [UK postcode] Southampton; [meteorology] southern oscillation;

special order; Staff Officer; standing order; Stationery Office; statistical office; suboffice; supply officer; symphony orchestra

S/O section officer; seller's option; shipowner

So. *Sonntag* (German: Sunday); south; southern

so. sonata; south; southern

.so Somalia (in Internet address)

s.o. seller's option; shipping order; *siehe oben* (German: see above); strike out; substance of (weight of paper)

SOA Scottish Orienteering Association; state of the art

SoA Society of Authors

SOAD Staff Officer, Air Defence

SOAP [medicine] subjective, objective, analysis, plan (in patients' records)

SOAS School of Oriental and African Studies (University of London)

SOB [USA] Senate office building; [medicine] shortness of breath; [informal] silly old bastard; [informal] son of a bitch; state office building

s.o.b. [informal] son of a bitch

SOBHD Scottish Official Board of Highland Dancing

SOC Scottish Ornithologists' Club; [informal] slightly off colour

Soc. Socialist; [commerce] *società* (Italian: company); Society; Socrates (ancient Greek philosopher)

soc. social; socialist; society; sociology

SocCE(France) *Société des ingénieurs civils de France* (French: Society of Civil Engineers of France)

Soc. Dem. Social Democrat

sociol. sociological; sociologist; sociology

SOCO scene-of-crime officer

SOCONY Standard Oil Corporation of New York

SOCS Society of County Secretaries

soc. sci. social science; social scientist

Socy Society

sod. sodium

SODAC Society of Dyers and Colourists

SODEPAX Committee on Society, Development and Peace (from Latin *pax*)

SODS ship's operatic and dramatic society (in Royal Navy)

SOE Special Operations Executive (in World War II); state-owned enterprise

SOED Scottish Office Education Department; *Shorter Oxford English Dictionary*

SOEID Scottish Office Education and Industry Department

SOES [US finance] Small Order Execution System (of NASDAQ)

SOF share of freehold (in property advertisement); [chemistry] soluble organic fraction; [cinema] sound on a film

SOFAA Society of Fine Art Auctioneers

sofar sound fixing and ranging

SOFCS self-organizing flight-control system

SOFFEX Swiss Options and Financial Futures Exchange

SOFIA Stratospheric Observatory for Infrared Astronomy

S of S Secretary of State; [Bible] Song of Solomon; [Bible] Song of Songs

S of Sol. [Bible] Song of Solomon

S of T Sons of Temperance

S of TT School of Technical Training

SOGAT Society of Graphical and Allied Trades (became part of GPMU)

SOH sense of humour (in personal advertisement)

SOHC single overhead cam(shaft)

SOHIO Standard Oil of Ohio

SOHO Solar Heliospheric Observatory

SoHo small office/home office (furniture); [USA] South of Houston

Sohyo *Nihon Rodo Kumiai So Hygikai* (Japanese: General Council of Japanese Trade Unions)

SO(I) Staff Officer (Intelligence)

SOIC [electronics] small outline integrated circuit

SO-in-C Signal Officer-in-Chief

SOL [US slang] strictly (or shit) out of luck

Sol. Solicitor; [Bible] Song of Solomon

sol. solicitor; soluble; solution

s.o.l. [insurance] shipowner's liability

Solace Society of Local Authority Chief Executives

Sol-Gen Solicitor-General

soln solution

solr solicitor

solv. solvent

soly solubility

SOM Society of Occupational Medicine

Som. Somerset

SOMA Society of Mental Awareness

SOME Senior Ordnance Mechanical Engineer

SOMPA [USA] System of Multicultural Pluralistic Assessment (intelligence testing)

Som.Sh. [currency] Somali shilling

sonar sound navigation and ranging

SONET [computing] synchronous optical network

SO(O) Staff Officer (Operations)

SOP significant other person; sleeping-out pass; standard operating procedure; [computing] sum of products

sop. [music] soprano

Soph. Sophocles (ancient Greek writer)

soph. sophomore

SOR sale or return; Society of Radiographers

SORD submerged-object recovery device

SORG Stratospheric Ozone Review Group

SORP [accounting] Statement of Recommended Practice

SOS save our souls (international distress signal, letters chosen for ease and clarity of transmission in Morse code); Secretary of State; senior officers' school; services of supply

s.o.s. [medicine] *si opus sit* (Latin: if necessary) (in prescriptions)

SOSc Society of Ordained Scientists

SoSh [currency] Somali shilling

sost. [music] *sostenuto* (Italian: sustained)

SOT stay-on tab

Soton Southampton

SOTS Society for Old Testament Study

Sou. south; Southampton; southern

sou. south; southern

SOV [linguistics] subject-object-verb

Sov. Soviet

sov. sovereign

s.o.v. shut-off valve

Sov. Un. Soviet Union

Soweto Southwestern Townships (South Africa)

SP [vehicle registration] Dundee; [civil aircraft marking] Poland; *Saint-Père* (French: Holy Father); [UK postcode] Salisbury; *Sanctissimus Pater* (Latin: Most Holy Father); Self-Propelled (Antitank Regiment); service pistol; [military] service police; shore patrol; Sisters of Providence; Socialist Party; [building] soil pipe; spark(ing) plug; Staff Paymaster;

standard play (on video recorder); starting price (hence slang meaning 'latest information'); stirrup pump; [banking] stop payment; stop press; stretcher party; submarine patrol; *Summus Pontifex* (Latin: Supreme Pontiff, the pope); supply point; [finance] supra protest

Sp. Spain; Spaniard; Spanish

sp. space; special; specie; [biology] species; specific; specimen; speed; spelling; spirit; sport; *sposa* (Italian: wife)

s.p. self-propelled; [music] *senza pedale* (Italian: without pedal); *sine prole* (Latin: without issue); [electrical engineering] single phase; [advertising] special position; starting point; [banking] stop payment

SPA Saudi Press Agency; Scottish Pipers' Association; Scottish Pistol Association; Scottish Publishers' Association; [USA] Society for Personnel Administration; special protection area (for conservation of wild birds)

SpA [commerce] *società per azioni* (Italian: public limited company, plc)

SPAA Scottish Passenger Agents' Association

SPAB Society for the Protection of Ancient Buildings

SPAC Standing Pharmaceutical Advisory Committee (of NHS)

spac. spacious (in property advertisement)

Sp. Am. Spanish American

Span. Spaniard; Spanish

SPANA Society for the Protection of Animals in North Africa

SPANDAR space and range radar (in NASA)

SPAR member of US Coast Guard women's reserve (in World War II, from Latin motto *Semper paratus* = always ready); superprecision-approach radar

Sp. Ar. Spanish Arabic

SPARC [computing] scalable processor architecture

SPARKS Sport Aiding Medical Research for Kids

SPAS *Societatis Philosophicae Americanae Socius* (Latin: Fellow of the American Philosophical Society)

SPATC South Pacific Air Transport Council

SPBA Scottish Pipe Band Association

SPBP Society for the Preservation of Birds of Prey

SPBW Society for the Preservation of Beers from the Wood

SPC Secretariat of the Pacific Community; Society for the Prevention of Crime; Southern Pacific Commission (former name of the Pacific Community); [commerce] statistical process control; [telecommunications] stored program control

SPCA [USA] Society for the Prevention of Cruelty to Animals

SPCK Society for Promoting Christian Knowledge

SPD Salisbury Plain District; [astronomy] south polar distance; *Sozialdemokratische Partei Deutschlands* (German: Social Democratic Party of Germany)

spd speed (in car advertisement)

s.p.d. [finance] subject to permission to deal

SPDA single-premium deferred annuity

SPDL [computing] standard page description language

SPE Society for Pure English; [USA] Society of Petroleum Engineers; [electronics] solid-phase epitaxy

SPEC [Canada] Society for Pollution and Environmental Control; South Pacific Bureau for Economic Cooperation

spec [short form] specification; [short form] speculation (as in **on spec**)

spec. special; specialist; specially; specific; specifically; specification; specimen; spectrum

special. specialized

specif. specific; specifically; specification

SPECmark Systems Performance Evaluation Cooperative's benchmark

specs [short form] specifications; [short form] spectacles

SPECT [medicine] single photon emission compute(rize)d tomography

SPECTRE Special Executive for Counter-Intelligence, Revenge and Extortion (in James Bond stories by Ian Fleming)

Sp.Ed. [USA] Specialist in Education

SPES South Place Ethical Society

SPET [medicine] single photon emission tomography

SPF South Pacific forum; sun protection factor (in sunscreen)

SPF/DB [aeronautics] super-plastic forming/diffusion bonding (manufacturing method)

SPG Society for the Propagation of the Gospel (in Foreign Parts) (became part of USPG); Special Patrol Group

s.p.g. self-propelled gun

SPGA Scottish Professional Golfers' Association

SPGB Socialist Party of Great Britain

sp. gr. specific gravity

sp. ht specific heat

SPI [finance] selected period investment; [USA] Society of the Plastics Industry

SPIRE [navigation] spatial inertial reference equipment

spirit. [music] *spiritoso* (Italian: with spirit); spiritualism; spiritualistic

SPIW special-purposes individual weapon

SPKC Small Pig Keepers' Council

s.p.l. *sine prole legitima* (Latin: without legitimate issue)

SPLA Sudan People's Liberation Army

SPM scanning proton microscope; [music] short particular metre

s.p.m. *sine prole mascula* (Latin: without male issue)

SPMO senior principal medical officer

SPMU Society of Professional Musicians in Ulster

SPN stop press news

SPNC Society for the Promotion of Nature Conservation

SPNM Society for the Promotion of New Music

SPNR Society for the Promotion of Nature Reserves

SPO senior press officer

SPÖ *Sozialistische Partei Österreichs* (German: Austrian Socialist Party)

SPOA Scottish Prison Officers' Association

SPOD Sexual Problems of the Disabled

SPOE Society of Post Office Engineers

Spool simultaneous peripheral operation on-line

s/pool swimming pool (in property advertisement)

Spore Society for the Preservation of the Rainforest Environment

SPOT single property ownership trust

SPP [medicine] sub-pubic prostatectomy

spp. [biology] species (plural)

SPQR *Senatus Populusque Romanus* (Latin: the Senate and People of Rome); small profits and quick returns

SPR Society for Psychical Research; strategic petroleum reserve

Spr [military] Sapper

spr. spring; sprinkle; sprinkler; sprung

SPRC Society for the Prevention and Relief of Cancer

SPREd Society of Picture Researchers and Editors

SPRI Scott Polar Research Institute (Cambridge)

SPRINT solid-propellant rocket-intercept missile

SPRL Society for the Promotion of Religion and Learning

sprl [commerce] *société de personnes à responsabilité limitée* (French: limited company, Ltd)

SPS Scottish Painters' Society; [physics] Super Proton Synchrotron (at CERN); syndiotactic polystyrene (plastic)

s.p.s. *sine prole supersite* (Latin: without surviving issue)

SPSL Society for the Protection of Science and Learning

SPSO senior principal scientific officer

SPSP St Peter and St Paul

spt seaport; sport; support

sptg sporting

SPTL Society of Public Teachers of Law

SPUC Society for the Protection of the Unborn Child

SPURV self-propelled underwater research vehicle

SPVD Society for the Prevention of Venereal Disease

sp. vol. specific volume

SQ sick quarters; [meteorology] squall; [building] squint quoin; stereophonic-quadraphonic; survival quotient

Sq. Squadron; Square (in road name)

sq. sequence; *sequens* (Latin: the following (one)); squadron; square

SQA Scottish Qualifications Agency; [computing] software quality assurance

sq cm square centimetre

sqd squad

Sqdn Squadron

sqdn squadron

Sqdn Ldr Squadron Leader

sq ft square feet; square foot
sq in square inch
sq km square kilometre
SQL [computing] standard query language; [computing] structured query language
sq m square metre
sq mi square mile
sq mm square millimetre
SQMS Staff Quartermaster-Sergeant
Sqn Squadron
sqn squadron
Sqn Ldr Squadron Leader
SqnQMS Squadron Quartermaster-Sergeant
SqnSM Squadron Sergeant-Major
SqO Squadron Officer
sqq. *sequentia* (Latin: the following (ones))
squid [electronics] superconducting quantum interference device
sq yd square yard
SR [vehicle registration] Dundee; [currency] Saudi riyal; Saunders Roe (aircraft); [USA] Senate resolution; senior registrar; service rifle; [computing] set-reset; Socialist Revolutionary (Party) (in former USSR); Society of Radiographers; sodium ricinoleate (in toothpaste); [USA] Sons of the Revolution; [railways] Southern Region; [physics] special relativity; [military] Special Reserve; [taxation] standard rate; [psychology] stimulus–response; [fishing port] Stranraer; [UK postcode] Sunderland; *Sveriges Radio* (Swedish broadcasting corporation); [physics] synchrotron radiation; synthetic rubber
S/R sale or return
Sr *Senhor* (Portuguese: Mr, Sir); Senior; *Señor* (Spanish: Mr, Sir); *Signor* (Italian: Mr, Sir); Sir; Sister (title of nun); [chemical element] strontium
sr senior; steradian (unit of solid angle)
s/r sunroof (in car advertisement)
.sr Suriname (in Internet address)
s.r. self-raising; shipping receipt; short rate
SRA Squash Rackets Association
Sra *Senhora* (Portuguese: Mrs); *Señora* (Spanish: Mrs)
SRAC [finance] short-run average cost
SRAM short-range attack missile

SRAM [computing] static random-access memory
SR&CC [insurance] strikes, riot and civil commotion
SRAP Scottish Rent Assessment Panel
SRB solid rocket booster; [computing] source route bridge; [microbiology] sulphate-reducing bacteria
SRBC [medicine] sheep red blood cell(s)
SRBM short-range ballistic missile
SRBP synthetic resin-bonded paper
SRC sample return container; Science Research Council (former name of SERC); [commerce] *sociedad regular colectiva* (Spanish: partnership); solvent-refined coal; [chemistry] standard reference compound; [engineering] steam Rankine cycle; Students' Representative Council; Swiss Red Cross
SRCC [insurance] strikes, riot and civil commotion
SRCh State Registered Chiropodist
SRCN State Registered Children's Nurse (former name of RSCN)
SRD service rum diluted
SRDE Signals Research and Development Establishment
SRE *Sancta Romana Ecclesia* (Latin: Holy Roman Church)
S Rept [USA] Senate report
S Res. [USA] Senate resolution
SRG standard reformed gas; Strategic Research Group (market research company)
SRHE Society for Research into Higher Education
SRI *Sacrum Romanum Imperium* (Latin: Holy Roman Empire)
SRIS Science Reference Information Service
Srl. [commerce] *società a responsabilità limitata* (Italian: limited company, Ltd)
SRIs [currency] Saudi riyal
SRM short-range missile; speed of relative movement
SRN State Registered Nurse (former name of RGN)
SRNA Shipbuilders and Repairers National Association
sRNA [biochemistry] soluble ribonucleic acid
SRO Scottish Record Office; [finance] self-regulatory organization; [microbiology]

sex-ratio organism; [USA] single room occupancy; sold right out; standing room only; Statutory Rules and Orders; Supplementary Reserve of Officers

s/roof sunroof (in car advertisement)

SRP Society of Recorder Players; State Registered Physiotherapist; suggested retail price; supply refuelling point

SRPA Squash Rackets Professional Association

SRPS Scottish Railway Preservation Society

SRR Society for Research in Rehabilitation

SRS Scottish Record Society; *Societatis Regiae Sodalis* (Latin: Fellow of the Royal Society)

SRs [currency] Seychelles rupee

SRSA Scientific Research Society of America

SRSS [mathematics] square-root sum of squares

Srta *Senhorita* (Portuguese: Miss); *Señorita* (Spanish: Miss)

SRU Scottish Rugby Union

SRWS Scottish Rights of Way Society

SRY Sherwood Rangers Yeomanry

SS [vehicle registration] Aberdeen; *Sacra Scriptura* (Latin: Holy Scripture); Saints; *Santa Sede* (Italian: Holy See); *Sa Sainteté* (French: His Holiness); *Schutzstaffel* (German: protection squad) (Nazi organization); secondary school; Secretary of State; secret service; security service; short sleeves; [computing] single-sided (disk); social security; [chemistry] sodium sulphate; [UK postcode] Southend-on-Sea; Staff Surgeon; stainless steel; standard size; steamship; [fishing port] St Ives; *Strada Statale* (Italian: National Highway); Straits Settlements; Sunday school; surface-to-surface (missile)

S/S same size (of illustrations); silk screen (printing); steamship

SS. Saints; *sanctissimus* (Latin: most holy)

ss. sections; [medicine] *semis* (Latin: half) (in prescriptions); subsection

s.s. screw steamer; *sensu stricto* (Latin: in the strict sense); [music] *senza sordini* (Italian: without mutes); simplified spelling; steamship; *supra scriptum* (Latin: written above)

SSA Scottish Schoolmasters' Association; [computing] serial storage architecture; [USA] Social Security Administration; Society of Scottish Artists; standard spending assessment (in local government)

SSAC Scottish Sub-Aqua Club; Social Security Advisory Committee

SSADM [computing] structured systems analysis and design method

SSAE stamped self-addressed envelope

SSAFA Soldiers', Sailors' and Airmen's Families Association

SSAIB Security Systems and Alarms Inspection Board

SSAP Statement of Standard Accounting Practice

SSB Bachelor of Sacred Scripture (from Latin *Sacrae Scripturae Baccalaureus*); [telecommunications] single-sideband (transmission); [USA] Social Security Board

SSBN [US navy] strategic submarine, ballistic nuclear

SSC Scottish Ski Club; Scottish Sports Council; Sculptors' Society of Canada; [India] Secondary School Certificate; Short Service Commission; [USA] smallsaver certificate; *Societas Sanctae Crucis* (Latin: Society of the Holy Cross); [Scotland] Solicitor before the Supreme Court; Species Survival Commission; [physics] Superconducting Super Collider

SScD Doctor of Social Science

SSD Doctor of Sacred Scripture (from Latin *Sacrae Scripturae Doctor*); Social Services Department

SS.D *Sanctissimus Dominus* (Latin: Most Holy Lord, the pope)

ssDNA [biochemistry] single-stranded deoxyribonucleic acid

SSE Society of St Edmund; southsoutheast

SSEB South of Scotland Electricity Board

SSEC Secondary School Examinations Council

SSEES School of Slavonic and East European Studies (University of London)

SSEG Scottish Solar Energy Group

SSF single-seater fighter (aircraft); Society of St Francis

SSFA Scottish Schools' Football Association; Scottish Steel Founders' Association

SSgt Staff Sergeant

SSHA Scottish Special Housing Association

SSHC Society to Support Home Confinement

SSI Scottish Symphony Orchestra; site of scientific interest; [electronics] small-scale integration; Social Services Inspectorate; Society of Scribes and Illuminators; [USA] supplemental security income

SSJE Society of St John the Evangelist

SSL Licentiate in Sacred Scripture (from Latin *Sacrae Scripturae Licentiatus*)

SSLH Society for the Study of Labour History

SSM Saturday, Sunday, Monday; [telecommunications] single-sideband modulation; Society of the Sacred Mission; [commerce] soft systems methodology; Staff Sergeant-Major; surface-to-surface missile

SSMA Stainless Steel Manufacturers' Association

SSMH Scottish Society for the Mentally Handicapped

SSN severely subnormal; [USA] Social Security number; Standard Serial Number

SSO senior scientific officer; senior supply officer; Staff Signal Officer; Station Staff Officer

SSP Scottish Socialist Party; statutory sick pay

ssp. [biology] subspecies

SSPCA Scottish Society for the Prevention of Cruelty to Animals

SSPE [medicine] subacute sclerosing panencephalitis

SS.PP. *Sancti Patres* (Latin: Holy Fathers)

sspp. [biology] subspecies (plural)

SSPWB Scottish Society for the Protection of Wild Birds

SSQ [military] station sick quarters

SSR secondary surveillance radar; Small Ships Register; Soviet Socialist Republic

SSRA Scottish Squash Rackets Association

SSRC Social Science Research Council (former name of ESRC)

SSRI [pharmacology] selective serotonin reuptake inhibitor (used to treat depression); [USA] Social Science Research Institute

SSS Secretary of State for Scotland; [USA] Selective Service System (for military mobilization); [medicine] sick sinus syndrome; Simplified Spelling Society; single-screw ship; [fishing port] South Shields; standard scratch score (in golf)

SSSA Scottish Salmon Smokers' Association; Scottish Schools' Swimming Association

SSSI site of special scientific interest

SSSR *Soyuz Sovietskikh Sotsialisticheskikh Respublik* (Russian: Union of Soviet Socialist Republics, USSR)

SStJ Serving Sister, Order of St John of Jerusalem

SSSU Scottish Speed Skating Union

SST Scottish Scenic Trust; [telecommunications] single-sideband transmission; Society of Surveying Technicians; supersonic transport

SSTA Scottish Secondary Teachers' Association

SSTC sold subject to contract (in property advertisement)

SSU Sunday School Union

s/susp. sports suspension (in car advertisement)

SSV [microbiology] simian sarcoma virus

SSW Secretary of State for War; south-southwest; special security wing (of prison)

SSWA Scottish Society of Women Artists

ST [vehicle registration] Inverness; sanitary towel; septic tank; shipping ticket; (Hubble) Space Telescope; speech therapist; spring tide; Standard Time; [fishing port] Stockton; [UK postcode] Stoke-on-Trent; [civil aircraft marking] Sudan; Summer Time; *Sunday Times*; [building] surface trench; surtax

St Saint; stokes (unit of viscosity); Strait; Street

St [meteorology] stratus

St. Statute; Strait; Street

st seat; strait; street

st. stanza; state; statement; statute; stem; [printing] stet (instruction to restore or retain deleted text); [knitting] stitch; stone (unit of weight); strait; street; strophe (division of verse); [cricket] stumped (by)

s.t. select time; short ton; static thrust; steam trawler

STA Sail Training Association; [USA] Science and Technology Agency; Scottish Typographical Association; Society of Typographic Arts; Swimming Teachers' Association

Sta *Santa* (Italian, Portuguese or Spanish: Saint (female))

sta. station; stationary

StAAA St Andrew's Ambulance Association

stab. stability; stabilization; stabilized; stabilizer; stable

stacc. [music] *staccato* (Italian: detached)

Staffs Staffordshire

STAGS Sterling Transferable Accruing Government Securities

stalag *Stammlager* (German: base camp) (World War II prisoner-of-war camp)

STANAG Standard NATO Agreement

stand. standard

St And. St Andrews (Scotland)

STARCAT Space Telescope Archive and Catalogue

START Strategic Arms Reduction Talks

stat. static; statics; [medicine] *statim* (Latin: immediately) (in prescriptions); stationary; statistic(s); statistical; statuary; statue; statute

STATE [military] simplified tactical approach and terminal equipment

Stat. Hall Stationers' Hall (London)

stats [short form] statistics

STAUK Seed Trade Association of the United Kingdom

STB Bachelor of Sacred Theology (from Latin *Sacrae Theologiae Baccalaureus*); Scottish Tourist Board

stbd starboard

stbt steamboat

STC Samuel Taylor Coleridge (British poet); satellite test centre; Senior Training Corps; Short-Title Catalogue; Standard Telephones and Cables Limited; state total cost; [India] State Trading Corporation; subject to contract (in property advertisement)

STD Doctor of Sacred Theology (from Latin *Sacrae Theologiae Doctor*); salinity-temperature-depth (sensor system); [medicine] sexually transmitted disease; Society of Typographic Designers; [computing] state transition diagram; [New Zealand] subscriber toll dialling; subscriber trunk dialling

Std. *Stunde* (German: hour)

std standard; started

STE Society of Telecom Executives

Ste *Sainte* (French: Saint (female))

Sté [commerce] *société* (French: company, Co.)

STEL short-term exposure level (of radiation); short-term exposure limit (of radiation)

STEM scanning transmission electron microscope (or microscopy)

Sten Shepherd and Turpin (inventors of Sten gun)

sten. stenographer; stenographic(al); stenography

steno. stenographer; stenographic(al); stenography

stenog. stenographer; stenographic(al); stenography

STEP Solar/Terrestrial Energy Programme; Special Temporary Employment Programme

ster. stereophonic; stereotype; sterling

stereo [short form] stereophonic

stereo. stereotype

St. Ex. Stock Exchange

stg seating; sterling

StGB *Strafgesetzbuch* (German: Penal Code)

stge storage

STGWU Scottish Transport and General Workers' Union

STH [biochemistry] somatotrophic hormone

STh Scholar in Theology

Sth South

sthn southern

STI Straits Times Index (of Singapore Stock Exchange)

STIM scanning transmission ion microscope

STINGS [aeronautics] stellar inertial guidance system

stip. stipend; stipendiary; stipulation

Stir. Stirling(shire)

s.t.i.r. surplus to immediate requirements

stk stock

STL Licentiate in Sacred Theology (from Latin *Sacrae Theologiae Licentiatus*); *Sacrae Theologiae Lector* (Latin: Reader in Sacred Theology); Standard Telecommunications Laboratories; [telecommunications] studio-to-transmitter link

stlg sterling

STLO Scientific Technical Liaison Office; Scientific Technical Liaison Officer

STLV [microbiology] simian T-lymphotropic virus

STM Master of Sacred Theology (from Latin *Sacrae Theologiae Magister*); scanning tunnelling microscope (or microscopy); scientific, technical and medical (as in **STM publishing**); [psychology] short-term memory; [computing] synchronous transfer module

STMS [finance] short-term monetary support (in EMS)

stmt statement

stn stain; station

STO sea transport officer; senior technical officer; standing order

Sto *Santo* (Portuguese: Saint)

STOL [aeronautics] short take-off and landing

STOLVCD [aeronautics] short take-off and landing, vertical climb and descent

S'ton Southampton

STOP Students Tired of Pollution; suction termination of pregnancy

STOPP Society of Teachers Opposed to Physical Punishment

S to S ship to shore; station to station

STP [informal] hallucinogenic drug related to mescaline (from its energizing effect, facetiously compared to that of the oil substitute STP); Professor of Sacred Theology (from Latin *Sacrae Theologiae Professor*); [trademark] scientifically treated petroleum (oil substitute); sewage treatment plant; [computing] shielded twisted pair; standard temperature and pressure

s.t.p. standard temperature and pressure

STPMA Scottish Theatrical Proprietors' and Managers' Association

Str. Strait; *Strasse* (German: Street); Street

str seater; steamer

str. straight; strait; street; strength; [music] string(s); [music] stringed; stringer (in journalism); [rowing] stroke (oar); strong; structural; structure

s.t.r. surplus to requirements

STRAC [USA] strategic air command; strategic army corps

STRAD signal transmitting, receiving and distribution

Strad [short form] Stradivarius (violin)

stratig. stratigraphy

strd stranded

strep. streptococcal; streptococcus

STRG Scottish Tory Reform Group

STRICOM [USA] Strike Command

string. [music] *stringendo* (Italian: compressing, with increasing speed)

STROBE satellite tracking of balloons and emergencies

STS Scottish Tartan Society; Scottish Text Society; [astronautics] space transportation system

Sts Saints

STSF Scottish Target Shooting Federation

STSO Senior Technical Staff Officer

st. st. [knitting] stocking stitch

STTA Scottish Table Tennis Association

STUC Scottish Trades Union Congress

stud. student

Stuka *Sturzkampfflugzeug* (German: dive bomber)

STV Scottish Television; single transferable vote; standard test vehicle; [USA] subscription television

stvdr. stevedore

stwy stairway

SU [civil aircraft marking] Egypt; [vehicle registration] Glasgow; Scripture Union; [fishing port] Southampton; Soviet Union; [physics] strontium unit

Su. Sudan; Sudanese; Sunday

s.u. set up; *siehe unten* (German: see below)

SUA [USA] State Universities Association

SUB [USA] supplemental unemployment benefits

sub [short form] sub-edit; [short form] submarine; [short form] subscription

sub. subaltern; [music] *subito* (Italian: immediately, suddenly); subject; [grammar] subjunctive; submarine; subordinate; subordinated; subscription; subsidiary; subsidy; subsistence; [grammar] substantive; substitute; suburb; suburban; subvention; subway

SUBAW Scottish Union of Bakers and Allied Workers

subd. subdivide; subdivision

sub-ed. sub-edit; sub-editor

subj. subject; subjective; subjectively; [grammar] subjunctive

SUBLANT [US navy] Submarine Forces, Atlantic

Sub-Lieut. Sub-Lieutenant

Sub-Lt Sub-Lieutenant

subord. [grammar] subordinate; [grammar] subordinating

SUBPAC [US navy] Submarine Forces, Pacific

SUBROC submarine rocket

subs [short form] subscription

subs. subsidence; subsidiary; subsistence

subsc. subscription

subsec. subsection

subseq. subsequent; subsequently

subsp. [biology] subspecies

subspp. [biology] subspecies (plural)

subsq. subsequent; subsequently

subst. [grammar] substantive; substantively; substitute; substitution

substand. substandard

suc. succeed; success; successor; suction

succ. succeed; succeeding; success; successive; successor

SUD [international vehicle registration] Sudan

SUDS [medicine] sudden unexplained death syndrome

suf. [grammar] suffix

Suff. Suffolk; Suffragan

suff. sufficient; [grammar] suffix

suffoc. suffocation

Suffr. Suffragan

sug. suggest; suggestion

SUIT Scottish and Universal Investment Trust

suiv. *suivant* (French: following)

Sult. Sultan

SUM surface-to-underwater missile

sum. [medicine] *sumat* (Latin: let her/him take it) (in prescriptions); [medicine] *sumendum* (Latin: let it be taken) (in prescriptions); summary; summer

sums. summons

Sun. Sunday

Sund. Sunday

SUNFED Special United Nations Fund for Economic Development

SUNS sonic underwater navigation system

SUNY State University of New York

sup. superficial; superfine; superior; superlative; [grammar] supine; supplement; supplementary; supply; support; supporter; *supra* (Latin: above); supreme

sup. ben. supplementary benefit

Sup. Ct Superior Court; Supreme Court

Supdt Superintendent

super. superficial; superfine; superior; supernumerary

superl. superlative

SUPLO Scottish Union of Power Loom Overlookers

supp. supplement; supplementary

suppl. supplement; supplementary

Supp. Res. Supplementary Reserve (of officers)

supr superior; supervisor

supr. superior; supreme

Supt Superintendent

supvr supervisor

SUR [commerce] set-up reduction

Sur. Surrey

sur. surface; surplus

SURF spent unreprocessed fuel

surg. surgeon; surgery; surgical

Surg. Cdr Surgeon Commander

Surg. Comdr Surgeon Commander

Surg. Gen. Surgeon General

Surg. Lt-Cdr Surgeon Lieutenant-Commander

Surg. Maj. Surgeon Major

Surr. Surrey

surr. surrender; surrogate

surro. surrogate

SURV standard underwater research vessel

surv. survey; surveying; surveyor; survive; surviving; survivor

Surv-Gen Surveyor-General

SUS Scottish Union of Students; Students' Union Society

Sus. [Bible] Susanna (book of Apocrypha); Sussex

sus [short form] suspicious

SUSI Sydney University Stellar Interferometer

susp. suspend; suspension

Suss. Sussex

Sustrans Sustainable Transport

SUT Society for Underwater Technology

Suth. Sutherland

SUV [USA] sport-utility vehicle

SV safety valve; *Sancta Virgo* (Latin: Holy Virgin); *Sanctitas Vestra* (Latin: Your Holi-

ness); [microbiology] simian virus; stroke
volume (of engine)

Sv sievert (unit of radiation dose
equivalent)

s/v [insurance] surrender value

.sv El Salvador (in Internet address)

s.v. sailing vessel; side valve; *sub verbo*
(Latin: under the word) (in reference
book); *sub voce* (Latin: under the word)
(in reference book); [insurance] surrender value

SVA Scottish Volleyball Association

SVC [medicine] superior vena cava; [com-
puting] supervisor call

svc. service

svce service

SVD [veterinary science] swine vesicular
disease

svg saving

SVGA [computing] super video graphics
array

svgs savings

SVO Scottish Variety Orchestra; [linguis-
tics] subject-verb-object; superintending
veterinary officer

SVP saturated vapour pressure

s.v.p. *s'il vous plaît* (French: (if you)
please)

SVQ Scottish Vocational Qualification

s.v.r. [medicine] *spiritus vini rectificatus*
(Latin: rectified spirit of wine) (in prescriptions)

SVS still-camera video system

SVTP sound velocity, temperature,
pressure

s.vv. *sub verbis* (Latin: under the words)
(in reference book)

s.v.v. *sit venia verbo* (Latin: pardon the
expression)

svy survey

SW [vehicle registration] Carlisle; [vehicle
registration] Glasgow; senior warden;
shipper's weight; shock wave; [radio]
short wave; small women's (clothing
size); South Wales; southwest; south-
western; [UK postcode] southwest
London; standard weight

S/W [computing] software

Sw. Sweden; Swedish; Swiss

s/w salt water; sea water; seaworthy

sw. switch

s.w. salt water; sea water

Swab. Swabia; Swabian

SWACS space warning and control
system

SWALK sealed with a loving kiss (on
envelope of love letter)

SWANU South West Africa National
Union

SWANUF South West Africa National
Union Front

SWAP Scottish Women Against Pornography

SWAPO South West Africa People's
Organization

SWAS Submillimetre Wave Astronomy
Satellite

SWAT [USA] Special Weapons and Tac-
tics (police unit)

SWB [military] South Wales Borderers

s.w.b. short wheelbase (in car advertisement)

swbd switchboard

SWCI [computing] software configuration
item

swd [bookbinding] sewed

SWE [USA] Society of Women Engineers

SWEB South Wales Electricity Board;
Southwest Electricity Board

Swed. Sweden; Swedish

SWET Society of West End Theatre(s)

SWF single white female (in accommodation advertisement)

SwF [currency] Swiss franc

SWFA Scottish Women's Football
Association

SWG Song Writers' Guild of Great Britain;
standard wire gauge

SWH solar water heating

SWHA Scottish Women's Hockey
Association

SWIE South Wales Institute of Engineers

SWIFT Society for Worldwide Interbank
Financial Transactions

Swing [finance] Sterling Warrant into
Gilt-edged Stock

Swit. Switzerland

Switz. Switzerland

SWL safe working load

SWLA Society of Wildlife Artists

SWM single white male (in accommodation advertisement)

SWMF South Wales Miners' Federation

SWO Station Warrant Officer

SWOA Scottish Woodland Owners'
Association

SWOPS single-well oil-production system

SWOT [marketing] strengths, weaknesses, opportunities and threats (of new product)

SWP safe working pressure; Socialist Workers' Party

SWPA South-West Pacific Area

SWPF single white professional female (in accommodation advertisement)

SWPM single white professional male (in accommodation advertisement)

SWR [telecommunications] standing-wave ratio

SWRB Sadler's Wells Royal Ballet (former name of Royal Ballet)

SWRI Scottish Women's Rural Institute

SWS static water supply

SWSWU Sheffield Wool Shear Workers' Union

SWT Scottish Wildlife Trust

Swtz. Switzerland

SWWJ Society of Women Writers and Journalists

SX [vehicle registration] Edinburgh; [civil aircraft marking] Greece; soft X-rays; [shipping] Sundays excepted

Sx Sussex

SXR soft X-radiation; soft X-rays

SXT sextant

SY [international vehicle registration] Seychelles; [UK postcode] Shrewsbury; steam yacht; [fishing port] Stornoway

Sy supply; Surrey

Sy. Seychelles; Syria

.sy Syria (in Internet address)

SYB Statesman's Yearbook

S Yd Scotland Yard

Syd. Sydney

SYHA Scottish Youth Hostels Association

syl. syllable; syllabus

Sylk [computing] symbolic link

syll. syllable; syllabus

sym. symbol; symbolic; symmetrical; symmetry; symphonic; symphony; symptom

symp. symposium

symph. symphony

syn. synchronize; synod; synonym; synonymous; synonymy; synthetic

sync [short form] synchronization (as in **out of sync**)

sync. synchronization; synchronize; synchronized; synchronous

Syncom synchronous communications satellite

synd. syndicate; syndicated

synon. synonymous

synop. synopsis

synth. [music] synthesizer; synthetic

Sy PO Supply Petty Officer

SYR [international vehicle registration] Syria

Syr. Syria; Syriac; Syrian

syr. [pharmacology] syrup

sys. system

syst. system; systematic

SZ [vehicle registration] Down

sz. size

.sz Swaziland (in Internet address)

T

T [physics] surface tension; table-spoon(ful); [music] *tace* (Italian: be silent); tanker; target; [chemistry] tautomeric effect; [horticulture] tea (rose); teacher; telegraph; telegraphic; telephone; temperature; [music] tempo; temporary; [music] tenor; tera- (indicates 10^{12}, as in **Tm** = terametre); Territorial; Territory; tesla (unit of magnetic flux density); Testament; [international vehicle registration] Thailand; thermometer; [advertising] third of a page (area of type); Thursday; [immunology] thymus (as in **T-cell**); time; torpedo; [photography] total light transmission (as in **T-number**); trainer (aircraft); [fishing port] Tralee; transaction(s); translation; transport; transportation; [obstetrics] transverse (presentation); Treasury; Trinity; [chemistry] tritium; [shipping] tropical (load line); true; Tuesday; Turkish; [knitting] twist

T [physics] kinetic energy; [physics] period;

[physics] thermodynamic temperature; [engineering, physics] torque

t [astronomy] hour angle; [music] te (in tonic sol-fa); thickness; [meteorology] thunder; tonne; [physics] top (quark flavour)

t Celsius temperature; [chemistry] tertiary (isomer); [chemistry] transport number

t. table; tabulated; [sports] tackle; taken (from); [commerce] tare; teaspoon(ful); teeth; temperature; [music] tempo; *tempore* (Latin: in the time of); [music] tenor; [grammar] tense; terminal; territorial; territory; thunder; time; *tome* (French: volume (of book)); ton; tonne; *tonneau* (French: ton); town; township; transit; [grammar] transitive; troy (weight); tun; turn

T2 [civil aircraft marking] Tuvalu

T3 [civil aircraft marking] Kiribati

T7 [civil aircraft marking] San Marino

5T [civil aircraft marking] Mauritania

7T [civil aircraft marking] Algeria

TA [vehicle registration] Exeter; [taxation] table of allowances; [UK postcode] Taunton; [USA] teaching assistant; telegraphic address; temporary admission; [computing] terminal adapter; Territorial Army; [physics] thermal analysis; tithe annuity; training adviser; Training Agency (formerly TSA); [psychology] transactional analysis; [USA] transit authority; travel(ling) allowance; Tricycle Association

T/A technical assistant; temporary assistant

Ta [chemical element] tantalum

ta. tableau; tablet

t.a. target area; time and attendance; true altitude

TAA Territorial Army Association; test of academic aptitude; Trans-Australia Airlines; Transportation Association of America

TA&VRA Territorial Auxiliary and Volunteer Reserve Association

TAB tabulator (key) (on typewriter); Technical Assistance Board (of UN); Total Abstinence Brotherhood; [Australia, New Zealand] Totalizator Agency Board; [medicine] typhoid, paratyphoid A, paratyphoid B (vaccine)

tab. table; tableau; tablet; tabulate; tabulation; tabulator

TABA Timber Agents' and Brokers' Association of the United Kingdom

TABMAC The All British Martial Arts Council

TAC [US air force] Tactical Air Command; Technical Assistance Committee (of UN); Television Advisory Committee; The Athletics Congress; Theatres Advisory Council; Tobacco Advisory Committee; Trades Advisory Council

Tac. (Publius Cornelius) Tacitus (Roman historian)

TACAN tactical air navigation

tach. tachometer

tacho [short form] tachograph

TACL Training for Action-Centred Leadership

TACMAR tactical multifunction array radar

TACS tactical air-control system

TACV tracked air-cushion vehicle; *Transportes Aéreos de Cabo Verde* (Portuguese: Cape Verde airline company)

Tads [military] target acquisition and designation sight

TAF Tactical Air Force

TAFE technical and further education

tafu [slang] things are fouled (or fucked) up

tafubar [slang] things are fouled (or fucked) up beyond all recognition

TAG [USA] The Adjutant-General; Towpaths Action Group

Tag. Tagalog (language)

T/Agt [USA] transfer agent

TAH [medicine] total abdominal hysterectomy

TAI *temps atomique international* (French: International Atomic Time, IAT)

Tai. Taiwan

TAL [insurance] traffic and accident loss

Tal. Talmud

tal. *talis* (Latin: such)

Talisman [stock exchange] Transfer Accounting Lodgement for Investors and Stock Management

tal. qual. *talis qualis* (Latin: average quality)

TAM tactical air missile; Television Audience Measurement

Tam. Tamil (language)

Tamba Twins and Multiple Births Association

tan [mathematics] tangent

TANCA Technical Assistance to Non-Commonwealth Countries

T&A [US slang] tits and ass; [medicine] tonsillectomy and adenoidectomy; [medicine] tonsils and adenoids

T&AFA Territorial and Auxiliary Forces Association

T&AVR Territorial and Army Volunteer Reserve

t&b top and bottom

T&CPA Town and Country Planning Association

T&E test and evaluation; [informal] tired and emotional (i.e. drunk); travel and entertainment; trial and error

T&G Transport and General Workers' Union

t&g tongue(d) and groove(d) (in wood-working)

t&o taken and offered (in betting)

t&p [insurance] theft and pilferage

T&RA Tennis and Rackets Association

T&S transport and supply

t&s toilet and shower (in property or accommodation advertisement)

T&SG Television and Screenwriters' Guild

T&T taxed and tested (in car advertisement); Trinidad and Tobago

Tang. Tangier

tanh [mathematics] hyperbolic tangent

TANS terminal-area navigation system; Territorial Army Nursing Service (became part of QARANC)

TANU Tanganyika African National Union

TAO Technical Assistance Operations (of UN)

TAOC [USA] Tactical Air Operations Center

TAP [USA] Technical Assistance Program; *Transportes Aéreos Portugueses* (Portuguese airline company)

Tapi [trademark] telephony application programming interface

Tapline Trans-Arabian Pipeline Company

TAPPI [USA] Technical Association of the Pulp and Paper Industry

TAPS Trans-Alaska Pipeline System

TAR terrain-avoidance radar; Territorial Army Regulations; [accounting]

throughput accounting ratio; thrust-augmented rocket

tar. tariff; tarpaulin

TARA Technical Assistant, Royal Artillery; Territorial Army Rifle Association

TARAN test and replace as necessary

TARDIS time and relative dimensions in space (Doctor Who's time machine used in BBC science fiction series)

tarfu [slang] things are really fouled (or fucked) up

TARO Territorial Army Reserve of Officers

TARS Technical Assistance Recruitment Service; The Arthur Ransome Society

TAS torpedo antisubmarine (course); [aeronautics] true air speed

Tas. Tasmania; Tasmanian

TASI [telecommunications] time-assignment speech interpolation

TASM tactical air-to-surface missile

Tasm. Tasmania; Tasmanian

TASMO tactical air support of maritime operations

TASR terminal area surveillance radar

TASS Technical, Administrative and Supervisory Section (of AEU); Transport Aircraft Servicing Specialist (in RAF)

Tass *Telegrafnoye Agentstvo Sovetskovo Soyuza* (Russian: Telegraph Agency of the Soviet Union)

TAT [psychology] thematic apperception test; [medicine] tired all the time; trans-atlantic telephone (cable)

TATSA transportation aircraft test and support activity

Tau [astronomy] Taurus

TAUN Technical Assistance of the United Nations

TAURUS [stock exchange] Transfer and Automated Registration of Uncertified Stock

taut. tautology

t.-à-v. *tout-à-vous* (French: yours ever) (at end of letter)

tav. tavern

TAVR Territorial and Army Volunteer Reserve

TAVRA Territorial Auxiliary and Volunteer Reserve Association

t.a.w. twice a week

tax. taxation

taxn taxation

TB [vehicle registration] Liverpool; [computing] terabyte; torpedo boat; torpedo bomber; training battalion; training board; Treasury bill; [book-keeping] trial balance; [medicine] tubercle bacillus; [medicine] tuberculosis

Tb [computing] terabyte; [chemical element] terbium (formerly Tr)

t.b. [printing] take back; temporary buoy; [baseball] total bases; [book-keeping] trial balance; true bearing

TBA tyres, batteries and accessories

t.b.a. [commerce] to be advised; to be agreed; to be announced

tb&s top, bottom and sides

TBCEP tri-beta-chloroethyl phosphate (flame retardant)

t.b.c.f. to be called for

TBD torpedo-boat destroyer

t.b.d. to be decided; to be determined

TBF Teachers' Benevolent Fund

TBI [engineering] throttle-body injection; [medicine] total body irradiation

T-bill Treasury bill

TBL through bill of lading

t.b.l. [knitting] through back of loop

TBM tactical ballistic missile; [surveying] temporary benchmark; [medicine] tuberculous meningitis; tunnel-boring machine

TBO [aeronautics] time between overhauls; [theatre] total blackout

T-bond Treasury bond

TBS talk between ships (radio apparatus); [computing] tape backup system; tight building syndrome; training battle simulation

tbs. tablespoon(ful)

tbsp. tablespoon(ful)

TBSV [microbiology] tomato bushy stunt virus

TBT tributyl tin (antifouling agent in marine paint)

TC [vehicle registration] Bristol; Tank Corps; [USA] Tariff Commission; [law] Tax Cases; technical college; temporary clerk; Temporary Constable; tennis club; touring club; town clerk; town council; town councillor; training centre; training college; training corps; [military] Transport Command; traveller's cheque; [music] *tre corde* (Italian: three strings) (instruction to release soft pedal of piano); Trinity College; (Order of the)

Trinity Cross (in Trinidad and Tobago); [meteorology] tropical cyclone; Trusteeship Council (of UN); tungsten carbide; [civil aircraft marking] Turkey; twin carburettors

Tc [chemical element] technetium

tc. [music] tierce (organ stop)

t.c. temperature control; terracotta; till cancelled; time check; [navigation] true course

TCA trichloroacetic acid (herbicide); [pharmacology] tricyclic antidepressant

TCB [US slang] take care of business; Thames Conservancy Board; [medicine] tumour cell burden

TCBM transcontinental ballistic missile

TCC [telecommunications] time compression coding; Transport and Communications Commission (of UN); Trinity College, Cambridge; [USA] Troop Carrier Command

TCCB Test and County Cricket Board

TCD Trinity College, Dublin

TCDD tetrachlorodibenzodioxin (environmental pollutant)

TCE trichloroeth(yl)ene (solvent)

TCF Temporary Chaplain to the Forces; time-correction factor; *Touring Club de France* (French: French Touring Club)

tcf [USA] trillion cubic feet (used to measure natural gas)

TCFB Transcontinental Freight Bureau

TCGF [immunology] T-cell growth factor

TCH [international vehicle registration] Chad (from French *Tchad*)

tchg teaching

tchr teacher

TCI *Touring Club Italiano* (Italian: Italian Touring Club)

TCJCC Trades Council Joint Consultative Committee

TCL Trinity College (of Music) London

T-CLL [medicine] T-cell chronic lymphatic leukaemia

TCM Trinity College of Music (London)

TCMA Telephone Cable Makers' Association

TCO test control office; *Tjänstemännens Centralorganisation* (Swedish: Central Organization of Salaried Employees) (Swedish trade union); Trinity College, Oxford

TCP [computing] transmission control

protocol; [trademark] trichlorophenylme-
thyliodisalicyl (antiseptic)

TCPA Town and Country Planning Association (or Act)

TCP/IP [computing] transmission control protocol/Internet protocol

TCR [immunology] T-cell receptor; [physics] temperature coefficient of resistance

TCRE [medicine] transcervical resection of the endometrium

TCS target cost system; [USA] traffic control station

tctl tactical

TCU [USA] Transportation, Communications, International Union

TD [UK postcode] Galashiels; [vehicle registration] Manchester; [military] Tactical Division; tank destroyer; [medicine] tard-(at)ive dyskinesia; Teaching Diploma; [Ireland] *Teachta Dála* (Gaelic: Member of the Dáil); technical development; technical drawing; Territorial (Efficiency) Decoration (in Territorial Army); Tilbury Docks; torpedo depot; [sports] touchdown; [USA] traffic director; [USA] Treasury Department; trust deed; [currency] Tunisian dinar

td. touchdown

.td Chad (in Internet address)

t.d. technical data; [medicine] *ter in die* (Latin: three times a day) (in prescriptions); test data; time delay; tractor-drawn

TDA tax-deferred annuity; Timber Development Association

TDB *temps dynamique barycentrique* (French: barycentric dynamical time); total disability benefit

TDC Temporary Detective Constable; through-deck cruiser

t.d.c. [engineering] top dead centre

TDD telecommunications device for the deaf; Tubercular Diseases Diploma

TDDL [telecommunications] time-division data link

TDE total digestible energy

TDG Timeshare Developers Group; twist drill gauge

TDH tall, dark and handsome (in personal advertisement)

TDK *Tokyo Denkikagaku Kogyu KK* (Japanese electronics company)

TDL tunable diode laser

TDM telemetric data monitor; [telecommunications] time-division multiplexing

TDMA [telecommunications] time-division multiple access

TDN total digestible nutrients

T-DNA [genetics] transferred deoxyribonucleic acid

TDP technical development plan

TDR [computing] time domain reflectometer; [finance] Treasury deposit receipt

t.d.r. *touts droits réservés* (French: all rights reserved)

TDRSS tracking and data-relay satellite system

TDS [computing] tabular data stream

t.d.s. [medicine] *ter (in) die sumendus* (Latin: to be taken three times a day) (in prescriptions)

TDT [astronomy] terrestrial dynamical time

TE [vehicle registration] Manchester; telecommunications engineering; [biochemistry] trace element; trade expenses; [telecommunications] transverse electric

Te [chemical element] tellurium

t/e time-expired; twin-engined

t.e. thermal efficiency; tinted edge (of paper); trailing edge; trial and error; turbine engine

TEA Terminal Education Age

TEAC Technical Educational Advisory Council

TEACH Teacher Education Admissions Clearing House

Tear The Evangelical Alliance Relief (Fund)

TEC Training and Enterprise Council

tec [short form] detective

tech [short form] technical college

tech. technical; technically; technician; technique; technological; technology

Tech(CEI) Technician (Council of Engineering Institutions)

techn technician

techn. technical; technique

technol. technological; technologically; technologist; technology

Tedco Thames Estuary Development Company

TEDIS Trade Electronic Data Interchange System

TEE Telecommunications Engineering Establishment; Torpedo Experimental Establishment; total energy expenditure; [railways] Trans-Europe Express

TEF Textile Employers' Federation; toxicity equivalence factor

TEFL teaching (of) English as a foreign language

t.e.g. [bookbinding] top edges gilt

Teh. Tehran

TEL tetraethyl lead (petrol additive); [astronautics] transporter-erector-launcher

Tel [astronomy] Telescopium

tel. telegram; telegraph; telegraphic; telephone

telecom. telecommunication(s)

teleg. telegram; telegraph; telegraphic; telegraphy

teleph. telephone; telephony

telex teleprinter exchange

telly [short form] television

TELNET [computing] teletype network

tel. no. telephone number

TELO Tamil Eelam Liberation Organization

TEM Territorial Efficiency Medal; transmission electron microscope (or microscopy); [telecommunications] transverse electromagnetic

TEMA Telecommunications Engineering and Manufacturing Association

temp [short form] temporary (worker)

temp. temperance; temperate; temperature; [music] tempo; temporal; temporary; *tempore* (Latin: in the time of)

Templar tactical expert mission planner (military computer)

temp. prim. [music] *tempo primo* (Italian: at the original speed)

tempy temporary

ten. tenant; tenement; [music] tenor; [music] *tenuto* (Italian: held, sustained)

tency tenancy

Tenn. Tennessee

TENS [medicine] transcutaneous electrical nerve stimulation

tepid [informal] tastes expensive, pension inadequate, dammit

TEPP tetraethyl pyrophosphate (pesticide)

Ter. Terence (Roman writer); Terrace (in road name); Territorial; Territory

ter. terrace; territorial; territory

terat. teratology

TERCOM [aeronautics] terrain contour matching (or mapping)

term. terminal; terminate; termination; terminology

Terr. Terrace (in road name); Territorial; Territory

terr. terrace; territorial; territory

terrd terraced (in property advertisement)

tert. tertiary

TES thermal-energy storage; *Times Educational Supplement*

Tesco T. E. Stockwell and J. Cohen (supermarket chain)

TESL teaching (of) English as a second language

TESOL teaching of English to speakers of other languages

TESSA Tax-Exempt Special Savings Account (replaced by ISA)

test. testament; testator; testatrix; testimonial; testimony

TET Teacher of Electrotherapy

T-et-G Tarn-et-Garonne (French department)

TETOC technical education and training for overseas countries

tet. tox. tetanus toxin

TEU [shipping] twenty-foot equivalent unit

Teut. Teuton; Teutonic

TeV teraelectronvolt

TEWT [military] tactical exercise without troops

Tex. Texan; Texas

text. textile(s); textual

text. rec. *textus receptus* (Latin: the received text)

TF [civil aircraft marking] Iceland; [vehicle registration] Reading; task force; [UK postcode] Telford; Territorial Force; [electronics] thin film; [biochemistry] transcription factor; [shipping] tropical freshwater (load line)

t.f. tabulating form; tax-free; training film; *travaux forcés* (French: hard labour)

TFA Tenant Farmers' Association; [biochemistry] total fatty acids

TFAP Tropical Forestry Action Plan

tfc traffic

TFD [electronics] thin-film detector

TFECG Training and Further Education Consultative Group

TFEL [computing] thin-film electroluminescent display
TFOF Taxi Fleet Operators' Federation
TFR Territorial Force Reserve; total fertility rate
tfr transfer
TFS [medicine] testicular feminization syndrome
TFSC Turkish Federated State of Cyprus
TFSK Turkish Federated State of Kibris (Turkish name for Cyprus)
TFSR Tools for Self Reliance
TFT [electronics] thin-film transistor
TFTA Traditional Farm-Fresh Turkey Association
TFTR [nuclear technology] Tokamak Fusion Test Reactor
TFU telecommunications flying unit
TFW [military] tactical fighter wing
TFX tactical fighter experimental (aircraft)
TG [vehicle registration] Cardiff; [civil aircraft marking] Guatemala; Tate Gallery; temporary gentleman; [informal] thank God; [USA] Theater Guild; [international vehicle registration] Togo; Townswomen's Guild; training group; transformational-generative (grammar); transformational grammar; Translators' Guild
tg [mathematics] tangent
.tg Togo (in Internet address)
t.g. tail gear; [biology] type genus
TGA [chemistry] thermal gravimetric analysis
TGAT [education] Task Group on Assessment and Testing
T-gate [computing] ternary selector gate
TGB *très grande bibliothèque* (French: very large library) (popular name for French national library)
t.g.b. tongued, grooved and beaded (in woodworking)
TGE [medicine] transmissible gastroenteritis
TGF [medicine] transforming growth factor
TGI [marketing] Target Group Index
TGIA Toy and Giftware Importers' Association
TGIF [informal] thank God it's Friday
TGM torpedo gunner's mate
TGMV [microbiology] tomato golden mosaic virus

T-group training group
TGT [aeronautics] turbine gas temperature
tgt target
TGV *train à grande vitesse* (French: high-speed train)
TGWU Transport and General Workers' Union
TH [vehicle registration] Swansea; *Technische Hochschule* (German: technical college, technical university); [fishing port] Teignmouth; Territory of Hawaii; [numismatics] toothed border; town hall (on map); Toynbee Hall; Transport House; Trinity House
Th [chemical element] thorium
Th. Theatre; Theology; Thursday
th. thermal
.th Thailand (in Internet address)
Thai. Thailand
thanat. thanatology
ThB Bachelor of Theology (from Latin *Theologiae Baccalaureus*)
THC tetrahydrocannabinol (active component of cannabis); [New Zealand] Tourist Hotel Corporation
THD total harmonic distortion (in recording)
ThD Doctor of Theology (from Latin *Theologiae Doctor*)
THE Technical Help to Exporters (division of British Standards Institution)
theat. theatre; theatrical
THELEP Therapy of Leprosy
Theoc. Theocritus (ancient Greek poet)
theol. theologian; theological; theology
Theoph. Theophrastus (ancient Greek philosopher)
theor. theorem; theoretical; theory
theoret. theoretical
theos. theosophical; theosophist; theosophy
therap. therapeutic; therapeutics
therapeut. therapeutic; therapeutics
therm. thermometer; thermometry; thermostatic
thermochem. thermochemical; thermochemistry
thermodyn. thermodynamic; thermodynamics
thermom. thermometer; thermometry
THES *Times Higher Education Supplement*
thes. thesis
thesp. thespian

Thess. [Bible] Thessalonians; Thessaly

THF Trusthouse Forte plc

THI temperature–humidity index

t.h.i. time handed in

thk thick

ThL Licentiate in Theology

ThM Master of Theology (from Latin *Theologiae Magister*)

tho' though

thor. thoracic; thorax

thoro. thoroughfare

Thos. Thomas

thou. thousand

thp thrust horsepower

THR [medicine] total hip replacement

thr their

thr. through; thrust

throt. throttle

ThSchol Scholar in Theology

THT Terrence Higgins Trust

Thu. Thursday

Thuc. Thucydides (ancient Greek historian)

Thur. Thursday

Thurs. Thursday

THWM Trinity (House) high-water mark

THz terahertz

TI [civil aircraft marking] Costa Rica; technical inspection; technical institute; temperature indication; temperature indicator; Texas Instruments; thermal imaging; tourist information

T/I target identification; target indicator

Ti [chemical element] titanium

Ti. Tiberius (Roman emperor); Tibet

TIA Tax Institute of America; Telecommunications Industry Association; [medicine] transient ischaemic attack (minor stroke)

TIB tourist information bureau

Tib. Tibet; Tibetan

TIBC [medicine] total iron-binding capacity

TIBOR [finance] Tokyo Inter-Bank Offered Rate

TIC [law] taken into consideration; Timber Industries Confederation; total inorganic carbon; tourist information centre

TICCIH The International Committee for the Conservation of the Industrial Heritage

t.i.d. [medicine] *ter in die* (Latin: three times a day) (in prescriptions)

TIE Theatre in Education

tier. [music] tierce (organ stop)

TIF [computing] tagged image format; telephone influence factor; telephone interference factor; Theatre Investment Fund; [biochemistry] transcription initiation factor; *Transports internationaux par chemin de fer* (French: International Rail Transport)

TIFF [computing] tagged image file format

TIG tungsten inert gas (in welding)

TIGR Treasury Investment Growth Receipts (type of bond, pronounced 'tiger')

TIH Their Imperial Highnesses

TIIAL The International Institute of Applied Linguistics

TIL [medicine] tumour-infiltrating lymphocyte

TILS Technical Information and Library Service

TIM transient intermodulation distortion (in recording)

Tim. [Bible] Timothy

t.i.m. time is money

timp. [music] timpani

timps [short form] timpani

TIMS The Institute of Management Sciences

TIN [USA] taxpayer identification number

TINA [informal] there is no alternative (phrase originally associated with Margaret Thatcher)

tinct. tincture

TIO technical information officer

TIP [computing] terminal interface processor

Tip. Tipperary

Tipp. Tipperary

TIR [optics] total internal reflection; *Transport international routier* (French: International Road Transport)

TIRC Tobacco Industry Research Committee

TIROS television and infrared observation satellite

TIS technical information service

tis. tissue

Tit. [Bible] Titus

tit. title; titular

TIU Telecommunications International Union

TJ [civil aircraft marking] Cameroon; [vehicle registration] Liverpool; [international vehicle registration] Tajikistan; talk jockey; terajoule; [athletics] triple jump

.tj Tajikistan (in Internet address)

TJR [currency] Tajik rouble

TK [vehicle registration] Exeter

Tk [currency] taka (used in Bangladesh)

tk tank; truck

tkg taking

tkgs takings

TKO [boxing] technical knockout

tkr tanker

tks thanks

tkt ticket

TL [civil aircraft marking] Central African Republic; [vehicle registration] Lincoln; target language; [physics] thermoluminescence; [physics] thermoluminescent (as in **TL-dating**); Torpedo Lieutenant; [insurance] total loss; [US informal] trade-last (exchange of compliments); transmission line; [currency] Turkish lira

T/L [banking] time loan; [insurance] total loss

Tl [chemical element] thallium

tl [meteorology] thunder and lightning

t.l. test link; [engineering] thrust link; time length; title list; total load; [insurance] total loss; trade list

TLA three-letter abbreviation (or acronym); Toy Libraries Association

TLB [computing] translation look-aside buffer

t.l.b. temporary lighted buoy

TLC tender loving care; [chemistry] thin-layer chromatography; [medicine] total lung capacity; [Australia] Trades and Labour Council

tld tooled

TLEH true love and everlasting happiness (in personal advertisement)

TLF transferable loan facility

TLG Theatrical Ladies' Guild

TLMI The Leprosy Mission International

TLO technical liaison officer

t.l.o. [insurance] total loss only

TLP [astronomy] transient lunar phenomenon

TLR Times Law Reports; [photography] twin-lens reflex

tlr tailor; trailer

TLRS Tramway and Light Railway Society

TLS *Times Literary Supplement*; typed letter, signed

tltr translator

TLU [computing] table look-up

TLV [electronics] threshold-limit value

TLWM Trinity (House) low-water mark

TM [vehicle registration] Luton; tactical missile; technical manual; technical memorandum; test manual; Their Majesties; [telecommunications] tone modulation; trademark; trained man; training manual; transcendental meditation; [telecommunications] transverse magnetic; trench mortar; tropical medicine; [computing] Turing machine; [international vehicle registration] Turkmenistan

Tm [chemical element] thulium

.tm Turkmenistan (in Internet address)

t.m. temperature meter; true mean

TMA Theatrical Management Association; Trans-Mediterranean Airways (Lebanese airline company)

TMB travelling medical board

TMBA Twins and Multiple Births Association

tmbr timber

TMC [USA] Tanglewood Music Center; The Movie Channel

TMD [military] theatre missile defence

TMI [USA] Three Mile Island

TMJ [medicine] temporomandibular joint

tmkpr timekeeper

TML [chemistry] tetramethyl lead; [shipping] three-mile limit

TMMG Teacher of Massage and Medical Gymnastics

TMO telegraph(ic) money order

TMP thermomechanical pump

TMPDF Trade Marks, Patterns and Designs Federation

tmpry temporary

tmr timer

TMS Tramway Museum Society

TMT turbine motor train

TMV [microbiology] tobacco mosaic virus; true mean value

TN [civil aircraft marking] (Republic of)

Congo; [vehicle registration] Newcastle upon Tyne; [US postcode] Tennessee; [UK postcode] Tonbridge; tradename; [fishing port] Troon; true north; [international vehicle registration] Tunisia

tn ton; tonne; town; train; transportation

.tn Tunisia (in Internet address)

t.n. technical note; telephone number

TNA Tamil National Army

TNC Theatres National Committee; total numerical control; transnational corporation

TNF [military] theatre nuclear forces; [medicine] tumour necrosis factor

TNG [USA] The Newspaper Guild

tng training; turning

TNIP [South Africa] Transkei National Independence Party

TNM tactical nuclear missile; [medicine] tumour, node, metastasis

T-note [finance] Treasury note

TNP *Théâtre national populaire* (French: National Popular Theatre)

TNPG The Nuclear Power Group

tnpk. turnpike

TNT trinitrotoluene (explosive)

TNTC too numerous to count

TNW tactical nuclear warfare; [military] theatre nuclear weapon

TO [vehicle registration] Nottingham; [commerce] table of organization; tax officer; technical officer; telegraphic order; telegraph office; telephone office; telephone order; Torpedo Officer; trained operator; transport officer; [fishing port] Truro; turn over (page)

T/O turnover

To. Togo

.to Tonga (in Internet address)

t.o. take-off; [printing] take over; turnover

TOB temporary office building

ToB [cycling] Tour of Britain

Tob. [Bible] Tobit (book of Apocrypha)

tob. tobacco; tobacconist

TobRV [microbiology] tobacco ringspot virus

TOC total organic carbon

Toc H Talbot House (original headquarters of society, from former telegraphic code for TH)

TOD time of delivery; trade and operations division

TOE [physics] theory of everything

t.o.e. ton oil equivalent

TOEFL test(ing) of English as a foreign language

TOET test of elementary training

TOF [physics] time of flight

TOFC trailer on flat car (freight container)

TOFPET [medicine] time-of-flight positron-emission tomography

tog. together

togr together

Tok. Tokyo

TOL Tower of London

TOM *territoire d'outre mer* (French: overseas territory); total organic matter

tom. tomato; *tomus* (Latin: volume (of book))

tomat. tomato

TOMCAT theatre of operations missile continuous-wave antitank weapon

TOMS Total Ozone Mapping Spectrometer

TON total organic nitrogen

tonn. tonnage

TOO time of origin; [commerce] to order only

TOP [computing] technical office protocol; temporarily out of print; termination of pregnancy

TOPIC [stock exchange] Teletext Output Price Information Computer

topog. topographer; topographical; topography

topol. topological; topology

TOPS Theatre Organ Preservation Society; Training Opportunities Scheme

TOR Tertiary Order Regular of St Francis

Tor. Toronto

t.o.r. time of receipt; time of reception

torn. tornado

torp. torpedo

t.o.s. temporarily out of service; temporarily out of stock; terms of service

TOSD Tertiary Order of St Dominic

TOSF Tertiary Order of St Francis

Toshiba *Tokyo Shibaura Denki KK* (Japanese electrical corporation)

tot. total; totally

t.o.t. time on target; time over target

TOTC time-on-target computation (military computer)

tote [short form] totalizator

TOTP *Top of the Pops* (BBC television programme)

tour. tourism; tourist

tourn. tournament

TOW tube-launched optically tracked wire-guided (antitank missile); tug-of-war

tox. toxicological; toxicology

toxicol. toxicological; toxicologist; toxicology

TP [vehicle registration] Portsmouth; target practice; taxpayer; teaching practice; technical paper; technical publication; teleprinter; [computing] teleprocessing; [music] *tempo primo* (Italian: at the original speed); *tempore Paschale* (Latin: at Easter); test panel; [insurance] third party; town planner; town planning; [computing] transaction processing; Transvaal Province; treaty port; trig point; true position; turning point

tp township; troop

t.p. *timbre-poste* (French: postage stamp); title page; to pay; toilet paper; [commerce] *tout payé* (French: all (expenses) paid)

TPA [medicine] tissue plasminogen activator

TPC [USA] The Peace Corps; [Australia] Trade Practices Commission; Transaction Processing Council

tpd tons per day

tph tons per hour

TPI tax and price index; [computing] terminal phase initiation; [Australia] totally and permanently incapacitated; Town Planning Institute; transpolyisoprene (synthetic rubber); Tropical Products Institute

tpi [engineering] teeth per inch; [engineering, textiles] threads per inch; [shipping] tons per inch (immersion); [computing] tracks per inch; [engineering] turns per inch

tpk. turnpike

TPLF Tigrean People's Liberation Front

TPM third-party maintenance; [commerce] total productive management

tpm tons per minute

TPN [medicine] total parenteral nutrition

TPO travelling post office; Tree Preservation Order

TPR [medicine] temperature, pulse, respiration

Tpr Trooper

tpr teleprinter

TPS Tax Payers' Society; Thomas Paine Society; toughened polystyrene

tpt transport; trumpet

tptr trumpeter

TQ [banking] tel quel (exchange rate); [computing] text quality; [UK postcode] Torquay; [commerce] total quality

TQM [commerce] total quality management

TR [civil aircraft marking] Gabon; [vehicle registration] Portsmouth; target rifle; tariff reform; Telephone Rentals plc; *tempore reginae* (Latin: in the time of the queen); *tempore regis* (Latin: in the time of the king); Territorial Reserve; test run; Theodore Roosevelt (US president); tons registered; tracking radar; transmit–receive; [UK postcode] Truro; trust receipt; [international vehicle registration] Turkey

T/R transmitter–receiver

Tr [chemical element] terbium (former symbol, replaced by Tb); [geology] Triassic

tr. [medicine] *tinctura* (Latin: tincture); trace; track; tragedy; train; trainee; transaction(s); transfer; [grammar] transitive; translate; translated; translation; translator; transport; transportation; [printing] transpose; transposition; treasurer; [music] treble; [music] trill; troop; truck; trumpet; trumpeter; trust; trustee

.tr Turkey (in Internet address)

TRA [USA] Thoroughbred Racing Association

TrA [astronomy] Triangulum Australe

trac. tracer; tractor

TRACALS [aeronautics] traffic control and landing system

TRACE task reporting and current evaluation; [aeronautics] test equipment for rapid automatic checkout evaluation

trad [short form] traditional

trad. tradition; traditional; *traducteur* (French: translator); *traduction* (French: translation); *traduttore* (Italian: translator); *traduzione* (Italian: translation)

TRADA Timber Research and Development Association

trag. tragedian; tragedy; tragic

TRAM [medicine] transverse rectus abdom-

inus myocutaneus (breast reconstruction)
TRAMPS temperature regulator and
missile power supply
trannie [short form] transistor (radio)
Trans. Transvaal
trans. transaction(s); transfer; transferred;
transit; [grammar] transitive; transitory;
translate; translated; translation; translator; transparent; transport; transportation; [printing] transpose; transposition;
transverse
transcr. transcribed; transcription
transf. transfer; transference; transferred
transl. translate; translated; translation;
translator
translit. transliterate; transliterated; trans-
literation
transp. transport; transportation;
[printing] transpose
trany transparency
trav. travel; traveller; travels
Trb. Tribune
trbn. trombone
TRC Thames Rowing Club; Tobacco
Research Council
tr. co. trust company
tr. coll. training college
Trd Trinidad
TRDA Timber Research and Development
Association
Treas. Treasury
treas. treasurer; treasury
trem transport emergency (card) (carried
by chemical tankers)
trem. [music] *tremolando* (Italian: trem-
bling); [music] tremulant (organ device)
TRF [biochemistry] thyrotrophin-releasing
factor; tuned radio frequency
trf tariff
trf. transfer
TRG Tory Reform Group
trg touring; training
trg. [music] triangle
trge [music] triangle
TRH Their Royal Highnesses; [biochem-
istry] thyrotrophin-releasing hormone
TRI Television Reporters International;
[USA] Textile Research Institute; Thrombosis Research Institute
Tri [astronomy] Triangulum
trib. tribal; tribunal; tributary; tribute
TRIC Television and Radio Industries

Club; [medicine] trachoma inclusion
conjunctivitis
trid. [medicine] *triduum* (Latin: three days)
(in prescriptions)
trig [short form] triangulation (as in **trig
point**)
trig. trigger; trigonometric(al); trigonometry
TRIGA [engineering] training, research
and isotope-production reactors –
General Atomic
trigon. trigonometric(al); trigonometry
trike [short form] tricycle
trim. trimester
Trin. Trinidad; Trinidadian; Trinity
Trip. Tripos (final examination at Cambridge University)
tripl. triplicate
trit. triturate
TRJ turboramjet (engine)
TRLFSW tactical range landing-force support weapon
trlr trawler
TRM trademark
trml terminal
t.r.n. technical research note
tRNA [biochemistry] transfer ribonucleic
acid
TRNC Turkish Republic of Northern
Cyprus
trng touring; training
TRO [law] temporary restraining order
TROBI Tree Register of the British
Isles
trom. trombone
tromb. trombone
trombst trombonist
Tron [computing] the real-time operating
system nucleus
trop. tropic; tropical
Trop. Can. Tropic of Cancer
Trop. Cap. Tropic of Capricorn
trop. med. tropical medicine
trp troop
TRRL Transport and Road Research Laboratory
TRS [computing] term rewriting system;
Torry Research Station (Scotland)
trs. transfer; [printing] transpose; trustees
TRSB time reference scanning beam
trsd transferred; transposed
trsp. transport
TRSR taxi and runway surveillance radar

TRSSGM tactical range surface-to-surface guided missile

TRSSM tactical range surface-to-surface missile

trt turret

Truron. *Truronensis* (Latin: (Bishop) of Truro)

try. truly

TS [UK postcode] Cleveland; [vehicle registration] Dundee; [music] *tasto solo* (Italian: one key alone); Television Society; Theosophical Society; Tolkien Society; tool steel; [slang] tough shit; [medicine] Tourette's syndrome; training ship; [chemistry] transition state; transsexual; Treasury Solicitor; [medicine] tuberous sclerosis; tub-sized (paper); [civil aircraft marking] Tunisia; typescript

T/S transshipment

t.s. temperature switch; tensile strength; test summary; till sale; turbine ship; twin screw; type specification

TSA The Securities Association Limited; [statistics] time-series analysis; total surface area; Training Services Agency (former name of TA); Training Support Agency; [medicine] tumour-specific antigen

TSAPI telephony services application programming interface

TSB Trustee Savings Bank

TSBA Trustee Savings Banks Association

TSD Tertiary of St Dominic

TSDS two-speed destroyer sweeper

TSE Tokyo Stock Exchange; Toronto Stock Exchange; [medicine] transmissible spongiform encephalopathy

TSF two-seater fighter

TSFA The Securities and Futures Authority

tsfr transfer

TSgt Technical Sergeant

TSH Their Serene Highnesses; [biochemistry] thyroid-stimulating hormone

Tsh [currency] Tanzanian shilling

TSH-RF [biochemistry] thyroid-stimulating-hormone-releasing factor

TSH-RH [biochemistry] thyroid-stimulating-hormone-releasing hormone

tsi tons per square inch

TSO The Stationery Office (replacement for HMSO); town sub-office; trading standards officer

TSP textured soya protein; [computing] travelling salesman problem

tsp. teaspoon(ful)

TSR tactical strike reconnaissance; terminate but stay resident (computer program); torpedo-spotter reconnaissance; Trans-Siberian Railway

TSRB Top Salaries Review Body

TSS time-sharing system; [medicine] toxic shock syndrome; turbine steamship; twin-screw steamship; typescripts

TSSA Transport Salaried Staffs Association

tstr tester

t.s.u. this side up

TSV [microbiology] tobacco streak virus

t.s.v.p. *tournez s'il vous plaît* (French: please turn over, PTO)

TSW Television South West

TT [civil aircraft marking] Chad; [vehicle registration] Exeter; [fishing port] Tarbert; technical training; teetotal; teetotaller; [banking] telegraphic transfer; [geology] Tertiary; tetanus toxoid; [cycling] time trial; torpedo tube; Tourist Trophy (motorcycle race); transit time; [international vehicle registration] Trinidad and Tobago; Trust Territories; tuberculin-tested (milk)

.tt Trinidad and Tobago (in Internet address)

TTA Teacher Training Agency; Travel Trade Association

TTAW Table Tennis Association of Wales

TTB tetragonal tungsten bronze

TTBT Threshold Test Ban Treaty

TTC teachers' training course; technical training centre; [military] Technical Training Command; [medicine] transcutaneous transhepatic cholangiography

TTF Timber Trade Federation

TTFN [informal] ta-ta for now

TTL [photography] through the lens; to take leave; [electronics] transistor-transistor logic; tribal trust land (in Zimbabwe)

TTM [commerce] time to market

Tto Toronto

TTRA Tourist Trophy Riders' Association

TTS teletypesetter; teletypesetting; [acoustics] temporary threshold shift; [computing] text-to-speech

TTT [cycling] team time trial; [banking] telegraphic transfer; Tyne Tees Television Limited

TTTA Timber Trade Training Association

TTY [USA] teletypewriter

TU [vehicle registration] Chester; [civil aircraft marking] Côte d'Ivoire (Ivory Coast); thermal unit; toxic unit; trade union; [telecommunications] traffic unit; training unit; [telecommunications, acoustics] transmission unit; Tupolev (former Soviet aircraft, as in **TU-144**)

Tu. Tudor; Tuesday

TUA Telecommunications Users' Association

TUAC Trade Union Advisory Committee

tub. [cycling] tubular (tyre)

TUBCS Trade Union Badge Collectors' Society

TUBE The Union of Bookmakers' Employees

tuberc. tubercular; tuberculosis

TUC Trades Union Congress

Tuc [astronomy] Tucana

TUCC Transport Users' Consultative Committee (or Council)

TUCGC Trades Union Congress General Council

Tue. Tuesday

Tues. Tuesday

TUG Telephone Users' Group

TUI Trade Unions International of Public and Allied Employees

TUIAFPW Trade Unions International of Agricultural, Forestry and Plantation Workers

TUIREG Trade Unions International Research and Education Group

TUIWC Trade Unions International of Workers in Commerce

TUIWE Trade Unions International of Workers in Energy

TULF Tamil United Liberation Front

TULRA Trade Union and Labour Relations Act

TUM Trades Union Movement

TUPE Transfer of Undertakings (Protection of Employment) Regulations

TUR [medicine] transurethral resection

TURB [meteorology] turbulence

turb. turbine

Turk. Turkey; Turkish

TURP [medicine] transurethral resection of the prostate

turps [short form] turpentine

TV [vehicle registration] Nottingham; television; [finance] terminal value; [informal] transvestite

.tv Tuvalu (in Internet address)

t.v. terminal velocity; test vehicle

TVA *taxe à la valeur ajoutée* (French: value-added tax, VAT); Tennessee Valley Authority

TVE Television Trust for the Environment

TVEI Technical and Vocational Educational Initiative

Tvl Transvaal

tvl travel

TVO tractor vaporizing oil

TVP textured vegetable protein (meat substitute)

TVR television rating; [physics] temperature variation of resistance; Trevor (Wilkinson) (founder of sports car company)

TVRO television receive only (type of aerial)

TW [vehicle registration] Chelmsford; [telecommunications] travelling wave (as in **TW antenna**); [UK postcode] Twickenham

.tw Taiwan (in Internet address)

t.w. tail wind

TW3 *That Was The Week That Was* (former television comedy series)

TWA Thames Water Authority; time-weighted average; Trans-World Airlines

TWh terawatt hour

TWI The Welding Institute

TWIF Tug of War International Federation

TWIMC to whom it may concern

TWN teleprinter weather network

TWO this week only

TWOC taking without owner's consent (theft of car)

twp township

TWR Trans World Radio

TWT transonic wind tunnel; [electronics] travelling-wave tube

TWU Tobacco Workers' Union; Transport Workers' Union of America

TWX [USA] teletypewriter exchange service

twy twenty

TX [vehicle registration] Cardiff; [US postcode] Texas
Tx transmission (in broadcasting)
tx tax; taxation; thanks
TY [civil aircraft marking] Benin; [vehicle registration] Newcastle upon Tyne
Ty Territory
ty truly (in correspondence)
TYC Thames Yacht Club
TYMV [microbiology] turnip yellow mosaic virus
t.y.o. [horseracing] two-year-old
typ. typical; typically; typing; typist; typographer; typographic(al); typography

typh. typhoon
typo [short form] typographical error
typo. typographer; typographic(al); typography
typog. typographer; typographic(al); typography
typw. typewriter; typewriting; typewritten
Tyr. Tyrone
Tyrol. Tyrolean; Tyrolese
TYVM thank you very much
TZ [vehicle registration] Belfast; [civil aircraft marking] Mali
.tz Tanzania (in Internet address)

U

U rate of heat loss; Union; Unionist; Unit; United; [cinema] universal (film classification); University; unsatisfactory; upper; [informal] upper class (as in **U and non-U**); [chemical element] uranium; urinal; Utah; you (phonetic spelling, as in **while U wait**)
U [physics] potential difference
u [meteorology] ugly threatening sky; [chemistry] unified atomic mass unit; [physics] up (quark flavour)
u [physics] instantaneous potential difference
u. uncle; *und* (German: and); unit; unsatisfactory; *unter* (German: under, among); upper; utility
U3A University of the Third Age
5U [civil aircraft marking] Niger
9U [civil aircraft marking] Burundi
UA [vehicle registration] Leeds; [international vehicle registration] Ukraine; Ulster Association; United Artists Corporation; University of Alabama
U/a [insurance] underwriting account
.ua Ukraine (in Internet address)
u.a. unauthorized absence; under age; *unter anderem* (German: among other things); *usque ad* (Latin: as far as)
UAA United Arab Airlines
UAB Unemployment Assistance Board; Universities Appointments Board; University of Alabama in Birmingham

UABS Union of American Biological Societies
UAC Ulster Automobile Club
UADW Universal Alliance of Diamond Workers
UAE United Arab Emirates
UAI *Union des associations internationales* (French: Union of International Associations)
UAL United Airlines
UAM underwater-to-air missile
u&o use and occupancy
UAOD United Ancient Order of Druids
UAOS Ulster Agricultural Organization Society
UAP United Australia Party
UAPT *Union africaine des postes et télécommunications* (French: African Postal and Telecommunications Union)
UAR United Arab Republic (former official name of Egypt)
UARS upper-atmosphere research satellite
UART [computing, electronics] universal asynchronous receiver/transmitter
UAS University Air Squadron
u.a.s. upper airspace
UAU Universities Athletic Union
UAV unmanned air vehicle
UAW [USA] United Automobile Workers (United International Union of Automobile, Aerospace and Agricultural Implement Workers of America)

u.A.w.g. *um Antwort wird gebeten* (German: an answer is requested)

UB [vehicle registration] Leeds; United Brethren; [UK postcode] Uxbridge

UB40 registration card for unemployment benefit

UBA [medicine] ultrasonic bone analysis

UBC University of British Columbia (Vancouver)

UBF Union of British Fascists

UBI Understanding British Industry

U-boat German submarine (from German *Unterseeboot*)

UBR [taxation] Uniform Business Rate; University Boat Race

UBS United Bible Societies

UBV [astronomy] ultraviolet, blue, visual

UC [vehicle registration] central London; [music] *una corda* (Italian: one string) (instruction to use soft pedal of piano); under construction; undercover; University College; upcast shaft (in civil engineering); [theatre] up centre (of stage); Upper Canada; urban council; *urbe condita* (Latin: the city being built); [obstetrics] uterine contraction

Uc [cinema] universal, particularly suitable for children (film classification)

u/c [commerce] undercharge

u.c. [printing] upper case

UCA United Chemists' Association

UCAE Universities' Council for Adult Education

UCAR Union of Central African Republics

UCAS Universities and Colleges Admissions Service

UCATT Union of Construction, Allied Trades and Technicians

u.c.b. unless caused by

UCBSA United Cricket Board of South Africa

UCC Union Carbide Corporation; Universal Copyright Convention; University Computing Company

UCCA Universities' Central Council on Admissions (became part of UCAS)

UCCD United Christian Council for Democracy

UCD University College, Dublin; upper critical depth (in oceanography)

UCET Universities Council for Education of Teachers

UCG underground coal gasification

UCH University College Hospital (London)

UCHD usual childhood diseases

UCI *Union cycliste internationale* (French: International Cycling Union); United Cinemas International; University of California, Irvine

UCITS [finance] Undertakings for Collective Investment in Transferable Securities

UCJG *Alliance universelle des unions chrétiennes de jeunes gens* (French: World Alliance of Young Men's Christian Associations)

UCL University College London; upper control limit

u.c.l. [engineering] upper cylinder lubricant

UCLA University of California at Los Angeles

UCM University Christian Movement

UCMJ [USA] uniform code of military justice

UCMSM University College and Middlesex School of Medicine

UCNS Universities' Council for Non-academic Staff

UCNW University College of North Wales

UCR [psychology] unconditioned reflex; [psychology] unconditioned response; [computing] under-colour removal; [USA] Uniform Crime Report

UCS [psychology] unconditioned stimulus; Union of Concerned Scientists; [computing] universal multiple-octet coded character set; University College School (London); Upper Clyde Shipbuilders

UCSB University of California, Santa Barbara

UCSD University of California, San Diego

UCSW University College of South Wales

UCTA United Commercial Travellers' Association

UCV [USA] United Confederate Veterans

UCW Union of Communication Workers; University College of Wales

UCWRE Underwater Countermeasures and Weapons Research Establishment

UD [vehicle registration] Oxford; United Dairies

U/D [USA] under deed

u.d. unfair dismissal; [medicine] *ut dictum* (Latin: as directed) (in prescriptions)

UDA Ulster Defence Association

UDAG [USA] Urban Development Action Grant

UDC [USA] United Daughters of the Confederacy; universal decimal classification; Urban Development Corporation; urban district council

u.d.c. upper dead centre

UDCA Urban District Councils' Association

UDE Underwater Development Establishment

UDEAC *Union douanière et économique de l'Afrique centrale* (French: Central African Customs and Economic Union)

UDEAO *Union douanière des états d'Afrique d'Ouest* (French: Customs Union of West African States)

UDF Ulster Defence Force; [South Africa] Union Defence Force; Union of Democratic Forces (in Bulgaria); *Union pour la Démocratie Française* (French: French Democratic Union) (political party); [South Africa] United Democratic Front

u.d.f. *und die folgende* (German: and the following)

u. dgl. *und dergleichen* (German: and the like)

UDHR Universal Declaration of Human Rights

UDI unilateral declaration of independence

UDM Union of Democratic Mineworkers

UDN [veterinary science] ulcerative dermal necrosis (disease of fish)

UDP United Democratic Party

UDR Ulster Defence Regiment; *Union des démocrates pour la république* (French: Union of Democrats for the Republic) (former name of RPR)

UDSR *Union démocratique et socialiste de la résistance* (French: Democratic and Socialist Union of the Resistance)

UDT United Dominions Trust

UDUP Ulster Democratic Unionist Party

UE [vehicle registration] Dudley; university entrance (examination)

UEA Universal Esperanto Association; University of East Anglia

UED University Education Diploma

UEF *Union européenne des fédéralistes*

(French: European Union of Federalists); *Union européenne féminine* (French: European Union of Women)

u.e.f. universal extra fine (screw)

UEFA Union of European Football Associations

UEI Union of Educational Institutions

UEIC United East India Company

UEL United Empire Loyalists

UEMOA *Union économique et monétaire ouest-africaine* (French: West African Economic and Monetary Union)

UEO *Union de l'Europe occidentale* (French: Western European Union, WEU); unit education(al) officer

UEP *Union européenne de paiements* (French: European Payments Union); [genetics] unit evolutionary period

UEPS *Union européenne de la presse sportive* (French: European Sports Press Union)

UER *Union européenne de radiodiffusion* (French: European Broadcasting Union, EBU); university entrance requirements; unsatisfactory equipment report

UETA [USA] universal engineer tractor, armoured

UETRT [USA] universal engineer tractor, rubber-tyred

UF [vehicle registration] Brighton; United Free (Church of Scotland); [India] United Front; urea–formaldehyde (as in **UF resin**); utilization factor (of electric light)

u/f unfurnished (in accommodation advertisement)

UFA *Universum Film-Aktiengesellschaft* (European media company); [biochemistry] unsaturated fatty acid

UFAW Universities Federation for Animal Welfare

UFC United Free Church (of Scotland); Universities Funding Council

UFCW [USA] United Food and Commercial Workers International Union

UFF Ulster Freedom Fighters

uff. *ufficiale* (Italian: official)

UFFI urea–formaldehyde foam insulation

UFO unidentified flying object

u.f.p. unemployed full pay

UFT [physics] unified field theory; [USA] United Federation of Teachers

UFTAA Universal Federation of Travel Agents' Association

UFTU Union of Free Trades Union (in Romania)

UFU Ulster Farmers' Union

UFW United Farm Workers of America

UG [vehicle registration] Leeds

Ug. Uganda; Ugandan

u/g underground

.ug Uganda (in Internet address)

Ugan. Uganda; Ugandan

UGC underground gasification of coal; University Grants Committee

UGLE [Freemasonry] United Grand Lodge of England

UGT *Unión General de Trabajadores* (Spanish: General Union of Workers)

UGWA United Garment Workers of America

UH [vehicle registration] Cardiff

UHA [South Africa] Union House of Assembly

UHB [informal] urban haute bourgeoisie

UHCC Upper House of the Convocation of Canterbury

UHCY Upper House of the Convocation of York

UHF [radio] ultrahigh frequency

UHT ultra-heat-treated (as in **UHT milk**); ultrahigh temperature

UHV ultrahigh vacuum; ultrahigh voltage

UI [vehicle registration] Londonderry; [USA] unemployment insurance; [computing] user interface

u/i under instruction

u.i. *ut infra* (Latin: as below)

UIA Union of International Associations

UIAA *Union internationale des associations d'alpinisme* (French: International Union of Mountaineering Associations)

UIC *Union internationale des chemins de fer* (French: International Union of Railways)

UICC *Union internationale contre le cancer* (French: International Union against Cancer)

UICN *Union internationale pour la conservation de la nature et ses resources* (French: International Union for Conservation of Nature and Natural Resources)

UICPA *Union internationale de chimie pure et appliquée* (French: International Union of Pure and Applied Chemistry, IUPAC)

UIE *Union internationale des étudiants* (French: International Union of Students)

UIEO Union of International Engineering Organizations

UIHPS *Union internationale d'histoire et de philosophie des sciences* (French: International Union of the History and Philosophy of Science)

UIJS *Union internationale de la jeunesse socialiste* (French: International Union of Socialist Youth)

UIL *Unione Italiana del Lavoro* (Italian: Italian Federation of Trade Unions); United Irish League

UIMS [computing] user-interface management system

UIP *Union internationale de patinage* (French: International Skating Union); *Union interparlementaire* (French: Inter-Parliamentary Union)

UIPC *Union internationale de la presse catholique* (French: International Catholic Press Union)

UIPM *Union internationale de pentathlon moderne* (French: International Modern Pentathlon Union)

UIPPA *Union internationale de physique pure et appliquée* (French: International Union of Pure and Applied Physics, IUPAP)

UIS *Union internationale de secours* (French: International Relief Union)

UISB *Union internationale des sciences biologiques* (French: International Union of Biological Sciences)

UISM *Union internationale des syndicats des mineurs* (French: Miners' Trade Unions International)

UISPP *Union internationale des sciences préhistoriques et prohistoriques* (French: International Union of Prehistoric and Prohistoric Sciences)

UIT *Union internationale des télécommunications* (French: International Telecommunications Union, ITU); unit investment trust

UITF [accounting] Urgent Issues Task Force

UITP *Union internationale des transports publics* (French: International Union of Public Transport)

UIU Upholsterers' International Union of North America

UJ [vehicle registration] Shrewsbury; Union Jack; [engineering] universal joint

UJC Union Jack Club (London)

UJD Doctor of Canon and Civil Law (from Latin *Utriusque Juris Doctor*)

UK [vehicle registration] Birmingham; United Kingdom; [civil aircraft marking] Uzbekistan

.uk United Kingdom (in Internet address)

UKA Ulster King of Arms; United Kingdom Alliance

UK(A) [athletics] United Kingdom Allcomers

UKAC United Kingdom Automation Council

UKADGE United Kingdom Air Defence Ground Environment

UKAEA United Kingdom Atomic Energy Authority

UKAPE United Kingdom Association of Professional Engineers

UKBG United Kingdom Bartenders' Guild

UKCC United Kingdom Central Council for Nursing, Midwifery and Health Visiting (replacement for GNC)

UKCIS United Kingdom Chemical Information Service

UKCOSA United Kingdom Council for Overseas Students' Affairs

UKCSBS United Kingdom Civil Service Benefit Society

UKCTA United Kingdom Commercial Travellers' Association

UKDA United Kingdom Dairy Association

UKFBPW United Kingdom Federation of Business and Professional Women

UKgal United Kingdom gallon

UKIAS United Kingdom Immigrants' Advisory Service

UKIRT United Kingdom Infrared Telescope (Mauna Kea, Hawaii)

UKISC United Kingdom Industrial Space Committee

UKLF United Kingdom Land Forces

UKMF(L) United Kingdom Military Forces (Land)

UKMIS United Kingdom Mission

UK(N) [athletics] United Kingdom National

UKOOA United Kingdom Offshore Operators Association

UKOP United Kingdom Oil Pipelines

UKPA United Kingdom Pilots' Association

UKPIA United Kingdom Petroleum Industry Association Limited

Ukr. Ukraine; Ukrainian

UKSATA United Kingdom South Africa Trade Association

UKSLS United Kingdom Services Liaison Staff

UKSMA United Kingdom Sugar Merchant Association Limited

UKST United Kingdom Schmidt Telescope (Siding Spring, Australia)

UKW *Ultrakurzwelle* (German: ultrashort wave)

UL [vehicle registration] central London; [fishing port] Ullapool; [USA] Underwriters' Laboratories (on electrical appliance labels); university library; [biochemistry] unsaturated lipid; [theatre] up left (of stage); [computing] upload (on Internet); [medicine] upper limb

u.l. upper left; upper limit

ULA [computing] uncommitted logic array

ULC [theatre] up left centre (of stage)

ULCC ultralarge crude carrier (oil tanker); University of London Computer Centre

ULCI Union of Lancashire and Cheshire Institutes

ULF [radio] ultralow frequency; upper limiting frequency

ULICS University of London Institute of Computer Science

ULM ultrasonic light modulator; universal logic module

ULMS underwater long-range missile system

ULP University of London Press

ULS [finance] unsecured loan stock

ULSEB University of London School Examinations Board

ULT United Lodge of Theosophists

ult. ultimate; ultimately; *ultimo* (Latin: in the last (month), of the last (month)) (used in formal correspondence)

ulto *ultimo* (Latin: in the last (month), of the last (month)) (used in formal correspondence)

ult. praes. [medicine] *ultimum praescriptum* (Latin: last prescribed)

ULTRA Unrelated Live Transplant Regulatory Authority

ULV ultralow volume

UM [vehicle registration] Leeds; [currency] ouguiya (used in Mauritania); unaccompanied minor (on aircraft); University of Minnesota

u/m undermentioned

um. unmarried

UMA *Union du Maghreb Arabe* (French: Arab Maghreb Union) (customs union)

UMa [astronomy] Ursa Major

UMB *Union mondiale de billard* (French: World Billiards Union); [computing] upper memory block

umbl. umbilical

UMC University of Missouri, Columbia

UMCP University of Maryland, College Park

UMDS United Medical and Dental Schools

UMEJ *Union mondiale des étudiants juifs* (French: World Union of Jewish Students)

UMF Umbrella Makers' Federation

UMFC United Methodist Free Churches

UMi [astronomy] Ursa Minor

UMIST University of Manchester Institute of Science and Technology

UMNO United Malaysia National Organization

ump. umpire

UMT universal military training

UMTS universal military training service (or system)

UMW United Mine Workers (of America)

UMWA United Mine Workers of America

UN [vehicle registration] Exeter; [civil aircraft marking] Kazakhstan; United Nations

un. unified; union; united; unsatisfactory

UNA United Nations Association

UNAA United Nations Association of Australia

unab. unabridged

UNACC United Nations Administrative Committee and Coordination

unacc. unaccompanied

unaccomp. unaccompanied

UNACOM universal army communication system

unan. unanimous

UNARCO United Nations Narcotics Commission

unasgd unassigned

unatt. unattached

unattrib. unattributed

UNAUS United Nations Association of the United States

unauth. unauthorized

unauthd unauthorized

UNB universal navigation beacon; University of New Brunswick

unb. unbound

unbd unbound

UNBRO United Nations Border Relief Operation

UNC [numismatics] uncirculated; *Union National Camerounaise* (French: Cameroon National Union); United Nations Command; University of North Carolina

unc. uncertain; uncle

UNCAST United Nations Confederation on the Applications of Science and Technology

UNCC United Nations Cartographic Commission

UNCCP United Nations Conciliation Commission for Palestine

UNCDF United Nations Capital Development Fund

UNCED United Nations Conference on Environment and Development

UNCID Uniform Rules of Conduct for Interchange of Trade Data by Teletransmission

UNCIO United Nations Conference on International Organization

uncir. uncirculated

uncirc. uncirculated

UNCITRAL United Nations Commission on International Trade Law

unclas. unclassified

unclass. unclassified

UNCLE United Network Command for Law and Enforcement (in 1960s television series *The Man from UNCLE*)

UNCLOS United Nations Conference on the Law of the Sea

uncond. unconditional

uncor. uncorrected

UNCSTD United Nations Conference on Science and Technology for Development

UNCTAD United Nations Conference on Trade and Development

UND University of North Dakota

UNDC United Nations Disarmament Commission

UNDCP United Nations Drug Control Programme

undergrad [short form] undergraduate

UNDOF United Nations Disengagement Observer Force (peacekeeping force in Syria)

UNDP United Nations Development Programme

UNDRO United Nations Disaster Relief Organization

undsgd undersigned

undtkr undertaker

UNE underground nuclear explosion

UNEC United Nations Education Conference

UNECA United Nations Economic Commission for Asia

UNEDA United Nations Economic Development Administration

UNEF United Nations Emergency Force

UNEP United Nations Environment Programme

UNESCO United Nations Educational, Scientific and Cultural Organization

UNETAS United Nations Emergency Technical Aid Service

unexpl. unexplained; unexploded; unexplored

UNFAO United Nations Food and Agriculture Organization

UNFB United Nations Film Board

UNFC United Nations Food Conference

UNFICYP United Nations (Peacekeeping) Force in Cyprus

UNFPA United Nations Fund for Population Activities

unfurn. unfurnished (in accommodation advertisement)

ung. [medicine] *unguentum* (Latin: ointment)

UNGA United Nations General Assembly

UNHCR United Nations High Commissioner for Refugees

UNHQ United Nations Headquarters

UNI *Ente Nazionale Italiano di Unificazione* (Italian: Italian Standards Association); United News of India

uni [short form] university

UNIC United Nations Information Centre

UNICA *Union internationale du cinéma d'amateurs* (French: International Union of Amateur Cinema)

UNICE *Union des industries de la communauté européenne* (French: Union of Industries of the European Community)

UNICEF United Nations Children's Fund (formerly United Nations International Children's Emergency Fund)

UNICOM universal integrated communication system

UNIDO United Nations Industrial Development Organization

UNIDROIT *Institut international pour l'unification du droit privé* (French: International Institute for the Unification of Private Law)

unif. uniform

UNIFIL United Nations Interim Force in Lebanon

UNIKOM United Nations Iraq–Kuwait Observation Mission (peacekeeping force)

UNIMA *Union internationale des marionettes* (French: International Union of Puppeteers)

UNIO United Nations Information Organization

UNIP United National Independence Party (in Zambia)

UNIPEDE *Union internationale des producteurs et distributeurs d'énergie électrique* (French: International Union of Producers and Distributors of Electrical Energy)

UNIS United Nations International School

unis. [music] unison

UNISCAT United Nations Expert Committee on the Application of Science and Technology

UNISIST Universal System for Information in Science and Technology

Unit. Unitarian; Unitarianism

UNITA *União Nacional para a Independência Total de Angola* (Portuguese: National Union for the Total Independence of Angola)

UNITAR United Nations Institute for Training and Research

Univ. Universalist; University

univ. universal; universally; university

UNIVAC universal automatic computer

UNIX [trademark] type of computer operating system (originally Unics, short for Uniplexed Information and Computing System)

UNJSPF United Nations Joint Staff Pension Fund

unkn. unknown

UNLC United Nations Liaison Committee

UNM University of New Mexico

unm. unmarried

UNMC United Nations Mediterranean Commission

UNMIBH United Nations Mission in Bosnia-Herzegovina (peacekeeping force)

unmod. unmodernized (in property advertisement)

UNMOGIP United Nations Military Observer Group in India and Pakistan (peacekeeping force)

UNO United Nations Organization

UNOG United Nations Office at Geneva

UNOMA United Nations Observer Mission in Angola (peacekeeping force)

UNOMIG United Nations Observer Mission in Georgia (peacekeeping force)

UNOMIL United Nations Observer Mission in Liberia (peacekeeping force)

unop. unopened; unopposed

UNOSOM United Nations Operation in Somalia

UNOV United Nations Office at Vienna

UNP United National Party (in Sri Lanka)

unp. unpaged; unpaid

UNPA United Nations Postal Administration

UNPC United Nations Palestine Commission

unpd unpaged; unpaid

UNPREDEP United Nations Preventive Deployment Force (peacekeeping force in FYROM)

UNPROFOR United Nations Protection Force (in former Yugoslavia)

unpub. unpublished

unpubd unpublished

UNREF United Nations Refugee Emergency Fund

UNRISD United Nations Research Institute for Social Development

UNRRA United Nations Relief and Rehabilitation Administration

UNRWA United Nations Relief and Works Agency (for Palestine Refugees in the Near East)

unsat. unsatisfactory; unsaturated

UNSC United Nations Security Council; United Nations Social Commission

UNSCC United Nations Standards Coordinating Committee

UNSCCUR United Nations Scientific Conference on the Conservation and Utilization of Resources

UNSCOM United Nations Special Commission

UNSF United Nations Special Fund for Economic Development

UNSG United Nations Secretary-General

UNSR United Nations Space Registry

UNSSM United Nations Special Services Medal

unst. unstable

UNSW University of New South Wales

UNTAA United Nations Technical Assistance Administration

UNTAB United Nations Technical Assistance Board

UNTAC United Nations Transitional Authority in Cambodia

UNTAG United Nations Transition Assistance Group (in Namibia)

UNTAM United Nations Technical Assistance Mission

UNTC United Nations Trusteeship Council

UNTSO United Nations Truce Supervision Organization (peacekeeping force)

UNTT United Nations Trust Territory

UNU United Nations University

UNV United Nations Volunteers

UNWCC United Nations War Crimes Commission

UO [vehicle registration] Exeter

u.ö. *und öfters* (German: and often)

u.o.c. ultimate operating capability

UOD ultimate oxygen demand (in water conservation)

U of A University of Alaska

U of NC University of North Carolina

U of S University of Saskatchewan

U of T University of Toronto

UOM Union of Myanmar

UP [vehicle registration] Newcastle upon Tyne; Ulster Parliament; Union Pacific; United Party; United Presbyterian; United Press (news agency); United Provinces (former name of Uttar Pradesh); University of Paris; University of Pennsylvania; University of Pittsburgh; University Press; unsaturated polyester; [USA] Upper Peninsula; Uttar Pradesh

up. upper

u.p. underproof (of alcohol)

UPA *Union postale arabe* (French: Arab Postal Union); United Productions of America (company producing animated films)

UPC Uganda People's Congress; *Union des Populations Camerounaises* (French: Union of the Populations of Cameroon); United Presbyterian Church; Universal Postal Convention; universal product code (bar code)

UPD united port district; Urban Planning Directorate

upd unpaid

UPF untreated polyurethane foam

UPGC University and Polytechnic Grants Committee

UPGWA United Plant Guard Workers of America

uphd uphold

uphol. upholsterer; upholstery

UPI United Press International

UPIGO *Union professionelle internationale des gynécologues et obstétriciens* (French: International Union of Professional Gynaecologists and Obstetricians)

UPIU [USA] United Paperworkers International Union

UPNI Unionist Party of Northern Ireland

UPOA Ulster Public Officers' Association

UPOW Union of Post Office Workers (became part of UCW)

UPP United Peasant Party (in Poland)

UPPP [medicine] uvulopalatopharyngoplasty

UPR [insurance] unearned premiums reserve; Union Pacific Railroad

UPS uninterruptible power supply; [trademark] United Parcel Service; United Publishers' Services

UPU Universal Postal Union (formerly GPU)

UPUP Ulster Popular Unionist Party

uPVC unplasticized polyvinyl chloride

UPW Union of Post Office Workers (became part of UCW)

UR [vehicle registration] Luton; [civil aircraft marking] Ukraine; [psychology] unconditioned reflex; [psychology] unconditioned response; uniform regulations; [theatre] up right (of stage); urban renewal

Ur. Urdu; Uruguay; Uruguayan

ur. [medicine] urine

URA Urban Regeneration Agency; [USA] Urban Renewal Administration

Uran. Uranus

urb. urban

URBM ultimate-range ballistic missile

URC United Reformed Church; [theatre] up right centre (of stage)

Urd. Urdu

URF *Union des services routiers des chemins de fer européens* (French: Union of European Railways Road Services); uterine relaxing factor

urg. urgent; urgently

URI [medicine] upper respiratory infection

URL [computing] Uniform Resource Locator (address of Internet location); Unilever Research Laboratory

urol. urologic(al); urology

URSI *Union radio scientifique internationale* (French: International Scientific Radio Union)

URT upper respiratory tract

URTI [medicine] upper respiratory tract infection

URTU United Road Transport Union

Uru. Uruguay; Uruguayan

Urupabol Uruguay, Paraguay and Bolivia (commission for international cooperation)

URW United Rubber, Cork, Linoleum and Plastic Workers of America

US [vehicle registration] Glasgow; *ufficio stampa* (Italian: press office); [medicine] ultrasonic scanning; [medicine] ultrasound scanning; [USA] Uncle Sam; [psychology] unconditioned stimulus; undersecretary; [USA] United Service; United States (of America); United States highway (as in **US66**); unsaleable

u/s unserviceable; useless

.us United States of America (in Internet address)

u.s. *ubi supra* (Latin: where (mentioned) above); *ut supra* (Latin: as above)

USA United States Army; United States of America; [international vehicle registration] United States of America; United Synagogue of America

USA/ABF United States of America Amateur Boxing Federation

USAC United States Air Corps; United States Auto Club

USAEC United States Atomic Energy Commission

USAF United States Air Force

USAFA United States Air Force Academy

USAFC United States Army Forces Command

USAFE United States Air Forces in Europe

USAFI United States Armed Forces Institute

USAFR United States Air Force Reserve

USAID United States Agency for International Development

USAMC United States Army Materiel Command

USAMedS United States Army Medical Service

USAR United States Army Reserve

USASA United States Army Security Agency

USASigC United States Army Signal Corps

USASMC United States Army Supply and Maintenance Command

USAT United States Army Transport

USATDC United States Army Training and Doctrine Command

USATEC United States Army Test and Evaluation Command

USAWC United States Army Weapons Command

USB [computing] universal serial bus

USBC United States Bureau of the Census

USBM United States Bureau of Mines

USC Ulster Special Constabulary; United Services Club; United Somali Congress; United States Code; United States Congress; United States of Colombia; University of South Carolina; University of Southern California

USCA United States Code Annotated

USCC United States Circuit Court

USCCA United States Circuit Court of Appeals

USCG United States Coast Guard

USCGA United States Coast Guard Academy

USCGC United States Coast Guard Cutter

USCGR United States Coast Guard Reserve

USCGS United States Coast and Geodetic Survey

USCL United Society for Christian Literature

USCRC United States Citizens Radio Council

USCSC United States Civil Service Commission

USD US dollars

USDA United States Department of Agriculture

USDAW Union of Shop, Distributive and Allied Workers

USDOE United States Department of Energy

USEA United States Energy Association

U/sec. Undersecretary

USECC United States Employees' Compensation Commission

USES United States Employment Service

USF United States Forces

usf. *und so fort* (German: and so on, etc.)

USFL United States Football League

USG United States Government; United States Standard Gauge

USGA United States Golf Association

USgal United States gallon

USGPO United States Government Printing Office

USGS United States Geological Survey

Ush [currency] Uganda shilling

USHA United States Housing Authority

USI United Schools International; United Service Institution; United States Industries

USIA United States Information Agency

USIS United States Information Service

USITC United States International Trade Commission

USL United States Legation; United States Lines

USLTA United States Lawn Tennis Association

USM ultrasonic machining; underwater-to-surface missile; United States Mail; United States Marines; United States Mint; [stock exchange] unlisted securities market

USMA United States Military Academy

USMC United States Marine Corps; United States Maritime Commission

USMH United States Marine Hospital

USMS United States Maritime Service

USN United States Navy

USNA United States National Army; United States Naval Academy
USNC United States National Committee
USNG United States National Guard
USNI United States Naval Institute
USNO United States Naval Observatory
USNR United States Naval Reserve
USNRC United States Nuclear Regulatory Commission
USNS United States Navy Ship
USO [USA] United Service Organization
US of A [informal] United States of America
USP unbleached sulphite pulp (for papermaking); [advertising] unique selling proposition (distinctive feature of product); United States Patent; United States Pharmacopeia
USPat. United States Patent
USPC Ulster Society for the Preservation of the Countryside
USPCA Ulster Society for the Prevention of Cruelty to Animals
USPG United Society for the Propagation of the Gospel
USPHS United States Public Health Service
USPO United States Post Office
USPS United States Postal Service
USR United States Reserves; Universities' Statistical Record
USRA [USA] Universities Space Research Association
USRC United States Reserve Corps
USS [medicine] ultrasound scanning; Undersecretary of State; *Union Syndicale Suisse* (French: Swiss Federation of Trade Unions); United States Senate; United States Service; United States Ship; United States Steamer; United States Steamship; Universities Superannuation Scheme
USSAF United States Strategic Air Force
USSB United States Shipping Board
USSC United States Supreme Court
USSCt United States Supreme Court
USSR Union of Soviet Socialist Republics
USSS United States Steamship
UST undersea technology
USTA United States Tennis Association; United States Trademark Association
USTC United States Tariff Commission
USTS United States Travel Service

usu. usual; usually
USV United States Volunteers
USVA United States Volleyball Association
USVB United States Veterans' Bureau
USVI United States Virgin Islands
USW [radio] ultrashort wave; ultrasonic waves; underwater sea warfare
usw. *und so weiter* (German: and so forth, etc.)
USWA United Steelworkers of America
USWB United States Weather Bureau
USWI United States West Indies; urban solid-waste incinerator
UT [vehicle registration] Leicester; ultra-sonic testing; ultrasonic transducer; [India] Union Territory; unit trust; Universal Time (= GMT); University of Texas (at Austin); [medicine] urinary tract; [US postcode] Utah
U/T under trust
Ut. Utah
ut. untrained; utility
u.t. universal trainer; user test
UTA Ulster Transport Authority; *Union de Transports Aériens* (French airline company); Unit Trust Association
UTC Universal Time Coordinated; University Training Corps
Utd United
UTDA Ulster Tourist Development Association
ut dict. [medicine] *ut dictum* (Latin: as directed) (in prescriptions)
utend. [medicine] *utendus* (Latin: to be used)
UTI [medicine] urinary-tract infection
util. utility room (in property adver-tisement)
ut inf. *ut infra* (Latin: as below)
UTK University of Tennessee, Knoxville
UTP [computing] unshielded twisted pair
UTS ultimate tensile strength
ut sup. *ut supra* (Latin: as above)
UTU Ulster Teachers' Union; [USA] United Transportation Union
UTW Union of Textile Workers
UTWA United Textile Workers of America
UU [vehicle registration] central London; Ulster Unionist
u.U *unter Umständen* (German: circum-stances permitting)

UUA [USA] Unitarian Universalist Association

UUCP [computing] UNIX-to-UNIX copy

UUM underwater-to-underwater missile

UUP Ulster Unionist Party

UUUC United Ulster Unionist Coalition; United Ulster Unionist Council

UUUP United Ulster Unionist Party

u.u.V *unter üblichem Vorbehalt* (German: errors and omissions excepted)

UV [vehicle registration] central London; ultraviolet

UVA ultraviolet radiation of wavelength 320–380 nanometres

UVAS ultraviolet astronomical satellite

uvaser ultraviolet amplification by stimulated emission of radiation

UVB ultraviolet radiation of wavelength 280–320 nanometres

UVF Ulster Volunteer Force

UVL ultraviolet light

UVR ultraviolet radiation

UW [vehicle registration] central London; underwater; University of Washington; unladen weight

U/W [law] under will; underwriter

u/w underwater; unladen weight

UWA University of Western Australia

UWC Ulster Workers' Council

UWCE Underwater Weapons and Counter-measures Establishment

UWI University of the West Indies

UWIST University of Wales Institute of Science and Technology

UWT Union of Women Teachers (became part of NAS/UWT)

UWUA Utility Workers Union of America

UWUSA United Workers' Union of South Africa

UX [vehicle registration] Shrewsbury

ux. *uxor* (Latin: wife)

UXB unexploded bomb

UY Universal Youth; [vehicle registration] Worcester

.uy Uruguay (in Internet address)

UZ [vehicle registration] Belfast; University of Zürich

Uz. Uzbek; Uzbekistan

.uz Uzbekistan (in Internet address)

V

V [Roman numeral] five; Valiant (aircraft) (as in **V bomber**); [chemical element] vanadium; [immunology] variable region (of immunoglobulin chain); [international vehicle registration] Vatican City State; [currency] vatu (used in Vanuatu); Venerable; *Vergeltungswaffe* (German: reprisal weapon, as in **V-1**, **V-2**); version; Very (in titles); very; vespers; *Via* (Italian: Street); Vicar; Vice (in titles); Victor (aircraft) (as in **V bomber**); victory (as in **V-sign**); Viscount; Viscountess; volt; [music] *volti* (Italian: turn over); voltmeter; Volunteer(s); Vulcan (aircraft) (as in **V bomber**)

V electric potential; [physics] luminous efficiency; [physics] potential difference; [physics] potential energy; volume (capacity)

v [Roman numeral] five; variable absorption (in spectroscopy); [meteorology] (abnormally good) visibility; [physics] (instantaneous) voltage

v [physics] instantaneous potential difference; [chemistry] specific volume; [physics] velocity; *versus* (Latin: against); [chemistry] vibrational quantum number

v. vacuum; vagrant; vale; valley; valve; vein; *vel* (Latin: or); ventilator; ventral; [grammar] verb; verbal; verse; version; [printing] verso (left-hand page); versus; vertical; very; via; vicar; vicarage; *vice* (Latin: in place of); victory; *vide* (Latin: see); village; violin; virus; visibility; [medicine] vision; [grammar] vocative; [music] *voce* (Italian: voice); [music] voice; volcano; volume; *von* (German: of) (in names); *votre* (French: your); vowel

V-1 *Vergeltungswaffe 1* (German: reprisal weapon 1) (World War II flying bomb)

V¹ [music] *violino primo* (Italian: first violin)

V2 [civil aircraft marking] Antigua

V-2 *Vergeltungswaffe 2* (German: reprisal weapon 2) (World War II ballistic missile)

V² [music] *violino secondo* (Italian: second violin)

V3 [civil aircraft marking] Belize

V5 [civil aircraft marking] Namibia

V6 car engine with six cylinders arranged in V-shape

V8 [civil aircraft marking] Brunei; car engine with eight cylinders arranged in V-shape

5V [civil aircraft marking] Togo

6V [civil aircraft marking] Senegal

9V [civil aircraft marking] Singapore

VA [vehicle registration] Peterborough; value-added; [commerce] value analysis; [medicine] ventricular arrhythmia; [USA] Veterans' Administration; Vicar Apostolic; Vice-Admiral; (Order of) Victoria and Albert; [US postcode] Virginia; [medicine] visual acuity; Voice of America; Volunteer Artillery; Volunteers of America; *Vostra Altezza* (Italian: Your Highness); *Votre Altesse* (French: Your Highness); *Vuestra Alteza* (Spanish: Your Highness)

V/A voucher attached

Va Virginia (US state)

va [music] viola

.va Vatican City State (in Internet address)

v.a. [commerce] value analysis; [grammar] verb active; [grammar] verbal adjective

VAB [astronautics] vehicle assembly building (of NASA)

VABF Variety Artists' Benevolent Fund

VABM [surveying] vertical angle benchmark

VAC vector analogue computer

vac [short form] vacation

vac. vacancy; vacant; vacation; vacuum

vacc. vaccination; vaccine

VAD Voluntary Aid Detachment

VADAS [medicine] voice-activated domestic appliance system

V-Adm Vice-Admiral

VAF Variety Artists' Federation

VAFC [computing] VESA advanced feature connector

vag. vagabond; vagina; vaginal; vagrancy; vagrant

VAH [USA] Veterans' Administration Hospital

val. valley; valuable; valuation; value; valued

valid. validate; validation

valn valuation

Valpo Valparaiso

vamp. vampire

VAN [computing] value-added network

van [short form] advantage (in tennis); [short form] vanguard

van. vanilla

Vanc. Vancouver

V&A Victoria and Albert Museum

V&L vodka and lime

V&M Virgin and Martyr

V&T vodka and tonic

V&V [computing] verification and validation

VANS [computing] value-added network service

VAPI [aeronautics] visual approach path indicator

vapor. vaporization

VAR [computing] value-added reseller; visual aural range; Volunteer Air Reserve; *Votre Altesse Royale* (French: Your Royal Highness)

var. variable; variant; variation; [botany] variety; variometer; various

VARIG *Viação Aérea Rio Grandense* (Portuguese: Brazilian airline company)

var. lect. *varia lectio* (Latin: variant reading)

varn. varnish

VAS [medicine] ventricular-atrial shunt

vas. vasectomy

VASARI [computing] Visual Art System for Archiving and Retrieval of Images

vasc. vascular

Vascar visual average speed computer and recorder

VASI [aeronautics] visual approach slope indicator

VASP *Viação Aérea São Paulo* (Portuguese: Brazilian airline company)

VAT value-added tax

Vat. Vatican

VATE versatile automatic test equipment

Vat. Lib. Vatican Library

vaud. vaudeville

v. aux. [grammar] auxiliary verb

VAV variable air volume (in air-conditioning system)

VAWT vertical-axis wind turbine

VAX [trademark, computing] virtual address extension (range of computers)

VB [vehicle registration] Maidstone; [chemistry] valence bond; volunteer battalion

vb [grammar] verb

vb. verbal

v.b. vehicle borne; vertical bomb

VBI [medicine] vertebrobasilar insufficiency

vbl verbal

V bomber Valiant bomber; Victor bomber; Vulcan bomber

VBR [computing] variable bit rate

VBRA Vehicle Builders and Repairers Association Limited

VC [vehicle registration] Coventry; [engineering] vapour compression; Vatican City; [cycling] velo club; [finance] venture capital; [USA] Veterinary Corps; Vice-Chairman; Vice-Chamberlain; Vice-Chancellor; Vice-Consul; Vickers Commercial (aircraft) (as in **VC10**); Victoria Cross; Viet Cong; [chemistry] vinyl chloride; [physiology] vital capacity

vc. (violon)cello

.vc St Vincent and the Grenadines (in Internet address)

v.c. valuation clause; vehicular communication; visual communication

VCA [chemistry] vinyl carbonate; [medicine] viral capsid antigen; [USA] Volunteer Civic Association

VCAS Vice-Chief of Air Staff

VCC Veteran Car Club of Great Britain; Vice-Chancellors' Committee

VCCS [electronics] voltage-controlled current source

VCDS Vice-Chief of the Defence Staff

VCE variable-cycle engine

Vce Venice

VCG vertical centre of gravity; Vice-Consul-General

VCGS Vice-Chief of the General Staff

VCH *Victoria County History* (reference book)

v.Chr. *vor Christus* (German: before Christ, BC)

VCI volatile corrosion inhibitor

vcl. (violon)cello; vehicle

VCM vinyl chloride monomer (plastic)

vcm vacuum

VCNS Vice-Chief of Naval Staff

vcnty vicinity

VCO [India] Viceroy's Commissioned Officer; voltage-controlled oscillator; voluntary county organizer (in Women's Institute)

VCPI [computing] virtual control program interface

VCR video cassette recorder; visual control room (at airfield)

Vcr Vancouver

vcs voices

VCT venture capital trust

V Cz Vera Cruz (Mexico)

VD [medicine] vascular dementia; venereal disease; Victorian Decoration; Volunteer Decoration

vd void

v.d. vapour density; various dates

V-Day Victory Day

VDC Volunteer Defence Corps

Vdc volts direct current

VDF [computing] voice data fax

VDH [medicine] valvular disease of the heart

VDI [computing] virtual device interface

VDJ video disc jockey

VDM *Verbi Dei Minister* (Latin: Minister of the Word of God); [computing] Vienna Development Method (notation)

VDQS *vin délimité de qualité supérieure* (French: superior-quality wine)

VDR variable-diameter rotor; video-disc recording

VDRL Venereal Disease Research Laboratory (test)

VDS variable-depth sonar

VDT [computing] visual display terminal; [computing] visual display unit

VDW [chemistry] van der Waals (as in **VDW force**)

VE [vehicle registration] Peterborough; [medicine] vaginal examination; [chemistry] valence electron; valve engineering; Victory in Europe (as in **VE Day**); vocational education; *Vostra Eccellenza* (Italian: Your Excellency); *Votre Éminence* (French: Your Eminence); *Vuestra Excelencia* (Spanish: Your Excellency)

ve. *veuve* (French: widow)

.ve Venezuela (in Internet address)

VEB *Volkseigener Betrieb* (German: People's Concern) (state-owned company in former East Germany)

vec. vector

ved. *vedova* (Italian: widow)

VE Day Victory in Europe Day (8 May 1945)

veg [short form] vegetable(s)

veg. vegetable; vegetarian; vegetation

veh. vehicle; vehicular

Vel [astronomy] Vela

vel. vellum; velocity; velvet

Ven. Venerable; Venetian; Venezuela; Venezuelan; Venice

ven. *vendredi* (French: Friday); veneer; *venerdi* (Italian: Friday); venereal; venery; venison; venom; venomous; ventral; ventricle

Venet. Venetian

Venez. Venezuela; Venezuelan

vent. ventilate; ventilation; ventriloquist

Ver. [commerce] *Verein* (German: association, company)

ver. verification; verify; vermilion; verse; version

VERA versatile reactor assembly; vision electronic recording apparatus

verb. *verbessert* (German: improved, revised)

verb. et lit. [law] *verbatim et literatim* (Latin: word for word and letter for letter)

verb. sap. *verbum sapienti* (*sat est*) (Latin: a word (is enough) to the wise)

verb. sat *verbum sapienti sat est* (Latin: a word is enough to the wise)

Verf. *Verfasser* (German: author)

Verl. *Verlag* (German: publisher)

verm. vermiculite; vermilion

vern. vernacular

vers [mathematics] versed sine; [mathematics] versine

vers. version

vert. vertebra; vertebral; vertical; vertigo

VES Voluntary Euthanasia Society

ves. [medicine] *vesica* (Latin: bladder); [medicine] *vesicula* (Latin: blister); [medicine] *vespere* (Latin: in the evening) (in prescriptions); vessel; vestry

VESA Video Electronics Standards Association

vesp. [medicine] *vespere* (Latin: in the evening) (in prescriptions)

VESPER Voluntary Enterprises and Services and Part-time Employment for the Retired

vet [US short form] veteran; [short form] veterinary surgeon

vet. veteran; veterinarian; veterinary

Vet. Admin. [USA] Veterans' Administration

veter. veteran; veterinarian; veterinary

VetMB Bachelor of Veterinary Medicine

vet. sci. veterinary science

vet. surg. veterinary surgeon; veterinary surgery

VF [vehicle registration] Norwich; [medicine] ventricular fibrillation; [Roman Catholic Church] Vicar Forane; video frequency; [telecommunications] voice frequency

v.f. very fair; very fine

VFA [Australia] Victorian Football Association; [chemistry] volatile fatty acid

Vfat [computing] virtual file allocation table

VFD [computing] vacuum fluorescent display; verified free distribution; [USA] volunteer fire department

VFL [Australia] Victorian Football League

VFM value for money; variable-frequency oscillator

VFOAR [US air force] Vandenberg Field Office of Aerospace Research

VFR [aeronautics] visual flight rules

VFT [Australia] very fast train

VFU [computing] vertical format unit

VFW [USA] Veterans of Foreign Wars

vfy verify

VG [vehicle registration] Norwich; *vaisseau de guerre* (French: warship); very good; Vicar-General; [Freemasonry] Vice Grand; *Votre Grâce* (French: Your Grace); *Votre Grandeur* (French: Your Highness)

Vg. [ecclesiastical] Virgin

.vg Virgin Islands (British) (in Internet address)

v.g. *verbi gratia* (Latin: for example); *verbi gracia* (Spanish: for example); very good

VGA [computing] video graphics adapter; [computing] video graphics array

v.g.c. very good condition (in advertisement)

VGH very good health

VGL very good-looking (in personal advertisement)

vgl. *vergleiche* (German: compare)

VGPI [aeronautics] visual glide path indicator (in World War II)

VGSOH very good sense of humour (in personal advertisement)

VH [civil aircraft marking] Australia; [vehicle registration] Huddersfield; *Votre Hautesse* (French: Your Highness)

v.h. vertical height; very high

v.h.b. very heavy bombardment

VHC very highly commended

VHD [computing] very high density; video high density (system)

VHE very high energy

VHF very high fidelity (in sound recording); [radio] very high frequency

VHLW vitrified high-level (radioactive) waste

VHN [engineering] Vickers hardness number

VHO very high output

VHP [India] Vishwa Hindu Parishad (militant group)

VHS [trademark] Video Home System

VHT very high temperature

VHV very high vacuum

VI Vancouver Island; [cartography] vertical interval; Virgin Islands; virgo intacta; viscosity index; volume indicator

.vi Virgin Islands (US) (in Internet address)

v.i. [grammar] verb intransitive; *vide infra* (Latin: see below)

VIA [computing] versatile interface adapter; Visually Impaired Association

viad. viaduct

VIASA *Venezolana Internacional de Aviación, Sociedad Anónima* (Spanish: Venezuelan International Airways Limited)

VIB vertical integration building

vib. [music] vibraphone; vibrate; vibration

VIC Victoria Institute of Colleges

Vic. Vicar; Victoria; Victorian

vic. vicar; vicarage; vicinity; victory

Vict. Victorian

VID [computing] virtual image display

vid. *vide* (Latin: see); [law] *vidua* (Latin: widow)

Vien. Vienna; Viennese

vier. *viernes* (Spanish: Friday)

VIF variable import fee

vig. vignette

vign. vignette

vil. village

vill. village

v. imp. [grammar] verb impersonal

v. imper. [grammar] verb imperative

VIN [USA] vehicle identification number

vin. vinegar

vind. vindicate; vindication

vini. viniculture

VIO Veterinary Investigation Officer

VIP [medicine] vasoactive intestinal peptide; very important person

VIR *Victoria Imperatrix Regina* (Latin: Victoria Empress and Queen)

Vir [astronomy] Virgo

Vir. Virgil (Roman poet)

vir. *viridis* (Latin: green)

Virg. Virgil (Roman poet); Virginia (USA)

v. irr. [grammar] verb irregular

Vis. Viscount; Viscountess

vis. viscosity; visibility; visible; visiting; visual

Visc. Viscount; Viscountess

visc. viscosity

Visct Viscount; Viscountess

VISS VHS index search system

VISTA Volunteers in Service to America

vit. vital; vitamin; vitreous

VITA Volunteers for International Technical Assistance

viti. viticulture

vitr. *vitreum* (Latin: glass)

vit. stat. vital statistics

viv. [music] *vivace* (Italian: lively, animated)

vivi. vivisection

vix. *vixit* (Latin: (he/she) lived)

viz *videlicet* (Latin: namely)

VJ [vehicle registration] Gloucester; [Australia] Vaucluse Junior (yacht); Victory over Japan (as in **VJ Day**); video jockey

v.J *vorigen Jahres* (German: last year)

VJ Day Victory over Japan Day (15 August 1945)

VK [vehicle registration] Newcastle upon Tyne

v.k. vertical keel

VL [vehicle registration] Lincoln; Vulgar Latin

vl. violin

v.l. *varia lectio* (Latin: variant reading)

VLA [astronomy] Very Large Array (of radio telescopes in New Mexico)

vla [music] viola

Vlad. Vladivostok

VLB vertical-lift bridge; [computing] VESA local bus

VLBA [astronomy] very long baseline array

VLBC [shipping] very large bulk carrier

VLBI [astronomy] very long baseline interferometry

VL-Bus [computing] VESA local bus

VLBW [medicine] very low birth weight

VLCC [shipping] very large crude carrier

VLCD very low calorie diet

VLDB [computing] very large database

VLDL [biochemistry] very low-density lipoprotein

VLE [chemistry] vapour–liquid equilibrium

vle [music] violone (double-bass viol)

VLF [radio] very low frequency

VLFMF very low-frequency magnetic field

VLIW [computing] very long instruction word

VLLW very low-level (radioactive) waste

vln violin

VLR very long range (aircraft); Victoria Law Reports

VLS [physics] vapour–liquid–solid

VLSI [electronics] very large-scale integration

VLT very large telescope

vltg. voltage

vlv. valve; valvular

VM [vehicle registration] Manchester; [physics] velocity modulation; Victory Medal; Viet Minh; Virgin Mary; [computing] virtual machine; [computing] virtual memory; [chemistry] volatile matter; *Votre Majesté* (French: Your Majesty)

v.M *vorigen Monats* (German: of last month)

VMC [computing] VESA medium channel; [aeronautics] visual meteorological conditions

VMCCA Veteran Motor Car Club of America

VM/CMS [trademark, computing] virtual machine, conversational monitor system

VMD Doctor of Veterinary Medicine (from Latin *Veterinariae Medicinae Doctor*)

VME [trademark, computing] Versa Module Eurocard (bus)

VMH Victoria Medal of Honour (Royal Horticultural Society award)

VMO [astronomy] very massive object

VMS vertical marketing system; [computing] virtual machine system; Voluntary Medical Services

v.m.t. very many thanks

VN [vehicle registration] Middlesbrough; Vietnam; [international vehicle registration] Vietnam; Vietnamese

vn violin

.vn Vietnam (in Internet address)

Vna Vienna

VNM [Canada] Victoria National Museum

VNTR [genetics] variable number tandem repeat

VO [vehicle registration] Nottingham; valuation officer; verbal order; very old (brandy etc.); veterinary officer; (Royal) Victorian Order; voice-over

vo. [printing] verso (left-hand page)

VOA Voice of America; Volunteers of America

VOC Vehicle Observer Corps; volatile organic chemical; volatile organic compound

voc. vocal; vocalist; vocation; vocational; [grammar] vocative

vocab. vocabulary

VOCAL Voluntary Organizations Communication and Language

vocat. [grammar] vocative

voc. ed. vocational education

voctl vocational

VOD velocity of detonation

VODAT voice-operated device for automatic transmission

VOH Vehicle on Hire (certificate)

Vol [astronomy] Volans

Vol. volume (of book); Volunteer

vol. volatile; volcanic; volcano; volume; voluntary; volunteer

volc. volcanic; volcano

Vols volumes

vols volumes

volum. volumetric

voly voluntary

VONA vehicle of the new age (rapid shuttle)

VOP very oldest procurable (brandy etc.)

VOR [navigation] very-high-frequency omnidirectional radio range

vorm. *vormals* (German: formerly); *vormittags* (German: in the morning, a.m.)

Vors. *Vorsitzender* (German: chairman)

vou. voucher

vox pop [short form] *vox populi* (Latin: voice of the people)

VP [vehicle registration] Birmingham; [civil aircraft marking] British Colonies and Protectorates; [physics, chemistry] vapour phase; [building] vent pipe; [grammar] verb phrase; Vice-President; Vice-Principal; victory points; *vita patris* (Latin: during the life of her/his father)

v.p. [photography] vanishing point; vapour pressure; variable pitch; [grammar] verb passive

VPC *vente par correspondence* (French: mail order)

vpd vehicles per day

vph vehicles per hour

v.ph. vertical photography

VPL visible panty line

vpm vehicles per mile

VPO Vienna Philharmonic Orchestra

Vpo Valparaiso

VPop [computing] virtual point of presence

VPP [India] value payable post; [veterinary science] virus pneumonia of pigs; Volunteer Political Party

VPRGS Vice-President of the Royal Geographical Society

VPRP Vice-President of the Royal Society of Portrait Painters

VPRS Vice-President of the Royal Society

vps vibrations per second

VPZS Vice-President of the Zoological Society

VQ [civil aircraft marking] British Colonies and Protectorates

VQMG Vice-Quartermaster-General

VR [civil aircraft marking] British Colonies and Protectorates; [vehicle registration] Manchester; variant reading; [physics] velocity ratio; [medicine] ventricular reflux; Vicar Rural; *Victoria Regina* (Latin: Queen Victoria); [computing] virtual reality; voltage regulator; Volunteer Reserve; vulcanized rubber

v.r. variant reading; *vedi retro* (Italian: please turn over, PTO); [grammar] verb reflexive

VRA [USA] Vocational Rehabilitation Administration

VRAM [computing] video random-access memory

VRB [meteorology] variable

VRC Vehicle Research Corporation; Volunteer Rifle Corps

VRD Royal Naval Volunteer Reserve Officers' Decoration

v. refl. [grammar] verb reflexive

V Rev. Very Reverend

VRG [biochemistry] vaccinia rabies glycoprotein

vrg [meteorology] veering

VRI *Victoria Regina et Imperatrix* (Latin: Victoria Queen and Empress); [medicine] viral respiratory infection; [aeronautics] visual rule instrument (landing)

VRM [USA] variable-rate mortgage

VRN [finance] variable-rate note

VRO vehicle registration office

Vry Viceroy

VS [vehicle registration] Luton; [Freemasonry] Venerable Sage; veterinary surgeon; *vieux style* (French: Old Style) (in dates); [chemistry] volatile solid; [music] *volti subito* (Italian: turn over quickly); *Vostra Santità* (Italian: Your Holiness); *Votre Sainteté* (French: Your Holiness)

vs. versus

v.s. variable speed; *vide supra* (Latin: see above); [music] *volti subito* (Italian: turn over quickly)

VSAM [computing] virtual storage access method

VSB [telecommunications] vestigial sideband

vsby visibility

VSC Volunteer Staff Corps

VSCC Vintage Sports Car Club

VSD vendor's shipping document; [medicine] ventricular septal defect

VSI [navigation] vertical speed indicator

VSL Venture Scout leader

VSM [telecommunications] vestigial sideband modulation

vsn vision

VSO [linguistics] verb-subject-object (as in **VSO language**); [computing] very small outline; very superior old (brandy etc.); Vienna State Opera; Voluntary Service Overseas

VSOP very special old pale (brandy etc.); very superior old pale (brandy etc.)

VSQ very special quality

VSR very short range; very special reserve (wine)

VSS [medicine] vital signs stable

vst violinist

VSTOL [aeronautics] vertical and short take-off and landing

VSUK Vegetarian Society of the United Kingdom Limited

VSV [medicine] vesicular stomatitis virus

VSW vitrified stoneware

VSWR [telecommunications] voltage standing-wave ratio

VT [civil aircraft marking] India; [vehicle registration] Stoke-on-Trent; variable time; [currency] vatu (used in Vanuatu); [medicine] ventricular tachycardia; [US postcode] Vermont

Vt Vermont

v.t. vacuum technology; variable transmission; [grammar] verb transitive

VTC Volunteer Training Corps; voting trust certificate

VTE [psychology] vicarious trial and error

Vte *Vicomte* (French: Viscount)

Vtesse *Vicomtesse* (French: Viscountess)

VTFL [computing] variable-to-fixed length (code)

vtg voting

VTL [computing] variable threshold logic

VTMoV [microbiology] velvet tobacco mottle virus

VTO [aeronautics] vertical take-off

VTOHL [aeronautics] vertical take-off, horizontal landing

VTOL [aeronautics] vertical take-off and landing

VTOVL [aeronautics] vertical take-off, vertical landing

VTR videotape recorder; videotape recording

VTVL [computing] variable-to-variable length (code)

VU [vehicle registration] Manchester; [medicine] varicose ulcer; [acoustics] volume unit

.vu Vanuatu (in Internet address)

Vul [astronomy] Vulpecula

Vul. Vulgate

Vulg. Vulgate

vulg. vulgar; vulgarly

VV [vehicle registration] Northampton

vv. verbs; verses; [music] (first and second) violins; [music] voices; volumes

v.v. vice versa; viva voce

VVD *Volkspartij voor Vrijheid en Democratie* (Dutch: People's Party for Freedom and Democracy)

vve *veuve* (French: widow)

vv.ll. *variae lectiones* (Latin: variant readings)

VV.MM. *Vos Majestés* (French: Your Majesties)

VVO very very old (brandy etc.)

VW [vehicle registration] Chelmsford; [computing] van Wijngaarden (grammar); Very Worshipful; *Volkswagen* (German vehicle manufacturer)

VWH Vale of the White Horse

VX [vehicle registration] Chelmsford

vx vertex

VY [vehicle registration] Leeds

vy very

v.y. [bibliography] various years

VYAH very young at heart (in personal advertisement)

VZ [vehicle registration] Tyrone

VZIG [immunology] varicella zoster hyperimmune globulin

W

W [genetics] sex chromosome of birds and insects; [chemical element] tungsten (from former name wolfram); Wales; Warden; [fishing port] Waterford; watt; Wednesday; Welsh; Wesleyan; west; western; [UK postcode] west London; white; wide; widow; widowed; widower; width; [shipping] winter (load line);

women; women's (clothing size); [currency] won (used in Korea)

W [engineering] load; [physics] weight; [physics] work

w [meteorology] dew

w [chemistry] mass fraction

w. waist; wall; war; warm; waste; water; weather; week; weight; wet; white; [cricket] wicket; [cricket] wide; width; wife; win; wind; wire; with; woman; won; wooden; word; work; wrong

5W [civil aircraft marking] Samoa

6W [civil aircraft marking] Senegal

WA [vehicle registration] Sheffield; [UK postcode] Warrington; [US postcode] Washington; [USA] Welfare Administration; West Africa; West African; Western Australia; Westminster Abbey; [fishing port] Whitehaven; [netball] wing attack; [insurance] with average; [US banking] withholding agent; Woodworkers of America

w.a. with answers

WAA Women's Auxiliary Association

WAAA Women's Amateur Athletic Association

WAAAF Women's Auxiliary Australian Air Force

WAAC Women's Army Auxiliary Corps

WAAE World Association for Adult Education

WAAF Women's Auxiliary Air Force; Women's Auxiliary Australian Air Force

WAAS Women's Auxiliary Army Service; World Academy of Art and Science

WAC [USA] Women's Army Corps (in World War II); World Aeronautical Chart

WACB World Association for Christian Broadcasting

WACC [accounting] weighted average cost of capital; World Association for Christian Communications

WACCC Worldwide Air Cargo Commodity Classification

WACSM [USA] Women's Army Corps Service Medal

WADEX word and author index

WADF [USA] Western Air Defense

WADS wide-area data service

w.a.e. when actually employed

WAF West African Forces; [USA] Women in the Air Force

w.a.f. with all faults

WAFC West African Fisheries Commission

W Afr. West Africa; West African

WAFS [USA] Women's Auxiliary Ferrying Squadron; Women's Auxiliary Fire Service

WAG [international vehicle registration] (West Africa) Gambia; Writers' Action Group; Writers' and Artists' Guild

WAGBI Wildfowl Association of Great Britain and Ireland

WAGGGS World Association of Girl Guides and Girl Scouts

WAIF World Adoption International Fund

WAIS [psychology] Wechsler Adult Intelligence Scale; [computing] wide-area information service

WAL [international vehicle registration] (West Africa) Sierra Leone

Wal. Walloon

WAM wife and mother; work analysis and measurement; [USA] wrap-around mortgage

WAN [computing] wide-area network

w&i weighing and inspection

W&L [USA] Washington and Lee University

W&M William and Mary (joint sovereigns of England)

W&S whisky and soda

w&t wear and tear

WANS Women's Australian National Service

WAOS Welsh Agricultural Organization Society

WAP work assignment plan; work assignment procedure

WAPC Women's Auxiliary Police Corps

WAPOR World Association for Public Opinion Research

WAR West Africa Regiment

War. Warsaw; Warwick(shire)

war. warrant

WARC [USA] Western Air Rescue Center; World Administrative Radio Conference; World Alliance of Reformed Churches

WARI [Australia] Waite Agricultural Research Institute

Warks Warwickshire

warn. warning

warr. warranty

warrty warranty

WASA Welsh Amateur Swimming Association

Wash. Washington

WASP [USA] White Anglo-Saxon Protestant; [USA] Women Airforce Service Pilots

WAST Western Australia Standard Time

WAT [aeronautics] weight, altitude, temperature; [psychology] word association test

Wat. Waterford

WATA World Association of Travel Agencies

WATFOR [computing] University of Waterloo Fortran

WATS [USA] Wide Area Telephone Service

W Aus. Western Australia

W Aust. Western Australia

WAV [computing] waveform

WAVES [US navy] Women Accepted for Volunteer Emergency Service

WAWF World Association of World Federalists

WAY World Assembly of Youth

WAYC Welsh Association of Youth Clubs

WB [vehicle registration] Sheffield; warehouse book; Warner Brothers (film studio); water board; [telecommunications] waveband; [commerce] waybill; weather bureau; [psychology] Wechsler–Bellevue (Intelligence Scale); [insurance] weekly benefits; World Bank

W/B warehouse book; [telecommunications] waveband; [commerce] waybill

Wb weber (unit of magnetic flux)

w.b. wage board; waste ballast; water ballast; [commerce] waybill; wheel base; [knitting] wool back

WBA West Bromwich Albion (football club); whole-body activity; World Boxing Association

WBAFC [USA] Weather Bureau Area Forecast Center

WBAN [USA] Weather Bureau, Air Force and Navy

WBC [medicine] white blood cell; [medicine] white blood (cell) count; World Boxing Council

WBF World Bridge Federation

WBGT [meteorology] wet-bulb globe temperature; [meteorology] wet-bulb globe thermometer

WBI [medicine] whole-body irradiation

w.b.i. will be issued

WbN west by north

WBR [medicine] whole-body radiation

WBS [medicine] whole-body scan; [physics] wide-band spectrometer; [physics] wide-band spectrum

WbS west by south

w.b.s. [engineering] walking-beam suspension; [insurance] without benefit of salvage

WBT [meteorology] wet-bulb temperature

WC [vehicle registration] Chelmsford; walking club; war cabinet; war council; water closet (= toilet); Wesleyan chapel; [UK postcode] west central London; [military] Western Command; working capital; [computing] world coordinates

W/C Wing Commander

w.c. watch committee; water closet (= toilet); water cock; wheelchair; without charge

WCA Wholesale Confectioners' Alliance; Wildlife and Countryside Act; Women's Christian Association

w.c.a. worst-case analysis

WCAT Welsh College of Advanced Technology

WCC War Crimes Commission; World Council of Churches

W/Cdr Wing Commander

WCEU World Christian Endeavour Union

WCF World Congress of Faiths

WCL World Confederation of Labour

WCP World Climate Programme; World Council of Peace

WCRA [USA] Weather Control Research Association; Women's Cycle Racing Association

WCT World Championship Tennis

WCTU [USA, Canada] Women's Christian Temperance Union

WCWB World Council for the Welfare of the Blind

WD [international vehicle registration] (Windward Islands) Dominica; [vehicle registration] Dudley; War Department; [UK postcode] Watford; [fishing port] Wexford; [astronomy] white dwarf; [netball] wing defence; Works Department

wd ward; warranted; weed; wood; word; would; wound

W/D wind direction; [banking] withdrawal

w/d warranted; well developed

2WD two-wheel drive

4WD four-wheel drive

WDA Welsh Development Agency; Women's Diocesan Association; [taxation] writing-down allowance

WDC War Damage Commission; [USA] War Damage Corporation; Woman Detective Constable; World Data Centre

w.d.f. wood door and frame

wdg winding

WDM [telecommunications] wavelength division multiplex

Wdr Wardmaster

WDS Woman Detective Sergeant

wd sc. wood screw

WDSPR [meteorology] widespread

WDV [taxation] written-down value

WE [vehicle registration] Sheffield; War Establishment

w/e weekend; week ending

WEA (Royal) West of England Academy; Workers' Educational Association

wea. weapon; weather

WE&FA Welsh Engineers' and Founders' Association

WEARCON weather observation and forecasting control system

WEC wave energy converter; wind energy converter; World Energy Conference

WECOM [USA] Weapons Command

Wed. Wednesday

WEDA Wholesale Engineering Distributors' Association

Wednes. Wednesday

Weds. Wednesday

w.e.f. with effect from

WEFC World European Fisheries Conference

WEFT [aeronautics] wings, engine, fuselage, tail

Wel. Welsh

weld. welding

Well. Wellington (New Zealand)

WEN Women's Environmental Network

w/end weekend

WES Women's Engineering Society; World Economic Survey

Wes. Wesleyan

WES/PNEU Worldwide Education Service of Parents' National Educational Union

west. western

Westm. Westmeath; Westminster; Westmorland

WET Western European Time

WETUC Workers' Educational Trade Union Committee

WEU Western European Union (replacement for BTO)

Wex. Wexford

Wexf. Wexford

WF [vehicle registration] Sheffield; [UK postcode] Wakefield; [physics] wave function; [USA] Wells Fargo and Company; white female

w.f. [sports] wing forward; [knitting] wool forward; [printing] wrong font

WFA White Fish Authority; Women's Football Association; World Friendship Association

WFB World Fellowship of Buddhists

WFC World Food Council (of UN)

WFD World Federation of the Deaf

w.fd [knitting] wool forward

WFDY World Federation of Democratic Youth

WFEO World Federation of Engineering Organizations

WFF [logic] well-formed formula; World Friendship Federation

WFGA Women's Farm and Garden Association

WFL Women's Freedom League

Wfl Worshipful

WFMH World Federation for Mental Health

WFMW World Federation of Methodist Women

WFN World Federation of Neurology

WFP World Food Programme (of UN)

WFPA World Federation for the Protection of Animals

WFSW World Federation of Scientific Workers

WFTC Working Families Tax Credit

WFTU World Federation of Trade Unions (replacement for IFTU)

WFUNA World Federation of United Nations Associations

WG [international vehicle registration] (Windward Islands) Grenada; [vehicle registration] Sheffield; water gauge;

weight guaranteed; Welsh Guards; West Germanic (language group); [informal] W(illiam) G(ilbert) Grace (British cricketer); wire gauge; working group

wg weighing; wing

w.g. water gauge; weight guaranteed; wire gauge

WGA Writers' Guild of America

WGC Welwyn Garden City; World Gold Council; [Freemasonry] Worthy Grand Chaplain

Wg/Cdr Wing Commander

WGer West Germanic (language group)

WGG [Freemasonry] Worthy Grand Guardian; [Freemasonry] Worthy Grand Guide

WGGB Writers' Guild of Great Britain

WGI world geophysical interval

w. gl. wired glass

W Glam. West Glamorgan

WGM [Freemasonry] Worthy Grand Master

WGmc West Germanic (language group)

WGPMS warehouse gross performance measurement system

WGS [Freemasonry] Worthy Grand Sentinel

WGU Welsh Golfing Union

WH [vehicle registration] Manchester; water heater; [fishing port] Weymouth; [cycling] wheelers; [USA] White House; [banking] withholding

Wh watt hour

w/h [banking] withholding

wh. wharf; which; whispered; white

w.h. [sports] wing half

WHA World Health Assembly (of WHO); World Hockey Association

W'hampton Wolverhampton

w.h.b. wash-hand basin

whd warhead

WhF Whitworth Fellow

whf wharf

whfg. wharfage

whfr wharfinger

Whi. Whitehall (London)

whis. whistle

whmstr weighmaster

WHO [USA] White House Office; World Health Organization

WHOA! [USA] Wild Horse Organized Assistance

WHOI [USA] Woods Hole Oceanographic Institution

whp water horsepower

whr whether

WHRA World Health Research Centre

whs. warehouse

WhSch Whitworth Scholar

whse warehouse

whsle wholesale

whsmn warehouseman

whsng warehousing

WHT William Herschel Telescope (La Palma)

WHTSO Welsh Health Technical Services Organization

w.h.y. what have you

WI West Indian; West Indies; Windward Islands; [fishing port] Wisbech; [US postcode] Wisconsin; Women's Institute; wrought iron

w.i. [finance] when issued

WIA wounded in action

WIBC [USA] Women's International Bowling Congress

WICA Warsaw International Consumer Association

Wick. Wicklow

WID West India Docks (London)

wid. widow; widower

WIDF Women's International Democratic Federation

WIF West Indies Federation

Wig. Wigtownshire

Wigorn. *Wigorniensis* (Latin: (Bishop) of Worcester)

wilco will comply (in radio communications)

WILPF Women's International League for Peace and Freedom

Wilts Wiltshire

WIMP [physics] weakly interacting massive particle; [computing] windows, icons, menus and pointers

WIN [USA] Work Incentive

Winch. Winchester

W Ind. West Indian; West Indies

Wind. I Windward Islands

Wings [finance] warrants in negotiable government securities

Winn. Winnipeg

wint. winter

Winton. *Wintoniensis* (Latin: (Bishop) of Winchester)

WIP waste incineration plant; work in progress

WIPO World Intellectual Property Organization

WIRA Wool Industries Research Association

WIRDS weather information reporting and display system

Wis. Wisconsin

WISC [psychology] Wechsler Intelligence Scale for Children

Wisd. [Bible] Wisdom of Solomon (book of Apocrypha)

Wisd. Wisden (Cricketers' Almanack)

WISP wide-range imaging spectrometer

wit. witness

WITA Women's International Tennis Association

withdrl withdrawal

witht without

Wits. Witwatersrand

WIZO Women's International Zionist Organization

WJ [vehicle registration] Sheffield

WJC World Jewish Congress

WJEC Welsh Joint Education Committee

WK [vehicle registration] Coventry; [fishing port] Wick

Wk Walk (in road name)

wk weak; week; work; wreck

w.k. warehouse keeper; well known

wkg working

wkly weekly

WKN [meteorology] weakening

wkr walker; worker; wrecker

wks weeks; works

wks. workshop

wkt [cricket] wicket

WL [vehicle registration] Oxford; [international vehicle registration] (Windward Islands) St Lucia; wagon-lit (French: sleeping car); waiting list; water line; wavelength; West Lothian; Women's Liberation

W/L wavelength

wl wool

w.l. water line

WLA Women's Land Army

WLAN [computing] wireless local area network

WLB [USA] War Labor Board

Wld World

wld would

wldr welder

WLF Women's Liberal Federation

wl fwd [knitting] wool forward

WLGS Women's Local Government Society

WLHB Women's League of Health and Beauty

WLI workload index

WLM Women's Liberation Movement

Wln Wellington (New Zealand)

W Long. west longitude

W Loth. West Lothian

WLPSA Wild Life Preservation Society of Australia

WLR Weekly Law Reports

WLRI World Life Research Institute

WLS [statistics] weighted least squares

WLTBU Watermen, Lightermen, Tugmen and Bargemen's Union

WLTM would like to meet (in personal advertisement)

WLU World Liberal Union

WLUS World Land Use Survey

wly westerly

wlz waltz

WM [vehicle registration] Liverpool; war memorial; washing machine (in accommodation advertisement); wattmeter; well maintained (in advertisement); white male; wire mesh; [Freemasonry] Worshipful Master

W/M [shipping] weight or measurement

Wm. William

WMA Working Mothers' Association; World Medical Association

WMAA Whitney Museum of American Art

WMC [USA] War Manpower Commission (in World War II); Ways and Means Committee; working men's club; Working Men's College; World Meteorological Centre; World Methodist Council

WMCIU Working Men's Club and Institute Union Limited

WMF [trademark, computing] Windows metafile format

wmk watermark

WMM World Movement of Mothers

WMO World Meteorological Organization

WMP with much pleasure

WMS Wesleyan Missionary Society; World Magnetic Survey

WMTC Women's Mechanized Transport Corps

WN [vehicle registration] Swansea; [UK postcode] Wigan; [fishing port] Wigtown

WNA [shipping] winter North Atlantic (load line)

WNB weekly news bill

WNCCC Women's Nationwide Cancer Control Campaign Limited

w.n.d.p. with no down payment

wndw window

WNE Welsh National Eisteddfod

WNL within normal limits

WNLF Women's National Liberal Federation

WNO Welsh National Opera

WNP Welsh National Party

WNW west-northwest

WO [vehicle registration] Cardiff; walkover; War Office; Warrant Officer; welfare officer; wireless operator; [fishing port] Workington; [commerce] written order

w/o without; [accounting] written off

w.o. walkover; *wie oben* (German: as mentioned above); [commerce] written order

WOA Wharf Owners' Association

w.o.a. without answers

WOAR Women Organized Against Rape

w.o.b. washed overboard

WOC [building] waiting on cement (setting)

w.o.c. without compensation

WOCA world outside centrally planned economic areas

WOCS [building] waiting on cement setting

w.o.e. without equipment

WOF [New Zealand] Warrant of Fitness (for vehicles)

w.o.g. water, oil or gas; with other goods

w.o.l. wharf-owner's liability

WOM wireless operator mechanic

WOMAN World Organization for Mothers of All Nations

w.o.n. [knitting] wool on needle

WOO Warrant Ordnance Officer; World Oceanographic Organization

WoO *Werke ohne Opuszahl* (German: works without opus number) (works by Beethoven not listed in standard catalogue)

woopie [informal] well-off older person

w.o.p. with other property; without personnel

w.o.p.e. without personnel or equipment

WOR without our responsibility

Wor. Worshipful

WORC [USA] Washington Operations Research Council

Worcs Worcestershire

WORM [computing] write once, read many (times)

WOSAC worldwide synchronization of atomic clocks

WOSB War Office Selection Board

wotcha [informal] wonderful old thing, considering her/his age

WOW waiting on weather; War On Want; Women Against the Ordination of Women

WP Warsaw Pact; weather permitting; West Point (US military academy); Western Province (South Africa); White Paper (government report); [USA] wire payment; [law] without prejudice; [vehicle registration] Worcester; word processing; word processor; working paper; working party; working pressure; [Freemasonry] Worthy Patriarch; [Freemasonry] Worthy President

Wp. Worship; Worshipful

w.p. waste paper; waste pipe; weather permitting; [baseball] wild pitch(es); will proceed; [law] without prejudice; word processing; word processor

WPA Water Polo Association; Western Provident Association; [insurance] with particular average; [USA] Work Progress Administration; [USA] Work Projects Administration; World Parliament Association; World Pool–Billiard Association; World Presbyterian Alliance

WPB [USA] War Production Board (in World War II); wastepaper basket

w.p.b. wastepaper basket

WPBL [USA] Women's Professional Basketball League

WPBSA World Professional Billiards and Snooker Association

WPC War Pension(s) Committee; Woman Police Constable; wood–plastic composite; wood–polymer composite; World Petroleum Congress

WPCA [USA] Water Pollution Control Administration

WPCF [USA] Water Pollution Control Federation

WPE white porcelain enamel

WPFC West Pacific Fisheries Commission

Wpfl Worshipful

wpg waterproofing

WPGA Women's Professional Golfers' Association

WPHC Western Pacific High Commission

WPI wholesale price index; World Press Institute

WPL warning-point level

wpm words per minute

WPMSF World Professional Marathon Swimming Federation

wpn weapon

WPPSI [psychology] Wechsler Preschool and Primary Scale of Intelligence

WPRL Water Pollution Research Laboratory

w.p.s. with prior service

WPT Women's Playhouse Trust

WR [vehicle registration] Leeds; wardrobe; ward room; warehouse receipt; war reserve; [medicine] Wassermann reaction; [railways] Western Region; West Riding (former division of Yorkshire); *Wilhelmus Rex* (Latin: King William); [astronomy] Wolf–Rayet (stars); [UK postcode] Worcester

w.r. warehouse receipt; [insurance] war risk; water repellent

WRA [USA] War Relocation Authority; Water Research Association; [horticulture] Wisley Rose Award

WRAAC Women's Royal Australian Army Corps

WRAAF Women's Royal Australian Air Force

WRAC Women's Royal Army Corps

WRAF Women's Royal Air Force

WRAM [computing] Windows random-access memory

WRANS Women's Royal Australian Naval Service

WRAP [USA] weapons readiness analysis program

WRC Water Research Centre; [USA] Welding Research Council

WRE [Australia] Weapons Research Establishment

w. ref. with reference (to)

w. reg. with regard (to)

WRI war risks insurance; Women's Rural Institute

w.r.n. [knitting] wool round needle

WRNG [meteorology] warning

WRNR Women's Royal Naval Reserve

WRNS Women's Royal Naval Service (hence informal name Wrens)

wrnt warrant

WRO Weed Research Organization

w.r.o. [insurance] war risks only

WRP Workers' Revolutionary Party

WRRA [cycling] Women's Road Records Association

wrt wrought (iron)

w.r.t. with respect to

WRU Welsh Rugby Union; Wesleyan Reform Union; who are you?

WRVS Women's Royal Voluntary Service (formerly WVS)

WS [vehicle registration] Bristol; [international vehicle registration] (Western) Samoa; [UK postcode] Walsall; water-soluble; weapon system; West Saxon; wind speed; [Scots law] Writer to the Signet [Scotland]

.ws Samoa (in Internet address)

WSA [USA] War Shipping Administration

W Sam. Western Samoa

WSC World Series Cricket

WSCF World Student Christian Federation

WSF Wake Shield Facility; [chemistry] water-soluble fraction

w/shop workshop

WSI Writers and Scholars International

WSJ *Wall Street Journal*

WSL Warren Spring Laboratory (Stevenage, Hertfordshire)

WSM Women's Suffrage Movement

WSP water supply point

WSPU Women's Social and Political Union

WSSA Welsh Secondary Schools Association

WSTN World Service Television News

WSTV World Service Television

WSU Wichita State University

WSW west-southwest

WT [vehicle registration] Leeds; Warrant Telegraphist (in Royal Navy); war transport; watertight; weekly takings; [fishing port] Westport; wireless telegraphy; wireless telephony; withholding tax

W/T wireless telegraphy; wireless telephony

wt warrant; watertight; weight; without

WTA winner takes all; Women's Tennis Association; World Transport Agency

WTAA World Trade Alliance Association

WTAU Women's Total Abstinence Union

WTB Welsh Tourist Board

Wtb. *Wörterbuch* (German: dictionary)

WTC Wheat Trade Convention

WTD watertight door

wtd wanted; warranted; watered

Wtf. Waterford

WTG wind turbine generator

WTH whole-tree harvesting

wthr weather

WTIS World Trade Information Service

WTMH watertight manhole

WTN Worldwide Television News

WTO Warsaw Treaty Organization; World Tourism Organization; World Trade Organization (replacement for GATT)

WTP willingness to pay; willing to pay (in advertisement)

wtr water; winter; writer

WTRC Wool Textile Research Council

WTS Women's Transport Service

WTT World Team Tennis

WTTA Wholesale Tobacco Trade Association of Great Britain and Northern Ireland

WTTC World Travel and Tourism Council

WTUC World Trade Union Conference

WTUL Women's Trade Union League

WU [vehicle registration] Leeds; Western Union

WUCT World Union of Catholic Teachers

WUF World Underwater Federation

WUJS World Union of Jewish Students

WUPJ World Union for Progressive Judaism

WUS World University Service

WUSL Women's United Service League

WV [vehicle registration] Brighton; [international vehicle registration] (Windward Islands) St Vincent; water valve; [US postcode] West Virginia; [UK postcode] Wolverhampton

w/v water valve; [chemistry] weight in volume (of solution)

WVA World Veterinary Association

W Va West Virginia

WVD *Wereldverbond van Diamant Bewerkers* (Dutch: Universal Alliance of Diamond Workers)

wvd waived

WVF World Veterans' Federation

WVS Women's Voluntary Service (former name of WRVS)

WVT water vapour transfer; water vapour transmission

WVU West Virginia University

WW [vehicle registration] Leeds; wall-to-wall (in property advertisement); walnut wood (trim) (in car advertisement); warehouse warrant; warrant writer; whitewall (tyre); *Who's Who*; World War; worldwide

W/W wall-to-wall (in property advertisement); warehouse warrant

w/w weight for weight

WW1 World War One

WW2 World War Two

WWDC World War Debt Commission

WWDSHEX [shipping] weather working days, Sundays and holidays excluded

Wwe *Witwe* (German: widow)

WWF Worldwide Fund for Nature (formerly World Wildlife Fund); World Wrestling Federation

WWI World War One

WWII World War Two

WWMCCS World Wide Military Command and Control System

WWO Wing Warrant Officer

WWSSN worldwide standard seismograph network

WWSU World Water Ski Union

WWW *Who Was Who*; World Weather Watch (of WMO); [computing] World Wide Web

WWY (Queen's Own) Warwickshire and Worcestershire Yeomanry

WX [vehicle registration] Leeds; women's extra (large) (clothing size)

WY [vehicle registration] Leeds; [fishing port] Whitby; [US postcode] Wyoming

Wy Way (in road name)

Wy. (John) Wycliffe (English religious reformer); Wyoming

Wycl. (John) Wycliffe (English religious reformer)

Wyo. Wyoming

WYR West Yorkshire Regiment

wysiwyg [computing] what you see is what you get

WZ [vehicle registration] Belfast; *Weltzeit* (German: universal time)

Wz. *Warenzeichen* (German: trademark)

WZO World Zionist Organization

X

X Christ (transcription of Greek letter chi); Cross (as in **Charing X**); error; exchange; experiment; experimental; explosive; extension; extra; extraordinary; [cinema] for over-18s only (former film classification); [chemistry] halogen; kiss (on letter, card, etc.); location on map; [genetics] sex chromosome; [Roman numeral] ten; unknown person or thing; X-ray; xylonite (plastic)

X [physics] exposure dose

x cross (as in **x-section**); [commerce] ex (= from); [finance] ex (= without); extra; [meteorology] hoar-frost; [Roman numeral] ten; trans- (as in **xformer**)

x [mathematics] algebraic variable; [mathematics] (horizontal) coordinate (as in **x-axis**)

3X [civil aircraft marking] Guinea

4X [civil aircraft marking] Israel

5X [civil aircraft marking] Uganda

XA [civil aircraft marking] Mexico

xa [finance] ex all (i.e. without any benefits)

XB [civil aircraft marking] Mexico

xb [finance] ex bonus

Xber December

XBT expendable bathythermograph

xbt exhibit

XC [USA, Canada] cross-country (as in **XC skiing**); [civil aircraft marking] Mexico

xc [finance] ex capitalization; [finance] ex coupon (i.e. without interest on coupon)

x.c.l. [insurance] excess current liabilities

xcp [finance] ex coupon (i.e. without interest on coupon)

xcpt except

XCT [medicine] X-ray compute(rize)d tomography

XD [physics] X-ray diffraction

xd [finance] ex dividend

x'd crossed; executed

xdiv [finance] ex dividend

XDR extended dynamic range (of cassettes)

Xdr crusader

Xe [chemical element] xenon

Xen. Xenophon (ancient Greek historian)

xf extra fine

xfer transfer

xfmr transformer

xg crossing

XGA [computing] extended graphics array

XG Midi extended general musical instrument digital interface

xhst exhaust

xhy extra heavy

XI [vehicle registration] Belfast; [medicine] X-ray imaging

xi [finance] ex interest

xin [finance] ex interest

XL extra large (clothing size)

xlnt excellent

x.l.w.b. extra-long wheelbase

XM experimental missile

Xmas Christmas

xmit transmit

XML [computing] extensible markup language (used on Internet)

XMS [computing] extended memory specification

xmsn transmission

xmtr transmitter

Xn Christian

xn [finance] ex new (i.e. without right to new shares)

x/nt excellent

Xnty Christianity

XO cognac of superior quality; executive officer

XP Christ (transcription of Greek letters chi and rho); Christianity; express paid; [medicine] xeroderma pigmentosum

x.p. express paid

xpl. explosive

xplt exploit
xpn expansion
xq cross-question
XR X-ray(s)
Xr examiner
xr [finance] ex rights
X-ray electromagnetic radiation of very short wavelength (from originally unknown nature of this radiation)
XRD [physics] X-ray diffraction
Xrds crossroads
XRE X-ray emission
x-ref. cross-refer; cross-reference
XRF X-ray fluorescence
XRM [medicine] X-ray mammography
XRMA X-ray microprobe analysis
XRT [medicine] X-ray therapy
XRT [medicine] X-ray tomography
xrts [finance] ex rights
XS cross-section; excess
xs expenses
XT [civil aircraft marking] Burkina Faso; extended technology

Xt Christ
xtal crystal
XTE [astronomy] X-ray Timing Explorer
X-tgd [building] cross-tongued
Xth tenth
Xtian Christian
xtra extra
xtry extraordinary
Xty Christianity
XU [civil aircraft marking] Cambodia
XUI [computing] X user interface
XUV [astronomy] extreme ultraviolet
xw [finance] ex warrants
x/wb extra-long wheelbase
XX double-strength beer
XXX triple-strength beer
XY [civil aircraft marking] Myanmar (formerly Burma)
xyl. xylophone
XZ [vehicle registration] Armagh; [civil aircraft marking] Myanmar (formerly Burma)

Y

Y [genetics] sex chromosome; [currency] yen (used in Japan); Yeomanry; [fishing port] Youghal; [chemical element] yttrium; [currency] yuan (used in China); Yugoslavia
Y [physics] hypercharge
y [meteorology] dry air
y [mathematics] algebraic variable; altitude; [mathematics] (vertical) coordinate (as in **y-axis**); [aeronautics] lateral axis
y. yacht; yard; year; yellow; young; youngest
Y2K Year 2000
5Y [civil aircraft marking] Alaska
6Y [civil aircraft marking] Jamaica
9Y [civil aircraft marking] Trinidad and Tobago
YA [civil aircraft marking] Afghanistan; [vehicle registration] Taunton; [insurance] York–Antwerp (Rules); [USA] young adult
YABA Young American Bowling Alliance
YAC [genetics] yeast artificial chromosome(s)

YACC [computing] yet another compiler-compiler
YAG [electronics] yttrium–aluminium garnet
YAH young at heart (in personal advertisement)
YAL Young Australia League
Y&LR York and Lancaster Regiment
YAR [international vehicle registration] Yemen (Arab Republic); [insurance] York–Antwerp Rules
Y-ARD Yarrow-Admiralty Research Department
YAS Yorkshire Agricultural Society
YAVIS [US informal] young, attractive, verbal, intelligent and successful
YB [vehicle registration] Taunton; yearbook
Yb [chemical element] ytterbium
y.b. [knitting] yarn back
YC [vehicle registration] Taunton; yacht club; [USA] Yale College; Young Conservative; youth club
YCA Youth Camping Association

YC&UO Young Conservative and Unionist Organization

YCL [USA] Young Communist League

YCNAC Young Conservative National Advisory Committee

YCS (International) Young Catholic Students

yct yacht

YCW [informal] you can't win; (International) Young Christian Workers

YD [vehicle registration] Taunton

yd yard (unit of length)

y'day yesterday

ydg yarding

yds yards (unit of length)

YE [vehicle registration] central London; [civil aircraft marking] Yemen; Your Excellency

.ye Yemen (in Internet address)

YEA [USA] Yale Engineering Association

yearb. yearbook

YEB Yorkshire Electricity Board

yel. yellow

Yel. NP [USA] Yellowstone National Park

Yem. Yemen; Yemeni

YEO Youth Employment Officer

yeo. yeoman; yeomanry

YER [finance] yearly effective rate (of interest)

YES Youth Employment Service; Youth Enterprise Scheme

yesty yesterday

YF [vehicle registration] central London

y.f. [knitting] yarn forward

YFC Young Farmers' Club; Youth for Christ

YFCU Young Farmers' Club of Ulster

YFG [electronics] yttrium–ferrite garnet

YG [vehicle registration] Leeds

YH [vehicle registration] central London; [fishing port] Yarmouth; [numismatics] young head (of Queen Victoria); youth hostel

YHA Youth Hostels Association

YHANI Youth Hostels Association of Northern Ireland

YHVH Hebrew name for God (the Tetragrammaton)

YHWH Hebrew name for God (the Tetragrammaton)

YI [civil aircraft marking] Iraq

Yi. Yiddish

Yid. Yiddish

YIG [electronics] yttrium–iron garnet

YIP [USA] Youth International Party

Yippie [US informal] member of Youth International Party

YJ [vehicle registration] Brighton; [civil aircraft marking] Vanuatu

YK [vehicle registration] central London; [civil aircraft marking] Syria

YL [vehicle registration] central London; [civil aircraft marking] Latvia; yield limit

YLI Yorkshire Light Infantry

YM [vehicle registration] central London

YMBA Yacht and Motor Boats Association

YMCA Young Men's Christian Association

YMCath.A [USA] Young Men's Catholic Association

YMCU Young Men's Christian Union

YMFS Young Men's Friendly Society

YMHA Young Men's Hebrew Association

YMV [microbiology] yellow mosaic virus

YN [vehicle registration] central London; [civil aircraft marking] Nicaragua

YNP [USA] Yellowstone National Park

YO [vehicle registration] central London; [UK postcode] York

y.o. [knitting] yarn over; year(s) old

y.o.b. year of birth

YOC Young Ornithologists' Club (of RSPB)

y.o.d. year of death

y.o.m. year of marriage

YOP Youth Opportunities Programme (former government scheme)

Yorks Yorkshire

YP [vehicle registration] central London; yield point (in mechanics); young people; young person; young prisoner

y.p. year's purchase

YPA Young Pioneers of America

YPFB *Yacimientos Petroliferos Fiscales Bolivianos* (Spanish: Bolivian state petroleum organization)

YPSCE [USA] Young People's Society of Christian Endeavour

YPSL [USA] Young People's Socialist League

YPTES Young People's Trust for Endangered Species

YR [vehicle registration] central London; [civil aircraft marking] Romania

yr year; younger; your

YRA Yacht Racing Association

yrbk yearbook
YRls [currency] Yemeni riyal
yrly yearly
Yrs Yours
yrs years
YS [civil aircraft marking] El Salvador; [vehicle registration] Glasgow; yield strength (in mechanics); Young Socialists
Ys. Yugoslavia; Yugoslavian
YSA Young Socialist Alliance
YSAG [electronics] yttrium–scandium–aluminium garnet
YSO [astronomy] young stellar object
yst youngest
YT [vehicle registration] central London; Yukon Territory
yt yacht
YTD [accounting] year to date
YTS Youth Training Scheme
YTV Yorkshire Television
YTYTK you're too young to know
YU [vehicle registration] central London; [USA] Yale University; [civil aircraft marking] Yugoslavia; [international vehicle registration] Yugoslavia

.yu Yugoslavia (in Internet address)
Yugo. Yugoslavia; Yugoslavian
Yuk. Yukon
YUP Yale University Press
yuppie [informal] young upwardly-mobile professional; [informal] young urban professional
YV [vehicle registration] central London; [civil aircraft marking] Venezuela; [international vehicle registration] Venezuela
YVF Young Volunteer Force
YVFF Young Volunteer Force Foundation
YW [vehicle registration] central London
YWCA Young Women's Christian Association
YWCTU Young Women's Christian Temperance Union
YWF Young World Federalists
YWHA Young Women's Hebrew Association
YWS Young Wales Society; Young Workers' Scheme
YX [vehicle registration] central London
YY [vehicle registration] central London
YZ [vehicle registration] Londonderry

Z

Z [genetics] sex chromosome of birds and insects; [international vehicle registration] Zambia; *Zeit* (German: time); zero (as in **Z-hour**); [civil aircraft marking] Zimbabwe; Zion; Zionist; *Zoll* (German: customs); zone
Z [physics] proton number
z [meteorology] haze
z [mathematics] algebraic variable; [chemistry] charge number; [mathematics] coordinate (as in **z-axis**)
z. zenith; zero; zone
ZA [civil aircraft marking] Albania; [international vehicle registration] South Africa (from Afrikaans *Zuid Afrika*)
za. *zirca* (German: approximately)
.za South Africa (in Internet address)
Zag. Zagreb
Zam. Zambia
ZAMS [astronomy] zero-age main sequence

Zan. Zanzibar
ZANU Zimbabwe African National Union
ZANU(PF) Zimbabwe African National Union (Patriotic Front)
Zanz. Zanzibar
ZAP [military] zero anti-aircraft potential
ZAPU Zimbabwe African People's Union
ZB Zen Buddhism; Zen Buddhist
z.B *zum Beispiel* (German: for example, e.g.)
ZBB [US finance] zero-base(d) budgeting
ZC Zionist Congress
ZCCT Zoo Check Charitable Trust
ZD [electronics] Zener diode; [astronomy] zenith distance; zero defect(s)
Z-DNA [biochemistry] zigzagged deoxyribonucleic acid
ZE [UK postcode] Lerwick
ZEBRA [nuclear technology] zero-energy breeder-reactor assembly
Zech. [Bible] Zechariah

ZEEP [nuclear technology] zero-energy experimental pile

ZEG zero economic growth

zen. zenith

ZENITH [nuclear technology] zero-energy nitrogen-heated thermal reactor

Zeph. [Bible] Zephaniah

zepp. zeppelin

ZETA [nuclear technology] zero-energy thermonuclear apparatus (or assembly)

ZETR [nuclear technology] zero-energy thermal reactor

ZF zero frequency; [military] zone of fire

ZFGBI Zionist Federation of Great Britain and Ireland

ZG zero gravity; zoological gardens

z-g zero gravity

ZH zero hour

z.H *zu Händen* (German: for the attention of, f.a.o., care of, c/o)

ZHR [astronomy] zenithal hourly rate

ZI [military] zone of interior

Ziana Zimbabwe Inter-Africa News Agency

ZIF [electronics] zero insertion force

ZIFT [medicine] zygote intrafallopian transfer (infertility treatment)

ZIL [computing] zigzag in-line

zip [computing] zigzag in-line package; [USA] zone improvement plan (as in **zip code**, US postcode)

ZK [civil aircraft marking] New Zealand

ZL [civil aircraft marking] New Zealand

Zl [currency] zloty (used in Poland)

ZM [civil aircraft marking] New Zealand

.zm Zambia (in Internet address)

ZN [civil aircraft marking] New Zealand

Zn [chemical element] zinc

ZO Zionist Organization

ZOA Zionist Organization of America

zod. zodiac

zoo [short form] zoological garden

zool. zoological; zoologist; zoology

ZP [civil aircraft marking] Paraguay

ZPG zero population growth

Zr [chemical element] zirconium

.zr Democratic Republic of Congo (formerly Zaïre) (in Internet address)

ZS [civil aircraft marking] South Africa; Zoological Society

Zs. *Zeitschrift* (German: periodical, journal)

ZSI Zoological Society of Ireland

ZSL Zoological Society of London

ZST zone standard time

ZT [civil aircraft marking] South Africa; zone time

z.T *zum Teil* (German: partly)

Ztg *Zeitung* (German: newspaper)

ZU [civil aircraft marking] South Africa

Zulu. Zululand

ZUM Zimbabwe Unity Movement

Zür Zürich

ZV zoomed video

ZW [international vehicle registration] Zimbabwe

zw. *zwischen* (German: between, among)

.zw Zimbabwe (in Internet address)

ZZ [vehicle registration] vehicle temporarily imported by foreign visitor

Zz. [medicine] *zingiber* (Latin: ginger)

z.Z *zur Zeit* (German: at present)

zz zigzag

READ MORE IN PENGUIN

In every corner of the world, on every subject under the sun, Penguin represents quality and variety – the very best in publishing today.

For complete information about books available from Penguin – including Puffins, Penguin Classics and Arkana – and how to order them, write to us at the appropriate address below. Please note that for copyright reasons the selection of books varies from country to country.

In the United Kingdom: Please write to *Dept. EP, Penguin Books Ltd, Bath Road, Harmondsworth, West Drayton, Middlesex UB7 ODA*

In the United States: Please write to *Consumer Sales, Penguin Putnam Inc., P.O. Box 12289 Dept. B, Newark, New Jersey 07101-5289*. VISA and MasterCard holders call 1-800-788-6262 to order Penguin titles

In Canada: Please write to *Penguin Books Canada Ltd, 10 Alcorn Avenue, Suite 300, Toronto, Ontario M4V 3B2*

In Australia: Please write to *Penguin Books Australia Ltd, P.O. Box 257, Ringwood, Victoria 3134*

In New Zealand: Please write to *Penguin Books (NZ) Ltd, Private Bag 102902, North Shore Mail Centre, Auckland 10*

In India: Please write to *Penguin Books India Pvt Ltd, 11 Community Centre, Panchsheel Park, New Delhi 110017*

In the Netherlands: Please write to *Penguin Books Netherlands bv, Postbus 3507, NL-1001 AH Amsterdam*

In Germany: Please write to *Penguin Books Deutschland GmbH, Metzlerstrasse 26, 60594 Frankfurt am Main*

In Spain: Please write to *Penguin Books S. A., Bravo Murillo 19, 1° B, 28015 Madrid*

In Italy: Please write to *Penguin Italia s.r.l., Via Benedetto Croce 2, 20094 Corsico, Milano*

In France: Please write to *Penguin France, Le Carré Wilson, 62 rue Benjamin Baillaud, 31500 Toulouse*

In Japan: Please write to *Penguin Books Japan Ltd, Kaneko Building, 2-3-25 Koraku, Bunkyo-Ku, Tokyo 112*

In South Africa: Please write to *Penguin Books South Africa (Pty) Ltd, Private Bag X14, Parkview, 2122 Johannesburg*

PHILOSOPHY

Brainchildren Daniel C. Dennett

Philosophy of mind has been profoundly affected by this century's scientific advances, and thinking about thinking – how and why the mind works, its very existence – can seem baffling. Here eminent philosopher and cognitive scientist Daniel C. Dennett has provided an eloquent guide through some of the mental and moral mazes.

Language, Truth and Logic A. J. Ayer

The classic text which founded logical positivism and modern British philosophy, *Language, Truth and Logic* swept away the cobwebs and revitalized British philosophy.

The Penguin Dictionary of Philosophy Edited by Thomas Mautner

This dictionary encompasses all aspects of Western philosophy from 600 BC to the present day. With contributions from over a hundred leading philosophers, this dictionary will prove the ideal reference for any student or teacher of philosophy as well as for all those with a general interest in the subject.

Labyrinths of Reason William Poundstone

'The world and what is in it, even what people say to you, will not seem the same after plunging into *Labyrinths of Reason* ... holds up the deepest philosophical questions for scrutiny in a way that irresistibly sweeps readers on' *New Scientist*

Metaphysics as a Guide to Morals Iris Murdoch

'This is philosophy dragged from the cloister, dusted down and made freshly relevant to suffering and egoism, death and religious ecstasy ... and how we feel compassion for others' *Guardian*

Philosophy Football Mark Perryman

The amazing tale of a make-believe team, *Philosophy Football* is the story of what might have happened to the world's greatest thinkers if their brains had been in their boots instead of their heads ...

READ MORE IN PENGUIN

LITERARY CRITICISM

The Penguin History of Literature

Published in ten volumes, *The Penguin History of Literature* is a superb critical survey of the English and American literature covering fourteen centuries, from the Anglo-Saxons to the present, and written by some of the most distinguished academics in their fields.

New Bearings in English Poetry F. R. Leavis

'*New Bearings in English Poetry* was the first intelligent account of the work of Eliot, Pound and Gerard Manley Hopkins to appear in English and it significantly altered critical awareness . . . Leavis gave to literary criticism a thoroughness and respectability that has never since been equalled' Peter Ackroyd, *Spectator*. 'The most influential literary critic of modern times' *Financial Times*

The Uses of Literacy Richard Hoggart

Mass literacy has opened new worlds to new readers. How far has it also been exploited to debase standards and behaviour? 'A vivid inside view of working-class culture and one of the most influential books of the post-war era' *Observer*

Epistemology of the Closet Eve Kosofsky Sedgwick

Through her brilliant interpretation of the readings of Henry James, Melville, Nietzsche, Proust and Oscar Wilde, Eve Kosofsky Sedgwick shows how questions of sexual definition are at the heart of every form of representation in this century. 'A signal event in the history of late-twentieth-century gay studies' Wayne Koestenbaum

Dangerous Pilgrimages Malcolm Bradbury

'This capacious book tracks Henry James from New England to Rye; Evelyn Waugh to a Hollywood as grotesque as he expected; Gertrude Stein to Spain to be mistaken for a bishop; Oscar Wilde to a rickety stage in Leadsville, Colorado . . . The textbook on the the the transatlantic theme' *Guardian*

READ MORE IN PENGUIN

LITERARY CRITICISM

The Practice of Writing David Lodge

This lively collection examines the work of authors ranging from the two Amises to Nabokov and Pinter; the links between private lives and published works; and the different techniques required in novels, stage plays and screenplays. 'These essays, so easy in manner, so well-built and informative, offer a fine blend of creative writing and criticism' *Sunday Times*

A Lover's Discourse Roland Barthes

'May be the most detailed, painstaking anatomy of desire we are ever likely to see or need again ... The book is an ecstatic celebration of love and language ... readers interested in either or both ... will enjoy savouring its rich and dark delights' *Washington Post*

The New Pelican Guide to English Literature Edited by Boris Ford

The indispensable critical guide to English and American literature in nine volumes, erudite yet accessible. From the ages of Chaucer and Shakespeare, via Georgian satirists and Victorian social critics, to the leading writers of the twentieth century, all literary life is here.

The Structure of Complex Words William Empson

'Twentieth-century England's greatest critic after T. S. Eliot, but whereas Eliot was the high priest, Empson was the *enfant terrible* ... *The Structure of Complex Words* is one of the linguistic masterpieces of the epoch, finding in the feel and tone of our speech whole sedimented social histories' *Guardian*

Vamps and Tramps Camille Paglia

'Paglia is a genuinely unconventional thinker ... Taken as a whole, the book gives an exceptionally interesting perspective on the last thirty years of intellectual life in America, and is, in its wacky way, a celebration of passion and the pursuit of truth' *Sunday Telegraph*

READ MORE IN PENGUIN

LANGUAGE/LINGUISTICS

Language Play David Crystal

We all use language to communicate information, but it is language play which is truly central to our lives. Full of puns, groan-worthy gags and witty repartee, this book restores the fun to the study of language. It also demonstrates why all these things are essential elements of what makes us human.

Swearing Geoffrey Hughes

'A deliciously filthy trawl among taboo words across the ages and the globe' *Observer*. 'Erudite and entertaining' Penelope Lively, *Daily Telegraph*

The Language Instinct Stephen Pinker

'Dazzling ... Pinker's big idea is that language is an instinct, as innate to us as flying is to geese ... Words can hardly do justice to the superlative range and liveliness of Pinker's investigations' *Independent*. 'He does for language what David Attenborough does for animals, explaining difficult scientific concepts so easily that they are indeed absorbed as a transparent stream of words' John Gribbin

Mother Tongue Bill Bryson

'A delightful, amusing and provoking survey, a joyful celebration of our wonderful language, which is packed with curiosities and enlightenment on every page' *Sunday Express*. 'A gold mine of language-anecdote. A surprise on every page ... enthralling' *Observer*

Longman Guide to English Usage
Sidney Greenbaum and Janet Whitcut

Containing 5000 entries compiled by leading authorities on modern English, this invaluable reference work clarifies every kind of usage problem, giving expert advice on points of grammar, meaning, style, spelling, pronunciation and punctuation.

READ MORE IN PENGUIN

REFERENCE

The Penguin Dictionary of the Third Reich
James Taylor and Warren Shaw

This dictionary provides a full background to the rise of Nazism and the role of Germany in the Second World War. Among the areas covered are the major figures from Nazi politics, arts and industry, the German Resistance, the politics of race and the Nuremberg trials.

The Penguin Biographical Dictionary of Women

This stimulating, informative and entirely new Penguin dictionary of women from all over the world, through the ages, contains over 1,600 clear and concise biographies on major figures from politicians, saints and scientists to poets, film stars and writers.

Roget's Thesaurus of English Words and Phrases
Edited by Betty Kirkpatrick

This new edition of Roget's classic work, now brought up to date for the nineties, will increase anyone's command of the English language. Fully cross-referenced, it includes synonyms of every kind (formal or colloquial, idiomatic and figurative) for almost 900 headings. It is a must for writers and utterly fascinating for any English speaker.

The Penguin Dictionary of International Relations
Graham Evans and Jeffrey Newnham

International relations have undergone a revolution since the end of the Cold War. This new world disorder is fully reflected in this new Penguin dictionary, which is extensively cross-referenced with a select bibliography to aid further study.

The Penguin Guide to Synonyms and Related Words
S. I. Hayakawa

'More helpful than a thesaurus, more humane than a dictionary, the *Guide to Synonyms and Related Words* maps linguistic boundaries with precision, sensitivity to nuance and, on occasion, dry wit' *The Times Literary Supplement*